The Younge.

John Ehrman, F.B.A, F.S.A., F.R.Hist.S., was born in 1920 and educated at Charterhouse and Trinity College, Cambridge. After the war, in which he served in the Royal Navy, he returned to Cambridge as a Fellow of his old College, Trinity. He was the Lees Knowles Lecturer, Cambridge, 1957-8, and James Ford Special Lecturer, Oxford, 1976–7.

By the same author

The Younger Pitt published in four volumes

The Younger Pitt: The Years of Acclaim
The Younger Pitt: The Reluctant Transition
The Younger Pitt: The Consuming Struggle, vol III and vol IV

THE
YOUNGER PITT

THE CONSUMING STRUGGLE
Vol. III

JOHN EHRMAN

CONSTABLE

This digital edition printed 2004 by
Constable & Robinson Ltd

Constable
An imprint of
Little, Brown Book Group
Carmelite House
50 Victoria Embankment
London EC4Y 0DZ

An Hachette UK Company
www.hachette.co.uk

www.littlebrown.co.uk

First published in Great Britain 1996
by Constable and Company Limited

This paperback edition first published 1986
Reprinted 1996
All rights reserved
ISBN 1 84529 142 5

A CIP catalogue record for this book
is available from the British Library

To Susan

AS AT THE START
SO WITH MY LOVE
AT THE END

Due to constraints of binding a large volume, *The Consuming Struggle* is printed and bound in two volumes.

The contents, acknowledgements, source references and the index have been printed in both volumes and should be used in reference to both volumes.

Volume III includes pages 1–492
Volume IV includes pages 493–855

Contents

Contents

PART FIVE

Illustrations

ix

Illustrations

Introduction

In Pitt's last nine years, from 1797 to January 1806, the cumulation of events was on a different scale from anything he had known. A sudden financial crisis struck and was met. Unrest and disaffection rumbled and flared, even affecting the home fleets at a dangerous moment. The problems of Ireland erupted in the rising of 1798. Preparations for invasion were set on foot in France, rising towards a peak from the start of the Napoleonic War. Three Allied Coalitions collapsed in succession, the third after high hopes. And Pitt himself resigned without warning in 1801, introducing a pattern of political uncertainty which, despite his return three years later, lasted to his death.

The final months of all in the story soon passed into national legend: the Army of Invasion poised in the camp of Boulogne with the landing barges massed below; Nelson dying in the hour of victory amid the thunder of Trafalgar; Napoleon at Austerlitz watching the rout of the two most imposing European Empires, Britain's two allies, and the Emperors themselves retreating from the field. Such scenes had an epic quality. But the preceding years had their own share of drama; and in perspective they were highly significant, for some of the developments had formative effects well beyond the immediate concerns. The fears of invasion, vivid at either end of the period and seldom far away meanwhile, did much to forward a surge of patriotic sentiment which remained a historic memory – it was to these years that the country looked back almost a century and a half later. And there were other consequences for the medium and indeed the long term. The financial alarm brought about a suspension of the convertibility of the pound which continued as a restriction for over twenty years, prompting the start of a public debate on monetary and banking policy whose influence was felt for a further century at least. Wartime needs also led Pitt by stages to change the basis of wartime taxation with the first clearly entitled direct income tax. The Irish rebellion led to the Union. In the war itself, Bonaparte's expedition to Egypt in 1798 raised questions for the British position in India which had mounting implications, stretching from south-east Europe to Arabia and central Asia, for the transition of a colonial into a genuinely imperial Power. And the political transactions in the five years following Pitt's sudden stepping down did much to mould the identities and conceptions of party emerging over the next two decades. It proved a notable period for the nation, at home and overseas. For Pitt himself it was mostly one of consuming pressure, not the less so for recurring visions of success, and in its later years of an adjustment to a personal situation which he had not encountered before.

For in 1801 it was indeed a long time – seventeen years – since Pitt had been anything other than First Minister, in an Administration of which he was soon the acknowledged focus and with Parliamentary majorities that after a decade changed from normally comfortable to normally commanding. His resignation exposed him to the unaccustomed experience of being out of office, and possibly disposable by others as one piece on the board. He dealt with that unattractive prospect in his own way. Nonetheless when he reassumed his old post he found himself hampered by the conditions which had changed in the interval since he had chosen to retire. His thoughts and conduct in those years accordingly present an interest of their own; and, it may be argued, particularly in the interval itself. For if Pitt by temperament and inclination was above all a man for government, it was in the unfamiliar freedom from the daily constrictions of power that he then formulated his aims, and acted in what proved in fact to be an exchange of one set of limits for another. The course of his path, the effort to reconcile a high and visible pursuit of 'character' with the reasons and inducements in favour of his return, comes as close perhaps as any passage in other phases of his life towards yielding an insight into his nature and his conception of himself. He died less than two years into his second Ministry, at a moment of disaster and the lowest point in his career. But the news stunned and awed supporters and opponents alike. His colleagues resigned, unwilling to face an imminent Parliamentary challenge without him; and Fox himself was heard to say that it seemed as if something was missing from the world.

I have tried throughout these volumes to show Pitt as a man moving among men on a busy stage. Their assumptions and attitudes were a frame for his own; and given the state of his papers theirs have often had to do duty for his. I must record my acknowledgments to owners and custodians for leave to consult their collections. Her Majesty The Queen gave gracious permission for me to inspect and cite a document acquired for the Royal Archives. I am very grateful also to the Duke of Buccleuch and Queensberry, the Marquess of Normanby, Earl Bathurst, the Earl of Harewood (and Dr W.J. Connor), the Earl of Harrowby (and Mrs Jane Waley), Viscountess Eccles, Viscount Sidmouth, Lord Kenyon, the Administrative Trustees of the Chevening Estate, Mr Giles Adams, Mrs Mark and Mr Nicholas Bence-Jones, Mr N.J. Llewellen Palmer, the late Mr W.H. Saumarez Smith, Mr K.J.M. Maddox Wright, and the owner of the Loan 72 papers at the British Library. The Spencer papers which I earlier failed to see at Althorp are now in the possession of the British Library. I wish to make similar acknowledgments to the authorities of that library (particularly to Mr Michael Borrie and Dr Frances Harris), of the Bodleian Library (and particularly Mrs Penelope Sturgis), the Cambridge University Library, the County Archives or Record Offices of Devon, Hampshire and Suffolk (Ipswich) and the Centre for Kentish Studies, Coutts and Company, the House of Lords Record Office, the John Rylands Library of the University of Manchester, the National Library of Scotland, the National Maritime Museum Greenwich (particularly Dr Roger Knight), the National Trust, Nottingham University Library, Pembroke College Cambridge, the Public Record Office, the Scottish Record Office, the Sir John Soane Museum, the William L. Clements Library of Michigan University, Duke University North Carolina, and the Huntington Library and Art Gallery California. I must also record my thanks for permission to read unpublished theses by I.S. Asquith, R.A. Cooper, C.J. Fedorak, G.B.A. Fremont, S.R. Cope, Michael Duffy, Clive Emsley, A.D. Harvey, Austin Vernon Mitchell, P.K. O'Brien, Christopher Oprey, Norman Frank Richards, W.A.L. Seaman, T. Naff, James Walvin, and the late J.R. Western.

Changed circumstances have led me to lean more heavily on research assistance than was the case in the two earlier volumes. I have been particularly fortunate in finding a series of meticulous medievalists, whose training proved very well adapted (though not confined) to examining the massed volumes of Foreign Office papers. First and foremost has been Dr Anthony Smith, to whose skilled labours over several years I would like to pay grateful tribute; and I would also thank warmly Drs Richard Brent (not a medievalist), Simon Payling, and Colm McNamee. Mrs Rosemary Bigwood continued assiduously to search papers in Scotland. Mr Douglas Matthews kindly agreed to undertake the index.

It is a pleasure once more to acknowledge help received, from those who have answered questions, provided information, or read parts of the book. I would like to thank Miss Myrtle Baird, Mr Giles Barber, Professor Daniel Baugh, Mr E.M.G. Belfield, Lord Blake (and Mr D.L. Jones of the House of Lords Library), Mr T.G.J. Brightmore, Mr Adrian Burchall, Professor Ian Christie, Professor J.C.D. Clark, Miss P.M. Clark, Dr J.E. Cookson, Dr J.G. Denholm, Miss Rosemary Dunhill, Professor Michael Durey, my daughter-in-law Mrs Edwina Ehrman, Dr C.J. Fedorak, Dr G.B.A. Fremont, Mr John Fuggles, Professor Norman Gash, Dr A.D. Harvey, Dr Peter Jupp, Mr J.B. Lewis, Dr Piers Mackesy, Mr Charles Maisey, Dr Peter Mathias, Professor P.J. Marshall, Dr Jennifer Mori, Professor Patrick O'Brien, Dr Richard Olney, Captain C.H. Owen, Dr D.B. Robinson, Dr Nicholas Rodger, Professor H.G. Roseveare, Dr John Rule, Viscount Sandon, the late Sir Robert Somerville, Mrs Elizabeth Sparrow, the late Miss Dorothy Stroud, Mr Richard Walker, Mr S.G.P. Ward, Dr Roger Wells, Mr and Mrs David Wilkinson, Dr Philip Williamson, Dr W.H. Zawadzki.

Illustrations have been reproduced by gracious permission of Her Majesty The Queen (fig. 7) and kind permission of the Trustees of the National Portrait Gallery (frontispiece, figs. 2a, 2b, 5c, 8, 9b, 12, 15a, 17a, 18b), the Trustees of the British Museum (figs. 1, 10, 13b), the Governing Body of Christ Church, Oxford (fig. 3b), the Trustees of Sir John Soane's Museum (fig. 4), the Master and Fellows of Trinity College, Cambridge (fig. 5a), Lord Braybrooke and English Heritage (fig. 5b), the Trustees of the National Maritime Museum (fig. 15b), the Bishop of Lincoln (fig. 17b), the Earl of Harrowby (fig. 18a).

I would add two special words of gratitude at the close. First to Jennifer Martin, whose contribution extended far beyond the call of duty, typing impeccably and promptly large quantities of almost indecipherable manuscript for this volume, as she did for part of its predecessor, and enlisting the aid of her daughter-in-law Christine Martin at moments when the stream threatened to over flow. And finally to my publisher Ben Glazebrook, who has never shown the slightest hint of an impatience which he must have felt over the years, and whose forebearance, personal kindness and ccare for the volumes I can only salute.

July 1995   J.E.

This reprint contains some corrections, mainly in the footnotes.

August 1996   J.E.

This digital edition is published in two volumes, this introduction, the contents and illustrations, sources and index to both appearing respectively in III and IV.

September 2004   J.E.

Abbreviations

I	John Ehrman, *The Younger Pitt, The Years of Acclaim* (1969).
II	John Ehrman, *The Younger Pitt, The Reluctant Transition* (1983).
A.C.	*The Journal and Correspondence of William, Lord Auckland*, ed. The Bishop of Bath and Wells (4 vols., 1861–2).
B.L.	British Library.
Buckingham	The Duke of Buckingham and Chandos, *Memoirs of the Courts and Cabinets of George the Third* (4 vols., 1853–5).
Ec.H.R.	*The Economic History Review.*
E.H.R.	*The English Historical Review.*
H of P	*The History of Parliament: The House of Commons 1790–1820*, ed. R.G. Thorne (5 vols., 1986).
H.C.J.	*Journals of the House of Commons.*
H.J.	*The Historical Journal.*
H.L.J.	*Journals of the House of Lords.*
H.M.C.	Publications of the Historical Manuscripts Commission.
Holland Rose, II	J. Holland Rose, *William Pitt and the Great War* (1911).
L.C.G. III	*The Later Correspondence of George III*, ed. A. Aspinall (5 vols., 1962–70).
N.L.S.	National Library of Scotland.
P.D.	*Cobbett's Parliamentary Debates* (1803–04).
P.H.	*Parliamentary History* (1812 et seq.).
P.R.	*The Parliamentary Register: or History of the Proceedings and Debates of the House of Commons [House of Lords], 3rd–4th series*, ed. John Debrett (to 1804); (*Stockdale*), 1804.
P.R.O.	Public Record Office.
R.O.	Record Office.
S.R.O.	Scottish Record Office.
Stanhope	Earl Stanhope, *Life of the Right Honourable William Pitt* (4 vols., 1861–2).

For Volume III and Volume IV

Part One

CHAPTER I

Point of Crisis: the Bank and the Fleets

I

The year 1797 by tradition is a dark year in British history. It was viewed as exceptional while it was under way. When *The Annual Register* shortly afterwards surveyed the events, it found them 'more striking and alarming than those of any year' in its four decades. '"Without were fightings, within were fears": Not only the British constitution trembled on the pivot of fortune, but the political balance of Europe.' The *Register* held Burkean overtones, as it had done from the start.[1] But this impression was very widely shared. Of course there had been plenty of alarms in recent times: in 1795, in the midst of dearth and discontent, Pitt was said to have expected 'a civil broil',[2] and thanks largely to the subsequent measures there were fewer riots and meetings now. But the public events in 1797 were of a different order. A year which saw a run on the Bank of England, two major mutinies in the fleets, the final collapse of an Allied Coalition, was exceptional indeed.

The sense of alarm was the keener because the events followed one another closely. The crisis for the Bank came in February, the mutinies lasted from April into June, Preliminaries of peace between France and Austria were signed at Leoben in April. The worst in point of fact was over, though it scarcely seemed so, in the middle of the year. Nor was the domestic danger in retrospect as great as it seemed at the time. The seamen's actions, if frightening, held their own constraints, and while the financial pressure was dramatic it proved not to have represented a basic economic threat. That does not mean that the crisis was unreal: its reality lay in the feeling of crisis, aroused easily enough in a period of uncertainty and growing doubt. For the state of the war as seen from London in the New Year was bleak. The attempt at peace talks, pursued since October, had failed in December, and the envoy Lord Malmesbury, sent packing from Paris, brought a tale of frustration when he dined with Pitt on the day of his return.[3] Spain, once

---

1. *The Annual Register . . . for the Year 1797* (1798), iv. It was still compiled in part by a group of Burke's friends, following his retirement in 1788 after thirty years of involvement in its affairs.

2. See II, 457.

3. Op. cit., 636, 645–50; *Diaries and Correspondence of James Harris First Earl of Malmesbury*, ed. by His Grandson, III (1844), 367: hereafter cited as *Malmesbury*.

3

our ally, was now an enemy joined with France and Holland. Prussia, once an ally, was unreliably neutral. Our partners in Italy – Sardinia and the The Two Sicilies, which geographically meant Piedmont and Naples – had laid down arms, and the ports of convenience in Tuscany and Genoa were likewise under threat. By the end of January there was no British naval force in the Mediterranean. And of our two remaining allies, Russia seemed likely to stay on the sidelines, after some belated signals of effective co-operation; while Austria, the only real hope of a further Continental campaign, might need little more, despite some recent successes, to push her into a unilateral peace.[1]

If that were to happen, it would be the worst reverse so far. In the first place, it would undermine the chance of a joint Allied settlement. It would also mean that Britain would be confined to sustaining the war immediately by sea alone, which might well not be enough against a Power itself 'not possessing the command of the sea'. 'This country had never so successfully combated [France] as when its maritime strength had been aided by the judicious application of a land force on the continent'; and our own army, needing friendly bases in any case, could not carry the bulk of that burden.[2] Such a strategy, which had finally crowned the last of our victorious wars, under Chatham, and to which his son had been turning, without much forethought, after the first year of the current war, appeared no less desirable as its prospects declined. If Austria withdrew, we would doubtless seek to resuscitate some action in Europe, presumably by turning once more to Russia and even Prussia. But the prospects in either case were hardly promising, our own attempts at landings had proved disastrous, and in the short term we would have to rely on blockade and colonial gains. This last policy would find some favour with the public, for a time; and also in some influential quarters, including now the Secretary of State for War, Henry Dundas. No doubt we could 'make our party good' on that basis.[3] But the problems were evident. The neutral Baltic Powers, Sweden and Denmark, might think it wise to join the hostile combination, with serious effects on our naval supplies and capacity for blockade itself. And experience of operations in distant waters was mixed: the war in the East had gone satisfactorily on a minor scale, but expensive efforts in the West Indies had not produced lasting results and were notoriously severe in losses from disease.[4] The

1. II, Chs. XIV, XV *passim*. I omit Portugal here, since she was an 'auxiliary' ally only (op. cit., 280).

2. See Pitt's statements in the Commons of 3 February 1794 (op. cit., 348) and 5 February 1795 (*P.R.*, XL (1795), 397).

3. Pitt's phrase, in June 1796 (II, 624). For Dundas's views – held in a less firm framework than has often been represented – see op. cit., 578–9, 609, 611–14, 635–6.

4. Op. cit., 624 for Pitt's view of the Baltic Powers; op. cit., 560–7, 589–90, 596, 612–14, 634, 644 for overseas operations from 1795; David Geggus, 'The Cost of Pitt's Caribbean Campaigns, 1793–1798' (*The Historical Journal*, Vol. 26, No. 3), 699–704 for losses in that region.

struggle in any case would probably be a long one, and that was unwelcome – profoundly so to Pitt himself, facing the strain on his cherished finances and rising signs of dissatisfaction among the 'respectable' interests on which Government relied to contain threats of popular unrest.[1]

Such was the broad prospect, if Austria were to go. But there was a closer, independent danger. In the past few weeks, towards the end of December 1796, the French had tried to land a force in southern Ireland. The attempt misfired, but thanks to winter weather rather than the Channel fleet. The expedition had not been intercepted, and public fears of a descent, on Ireland or even England, reached a new height at the turn of the year.[2] Government itself had wind of a plan for a further attempt, to follow a concentration of the French and Spanish fleets at Brest, with perhaps a sortie from the Texel and activity from Dunkirk. On 18 February it took the precaution of ordering farming stock to be driven from the coasts,[3] and in a nervous atmosphere this sparked off the latent alarm. Farmers in Northumberland – scarcely the front line – descended on Newcastle demanding their money, and on the 20th two banks closed their doors. Country banks elsewhere soon came under pressure, and while no further failure occurred in that month there was a sharp reduction in their note issues, and urgent calls to the Bank of England for coin.[4] And then on Saturday 25th news of an actual descent reached the capital:[5] French troops had landed at Fishguard Bay in Pembrokeshire three days before. The episode in point of fact was brief and unimportant. A motley force of some 1,400 men, many taken from the gaols, placed under an elderly American adventurer, surrendered to the militia the next day. Nonetheless it seemed a startling event, details at first were naturally scarce, and following a week of rumour and unease it was almost bound to cause a fright. The stocks had been falling in the past month, the 3 per cents in fact reaching a new low of $51^1/_2$,[6] and cash was now being hoarded in London. In the past two days over £200,000 had been withdrawn from the Bank of England. What would happen on Monday when it opened its doors?

For the Bank's reserves were at a low ebb. Its holdings of bullion had

---

1. See II, 615–24, 638–41.

2. Op. cit., 641–2, and for earlier apprehensions 323, 328, 611–12.

3. For 'driving' see op. cit., 261. Official preparations were in hand, by districts, by the start of the year.

4. There was one failure in March, in Suffolk. For the fall in note issues by a cross-section of local banks see L.S. Pressnell, *Country Banking in the Industrial Revolution* (1956), 460.

5. Known actually in the Admiralty by nightfall on the 24th.

6. *The Annual Register for 1797*, Appendix to the Chronicle, 162. T.S. Ashton, in *Economic Fluctuations in England 1700–1800* (1959), 135 gives a figure of 53; but this is a mean of levels in the two halves of the month.

been sinking in the past year, and in January they fell dramatically to less than £1,200,000 – the worst figure since the immediate aftermath of the American War. Around the close of that month, the Governor and his Deputy called on Pitt three times for intervention. But he in turn was calling for more specie desperately wanted to pay the troops in Ireland, and while he told them that he was planning his moves in case of need he was not prepared to act until he reckoned that point had been reached.[1] On 24 February he disclosed what such measures would be;[2] the news the next day certainly showed that the time had come. Fortunately there was a Sunday's grace. The Cabinet met at noon on the Saturday, and after, apparently, a second meeting, probably now under pressure from Pitt, the Minister wrote to the King requesting his presence in town the next day.[3] Such a step – quite exceptional if not unique in living memory – found a ready response. George III was at the Queen's House – Buckingham House – for a meeting at one o'clock on Sunday, at which an Order in Council and a Royal Message to Parliament were agreed. The Cabinet itself seems to have been in session, formally or informally, for most of the day, in the course of which news of the French surrender was received.[4] The Order in Council was sent to the Bank of England in the evening, and its contents were published first thing on Monday 27th. The Bank was directed to suspend payments in cash 'until the sense of Parliament can be taken'. When crowds flocked to Threadneedle Street that morning to demand their money, they found copies posted up on the walls.[5]

The action, severe when it came, did much to rally sentiment. At the

---

1. Important extracts from Pitt's correspondence with the Bank, and its reports of meetings with him, dating back to January 1795, are given in the Third Report of the Committee of Secrecy of the House of Commons 'on the Outstanding Demands of the Bank of England . . .' of 21 April 1797 (see *Reports from Committees of the House of Commons*, XI (1803), 20–92); and also in *P.H.*, XXXIII (1818), cols. 294–324.

2. *Reports from Committees . . .*, XI, 180.

3. The letter was written at 9 pm, which tends to support the statements of the 27th in *The Times* and *The True Briton* newspapers (both in receipt of Treasury money) that there was a second meeting.

Wilberforce, who was seeing Pitt at this time, was struck by a report the next day (from Samuel Thornton, a Director of the Bank of England) that the Cabinet had been 'averse' to making itself responsible for the measure until impelled by '*General*', as he described the Minister (Robert Isaac Wilberforce and Samuel Wilberforce, *The Life of William Wilberforce*, II (1838), 194).

4. For the Council see *L.C.G. III*, II (1962), no. 1507. Accounts of attendance (which differ from each other) appear in *The Morning Chronicle* and *The Times* of 27 February. Some of those mentioned by the latter, however, may have been called only to the sessions in Downing Street, for which see also *The Diary of the Right Hon. William Windham* [Secretary at War] . . ., ed. Mrs Henry Baring (1866), 353.

5. The text is given in, *inter alia*, *P.R., 3rd series*, I (1797), 642; that of the Royal Message, op. cit., 641.

The expression 'The Old Lady of Threadneedle Street' has been taken in the Bank itself as dating from this time, from a passage in Sheridan's speech in a Commons' debate of 24 March in which he spoke of 'an *elderly lady* in the City' falling 'into [Pitt's] bad company' (W. Marston Acres, *The Bank of England from Within, 1694–1900*, I (1931), 283).

start of the day one of the Treasury Commissioners noted 'the gloom that prevails among all ranks and classes'.[1] Some hours later a 'respectable meeting' at the Mansion House agreed unanimously to accept and circulate the Bank's notes as usual. The Directors for their part raised the discounts in order to sustain credit, and by nightfall Pitt could announce that 'Confidence . . . revives, and things in the City wear a better aspect than for some time'. This reassurance was given to a nervous Lord Lieutenant in Ireland.[2] As far as it went, it was perfectly true. There remained much caution and uneasiness over the next few weeks; but commercial operations were able to continue, and after a time indeed to expand, and the Bank was able steadily to recoup its reserves of specie. The impact of the crisis beyond the Square Mile, taken broadly, took longer to subside. The suspension applied only to the Bank of England; but the Bank was 'the Head of all Circulation' in the last resort,[3] and if substantial interests in London were prepared to honour its notes that was not always the case in the country. Credit did not revive so fast everywhere, and banks' deposits suffered in the provinces. Nor did Government Funds recover their earlier levels for the rest of the year. The 3 per cents in fact sank farther, below the hitherto inviolate level of 50, though this had more to do with wartime events than with the strictly financial situation. Nevertheless the worst was over: the crisis burned out. The Bank of England's pivotal position, which had brought to a head a growing loss of confidence, supported a recovery which, more slowly, spread outwards from itself.

The immediate cause of the shock was fear of invasion. But immediate causes do not stand by themselves. The drain on specie took place at a time when the quantities of coin and of bullion were low for a system of credit which itself had been coming under strain. Within the next month Pitt was giving evidence before Secret Committees of the Lords and Commons set up, at his instance, to examine 'the outstanding demands of . . . the Bank'.[4] In his notes on the crisis, made perhaps for that occasion, he summarised 'Immediate & remote Causes'.

1. And which 'increases every day'; *The Diaries of Sylvester Douglas (Lord Glenbervie)*, ed. Francis Bickley, I (1928), 129. For Douglas see II, 406–7, 473. He had been a member of the Board of Control for India since 1795, and was appointed to the Treasury Board in addition in January 1797.

2. Pitt to George III, 27 February 1797 (*L.C.G. III*, II, no. 1507); same to Earl Camden, sd (copy in P.R.O. 30/8/195). A City meeting, to give a show of confidence, had been suggested to Pitt by the Bank on 24 February, for the 28th or 29th.

See also *Life of William Wilberforce*, II, 194.

3. The phrase was that of the Committee of Secrecy of the House of Lords (see below), report of 27 April 1797 (*H.L.J.*, XLI (nd), 257–8).

4. He had disclosed this possibility – to follow an Order in Council – to the Bank of England late in January (cf. p. 6 above), and he moved for a Committee of the Commons on 28 February (*P.R.*, *3rd ser.*, I, 656). For its Reports, including his evidence, see p. 6, n1 above; for that of the Lords' Committee, *H.L.J.*, XLI, 186–262.

Immediate
Demands from the Country –occasioned by local or particular Alarms
of Invasion – No general Distrust especially in London

Remote – General Insufficiency of Medium in Circulation in the
Country – or Embarrassments and Apprehension occasioned by
either
 Inadequacy of the whole cash to the Demands
 Discredit of Country Bank Notes
 Diminution of Discounts
 High Price of Government Securities
 Arrears owing by Government
 Low Price of the Funds
 Political Circumstances[1]

Some of these factors were more basic than others. The two root elements
had been visible for well over a year. In the first place, the minting of coin
had fallen drastically in 1795 and declined again in 1796, while reserves of
bullion at the Bank in that period sank by some sixty per cent.[2] Pitt listed
the reasons for this last: certain aspects of the balance of trade as measured by the exchanges, and above all the wartime needs for remittances
overseas – for British forces and secret services, subsidies and loans to
allies, the exceptional demands of Ireland for imports of corn and for
defence.[3] This drain had been the subject of complaints from the Bank
since 1795, when there was a particularly massive loan for Austria, even
producing threats to withhold advances to the Treasury.[4] And it compounded the effects of a reduced supply of coin for domestic use. For – and
this was the second element – while the bullion reserves were falling
demands on credit were still pressing, within an economy which had
expanded in volume during the war. An 'Encrease of Active Capital' had
led to an 'Encrease of Bank Paper', whose accelerating ratio to specie then
alarmed the Directors and caused them to reduce the quantity of their
notes and the level of discounts.[5] In uneasy 'Political Circumstances' this

---

1. Nd; P.R.O. 30/8/196, ff. 211–v. The remark about 'Distrust' is carefully qualified, but
questionable even so: cf. the scale of withdrawals in London (p. 5 above), Douglas's
impression (p. 7 above), and also that of William Huskisson [Under Secretary at War] a
few days earlier of a 'dangerous & unjustifiable despondency [that] threatens to prevail'
(draft to Earl of Carlisle, 22 February 1797; B.L. Add. Ms 38734).
2. Minting fell from £2,558,000 of gold in 1794 to £493,000 (and £300 of silver)
in 1795, and £464,700 in 1796 (II, 618n4); reserves of bullion (as measured by an aggregate of the figures at February and August) from £5,632,000 in 1795 to £2,331,000 in
1796 (B.R. Mitchell and Phyllis Deane, *Abstract of British Historical Statistics* (1962),
ch. XV, table 2), before reaching the highly alarming figure of January 1797 (p. 6
above).
3. P.R.O. 30/8/196, ff. 209v–10v.
4. See II, 519–20, 617–18.
5. Op. cit., 617–18. The quotations are from P.R.O. 30/8/196, ff. 210v–11.

facilitated a run: a stagnation of credit lay behind the fear which starkly revealed a shortage of cash.[1]

Embedded in this complex were the 'Arrears owing by Government'.[2] The war had been financed, as always, by borrowing, and the loan system was under mounting strain. It had achieved remarkable results, rising from receipts of £6.7 million in 1793 to £32.5 million in 1796. But the market's terms were growing more adverse, and an alternative approach direct to the public – the Loyalty Loan of 1796 – had itself sunk into discount, discouraging hopes of a successor.[3] The 'High Price of Government Securities' for the borrower and 'Low Price of the Funds'[4] for the lender were affecting commercial transactions, the Treasury's outlook for the future, and the very conduct of the war. They were making life difficult with the surviving allies, particularly with Austria, and had recently led Pitt to sound out prospects for peace.[5] Such deep-seated problems, underlying the shock of February 1797, could not be expected to disappear with itself.

Meanwhile however measures must be framed to meet the immediate need; and these were found to be problematical. For of course Suspension could be only the first step. It was a holding operation 'until the sense of Parliament can be taken',[6] and no precedent existed to show what should be done. There had never been a situation in which the Bank's paper was wholly inconvertible.[7] Prophets of doom were not lacking, and Pitt was steering a poorly charted course. Two decisions had to be made quickly. Should bank notes of small denomination be issued to meet the shortage of coin? And should the Bank of England's notes, of whatever value, be specified as legal tender? The first was settled without any trouble. The lowest permissible denomination of notes, after legislation in the 1770s, was £5. The Bank's Directors were now prepared to issue notes for £1 and £2, and on 28 February Pitt brought in a bill giving sanction until 1 May. It passed all its stages in two days, and on 10 March the earlier statutory constraints were suspended for the same period, thereby authorising country banks as well to issue notes of small value.[8] The terminal date was extended when the time came, and this was regularly repeated: the low denomination note, a feature of the earlier years of the century, had in

---

1. Pitt himself in his notes wondered if 'Advances to the Public' might not have been made in another 'Shape' which would have avoided a 'positive danger of Run on the Bank' (loc. cit., f. 211).

2. P. 8 above.

3. II, 523, 617 (and n5 for a brief temporary drop in the interest rate), 638–41.

4. P. 8 above.

5. II, Chs. XV, XVI *passim*.

6. P. 6 above.

7. Almost exactly a century earlier, in a run on the Bank in 1696, it had made a partial payment of cash on presentation of notes, the rest to follow later.

8. The measures were 37 Geo. III, cs 28, 32; the suspended Acts, 17 Geo. III, c 30 – which was held to be ambiguous – and 15 Geo. III, c 51. For an earlier issue of £5 notes at Pitt's behest see II, 387.

fact now come to stay. The question of legal tender was a trickier one, particularly for a Minister who had long forecast a French collapse from printing money without relation to a specie standard.[1] He could appear to be in danger – as Sheridan predictably taunted from the Opposition benches – of producing his own *assignats*; and in fact this was a charge he was determined to rebut. Having obtained 'the security of Parliament to the notes of the Bank', as he had assured the Directors, he enlisted the support of the Commons to let the matter rest at that.[2] There was some disagreement, most notably from the veteran Francis Baring, who published his interesting arguments for legal tender later in the year.[3] But Pitt rested his case on the fact that the notes were the Bank's, not the Government's, and that 'general consent' was preferable to the hazards of a general statutory support.[4] On that basis he specified the ends to which the instruments might be applied: to payment of taxes, and to a tender of payment of debts (which would thereby preclude imprisonment). For normal transactions, payments would be valid provided that the notes were accepted as cash; and in all such cases the paper was legal tender only at the Bank of England. The measure thus did not give statutory protection to dealings between individuals or institutions, relying instead, beyond the purposes stated, on customary risk-bearing agreement.[5]

These provisions formed part of the Act which, after much debate and the reports from the Committees of Secrecy, confirmed the Order in Council of 26 February. In so doing it converted Suspension into Restriction; and regularised an emergency action which, as Pitt confessed, was otherwise 'certainly . . . illegal'.[6] As in the Act for notes of low value, there was a time limit, set in this instance at 24 June. As in that case, the limit was extended on more than one occasion, and in the event for a very long time. The Restriction Period, as it came to be known, lasted indeed for twenty-four years: prolonged throughout the Revolutionary War, then to a date six months after its legal ending, coming finally to a close in 1821.[7]

---

1. Eg II, 479, 541, 558, 580, 593.

2. Speech of 27 March (*P.R., 3rd ser.*, II (1797), 155). His assurance to the Bank, in the case of his taking action, was given on 24 February (*Reports from Committees*, XI, 180).

3. *Observations on the Establishment of the Bank of England*. For his contacts with Pitt from early in the latter's career see I, 242, 244, 296, 458, 463.

4. Speech of 27 March 1797 (see n2 above).

5. It was passed on 5 May; 37 Geo. III, c 45, sections 2, 8, 9, 10. There are marginal remarks by Pitt on these points in a memorandum of 18 March bearing on the comparable position of the Irish Government (P.R.O. 30/8/196, ff. 237–40v).

The Act also enabled persons depositing coin with the Bank of England worth more than £500 to withdraw up to three-quarters, when desired, in coin, the rest being in notes. Pitt had tried to persuade the Directors to include other forms of specie as well; even so the provision brought in more than £1 million net over the next eight months.

6. Speech of 9 March (*P.R., 3rd ser.*, II, 796).

7. By 37 Geo. III c 91, 38 Geo. III c 1, 42 Geo. III c 40, 43 Geo. III c 18, 44 Geo. III c 1, 55 Geo. III c 6, 56 Geo. III c 21, 58 Geo. III c 37, 59 Geo. III c 23, 49, 1 & 2 Geo. IV c 26, 27. Cf. p. 6 above.

The emergency action of February 1797 was to have a long and highly significant history.

Such a result would have surprised most people at the time. Very few, naturally, could look beyond the needs of the near future. The Bank itself felt able to re-establish convertibility within a few months. But it was content – quite content probably – to let 'political circumstances' decide; and it did so in the knowledge that Pitt by then had shown a wish for Restriction to continue.[1] This did not mean that he was happy with it – let alone, as was later alleged, that he intended 'permanency' from the start.[2] The stoppage came too close for comfort to the abandonment of a specie standard, and it went against many of the instincts derived from his early studies. He had shown himself wary the year before of too sharp a rise in the volume of paper, and proved distinctly reluctant in February to act until the need was very clear. The eventual decision indeed was said later, by a colleague who turned against it, to have caused him 'the most painful day . . . of his . . . political life'.[3] He would not have cared to be remembered by the contemporary verse:

> Of Augustus and Rome
> The poets still warble
> How he found it of brick
> And left it of marble.

> So of Pitt and of England
> Men say without vapour
> How he found it of gold
> And left it of paper.[4]

Rather he opted for continuation because it seemed safest, at a time when the country at large had still to adjust from a feeling of crisis and was shaken moreover by fresh events beyond the strictly financial sphere.[5] It was the largely unexpected success of the policy in the period which followed, in circumstances which in fact remained favourable for the next two years, that turned an enforced expedient into an engine of wartime finance.

1. The correspondence on this question, from Pitt in June 1797 and between him and the Directors in October and November, is clarified by Richard A. Cooper in 'British Government Finance, 1796–1807 . . .' (Ph.D. thesis, University of North Carolina (1976), 133–5).

2. Burke and his correspondent French Laurence, however, perceptively forecast 'something' of the kind at the time (*The Correspondence of Edmund Burke*, IX, ed. R.B. McDowell (1978), 271, 276).

3. Lord Grenville, in a Lords' debate of 2 July 1811 (Hansard's *Parliamentary Debates*, XX (1812), col. 824). They had studied Adam Smith together as young men (see I, 132). For Pitt's wariness in 1796 see II, 619–21.

4. Quoted in Stanhope, III (1862), 20.

5. For the former see pp. 3–4 above; for the latter, section II below.

Pitt did not hide his uncertainty about the effects of Suspension. Of course he kept his end up, surviving the Parliamentary debates tolerably well.[1] Opposition were seldom strong on finance, other acknowledged speakers in this instance proved mostly unimpressive – old Sir William Pulteney and the prolific Sir John Sinclair in particular – and he himself was not easily thrown in matters of this kind. But in his evidence to the Commons' committee he did not pretend to have all the answers: less so in fact than Pulteney and Sinclair on the floor of the House. This was sensible. For not only did Suspension give rise to new and maybe temporary problems, but such monetary and banking theory as existed was sketchy here on its own terms. Adam Smith, as usual, had attended to the subject, more extensively than anyone since Law; but his treatment in this case was scarcely rigorous, as would soon be shown. Pitt may have felt the distinguished influence, in background and maybe in detail: like Smith he was inclined for instance to count on a self-regulating relationship between the volume of commercial transactions and the volume of notes. But he had long taken from 'that great author' only what he found suitable; he specifically disagreed now with a passage that did not help his case – Smith's arguments 'though always ingenious' were 'sometimes injudicious'; and while he was gathering his ideas about causes of the crisis he confessed to caution and sometimes to ignorance in assigning them relative weight.[2] He was not prepared, or equipped, at that point for a structured analysis. Nor indeed did one emerge – from a source critical of his management – until conditions changed further after another few years.

The measures in 1797 supported an alternative to coin. There was also the need to attend to the shortage of coin itself. The 'extraordinary Phenomenon' of the 'Scarcity of Money', worrying since the previous autumn,[3] clearly required urgent treatment now which would tackle both its elements. Pitt indeed criticised an attack from Opposition on the

1. Though Opposition newspapers claimed that his style of speaking since February was noticeably 'unintelligible' and 'obscure' (*The Morning Post*, 11 April; *The Morning Chronicle*, 15 April 1797). Canning noted his defensive tone in the early stages (see *L.C.G. III*, II, no. 1521 n3) and another friend, Bathurst, the effect of a 'violent' and exhausting cough (op. cit., xxiii).

2. Pitt made his remark about Adam Smith (referring to a statement of the true constitution of the balance of trade) in the Commons on 16 May (*P.R., 3rd ser.*, II, 490); and cf. I, 167, 277, 511 12, II, 447, 467, and p. 11, n3 above. His opinion on the self-regulation of note issues may be seen in *P.R., 3rd ser.*, II, 19, 101, 489 and *Reports from Committees*, XI, 153, 156. For his ideas on causes of the crisis see pp. 8–9 above; for instances of caution, *P.R., 3rd ser.*, II, 155 and *Reports from Committees*, XI, 151–3, 156–7. The printed account of his evidence may be compared with an undated ms in P.R.O. 30/8/276, endorsed (not in his hand) 'Challor of the Exchequer's Examination' on 'Stoppage of Cash Payments at the Bank 1797'.

3. Cf. Dundas to Pitt, 3 September 1796 (II, 621).

potential increase of paper by pointing out that their statement would not in itself provide for an increase of coin.[1] Government by then was taking steps. On 3 March it gained support from the Commons for the provision of 'a new copper coinage', such as would be best adapted in particular to help 'the Laborious Poor'; and on that same day Pitt received the outline of a plan, for which the services of the experienced Matthew Boulton would be sought.[2]

Meanwhile an immediate expedient of a different kind was put in hand. Among the specie lying in the vaults of the Bank of England was a quantity of silver dollars taken from Spanish ships. They were now issued, from 9 March, at a value of 4s 9d, with a small effigy of George III stamped over the larger one of Charles IV –

> The Bank to make their Spanish Dollar pass
> Stamped the head of a fool on the neck of an Ass.[3]

This experiment, however, did not 'pass' well. Although more than two million of the Bank tokens – for they were not statutory currency – were stamped in the next six months, only some sixteen per cent was put into circulation. The surcharged head proved easy to counterfeit, there were many base dollars scattered through Europe, and in September the bad money drove out the comparatively good. The latter was called in, and soon replaced by an issue of gold coins at a third of a guinea – a denomination which the Bank had long wished to introduce.

Such currency, whether good or bad, was not however directed to the poor, laborious or not. Arrangements for the new copper coinage were made in the summer. A contract was signed with Boulton in June to mint five hundred tons of pennies and twopences, valid as legal tender for payments up to a shilling. The twopences, containing like the pennies their full weight of metal,[4] were cumbrous pieces – 'cartwheels' as they became known. But not many of them were produced, and further relief came in 1799 with the supply of 550 tons of halfpennies and farthings, to be legal tender for payments up to sixpence.[5] Over a thousand tons of coin of low denomination was thus provided for in under two and a half years.

---

1. 10 March 1797 (*P.R., 3rd ser.*, II, 20).
2. *H.C.J.*, 52 (nd), 364. Pitt's approval on 3 March of the approach to Boulton, suggested by the Earl of Liverpool [President of the Committee (or Board) of Trade], appears from an endorsement on the latter's draft of a letter to Boulton sent the same day (B.L. Add. Ms 38192). There are notes in Pitt's hand on possible quantities of coin, endorsed (in another hand) 'Copper March 27th 1797', in P.R.O. 30/8/197. The plan was brought to the Privy Council in the next few days (George III to Earl of Chatham [Lord President of the Council], 28 March 1797; *L.C.G. III*, II, no. 1524).
3. See Acres, op. cit., I, 279.
4. Ie, not lightened to allow for the cost of minting. Boulton's contract did however allow for costs of distribution.
5. For the need and some of the prospective problems of this last see Liverpool to Pitt, 8 December 1798 (P.R.O. 30/8/152).

The size of the operation was not aimed solely at the quantity of cash. It was designed also to improve the quality. The currency overall had long been in a poor – by Victorian standards a parlous – state, resisting efforts for improvement over successive decades. Indeed the demands of a growing economy were if anything making the situation worse. Much coin of all metals was worn out or debased; some was originally of light value; but the worst of all was the copper 'people's money'.[1] Small transactions were served largely by a range of 'irregular' pieces,[2] some initially from the Royal Mint, some from private mints beyond effective control, mixed with counterfeits and not least a range of private traders' tokens. The new recoinage was thus the latest, but also the most ambitious attempt to reduce the familiar obstacles to a valid popular means of exchange.

As such, like the Restriction itself, it had some marked immediate success. The size of the undertaking produced a sizeable effect; and it was accordingly extended, like the Restriction, under more debatable circumstances. In the eyes of its main exponent, however, the operation did not stand alone. It was meant to form part of a wider review, to be energetically pursued.

Such an approach was to be expected from the author. For a familiar figure was active once more. Liverpool – the Earl of Liverpool, as the Hawkesbury of earlier days had recently been made[3] – had long joined to his strictly official concerns an interest in currency questions. In fact he had inspired the last recoinage of gold, in the 1770s, and he quickly recognised a chance to intervene now. Success however, as he knew by experience, must depend finally on Pitt's support; and he could not be sure of counting on that. For if Liverpool was a powerful figure, as the Ministry's expert on all matters of trade, he came from a different political background and a different school of economic thought, and these constrictions were not eased by personal warmth. Stiff, rather awkward, by now rather pompous, he was not equipped to breach Pitt's own reserve: he was the indispensable odd man out, never one of an inner circle. And while none of these facts had stopped the two men from working together effectively, while wartime pressures moreover were leading to a growing approximation of economic views, the same preoccupations lessened the chances of regular contact, and Liverpool in any case was well aware that he could be overborne or, worse, ignored.[4] Keenly alive to the need for Pitt's attention – itself always apt to be volatile – he did his best to hold it once the new recoinage was under way. Apologising but insistent, he wanted a 'Conversation'. With copper in

1. See Peter Mathias, 'The people's money in the eighteenth century . . .' (republished as ch. 10 in his *The Transformation of England . . .* (1979)).

2. The Mint's phrase, on a sampling of such coins in 1787.

3. See II, 640n1.

4. Cf. I, 330–2, 359n2, 433, and Chs. XII–XIV *passim*; II, 411, 413 and n6, 465n2, 513–14.

hand, he wished the Minister now 'to think of a Silver Coinage', and in the process to tackle a reform of the Mint.[1]

Liverpool always prided himself on being realistic. He expected the former task to be 'a long Operation', but the latter to yield to 'high & proper Authority'.[2] He proved right in his forecasts, though it all took longer than even he could have thought; and Pitt for a start did not do much to help. A year later however, in February 1798, the Minister gave the process a fair wind. Following continued pressure from Liverpool a new Committee on Coin was then set up, taking over from a body of that title established in 1787 under the perennially useful umbrella of the Privy Council. Liverpool himself, as before, was merely one of a large membership which included, like most Council committees, an assortment of Ministers and dignitaries as well as some more expert figures. But the objects were framed as he wished, and he was the moving spirit throughout. Even so it did not prove easy, as he had feared, to move fast on the question of silver. Although he kept in touch with Pitt, and sent a long report – 'a work of great Labour' – which recommended employing the metal as a standard jointly with gold, Pitt did not read the document and Liverpool had to admit that he could not gain a concerted view from the Committee itself. [3] The subject, one may suspect, was too technical for most of his colleagues; certainly they were not prepared to hurry, and the years went by until at last, in 1805, Liverpool published his findings on his own. Still there was no visible effect. It was not until 1816, after his death, that the proposals were accepted and, under his son as Prime Minister, passed into law.[4] Meanwhile however, if also slowly, the Mint had been transformed. A thorough examination was set on foot in April 1798, which unlike the review of silver was not allowed wholly to drop. The Royal Society and the Royal Academy were asked to advise on improvements to coins, new machinery was put in hand, the office itself, after fierce resistance, moved from its ancient home in the Tower. Staff and pay were then reorganised. The whole exercise took some fourteen

---

1. 24 March 1797 (P.R.O. 30/8/152). He wrote, typically, in the third person.
2. Loc. cit.
3. Liverpool to Pitt, 5 May, 8 December 1798, 23 March 1799 (P.R.O. 30/8/152). The report as then sent was to be part of a larger document (for Pitt's failure to read this from lack of time, see Lord Hawkesbury to Liverpool, 7 October 1799; B.L. Loan Ms 72, vol. 54). A printed draft with ms marginalia can be found in B.L. Add. Ms 38192.

The Bank of England was itself uneasy about the lack of silver coin (eg Henry Thornton to Liverpool, 18 August 1797, loc. cit.; Governor and Deputy Governor to Pitt, 12 January 1798, P.R.O. 30/8/276). But as Liverpool himself acknowledged, 'no one' would agree what should be done.

4. 56 Geo. III, c 68. The publication was *A Treatise on the Coins of The Realm in a Letter to the King*. Liverpool had thought of producing it, in that form, in 1799, and Pitt had not objected (Hawkesbury to Liverpool, 7 October, 15 November, 1 and 17 December 1799; B.L. Loan Ms 72, vol. 54). He presumably refrained in the hope that he might still persuade the Committee.

years; but by the end the institution could truly be said to have been 'refounded'.[1]

The undertaking was kept firmly within the Committee's grasp. Liverpool and Pitt alike were clear that this should be so. The former indeed was nervous at the start that there could be a rival inquiry, and he sought the latter's help in blocking any such move. He wanted Government – himself – to reap the credit for any reform of the Mint; he also feared 'a very rough hand' if others were let loose.[2] He had a point. For a potential rival did in fact exist, and one coming from a quarter which he always instinctively disliked.

This development had arisen, like others, out of the Suspension. On 10 March 1797 Pitt proposed the appointment of a Commons' Select Committee (in addition to the Committee of Secrecy) to report on the state of the finances – debt, expenses, revenue – as that had developed in the past four years. His object was to reassure the country that a collapse need not be feared. But three days later Opposition scented an opening for an advantage. A motion was introduced for the reduction of 'useless places and sinecure offices'; and while this was defeated in the form it stood, the Minister felt obliged – indeed he claimed to have been waiting – to agree that the Committee should 'exercise a full power' in reaching conclusions on control of expenditure.[3] The House now had an opportunity to range far afield; and though a Ministerial majority was of course assured on the Select Committee, the members hastened to make the most of their luck. Thirty-six reports appeared between March 1797 and June 1798; detailed and thorough, they also covered offices not scrutinised before. The result laid before the Commons 'for the first time in history . . . a really adequate statement of current revenue and expenditure'.[4] Equally significantly, the reports when published stated how far the Executive had followed them up.[5] The Commons did not examine the Mint itself, once the Privy Council Committee was reshaped. But in the scope and quality of the work, and the fact that this sprang from successful pressure, the great Finance Committee of 1797–8 joined the other bodies of investigation, Parliamentary and official, in extracting from a passing shock materials for the longer term.

1. Sir John Craig, *The Mint* (1953), 277.

2. Liverpool to Pitt, Private, 'Sunday', endorsed 'Feb. 1798' (P.R.O. 30/8/152).

3. *P.R., 3rd ser.*, I, 807, II, 1–2, 27–31, 35. The motion of 13 March came from the regular Opposition Member John Harrison. It was defeated by 169 to 77. For the Committee of Secrecy see p. 7 above.

No doubt Pitt *was* ready to speak on the lines he claimed. But his defence for not doing so in the earlier debate – that the Committee had not yet been set up – is scarcely convincing.

4. J.E.D. Binney, *British Public Finance and Administration 1774–92* (1958), 19. It is instructive to note how far this standard account stresses the achievements of a body lying beyond its chronological term.

5. They were published in 1803, in *Reports from Select Committees*, XII–XIII.

II

Easter in 1797 fell on 16 April. Shortly after midnight that night Rear Admiral Charles Pole, sent posthaste to London from Spithead, roused the Secretary of the Admiralty, who in turn roused the First Lord. He brought the news that the Channel fleet was in a state of mutiny. A few hours later the First Lord, Spencer, went to tell Pitt and then Dundas. In the late afternoon he informed the King that he was setting off for Portsmouth with two members of the Board.[1]

As George III remarked a few days later, with his usual shrewdness, 'How this could break out at once without any suspicion before arising seems unaccountable'.[2] The lack of warning fell on the public, let alone the Government, as a stunning blow. It appeared the more shocking after a recent triumph which, set against the failures off Ireland, showed the navy again as the first line of defence. For the only relief in the depressing months at the start of the year came when Sir John Jervis and the Mediterranean fleet (as it had lately been) beat the Spanish fleet, of almost twice the size and power, off Cape St Vincent on 14 February.[3] Their achievement not only prevented the junction planned with the French at Brest, to clear the Channel with Dutch assistance and open the way to invasion;[4] it was also deeply heartening in its own right. As Jervis himself was heard to say while the line sailed into battle, 'A victory is very essential for England at this moment'. The renewed proof of fighting prowess, with the tales of the Admiral and his subordinate Nelson, was soon circulating through the country and struck a resounding chord. Government made the most of it: the celebrations were given full backing, honours freely distributed and Jervis – not politically a favourite – awarded an Earldom in one step.[5] Coming so soon therefore after all this jubilation, mutiny embracing a fleet was scarcely to be believed.

But why did the event so greatly surprise Ministers? There was no suspicion among the officers themselves until almost the last moment;[6]

1. *Private Papers of George, second Earl Spencer . . . 1794–1801*, ed. Julian S. Corbett, II (1914), 109–10; *L.C.G. III*, II, no. 1530. They left, with the Second Secretary of the Admiralty, at 5 pm. Dundas, it will be recalled (p. 4 above), was Secretary of State for War; for Spencer's appointment see II, 379, 417.

2. To Henry Dundas, 21 April (*L.C.G. III*, II, no. 1532).

3. The news of the battle reached London on 3 March. For the withdrawal from the Mediterranean see II, 630–6, 643.

4. P. 5 above.

5. A most unusual occurrence, sanctioned because he was already in line for a Barony for his services in the Mediterranean (Earl Spencer to Pitt, 9 February 1797; B.L.Add. Ms temporary Althorp 9197). See II, 357–8 for the Admiral's political background and an earlier difficulty with the Ministry.

6. For their sudden belated recognition of unrest, possibly from late on 12 April and certainly by the 15th, see Conrad Gill, *The Naval Mutinies of 1797* (1918), 16–19, and G.E. Manwaring and Bonamy Dobrée, *The Floating Republic . . .* (1935), 26–30. The acting Commander-in-Chief, Lord Bridport (see p. 18, n1 below), had gone on leave for the first ten days of the month.

nonetheless some evidence existed that all was not well. One warning had come as long ago as 1795; more to the point, signs had not been wanting in the past few months. As so often during the century, they centred on discontent over pay. In December 1796 Spencer received a letter to this effect from a Captain at Portsmouth, and at much the same time the Admiralty was sent at least one other such warning from the Nore. In December, too, seamen in the Channel fleet addressed some petitions to the Board, and a further batch went to the veteran Admiral Howe, taking the waters at Bath. He was an obvious recipient: the Channel fleet's Commander-in-Chief at the Glorious First of June, known within that fleet as the sailors' friend, a former First Lord of the Admiralty, a national hero.[1] But though Spencer was made uneasy by the letter he was more disturbed by the financial implications;[2] and in general the portents were played down. After all, the authorities could argue, there had been scattered instances of trouble in individual ships since the war began; but only two, both in 1794, had led to actual mutiny. Nor indeed was collective mutiny itself, in single ships, looked on as necessarily disastrous: as with other forms of unrest, unwritten assumptions could apply. An outbreak of course must not take place at sea, or personal violence be offered. But given these facts, certain types of ill treatment by officers could mitigate the offence; mutiny could then indeed be regarded sometimes even as an accepted form of complaint.[3] Furthermore, it was not a consequence normally of unsatisfied representations on conditions or pay to the Admiralty direct; those were apt to be headed off or suppressed without matters reaching the ultimate stage. Conditions by and large had been much the same for generations; and grousing, desertions, even the odd outbreak, were likewise familiar enough. The Department now did not suspect anything new: the latest petitions to the Board were not even shown to Spencer; and though Howe passed on those which he received, he did so with some demur. For, struck by similarities of phrasing and handwriting, the Admiral was inclined to ascribe them to a single author, and his scepticism was heightened by a reassuring report from a member of the Board on a recent visit to Portsmouth. The First Lord himself was rather more uneasy; but not significantly so. Ministers always kept an eye for signs of disaffection in the armed forces, potentially the worst danger in times of unrest. But attention had been concentrated chiefly on the army and the militia;[4] every one, or almost every one, underestimated the seamen now.

The assumption that the present was altogether like the past might

---

1. See I, 131, 315; II, 349. He was indeed nominally still Commander-in-Chief of the Channel fleet, though owing to ill health he had not flown his flag since the spring of 1795. George III had insisted that he should officially retain the post.

2. To Captain Thomas Pakenham, 12 December 1796 (*Private Papers of Spencer*, II, 108).

3. For an illuminating discussion of this whole subject see N.A.M. Rodger, *The Wooden World . . .* (1986), 237–44. It applies admittedly to decades before the 1790s themselves. But the Admiralty was a conservative institution, for good as well as ill.

4. Cf. II, 156, 402, 451.

however have been checked against three developments, which together could have set it in a different perspective. In the first place there had been an unprecedented bout of inflation in the past two years. Hitting the population at large, it fell with particular cruelty on men whose wages – themselves generally in arrears – had remained unchanged since Cromwell's day.[1] The familiar complaints thus acquired a new edge. And they were raised moreover in a wider context brought about by the pressures of this unusual war. For naval recruitment now drew on two elements not hitherto tapped in the same way. In 1795 Pitt had introduced his Quota scheme, which included men from the inland regions, officially as volunteers under offer of bounties and not confined, for the first time inland, to 'idle, disorderly and vagrants' in moments of need. This represented therefore a fresh source, to set alongside men recruited from the coasts. The Acts applied to Britain;[2] but in practice there had been a growing dependence since 1793 on Ireland as well. Of course Irishmen had entered the fleets before; but not in such numbers. Nor had they left their country in the state it was reaching in those same troubled years.

For it was not a matter only of the numbers from such sources: it was also a question of their backgrounds and quality. The figures themselves were not insignificant. The Quota men comprised those supplied under the scheme by coastal as well as inland areas, so that many of them may have been of broadly familiar types. But it has been reckoned that in all some 31,000 were provided in 1795, with markedly lower numbers in the two following years.[3] In Ireland, the recruiting service itself did not always produce high returns: only some 2,400 men for instance in the year from May 1797, though this may have been low because it followed the mutinies. But that was far from being the only source. There were always Irishmen in England and aboard British merchant vessels; and the Irish Government itself was using the navy as a repository for men taken up on suspicion or proof of sedition. One cannot be sure of the Irish numbers in total. In November 1796 the Chief Secretary in Dublin gave them as some fifteen thousand since the outbreak of war, though he had later to admit that this was inaccurate;[4] and in the year following the mutiny there were

1. For the rise in prices' and wages' movements in general, see op. cit., 443–4, 451–2. While the inflation drove men into the armed forces out of need (op. cit., 485), the impact on the navy was heightened by the fact that the regular land troops received a rise in pay (op. cit., 490–1).

2. Op. cit., 497.

3. See Christopher Oprey, 'Schemes for the Reform of Naval Recruitment, 1793–1815' (Ph.D. thesis, University of Liverpool, 1961), 127–8.

4. R.B. McDowell, *Ireland in the Age of Imperialism and Revolution 1760–1801* (1979), 493, 495; and cf. Marianne Elliott, *Partners in Revolution, The United Irishmen and France* (1982), 138 with Roger Wells, *Insurrection, The British Experience 1795–1803* (1983), 82. Suspects as well as men found guilty in the Courts could legally be so shipped by the Irish Parliament's Insurrection Act of 1796, but the practice had been common before that.

At Trafalgar in 1805 about a quarter of the men on the lower deck in the ships of the line were Irish.

over two thousand seamen and Marines classified as Irish on the books of the Channel fleet. Such figures, taken all together, may be measured against the provision for a navy of 100,000 in 1796–7, which in the event was probably not very different from the serving strength.[1]

The proportions of supply from these origins raise an obvious question. They suggest the presence, within a doubtless amorphous mass, of politically conscious men. How far this was so, and how great the influence, has long been debated. The evidence is complicated and often uncertain, and judgment had best be cautious in a case which, like that of unrest in general, has been shot with passion at the time and since. The Quota men have been favourite candidates – reviled or applauded – for incitement to mutiny; particularly because the most prominent leader to emerge was a product of that scheme. It is easy to surmise that they must have included some men of talent or education who resented being driven to the bounty and hated what they found on board. The more careful the examination, however, the harder it becomes to gauge the effects. Within a society of marked local variations entries came from a range of backgrounds: from highly diverse areas within the countryside, the seaports and the inland towns. They included the 'volunteers' responding to the inducements, and substitutes for others who could manage to stay out. There was no common type, though most of those from the counties have been found to be 'undoubtedly ordinary local workers' who, particularly in 1795, were going through hard times; the worst, by and large, to have been the urban volunteers, particularly from London.[2] Out of all these men, some, from later suggestions, may have been in touch with the radical Societies; and a good many of the substitutes in particular, equally significantly, were Irish. For whatever the attitudes of British recruits those of some from Ireland can hardly be doubted; and among recent batches in particular there were bitterly angry men. Of course the keenly disaffected were by no means the rule – and when battle came it showed that, whatever their sentiments, Irishmen as always relished a fight. But when all has been said – when much has been discounted – it would seem only natural that, given developments at home and the pattern of distribution through the fleets, the Irish dimension, while not decisive, should not be ignored.

Ignored however it seems to have been before the event; at any rate not brought into question as a persistent means of recruitment. Naval needs were too great by this stage to discourage any source of supply; the Admiralty did not distinguish too sharply, whatever it might have wished;

1. For one comparison of Parliamentary Votes with serving strengths, the latter always hard to ascertain precisely, see Michael Lewis, *A Social History of the Navy 1793–1815* (1960), 120. The provision for the following financial year was 110,000.

2. Oprey, loc. cit., 169–81, particularly 169–74. He is prepared even to *contrast* the former, 'usually decent', with the latter, 'often rough criminals'. It should be noted that all these categories exclude the men – few in number during these years – brought in by a separate fresh application of the Vagrancy Acts. For the importance of local variations as a factor in unrest see II, Ch. IV, particularly section I.

and if it was prepared to take men shipped over from political detention or suspicion, the Government in Dublin – and presumably in London – was content to have them out of the way.[1] The Quota scheme for its part seemed to have been working tolerably well: it was held to be an administrative success, and some recruiting officers at least were not displeased with the products. As they looked at the Channel fleet early in 1797, their Lordships did not expect any real change for the worse.

It was in such a frame of mind that, in deference presumably to the First Lord's mild misgivings or the sudden worries of senior officers on the spot, the Board decided nonetheless as a precaution to send the Channel fleet to sea. The cruising season was already under way, and while invasion was now less likely the French coasts had to be watched and further sorties to Ireland prevented. The fleet had in fact returned to Spithead a fortnight before. On 15 April the order was sent for it to sail again. The next day, to the general consternation, it refused.

Following their initial response, Ministers had now to wait for Spencer's news from Portsmouth.[2] From the 18th to the 21st messengers travelled up and down the well-worn road. He had set out with some small concessions on pay, which all concerned in London seem to have expected to do the trick.[3] But matters were not going to be settled as simply as that. The figures, put to the men through Bridport, were rejected the next day, and some firm and extended demands were in turn sent to the Board. They included (scarcely surprisingly) an improvement in the quality and weight of victuals, and in the pensions at Greenwich Hospital,[4] as well as a greater rise in pay including – adroitly – that of the Marines. The First Lord and his colleagues were affronted; but thoughts of total rejection died after a meeting with the senior officers. Instead the reply was a compromise. The demands for pay would be recommended, as the men insisted, to the King and Parliament (in all but one respect);[5] victuals would be provided in full measure, or short measure would be made up in money; no mention was made of their quality, or of the Greenwich

1. If the question were to be raised, it would have been likely to involve the Home Secretary as well, the normal – and superior – channel of communication with Ireland on matters of policy. There is no real sign that it had done so yet.

2. See p. 17 above.

3. This is indicated by the tone of a letter to him from Dundas on the 18th, talking in advance of 'what has been conceded by you' (*Private Papers of Spencer*, II, 111), and by that of the Ministerialist newspaper *The True Briton*, which on that same day announced that the discontent on wages had subsided.

4. See II, 494n4.

5. 'Landmen' – a category long known among the crew afloat – was now proposed as an official rating, at a wage lower than those of able and ordinary seamen. The men's objection to this (which they took to be a device to split them) was disregarded in London.

There was also a slight diminution of the figure demanded for ordinary (as distinct from able) seamen's pay.

pensions; the mutiny would be pardoned if the men returned to duty, failing which they would forfeit some money and be disqualified for pension. At first it looked as if this answer would be accepted; but following a sudden upset things took a turn for the worse. The men's leaders declared that only a pardon signed by the King would do; one of the Admirals lost his temper and was bundled ashore, ships' guns were manned and Bridport's flag was hauled down. Confronted by these scenes, the members of the Board left Portsmouth at midnight on the 21st, bent on securing the pardon from George III.[1]

Spencer had been alarmed by the extent of the concessions – 'I tremble when I state to you', he wrote to Pitt, 'the outline of what has been agreed'. But there was no disposition in London to argue; Pitt in fact conceded the rises in pay at once. 'The amount of the expence', he reassured his colleague, 'is comparatively of no consequence':[2] an unusual tribute to the sudden pace of events. The Admiralty delegation arrived back on the morning of 22 April. In the afternoon the Cabinet met, and Ministers then went down to Windsor for a Privy Council. That evening a Royal Proclamation assured the men that their demands, as accepted, would be recommended to Parliament, and that a pardon was granted to the fleet.[3] By midnight a hundred copies had been printed, and were carried at once down the Portsmouth road.

Surely therefore all would now be well. The Admiralty acted promptly and properly: it sent its recommendations to the Privy Council on the 22nd, to comply with the expected Proclamation. But 'the usual forms of business' then took over at the usual pace. The Council appointed a committee; the committee reported on 3 May, authorising an Estimate for a supplementary grant; Pitt gave notice in the Commons that this would be presented on the 5th; and the House agreed the money on the 8th, after the weekend.[4]

There was thus a pause of over a fortnight after the Proclamation reached Portsmouth. It proved enough to arouse more, and worse,

---

1. Spencer's diary for these days, and the main papers from both sides, are printed in Gill, op. cit., Appendix A.

2. Spencer to Pitt, 20 April 1797 (Dacres Adams Mss, formerly P.R.O. 30/58/2); Pitt to Spencer, midnight 20 April 1797 (*Private Papers of Spencer*, II, 115–16). Cf. p. 21 above.

3. Leading newspapers, Ministerialist and Opposition, published much the same detail on the 24th (a Monday): cf. *The True Briton, The Times, The Morning Herald, The Morning Post*. The information must have come by authority. For Spencer's own communication to the King and the Cabinet's Minute, see *L.C.G. III*, II, no. 1533.

4. The quotation is from Pitt's 'candid explanation' on 9 May (*P.R., 3rd ser.*, II, 427); and see also op. cit., 440–3 for 10 May. The Privy Council was involved because the Royal Proclamation under which the Admiralty set the ball in motion was issued by Order in Council. The Parliamentary Vote was for £372,000. It was followed at once, in view of its size – which Pitt now admitted (cf. above) was 'very considerable' (*P.R., 3rd ser.*, II, 419) – together with the seamen's demand for Parliamentary sanction (p. 21 above), by a confirmatory bill. This passed through both Houses without opposition and, in contrast to the recent lack of haste, became law on 9 May as 37 Geo. III, c 53. It has generally been known as the Seamen's Act.

trouble. The men went back to their duties; but the Admiralty doubted their immediate usefulness – 'The Channel fleet', wrote Spencer on 30 April, 'is now absolutely lost to the country as if it was at the bottom of the sea'[1] – and the growing wait made them increasingly uneasy. Their doubts were fanned by the reports of a Lords' debate brought by Opposition on 3 May, and an order from the Admiralty for heightened precautions also caused disquiet when its contents were discovered. Nonetheless, despite instances of tension the senior officers seemed not too apprehensive.[2] If this was really so they were again mistaken, for on the 7th the mutiny broke out afresh.

This time there was little indecision, and the mood was determined: the men after all had placed themselves even more at risk. Officers – over a hundred – were put ashore, there was an instance of bloodshed for the first time, and the fleet with one exception concentrated in the more distant anchorage of St Helens. The news of these extraordinary steps gave Ministers a nasty jolt. The supplementary Vote came up the next day – allowing Fox and Sheridan to give Pitt a rough time while they agreed to grant it.[3] When that was over, the Cabinet met and decided on a further step. Lord Howe should be asked to go down to the fleet.[4] Infirm and easily exhausted, the old Admiral did not hesitate. He set off on 10 May, and by noon on the 11th was with the ships at St Helens.

The move was awkward in one respect. It might seem to derogate from Bridport's position.[5] Pitt did his best to smooth the way: Howe came with 'a Civil Commission' bearing discretion to grant a fresh royal pardon, and no 'Naval Authority or Functions'.[6] But of course he overshadowed his junior, by virtue of his person and bearing as he did the King's pardon and news of the Seamen's Act.[7] His progress through the fleet was correspondingly successful. So confident indeed did he become that he

1. Quoted in *L.C.G. III*, II, xxiv.
2. Not at any rate in reporting to the Admiralty. On the 6th Spencer could write to Bridport, in contrast to his feelings a week before, of his relief 'to find that at length tranquillity and order seem to be perfectly established' (Manwaring and Dobrée, op. cit., 95).
3. As Pitt himself put it to the King, 'Mr Fox and Mr Sheridan, . . . without opposing the measure, tended as far as possible to lay ground for embarrassment' (8 May, 8 pm; *L.C.G. III*, II, no. 1541).

In some 'traditional' mutinies in single ships officers had been put on shore and the fact condoned by the Admiralty. But it had been accepted that they were removed without violence, and of course the numbers involved now were a different matter – as, above all, was the concentration of mutinous ships at sea.
4. Spencer to George III, 9 May, 4.30 pm (op. cit., no. 1542). It has been stated (*DNB*) that this was done on the King's initiative. By his note to Pitt later that day, however, (in Stanhope, III, Appendix vi–vii) it would seem probably not to have been so.
5. Particularly since Howe was titular Commander-in-Chief in the earlier part of the year (see p. 18, n1 above). He had however very recently insisted on resigning the post.
6. To Bridport, 10 May 1797 (copy in Pitt's hand, P.R.O. 30/8/102; see Holland Rose, II, 313–14). He signed himself, unusually even allowing for an old family friendship (see II, 463n5), 'sincerely & Affy'. Spencer, and Speaker Addington, also wrote.
7. See p. 22, n4 above.

decided to talk direct to the men's assembled delegates – which Spencer from principle had refused to do.[1] The event was watched eagerly in London: 'His Lordship going off. 16 Boats coming from St Helens' – so Pitt was informed through the Admiralty telegraph.[2] The meeting produced one final concession: officers whose crews had lodged written complaints of treatment would not return to their ships. When this was settled, and the delegates had been lectured and expressed suitable regret, the pardon (slightly altered) was given and on 15 May the mutiny came to an end.

It closed, under Howe's management, with great good humour all round. The ships' bands played 'Rule Britannia', Portsmouth was given over to jollifications, he himself was rowed round the fleet with the delegates, and that evening they all dined together. Officers returning aboard were treated respectfully, and on the 17th the Channel fleet put to sea. The crews, it seemed, were sound at heart once the grievances were met. And so indeed they had shown in many ways in the mutiny itself. Particularly before the pause in London, they were seldom needlessly obstructive; and they maintained discipline by their own management almost unbroken throughout. Bridport and Spencer, on the latter's visit, were able to escort the Prince of Württemburg, in England to marry George III's eldest daughter, ceremonially through the fleet. The dastardly deeds provided by rumour failed to occur,[3] and even when the red flag flew at Bridport's masthead expressions of loyalty were not dimmed.

This combination of actions and attitudes has long caused debate. Many historians have held, like a good many contemporaries, that the mutiny sprang from and was governed strictly by the grievance: that it did not express political disaffection, with which indeed no firm link could be proved at the time. Others, in varied degrees, have taken an opposite view. Perhaps it would be reasonable to suggest that the truth fell in between: that mutiny arose from anger over pay, to which other grievances could be added among a body of men collectively disposed to be patriotic within a national setting which contained widespread stringency and uneven, sometimes fierce, unrest. Naval conditions of course were peculiar by general standards. In one sense, social contrasts were heightened within the wooden walls; in another they could be redeemed by the needs of collective life at sea, by personal loyalties

1. P. 21 above.

2. '20 m.p. Noon, 13th May 1797' (P.R.O. 30/8/259). Messages by the same means from Howe on the 14th and 15th are also among Pitt's papers, in P.R.O. 30/8/146.

The famous telegraph stations were erected in 1795–6, linking the Admiralty roof by semaphore with Portsmouth, Deal and Sheerness. In the best conditions a message could pass between London and Portsmouth in seven and a half minutes.

3. Pitt's wild young cousin Camelford for instance (see I, 4, where I am ashamed to say 'nephew' is incorrect), then a naval lieutenant at Portsmouth, warned Spencer that he and his colleagues might find themselves 'detained' if they went aboard any of the mutinous ships (*Private Papers of Spencer*, II, 115).

at close quarters, and the prospect of meeting the foe. On this occasion the upshot suggested that the discontent had not in fact grown into coherent subversion; for when an attempt followed shortly afterwards to provoke a further rising, and one moreover now including a call for a change of Ministry or for peace, it had only a limited effect, being confined to some individual ships.[1] But whatever the verdict on the main event, one highly disquieting feature stood out. However one may judge the true balance of feelings in the ships at Spithead, the organisation emerging from the lower deck was something disturbingly new. The initial secrecy, the maintenance of unity, were quite unfamiliar on such a scale; they went quite beyond the authorities' conception of the average seaman's grasp. It was not therefore surprising that, despite the initial limits of evidence, Ministers should link such 'system' with seditious aims. It *was* surprising that, given this suspicion, they allowed the issue to drag on.[2]

The pause of over a fortnight furthermore may have had an added significance. It may have given room for the new trouble that followed elsewhere. There had been signs of contagion from the Channel mutiny among other units in the home fleets. A rather mild attempt to join the main action occurred late in April at Plymouth, and on 1 May Admiral Duncan's flagship in the North Sea squadron at Yarmouth made a show. This last did not get far; Duncan was highly popular, he was furious at the misconduct, and the men piped down at once. There seemed indeed no reason to fear any consequences in the ships under his command. But able, humane and experienced as he was, he too misread the general position. While he was still writing confidently from Yarmouth, trouble was being planned at the Nore.[3]

The Nore mutiny, and its spread to the North Sea force, proved much more dangerous than that at Spithead. The reason lay partly in the fact that a single more dominant leader appeared, in exactly the type of situation where a personality can sway events. It was perhaps fitting that he was thrown up in that base, for Richard Parker was a Quota man in the catchment area which may have supplied the worst of the Quota men – his presence indeed gave Duncan a point when he ascribed the

1. See the interesting treatment by Wells, who rates subversive sentiments in general more highly; op. cit., ch. 5 and particularly 100–2. An attempt to convey the particular quality of contemporary patriotism is made in my II, 157–8, and cf. 156.

2. As the King noted shrewdly once again (cf. p. 17 above), 'It would be idle to lament that the measures for increasing . . . pay have been delayed for two weeks coming forward in Parliament' (to Spencer, 9 May 1797; *Private Papers of Spencer*, II, 124); and see also Pitt in p. 22, n4 above. The earliest example I have found of Ministerial suspicion of subversion is in Dundas to Spencer on 18 April (op. cit., 110–11).

3. Like other senior officers, Duncan foresaw no real change from the past; see his letter to Spencer of 1 May (*Private Papers of Spencer*, II, 121). A second confident letter followed on the 7th (op. cit., 121–3).

trouble to them and the Irish.[1] The ships at the Nore moreover were a random collection at any one time. They were not a constituted body like the Channel fleet which, though its discipline was mild compared with that of the Mediterranean fleet under Jervis,[2] had its pride and loyalties and sense of identity. Given the circumstances, the men's own loyalties and discipline indeed could effectively aid their cause; on the other hand, the sparks could fly quickly in the looser atmosphere of Sheerness. The Admiral there was a port Admiral, Charles Buckner, of no great renown. Vessels were always coming and going on passage from and to their squadrons. The Medway was near the capital, in touch more directly with the outside world. It might be – suspectedly was – accessible to radical influences. Such conditions might possibly mean a lack of cohesion under pressure. But pressure would not be brought easily to bear at the start.

Nevertheless it seemed rather curious that this new mutiny developed as it did. The reason lay largely in the fact that no one for a time thought of it as new. Nor of course was it so in origin: the Channel fleet was showing the way. Its preparation began on 6 May at Sheerness, and trouble broke out on the 12th: the high period of the second outbreak at Spithead. The action at the Nore was therefore seen, correctly, as an offshoot of the main rising, and both the authorities in London and the local populace treated it with corresponding calm once that died down. A pardon on return to duty was granted on the 17th, and the same assurance respecting 'obnoxious' officers as had been given in the Channel affair. Howe himself while at Portsmouth had talked to a deputation that arrived from Sheerness, and like every one else he assumed that the fresh outburst was a passing incident. But that assumption gave time for the mutiny to gather confidence: caught by the agreement with the Channel fleet, but reluctant tamely to beg for pardon, and perhaps excited by their action, the leaders at Sheerness carried on. In so doing they would now of course have to outbid the men at St Helens; to show that they could wring greater concessions from Government. On 20 May they presented the port Admiral with eight demands: for confirmed inclusion in the Spithead pardon; for satisfaction of wages in arrears, an advance to pressed men – who could not receive the volunteers' bounty –, and a more just distribution of prize money; for leave to be allowed while in port; some changes in the Articles of War; and two points which in particular struck the authorities as insolent. Officers removed from the ships (and in this case there had already been a substantial ejection, with the rest moreover stripped of their duties on board) should not return without their crew's consent – a significant enlargement of Howe's

1. To Spencer, 14 May 1797 (op. cit., 131–2). And see pp. 19–20 above.
2. When it was rumoured later that Bridport was going to be succeeded by Jervis, one of his Captains was said to have given the toast, at the Admiral's table, 'May the discipline of the Mediterranean never be introduced into the Channel fleet'. Though applied to the officers, this certainly covered the fleet as a whole.

concession;[1] and any deserter rejoining the service should not be punished for his 'run'.

The document, combined with the men's air towards Buckner himself, was disturbing. The Admiralty rejected the demands, other than the first which they had granted already, and the next day the Sheerness garrison was strengthened. But Buckner was not the man to take risks, and he continued to hope that enough would be enough. He was very soon proved wrong. His flag was hauled down, the mutineers brought their ships together in formation, and Parker called for the presence of the Admiralty Board. This was rejected on the 24th. In the next two days things did not improve. The men were known to be planning a blockade of the Medway and the Thames, and they made efforts to gain other ships lying upriver towards Chatham. The shore guns at Tilbury had to be brought into action. It was clear, after a fortnight, that something effective must be done.

By 26 May Ministers were in fact becoming alarmed. Rumours of course were rife, and it was genuinely hard to tell what the mutineers might do. The Prince of Württemburg, now married to his English princess and due to take her to the Continent, was embarked at Harwich instead of in the Thames in case the vessel was seized passing the Nore.[2] On the same evening the Cabinet held 'a very long discussion', at which two preliminary soundings were agreed. An officer was sent to Yarmouth to see if Duncan thought he could put down the mutiny; and the experienced General Sir Charles Grey, called in with a view to commanding the Sheerness garrison, advised a firm stand and a visit with such a message by the Admiralty Board.[3] These steps were put in hand the next day. Duncan, though reluctant to use his men against their fellows, complied and was sent instructions. Grey went down to Sheerness, followed shortly by more troops. And on the evening of the 27th the same members of the Board that had travelled to Portsmouth set off from Whitehall down the Old Kent Road.[4]

For the first time therefore there was a definite response to what was now taken as a real threat. The Board's representatives went down with a fresh royal pardon on the one hand and on the other 'an express determination not to add to the concessions already made'.[5] This stance

1. See p. 24 above.

2. Correspondence between George III and Spencer, 26 May 1797 (*L.C.G. III*, II, no. 1555). Cf. for the Prince at Spithead in April, p. 24 above.

3. Spencer to George III, 'Midnight' 26 May; Dundas to same, '12 pm' sd (op. cit., nos. 1555–6). For Grey see II, 322n7, 325, 356–60, 490 n6, 491.

The officer sent to Yarmouth had some experience of mutiny. He was Captain Bligh, once of the *Bounty* and now commanding a ship at the Nore.

4. Including one, Lord Arden, who had vainly tried to resign his seat meanwhile (see Arden to Pitt, 10 May 1797; Dacres Adams Mss, formerly P.R.O. 30/58/2).

5. Spencer to George III, 27 May 1797 (*Private Papers of Spencer*, II, 136). The Lord Chancellor had pointed out the need for a new pardon, since that carried by Howe to the Channel fleet could not cover offences committed later (see op. cit., 133–4).

was maintained over the next two days, while the mutineers' delegates came and went and the Board refused to talk to them direct. The visit ended on the 29th, to all appearance with no result. But in fact, as Spencer suspected, it had shaken some of the men – several crews showed signs of giving up, though their hesitations proved ineffectual – and, perhaps equally important, it lessened initial local sympathy for the grievances. The ships' bands continued to play to all appearance undismayed, the red flags were hoisted, weaker brethren disciplined; but the shore parades died down, and the mutineers entered on a deeper isolation. It began to look not impossible that the affair might decline or collapse. But at that very time a fresh development placed it on a more dangerous plane.

For on 27 May mutiny broke out in the North Sea squadron at Yarmouth. Duncan sailed that day to maintain his constant necessary watch on the Dutch coast, though he had to leave two recalcitrant ships behind. But once out at sea he had a run of desertions, and within twenty-four hours his command was out of action bar his own flagship, one ship in company, and two loyal units in port. The story has often been told of his watch on the Texel over the next few days, stationed in the channel and signalling to a non-existent force over the horizon. Meanwhile the Ministry was faced by a potentially ugly crisis, with a hard core of men at the Nore who could now claim support from a more potent source.

The outbreak came in the worst place at what seemed to be the worst time. With retrospective knowledge of the state of affairs on the other side of the Channel, we can see that continuing fears of invasion – whether of Britain or Ireland – were exaggerated.[1] After Cape St Vincent the French wrote off Ireland for the first half of the year at least, and while the Dutch preparations at the Texel were real enough no target had been specified. There might be an attack on Scotland, or Ireland, or some of the colonies. Nonetheless, if the plans were not so far advanced as was suspected in London, towards the end of May the armament at the Texel looked ready to set out. It was in fact thought to be held only by continued adverse winds which had been blowing fortunately for some weeks. By the latest intelligence, Duncan's blockade was thus taken to be of vital importance, and the Admiralty and the Foreign Office swung into action at once. Six units of the Channel fleet were ordered to join him forthwith, and the small Russian squadron which had cruised in the North Sea on and off for the past two years, but was about to leave for a review in the Baltic, was requested and allowed to stay as a temporary reinforcement. These additions would be of some help. But they had still to arrive, no one in the navy thought much of the Russians, and if Duncan's own squadron was to be out of control the future could look black indeed.[2]

1. Cf. pp. 5, 17 above.

2. For the Russians in 1795 and 1796 and the British view of them, see II, 590, 611, 632; for their retention now, which was agreed on 5 June, P.R.O., F.O. 65/37 *passim* and *H.M.C.*, *Dropmore*, III (1899), 327–8; for intelligence on the Texel in the first half of May, F.O. 38/2.

Under these threats from without and within the first fortnight in June was tense. Government added to its legal powers. A royal message to Parliament on the 1st called on 'all . . . faithful Subjects to give their utmost Assistance in repressing such dangerous and criminal Proceedings', and on the 2nd and 3rd Pitt brought in two bills, the first for the prevention of seduction of sailors and soldiers and the second to restrain intercourse with the ships in mutiny. They passed swiftly through both Houses and became law on the 6th.[1] There was indeed a general rallying in the Commons – Sheridan himself made a speech in support –, and among the prosperous ranks of London, and the public at large. Shipowners in the River offered vessels and the East India Company all its resources, volunteers flocked to recruiting offices, the City set up subscriptions. The mutineers for their part put their plans for blockade into execution, meeting their needs as best they could from impounded storeships, intercepted coastal traffic and sporadic raids on the Isles of Grain and Sheppey. The leaders tried to keep up the spirit with the familiar demonstrations and speeches, and Pitt and Dundas were hanged in effigy from Parker's yardlines for shooting practice. But the pressures were telling. No comfort was now to be had from shore, the Sheerness garrison was in a state of defence, and following an Order in Council on 6 June the buoys and lights were removed from the channels. Escape was thus blocked; and while the men – and likewise Pitt himself[2] – considered the possibility of an attack on London, they lacked the cohesion for so bold a course. Signs of moral wear and tear indeed were growing, two ships escaped from their fellows on the 9th, and thereafter the mutiny was clearly approaching collapse. From the 10th ships started to surrender. By the 16th it was all ended. London, and the Government, could breathe safely again.

Once the Cabinet had decided to defy the mutiny, the executive departments had taken over: the Admiralty with Trinity House, Grey and the army at Sheerness. The relevant Ministers, Spencer and Dundas, were of course in final charge with Pitt himself.[3] He seems not to have lost his usual power to 'throw off all his Load'. Spencer told a story of having to wake him one night. Having obtained the reply, he remembered in the street a point he had wished to make; on returning and going upstairs, he

---

1. *P.R., 3rd ser.*, II, 698–702, 711–12; *H.C.J.*, 52, 634–5; *H.L.J.*, XLI, 342, 344. The Acts were 37 Geo. III cs 70, 71. A third Act, 37 Geo. III c123, forbidding unlawful oaths – such as the seamen had been taking – was passed shortly afterwards. Taken together, they had a not unimportant history. The first was still in force at the time of the Home Fleet's Invergordon mutiny in 1931, and it was under the third that the Tolpuddle Martyrs were condemned in 1834.

2. Pitt to Spencer, nd but 7 June 1797 (*Private Papers of Spencer*, II, 149–50).

3. Grenville too, who had become distinctly critical by June, seems to have been in touch at that point (*Diary of William Windham*, 366 and see also a letter to Pitt of 26 June complaining of 'weakness' in the conduct of business at home; Dacres Adams Mss, formerly P.R.O. 30/58/2).

found the Minister once more asleep.[1] This impressed him, as did Pitt's demeanour in general in the closing stage. Nonetheless the Government's handling of policy had proved patchy, surprised constantly by events. At Spithead, swift initial response was followed by a lack of urgency which in turn had to be followed by the recourse to Howe; at the Nore, a prolonged expectation, or hope, that the business would sort itself out, a reluctance to raise the temperature, preceded firm and effective measures. Mutinies of course can be hard to gauge, and turn all too easily on chance; reports in these instances came from officers who could not quite credit what was happening; and Pitt and his colleagues were deeply immersed in other pressing business for much of this time.[2] Such facts can help but not wholly explain why Ministers had no clear view, and only a belated grip on developments that continued for two months. Indecision, at one point inattention, lay at their own door. Like the officers themselves, they found it hard to come to terms with such an event.

One of the Government's greatest fears, particularly in May, was that of contagion in the army, not least among the Guards who formed the regular defence of the capital. For a time indeed it looked as if the worst might happen. Intelligence of an intended mutiny in the Household troops led to a Privy Council being held on 11 May for precautionary measures. The Secretary at War was thoroughly alarmed – the possibilities were 'too dreadful. There does not seem to be anything to prevent their being masters of the Tower, the Mint, the Palace and the Cabinet.'[3] On the 12th there were in fact signs of discontent in two battalions, and Ministers then moved to avert a calamitous blow. On the 15th the Guards were drawn up in St James's and Hyde Parks to hear a message read from the Commander-in-Chief, the Duke of York, that grievances would be heard and action taken after Parliament had been consulted.[4] The Government was prepared in point of fact to raise pay and allowances, including provision for a subsidy against a rise in the price of bread, and details were ready to present to the Commons on the

---

1. Stanhope, III, 39, perhaps drawing on Lord Holland's *Memoirs of the Whig Party*, I (1852), 96. And cf. I, 131, 589.
2. Which will be followed in Ch. II.
3. *Diary of William Windham*, 363. His gloom roused Canning the next day.

> Come Windham, celebrate with me
> This day of joy and jubilee,
> This day of *no* disaster!
> Our Government is *not* o'erturned –
> Huzza! – Our Fleet has *not* been burn'd,
> Our Army's *not* our master.

(*The Windham Papers . . .*, ed. the Earl of Rosebery, II (1913), 53.)
Only a week before, however, Canning himself had 'croaked' with Windham 'over the state of things (the Fleet)'; diary of 6 May 1797 (Canning Ms 29d; Leeds City Archives).
4. *The True Briton*, 17 May 1797.

24th.[1] By then information was coming in of scattered discontent among the forces in the provinces; and on the 26th the artillery rioted at Woolwich. Pitt was roused in the night and held a meeting with the military authorities – a few hours, it would seem, after the long Cabinet which had discussed the steps to be taken for the mutiny at the Nore.[2] The next day, in the accumulating troubles, he 'and others' were said to be 'convinced that things [were] *in extremis*'.[3] So far as the army was concerned, however, matters quietened down. The Guards and cavalry disarmed the artillery, the garrison at Sheerness remained steady, and while there were more reports of discontent Government was not confronted with the ultimate danger of mutiny spreading through the regular troops.

The military authorities and the Home Office were by now very largely convinced that the unrest was being excited from outside. The Admiralty and the Home Office already suspected the same in the navy; and to Pitt it was necessary 'only to connect the discontents on board the fleet with the other species of sedition upon shore, to pronounce them to be part of a fatal and deep digested system'. This conclusion underlay the severity shown to the Nore mutineers: the twenty-three executions and the lesser punishments which, in contrast to Spithead, were swiftly put into effect. It drew on the reports of 'emissaries being at work' and 'hand-bills . . . industriously circulated'; and it was echoed two years later when a Parliamentary Secret Committee examined the history of sedition as a whole.[4] Of course such things took place, and Government by this time had much better intelligence than in the early years of the war. Even so – and perhaps by the nature of the case – its agents found it difficult to measure the impact, at any rate for legal purposes. There is no doubt that connexions existed between the seamen at least and radical movements, the London Corresponding Society in particular; and it is also certain that the United Irishmen had cells in both the Channel and the North Sea fleets.[5] The two Societies seem to have collaborated on occasion; and until

---

1. Duke of York to George III, 22 May 1797 (*L.C.G. III*, II, no. 1549); anon., but George Rose [Joint Secretary to the Treasury] to [Pitt], note of Saturday, 2 o'clock, nd but endorsed 1797 (P.R.O. 30/8/173); *H.C.J.*, 52, 605–6. For compensation for the price of bread two years earlier see II, 490–1.

2. P. 27 above. There are different accounts here. Wilberforce, who was in touch with Pitt and records his being 'awaked', says that he 'went out to Cabinet' (*Life of Wilberforce*, II, 219). *The True Briton*, which with the evening paper *The Sun* was favoured by Government, says that he met York and Marquess Cornwallis [Master General of the Ordnance] at the Horse Guards at 4 am on the 27th, after which Cornwallis went down to Woolwich (27 May 1797). Since Dundas did not mention Woolwich in his letter to the King at midnight on the 26th, after the Cabinet meeting (p. 27, n3 above), I have opted for *The True Briton*.

3. *Life of Wilberforce*, II, 220. Wilberforce added sadly, 'yet no apparent sense of God'.

4. Pitt in the Commons, 2 June 1797 (*P.R.*, *3rd ser.*, II, 699). The Committee of 1799 is considered on pp. 304–5 below. Cf. p. 24 above for the initial suspicions of the Channel fleet.

5. For the former Society see II, 106–7, 393–5, 453–4, 459, 615; for the latter op. cit., 220, 641.

communications were stopped with the ships in the second naval mutiny, there was no bar on the sending of legal mail. As already suggested, that is not to say that such influences were responsible for the first naval out-break, though under that example they may well have been more active in the rest and among some of the discontented troops. But by the time the main troubles died down Government was tending towards one particular conclusion. It was paying more attention to the Irish factor. This process moreover gained strength in the next few months, when Irish seamen appeared to be prominent in scattered troubles which still occurred. For naval unrest did not subside in the aftermath without trace. There were further individual incidents in the Channel ships; the North Sea squadron was unsettled for some time; and short-lived mutinies in the summer and autumn took place in more distant waters, in some units of Jervis's fleet in the approaches to the Mediterranean, and among the formations in the West Indies and at the Cape of Good Hope. Officers on the spot attributed some of these episodes largely to the Irish, and there was already an exchange of views between London and Dublin on the hitherto unquestioned policy of sending disaffected men to serve in the fleets.[1] The practice was in fact dropped, and some were shipped instead to the army in the Caribbean – a sadly effective way of dealing with their discontent.

The Irish dimension would become an increasingly serious element over the next few years in assessments of British subversion extending beyond the Admiralty's concern at this point. But meanwhile, as the months wore on and the home squadrons cruised once more on their sta-tions, there was a growing feeling that co-ordinated mutiny had in fact been contained. Ministers could claim with relief that 'Jacobinism' had suffered a blow. For if they were right in believing that the outbreaks, actual and abortive, were connected, that they really were 'part of a deep digested system',[2] then the effort had failed, at the cost of concessions which were not indigestible – the great target of effectively inciting the armed forces to rebellion had been missed. A continuing alertness remained necessary; but the crisis had also indicated reserves of profes-sional and public sentiment from which considerable comfort could be drawn. And in the early autumn there was further room for reassurance. A bare four months after the mutiny in Duncan's squadron ended, he won a victory to set alongside Jervis's in the year that witnessed Spithead and the Nore.

1. See pp. 20–1 above.
2. P. 31 above.

CHAPTER II

Point of Crisis: Politics and Peace Talks

I

The cascade of bad news from February to June was highly damaging to Pitt's reputation. It brought him in fact to the lowest point of his career so far. Entering the war from a plateau of acclaim almost unmarked by depressions, he had ridden the first long phase of growing disappointments pretty well. A rising frustration at the lack of success in Europe in 1794 was offset by the increased revulsion from events in France, increased fear of subversion at home, and a level of prosperity which was broadly sustained. The next year saw the first real pressure, as bad harvests and inflation took their toll and unrest spread, this time to alarming proportions. The war itself too went badly, with the expulsion of the British army from the Continent followed by more setbacks in the West Indies, no clear naval success, and the tragic fiasco of the landing in the Vendée. The Minister's popularity slumped within the middling as well as the lower orders, and there were mutterings in Parliament across the spectrum of his Coalition. But the very fears of serious trouble served as a form of support, and with no clear focus of political challenge Pitt maintained his position in 1796: baffled in strategy, increasingly worried by unaccustomed financial strains, snubbed by the French in an attempt at peace talks, suffering spasmodic bouts of ill health. The magic of success had gone. But none of his colleagues rebelled, and there was no rival in sight beyond them with enough Parliamentary, or public, strength.[1]

For amid the reversals and unease Pitt's ascendancy was still real. In part this was due to one simple fact: the historic split in the earlier Opposition. When Fox denounced the Government's steps against unrest at the end of 1792, and the war thereafter, he handed his opponent a key to continued political fortune which turned the lock when the main Whig body joined the Ministry in 1794.[2] More than that, Ministers could thank him for potent aid when things went wrong. For it was the fear of his

---

1. See II, Chs. VIII–XII, XIV–XV. There were of course powerful constraints on the importance of either of the last two factors, as his own appointment to office had shown (I, Ch. VI).
2. II, Chs. VII section II, X section II.

coming into office that then helped guarantee their majorities, reinforcing the normal inducements and conventions which kept Administrations in being. By the same token, he had finally confirmed the King's suspicion and dislike. If there had ever been a time when, as Pitt was reported to have said in the summer of 1792, the disapproval of Fox was 'obliterated . . . from the *Royal memory*',[1] that time had been obliterated, seemingly beyond recall. As head of the Ministry, Pitt thus benefited from his former rival's chosen course. He had still to preserve himself at the head of such a Ministry.

There were two possible, interrelated, sources of danger. The King might himself try to find a replacement. He and Pitt had always had a guarded working relationship: neither had warmed to the other, though Pitt felt a greater sympathy after George III's illness in 1788. By and large however they had established a highly effective co-operation, in which the Minister achieved his success largely outside the areas of the royal prerogative while the King gained popularity from the Ministry and supplied his share of Parliamentary support. As was usually the case, endemic in varying degrees in the constitutional arrangement, neither party was prepared to trust the other too far; as happened with most First Lords of the Treasury dealing with a shrewd and watchful monarch, there had been disagreements over appointments and, open or muted, sometimes on policy. But these had not been serious enough to jeopardise a collaboration in which, generally speaking, each respected the other's role.[2] Sovereign and Minister indeed had become broadly linked in the public mind; and George III, so long as what he saw as his essential position was concerned, was not the man lightly to withdraw his countenance when the sun went in. He allowed for Pitt's wartime burdens, and had been giving him resolute backing. At the same time he was not impressed always by the Government's handling of strategy, he had been sharply upset by its treatment of his favourite son's command in Flanders, and more recently, when Pitt twice embarked on approaches to France for peace talks, had come seriously to doubt if the Minister shared his own brand of resolve.[3] Nor, while he knew his responsibilities, was he moved beyond that. Pitt was not particularly favoured at Court: he was too formidable and awkward, and a tendency, held earlier within firmer limits, to bypass forms and leave the monarch on the sidelines,[4] did not diminish as the years passed and the volume of business grew. The King would follow his duty, as he conceived it, by his throne and country. He dearly wished to have a Minister capable of meeting the needs of hard times. He would not welcome politicians associated too closely with his eldest son, and certainly would try to avoid anything beneficial to Fox. All

1. Op. cit., 179n1.
2. Cf. I, 635–43.
3. See II, 293, 318, 364, 374–5, 601, 604–7, 626, 636, 647n1.
4. Cf. op. cit., 31–2, 535.

these considerations supported an effective incumbent. But George III, experienced and lonely, had long been wary of personal attachments – one seasoned observer noted his 'total disregard of his public servants'[1] – and by these same tokens he would not necessarily be tied to any given man.

He was not likely to move, however, unless he thought the Minister a real liability: one who was forfeiting too much confidence within the Cabinet and the Commons. Even if he were to clash with Pitt over policy – above all on the question of peace talks – his position would be weak without co-operation from inside the Ministry; and early in 1797 there was no real sign that this would be found. For Pitt remained in charge, as he had long been, at the head of affairs. His control might be reduced over events, but not seriously over his colleagues: the position there had not changed in the past few years.[2] Since 1794 in fact, whatever some on the fringes might think, he had dominated a Coalition in which almost half the Cabinet came from his opponents, much as he had dominated the reconstructed Ministry of the preceding period. This is not at all to say that he overrode them throughout: no Government is likely to be contented or successful for long on that basis. It is rather to argue that, over a spell in which success was mixed increasingly with failure, he carried his associates with him to a remarkable extent.

Again, this is not to say that Ministers were now happy with the way things were going. Two members of the Cabinet indeed were distinctly aggrieved. Spencer, always prone to agitation 'when anything falls ill in his department', was already upset by defeats at the hand of Dundas over the West Indies and a recent disagreement over the Mediterranean. He now found himself at odds again, more disturbed than Dundas over possible invasion, and, forced publicly on the defensive by Bantry Bay and Fishguard, felt he lacked influence with Pitt and adequate support.[3] Windham, at the War Office, was under growing strain from the Ministry's refusal to succour the French royalists, let alone to place them, as he wished, at the centre of affairs. He had been the most openly unhappy at the decision to hold peace talks, and seemed now to be coming close to despair. Early in the year he was said to be 'running over with spleen against Pitt and Dundas', and by May to be 'violent' against

1. Sir James Bland Burges's notes for character sketches (Burges Mss, Box 74, Bodleian Library). He was not always an unprejudiced witness (cf. I 369, II 415n4); but he knew his political world and saw a good deal of the royal family, finally being given a sinecure place in the Household.

2. Cf. II, 461.

3. For the earlier disagreements see op. cit., 613, 642. His dissatisfaction, appearing clearly from his correspondence in B.L. Add. Ms temp. Althorp G30–1, was noted by the Opposition, and dismissed by the Ministerial, press in January and February. Sylvester Douglas (see p. 7, n1 above) remarked on his 'nervousness' when his department was in trouble (*Diary of . . . Glenbervie* (hereafter *Glenbervie*), I, 124, for 2 February 1797), a trait noted also (if by implication) by Bridport during the Spithead mutiny (to Pitt, 11 May 1797; Dacres Adams Mss, formerly P.R.O. 30/58/2); and cf. p. 22 above.

them.[1] But he was unique in the extent of his gloom, he had not shown weight in Cabinet, and his ideas on policy were not widely shared. The Secretaries of State themselves, 'normally the linchpins of an Administration',[2] remained broadly agreed in the first half of the year on a strategic and diplomatic policy which two of the three concerted with Pitt. The third, Portland at the Home Office, marginal to the conduct of war and deriving consideration from his leadership of the Old Whigs, worked unobtrusively but steadily for the unity of a Coalition which they acknowledged, with some reluctance, was essential to themselves. Of the more important pair, Dundas was loyal, both by need and inclination. He was identified with Pitt in running the war, had no solid following outside Scotland, and in any case, while holding his views and expressing them freely and at times forcefully, greatly admired Pitt's talents, had come to be genuinely fond of him, and did not really look on himself as a possible successor. Grenville's position was more independent. By family and connexions he was a credible First Lord of the Treasury, could more easily muster political strength – he had indeed his links with the Portland Whigs[3] – and both personally and in business maintained a certain reserve. He looked on himself as a cut above Dundas, and the two men had their disagreements. But he was firmly seized of the need for the triumvirate to work closely together, and while not simply a follower, and certainly no flatterer, was not disposed to supplant his cousin.[4] Pitt had had a series of reverses to report. The dangers now seemed greater; the future dark. To his colleagues, none of this removed their sense of his pre-eminence.

The acceptance was due not least to habit, and felt perhaps most strongly by his early associates: Spencer and Windham from the old Opposition were more recent recruits. But it pervaded the Ministry as a whole, and it was well entrenched. After all, Pitt had now been in Downing Street uninterruptedly for some thirteen years, a period unequalled, if approached by Pelham and North, since the days of Walpole. Allowing for the limits set by a more dispersed system of government, tenure of that length in any age is bound to leave a mark.[5] And in Pitt's case he had long stamped his style unmistakably on his office. For of

1. See II, 592n3, 600, 649 for the peace talks; Windham to Addington, 6 February 1797 (B.L. Add. Ms 37876) for his despair – and cf. p. 30 above for May; Douglas's diary of 10 January for his spleen (*Glenbervie*, I, 121), and Sir Gilbert to Lady Elliot, 23 May 1797, for his violence (*The Life and Letters of Sir Gilbert Elliot, First Earl of Minto, from 1751 to 1806*, ed. by his Great Niece the Countess of Minto, II (1874), 396).
  Liverpool too probably had his misgivings, like his royal master, but confined himself more strictly to his departmental concerns.
  2. I, 184.
  3. To look no farther, his brother Thomas, earlier employed on a mission to Vienna, was of Portland's connexion (see II, 32n5, 189n2, 343).
  4. Nor for that matter was George III particularly well disposed towards him.
  5. North, it should be remembered, became ineffectual only in his last few years. For the system and habits of government see I, Ch. VII, sections III, IV.

course it was the quality he had brought to his tenure that gave the latter
its impact. Whatever constraints might emerge in practice, he looked and
was a masterful First Minister. He was capable, when necessary, of speaking to colleagues 'in as full tone as ever used by Lord Chatham';[1] and such
occasions reinforced the impression of an ability which justified his claim.
Bagehot once observed that there were two kinds of statesmen produced
by 'representative government': the 'dictators' who were called in circumstances of danger 'to save the State', and the 'great [as sharply distinguished from 'ordinary'] administrators', those who were 'concerned
with the far-seeing regulation of future conduct, as well as with the limited
management of the present.' Pitt, he concluded, 'had in the most complete perfection the faculties of a great administrator, and . . . added to it
the commanding temperament, though not the creative intellect, of a
great dictator.'[2] There is a Victorian sweep to this summing-up. But in its
very contrasts it points to elements that spanned the divide in the
Minister's career.[3] For the commanding temperament had always laid its
impress on the talents of the 'great administrator', which themselves continued to be applied while he faced an unfamiliar scene. Pitt's significant
failure in the early war years, one may argue, lay in his inability to marry
an appreciation of resources, in training and readiness as well as numbers,
to a strategy which would take them into proper account. It was here, in
this vital area, that his limitations were exposed, within the demands of an
Alliance whose partners' incompatibilities made success in any case
unlikely against the enemy's recuperative powers. He had not understood
the components of military affairs: the uncertainties of intelligence, the
many constraints on planning. And this being so, the optimism which had
always, often beneficially, sustained him, compounded all too often the
inherent defects. His strengths persisted elsewhere: in maintaining a
national capacity and a constant diplomatic effort in which the strategy
was enmeshed. The familiar talents were deployed across the whole field
of government; and while they could by no means always be effective, he
focused its work on himself with powers still largely unimpaired. There
was the same rapid grasp of varied factors over a range of issues, the same
thrust and balance in reaching an answer, the same skill in exposition. He
could be slow – it was part of his optimism – to admit that tried methods
were proving ineffective. But he had not lost the will to reshape or inno-
vate when convinced of the need: in schemes of recruitment, the supply of
foodstuffs, provision of credit, provision for the poor.[4] Fertile in expedients
and by now deeply versed in business – he knew the pitfalls, and was adept
at avoiding them – his response was not always adequate, but he was
seldom inept. The level – perhaps as telling, the potential – of performance

1. *Diary of William Windham*, 386.
2. *Biographical Studies*, ed. Richard Holt Hutton (1889), 118–20. The piece was written in 1861, as a review of Stanhope's *Life*.
3. Others are outlined in II, ix x.
4. See op. cit., 486–7 and 497, 464–5, 386–7, 471–5.

remained high, where interest and knowledge were really engaged: the failures and omissions occurred more often where they were not, or attention was spasmodic. These powers, essentially of the type appreciated in daily action, were illuminated for those who worked with him by a poise of mind, a lack of prejudice, a resilience and high dedication which could sometimes captivate and could not but impress. The combination brought others to accept his own conception of his role – a central element of his being, the prop and object of his pride. And that in turn, while it brought – or reintroduced – a singular flavour to his office, made him, as it had made his father while in office, the more formidable.

He also remained a dominating politician in this setting of acknowledged primacy, and now of a Coalition whose Parliamentary advantage outweighed any weakening effect on the conduct of government.[1] Much of his strength indeed continued to derive from his handling of the Commons. His attitude to his role, which was real enough to himself, had a reality also for them. The effect was not limited to any one quarter: associates and supporters could encounter its less comfortable aspects as readily as opponents – 'that high indignant stare which sometimes marked his countenance'.[2] The ascendancy was expressed by – owed its force to – debating powers which maintained an authority, in conditions of frequent pressure, that none of his colleagues was likely to match. Forced now more often onto the defensive, the style was the same. He rang the changes as he always had done: elevated, caustic, conciliatory, crushing as the case might be.[3] Wartime conditions moreover heightened one advantage to set against their pressures: a knowledge of confidential information which Opposition could not fully share. He was assisted, as he would soon be increasingly, by some competent performers: Dundas remained capable, Windham on his day was good, and there were some younger men of promise – Hawkesbury, Perceval, Canning – who however did not often speak as yet. But if the reports are to be believed, he himself was on his legs much more, as he had been from the start, than any other Government spokesman.[4]

---

1. The disadvantages of the junction were probably greatest in point of fact at the start; and then they were balanced by the introduction of desirable talent into the important range of posts beyond the Cabinet (see II, 419). For a sharply adverse impression of the arrangement's effect on government see op. cit., 429, 536.

2. *Life of Wilberforce*, II, 327. The victim indeed on the occasion cited was the Lord Chancellor of Ireland, Lord Clare, under Pitt's visiting gaze in a Lords' debate.

3. Cf. I, 53–6, 611–12. A well known target of his sarcasm was the militia, of which he never had a high opinion. In one wartime debate which led a Member to demand the retention of the law that its troops should not be allowed to leave the kingdom (cf. II, 488), the Minister 'immediately arose, and with sarcastic smile said, "Except in case of invasion"' (*Records of My Life by the late John Taylor, Esquire . . .*, I (1832), 183).

4. The position in fact remained much as it had been in the Parliament of 1790–6, when nineteen 'leading speakers' were responsible for over 5,100 out of more than 9,000 recorded contributions to debate, and of those nineteen three (Pitt, Dundas and Windham) were Cabinet Ministers and Pitt spoke the most (*H of P*, I, 344). For the quality of the reports see I, 53–4.

He still appeared indispensable: one could hardly imagine another in his seat. It was indeed noted at this time, when his fortunes were at a low ebb and some in Opposition disposed to underrate him, that Fox continued to speak of him 'always' 'as a great man'.[1] Supporting and supported by his standing within the Ministry, his Parliamentary position indeed remained unique.

Nevertheless it was from the Commons that threats came in the spring and early summer of 1797. Those that had embarrassed Pitt most in the past four years had been weathered without too much trouble: Wilberforce's call for peace talks at the end of 1794, discontent over the Prince of Wales's finances the next year, were subdued by firmness and conciliation respectively, and the majorities by and large had held very well throughout. Results in the division lobbies of course were not necessarily the whole story in a body where feelings could also be shown by other means. Deliberate absenteeism, the tone of speeches as distinct from the votes, above all reactions from independents and the county Members – not coterminous types, but together deemed the most respectable and representative: such signs were important to a Ministry which might not fall to numerical attack, but could be weakened from within by ignoring movements of sentiment. It was not least in such ways that the Commons, unrepresentative by franchise, could reflect or at least refract opinions 'out of doors'.[2] And both were giving cause for disquiet in the first half of this dangerous year.

The speed of the fluctuations could be disconcerting. At the start of 1797 one Opposition newspaper lamented 'the indifference of the present times';[3] but the gathering disillusionment with the war, earlier unfocused, found specific targets in the next few months. Pitt's prestige in the country rested to an unusual extent on trust in his competence. If he could not stop the French from landing, or a run on the Bank of England, or mutinies in the fleets, was he still capable of success? It was one thing for him to be under fire from old opponents and sceptics; but the doubts were spreading now into more unaccustomed quarters. 'Monied men', perhaps particularly in the Midlands, were showing broader signs of discontent. Rural societies, particularly near the coasts, were becoming divided over the Ministry's efforts. In London, among respectable men 'well disposed to Government, no democrat[s]', there was talk of his mismanagement and the case for his going.[4] In this atmosphere of growing unease the old

1. The observation came in March from Richard Payne Knight, the Foxite MP and connoisseur (*The Diary of Joseph Farington*, ed. Kenneth Garlick and Angus Macintyre, III (1979), 794); the phrasing may be Farington's.
2. An extended consideration of this whole subject has been attempted in I, Ch. II and 144–6.
3. *The Morning Chronicle*, 12 January 1797.
4. The quotation comes from *The Diary of Farington*, III, 805; see also 780, 833, 844.

petitioning spirit revived, as it tended to do in dispiriting times, most recently in 1795.[1] London provided the first test. In the last week of March the City's Common Council – the Common Hall of the Livery – voted to address the King for peace and a change of Ministers. The move led to a struggle with the Corporation – the Lord Mayor, aldermen and sheriffs – which opposed the petition with procedural tactics and ended by dissolving a Common Hall meeting. Meanwhile the King declined to receive an address from the Livery in form on the throne, since he did so only when one was presented by or with the Corporation. The affair intensified an interest already stirring throughout the country. Westminster and Southwark sprang into life at the beginning of April, and by the last week in the month twenty-six similar addresses (some from Scotland and Ireland) were said to have been voted.[2] More followed in May, as the naval mutinies dragged on. A good many of course stemmed from likely sources: from towns or regions where support for Pitt's Ministry was usually contested or weak. Some efforts moreover had been defeated outright, and there were counter-addresses, some in cases where a majority had been slender or disputed. The numbers in all seem not to have approached those in 1795, though this perhaps was not surprising since the latter had called for relief of distress as well as, often but more controversially, for peace.[3] And the potential impact was sometimes weakened in advance by divisions of object, particularly when campaigners for Parliamentary reform, themselves reviving in these circumstances, fought to impose that nostrum on the more widely felt aims. Nevertheless the wave of addresses could certainly not be dismissed, if only because it included ten at least from the English counties – always the weightiest source, and totalling more on this occasion than in 1795.[4] The movement's limitations were significant, as such movements' often were. It also showed a genuinely widespread feeling that all was far from well.

That feeling supported and was partly supported by signs of restiveness in Parliament. Opposition had been listless in the last quarter of 1796. It

---

1. Showing indeed by its reappearance that it had not been killed by the legislation of that year; cf. Pitt's claim in then moving the Seditious Meetings bill (II, 456).

2. *The Morning Chronicle*, 26 April 1797. Newspapers, particularly the Opposition press, followed these events from the last ten days of March to the first half of June.

3. See II, 452n4, 459, 475.

4. Cf. op. cit., 459. One was even from Hampshire, normally considered a 'citadel of Ministers' (*The Morning Chronicle*, 21 April 1797).

It is hard to give precise numbers. Newspapers seem to have stopped listing totals after April, and *The Annual Register* for the year, which was distinctly anti-Ministerial, ends its list, for 'the spring', at 24 plus '&c. &c.' (Occurrences, 69–70). J.E. Cookson, *The Friends of Peace . . ., 1793–1815* (1982), 161, gives twelve (unnamed) counties in all. His account is instructive on the mixed fortunes of the efforts.

The movement, not surprisingly, aroused suggestions to Ministers for organising efforts in their support. Equally unsurprisingly, John Reeves emerged to suggest a repetition of 1792. He gained some sympathy from Dundas, but not from Pitt (Dundas to Pitt, nd, enclosing Reeves's letter of 11 April 1797, P.R.O. 30/8/157; Reeves to Pitt, 27 December 1797, P.R.O. 30/8/170). Cf. II, 229–33, 458.

had seldom mustered more than 50 votes in a major debate – only 37 when Fox brought a motion of censure on 30 December on the conduct of the war.[1] The succeeding months however, at least into April, saw a marked change. In March one of Pitt's friends noted 'slack attendancies' and 'support reluctant' on the Ministry's back benches;[2] and the uneasiness, though held in check by the very threat of damage, did not disappear as the session wore on. Personal attacks on Pitt, it is true, were pronounced failures. On 10 May the Foxite Samuel Whitbread brought a motion of censure on him for the delay in the seamen's grant,[3] and nine days later the radical Alderman Combe moved for the dismissal of Ministers. Neither attracted a full vote from the combined elements of Opposition – 63 in the first case, 59 in the second – while the Ministry maintained figures, not untypical, of 237 and 242 respectively. But in the latter instance there were special circumstances: the motion came, as an offshoot of the public petitions and particularly the struggle in the City of London, from a Member of no standing outside the City, unsupported directly by the Opposition leaders. The attack moreover raised no significant hopes or fears.[4] And in point of fact the debating thrust from Opposition, with one great exception, was again on the wane in May. Over the previous six weeks it had succeeded in bringing its regular strength, with some of the independents, to an unusual point. On 13 March the minority vote on Harrison's motion on sinecures[5] was 77, on the 23rd it was 84 on a motion by Fox on the state of Ireland, on the 24th 88 on an amendment by him to the Bank Restriction bill, on 4 April 87 on Sheridan's motion against a loan to Austria. On 10 April a motion calling for peace, brought by the young and unimportant member Augustus Pollen, secured a minority vote of 85. Of course support remained as always subject to the matter in hand: while Fox gained 88 votes on 24 March for one alteration to the Bank bill, he could attract only 45, on 5 April, for another. Such figures, however, contrasted strongly with the run in the previous year, and they were indeed highly respectable.[6] But from

1. The vote rose to 58 in a debate on the Budget, and once, exceptionally, to 81 on Fox's motion of censure on Ministers for advancing money to Austria without the consent of Parliament (both in December). This last elicited a Ministerial vote of 285 (see *P.R., 3rd ser.*, I, *passim*).

2. Earl Bathurst to Earl Camden, 29 March [endorsed 1797], (Camden Ms 226/4, Kent AO).

3. P. 33 above. The motion was amended during the debate, with Fox's concurrence, to censure on Ministers.

4. Cf. the Tory historian John Adolphus, in his *The History of England from the Accession to the Decease of King George III* (1843), 593–4: 'none of the great leaders appeared on either side, and the debate was confined to London aldermen and country gentlemen'. Pitt himself remarked that the motion 'was resisted by many persons who seldom take part' (to George III, 19 May 1797; *L.C.G. III*, II, no. 1546).

5. P. 16 above.

6. For the composition and attendance of Opposition on different occasions see *H of P*, I, 151–3; for division figures, *P.R., 3rd ser.*, II, *passim*. As throughout, they exclude the tellers.

late in April they generally fell away. On the 26th a motion by Fox on the Austrian loan gathered 45 votes in a thin House, on 1 May his motion on a Vote of Credit for Austria and Ireland gained 58, there were 66 on 16 May for a motion by Grey on the Bank's earlier advances to Government, and 52 on the 19th on a motion by Fox to repeal the Treason and Sedition Acts of 1795. Most of these causes were as important as those raised in the preceding weeks. It was against such a background that Whitbread's and Combe's motions failed.

On the face of it, then, the Ministry was not going to be undermined. Against Opposition's challenges in a rising crisis it held its votes, whatever the reluctance, fairly steadily throughout, and particularly on most of the more significant debates. They numbered 169 on Harrison's motion of 13 March; but 220 on the 23rd, 218 on the 24th, 266 on 4 April, 291 (the highest) on Pollen's motion for peace on 10 April, 193 on 1 May, 237 on the 10th, 206 on the 16th, 242 and 260 on the 19th.[1] This was in fact the trend that led Fox in May to take his famous decision – suggested perhaps by others – that opposition was futile, and that he would not attend the House in the next session. But it was announced, paradoxically, in a debate whose result gave the Government a sudden shock. On 26 May – the day on which Ministers held their long meeting on the Nore mutiny, and the artillery rioted at Woolwich[2] – Charles Grey brought a motion for Parliamentary reform. Considering that his last attempt, in May 1793, had been lost by 282 to 41, one might have expected that at this time of greater danger, and when the new plan was distinctly more far-reaching, such a proposal would have been equally convincingly crushed. Government duly mustered 256 votes. But the minority vote was 91, the largest so far in the year.[3] The Ministry was surprised and perturbed: George Rose at the Treasury – by definition the expert – confessed that the figure was much higher than expected, and to his 'utter Astonishment' it included 'about a Dozen of our Friends'.[4] The result was doubtless affected by some particular factors. Fox made a special effort to rally his forces, based precisely on the prospect of his future withdrawal.[5] He also made one of his greatest speeches, which held the Commons enthralled. Government for its part seems to have made no unusual arrangements to

1. Op. cit., *passim.*

2. Pp. 27, 31, above.

3. *P.R., 3rd ser.*, II, 656. For 1793 see II, 387–8. The motion now included proposals for household franchise and to remodel the borough representation through new urban constituencies.

4. To Thomas Pelham [Secretary to the Lord Lieutenant of Ireland], 27 May 1797 (B.L. Add. Ms 33104). Cf. George III's comments of sd to Pitt, in J. Holland Rose, *Pitt and Napoleon. Essays and Letters* (1912), 241.

5. Though he and others were said, in one anonymous report, to be lukewarm in advance (22 May; *The Correspondence of George, Prince of Wales 1770–1812*, III, ed. A. Aspinall (1965), no. 1264). His nephew made the same point later, not mentioning Fox himself (Lord Holland to Lord John Russell, 13 August 1810; *The Early Correspondence of Lord John Russell*, ed. Rollo Russell, I (1913), 131).

preserve its ranks, and Pitt's own speech was said to have been 'flat'.[1] But the open loss of the normal supporters on such an issue was worrying,[2] and all the more since it came when there was already a move on the back benches to topple the Ministry.

This was not in fact the first such attempt, though it was the best organised. It emerged, strictly speaking, on the heels of a rather different kind of effort. Early in March, following the Bank Suspension, a number of MPs thought of forming a 'Third Party' or 'Armed Neutrality' – a not unfamiliar proclamation of the old ideal of independence which was apt to surface at moments of extreme Parliamentary conflict or national misfortune.[3] Centred on the zealous figure of Sir John Sinclair, who had been involved in both of the last two such groupings, and was now dissatisfied with Pitt on personal as well as public grounds,[4] it included at least nineteen and more likely twenty-two or twenty-three Members, and some of those figured in the Treasury's lists of the 'well disposed'.[5] The attempt came to nothing, as such attempts did when confined to the more independent backbenchers; and in any case it was designed to produce a pressure group rather than a new Administration. But there were also stirrings towards that second goal. Lansdowne, as so often, was said to be involved; Thurlow was likewise the subject of rumour; Leeds, late in the day, was named as willing to 'lend his feeble aid'. It was natural to speculate on former Ministers who had parted or been parted from Pitt, though there may not have been much to the reports at least on the last two.[6] More positive manoeuvres however were in the wings.[7] Lansdowne in fact, probably with others, approached another discontented grandee, the Duke of Northumberland – a kite that soon showed signs of falling to the ground. And in the first half of May a rather more credible scheme emerged.

For the candidate found in this instance was the Earl of Moira; and Moira was a more substantial choice. A man of talents – as Marquess of Hastings he was the renowed Governor General of India two decades later – his relations with Pitt had been ambivalent over the past few years. As a military commander he had been sometimes in close touch with the

1. Canning's description, in his diary for 27 May 1797 (Canning Ms 29d).

2. I put it like this because there had earlier been some desertions following the Bank stoppage (see *H of P*, I, 151).

3. Cf. I, 31; op. cit., 655 for the most recent instance of an Armed Neutrality, in 1788; II, 402–3 for the Third Party of 1793, which however was a more important and by no means strictly analogous connexion.

4. See II, 638n4 and cf. I, 615, 660 n3. *The Times* (11 and 13 March 1797), which reported the emergence of the group, was well informed of his resentment of Pitt's neglect.

5. *L.C.G. III*, II, xxiii, n1; *H of P*, I, 152–3. Names were given by the MP Charles Abbot, not himself involved, in his diary for 9 March (P.R.O. 30/9/32).

6. *The Times*, 11 March, *The Morning Post*, 30 March, *The True Briton*, 31 March 1797. See I, 87–9; II, 174–6; I, 570, II, 26 for the past history in each case.

7. The following account rests on Arthur Aspinall's in *L.C.G. III*, II, xxv–xxix and *The Correspondence of George, Prince of Wales 1770–1812*, III, 306–8, in which volumes the main correspondence is published.

Minister, with mixed results;[1] as a politician – in the Irish Commons until he succeeded to a British title in the early eighties, and thereafter active intermittently in the House of Lords – his affinities since the later eighties were Whiggish, based mainly on friendship with the Prince of Wales. He had recently made a controversial speech in the Lords criticising the severity of measures in Ireland. In point of fact he seemed to fill the bill quite well: intelligent and forceful, distinct from Fox but on cool terms with the Ministry, associated with the Prince of Wales but also with the Duke of York.[2] By mid-May he had held conversations with 'a formidable body' of MPs: 'not Sir J. Sinclair's set, but an association of much greater weight', though its existence was not yet suspected.

> They are violent against Pitt, though they vote with him, but they will not bear the Opposition as a party. Their object is to make some effort to save the country from the evident ruin into which it is most rapidly running.[3]

Allowing for Moira's typically cogent style, there seemed enough here to test matters farther, and over the next fortnight there was much movement among those concerned. He himself had preliminary thoughts of a necessary alliance, on strict terms, with Fox; but those were soon dropped, and the Prince of Wales, who had lately been favouring Opposition more openly, was likewise held politely at arm's length. Fox himself in fact aided the plans when he got wind of them; on 24 May he indeed went so far as to seek an audience of the King, and declared his willingness to stand aside in any change. By the 29th the indefatigable Sinclair could claim 'great progress in the House', and Moira reckoned the next day that 'the neutrals' had 'gained ground prodigiously'.[4] His ideas by then were defined: talks for an immediate peace, a 'just and lenient system' in Ireland, 'heavy contributions' to restore the finances, and appointments covering but confined to those 'immediately connected with Ministerial function'. On 2 June he in turn wrote to the King, in more general terms, enclosing a letter and an Address to the Throne from five leaders of the group.[5]

The effort was foredoomed. Northumberland, and indeed Moira at first, had predicted that no arrangement could stand if both Pitt and Fox were against it. But while Fox appeared sympathetic, he did not commit

1. II, 322–3, 370, 573–6.
2. For the latter see op. cit., 323.
3. Moira to Northumberland, suggesting co-operation, 15 May (*L.C.G. III*, II, xxv). Sinclair however was not long kept out.
4. Some even supporting Grey's motion for Parliamentary reform. Fox sought an audience of George III in his capacity as a Privy Councillor.
5. *L.C.G. III*, II, no. 1565. Sinclair was one of the signatories. Moira's ideas, and his retrospective account of events, are given in a memorandum (for Colonel McMahon, an intimate of the Prince's) of 15 June (*Correspondence of Prince of Wales*, III, no. 1270).

himself; and Ministers for their part were united against a challenge.[1] Its Parliamentary fate therefore must be reckoned doubtful. But before it could be seriously mounted the King must take notice of Moira's letter, and the King was not prepared at this point to encourage a change of this kind. Pitt might have lost much goodwill in the Commons; but that was not enough to dispose George III towards risking confusion, which more-over – given Moira's position – might benefit his heir. By the middle of June, despite fresh troubles for the Cabinet by then, the affair was 'extinct',[2] and the Minister was still in the saddle as the long Parliamentary recess approached.

These months of political unease are instructive on several counts. They showed the most overt signs of discontent from the Commons in the course of Pitt's first Administration. The threat proved notably ineffectual as an attempt to displace him: the Cabinet held together, the King was unresponsive, the dissatisfied Members – as Moira noted[3] – refrained from anything like collective rebellion in the lobbies. Most of them indeed stayed discreetly out of sight, while they gauged the strength of an assault that in turn awaited a recognised source of power.

Nonetheless the signs of alientation, in Parliament and beyond, made their impact. If they did not remove the Minister they affected his policy – in fact, paradoxically, ended by strengthening his hand. The indications of trouble, with rumours of his dismissal, worried Pitt's friends at least at times,[4] and the former were taken seriously by Pitt himself. The public petitions called for a change as a necessary means of reaching a peace. Early in April, when he was under urgent pressure from fresh events in the war, he cited 'the gradual and increasing difficulties of finance . . . as well as the effect of the impressions which they may produce in Parliament and with the public', as 'long an object of his anxious attention' in weigh-ing the merits of fresh talks.[5] In the same vein he is said to have remarked later that the petitioning movement had influenced his course.[6] On

---

1. Whether, as it seemed in most cases, by a resolve to fight 'to stay in' (Portland's phrase) or, if a change came, by 'a refusal' to co-operate (Dundas, as reported); see *L.C.G. III*, II, xxviii. These sentiments may be compared interestingly with Moira's own views in his memorandum of p. 44, n5 above.

2. Moira's word. The Cabinet's difficulties in June are followed in section IV below.

3. P. 44 above.

4. For some of the rumours see *The Morning Post* of 30 March, *The Morning Chronicle* and *The True Briton* of 31 March 1797.

5. To George III, 9 April 1797 (Stanhope, III, Appendix, iv–v).

6. The source here is Fox, writing on 28 April 1801. 'The petitions in 1797 produced, as Mr. Pitt says (and I suspect he says truly) the [subsequent] negotiation' (*Correspondence of the late Gilbert Wakefield . . . with the late Right Honourable Charles James Fox, . . . 1796–1801* (1813), 214).

Fox may have been referring to a Parliamentary speech, perhaps in 1801 itself; but if so I have not found the statement.

27 May, after several weeks of thought, he announced himself 'convinced
at length' of the need to try again.[1] Circumstances on the Continent had
by then deteriorated farther; things seemed in that week '*in extremis*' at
home. It may also be noted that Pitt spoke on the morrow of the debate on
Parliamentary reform.[2] Foreign and domestic developments were pointing him in the same direction. It was one in which, impelled by both, he
was increasingly prepared to advance.

II

The extent of his readiness is in fact suggested by an episode that had
probably occurred by then: almost certainly in the first half of the year,
and arguably in the first quarter. At some point seemingly in that period
Pitt considered resigning, and took steps to prepare for a successor. He did
so on the ground that the French might make peace more easily if he was
not in office, and his intention, if held briefly, appears to have been real.
Evidence for the episode itself looks indisputable; evidence for period, if
more open, persuasive. The earliest statement to be published came in
1847, in Pellew's *Life* of Addington. Referring to January–February 1797,
he remarked

> . . . probably this was the period to which Lord Sidmouth alluded in the
> following statement, which many years afterwards he made to the
> author: – 'Pitt told me, as early as 1797, that I must make up my mind to
> take the government.'[3]

An account from Pitt's quarter, written earlier by Bishop Tomline
(Pretyman) in his *Life*, but in the final part not then published, was printed
by Lord Rosebery in 1903.[4]

> . . . it was imagined, though probably without foundation, that the
> French Government would be more disposed to make peace with a new
> Minister than with Mr. Pitt, and Mr. Pitt, therefore, entertained some
> idea of resigning. He submitted these circumstances to the King, and

1. By Wilberforce in his diary, after seeing Pitt that evening (*Life of Wilberforce*, II, 220).
He had been pressing the Minister without marked success during the month.
2. Pp. 31, 42, above, 50–1 below.
3. The Hon. George Pellew, *The Life and Correspondence of the Right Honble Henry Addington,
First Viscount Sidmouth*, I (1847), 183. Addington was given the peerage in 1805.
4. 'Bishop Tomline's Estimate of Pitt together with Chapter XXVII from the
Unpublished Fourth Volume of the Life' (*The Monthly Review*, August 1903). This was
reprinted as a separate publication in the same year. Pretyman assumed the name Tomline
(see I, 13) in 1803.
    In what are probably his most complete drafts, Pretyman wrote in the last sentence that
'this was known [to Addington] & scarcely to any other person' (B.L. Add. Ms 45107(H),
f. 14; loc. cit., 45108(F), f. 17).

had several conferences with His Majesty upon the subject. After much deliberation the plan was abandoned on the ground that a new, strong administration, consisting of persons of true constitutional principles, could not then be formed, and Mr. Pitt remained in office; but the consideration of this business had gone so far that it was settled, in case of Mr. Pitt's resignation that he should be succeeded by Mr. Addington, Speaker of the House of Commons, and this was known at the time to Mr. Addington, and to very few other persons.

The Bishop could not recall, over twenty years later, precisely when the idea was mooted: 'I believe', he noted in the margin of a draft, 'it was in 1797'.[1] But in point of fact he himself had not heard the details at first hand. The primary source was his wife, who was told at the time by Pitt's great friend and brother-in-law Edward Eliot.[2] She passed on the news to her husband at once, and wrote a full account in November 1801.[3]

> In 1796 and 1797 things were critical *for the Country*, Bank of England, naval mutiny, &c., and Mr Pitt, *ever ready to sacrifice himself for what he thought the good of his Country*, had serious thoughts of *resigning his situation* hoping the French would make peace with another Minister rather than with him – We were at Buckden[4] while this idea & consequent plan was upon the Tapis. But we heard constantly from Mr. Eliot . . . *Details* could not mentioned in letters, and *this* plan was of a nature too delicate to be trusted to the Post. We knew nothing of it therefore till we went to Town which happened to be 2 days after it was given up – Mr Eliot came to the Deanery[5] an hour after our arrival – The Bishop was engaged with a person upon business and Mr Eliot afraid of not being in time for the House of Commons told me the whole surprising Story before the Bishop came up – He told me what I have related, of *Mr. Pitt's idea and proposal*, and that he thought he could make *a very tolerible* [*sic*] *Administration without himself & a few others so as to keep Fox and the Jacobins entirely* [?] *out* – Upon my asking eagerly '*who* could be found as *Mr Pitt's Successor*' Mr Eliot answered '*Addington*' –

Mrs Pretyman was astonished – 'Addington! (exclaimed I instantly) . . . *Are you all mad?*' – and, so she claimed later and probably truthfully, said that she distrusted him. But Eliot was unperturbed. 'Oh no,' he answered her 'smilingly',

1. B.L. Add. Ms 45107(H), f. 13v.
2. For whom see I, 17, 111, 582.
3. Notes, October and November 1801 (Stanhope Ms U1590, S5/C41 (Maidstone)). In the ms the words 'and 1797', 'Bank of England, naval mutiny, &c.', '& a few others', and 'Mr. Pitt would have' are inserted. The underlinings are typical.
4. Buckden Palace in Huntingdon, a residence of the Bishop of Lincoln, which Pretyman then was.
5. Of St Paul's. Pretyman was Dean of the Cathedral as well as Bishop of Lincoln (see I, 13).

'Addington would do very well *under the direction of Mr. Pitt, – for a time – It would not do for ever*, but it would do Mr. Pitt good to be out of Office for a little while' . . . 'But [he continued] you may make yourself easy, for the thing is not to be – Everything is now settled and we are to remain as we are – the Storm is over.' 'Does Addington know what was intended?' [Mrs Pretyman asked] 'Yes.' – 'Does the King know? Did it go so far as that?' – 'Yes – He certainly did *not like the Change*, but what could he do the present Ministers thought it necessary?' '*Did Addington readily agree to the new Arrangement?*' '*Certainly, how could he do otherwise at Mr. Pitt's request? He owes* everything to Mr. Pitt and Mr. Pitt would have *directed* had he taken the situation, so that he would not have been under *great* difficulties. Besides, I really do not think so ill of his abilities . . .'

Mrs Pretyman was a forceful woman with strong feelings, but in general she is a credible witness, and the circumstances of her account can hardly have been invented. Were it not for them, one might have attributed the episode to later in 1797, when the peace talks which by then had opened had decisively failed.[1] But Edward Eliot died just before that outcome, in the third week of September, which gives a *terminus ad quem*; and an earlier limit must surely have lain in the middle of June, when the Cabinet, with Pitt very much in charge, agreed finally on direct talks.[2] A more problematical limit might be said to lie early in April, for Pitt then recommended a joint approach to France with Austria, and with considerable force.[3] It could be argued that if he gained his point, that would have been the time for him to suggest his replacement. But conversely, he may have so committed himself because the initial idea had by then been withdrawn. Other considerations reinforce the argument for a date earlier than that. Mrs Pretyman, it is true, mentioned 'Bank of England, naval mutiny &c.', which could thus have covered a period from February to June. But that might have arisen from her recollection of a 'critical' time in general, and one may doubt very much if Pitt would have retired while the mutinies were under way. Nor indeed, it might be thought, would he have gone once the Bank crisis broke; and in that case one is left, as Pellew surmised, with the period of January to late February. Such a date may receive some further support from Mrs Pretyman's reference to '1796' – which she repeated[4] – as well as 1797, suggesting an early period if the episode occurred in the latter year. 1796 itself seems, on the face of it, unlikely: the unsuccessful peace talks of that year ended suddenly as late as 18–19 December.[5] Unless Eliot's news was

1. See section IV below.
2. P. 58 below.
3. Pp. 52–3 below.
4. When stressing slightly later in the Notes that she had expressed her feelings about Addington during the conversation. As stated in p. 47, n3 above, '1797' was added to 1796 in her opening dating.
5. II, 649. And Mrs Pretyman was certainly at Buckden on the 27th, when she wrote to Pretyman in London (Pretyman Ms 435/45; Suffolk RO, Ipswich).

Pitt and the Bank of England, 1797, by James Gillray

Earl Spencer, *by John Singleton Copley*

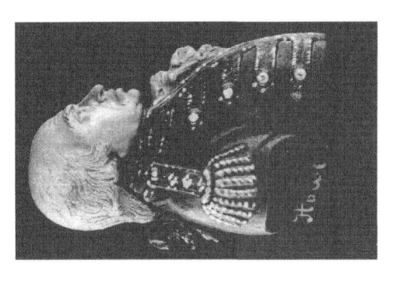

Earl Howe. *Wax Relief*

conveyed some months earlier still, before that approach was prepared in September – which seems out of the question – one might therefore opt, with due caution, for a point in 1797 before late February: a time when the memory of failure in Paris was still keen.

Mrs Pretyman was only the first person to find Pitt's idea 'surprising'. Historians in the nineteenth century were inclined to dismiss Pellew's report as too strange to be true. In this century, since Pretyman's (Tomline's) passage was published, the response has again been one of surprise. Addington had been a successful Speaker since Pitt caused him to be placed in the Chair in 1789. He had been consulted, thanks perhaps to a friendship with Grenville, on matters of policy during the war, and, it would appear, had even been thought of as a Secretary of State towards the end of 1793.[1] But in the event he had not held any office, he was scarcely known as a debater, and neither by experience nor by social position, personality or known attainments, seemed in the least fitted for such a post, and at such a time. 'Are you all mad?' was indeed a natural instant response.

The word 'all' however poses a further question, taken on the one hand with Eliot's comment about the King's position when 'the present Ministers thought it [the step] necessary', and on the other with the Bishop's statement that 'very few other persons', or 'scarcely . . . any other person', than Addington knew of the 'plan'.[2] The alleged mention of 'a few others' resigning can itself be taken in one of two ways: as a statement of something already agreed, or as a proposal still to be put. If it was the former, as Eliot implied, it was curious; for Addington would have seemed an extraordinary choice, and one cannot see any one taking happily to the prospect of resigning to make way for him. How would Grenville, for instance – the most likely victim, even if a friend of the Speaker – have responded?[3] But whether he and others had in fact been approached, or would have been sounded as matters progressed, the idea is revealing of Pitt's confidence in supposing he could call on them to comply. And if Mrs Pretyman got it wrong – which seems rather unlikely from her specific statement, and also from the Bishop's remark about 'a new, strong administration'[4] – and Pitt was proposing to leave on his own, the same self-confidence was evident in the plan that he would continue to 'direct' – a key element – and the implication that he might return a little later. That he should make such assumptions showed his attitude to his colleagues, himself, and his successor: no one was disposing of him; he was disposing

1. See Philip Ziegler, *Addington* . . . (1965), 69, 71.
2. Pp. 48, 46n4, 47 above.
3. The statement about other Ministers was made in Mrs Pretyman's account, which he, or they, would presumably not have seen. But there are no recorded comments from any one, so far as I know, on the Bishop's account of the episode for his *Life of Pitt*. It is possible however that no one concerned saw the later, unpublished chapters, though Grenville at least was consulted on an earlier part of the work.
4. P. 47 above.

them. That he should have thought of stepping down, if only for a time, showed the importance he attached to fresh peace talks. Compounded of anxiety about events and a lack of anxiety about his own position, the plan casts some light on his view of a sombre scene. It also throws its shadow forward, to an event in which the same actors would be involved.

III

At whatever point Pitt thought on these lines in such a period, the war itself gave ample cause for gloom. By the end of March 1797, as the peace petitions gathered, the position was even worse than at the start of the year.[1] The reason, simply, was Bonaparte once more.[2] Amid all his triumphs in the past year in Italy he had failed to take the key fortress of Mantua,[3] and in January the Austrians regrouped to lift the siege. Their reward was a shattering defeat, and on 2 February the loss of the city. Bonaparte then turned to the Papal States, achieving their surrender on the 19th; and thereafter against the Archduke Charles, the most successful of the Austrian commanders, who had now been sent down into the Lombard plain. A series of engagements in March drove him back into the mountains, and on the 30th the French, never slackening, were across the frontier. On the last day of the month Bonaparte suggested a local armistice, which though due in part to a lack of reinforcements sought from the Rhine front, came as the culmination of a further spate of headlong assaults.

The appearance of the enemy on Austrian soil heightened a mounting crisis in Vienna, one of the main aspects of which was the state of relations with Britain. Ever shifting all too easily, these were now increasingly acrimonious. Each Power needed the other if the First Coalition was to survive, the Emperor representing for Britain the only major fighting army in Europe, Britain the only source for the Emperor of essential war funds. But for some time each had been faltering in its role. Although Austria had gained ground in Germany in 1796, the Italian campaign was demoralising and now draining her forces in Germany itself; and if Britain was providing funds, the amounts and the terms were bitterly argued, while the remittances themselves were falling increasingly into arrears.[4] Springing from these problems, the continuous tension bore witness to the limits of the interests common to both parties. In one, bad, respect matters had improved, with the final partition of Poland which

1. Pp. 33, 39–40 above.
2. He changed the spelling from Buonaparte (the form used in II) in 1796.
3. See II, 607, 627, 633, 646.
4. Op. cit., 633–4, 645–6 for the Austrians in Germany; 595, 609, 627, and M. Duffy, 'British War Policy: the Austrian Alliance, 1793–1801' (D. Phil. thesis, Oxford, 1971, 273n2), for the British payments in policy and practice, background to which may be found in II, 362–3, 377, 519–20, 551–2, 557, 591–2.

allowed Austria to concentrate more freely on the war against France. But the range of the Emperor's commitments in the latter cause – in Germany, Italy, and the Low Countries – had its diplomatic drawbacks for London as well as its advantages, particularly in his ambition to exchange the Austrian Netherlands for Bavaria, which ran contrary to British policy and was accepted only with great reluctance.[1] 'The Old Alliance' had much to commend it to both members, if placed against other choices. But when those choices were removed from a system designed in London to contain them all – when Austria's rival Prussia had defected, and Russia would not provide troops – the effective survivors were locked in, rather than able to build on, their partnership.

And now the strain was extreme. Bonaparte and the Bank Suspension had brought Austria dangerously close to despair. At the turn of the year a new British offer of funds followed the end of the peace talks in Paris. But the news took some six weeks to reach Vienna, by then Mantua had fallen, and the proposals – both figures and conditions – were rejected.[2] Less than three weeks later the financial crisis broke in London, and the future of agreed advances, let alone fresh support, was in doubt.[3] As April opened, Bonaparte drove on to the north. Within ten days he was in Leoben, less than ninety miles from Vienna. The city was in a turmoil, and the Archduke Charles could see no hope. On the 8th a brief truce was agreed. It was then extended. And on 18 April, at Leoben, Preliminaries of Peace were signed.

Unable to affect operations, and hampered in its finances, the British Government was meanwhile confined to diplomatic efforts. It did what it could in Europe to limit the damage in the first quarter of the year. The main exertions naturally were focused on Russia. There was little hope of direct armed support from the new Emperor Paul; but care was taken to try to dissuade him from countenancing overtures from the suspect Prussia, to hold him firmly in the Coalition, and keep him informed of British views. These attentions seemed not unsuccessful, for a time; Russia proved helpful in the naval mutinies; and talks on an early renewal of the commercial Convention of 1793, which the British thought expedient to start, went ahead with unusual speed.[4] But none of this could help Austria directly, and still less could diplomacy in other quarters.

1. See I, 473, II, 198, 253, 265, 273, 598, 606, 625, 628, 646–7 for this aim.
2. The offer settled at £2.4 million; the Austrians wanted £3 million, as they had demanded earlier (see II, 595), by way of loan. Duffy follows the despatches from 27 December 1796 to 8 February 1797 in 'War Policy', 274–5.
3. Loc. cit., 276 for the delay in the latest remittance and for Grenville's forebodings to Sir Morton Eden [Minister in Vienna] on 28 February and 3 March. ´
4. P.R.O., F.O. 65/36 for January–March 1797; *H.M.C., Dropmore*, III, 292–3, 306, 308. See p. 28 above for the Russian naval squadron. The commercial talks began on 12 January, and a text was approved for ratification, subject to some prospective amendments, by 24 March. The Emperor had earlier seemed disposed to suspend some protective tariffs (II, 645n1). For the Convention of 1793, which in point of fact had two years to run, see op. cit., 275–6, 503.

British envoys in parts of Germany and Italy did their best to keep matters in check, and at the other end of the arc, in Portugal, to see if Spain could be weaned from France.[1] Prussia, the joker in the pack, was treated with caution, in a situation of which, on her record, she might be expected to make greatest use. Sure enough, in February there was a suggestion from Berlin for an Anglo-Prussian démarche to France for peace talks, which if then unsuccessful might lead Prussia to rejoin the war with the Allies. In return for that she would claim a subsidy, but not, it was said, territorial gain. The Foreign Secretary however was sceptical: he scented fear of a Franco-Austrian peace which might promise Bavaria to the Emperor and sustain him in the German Empire; and his reaction in fact was very soon proved right. News leaked out in March that Prussia had signed a secret treaty with France seven months before, giving her the lands of the bishopric of Münster, adjoining Hanover and Holland, at a general peace. The Foreign Office rubbed in the lesson, in other German states and above all at St Petersburg. While Ministers believed, as they had done so often, in the value of real aid from Berlin, they were 'full of distrust' once more 'as to the sincerity of all the professions'.[2]

They were moreover still not prepared at that point to risk the bird, however frail, in the hand: 'to lose Austrian realities in pursuing Prussian expectations'.[3] As April succeeded March, however, the priorities changed. Fading hopes of military resistance were perforce being overtaken by the urgent need for a joint negotiating stance. There was one belated step to give some armed support, by a decision early in the month to send a force of frigates into the Mediterranean for the upper Adriatic, in response to pressing demands from Vienna for the return of a fleet.[4] At the same time the Ministry defeated an attempt in the Commons to withdraw financial aid: a challenge which caused less trouble than had been feared.[5] But all such palliatives were being swept away, and the great object now must be to dissuade Austria from making a hasty unilateral peace. Only a united approach to talks could bring about an acceptable settlement – a course which the British had earlier interpreted according to their own lights.[6] Pitt was addressing himself to the question in the first few days of April. On the 6th the news was received that the French were

---

1. See in particular P.R.O., F.O. 68/11 (Saxony), 79/15 (Tuscany), 63/24 (Portugal) for January to March 1797.

2. Grenville to Earl of Elgin [Minister in Berlin – the Elgin of the Marbles], 2 March 1797 (*H.M.C., Dropmore*, III, 298). The despatches are in P.R.O., F.O. 64/43–4. See II, 627 for the Franco-Prussian secret Convention.

3. *H.M.C., Dropmore*, III, 298. As late as 20 March Grenville doubted if the French could advance farther for the time being (to Marquess of Buckingham; Buckingham, II, 367).

4. Which had been reiterated over the past two months. The news was sent in Grenville to Eden, no. 22, Secret, 4 April 1797 (P.R.O., F.O. 7/48).

5. See pp. 41–2 above, and *L.C.G. III*, II, no. 1526 with n3.

6. Cf. II, 627–30, 637, 645–7 for shifts in attitude in the last quarter of 1796.

poised on Austrian soil. On the 8th, he sat down to explain his views to the King.[1]

Austria, Pitt argued, might now well feel 'exposed' to a separate negotiation. We should therefore propose to her a mediation by another Power for a general peace. The intermediary should be Russia, '(joined if necessary with Prussia)' – the last an eloquent reflection of the gravity of recent events. At the same time we must inform Austria of our own framework for peace talks and agree the terms for our participation; for a unilateral peace on her part 'would be the greatest aggravation of [our] difficulties ... which could possibly arise'. Of those, far the most dire was the fact that

> the *extreme* difficulty of providing even now for the pressing and indisputible [*sic*] exigencies of the public service, renders the pecuniary support necessary for the Emperor at least precarious, while it at the same time, proves that the continuance of the contest (in the event of a separate peace between France and Austria), would produce a pressure on this country which ought by all possible means to be avoided, though it is to be hoped that it will be met with fortitude ...

'Even the object of the [Austrian] Netherlands,' Pitt concluded, 'important as it is in every point of view, does not seem to be one which can be set against so many important and urgent considerations.'

This was a plain enough statement of Pitt's most acute fear. 'All modern Wars are a Contention of Purse', and even before the Suspension our 'great apparent Difficulty' had become finance.[2] He repeated the message the next day, stressing the political implications: the effects of the financial pressure on Parliament and the public.[3] This second letter, which was firmly worded, followed indeed a dusty answer to the first. For George III thoroughly disliked the whole idea. He 'lamented' 'the mode, but too often adopted of late years, of acting immediately on the impulse of the minute'; hated the prospect of another 'humiliating step' in approaching the French; thought the military reports too recent to draw sound conclusions; and reminded his Minister that if the Low Countries were lost 'one may talk of balances of power, but they cannot exist'. He had supposed that we would be continuing our financial support. But even if he was wrong, he would prefer a separate peace by Austria to a settlement which could prejudice our freedom to make our own terms.[4]

1. Pitt to George III, 8 April 1797 (*L.C.G. III*, II, no. 1526). See also Grenville to Eden, no. 21, 4 April 1797 (F.O. 7/48); same to same, Private, sd (*H.M.C., Dropmore*, III, 308).
2. Cf. Dundas to Pitt, 9 July 1794 (II, 412); Pitt to Earl of Chatham, 4 September 1796 (op. cit., 622).
3. Pitt to George III, 9 April 1797 (Stanhope, III, Appendix, iv–vi). And see p. 51 above. Over three years later, he told the Commons that it was the prospect of the failure of the funding system that had led the Government to seek a negotiation (3 February 1800; see *P.H.*, XXXIV, cols. 1349–50).
4. To Pitt, 9 April 1797 (Stanhope, III, Appendix, ii–iv).

53

The tone of the rejoinder was the severest expression so far of the King's dislike of Pitt's hankering for peace talks. He was clearly hoping to influence other Ministers;[1] but, once more, he could not gain them outright. The Cabinet, meeting on the 9th, resolved that it was 'indispensably necessary' to seek a joint approach with Austria for Russian mediation (Prussia not being mentioned). Instructions were ready to be taken to Vienna by a special envoy, bearing powers to act with the resident British Minister.[2] The man chosen was George Hammond, an Under Secretary in the Foreign Office who had been seasoned by an unsuccessful mission to Berlin the year before.[3] He conveyed terms markedly weaker, for Britain, than those last put to the French. The enemy would retain the Austrian Netherlands (and thus, obviously, control over Holland), indemnifying Austria in Germany or Italy – the last at the cost of Bonaparte's other victims. British gains overseas would be returned except for the Cape of Good Hope, Ceylon and Martinique; and Martinique, the envoys were told, was expendable in the last resort. The decision was one, wrote George III, 'that from the bottom of my heart I deplore'. But he perforce accepted it 'with . . . sorrow' the next day.[4]

The King indeed, as he remarked, had no choice, for the Ministers had been unanimous. They had agreed from a sense, in Pitt's words, of 'overruling necessity'.[5] The projected terms were correspondingly weighted to try to help Austria. But they also reflected pressures held to be falling on Britain itself. No Minister indeed seems to have had great confidence in the country's will to fight on alone: certainly the Foreign Secretary, normally robust, was despondent. The 'panic', he found, was too 'disgraceful' for people to 'be quiet and let themselves be saved'; and he gave an expert's typical view of the public.

> It is a curious speculation in history to see how often the good people of England have played this game over and over again, and how incorrigible they are in it. To desire war without reflection, to be unreasonably elated with success, to be still more unreasonably depressed by difficulties, and to call for peace with an impatience which makes suitable terms unattainable, are the established maxims and the regular progress of the popular mind in this country.

1. He stated that he wished his views to be made known in Cabinet.
He also wrote a further letter on the same day, which however he did not send, objecting in his capacity as a German Elector to the idea of including Prussia in a mediation. The text is printed in *L.C.G. III*, II, 560n1.
2. Minutes, in *H.M.C., Dropmore*, III, 310–11. Liverpool and Windham were not present.
3. See II, 37; and op. cit., 508–11 for his earlier, patchy time as Minister to the United States.
4. Grenville to Eden, nos. 23 and 24, 11 April 1797 (P.R.O. 7/48, 49 respectively), and Private, sd (*H.M.C., Dropmore*, III, 312–13); George III to Pitt, 10 April 1797 (Stanhope, III, Appendix, vi). Cf. II, 647 for the terms proposed in December 1796.
5. Pitt to George III, 9 April 1797 (ibid). For the absentees see n2 above.

'Yet,' he concluded, equally typically of his background and his time, 'such as it is, it is worth all the other countries of the world put together'.[1]

Grenville's emphasis was not identical with Pitt's. He did not put the financial problems in the front of his argument. Nor was he entirely convinced of the rightness of Hammond's mission, though he submitted to the need; he confessed to 'hardly know[ing]' what his wishes were about it.[2] He opted resignedly for a move pressed personally by his cousin. For the strength of Pitt's determination was shown by the fact that he wrote to the King direct, on a subject which officially did not lie within his province. Communications to the sovereign on foreign affairs were the Foreign Secretary's responsibility: it was exceptional for the First Lord of the Treasury so to intrude. The rule was not hard and fast; Pitt had followed this course before – once, at the end of 1785, in the trade talks with France that were nominally under the Foreign Office, through the Dutch crisis of 1787 and its sequel, in the Nootka Sound crisis of 1790, on the declaration at Toulon in 1793, on policy over Prussia in 1795 (when Grenville disputed it), on the decision to seek peace talks with France in the second half of 1796.[3] The occasions were few in number. In a system in which forms were closely watched, and the Foreign Secretary of the war years was far from complaisant, their appearances are suggestive.

The initiative was too late; not that it might ever have stood much chance. Hammond set off on 11 April. He reached Vienna on the 30th, three days after Eden received the first intimation of the possible British plan.[4] By then the Preliminaries of Peace had been signed;[5] and their terms set the scene. As late as 7–9 April, unprompted by London, Thugut[6] had in fact asked Russia to mediate. But that was pushed into the background by the events of the next ten days. For at Leoben Austria gained a much better prospect than might have been expected. The key lay in secret articles which, in return for the Austrian Netherlands and the Milanese, gave her the mainland territories of Venice in eastern Italy and across the Adriatic. Bonaparte had calculated that this would be the best inducement to a prompt end of the campaign; and he wrought better than he knew, for it had indeed long been Thugut's dream. Anxious not to forgo the prize, the Austrian Minister was now uninterested in a British

1. Grenville to Marquess of Buckingham, 28 April 1797 (Buckingham, II, 376).

2. To Buckingham (n1 above).

3. *L.C.G. III*, I, nos. 266; 368, 378, 382, 394, 403, 408, 451, 485; 589, 631; op. cit., II, nos. 938; 1223, 1233, 1236; 1430 (p. 498), 1446. There were a few other, marginal, occasions – see op. cit., I, no. 235, II, no. 974, on matters involving the King as Elector of Hanover; and I, nos. 378, 380. Reports of Commons' debates and drafts for King's Speeches affecting foreign affairs fell of course always within Pitt's compass.

4. Communicated by Grenville on the 4th (p. 52, n4 above). For Eden see p. 51, n3 above.

5. P. 51 above.

6. See II, p. 271.

offer. On the contrary, he could envisage trouble if the arrangement were to figure in a joint negotiation, and was correspondingly determined not to divulge the terms as a whole. He no longer wanted talks, or a mediation, and with his change of heart the unity in Vienna was to all intents complete. There were plenty of complaints of British treatment to be cited when assenting to *force majeure*. Meanwhile the Government in London waited for news on which to build an Allied diplomatic effort. The report of a provisional peace was received on 3 May, from the French newspapers. But no detail was forthcoming; Eden and Hammond themselves could get nowhere; and on the 9th the latter left Vienna empty-handed. It was late in the month before Ministers concluded that they were not going to hear any more and had been left to fend for themselves. By the 26th they decided to act on that assumption. On the 28th they learned that Russia, though not wishing to mediate in the form proposed by Austria, was prepared to call a Congress for a general peace.[1] But there no longer seemed to be any point, and on 1 June the British Government made an overture to France for peace talks between the two Powers direct.

IV

The Cabinet which approved this step, on the last day of May, did so at a very low moment. Much of its time was spent in fact on the urgent moves to be made for the Nore;[2] and wherever one looked in the weeks since Pitt had last argued the need for peace talks, dangers and threats had risen on every side. The Channel fleet, the ships at the Nore, the North Sea squadron had mutinied in turn. The Dutch at that moment were thought to be ready to sail with troops for a landing. Sections of the army seemed close to revolt, and Ireland perhaps not far from rebellion. Petitions for peace had been flowing in. And now Austria had left the war. The inner group of Ministers had been on the stretch almost continuously, some of them battling also in the spate of Commons' debates. No wonder if they were finding that 'things were *in extremis*'. Pitt, at the centre of the storm, had had no reason to alter his views.

The decision however did not really turn on these events. To some Ministers at least the threats might in fact have argued the other way. An approach to the French while ships were in mutiny, and under circumstances of apparent danger, could be taken as a sign of weakness which

1. Sir Charles Whitworth [Minister in St Petersburg] to Grenville, no. 24, 3 May 1797, endorsed received 28 May (P.R.O., F.O. 65/37).

2. Reports of two meetings on 31 May appear in *The Morning Chronicle* and *The Morning Post* of 1 June; the Nore is mentioned as the subject, but the discussion of the approach to France is outlined in Windham's diary for that day (*Diary of William Windham*, 365). There may also have been Cabinets devoted more to France on 30 May and 1 June (Canning's diary; Canning Ms 29d).

augured ill for talks.[1] The Government was now acting firmly at the Nore and gaining solid popular support. The very seriousness of the crisis was heightening resolve. But Pitt himself was thinking on other lines, guided by the reasons that already weighed with him: by his fear that financial resources might not continue to sustain a war for which public opinion seemed unlikely to provide larger supplies.[2] While he may have been heartened by the growing response to an immediate threat, he was chiefly concerned with a possible reluctance to support a further prolonged struggle.

The Minister's continuing eagerness for talks did not reassure earlier doubters. Grenville in particular was becoming increasingly restive. Uncertain at the prospect of a joint approach with Austria, he was much more unhappy now. He agreed to sound out the ground: to 'ascertain', as Pitt himself put it, 'whether the disposition of the enemy will admit of negotiation'.[3] But he was not pleased with the method chosen – a letter to the Foreign Minister, Delacroix, whose tone in the past had been objectionable – and a fortnight later he could claim to have been right. For while Delacroix's initial response was courteous, he then named the place for the talks – Lille – without an option, and sent a passport for an emissary specified as holding 'full powers . . . for concluding . . . a definitive and separate treaty of peace'. This of course prejudged the issue in its demand for a 'separate' settlement (with no reference to any allies), and the Foreign Secretary objected strongly. The message was received on 14 June, and the Cabinet met on that day and the next. Grenville argued that we could not afford to make such concessions: 'nothing but firmness' – so he was reported – 'could save us'.[4] He knew that he could probably enlist a minority of his colleagues, for Windham and Spencer had also voiced misgivings on 31 May.[5] He probably hoped to gain a majority with the support of the King, for George III on 1 June had again not concealed his views. On the contrary, he informed the Foreign Secretary 'in confidence' that

> the many humiliating steps I have been advised to take in the last nine months have taken so deep an impression on my mind that I undoubtedly feel this Kingdom much lowered in its proper estimation: . . . that I certainly look on the additional measure now proposed as a confirmation of that opinion . . . that if both Houses of Parliament are

1. I do not know of explicit evidence for this on 31 May, though one might make an inference from Grenville's letter to George III that night (*H.M.C., Dropmore*, III, 327). Some subsequent attitudes are compatible with it. Canning recorded 'violent disputes' in Cabinet on 1 June.
2. Cf. pp. 53–5, above.
3. Pitt to Earl of Carlisle, 4 June 1797 (Holland Rose, II, 322), who had written to him about the public's 'cry' for peace (1 June; P.R.O. 30/8/121).
4. *Diary of William Windham*, 14 and 15 June (op. cit., 367–8). See also Canning's diary of 14 June (Canning Ms 29d).
5. *Diary of Windham*, 365.

in as tame a state of mind as it is pretended, I do not see the hopes that either war can be continued with effect or peace obtained but of the most disgraceful and unsolid tenure.[1]

Here then was potential and powerful backing; even a hint of an open hint to Parliament. But the royal pressure was not forthcoming in the event. The Cabinet meeting on the morning of 15 June disclosed a 'complete opposition of opinion', and a second that night was said to have been a '*Séance orageuse*'.[2] Grenville's allies of 31 May were joined by Portland; Pitt held Dundas, Lord Chancellor Loughborough, Cornwallis, Chatham and 'ultimately' Liverpool.[3] By a slender majority it was therefore determined to accept the French reply, and a Note was drafted accordingly in which the scope of the talks was covered by a statement that Britain would not abandon the interests of her ally Portugal, and that those of Spain and Holland could be represented by France.[4]

When a Cabinet Minute, necessary in such an instance, was sent to the King, it contained a record of Grenville's dissent, as on an analogous occasion in 1795.[5] Grenville himself explained that if 'the present hour' had not been so critical he would have resigned.[6] But George III, acknowledging that his own view 'tallied' with his Foreign Secretary's, and complaining that the Cabinet's 'tone' was 'too low', accepted nonetheless that the answer must be sent.[7] With the potential obstacles thus removed, the negotiation could go ahead.

---

1. *H.M.C. Dropmore*, III, 327. The 'last nine months' of course took him back to the approach to France in September 1796 (see II, 630).

2. *Diary of William Windham*, 367–8, for 15 June states that there were two meetings – as indeed did *The Morning Chronicle* and *The Morning Post*. He himself did not attend the second, which apparently 'lasted till past twelve'. Canning too heard of the 'violence' (diary of 16 June; Canning Ms 29d).

3. *Diary of William Windham*, 367–8. Liverpool however, like Windham, did not sign an ensuing Minute, probably because he was not present, again like Windham, at the second meeting – an absence which the King ascribed to deliberate preference (to Pitt, 17 June 1797; *H.M.C., Dropmore*, III, 330).

4. Cabinet Minute, 16 June 1797 (*H.M.C., Dropmore* as in n3 above). The draft itself, said to have been 'settled' at the first of the two meetings (Canning's diary for 16 June; Canning Ms 29d), is in Pitt's hand among his notes in P.R.O. 30/8/196, ff. 205–6.

5. See II, 555. For the use of Minutes in peacetime see I, 629 with n5; for some other wartime examples, op. cit., II, 677.

6. Grenville to George III, 16 June 1797 (*H.M.C., Dropmore*, III, 329–30). He noted on his copy that this referred to the naval mutiny.
In a letter to his brother Thomas the day before he likewise dwelt on 'the most painful decision I can have to make': whether to accept 'a measure which I cannot approve' or to 'desert my station in a moment of danger' (15 June 1797; B.L. Add. Ms 41852). The depth of his distress is equally clear in a letter to Pitt of the 26th stating that he would carry on 'for the moment' (Dacres Adams Mss, formerly P.R.O. 30/58/2; cf. p. 55 above). Pitt told Canning a few days earlier that he himself had written to the Foreign Secretary to 'agree or *go out*. Ld. G. agreed' (note in diary, 23–25 June 1797; Canning Ms 29d).

7. George III to Grenville, 17 June 1797; same to [Pitt], sd (*H.M.C., Dropmore*, III, 330–1).

The Note to France, dated 17 June, gave the name of the emissary. It was that of Malmesbury once more.[1] Despite his own reservation that he might be unwelcome, and a recent illness, he was the obvious man and he was chosen at once. There was in fact some demur from Paris. But the Cabinet this time stood firm, and Malmesbury left at the end of the month, arriving in Lille on 4 July.[2]

He had made good arrangements to guard his back in London. The three main aides in his mission were well placed, as two of them had been the year before, for confidential liaison with the Department concerned. On this occasion indeed all three shared one strong connexion. All were friends, and one a great friend, of Canning at the Foreign Office.[3] Malmesbury had taken care in 1796 to cultivate the young hopeful, already known to him, who in that useful position was known to have Pitt's ear.[4] He now strengthened the link, with Canning's connivance or at his request. For the Under Secretary and the envoy clearly planned to keep privately in touch, and their agreement must have stemmed from the tension in this instance between Grenville and Pitt, superimposed on Canning's self-confidence and his zeal for his patron. Whether Pitt himself sponsored the arrangement one cannot be sure: he certainly made his own views clear to Malmesbury in private before the latter left.[5] In any case the Minister was soon profiting from Canning's reports, as well as hearing from the envoy direct,[6] and the management of the talks

---

1. See II, 636 for 1796.

2. See *Malmesbury*, III, 370–2, 375–9. He was reported to have attended the Cabinet on 14 and again possibly on 16 June (*The Times* of 15 June, *The True Briton* of the 15th and 17th).

3. The mission under Malmesbury consisted of Lord Morpeth, Lord Granville Leveson Gower, George Ellis, James Ross (private secretary), and for a time Henry Wesley – or Wellesley – as Secretary of the Mission. The first three formed a well-knit group. Morpeth, aged 23, was the eldest son of Lord Carlisle, a MP since 1795, and a friend of Canning's since Oxford days. So too was Leveson Gower, who was in fact one of Canning's greatest friends. Also aged 23 and a MP since 1795, he was a son of Lord Stafford, the former Cabinet Minister, step-brother of Lord Gower, the last Ambassador in Paris, and through his mother Morpeth's first cousin. In 1796 he had accompanied Malmesbury on the abortive peace talks. So also had George Ellis, a MP for the Cinque Ports since 1796, now aged 42 and enjoying a longer connexion with Malmesbury: a member of his staff at The Hague in the eighties, and a companion on the Grand Tour in 1791. His friendship with Canning derived from his younger cousin Charles, a close friend of the latter's since Eton.

Morpeth had a connexion in another important Department. His Parliamentary colleague for the borough of Morpeth, as his father's nominee, was William Huskisson, Dundas's Under Secretary for War. Malmesbury himself, however, did not like or trust Huskisson.

The mission's connexions endured. James Ross, who had also been with Malmesbury as his secretary in 1796, was in the Embassy at St Petersburg when Leveson Gower was Ambassador in 1804, and private secretary to Canning as Foreign Secretary in 1807.

4. See II, 648.

5. See Malmesbury's confirming note of their memories of the occasion in November 1802 (*Malmesbury*, IV (1804), 128).

6. A practice which he often took care to ensure in important issues of foreign affairs; cf. I, 325.

throughout bore witness to the fact. Grenville of course could not be ignored – far from it – or circumvented in the last resort. But he could be kept in check by what Canning once called '*most private*' communications,[1] including some during visits by Malmesbury's aides, Leveson Gower above all. The uncomfortable circumstances bore on all the parties principally concerned. Malmesbury had to deal with two ill-attuned masters – which by and large he did with great skill – while Canning stressed the need 'to give as little opportunity as can be helped to those who hate the work to revile the master workman'.[2]

In this atmosphere the two Ministers operated within a situation which in one respect, ironically, bound them more closely together than ever. For the negotiation was soon subject to an exceptional level of secrecy. In mid-July the Government was perturbed by a series of leaks to newspapers, coming, as Grenville told Malmesbury, 'within a few hours after your couriers arrive here'.[3] Quite apart from other dangers there seemed to be a risk of stockjobbing. On the 19th the Cabinet accordingly resolved that its members must observe complete security, and that the relevant papers were to be held, separate from others, by the two Under Secretaries in the Foreign Office, copies being made only to the members themselves.[4] Matters in point of fact were quietly taken farther. The copying was entrusted to Canning's colleague Hammond, now returned from Austria, whose handwriting was said to be so bad that Ministers in general might be put off; and when a little later a secret report was received on the position within the French Government, it was withheld from every one but Grenville, Pitt and the King.[5] All further intelligence of that kind was similarly restricted. Nonetheless within the close circle itself there was an added limitation, for when the French informant mentioned things likely to harden Grenville's attitude the passage was apt to be edited. The intimate arrangements thus did not remove the mutual doubts of the two leading Ministers, though one should not go so far as to say – as Malmesbury did in the end – that Grenville was '*against peace from the beginning*'.[6] Once the talks started, the Foreign Secretary pursued them in fact in a firm if sceptical effort for terms that he considered not too

---

1. To Malmesbury, 20 July 1797 (*Malmesbury*, III, 416).

2. To George Ellis, 27 July 1797 (op. cit., 438); the master workman being Malmesbury. Relations between Pitt and Grenville had just been strained farther (or their state perhaps was underlined) by the weakness of the support from Pitt's colleagues in the Lords to a bill, which he himself had not contested in the Commons, for enabling Roman Catholics and Dissenters to serve in the militia. 'Grenville and Pitt', noted Wilberforce on the matter, 'very like breaking friendship' (diary for 12 July; *Life of Wilberforce*, II, 223).

3. 20 July 1797 (*H.M.C., Dropmore*, III, 334). Couriers were of course distinct from members of the mission. The leaks – from whatever sources – may be seen in the newspapers, above all, suggestively, in *The True Briton*.

4. Order of Cabinet, 20 July 1797. There is a copy in *Private Papers of Spencer*, II, 213.

5. See *Malmesbury*, III, 416n (and for Hammond's return p. 56 above); *H.M.C., Dropmore*, III, 337–44.

6. *Malmesbury*, III, 595; diary of 4 October.

dangerous or disgraceful. Since however these proved stricter than Pitt's, mistrust did not disappear. Canning is not always a reliable witness; he ran to extremes. But his comments at least convey something of the atmosphere. The Cabinet's self-denying ordnance, as he saw it, was 'devised' by the Foreign Secretary

> to *tie up Pitt's tongue alone*, whom he suspected of communicating with other persons, and fortifying himself . . . against the opinions which might be brought forward in Council by those with whom he differed in his general view of the Negotiation.[1]

The strong differences in approach were bound to influence attitudes to the terms. At the start, these last followed official lines which could be broadly approved. That indeed was likely to be so. Pitt could hardly have gained his colleagues' consent to open talks without seeking their consent on conditions; and those had to include not only enough to give Grenville a prospect of 'firmness' but also the points on which Dundas – a necessary ally – set greatest store. In 1796 the Secretary for War had demanded retention of both Ceylon and the Cape of Good Hope, and he was said to be equally insistent now.[2] Both figured accordingly in Malmesbury's instructions, and as a *sine qua non*. He was also to seek retention of Cochin in India (possibly to be set against a return of Negapatam to the Dutch), and in the Caribbean of Trinidad or Demerara or Martinique or St Lucia or Tobago. If these last objects were refused the negotiation was not to be closed. But they were to be argued as part of the counterweight to France's increased influence in Europe, and to the concessions which we would make there: recognition of her sovereignty in the Austrian Netherlands (scarcely to be challenged when Austria had made peace), Nice and Savoy.[3]

Most of the demands fell on France's allies. Martinique, St Lucia and Tobago – whichever would be affected – had been French possessions: the rest had been Dutch, at the Cape and in the East, and Spanish or Dutch in the West. The British for their part intended to protect the interests of their own ally Portugal.[4] Although they claimed that France could speak for Spain and Holland, on the ground that these were client states, a bilateral negotiation would thus include matters of concern to other parties

1. To Malmesbury, 20 July 1797 (*Malmesbury*, III, 416). The system proved hard to follow completely, and one may doubt if Dundas for one was kept in such a degree of ignorance in practice.

2. To the point, it was believed in some quarters (probably wrongly), of resignation if necessary (*Life and Letters of Sir Gilbert Elliot*, II, 410). For Dundas in 1796 see II, 628n2; for Grenville on the need for firmness, *Diary of William Windham*, 368 for 15 June.

3. Grenville to Malmesbury, no. 1, 29 June 1797; and see also nos. 2–5, sd (P.R.O., F.O. 27/49). I, 427, 431, 433–4, II, 562 give background for Negapatam and Cochin respectively; II, 628–9, 647, the peace terms offered in 1796. For Austria's cession of her Netherlands see pp. 51, 54 above.

4. P. 58 above.

which – not least from its form, for a negotiation, so designated, was a full-dress affair – would make it more complex and less likely to be brief. This was unfortunate, for the Government was looking to steady and if possible rapid progress. It must thus hope that the minor partners would act as advised, and without much delay.

It must also hope that a Government in Paris would pay heed to the war weariness on which reports from France were being regularly received. But the situation there was not in fact easy to gauge. Different sources of intelligence differed, and it was hard to estimate the strength of the feelings, or the political currents and developments in Paris itself. British hopes of an effective challenge to the Directory, fluctuating in 1796, had been pinned on a second round of elections to the Assembly due in the spring of 1797.[1] London continued to support moves in diverse quarters: to reconcile the 'ultra' and 'moderate' royalists, to finance and direct the underground Paris Agency which the Minister in Berne, William Wickham, had been helping to fund for some time, and to encourage recruitment of 'respectable' republicans. There were successes and failures. Louis XVIII was brought in March to issue a much more tactful manifesto than he had done earlier, in 1795, before he received British advice.[2] On the other hand the Paris Agency was disrupted by the arrest of most of its members. The elections themselves moreover did not answer all the questions. The success of royalists and their sympathisers was again considerable – more so than even Wickham could have hoped. But that itself produced the all too familiar resurgence of internal quarrels, while the survivors of the Paris Agency offered little immediate promise. The Directory was at bay. But such an animal could be the more dangerous. The negotiation was about to take place in a highly uncertain domestic setting.

Nor was it easy to gauge exactly the course of French diplomacy in Europe. All reports from the capitals told of an expectant pause. France might seem to have the ball at her feet, from northern Germany to central Italy; but she still had to settle her policies, particularly in her dealings with Prussia. Above all it was impossible from London to tell how her final peace talks with Austria were going, based on the Preliminaries – their own terms unknown – negotiated at Leoben.[3] Progress at Lille was thus likely to depend, in whichever direction one looked, to an unusual extent on the course of events elsewhere.

And so it proved. Countering the British demands, the French led off with three of their own: renunciation by George III of his claim to the throne of France which still figured in his title, restoration or 'the equivalent' of their ships lost at Toulon in 1793, and abandonment of the British

1. See II, 609–10.

2. Op. cit., 582–4. The rest of this paragraph draws largely on Harvey Mitchell, *The Underground War against Revolutionary France . . . 1794–1800* (1965), chs. 6–10.

3. See pp. 55–6 above.

claim on the revenue of the Austrian Netherlands as part of the security for the loan to the Emperor. Although somewhat disconcerted, Ministers did not foresee unsurmountable difficulties; Pitt made jokes in private about the King's title – bad jokes too, Canning complained – and both he and Grenville were prepared if necessary to discuss at any rate the first two points.[1] A more disagreeable note however was sounded a week later, on 15 July, when the restoration of all British conquests was required before the negotiation could proceed. The Directory, it was explained, could not discuss its allies' possessions, the future of which was covered in wartime treaties, while those possessions remained in enemy hands. The demand was refused categorically; but Pitt was anxious for the talks to continue, and continue they did for the rest of that month and through August. The French plenipotentiaries proved content in practice to talk about those issues. But little of substance transpired in the ensuing weeks. It was clear that the delegation had no real freedom of manoeuvre; its members were closely dependent on Paris, and Paris, it was said, was in touch with Madrid and The Hague. The relevance of recent and earlier treaties became a leading subject of conferences which, amicably conducted, did not get very far.

Malmesbury however was not too depressed. He had been received politely – unlike the year before –, was on good terms with the French negotiators, and had come to believe, if cautiously, that there was a real chance of agreement. He was encouraged by the unusual courtesy, by the composition of the delegation on the whole – particularly the fact that it included Maret, the sensible official who had conferred with Pitt in 1792, and proved to be the source, through an intermediary, of the cherished secret information now[2] –, and by the regularity and usually the tone of the meetings. He took even greater comfort from the continuance of the intelligence itself: 'what is . . . passing ex-officially', he remarked, 'is so much more important than what passes officially'.[3] And finally he had arrived with some personal information which gave him a degree of manoeuvre. For on the eve of departure Pitt had told him in confidence that – despite the Cabinet's terms – one of the two demands *sine qua non*, either Ceylon or the Cape, might be conceded in return for a reasonable

---

1. But not the third, which they dismissed as no business of the French, who could talk to the Emperor if they wished. The basis of the claim over the ships was that Hood had occupied Toulon in trust for a legitimate French Government (see II, 309–11), and since the British were now treating with the Directory that declaration applied to itself. For Pitt's joking see Malmesbury to Ellis, 8 August 1797 (*Malmesbury*, III, 455).

The following account of the talks draws on Ephraim Douglass Adams, *The Influence of Grenville on Pitt's Foreign Policy 1787–1798* (1904) – with much of whose emphasis however I disagree –, on C. Ballot, *Les Négociations de Lille .   .* (1910), and above all on a paper prepared for me by Dr A.R. Smith.

2. The direct recipient was George Ellis, Malmesbury himself staying clear. For Maret in England in 1792–3 see II, 212, 233–5, 237, 254–5. He had suffered imprisonment in France for a time since.

3. To Grenville, 6 August 1797 (*H.M.C., Dropmore*, III, 345).

result. There would clearly be a serious quarrel in that case in London. It would presumably mean Grenville's resignation, and it would greatly strain Dundas's loyalty, thus creating real discord and threatening Pitt's slender majority on the talks in Cabinet. But he seemed prepared for the issue if it should arise: 'on this particular point,' he had told Malmesbury – as he reminded him a few years later – 'he, or Lord Grenville, *must* have gone out; and he added, *it would have been Lord Grenville.*'[1] The envoy could thus assume that he probably had a reserve position in prospect when attention fastened on those conquests in continuing talks.[2]

At the same time there were adverse developments, of whose force he was well aware. One unexpected setback occurred in August. It became known on the 12th that the Portuguese Minister in Paris had signed a peace treaty with France. He did so in point of fact without the overt authority of his Government, and a period of confusion followed, producing a flurry of despatches from London. But whatever might emerge it could not favour Malmesbury's case in the short term. There was a force under British command in Portugal, requested in 1796 against a threat from Spain. The British had stated that they would protect Portuguese interests during the talks.[3] Above all, the facilities of the Tagus were highly important to the blockade of Cadiz, the principal base of the Spanish fleet. Even if it was disavowed in due course in Lisbon – which was far from certain – the treaty marked a coup for France at an interesting point.

The news also served to underline the problems in Malmesbury's dealings with his base. He was perturbed by the reaction – he assumed Grenville's – to something he himself wished to play down. 'The Portuguese peace', he commented, 'seems to have made the Cabinet as mad as if they had been bitten by the Queen of that country';[4] and his misgivings were heightened soon afterwards when the Foreign Secretary instructed him to protest formally at a public statement in Paris which seemed to blame Britain for delays in the talks. That episode indeed brought to the surface his feelings about his position, sandwiched between 'the Minister under *whose orders I am bound to act*' and 'the Minister *with whom I wish to act*'.[5] In private he deplored what he saw as 'Pitt's weakness

1. *Malmesbury*, IV, 128. Malmesbury confirmed the accuracy of this statement in 1802.

2. According to the French later, indeed, he may have dropped a hint. Certainly they seem to have had some suspicion that a concession might be made; and some awkwardness arose in London when this became known to persons ignorant of Pitt's real views (see Huskisson to ?Dundas, Secret, 6 September 1797, and enclosure, which was sent also to Pitt; P.R.O. 30/8/147).

3. See II, 634; p. 58 above.

4. To Granville Leveson Gower, 22 August 1797 (P.R.O. 30/29/354). Cf. same to Canning, sd and 29 August 1797 (*Malmesbury*, III, 496–7, 512–16). The Queen was the unstable Maria.

5. To Canning, second letter of 29 August 1797 (op. cit., 517); and see also a third letter sd, op. cit., 518–19.

64

in regard to Lord Grenville';[1] and, bold as ever, he confined himself to verbal protest and did not present a Note. It all added to the difficulties of an inherently delicate mission, in which he became increasingly conscious of divided counsels at home.

But in the event all this was soon water under the bridge. For the most serious cause for worry in August remained the lack of substance in the talks themselves. No *contre-projet* was received in answer to the opening British statement: the month passed in polite discussion of the admissibility of existing treaties, and assurances that the Spaniards and Dutch were being consulted on the demands. The Dutch in particular were said to be recalcitrant; and no doubt they were. There may well have been substance in the French negotiators' claims of difficulties at The Hague. But it was becoming ever more clear that, whatever the diplomatic problems, any serious advance must depend on the outcome of troubles in Paris itself. For in the second half of the summer these were rising fast: a struggle was brewing in and around the Directory which seemed likely to move soon to a crisis. Both Malmesbury and Grenville acknowledged that the issue at Lille would turn on the outcome:[2] that the content of the negotiation could be subordinate to other events. It was an uncomfortable thought for a Ministry whose main aim, in Pitt's constant phrase, was 'security',[3] and which had committed itself to a process that might turn on a struggle beyond its control.

The question was answered on 4 September. The *coup d'état* of 18 Fructidor removed from the Directory the elements most disposed to continue the talks. On the 11th the French mission was recalled from Lille, and a fresh one appointed. Neither Malmesbury nor Pitt was prepared to give up, though Malmesbury saw very little hope; Pitt for his part was quick to confirm that his views remained 'unaltered . . . and my ultimate determination will be what I think you know'.[4] On the 16th however the new French negotiators presented a Note asking Malmesbury if he was authorised to treat on the principle of a return of all British conquests. Faced with this abrupt revival of a question thought to have been laid to rest, the British envoy answered simply that his powers were sufficient for negotiation, and that he was prepared to discuss the matter, which related to his instructions, at an appropriate point. He was thereupon required to leave Lille within twenty-four hours. After a further exchange he did so on the 18th, reaching London at midnight on the 19th.

1. In conversation with Ellis on 1 September (op. cit., 521). Canning claimed to have persuaded Pitt at various points to soften Grenville's draft despatches on Portugal (diary of 20 August, 1 and 10 September; Canning Ms 29d). If so, the results still failed to satisfy Malmesbury (see Canning to Pitt, 10 September 1797; P.R.O. 30/8/120).

2. Malmesbury to Grenville, 25 July 1797 (see *The Cambridge History of British Foreign Policy*, ed. Sir A.W. Ward and G.P. Gooch, I (1922), 278); Grenville to Malmesbury, 27 July 1797 (*H.M.C., Dropmore*, III, 335).

3. Cf. II, 302.

4. Malmesbury to Pitt, 9 September; Pitt to Malmesbury, 14 September 1797 (*Malmesbury*, III, 541–2, 560–1). That Pitt was referring to their conversation in June seems clear from another letter to Malmesbury, of the 11th (op. cit., 554).

Not every one was convinced even so that the negotiation was at an end. Malmesbury had made it clear that this surprising demand was unacceptable as it stood. But he left saying he would report to his Government, and the French claimed thereafter that it was not they who broke off the talks. They had indeed never specifically dropped the initial precondition,[1] although it had been tacitly buried in the subsequent conduct of business, and the British were convinced that its reappearance was a pretext. Some hopes lingered, however: Canning would not admit defeat, and remained disposed to more conciliatory language than Pitt himself was now inclined to adopt.[2] And while the Minister seemed to have virtually rejected an immediate resumption of talks, he had not abandoned the object; rather he now decided to pursue it by other means.[3]

For there was an epilogue. The negotiation from the start had given rise to suspicions of interested corruption in France. They had been partly responsible at least for the measures of secrecy in London in July,[4] and they did not diminish, particularly when Talleyrand, in the uneasy situation in Paris, replaced Delacroix as Foreign Minister at about that time. He was known, or thought, to be working for peace; but as so often both his motive and his practice seemed dubious, and the agreement with the Portuguese Minister was surrounded by rumours of bribery. The Directory was certainly anxious to find some money: it was failing to extract sums due from the Dutch, and the Portuguese payment may have been taken partly to compensate for that. But to British eyes the transaction was simply another example of native 'venality';[5] and the suspicion seemed to be confirmed by a comparable approach. For in mid-August a certain 'Mr Melville of Boston', who claimed to have secured the Portuguese peace, visited Malmesbury to offer a treaty in return for payment. Something of the kind indeed appears to have been heard

1. Canning in fact argued this point with Pitt, warning him of its formal validity before the Minister spoke in Parliament, and following up with a telling mock speech for Opposition (1 and 3 October 1797; P.R.O. 30/8/120).

Malmesbury himself, who thought success had been tantalisingly close (*Malmesbury*, III, 539, 541, 577), was anxious for a Note to be sent in answer on '*business*' which he had left '*unfinished* . . . and on purpose' (diary, 20 September; op. cit., 580, and see also 581). This was indeed done, and further self-exculpatory Notes were exchanged over the next fortnight.

2. Canning to Rev. William Leigh, 19 September 1797 (op. cit., 579); same to Pitt as in n1 above.

3. Pitt's attitude to any possible further negotiation in form emerges, I think, from a conversation with Malmesbury on 22 September in which that is made dependent on previous success through a different channel (op. cit., 582–3).

4. P. 60 above.

5. George III's word (to Pitt, 23 September 1797; Holland Rose, *Pitt and Napoleon*, 242).

earlier from another American, a Mr Potter;[1] but Melville (or Melvil) was possibly a more serious proposition, claiming to come from the notoriously self-seeking Barras, the most powerful of the Directors. He soon slipped over to England, and on 28 August talked to Pitt at Holwood,[2] bringing with him an apparently definite proposal that, in return for a payment of £450,000 to 'the different members of the French Government', the British could retain the Cape, Ceylon, Cochin and Trinidad in an immediate peace. Pitt was anxious to inquire further. He informed those Cabinet colleagues in reach, and the King on 6 September; and on the 9th George III agreed to see what might emerge.[3] Fructidor then followed, which plunged everything into confusion. But it did not witness the end of these particular thoughts. The processes however became murkier, and inherently less promising, for Melville, while apparently still involved, seems now to have become one of several channels, perhaps from several sources. A certain O'Drusse who was connected with Talleyrand, and an intermediary in touch with the banker Walter Boyd – himself well known to Pitt –[4] are glimpsed also in the more serious comings and goings. Nor was the offer the same: the cost had become £1,200,000 for Ceylon or £2 million for Ceylon and the Cape (Cochin and Trinidad presumably being thrown in). As George III observed, this was an 'enormous' sum, and strict confidentiality moreover must be reconciled with some form of Parliamentary approval. Malmesbury himself disliked the business, which he thought reeked of '*stock-jobbing*'. But Pitt was still anxious to follow it up, and with characteristic hope.[5] The problems in the event did not have to be faced, for by 20 October the plan

1. *Malmesbury*, III, 492 and n.
As early as the end of June indeed 'a man from Paris' called at the Foreign Office, 'undertaking' 'Terms of Peace'. Pitt declined to see him (Canning's diary for 29 June 1797; Canning Ms 29d).

2. Pitt's villa in Kent; see I, 3.

3. Pitt to Grenville, 28 August, 2 September 1797 (*H.M.C., Dropmore*, III, 360, 368); same to George III, 6 September 1797 (op. cit., 369); George III to Pitt, 9 September 1797 (Holland Rose, *Pitt and Napoleon*, 242). The Minister found Melville 'a very dull stupid Fellow', but well informed (to Canning, nd; Canning Ms 30). The agent in fact paid several more visits, collecting £10,000 for his pains.

4. See II, 377 with n5, and op. cit. 676.

5. Two notes by Pitt, 22 and 23 September 1797 (P.R.O. 30/8/101); Pitt to George III, 22 September 1797; George III to Pitt, 23 September 1797 (Stanhope, III, Appendix, vii–ix, the second letter completed in Holland Rose, *Pitt and Napoleon*, 242). See also Pitt's letters to Canning on the business, 6, 10 and (possibly relevant) 15 September 1797, together with six nd, in Canning Ms 30. Malmesbury found that among those 'in the secret' was Huskisson, whom he suspected of participating in the stockjobbing (*Malmesbury*, III, 583 and in general 580–4). Huskisson was in fact a friend of Boyd, and the rumour became quite widespread. It is interesting to note that he had warned his superior Dundas after Fructidor of 'the refinement of corruption . . . on the part of France' (11 September 1797; S.R.O., Melville Castle Muniments, GD 51/1/529/1).

collapsed.[1] It is hard to tell exactly why: something may have been compromised – Boyd at any rate lost Pitt's trust – and verifiable proof was no doubt elusive. While it lasted, however implausibly, the offer kept alive such hopes as remained; and when it died they finally disappeared.[2]

The episode closed not only a series of moves but a chapter in Pitt's career. From 1793 to 1796 he had looked, if latterly with less confidence, to peace within a measurable distance, and more often than not from the next campaign. The French rejection of terms at the end of that year faced him at last inescapably with the prospect that the war could be indefinitely prolonged. Throughout the first half of 1797 he made intense efforts to avoid that fate. Thoughts of resignation were followed (if the chronology is right)[3] by preparations for peace talks in conjunction with Austria. When Austria disappeared, he forced through a unilateral approach against the King, the Foreign Secretary and almost half the Cabinet. He was ready to face them again if necessary over terms which most would have wished to reject, and against which he expected Grenville himself to resign. When the possibility arose he was anxious to explore the effect of bribery, and though the cost soared and the likelihood shrank he persisted for as long as he could. 'When in war,' Dundas remarked at a later point of strain, 'his hopes and confidence are sanguine beyond all reason; and when aiming at peace there is no sacrifice which at times he has not been ready to make for the attainment of it'.[4] In the early autumn of 1797 it seemed clear that peace was unattainable. He turned again to war, but now with the knowledge that he must devise further measures to develop the nation's capacity for a struggle whose length could not be guessed.

1. See Canning to George Ellis, 10 October 1797 (Canning Ms 62); Malmesbury to Canning, 20 October 1797 (Malmesbury, III, 596); Canning's diary for a conversation with Pitt probably on the 22nd, by which time the Minister was 'determined to have done with it' (Canning Ms 29d).
There was at least one other, abortive, approach to Pitt direct – from a Monsieur Philip – which may or may not have been of this nature (Philip to Pitt, 9 September 1797; Canning to Philip, 12 September 1797, in P.R.O., F.O. 27/52). And when all in fact was over, William Beckford sent to the Duke of Portland [Home Secretary] 'certain overtures from France' made to his agent in Paris, David Williams, which to his annoyance received no attention (Beckford to Pitt, 11 December 1797, 27 March 1798 (Stanhope Ms S5 o6/6, Maidstone); and see also *Diary of Farington*, III, 922).
2. Boyd's letters to Pitt, from 14 September to 28 October, are in P.R.O. 30/8/115, and a copy of Pitt's apparently final reply, of 28 October, is in P.R.O. 30/8/102. One from Boyd to ?Dundas, nd, deploring a report of Pitt's 'tone of asperity' about his conduct in the affair is also in P.R.O. 30/8/115. His personal financial interest in peace is followed in S.R. Cope, *Walter Boyd* . . . (1983), 127–9, 145–6. Canning noted from his own conversation with Pitt on probably 22 October (n1 above) that the whole business had become 'utterly unsafe'.
For continuing, faint possibilities of reviving the direct negotiation at Lille see Grenville to Pitt, 8 October 1797; Pitt to Grenville, 18 October 1797 (*H.M.C., Dropmore*, III, 378–80, 382), and Pitt's final note on 18 October (P.R.O. 30/8/195).
3. Pp. 48–9 above.
4. To Spencer, 17 November 1800; quoted in Keith Grahame Feiling, *The Second Tory Party 1714–1832* (1938), 165–6.

CHAPTER III

A Private Life

I

At the very start of this worrying year Pitt had a worrying personal experience. He had to make it clear to those involved that he did not propose to get married. His own involvement caused some passing interest, and amusement. The reasons for his withdrawal have caused speculation since.

The reports of Pitt's supposed intention certainly surprised the London world. His lack of interest in women had been taken for granted since he first came to office, and remained a target, wearisomely familiar by now, of allusions and jokes. In the past few years moreover – from 1795 at least – he was largely withdrawn from society, passing his days mostly in Downing Street and the House of Commons when in session, his nights often at Dundas's at Wimbledon, with short forays to his retreat of Holwood in Kent and longer stays in the summer, and occasional visits, particularly in the late summer, to Walmer.[1] While enjoying company, he had never been immersed in the social round, though in the early nineties he perhaps took part rather more than before.[2] But as the war absorbed him increasingly his habits became ever more private, and in the first months of 1797 he was said to be 'seldom seen even by his intimate acquaintances except in public, the pressure of affairs occupies him entirely'.[3] This, if true, was exceptional; but exceptional only in degree. He was the last person to be the subject of rumour in the marriage market.

In point of fact, however, the episode stemmed from his very seclusion. Among the politicians and officials with houses in easy reach of London was Lord Auckland, based on Eden Farm at Beckenham since retiring from his

1. Dundas's hospitality began to replace Wilberforce's at Wimbledon in the second half of the eighties (see I, 105, 107–8, 578, 584). For Pitt's house at Holwood, by Hayes where he had been born and brought up, see op. cit., 105, 590–4; for Walmer Castle, his residence as Lord Warden of the Cinque Ports from 1792, II, 189, 202, 291–2, 461. His visits to each house can be followed broadly from his wine accounts in P.R.O. 30/8/203.
   For the impression of Pitt's attitude to women see I, 108–9.
2. Eg Sir George Beaumont, the MP and connoisseur, on Pitt's 'frequent' visits to White's (cf. I, 106, 580) and attendance at London dinners and parties in those years (*Diary of Joseph Farington*, III, 794).
3. Op. cit., 793–4, diary of 11 March. And see Archbishop of Canterbury to Auckland, 7 February 1797 (*A.C.*, III, 377); Canning's diary for February (Canning Ms 29d).

Embassy at The Hague in 1793.[1] This was less than five miles from Holwood, and he was not the man to waste propinquity, or be backward with advice on public affairs. Able, experienced, insatiably ambitious, politically unreliable, rather short of money – he ended with fourteen children – he did not neglect the Minister; and Pitt, generally disposed to make the best of those whom fortune brought within his habits of life, and to consult expert views and aid, often called in on his neighbour.[2] Among Auckland's many daughters the eldest was Eleanor, aged nineteen in 1796. Tall and fair, and by all accounts beautiful, lively and intelligent,[3] it was observed that Pitt enjoyed her company; and she, doubtless flattered, seemed – at least according to her father – to respond. By the turn of the year gossip was rising. There had already been paragraphs in the newspapers, more appeared now, and the Aucklands were contentedly discounting the rumours to their friends. In the first half of February Gillray produced a cartoon.[4] Had he but known it, he was then out of date. At some point, in the last days of December 1796 or the first week of the new year, Pitt seems to have spent much time with the family. He was back in London thereafter; but on 20 January he sent a letter.[5] It seemed, quite unexpectedly, to spell the end of the hopes.[6]

1. To which he had been appointed, after Madrid, in 1789 (see II, 13).

2. Auckland's career and character (as William Eden) are discussed in I, 484–5, and at greater length in John Ehrman, *The British Government and Commercial Negotiations with Europe 1783–1793* (1962), 33–9; Pitt's attitude to company in I, 587.

3. She became the favourite correspondent of her much younger sister Emily, the novelist. Even Hester Stanhope, no doubt bowing to Pitt's taste, said later that she admired her looks at the time (*Memoirs of the Lady Hester Stanhope . . .*, I (1845), 177–8).

4. That the Aucklands were writing or talking to some of their circle might be inferred from his later need to state that the rumours had been false (to Pitt, 23 January 1797; *Letters Relating to the Love Episode of William Pitt . . .*, ed. Lord Rosebery (1900), 27 [reprinted from *The Monthly Review*, December 1900]. Hereafter cited as *Love Episode*). There is one such letter in *A.C.*, III, 369.

5. Precise dating for the period before the letter is difficult. Auckland wrote to Pitt on 21 January, 'after the happy week that we all pass'd together, the separation of the last fortnight has been matter of evident regret to us all' (*Love Episode*, 8). It may not have been a full week. Pitt was held in London for much of December by the course and collapse of the peace talks with France, and seems to have been there on Christmas day and perhaps expected to be there again on the 28th (to Auckland, 24 December 1796; *A.C.*, III, 369–70). Whether or not this last turned out to be so he seems to have been back on New Year's day, and from correspondence, and newspaper reports of Cabinet meetings and other business if correct, was in London for much of the next three weeks. He was said however to have gone down to Beckenham to dine with Auckland on 1 January, leaving the next day (*The Times*, 2, 4 January 1797), and he certainly did so on the 7th, returning to London the next morning. On this last occasion, however, there was a large party (Canning's diary, 7–8 January 1797; Canning Ms 29d). The wine accounts show consumption at Holwood between 5 and 10 January (P.R.O. 30/8/203).

According to one, impressionistic, account (*Glenbervie*, I, 98–9, for 21–22 November 1796) Pitt had been going down or over to Eden Farm 'almost every day . . . in idleness and lounging' since 'the recess of Parliament' – meaning presumably the turn of September–October. On a visit himself on 5 December, Douglas noted the Minister's obvious attachment (op. cit., 102).

6. *Love Episode*, 1–5. The text was first published, from the Pretyman Mss, by Lord Ashbourne in *Pitt: some Chapters of his Life and Times* (1898), ch. VII. Rosebery published the

My dear Lord,

Altho' the anxious expectation of public business would at all events have made it difficult for me to leave town during the last ten days, you may perhaps have begun to think that it cannot have been the only reason which has kept me so long from Beckenham. The truth is that I have really felt it impossible to allow myself to yield to the temptation of returning thither without having (as far as might depend upon me) formed a decision on a point which I am sensible has remained in suspense too long already. Having at length done so, I should feel myself inexcusable if (painful as the task is) any consideration prevented me from opening myself to you without reserve. It can hardly, I think, be necessary to say that the time I have passed among your family had led to my forming sentiments of very real attachment towards them all, and of much more than attachment towards one whom I need not name. Nor should I do justice to my own feelings or explain myself as frankly as I think I ought to do, if I did not own that every hour of my acquaintance with the person to whom you will easily conceive I refer has served to augment and confirm that impression; in short, has convinced me that whoever may have the good fortune ever to be united with her is destined to more than his share of human happiness.

Whether, at any rate, I could have had any ground to hope that such might have been my lot, I am in no degree entitled to guess. I have to reproach myself for having ever indulged the idea on my own part as far as I have done without asking myself carefully and early enough what were the difficulties in the way of its being realised. I have suffered myself to overlook them too long, but, having now at length reflected as fully and as calmly as I am able on every circumstance that ought to come under my consideration (at least as much for her sake as for my own), I am compelled to say that I find the obstacles to it decisive and insurmountable. In thus conveying to you, my dear Lord, what has been passing in my mind, and its painful but unavoidable result, I have felt it impossible to say less.[1] And yet it would be almost a consolation to me to know that even what I have said is superfluous, and that the idea which I have entertained has been confined solely to myself. If this should be the case, I am sure this communication will be buried in

---

whole correspondence, at that time from the same source. The contents are now in two batches in the B.L., complementing each other: in Add. Ms 46491, ff. 161–74 (this letter in a copy – unlike the rest – at ff. 163–4v); and in Add. Ms 59704 (the original of the letter being there together with Pitt's corrected, and in places different draft, at ff. 1–10). Auckland returned Pitt's two main letters (here, and pp. 72–3 below) to him. Add. Ms 46491 was presented to the British Library in 1948 by a descendant of Emily Eden; Add. Ms 59704 was bequeathed, in 1976, having strayed from the Pretyman Mss at some time.

I have cited *Love Episode* throughout, following its orthography and punctuation except where I indicate otherwise.

1. The draft of this sentence reads, 'It is my first duty under these Circumstances to state to you thus plainly the Result. To enter into detail would be useless.' (B.L. Add. Ms 59704, f. 3v).

silence and oblivion. On any other supposition I know that I but consult the feelings of those who must be most in my thoughts by confiding it to your discretion. And in doing so I have every reason to rely on those sentiments of mutual friendship which I hope will not be affected by any change which may at the present moment be unavoidable in what have lately been the habits of our intercourse. For myself, allow me only to add that, separated as I must be for a time from those among whom I have passed many of my happiest moments, the recollection of that period will be long present to my mind. The greatest pleasure and best consolation I can receive will be if I am ever enabled to prove how deep an interest I must always take in whatever may concern them.

They will not, I am sure, be less dear to me through life than they would have had a right to expect from the nearest and closest connection.

Believe me, my dear Lord, under all circumstances,
Ever sincerely and faithfully yours,
W. Pitt.

If Pitt had expected thus to end the affair, at a stroke, he was disappointed. Auckland did not accept the verdict at once. Hardly surprisingly, he tried to probe the 'reserve' which Pitt disclaimed; and he put paid to any disclaimer of knowledge of the lady's feelings. The sentiments were '*most cordially*' mutual, and they 'were ripening into an attachment which might lay the foundation of a system of most perfect happiness, for the two persons' involved. If the 'circumstances' which Pitt mentioned were financial, they should not 'create an hour's interruption in . . . intercourse . . .; still less . . . affect the ultimate result', even if that had to be delayed. His daughter, he was sure, would wait; he only regretted he could not help much himself. But 'these small details' should not be followed further. Pitt should come to Beckenham as soon as convenient, '& especially in the eyes of observers as if nothing had happened.' They could 'talk about the whole at leisure & again & again'. Alternatively 'let the persons most concerned express themselves to each other'.[1]

This effort met with a firm repulse. The last thing Pitt wished to do was to talk the matter over 'again & again'.[2] Nor would he explain his decision 'at large'. 'The circumstances of every man's private and personal situation can often, on various accounts, be fully known and fairly judged of by no one but himself'. Despite all the inducements to the contrary, he could not 'distrust' his decision. 'Believe me, I have not lightly or easily sacrificed my best hopes and earnest wishes to my conviction and judgment.' And then the door was decisively shut.

1. 21 January, $^1/_2$ pt. 4 (*Love Episode*, 6–11). The original is in B.L. Add. Ms 46491, ff. 167–8v.

2. Two days later, in a letter to Addington, who like others of his friends had earlier been watching what was going on, Pitt described Auckland's reply as 'the most embarrassing possible' (quoted in Philip Ziegler, *Addington*, 83).

Believe me, also, that further explanation or discussion can answer no good purpose. And let me entreat you to spare me and yourself the pain of urging it further. It could only lead to prolonged suspense and increasing anxiety, without the possibility of its producing any ultimate advantage.[1]

That was undeniably that. Winding-up however proved not quite pleasant. The two men exchanged letters in the next forty-eight hours on the line to be taken with inquiries, and Pitt returned Auckland's two earlier missives, as Auckland suggested, leaving him to do likewise if he wished.[2] The tone at the start was friendly on either side. But as far as Auckland's was concerned, one reason became clear. It seems likely that, probably in the 'week' spent in company, he had asked Pitt to consider him for a Cabinet post. There was an existing vacancy, in the Office of Lord Privy Seal, open since the previous September when its incumbent Chatham had moved to the Lord Presidency of the Council on Lord Mansfield's death.[3] He now repeated his request, and when Pitt answered doubtfully responded in strong terms.[4] The appointment was '*now*' 'essential . . . to me and still more to mine'. It would give him and them 'as soon as possible an ostensible & honourable pretext for throwing ourselves once more into the full tide of courts and of London society', and distancing themselves from 'a place in which every idea for a time is poisoned'. Pitt's alleged difficulties, arising from a possible prior obligation, could surely be removed. And

I certainly did not say all. It is most important for all our sakes to shew to the Public what I am sure will be true in fact, tho' subject to severe difficulties in practice that there remains an undiminished friendship between us two at least . . .[5]

The manoeuvre did not succeed. No answer is afforded. But the post remained vacant for a further year, and on that note the episode closed.

1. 22 January 1797, 2 pm (*Love Episode*, 12–15). The original, again with the draft, is in B.L. Add. Ms 59704, ff. 11–17v. The second sentence in this last passage was added in the draft. So was the phrase 'on various accounts' in another sentence quoted above.
2. See p. 70, n6 above. Auckland to Pitt, 22 January 1797 (*Love Episode*, 16–18; original in B.L. Add. Ms 46491, ff. 169–v); Pitt to Auckland, 23 January 1797 [from Holwood] (*Love Episode*, 19–21; original in B.L. Add. Ms 46491, ff. 171–2v); Auckland to Pitt, sd, 8 pm (*Love Episode*, 24–30; original in B.L. Add. Ms 59704, ff. 19–20).
3. For Chatham's appointment see II, 463; for Mansfield, op. cit., 414, 418.
The suggested timing of Auckland's initial request is put forward on the basis of Pitt's statement (to Auckland, 23 January 1797, 3 pm; *Love Episode*, 22–3; original in B.L. Add. Ms 46491, ff. 173–4) that he had been 'turning it' over in his mind 'during the last Ten Days'.
4. Auckland's first letter, apparently of the 23rd morning, is missing. But its content can be deduced from the sequel in Pitt to Auckland, 23 January 1797, 3 pm and Auckland's second letter, sd, 8 pm as in n2 above.
5. 23 January 1797, 8 pm (n2 above).

What lay behind Pitt's decision? He had certainly gone so far as to raise expectations: he acknowledged this in his first long, embarrassed letter, and one at least of his intimates assumed that marriage was on the cards. '. . . Eden Farm – all off. I am surprized – & sorry,' wrote Canning shortly afterwards.[1] It may in fact have been the publicity that brought the Minister to the point, spreading in a way which, as Auckland observed, he had been slow to grasp.[2] When he faced the issue, several possible reasons can be cited for his behaviour. One simple if contributory factor might have been a reluctance to be linked too closely with the Aucklands in general, and in particular with Auckland himself. This was Hester Stanhope's partial explanation – fastening on Lady Auckland's chatter and match-making, though she also mentioned more broadly 'the family intrigues'. And while she is a highly unreliable witness, and was speaking after Pitt had broken later with Auckland, she may not have been entirely wide of the mark. Politically at any rate it could have been awkward to be allied to a man with a mixed reputation and, in such conditions, wearyingly near at hand. Lord Rosebery – no subscriber to Lady Hester's credibility – was himself inclined to put that weight, as an addition, in the scales.[3] However, Auckland had not shown his colours plainly in this instance before Pitt made up his mind, and their correspondence in general continued, on the surface amicably enough. Auckland indeed did not give up. Within a few months he was reminding the Minister of an 'inactivity ill suited to the whole frame . . . of my Mind', and in August Pitt, acknowledging that they had not met over a 'long interval', assured him of a wish still to find him a place.[4] In 1798 he did so, though not in the Cabinet, as joint Postmaster General. Any danger of an intimate relationship had by then disappeared; and if Pitt may perhaps have become more alert when the need to think closely arose, the problem of Auckland as a father-in-law might be thought nonetheless to have been subsidiary. There were other matters bearing on a 'private and personal situation', which could be known and judged by 'no one but himself'.[5]

1. Diary of 8 February 1797 (Canning Ms 29d). The information came to him in a 'Long letter' from Pitt, which seems to have disappeared.

2. To Pitt, 23 January 1797 (as in p. 73, n2 above).

3. *Memoirs of the Lady Hester Stanhope*, I, 179 & n1; Rosebery, introduction to *Love Episode*, ix–x, and, on Lady Hester, in his *Pitt* (1891), 265. And cf. *Glenbervie*, I, 102.

4. Auckland to Pitt, 20 April, endorsed (and from internal evidence) 1797; and again – 'You also know it [my mind] to be incompetent to many domestic considerations, claims & duties', 21 June, private & in confidence, endorsed 1797 (both in P.R.O. 30/8/110); Pitt to Auckland, Private, 27 August 1797 (B.L. Add. Ms 46519). Some other letters, on public affairs, had passed between them since late in February, when Pitt may also have seen Auckland in London (*A.C.*, III, 379).

According to Lord Stanhope in the 1860s, there was 'a complete estrangement' between the two men when the affair ended, which however was 'soon' composed through the efforts of Addington and the Archbishop of Canterbury, Dr Moore, who was Auckland's brother-in-law (notes in Stanhope Ms U1590 S5, C60/19).

5. P. 72 above.

II

One such, cited from Auckland's day to this, could have been money. Pitt's finances were certainly in a bad, and unpromising, way. As had been the case almost from the start, it is hard to tell exactly how confused they were; he gave them sparse attention in the nineties, as he had given virtually none before.[1] His income from official sources remained as it had been since August 1792, when the revenues – salary, fees and incidents – of the Lord Warden of the Cinque Ports were added to those of the First Lord of the Treasury and the Chancellor of the Exchequer. The total amounted to something under £10,000 when taxes and duties were deducted.[2] This was the situation (with one minor exception) until the second quarter of 1801, the sums reaching him on the whole – more so indeed than earlier – fairly promptly and regularly.[3]

An income of that size was by no means small in the circumstances of the age. Prices had recently been rising; but £5,000 a year was still a sum considered adequate for a 'man of high rank'.[4] Such private resources as Pitt had inherited could not usefully be added: on the contrary, they had mostly provided the means for his early recourse to loans. By 1782, when he was twenty-three, he had a nominal fortune of £10,244. But since this was by legacy from his father it was not going to be paid in full. In the event he received in cash just under £4,400, and by the time it reached him, in 1785, he had converted some capital (how found is uncertain) into an annuity of £300, was receiving another £600 in income, half of which was by grant from his brother, and had started borrowing on his expectations. The process continued, his official revenues being taken as security: between 1780 and 1792 Pitt seems to have raised some £37,400 in sums requiring specific payments through his bank, of which £8,000 was repaid.[5] He was paying interest on a mortgage for Holwood, purchased in 1785, on loans from his bankers Coutts and from Thomas Coutts himself, and from the middle nineties at least on an overdraft costing between some £500 and £950 a year. In June 1793 he assigned to Thomas Coutts his salary as First Lord of the Treasury.[6]

1. See I, 595, 598 for the eighties; p. 72 above for Auckland's query.
2. And, for the Cinque Ports, some subordinates' salaries. Cf. I, 595–6. The figures may be checked against the payments for 1792 to 1801 in Messrs Coutts' Ledgers (Coutts's Bank), which are also listed in the papers of Pitt's private secretary Joseph Smith (for whom see I, 578 & n2) in the possession of Mr W.H. Saumarez Smith. For Pitt's appointment as Lord Warden of the Cinque Ports see II, 189–90.
3. Cf. I, 597. The small item of the First Lord's ancient receipt of New Year's Gifts – worth less than £50 in Pitt's time – was abolished in October 1797.
4. Op. cit., 596. For prices see II, 451.
5. I put it like this because he probably borrowed elsewhere in ways that do not disclose payments of interest so readily. At some point probably in 1796, for example, he passed 'an edifying morning . . . chiefly with kind-hearted Jews' in an unknown transaction (Pitt to Auckland, nd; *A.C.*, III, 358); and this is unlikely to have been the only time.
6. See I, 19–20, 591 & n1, 595–8, 600–2 for developments up to that date.

One of the loans was almost certainly devoted in part to a purpose from which Pitt did not benefit. In 1786 he seems to have assigned to his mother the nominal balance – £5,800 – of his inheritance. This was generous, at a time when he was already embarrassed, and he probably moreover met the annual interest, which in better circumstances she should have done. In 1793 he managed to advance her £300, explaining that he could not do more because he must apply his new income as Lord Warden immediately to tradesmen's bills.[1] But it was those bills, and his approach to his affairs, that accounted for his state. Some of the expenditure was unexceptionable: from 1786 he had the upkeep of two houses and from 1792 of three, and while two of the three attracted no rent and some allowances and perquisites, they had to be looked after and run, according to whether he was there or not. The addition of Walmer Castle, the Lord Warden's residence, presumably explained for instance some of the expense on menservants, fifteen in 1794 compared with eleven in 1786, on whom Pitt was paying tax.[2] Extra costs there were unavoidable, to set against the increased income. But Walmer did not yet figure largely: it was Downing Street and Holwood that absorbed the funds; and while the former of course sustained costs such as the larger political and official dinners, which could take anything from £25 to £60 a time and amount to twenty-five a year,[3] both continued to swallow money, if not as ravenously as earlier, and in ways that were still largely uncontrolled.

It is correspondingly hard to tell exactly why the money went as it did. Various lists of figures survive; but we do have one attempt at a comprehensive answer for a given year in the middle nineties. Pitt's private secretary, Joseph Smith, writing at the time, gave details as he knew them for 1796. According to these, Pitt's current expenditure then was some £8,924: £1,942 on the 'table' for the three establishments, £1,136 on 'housekeeping' likewise, £543 on wines, £494 on clothes, £655 on servants' wages, £438 on board wages, £659 on 'servants' bills', £249 on their liveries, £299 on 'job horses', £175 on 'carriages' and £397 on 'stables'. 'Incidents', divided almost equally between London, the house at Holwood, and its farm, came to £1,116, 'labourers' pay' to £556, taxes to £263.[4] These figures, which were almost certainly much too low, were

1. Op. cit., 596–7.
2. P.R.O. 30/8/206, entry for 4 January 1794 – there appears to have been one less in 1793 (P.R.O. 30/8/219, f. 39); I, 599. By 1799 there seem to have been 19 or 20 male servants (P.R.O. 30/8/201), 14 of them in London (P.R.O. 30/8/217). While the proportion was small for Walmer, it included board wages separate from those for Downing Street and Holwood (household accounts for 1796, Saumarez Smith Mss; P.R.O. 30/8/202).
Pitt did not of course pay tax on female servants, having had to drop the idea, amid ribaldry, when he proposed it in 1785 (I, 250, 253 & n6). In 1793 there seem to have been nine of these (P.R.O. 30/8/219, Part 6).
3. Note in Pitt's hand, nd, in P.R.O. 30/8/197. P.R.O. 30/8/219, Part 6 contains some bills of fare from 1794 to 1797.
4. 'Expenses in yᵉ Year 1796 . . .', in Joseph Smith's hand (Saumarez Smith Mss). Figures in each case to the nearest £ account for a discrepancy of £3 for the total.

followed by others for 'Propos'd future Expenditure': 'table' £1,000, 'housekeeping' £700, cellar £500 (not too harsh a reduction), clothes £300, servants' wages £600 and board wages £700, servants' bills £400 and their liveries £150; 'job horses' £300, 'carriages' £150 and 'stables London' £250; incidental expenses £350 (£200 for London, £50 for Holwood, £100 for its farm); labourers' pay £250; taxes £265. They produced a total of £5,915, which Smith noted firmly 'appears to be even more than sufficient, & it is hoped that by Care & Attention it will fall considerably within y.ᵉ proposed Limits – it must not exceed them'. He commented further that by such an arrangement 'there is no Diminution whatever in y.ᵉ Establishment, nor any Retrenchments that will in any degree affect either Comfort or Appearance'.[1]

The account suggests certain points – and questions. Pitt's secretary, a shrewd – and devoted – man, concluded that his master could cut his current expenses by over a third without detracting from his way of life. As things stood in 1796, they exceeded his probable disposable income, private and official, by perhaps £2,500.[2] On the other hand, if the list is correct, earlier outgoings had been reduced: the astonishing outlay on the stables' account – £16,813 in 1783–4, £8,647 in 1785–6 – drastically so.[3] Even purchases of wine, if much the same as for recent years, seem to have been down on those of a decade before.[4] One must wonder however if Smith's efforts could produce a wholly accurate answer. They were not concerned of course with capital items – to take one example, Pitt spent some £1,400 on works and plans for the house at Holwood from 1795 to 1799.[5] But the confused state of the debts to tradesmen – not to servants, who as earlier were paid regularly – which reached £11,000 in 1801, suggests a rate of expenditure higher than was revealed by current estimates.[6]

There is a comparable account, but for the second half of the year only, for 1794. According to a later abstract, Pitt's man of business Dr Joseph Bullock disbursed totals of some £9,942 in 1795, £10,731 in 1796, and £9,871 in 1797 (Pretyman Ms 562:3; another copy is in Tomline Ms 35.11, Pembroke College, Cambridge). But these may not have covered precisely the same objects.

1. Saumarez Smith Mss.

2. Private income £600, net official income say £9,800 (I, 19–20, 596). But he had by then parted with his salary as First Lord of the Treasury (£4,022 less about £500 in duties and taxes; see op. cit., 595).

3. Cf. I, 599–600. And this despite the fact that in 1794 he was paying tax on three carriages, as compared with two in 1785. He was also paying on nine horses (P.R.O. 30/8/206). By 1799 the figures had risen to four and twelve respectively, plus six horses used 'in Trade' – presumably for farming (P.R.O. 30/8/217).

4. Which did not necessarily mean a comparable drop in consumption, if the cellars had been largely built up earlier. Cf. I, 598–9 for figures then.

5. Soane Mss, Ledger C (Sir John Soane's Museum, London). He had spent some £532 similarly between 1786 and 1791. The architect was paid in part in May 1803 and the rest soon after Pitt's death, in April 1806 (Ledger D).

6. Saumarez Smith Mss, 1801 and 1803. And this was after an exceptional crop of payments by Bullock of perhaps almost £19,000 in 1800 (cf. p. 76, n4 above). For payments of servants earlier see I, 602n5.

Even if Smith's account was correct, this latter figure reveals a situation which needed, and did not receive, further action on the lines he advised.

The lack of response was not due to a change in habits. Pitt's private style remained as simple as ever. His achievement indeed was to combine marked financial extravagance with a markedly unassuming standard of life. He was still a bachelor with a substantial, though now smaller income at his command. He does not seem to have indulged in cards or women, or with one possible exception in other familiar outlays. While keenly interested in architecture, he kept his building operations within bounds; and he formed no racing stable or great library or collection of works of art.[1] He was not in fact greatly concerned with material possessions. His highest expenditure in any one direction was on his farm and grounds at Holwood: totals of some £2,230 and £2,330 in 1799 and 1800. But the great bulk here went on the farming, and while he may well have lost money one does not know exactly how much.[2] Allowing for that, drink was the most visible item of conspicuous expenditure; and if it helped wreck his constitution it could not wreck his finances by itself. One must suspect that he continued to be robbed, to an unusual extent, by trades-men and servants[3] – scarcely surprisingly when the former had often to wait as long as they did – until a situation long out of hand could no longer be redeemed. His absorption in public business, and its increased pressures now, acted reciprocally on an indifference, both natural and induced, to his personal affairs. Example, temperament and circum-stances pointed the same way.[4] But if the influences were complementary, the result was in striking contrast to the assiduous labours of a great Chancellor of the Exchequer in the promotion and care of the national wealth.

Smith's account might have been made when Pitt was facing the ques-tion of marriage. It may also have been made in the period when he was considering resignation. If this last was so the financial prospect was par-ticularly bleak, with the First Lord of the Treasury's salary already assigned as security to Thomas Coutts.[5] But in any case the outlook was sombre. In 1796 Pitt paid £676 in interest on his overdraft, and some £940 on bank loans, and there may have been other similar obligations, hon-oured or postponed.[6] There was a mass of bills, mounting once more since

1. He did however spend a not insignificant proportion of his income on his books, including on their bindings in later years at least; though the sums themselves in any year were not large. This subject is discussed in Ch. XVI, section I below.

2. P.R.O. 30/8/201, 202; and cf. loc. cit., 214, 216, 217 for 1797–1800. These current expenditures amounted to broadly a fifth of the totals recorded for those two years (p. 79 below). The 'Garden' cost at the most a tenth of the 'Farm'.

3. Cf. I, 599 600.

4. For the impact of Chatham's example, and Pitt's own temperament, see op. cit., 7–9, 602–3.

5. See pp. 48–9, 75 above.

6. Coutts's Ledgers 118, 122; p. 75 above.

the settlement, or reduction, in 1793.[1] Marriage must mean some domestic enlargement – if perhaps a closer check on costs. And Auckland could not help much – unless he was found a rewarding post. No relief lay in sight, unless Holwood were to be sold, which would be a depressing start to marriage and would have met less than half of the capital needs. Even then, despite the saving on running costs, Pitt would be strained; and while this might not worry him for himself, it could – and should – have been another matter if a wife was involved. Looking to the strictly financial implications of such a future, there was ample reason for him to turn away.

As it was, he carried on very much as before: in fact, at least from 1798, more carelessly than in the past few years.[2] At the beginning of 1797 he made a first payment on a new loan of £10,000; later in the year he took out a second mortgage on Holwood of £7,000 – so much for sale; and, it would seem, at the end of the decade raised a loan of £10,437 in the names of himself and a certain Charles Townshend.[3] These further facilities were needed to help finance an expenditure that stood at well over £20,200 in 1799.[4] It was a period in which he began moreover to face higher taxes, of his own making as Chancellor: the increased Assessed Taxes and Voluntary Subscription in 1798, followed from 1799 by the Incomes' Tax.[5] Not surprisingly the interest on his bank overdraft, reduced in 1797–8, rose again in 1799 and 1800.[6] By the end of the century Pitt in fact seems to have abandoned any attempt to meet his situation. It did not disturb his habits or, at least for long, cause him undue distress.

III

One of the creditors from now on was Pitt's doctor, Sir Walter Farquhar, introduced, probably by Dundas, in 1795 or '96.[7] The Minister's health in

1. See p. 76 above.

2. There is a note, not in Pitt's hand, of items of expenditure to be reduced ('Mr Pitt's Wardrobe, Steward's Room, Stable') which seems to refer to that year (P.R.O. 30/8/196, f. 287v). The intention did not bear fruit, at any rate for long.

3. Coutts's Ledgers 122, 143 for the loans. The new mortgage figured in the Holwood estate papers, which were examined by Lord Cranworth, then owner of the property, for Lord Stanhope in 1860 (letter of 5 September; Stanhope Ms U1590 S5 60/6). Charles Townshend was Pitt's attorney (see P.R.O. 30/8/219, Part 4).

4. I have taken this figure, which nevertheless includes Walmer for only one quarter, in preference to a much lower one in P.R.O. 30/8/201, itself comparable in size and method of calculation with Joseph Smith's in 1796 (p. 76 above). There can be little doubt in point of fact that he failed to plumb the real depths of those, and succeeding, years (George Rose to Pretyman, 21 July 1801; Holland Rose, II, 475).

Similar accounts are not available for 1797 and 1798, though there are detailed lists of household expenses and wages in P.R.O. 30/8/212–16, and miscellaneous lists scattered (for all years) in P.R.O. 30/8/196–7, in Pretyman's papers at Ipswich and (marginally) at Pembroke College, Cambridge, and in the Stanhope Mss at Maidstone.

Dr Bullock apparently drew £11,376 from Coutts's in 1799 (Pretyman Ms 562: 3).

5. Discussed in Chs. IV, IX below.

6. Coutts's Ledgers 126, 131, 136, 143.

7. II, 461–2.

the later nineties was indeed causing concern to his friends; and it has been given as a further reason for him to reject marriage. In his letter to Addington about Eleanor Eden he wrote that he would 'not be wanting either to the calls of public duty or to what yet remains to me of the private relations of life'.[1] If, or in so far as, the last phrase referred to health it may have been a form of words, which given Pitt's resilience need not be taken too seriously: he often talked and behaved differently later when his constitution showed greater sign of strain.[2] But in the winter of 1796–7 he was certainly in a poor way: 'hoarse' and his face 'much swollen' as reported in February, 'with a violent cough which prevented his sleeping' then and in March. His 'bad Health' was partly responsible for 'his appearing to sink under the difficulties' which themselves had doubtless helped bring it on.[3] In point of fact he did not allow the pressure to depress his spirits for long, or the example of cheerfulness he always tried to set. Like his father, he acted as 'a cordial' at times when others were 'despondent', and the display of character was not absent now.[4] In any case he shortly revived, and the effect was visible, not least on the floor of the Commons. But those months furnished an example of a pattern that was to become familiar when 'unremitting attention upon subjects of anxiety and interest' bore on his physical state.[5]

The interaction had been noted, though not seriously, as early as 1793.[6] Exactly what was wrong was not clear. It was certainly aggravated by the amount that Pitt was drinking, with consequences now more serious for the physique it had helped undermine. One may put it like this because judging by the cellar books – sparse though the details are for London – consumption does not in fact seem to have risen from that of previous years. Port remained easily the main item, with madeira second; but on aggregate no more was drunk in the 'parlour' at Holwood and Walmer than before, and the 'steward's room' continued to account for more than half the totals.[7] Without knowing the size of the company one cannot be precise; taking port alone, the entries vary between one and five or six bottles for an evening. But so they had done for at least a decade, and the difference may have been that Pitt was now depending increasingly on a habit long indulged on much the same scale.[8]

1. 23 January 1797 (see p. 72, n2 above).
2. I have not therefore been disposed to cite fear for his health as an element in his thought of resigning in perhaps the early part of this year (Ch. II, section II above).
3. Archbishop of Canterbury to Auckland, 7 February (*A.C.*, III, 338); Bathurst to Camden, 29 March [endorsed 1797] (Camden Ms U840 226/4).
4. Canning's diary, 18 February 1797 (Canning Ms 29d). And cf. in general *Private Papers of William Wilberforce* . . . ed. A.M. Wilberforce (1897), 64.
5. Farquhar's retrospective account (*Letters Relating to the Love Episode of William Pitt together with an Account of his Health by his Physician Sir Walter Farquhar*, 27); see II, 462.
6. See I, 461.
7. Largely because wine was drunk there, as earlier, whether Pitt was in residence or not. Cf. I, 586.
8. This paragraph, like that in I, 586 for earlier years, is based primarily on the contents of P.R.O. 30/8/203. To take a fairly typical list, of the cellar at Walmer at the end of

George Canning, *by Thomas Lawrence*

Eleanor Eden. *Unknown*

Holwood House. *Design, unexecuted, by John Soane*

The prescription of port for his 'gouty tendency' as a boy, the long sessions with Dundas in particular, had ensured that he 'liked a glass of port wine very well, and a bottle still better'. 'Now Pitt', Addington recalled saying, 'you shall not have another drop'; but any 'promise of abstinence was seldom long remembered'. Farquhar observed, in an effort to curb him in 1798, that 'As one is apt, by the Society of Friends and the Eagerness of Conversation . . ., to forget Quantity', it would be wise to place a pint bottle on the table and confine himself to that. His portion would otherwise often have been more; but the greatest change lay in the increasing effects, which even Pretyman, with whom Pitt was more restrained, noticed in that same year.[1]

The deterioration of which this formed a visible part had apparently advanced quite rapidly. After a troubled childhood, and improvement from puberty, Pitt had passed his first decade in office pretty well. But when Farquhar was summoned he found a measure of 'general debility', with 'the functions of the stomach greatly impaired' and the 'gouty tendency' long remarked.[2] Diffused gout, sharper from the end of the eighties, was certainly in evidence; what else there might be was less obvious, though some bouts of sickness were suggestive. An attempted diagnosis had best await a later stage of Pitt's life: here we may simply record a series of disturbing episodes. One came in September 1797, after he had complained of a 'tormenting' headache for a fortnight, and 'some degree of Cold'; when Malmesbury was dismissed from Lille, and then his brother-in-law Edward Eliot died, he had a violent abdominal attack. He was indeed badly shaken by the domestic blow – worrying also about his orphaned niece at a time when his mother herself seemed far from well – and while he quickly recovered from the worst he was under the weather for some time. A spell at Walmer, always a favourite place, and some medicine from Farquhar set him up.[3] But there was another bout of ill-health the next summer. Wilberforce reported him 'seriously ill' at the beginning of June 1798, and though again he recovered quite fast – Rose described him as 'much better' within a week – he again took time to shake off the effects. He did not attend the Commons throughout that last month of the session, and at the end of July he seemed to Auckland better but 'much

September 1798, it held (to the nearest dozen) 16 dozen madeira, 23 of claret, 3 of burgundy, 144 of port, 2 of champagne, 2 of red and 4 of white 'hermitage', 7 of hock, 2 of barsac, 3 of constantia (from the Cape), plus 3 bottles of sherry, 1 of rum and 3 of brandy. Cf. I, 586n2 for 1784–5. Consumption in Downing Street in 1796 was 204 dozen of port, 35 of madeira, 15 of claret, and smaller quantities of other wines. This list would seem to have referred to private occasions (Saumarez Smith Mss). Cf. also p. 78 above.

1. See I, 12, 584–5; Pellew, *Life of Sidmouth*, I, 152–3; Farquhar to Pitt, 10 October 1798 (P.R.O. 30/8/134). One must of course take into account that port was then a lighter wine, in a smaller bottle.

2. See II, 462, and for earlier years I, 9, 12, 29, 105–6, 594–5.

3. There is a fair amount of information in letters and diaries about the attack in September; a good summary is in Robin Reilly, *Pitt the Younger* . . . (1978), 276. For Eliot's death see p. 48 above; Rose, who was with Pitt when he learned of it, wrote to Wilberforce that 'the effect . . . was beyond description' (*Life of Wilberforce*, II, 417).

striken in his constitution'. Farquhar recommended ale instead of the wine and water he had prescribed earlier – a change duly noted by Opposition newspapers;[1] but 'Nourishment' was 'the Thing principally wanted', together with a change of air, and some rest, and some good news. Two of these were provided in the long recess, and the last in the late summer culminating with Nelson's victory at the Nile. But the attack had been severe enough to excite real fears in Pitt's circle, and he was persuaded to adopt 'improved . . . habits': not only the reduction in wine – which seems in fact to have settled at two glasses of madeira and 'nearly a pint of Port after, but not quite' – but also more food (to be taken in two separate dinners), glasses of Bath water at regular hours, and as much moderate exercise as possible, especially through riding.[2] Whether or not as a result of these precautions, he survived the Parliamentary 'Winter Campaign' without crisis;[3] nor, though he was indisposed and depressed in April, was there a comparable physical episode in 1799.[4] But in 1800 he had a severe relapse. At the end of July and again in October (perhaps starting in September) he was attacked by the 'old Complaint in the Bowels'. His weakness was all too visible on the second occasion: 'he cannot carry a Glass of Beer to his Mouth without the aid of his second Hand'. Farquhar then advised a spell in Cheltenham or Bath; but Pitt went instead to Addington's at Woodley, in Berkshire, one of the houses he was used to visit within easy reach. Put once more on a diet, he pulled round in the next three weeks. But he seems to have suffered something like a nervous breakdown, and returned distinctly shaken and further undermined.[5]

No one in these years doubted that the public pressures were largely

1. Eg *The Morning Post* for 28 June. *The Morning Chronicle* of 4 June reported that he was so weak he could scarcely walk across the room, and *The Courier* a little later announced for good measure that he had become insane. The attack was ascribed to gout in the stomach.

2. Hawkesbury to Liverpool, 29 May 1798 (B.L. Loan Ms 72, vol. 54); Grenville to Thomas Grenville, 30 May 1798 (B.L. Add. Ms 41852); Wilberforce's diary, 2 June, 12 July 1798 (*Life of Wilberforce*, II, 284, 297); Rose to Pretyman, 7 June, 12, 17 September 1798 (Pretyman Ms 435/44); statement by George Rose in the Commons, 13 June 1798 (*P.R., 3rd ser.*, VI (1798), 386, and see *passim* for June); Countess of Salisbury to Pitt, 'Thursday', endorsed as received 6 July 1798 (P.R.O. 30/8/175); *A.C.*, IV (1862), 11, 41, 42; Pitt to Hester Countess of Chatham, 12 July, 16, 26 September 1798 (P.R.O. 30/8/12); Lady Hawkesbury to Liverpool, 12 August 1798 (B.L. Loan Ms 72, vol. 54); Pitt to Pretyman, 24 October (Pretyman Ms 435/42); Farquhar to Pitt, 10 October 1798 (P.R.O. 30/8/134; cf. p. 81, n1 above). The King too expressed concern (to Pitt, 26 June 1798; Stanhope, III, Appendix, xvi).

It should be remembered that dinner was generally taken at four or five o'clock (see I, 577); the second dinner would presumably have replaced the normal late supper.

3. Farquhar to ?, 18 October 1798 (P.R.O. 30/8/134).

4. George Rose's daughter wrote of Pitt's 'depression of spirits' in the spring, ascribed to failing health. Her evidence is not perfect, for she dates his recuperation, at Addington's house in the autumn (see below), to that year rather than the next; *Diaries and Correspondence of . . . George Rose*, I, 212–13. But other reports speak of some trouble at the time.

5. Rose to Pretyman, 30 July, 10 October 1800 (Pretyman Ms 435/44); Pitt to Addington, 8 October 1800 (Stanhope III, 244); Pellew, *Life of Sidmouth*, I, 266–7; *Diary of*

responsible. Rest, however relative, and a change of surroundings gave a damaged but resilient physique a chance. But while the pressures persisted the difficulties of escape grew; as Pitt told Farquhar in 1800, he could not 'leave his Anxiety behind him'. In 1798 he recognised the damage of 'so long making Exertions beyond my real Strength', and that 'our Victories and the State of Revenue' had a good deal to do with his recovery. Two years later, when events were adverse, Farquhar was sure that the attack stemmed 'more from his Mind than anything else';[1] and if this was most marked at such points the hidden impact was always there. Pitt's resilience of spirit was very great: he was not easily cast down, and his optimism, excessive as it often was, had its beneficial side.[2] Nor, as the comments of his friends and the standard of his own letters suggest, did illness overturn the grasp of his attention to affairs. But by 1800 the burden was great, and the resilience strained.[3] And even earlier the signs could be seen as an unpromising prospect for married life.

IV

When an Opposition newspaper published a story in 1798 that Pitt was insane,[4] the remark was of course instantly denied, not only in the Ministerialist press. But the fact that there could be such a rumour probably reflected the knowledge that he came of a distinctly troubled inheritance. Chatham had been a manic depressive, at his worst in a formative period in the life of his favourite son. Nor was he the only unstable member of the family in that generation: his sisters Ann and Elizabeth, his brother Thomas, perhaps his sister Mary were also affected.[5] Fear of a possible transmission has been cited as a further reason for Pitt to shun marriage. And while this may seem far-fetched – it did not deter his own brother and sisters –, and the alleged condition would be raised again at a

---

Joseph Farington, IV, 1446 – according to this second-hand report, a bottle of port was allowed Pitt and Addington after dinner, but none after supper. And see Pitt to Pretyman, 2 November 1800 (Pretyman Ms 435/42) for uncertainty as to whether he could face the oncoming session due in the next nine days.

A list of dates for supplies of medicines from February 1797 to December 1800, from S. Chilver (who seems to have been unpaid during that time), is not uninstructive as a check; but the occasions are pretty regular even in the better periods (Saumarez Smith Mss).

1. Pellew, op. cit., I, 266; Rose to Pretyman, 30 July 1800 (Pretyman Ms 435/44), and see also his letter of 18 October; Pitt to same, 24 October [1798] (Pretyman Ms 435/42). In September 1798, on hearing the news that Nelson had missed the French in the Mediterranean, Rose feared for the effect on Pitt's health (to Pretyman, 12 September 1798; Pretyman Ms 435/44).

2. Cf. II, 543.

3. By then indeed a decline may be observed at least intermittently in his handwriting, so often a significant sign. I am indebted for this assessment, and what could follow from it, to the late Dr M.J. Mannheim.

4. P. 82, n1 above.

5. See I, 4.

more ominous time, it may at least be mentioned in considering his life at this stage.

The intense seclusion in 1797 wore off with the crisis;[1] but only to some extent, and the pattern of habits remained much as before. Outside Parliament and Whitehall and St James's Pitt was not widely seen. He was present of course on some ceremonial occasions – at a thanksgiving service for naval victories at St Paul's in 1797, in the procession at the opening of the West India docks in 1800, sometimes at the military reviews and exercises which were a feature of these years. But neither officially nor socially was he often in the public gaze: it caused a sensation when he went with Dundas to Drury Lane in 1799 to see Sheridan's new historical drama *Pisarro*.[2] His leisure in London indeed was confined largely to an intimate group: seeing a range of people on business, he saw quite few when he was free. They were of the familiar kind; the old friends who like himself had always been in public life, and now a rising genera-tion of the same type. When he 'threw off his load',[3] as he liked to do, it was in such company. The regular Cabinet dinners (not always restricted to the Cabinet) and the larger official entertainments were very different from the small, often impromptu dinners and suppers in a working day.[4] He was sometimes to be viewed in wider circles at formal occasions given elsewhere: by Trinity House, where he was Master for sixteen years from 1790 to his death, by the East India Company, the Marine Society, the City of London Volunteer Corps, the City itself at Lord Mayor's Banquets, sometimes at a Livery Company. He was also reported from time to time at a 'grand entertainment' – Lord Chesterfield's, the Duke of Montrose's, the Princess of Wales's at Blackheath, Lord Hood's at Greenwich, Lord Glenbervie's, the young Duke of Rutland's; even at an *al fresco* fête given by the Duchess of York at Oatlands, where there were country dances in unremitting rain. But these occasions seem to have been quite rare, and while of course he sometimes dined out it seems now to have been at a colleague's house more often than not. From one form of entertainment his 'tall, gaunt figure' was notably absent. He hardly ever graced a ball, and when he did he left early.[5]

Such was life when he was tied to Downing Street. Quite often he could drive or ride out for the night to Dundas's at Wimbledon, or to his old

1. Ie in the autumn.

2. This paragraph draws on reports in the London newspapers, which now followed Pitt's movements regularly, as well as on diaries and correspondence.

3. See I, 589.

4. Nonetheless he kept a good cook, whose subsequent transfer to the Princess of Wales was said to have noticeably improved the standard of her dinners (*Glenbervie*, I, 406). Perhaps he was the artist who was paid £100 a year – compared with the steward at £50 and the butler at £30 – at some undisclosed date (P.R.O. 30/8/197).

5. His old friend and hostess the Duchess of Gordon appears in fact to have been about the only person for whom he made an exception, and then he did not stay long. The description of him was by Lady Holland at a Drawing Room at St James's in 1797 (*The Journals of Elizabeth Lady Holland . . .*, ed. the Earl of Ilchester, I (1908), 153).

friend Pepper Arden's at Hampstead.[1] But whenever possible he took the longer road to Holwood, staying into the next day or even for more than one day. A deputation to Downing Street might find him still booted and spurred and in plain dress, returning from an often hurriedly snatched visit.[2] For Holwood remained Pitt's main solace: the place where he could work at his ease and relax and take chosen associates and friends. It was suited to many of his tastes, which had not changed over the years; giving opportunity for 'lounging' and reading, particularly of his favourite classics, for walking, and not least for his love of landscaping and architecture.[3] He had always been very much a man of his time – and his family – in both respects. The Grenvilles were builders and planters; Chatham had been likewise, and free with his advice; Thomas Pitt, the first Lord Camelford, was a prolific gentleman architect, and a more distant cousin, John Pitt, was likewise a talented amateur. The Younger Pitt himself is supposed to have designed the library for Henry Thornton's house in Clapham,[4] and while Holwood gave limited scope he did what he could, and planned more. His architect – one might almost say his more professional colleague – was the great John Soane, who had been introduced by the elder Camelford; and the connexion flourished beyond Holwood itself. A cluster of commissions from 1788 may reflect Pitt's influence with his friends – work for Lord Abercorn, Lord Carrington, Joseph Smith,

1. For the latter, Master of the Rolls since 1788, see I, 107.
2. *Diary of Farington*, II, 632; and cf. I, 594.
At the other end of the scale, at the royal Birthdays at St James's, he seems to have settled for a succession of brown coats embroidered with silver (once with 'leaves of light green intermixed', once together with 'stones'; *The Morning Post*, 19 January 1798, 5 June 1799 and 1800) – a more sober outfit than the black, green and pink velvet, 'embroidered with gold and silver spangles, with wreaths of silk flowers' which was described as 'neat, rather than elegant' on the Queen's Birthday in 1788 (op. cit., 19 January). Social historians may like to know that his tailor in 1799 and 1800 was William Morse, his breeches maker David Thomas, his hosiers were James Wood and then M. Klype, his hatter was Morys & Co., shoemaker F. Bristow, sword cutler R. Johnstone, jeweller Jeffries & Co. Nourse & Co. supplied lace ruffles; Emmot, the servants' liveries (P.R.O. 30/8/201–2; Saumarez Smith Mss). J. Macfarlane, described as perfumer, seems in fact to have been a servant (he appears in lists of servants in P.R.O. 30/8/201–2).
An idea of Pitt's formal dress on the Treasury bench in the Commons may be gained from Hickel's portrait of 1793–4, for which see Frontispiece to II.
3. Cf. I, 14–16, 592–4. His preferences in the other arts were limited. He had never had an ear for music, though fond of it at Cambridge (op. cit., 21), and remained indifferent to painting, though now on somewhat better terms with the Royal Academy (cf. op. cit., 579), probably through the influence of Charles Long and Addington. He does seem to have favoured the abortive plan to purchase the cream of the Orléans collection for the nation in 1799, and in 1800 was said to wish to 'contend' with France in supporting the arts if peace came. But like most Chancellors when brought, usually reluctantly, to a point, he appears to have approached the whole subject as a matter of prestige, and a possible aid to improving 'Manufacturers'' design (see *Diary of Farington*, III, 953, 955–62; IV, 1132, 1393).
4. A handsome bow-windowed room carried out in the early nineties. It is illustrated in E.M. Forster's *Marianne Thornton* . . . (1956).
Pitt knew the family well, officially (Henry himself and his brother Samuel being among other things Directors of the Bank of England) and privately through Wilberforce.

George Rose, Lord Mornington, Samuel Thornton, Canning, Lord Bridport, Lord Hawkesbury. Beyond that again, the Minister influenced Soane's appointment to the Surveyorship of the Bank of England in 1788 – which produced the one notable artistic monument to his patronage – and in 1790 to the Clerkship of the Works at St James's Palace, Westminster and Whitehall; a post which Soane however left in 1793. In 1797 the architect was also made Deputy Surveyor of the Crown's Woods and Forests, though there again he resigned two years later, partly it was said because of the King's known preference for James Wyatt. At about that time too he was said to have lost Pitt's goodwill, because of an 'ungrateful' vote in the East India Company which displeased Dundas.[1] But in point of fact this seems doubtful; and it was not inappropriate that a statue of Pitt should have been placed posthumously in the National Redemption Office, a building designed by Soane of which both, in their different ways, could be called the architects.[2]

Some modest enlargements had been made to Pitt's 'villa' after he bought it in 1785.[3] A new drawing room was built the next year with a bedroom above, and a portico outside the library; and servants' rooms were fitted up above the brew-house nearby.[4] But the house remained quite small, with six bedrooms for guests, and some of those rooms were themselves small – when Humphry Repton stayed a night in the nineties he was given a chamber which Pitt described as 'like a berth on board a ship', usually reserved for Lord Mulgrave.[5] Some further, very minor,

1. Dorothy Stroud, *Sir John Soane Architect* (1984), 60, 64, 68–9; H.M. Colvin, *A Biographical Dictionary of English Architects 1660–1840* (2nd edn., 1978), 765–72. For the political troubles in 1799 see *Diary of Farington*, IV, 1209, 1230, 1271; but although Soane confirmed that Dundas had been annoyed with him, the entries about Pitt's withdrawal of favour were made in April and May, and the architect continued to visit Pitt with plans for Holwood, still apparently on terms of personal friendship, in August (Soane's Journal No. 3; Soane Mss, Sir John Soane's Museum, London).

From an undated but obviously early letter, probably in the mid eighties, it would seem that Pitt may have supported Soane for some work for Cambridge University before the architect had undertaken 'any great public work' (J. Turner to John James Hamilton, nd, enclosed in Soane to Pitt, nd; P.R.O. 30/8/179).

2. Stroud, op. cit., 207. The building was demolished in 1900, and the life-size seated statue, by Westmacott, is now, after various adventures, at Pitt's Cambridge College, Pembroke. For his remodelling of the National Debt, see I, 260–9.

3. See I, 591. 'Villas' were defined in 1793 'first as the occasional and temporary retreats of the nobility and persons of fortune from what may be called their town residence, . . . in the vicinity of the metropolis; secondly, as the country houses of wealthy citizens and persons in official stations, which also cannot be far removed from the capital; and thirdly, as the smaller kind of provincial edifices, considered either as hunting seats or the habitations of country gentlemen of moderate fortune' (Charles Middleton, *Picturesque and Architectural Views of Cottages, Farm Houses and Country Villas*; quoted in Lawrence Stone and Jeanne C. Fawtier Stone, *An Open Elite? England 1540–1880* (1984), 404–5).

4. Soane's Ledger C, ff. 407–v (Soane Mss, Sir John Soane's Museum). Cf. I, 591, which needs this slight amplification.

5. Repton's memoirs, B.L. Add. Ms 62112, f. 56; Soane Ms 2/9, Plans of house, nd but before later plans. For Mulgrave see II, 316.

alterations were carried out in 1787–8, and in 1795 there were repairs to the roof and the front was stuccoed. There was still however too little room, and in fact comfort, and more extensive plans were drawn up in the next two years. Pitt may indeed have thought of building an entirely new house;[1] but, doubtless from the expense, he settled for a remodelling and enlargement. In August 1796 the architect produced drawings and plans, with the Minister's co-operation, for a new library, a new staircase hall which would have risen to the height of the house, and consequential alterations on both floors.[2] The designs were not carried out in full. The new library was completed in 1797, with some further repairs and painting elsewhere. But though Soane continued to produce modified plans for the rest, and noted them as 'finally settled' '& to be exḍ' in the summer of 1799, Pitt must have told him shortly afterwards that this depended on his finances, and in the event nothing more was done.[3]

When works or plans were in train the architect saw a certain amount of the Minister. He took drawings down to Holwood (or left them at Downing Street), discussing them with him if he was there and sometimes breakfasting if the hour was right.[4] The same easy, and advantageous, relationship applied to Pitt's other adviser, Humphry Repton, for the landscape plans.[5] Pitt may have sounded him out, through Rose and Long, towards the end of 1791, and Repton submitted some ideas at the end of 1792. The two men met the next year at Holwood, probably in May or July, and a Red Book, unfortunately missing, was soon completed. The works may have been carried out in 1793 and again in 1798, including plantations which, against Long's protests, disturbed the lines of an Iron Age fort, and a piece of 'water' which the more knowledgeable Bathurst thought Pitt 'mismanaged sadly'.[6] Repton was surprised by his client. He had expected a cold and obstinate man, and was much relieved to find instead 'a degree of cheerfulness and lightness in his Manner – which no one could suppose, from his natural dignity and stateliness of person'.

1. See Stroud, op. cit., 132. Soane remarked on the continued lack of comfort and convenience after the latest repairs (to Pitt, nd but 1795; P.R.O. 30/8/179).

2. See Soane Ms14/1 (Sir John Soane Museum). There is also a series of views, drawings and plans in Soane Ms 2/9.

3. Soane's Ledger C, and Journal No. 3 for 29 July, 2 August 1799 (Soane Mss); Stroud, op. cit., 132, quoting Soane in his *Public and Private Buildings*, of 1832, on Pitt's statement.

4. Journals Nos. 1 and 3 *passim* (Soane Mss). He took George Dance with him on one occasion, and Matthew Brettingham on another, in the summer of 1795; the former when Pitt was there (Journal No. 3, 6 August, 20 August 1795).

5. Between 1792 and 1794 Repton gained a crop of commissions in Cornwall, all from men connected personally or politically with Pitt. The first of the resulting Red Books – for Port Eliot, Edward Eliot's family seat – was in fact approved by Pitt himself (Dorothy Stroud, *Humphry Repton* (1962), 69–70).

6. Repton's Memoirs, B.L. Add. Ms 62112, ff. 54–5 (where he refers to *Charles* Rose and *George* Long); 'Memorandum from H. Repton for Visits to Holwood', 1792–9; 4 April 1803 (Saumarez Smith Mss); Frederick Sidney Gammon, *The Story of Keston, in Kent* (1934), 25. Repton mentioned Holwood in his *Observations on the Theory and Practice of Landscape Gardening* . . . of 1803 (p. 186). Cf. I, 592 for the camp.

When he called one day, not expecting the Minister to be there and lighting on a large party, he was bidden to stay the night, and later they all 'sallied forth' to see the improvements by moonlight. His memories of Pitt were of animated talk and sometimes a 'flow of merriment';[1] happy in his surroundings, lively and at ease.

Most of his spare energy in fact went into Holwood. His occupation of Walmer was of course on a different footing, as Lord Warden of the Cinque Ports and not a private owner. But he was fond of the place, not least, as his mother remarked, because 'he loves the sea'.[2] The little castle indeed commanded an important short stretch of coast, running from the South Foreland to Deal and the anchorage of the Downs which sheltered and was often alive with shipping and men of war. At a few miles' distance Pitt could see an embodiment of England's defence and wealth. He could also interest himself in the Cinque Port boatmen's affairs.[3] Sometimes he went sailing. He rode a good deal, shot a bit in season, and began the farming operations in which he was later fully engaged.[4] And it was probably something of a recreation as well as a change to pick up the threads of his duties as Lord Warden and Admiral of the Cinque Ports. He had been alert since 1795–6 to the possibility of invasion, and kept an eye on the defences when living in their midst.

Above all Walmer gave him extended opportunities to entertain his friends – and to lend his house in his absence occasionally, for instance to Dundas and his wife. He could put up a few people in the castle, he bought a cottage nearby to take an overflow, and he was seldom down there without company for long. Given the course of his life, he could not expect to travel much to others. He hardly even saw his mother at Burton Pynsent in the later nineties, he could not get to Belvoir for the coming of age of his ward the Duke of Rutland, he no longer went up to Cambridge as he had done in the past. His visits – to Addington in Berkshire, Carrington in Buckinghamshire, increasingly to Charles Long in Kent – were to houses within very easy reach of London.[5] Holwood and Walmer

1. B.L. Add. Ms 62112, ff. 56–7. Cf. p. 86 above for the bedroom.
One has to say that Repton, to judge from his memoirs, was not hard to please in the company of eminent persons. But his impressions reinforce those of others.
2. Hester Countess of Chatham to Thomas Coutts, 7 December 1798 (Correspondence, no. 3024, Coutts Mss).
3. Stephen Pritchard, *The History of Deal and Its Neighbourhood* (1864), 228.
4. This last seems to have been so at any rate by 1800, to judge by an account of sales of hay and produce starting in that year (Saumarez Smith Mss C(iii)).
In the summer of 1796 Pitt appears to have made use of the yacht stationed for his use by the Admiralty, lying off the castle for part at least of his stay (John Laker, *History of Deal* (1917), 309); in August 1798 he was looking forward to a 'a Water Party with a Fair Wind' (to Rose, 8 August 1798; B.L. Add. Ms 42772). In October 1797 Dundas, then at Walmer, reported good shooting prospects and awaited the arrival of Pitt's dogs (to Pitt, 13 October 1797; Dacres Adams Mss, formerly P.R.O. 30/58/2); and in 1799 the Minister had a shooting party there (*The Morning Post*, 17 & 18 October). Cf. I, 593n3.
5. Pitt went down to Burton Pynsent in the late summer of 1798. His absence from the festivities at Belvoir, which he had apparently meant to attend, was quite widely remarked

between them gave him the society he wanted, and the limited relaxation which was all he knew.

Pitt's circle of close friends was changing to some extent with the years, as happens to most people and particularly those in public life. The closest of all in frequency of contact remained Henry Dundas, already in the ascendant before the war and by force of events as well as character now the Minister's main confidant. Some earlier companions however were withdrawn in varying degrees. Pitt saw less of Wilberforce in the nineties – and then all too often it was to be lectured, though the affection endured –, Camden's absence in Ireland[1] for three years weakened ties which were not fully re-established for some time. Edward Eliot was removed suddenly by death. Henry Bankes and Tom Steele, too, were no longer such regular intimates, and Pretyman, more a familiar than a companion, was very largely in his diocese. Others remained closer: Dudley Ryder, Pepper Arden, J.C. Villiers, Bob Smith (Lord Carrington from 1796);[2] and so, from a slightly later vintage, did Lord Mornington until he went to India in 1797. But the balance shifted largely from circumstance, and some younger faces also were beginning to appear. In the older group – still mostly under forty – two men had become more prominent: Henry Addington the Speaker, and the joint Secretary of the Treasury Charles Long. The latter, a Cambridge friend who succeeded Steele in the post in 1791, had quickly proved himself, in confidential talks with the French during the final months of peace[3] and in the multifarious chores of the 'patronage' office which he shared with George Rose. A steady, reliable man of business, he also had private accomplishments – he formed a fine collection of paintings and painted himself, had a keen interest in architecture, and with his wife, a noted horticulturist, laid out a celebrated landscaped garden.[4] Cultivated, sensible, able to call on memories and some tastes in common with Pitt, he was of congenial aid as the decade progressed, and in its last years began to offer hospitality. Not the least of his assets proved a little later to be his friendship with Addington. For Addington was also now playing a bigger part in the Minister's life, though it is not clear exactly how this came about. He had been present

in January 1799. Pretyman in the autumn of 1799 reminded him that he had not been in Cambridge for more than three years (20 October 1799; Stanhope Ms U1590 S5 C34. He seems in fact to have gone there last for a few days in May 1796; expenses in P.R.O. 30/8/210). For his friendship with Rutland's father see I, 17–18, 20, 25, 601.

1. See II, 439.
2. Cf. I, 13, 17, 107–8, 109n1, 230, 584.
3. II, 211–12, 249. See I, 17 for Cambridge.
4. *D.N.B.* According to the article op. cit. on George Rose, Pitt started bringing Long at some stage (possibly in the eighties or early nineties) to the fish dinners which he enjoyed at Greenwich and to which he had earlier taken Camden, another Cambridge friend (see I, 581n5).

from the beginning; from the very beginning indeed, when his father was Chatham's doctor[1] and he and his brother sometimes saw the Pitt children. But there was a social difference, and while Pitt encouraged him in Parliament and in due course secured him the Speakership, their private lives in the eighties were not particularly close. In the nineties however this changed, as Addington took part in discussions on business, and by 1797 he had undoubtedly been drawn in. Pitt told him of Auckland's first letter at the time of the Emily Eden affair, in terms which showed that his reader knew all about the position; and in the same year he chose him as his recommended successor should he himself resign.[2] This was not exactly flattering, seeing that Pitt intended then to 'direct'. But the personal contacts doubtless benefited, he stayed sometimes with Addington at his country house, and was content to recuperate there after his illness in 1800.[3] The Speaker may not in point of fact have been as devoted as others in the circle.[4] That would not have been surprising given the background; and he was not in any case an emotional man. But he had a genuine regard for Pitt, and a genuine wish to help, and accepted what may well have been a somewhat light and routine affection.

Private and political ties in these two cases were indistinguishable. And, as so often, business was initially responsible for another personal development. Lord Mulgrave, a soldier and former MP, was called in often for military advice; he soon became a frequent and welcome visitor to Holwood. An easy, independent manner combined with good professional judgment and debating powers in the Lords to turn an earlier acquaintance into a friendship which deepened with the years.[5] In a different category was another man who in his way saw as much of Pitt as did any one, and, perhaps particularly in the later nineties, developed from a factotum into something more. Joseph Smith, succeeding Pretyman in 1787, was the Minister's private secretary for the next fourteen years. He fully earned the approbation shown in a bestowal of sinecure posts.[6] Troubled by the state of his master's affairs, and all the more so out of real affection, his efforts to take matters in hand as they grew increasingly serious[7] brought him into confidential touch with a group of Pitt's friends. He became in fact the trusted watchdog on the

1. I, 9.
2. See p. 72, n2; Ch. II, section II above; Ziegler, *Addington*, chs. 1–4 *passim*.
3. P. 82 above. Repton wrote in his memoirs of meeting Pitt at the house, Woodley at Sonning, as if this happened more than once and, by the tone, before the convalescence in 1800 (B.L. Add. Ms 62112, ff. 58–9).
4. It is interesting that two intelligent women suspected this, Pretyman's wife by 1797 (see p. 47 above), and George Rose's daughter in 1799 (*Diaries of George Rose*, I, 212–14).
5. See p. 86 above, and II, 316–17 for his influence in the Toulon operations of 1793. Succeeding his brother as an Irish peer in 1792 while sitting in the Commons, he ascended to the Lords after being given a British barony in 1794.
6. See I, 578 & n2. He was assisted and in fact largely replaced in day to day business from the late nineties by John Carthew, a Treasury Clerk.
7. Pp. 75n2, 76n4, 77 above.

private finances, so far as that was possible, continuing after he ceased to be employed and being involved eventually in their winding-up. Pitt, quite rightly, thought highly of him. He got on well with all his secretaries in turn; but 'Joe Smith' was probably his favourite – on a different footing from Pretyman, but for that very reason perhaps more comfortable to have around.

In their various ways these connexions had their origins in the past. But younger men were now coming along, and some of them were entering Pitt's life. In point of fact they were not so much younger; most of them by about ten years. But a decade counts, particularly when one party was Prime Minister while the other was at school. With a sole exception their impingement was still slight, though in each of those instances it soon grew; and they included four men of future note. Spencer Perceval, more nearly a contemporary than the rest, attracted interest as an able lawyer, and by the mid nineties was seeing a certain amount of Pitt, who was impressed and enjoyed his company. In 1796, when a Parliamentary seat had been found and a vacancy occurred in the Irish Chief Secretaryship, he was indeed offered the post; and while he declined on financial grounds, the Minister continued to look on him as destined for office.[1] The man who took the place instead, Lord Castlereagh, was also to be of consequence. Not well acquainted with Pitt at the time, in 1797 Irish affairs soon began to bring him into closer contact.[2] A near contemporary of his had opened his career better known to the Minister; for Robert Jenkinson, Lord Hawkesbury from 1796, was Liverpool's eldest son. As such, and as a promising MP, he had a claim to some attention, and in 1793 was given a seat on the India Board of Control. But there was a more personal link, for when the young man wanted to marry, against his father's wishes, Pitt and Dundas conspired to advise him on how to get his way. He did so, and his private life was happily secured. The connexion, public and private, may still have been occasional. But there are glimpses in these years of him at Holwood, and he spent time in the Cinque Ports, where he was Member for Rye and Pitt as Lord Warden gave him a commission in the Fencible cavalry.[3]

Hawkesbury's ties were his own. But he was also a close friend of

1. And even was rumoured to have named him as a possible successor as early as 1798, when Perceval was thirty-six (Spencer Walpole, *The Life of the Rt. Hon. Spencer Perceval*, I (1874), 51). The Minister was also taken with Mrs Perceval, whom he thought 'remarkably engaging' (Pretyman to Mrs Pretyman, nd but between July 1795 and April 1801; Pretyman Ms 435/45).

2. He was in point of fact made Chief Secretary formally in 1799, but had been carrying out the duties since 1797. He was born in 1769.

3. Born in 1770. See II, 461 for his entertainment by Pitt at Walmer as early as 1792; but also op. cit., 465n2 for an impression of his access on business by 1796. In the summer of 1798 he and his wife were lent the castle at Walmer while they looked for a house in the town (B.L. Loan Ms 72, vol. 54).

Pitt may indeed have been quite amused to assist in overcoming resistance from Liverpool, with whom he was always on ambivalent terms; see I, 330–1.

Canning; and among these younger men Canning's relations with Pitt were unique. Others of his friends indeed gained directly from the fact: Granville Leveson Gower – though he was eligible already – and more briefly John Hookham Frere. The process was unusually swift, though this was not wholly surprising, for Canning's introduction and claims were themselves, typically, unusual. Moving from a brilliant reputation at Oxford at once into Whig circles, and consorting with Sheridan and Fox, he transferred his allegiance in 1792 personally to Pitt. While the Minister had shown some interest, the initiative was indeed Canning's own – he wrote seeking an interview –, and unimportant though he was the move caused a minor stir in that small world.[1] It also placed the recruit on potentially profitable terms with his patron. A Parliamentary seat was supplied the next year, and Canning's sparkle and thrust did the rest; here was a new adherent in whom one could take interest and pride. Pitt was very soon responding to regular calls for advice, and in return giving clear support. Canning was chosen to second the Address at the opening of the session in January 1795, and a year later he was made an Under Secretary at the Foreign Office. From then on there was no holding him. He moved with brio into Government business, and the fortunate chance of peace negotiations in 1796–7 gave him access to the circle of power and, for a time, to Pitt's inner thoughts.[2]

The pace of the advance, and the closeness of contact between the two men, naturally caused comment. Canning was certainly seeing a great deal of Pitt from 1795–6 to at least the spring of 1799. He often dined or supped in London, and walked with the Minister in the park; and, particularly in 1797, paid frequent visits to Holwood.[3] There was obvious mutual sympathy. Of course Canning was highly ambitious, he depended on Pitt's favour and pressed his case. But that was far from being the whole story; he was drawn to Pitt himself. At the start he was reassured by the older man's lack of pretension in company: 'mixing in the conversation without attempting to lead it – laughing often and easily – and boyish enough . . . to discuss the history of Cock Robin'.[4] And as his brief diffidence, never marked, vanished in the warmth of his treatment, admiration for the Minister deepened into fervent attachment to the man. Pitt for his part was attracted by his disciple's quick intelligence and infectious spirits, and probably above all by this unique blend of unashamed devotion and lack of awe. Early success, at school and university, had removed any tendency in Canning to deference; his charm lay in a wit and ebullience directed at all alike, and such caution as he may have felt here quickly disappeared. As he himself remarked, 'I talk to him without reserve or hesitation . . . and laugh and make jokes'. Once he was even seen in the Commons to put his hand on the Minister's shoulder.[5] This

1. See II, 183–4.
2. Pp. 59–68, with notes, above; and see II, 648.
3. Diaries *passim*, Canning Ms 29d.
4. Quoted, from a description of his first dinner at Downing Street, in Dorothy Marshall, *The Rise of George Canning* (1938), 49.
5. Canning to Granville Leveson Gower; quoted op. cit., 90.

was not the way that others behaved to Pitt in public. But it seemed that to a shy and haughty man, accustomed since youth by circumstance and nature to erect barriers and assume primacy, his protégé's unconstrained self-confidence was accepted with delight. In that sense Canning was the privileged jester; he could talk and write to Pitt as no one else did.[1] And perhaps no one else could have drawn Pitt so readily into a journalistic venture, and provided such amusement, as Canning did with *The Anti-Jacobin* in 1797–8.[2]

Was there anything more than sympathy? No Whig *Rolliad* now flourished, to hint at a more intimate relationship as it had done with Pitt and Steele a decade before.[3] But while the jokes continued about the Minister's virginity, and Canning's behaviour and fortunes were watched, the comments may have fastened, as they have done since, on a possible homosexual love. Certainly there were still no hints that Pitt had any adventures with women. Opposition newspapers in 1798 had a joke about a birth by a servant at Holwood;[4] but the only other speculations of which I know surfaced after his death. Lord Holland in the 1830s relayed a story that 'Pitt used to go to brothels but was never known to have touched a woman'.[5] Of somewhat greater interest is the case of Elizabeth Williams, who died in attendance on Hester Stanhope in her Syrian retreat, had been in Pitt's (or Hester's) service in his last few years, and was in his house when he died.[6] Almost sixty years later the biographer Lord Stanhope was asked by two of her great-nephews about a family tradition that she had an 'affinity' to Pitt. He dismissed the tale, of which he had never heard; but Pitt had had some interest in the girl and her sister, paying for or towards their schooling from 1797 to early in 1801.[7] That seems to be all one knows, unless it is relevant that a William Williams was for

1. Even starting his letters, without a form of address, in the manner of a note.

There are two consecutive letters, forming one lengthy screed, which seem to me to convey something of his attraction for Pitt; contesting arguments which the Minister proposed to use in public if the peace approach to France finally failed, and delivering an imaginary 'Jacobin' reply from the Opposition benches (Private, 1 and 3 October 1797; P.R.O. 30/8/120). In their ingenuity, energy and unfettered tone one can see his allure – as also the thinness of the line separating verve from excitability and freedom of expression from a propensity to hector.

2. For which, and the extent of the Minister's involvement, see pp. 110–12 below.

3. I, 109n1.

4. Eg *The Morning Post*, 15 and 20 November, 25 December; *The Morning Herald*, 15 November.

5. To John Cam Hobhouse (diary, 2 March [1839]; B.L. Add. Ms 56560). I owe this information to Dr Richard Brent.

6. Aubrey Newman, *The Stanhopes of Chevening* (1969), 217; *Memoirs of the Lady Hester Stanhope*, II, 317, III, 165–6; list of servants in Pitt's pay at his death (where she figures as a housemaid), Pretyman Ms 562:1820. She does not appear in such lists up to and including 1800 (P.R.O. 30/8/201–17).

7. C. Moberley Bell and Major C.D.J. Dodd to Earl Stanhope, 23 August 1874, and reply, in Stanhope Ms C372/6; payments to C. Bradshaw for the Misses Williams, 'education' and expenses, one quarter each in 1797 and 1798 (P.R.O. 30/8/213, 215), to Mrs Tutty for 'schooling' and sundries for E & L Williams (names given in one instance), January 1799–March 1801 by quarters (P.R.O. 30/8/201, 202, 217).

Rumour of a secret marriage to Miss Williams was raised in 1880 (*Notes and Queries, 6th Series*, I, 376).

long in his employ as under butler and then house porter, being indeed the servant to whom in the late nineties the Christmas boxes were given for distribution.[1] Possibly more was on record in the papers bearing on Pitt's private affairs which were said to have been destroyed by Pretyman and also by Addington.[2] In their absence one can only guess. No such rumour seems to have spread in his lifetime. Perhaps the common verdict may be allowed to stand.[3]

If there was a homosexual relationship in Pitt's life Canning might appear the most obvious candidate. Some reports may be assembled to support the impression made by the younger man's familiarity. Pitt wrote Canning a 'wonderfully affectionate & confidential' letter on the occasion of breaking off from Eleanor Eden. He wished 'of all things' to put Canning into Rose's place at the Treasury – where he would of course be constantly in touch. He showed 'wonderful kindness' in their tête-à-têtes. Lady Hester Stanhope told Canning in 1804 that her uncle 'is attached to you in a way unlike what he feels about anybody else' (only Canning was not sure that the appropriate words then were not in fact 'was' and 'felt'). At the end, on his deathbed, after years in which they had had differences and seen less of each other, Pitt 'was very very kind, and seemed to have something on his mind that he wished to say to me but could not'.[4] And there was also his behaviour at Canning's marriage in 1800. On the way to the church, according to the later story of John Hookham Frere who was also in the carriage together with the clergyman, a man peered in and exclaimed 'What Billy Pitt and with a parson, too!'

I said, 'He thinks you are going to Tyburn to be hanged privately', which was rather impudent of me; but Pitt was too much absorbed, I believe, in thinking of the marriage, to be angry.

The absorption, and perturbation, continued in the church itself.

After the ceremony, he was so nervous that he could not sign as witness, and Canning whispered to me to sign without waiting for him. He

1. P.R.O. 30/8/201, 202, 208–11, 213, 216, 219 Part 6. He was not in the list at Pitt's death (see p. 93, n6 above). There was also an Edward Williams, in the stables, until late in 1797.

2. See I, 13 for Pretyman, and George Pellew to Earl Stanhope, 27 November 1861 (Stanhope Ms U1590 C405/1) for Addington.

3. For what it is worth, one may record that Dundas was quoted in Lord Holland's story as having said that 'he would give any one a place of £500 a year who could prove' that Pitt had ever 'touched a woman' (see p. 93 above).

4. Canning's diary, 8 February 1797 (the letter itself has disappeared), 4 May, 16 May 1797 (Canning Ms 29d); Canning to Granville Leveson Gower, 19 February 1804 (P.R.O. 30/29/8(3)); diary, 14 January 1806 (Canning Ms 29d). Some other possible allusions *might* be cited – eg talk about politics 'and all sorts of things' (diary, 30 July 1797); on a dinner at Dundas's which included the latter's daughter Mrs Drummond, 'q. does Pitt like her I hope not' (diary, 8 July 1797).

regarded the marriage as the one thing needed to give Canning the position to lead a party, and this was the cause of his anxiety, which I would not have believed had I not witnessed it, though I knew how warm was the regard he had for Canning. . . .[1]

Such accounts could be cited as suggestive, as perhaps could Canning's attitude towards Pitt throughout: always intense, proprietary and watchful. He looked on himself as the chosen disciple, perhaps the rightful heir, certainly the intimate; and he was correspondingly alert for any sign, or hint, of withdrawal. It is possibly indicative of a state of mind in which confidence rested on extreme sensitivity that at such a point the habitual 'Pitt' of the diary could turn back into 'Mr Pitt'.[2] He was very quick to scent disapproval; and, as in all his dealings, to resent the fact. He could also be markedly protective, adopting a bantering bullying tone which might be thought curious given the two men's relative positions.

Indications of this kind, valid for what they convey of Canning, must be placed in a context. It will have been noticed that they come mostly from himself; that we are seeing very largely through his eyes. The resulting emphasis is compelling, but it is not untypical; for neither Canning's manner nor mode of expression in this instance differed from his norm. Both were always apt to be extravagant, the first 'with people whom I like, . . . *caressing*',[3] the second, as the letters in his circle show, vehement and affectionate. One must remember that his generation saw the dawning of the romantic movement, and the phrasing of his youthful relationships owed something to an idiom that suited him well. Other considerations bear on some of the episodes themselves. Pitt's nervous preoccupation at Canning's wedding may have been deepened by the lurking exhaustion, which was soon in fact to surface again, amid pressing anxieties brought on by the war.[4] The unspoken words on his deathbed might have related to two recent events, when Canning had wished first to refrain from joining and later to leave his second Ministry, and been dissuaded: Canning himself in fact suspected as much.[5] And while the expression of a protective attitude was, again, peculiarly Canning's own, he was not alone in the attitude itself, which was widely shared. Dundas, from an

1. Gabrielle Festing, *John Hookham Frere and his Friends* (1899), 31.
2. Eg most noticeably in October and November 1804, after he caused Pitt trouble by quarrelling with Hawkesbury. The more usual 'Pitt' returned after 'much comfortable conversation' (diary, Canning Ms 29d).
3. To Granville Leveson Gower; Marshall, op. cit., 90.
4. See p. 82 above.
5. '. . . And I could not *now*, for the world, have persisted in my refusal to embark in the unfortunate Government which he was induced to form – nor have quitted him, upon whatever provocation, during the time that he was struggling to carry it on. He was fully sensible of this & wished to have *shewn* his sense of it – and upon this point I think it was that he felt an inclination to have said something more to me – had he had strength – &, not having so, to leave upon my mind the impression that he had something more to say' (to Granville Leveson Gower, 29 January 1806; P.R.O. 30/29/8(3)).

older generation, felt for Pitt 'all the fondness of a father'; Mulgrave, a contemporary, mourned his death with the 'sorrow of paternal feelings' and 'affection . . . of a brother'; and now a younger generation was touched in much the same way. 'P. with all that he had done, and thought, and seen', reflected Canning's friend Frere in 1801, was 'such pure nature' that in some ways he was 'an ingénue'.[1]

Observations of that kind lead one to the second half of the equation. For whatever Canning may have felt for Pitt, our business lies with what Pitt may have felt for Canning.[2] The pattern began to change in 1799, when Canning left the Foreign Office for a seat on the Board of Control for India, and then fell suddenly and violently in love with the girl he married the next year.[3] Pitt in point of fact played a notable part in this last event; Canning met her first at Walmer, the Minister approved and gave advice, taking in fact considerable trouble to forward his protégé's cause. As in Hawkesbury's case, he liked to be involved, and act the father himself when he could.[4] His attachment, real enough, was not possessive; that indeed was not the kind of adjective his friends ever used. Their descriptions rather were the same at the end of his life as those heard in his youth: simple, unassuming in private, cheerful, kind, considerate, pure.[5] Such epithets do not exclude sentiment. But they do not suggest possessive passion; and they may be viewed in the light of a less welcome fact, accepted sometimes charitably, sometimes not. For Pitt, affectionate and warm in his friendships, did not keep them actively in good repair. A bad correspondent from the start and then governed increasingly by daily business, if people were out of sight they could quite easily fall out of mind. He had always taken his companions from among those presented to him: he had not sought them out;[6] and relationships on such terms, while often strong, carried their connotations. Friendship was vitally important to Pitt; it was his comfort – a refuge – within the world at large, the more so because his family had not supplied that relief since Harriot's

---

1. Lady Anne Barnard on Dundas, in her memoirs quoted in Piers Mackesy, *War Without Victory* . . . (1984), 9; Mulgrave on 23 January 1806, quoted in *G.E.C.*, IX (1936), 394nb; Festing, op. cit., 55. Cf. I, 588.

2. For what it is worth, again, Hobhouse [p. 93, n5 above] 'asked Lord H[olland]' many years later 'if he had ever heard that C was not orthodox in his propensities he said *yes* & he heard the same of Pitt – but did not believe it either' (B.L. Ms 56560, for 2 March 1839).

3. The decline in visits and conversations can be seen in his diary (Canning Ms 29d).

4. Cf. p. 91 above. 'Pitt is almost all that *you* could be to me [in the affair], with the addition of as much of a father, as a person, so much above me' could be (Canning to Granville Leveson Gower, 30 August 1799; *Lord Granville Leveson Gower . . . Private Correspondence 1781 to 1821*, ed. *Castalia Countess Granville*, I (1916), 256), and see also op. cit., 250–5, and Festing, op. cit., 31.
   The Minister was the readier for the affair to succeed because of the girl's wealth which might help his protégé's political career (p. 95 above). Canning himself genuinely found the discrepancy in fortune rather embarrassing than otherwise.

5. Cf. I, 109, 587.

6. Cf. op. cit., 587, 603.

death.[1] He needed affection, and, perhaps increasingly, affectionate admiration.[2] But the essence of such companionship lay in easy, undemanding harmony and trust. Although happy enough on his own terms in the society of women, he found these qualities most readily in his 'Bachelor's Hall'.[3] In either case however one may doubt if he was prepared to look too far beneath the surface; possibly when he did so he was shaken by the result. Harriot's death, Edward Eliot's death, released a grief which alarmed those who saw it. It was quickly dammed, and life went on as before. As he sat absorbed on the road to Canning's wedding, there could have been much on which to reflect: the endless disappointments and dangers of the war, by then affecting relations with old colleagues, his precarious health, perhaps his ruined finances, his crowded but solitary life. Canning would remain; but no longer the free companion, more amusing and clever than the others, sympathetic and ardent, the renewal of Pitt's own youth. And he was going where Pitt himself had not gone, where probably he could not go: into a sexual region for which, perhaps in general, Pitt may not have been equipped.[4] On the verge of middle age, in the midst of his friends, the Minister remained alone. A few years later he told his niece that he must stay 'a single man' 'for my King and country's sake'.[5] The words, addressed to marriage, might be taken in a comprehensive sense. For Pitt in essence was indeed single, affectionate in private but fulfilled in public. He stood apart, untouched as a priest stands untouched at the centre of his avocations; a priest in this instance of politics and government.

1. Op. cit., 582, II, 463; and see p. 832, n3 below.
2. Cf. I, 587n4. Burges, cited there, suggested that this last desire grew with the years.
3. As Downing Street was described in the eighties (op. cit., 584).
4. Cf. I, 108–9.
5. *Memoirs of the Lady Hester Stanhope*, I, 179. One would be foolish to rely on her recollection of the exact phrasing, but the point is clear enough.

CHAPTER IV

The Base Reinforced

I

In the manner of successful politicians, Pitt spent little time in lamenting failure. When the search for peace seemed likely to collapse at Lille in September 1797, he was quick to turn the page. He did so moreover with a fresh zest, and in a highly practical way, for while he was still seeing if the French could not be brought to the table by bribery,[1] he was working on a new approach to produce the means for continued war. By the end of September he was convinced that he had an answer. 'Pitt in spirits', reported Malmesbury, returned from France less than a fortnight before; 'had provided supplies for two more campaigns'. His 'almost unremitting Attention to the . . . Business' aided his recovery from the recent bout of ill health and the shock of Eliot's death.[2] Always influenced sharply by the state of the finances, he was now as much comforted by the prospects as he had been earlier cast down.

A more immediate and dramatic event soon lifted his spirits farther. On 11 October Duncan defeated the Dutch fleet at Camperdown. The victory came, as St Vincent's had done, at a most useful time, and Government, as then, proceeded to make the most of it. The Tower guns were fired, church bells rung, illuminations put in hand. Pitt, who was going down to Walmer, planned to meet the ships returning to the Nore; and although this could not be done, since they were delayed by weather, he entertained the Admiral soon afterwards at the Castle.[3] A Viscountcy was bestowed at once, and the Minister was anxious still to go to the Nore, in company now with the King who had arranged to do so. 'Such a

1. Pp. 66–8 above.
2. See p. 81 above. Malmesbury's diary for 27 September (Malmesbury, III, 591); Rose to Pretyman, 26 September 1797 (Pretyman Ms 435/44). Rose was working with Pitt at Holwood.
3. Pitt to Hester Countess of Chatham, 22 October 1797 (Stanhope, III, 73–4). Duncan had in fact been a regular visitor to Walmer when Pitt was there and the squadron was in the Downs in the weeks before Camperdown.
Pitt liked the 'Venerable' Admiral (to Lord Carrington, 16 October 1797; Bodleian Library, Mss Films 1121), despite the fact that he was of a party in the navy not well disposed to the Pitts' old connexions the Hoods (see II, 463n5). He was however a relation by marriage of Dundas, and his services in the mutiny and the blockade of the Texel, and his genial and forthright personality, recommended him.

ceremony', as he remarked, 'will be no bad prelude for the opening of the Session'.[1] A service of thanksgiving had already been announced for the three great naval victories of the war, the Glorious First of June, Cape St Vincent and now Camperdown; and this was duly held in St Paul's on 19 December. Pitt's reception was variously described. Ministerial newspapers reported that inside the Cathedral he 'was received with peculiar marks of respect' – indeed with 'Acclamations, Clapping &c:', according, not surprisingly, to the Dean. The greetings outside seem to have been more mixed. Great 'Marks of Favour particularly from the People in the Houses' were noted; but his carriage was pelted and threatened while waiting in the churchyard, and he travelled back, in Steele's carriage, attended by the City Light Horse Volunteers.[2]

In the upshot however the Minister's supporters considered it 'a very glorious day for Mr Pitt at this moment of heavy Taxation'.[3] For by then his 'new scheme of finance' was occupying 'the thoughts of every political circle',[4] within the reassembled Parliament and beyond. Working fast, in the framework of ideas already floating, he was ready by 11 October with a long memorandum which formed a basis for a bill.[5] As such it was important. But the effect was not confined to the short term. For in its advocacy of a shift in direction the paper stands as a landmark, despite flaws in its specific proposals, along the road of fiscal policy.

Pitt's direct problem – the size of expenditure for the fiscal year 1798–9 – was itself expected in point of fact to be smaller than in the immediate past. After the expansion of recent years he expected naval costs to drop

1. To Hester Countess of Chatham (p. 98, n3 above). He did in fact get as far as Sittingbourne, together with the Dundases and Carrington. But continued bad weather stopped the King's visit, and the Minister carried on to town.

2. *The True Briton*, 20 December 1797; Pretyman to Mrs Pretyman, 'Wednesday 12 o'clock', endorsed 20 December, 1797 (Pretyman Ms 435/45). Cf. *Diary of Farington*, III, 950, 952–3. *The True Briton* stated that the attackers were stopped by other members of the crowd; and see op. cit. for the 21st. *The Morning Chronicle* (for the 20th) contented itself with observing that the cavalry was no doubt needed to protect him from the people's kindness.

For Pitt's dinners with the City Volunteers in these years see p. 84 above.

3. Pretyman to Mrs Pretyman (n2 above).

4. *The Morning Chronicle*, 11 November 1797.

5. It may be found in P.R.O. 30/8/273, ff. 26–46, and again in P.R.O. 30/8/302, ff. 152–74. There is a brief draft of ideas in Pitt's hand, dated 'Sept. 23ᵈ' in P.R.O. 30/8/197, ff. 120–1v; and a copy of the same date, '23 September 1797', endorsed 'Mr Pitt, Finance Scheme', is in Stanhope Ms S5 09/39. This, and the fact that Liverpool referred to 'Mr. Pitt's Paper' in one of his own in October containing a proposal for raising supplies (B.L. Add. Ms 38354, ff. 234–5), suggests very strongly that the final document, though not in Pitt's hand or endorsed in either copy, is by him.

In its introductory passage the memorandum alludes to 'the idea often discussed' (P.R.O. 30/8/273, f. 27), and the resulting proposal itself may in fact have been suggested as far back as the previous December by Auckland, though in the different context of an impost to be levied on persons not subscribing to the voluntary Loyalty Loan – for which see II, 638–41 (Richard A. Cooper, 'British Government Finance, 1793–1807', 157n22). He was almost certainly consulted in any case on the plan now (to Pitt, 7 October, endorsed 1797 (P.R.O. 30/8/110).

by nearly £2¹/₂ million, and those for the armed services in total by some £6.7 million. The army abroad would need no more than in 1797. And over and above such outlay there would be a further decline, particularly with Austria gone, in subsidies and loans to allies.[1] But welcome as such reductions might be they remained of limited significance: there would still be a gap of some £21 million – soon increased in his calculations to £22 million[2] – between the estimated expenditure and revenue. And it was in the method now designed to help meet this shortfall that the novelty – judged by the practice of the century – lay.[3]

For Pitt had decided to reduce as far as possible his dependence on loans. The mainstay of wartime finance, by and large successful until 1795,[4] they had proved increasingly hard to raise on favourable terms in the past two years. The market's rates had become adverse, the prices of the funds were low, and an alternative call directly on the public, for the Loyalty Loan, was likewise standing at a discount after the early vigorous subscription.[5] Neither Government nor its lenders were doing well out of recent transactions; while the funded National Debt was rising once more at an alarming pace. The Sinking Fund, Pitt's cherished arrangement for sustaining its credit and reducing its size, was accordingly demanding an ever growing revenue to feed a larger capital and a higher interest rate. Some figures show the position. The nominal amount of the unredeemed National Debt had risen since the start of the war from just under £243 to just over £359 million (the funded element taking £229¹/₂ and £351¹/₂ million). The 3 per cent Consols hovered at about 49, around their historical low. Government was having to borrow at some 6¹/₄ per cent – Pitt thought it might soon be 6.7 per cent – compared with 5 per cent and less at the turn of 1795–6.[6] The bill for annual interest was £13.2 million, compared with £9 million in 1793.[7] Pitt was deeply worried by this escape from his earlier control. He was determined to persist in the process of redemption through an inviolate Sinking Fund: that way alone, he still maintained, lay salvation for both the near and the longer future. But it could not succeed unless the wartime growth of debt capital could be restrained and the annual charges met without themselves contributing to that growth. The loan system as it stood was becoming

1. In the event, £0.2 million went to the British land forces overseas, as in 1797, and the same sum, compared with £1.4 million for the previous year, in payments to allies (P.K. O'Brien, 'Government Revenue, 1793–1815 . . .' (D. Phil thesis, Oxford, 1967), 531, table 37). Cf. II, 617, 520.

2. Speech of 24 November 1797 (*P.R., 3rd ser.*, IV (1798), 271). Another lengthy report of the speech, as usual with some differences, is in *The Senator . . .*, XIX (1798).

3. The qualification was made by Pitt himself (24 November 1797; op. cit., 272).

4. See II, 523; and p. 9 above.

5. P. 9 above.

6. Cf. II, 617n5. Pitt's memorandum of 11 October (P.R.O. 30/8/273, f. 36).

7. *The Annual Register for . . . 1797*, Appendix to the Chronicle, 282; Mitchell & Deane, op. cit., ch. XIV, table 5; O'Brien, loc. cit., 49, table 13. Figures of the Debt to the nearest £ half million.

dangerously out of hand, and he acknowledged the fact in a striking phrase.

> I am aware that it will be said (for it has often been said) and I agree to it, that it would be fortunate if the practice of funding had never been introduced; and that it is not terminated is much to be lamented . . .

One could only 'regret the extent to which it has been carried' by the war, and in that situation take steps 'to prevent the depreciation of our national securities'.[1]

The answer in principle was clear. From every point of view, current and prospective, we must go as far as we could towards 'raising the supplies within the year', which meant higher taxation. Equally clearly it would be 'impracticable' to raise them all by that means. The taxes and duties which must take the strain produced a net revenue of some £21.4 million in 1797, less than the deficit forecast for 1798 after their collection.[2] Their yield indeed had never been expected to meet the full expenses in recent wars: whatever the state of affairs in practice, it was a cardinal political aim to sustain the impression of low taxation, and in 1793 Pitt 'did not intend his . . . policy to pay for the war but to support the funding system which would pay for the war'.[3] While therefore he was resolved to call now for 'extraordinary exertion', this was in order to

> devise some expedient by which we may . . . render within equitable limits the accommodation of the funding system, and lay the foundation of that quick redemption which will prevent the dangerous consequences of an overgrown accumulation of our public debt.[4]

If the method had now to be adjusted, the object remained that of 1786.[5]

How best then to raise the taxes? Pitt had already increased some duties, and introduced others, in the course of the year. Spirits, sugar, some brands of tea, Scotch distillery licences, property at auction, bricks, a range of imports, stamp duties – the usual miscellany – figured in his first budget. In a second a few months later – by now an enforced habitual

1. Speech of 24 November 1797 (*P.R., 3rd ser.*, IV, 284, 272); and see p. 53, n3 above. See II, 523, 527-8 for his earlier wartime policy.
2. Mitchell & Deane, op. cit., ch. XIV, table 1 (figure here to the nearest £100,000); p. 100 above.
3. See II, 522, quoting Cooper. For the argument that Britain throughout much of the century had in fact suffered a higher level of taxation than France, but one levied in less politically obtrusive ways, cf. P. Mathias and P.K. O'Brien, 'Taxation in Britain and France 1715–1810' (*Journal of European Economic History*, vol. 5, no. 3, 601–49).
4. 24 November 1797 (*P.R., 3rd ser.*, IV, 272) – and cf. speech of 4 December (op. cit., 316-17); memorandum of 11 October (P.R.O. 30/8/273) for the phrases 'raising the supplies within the year' and 'extraordinary exertion'.
5. Cf. I, 158 for the remodelling of the Sinking Fund in that year, to face the rise in debt caused by the American War.

recourse – increased levies were added on houses, on servants, legal deeds, and horses for farming and business.[1] By then however he was 'a good deal at a loss' to know how to spread such imposts farther. His new plan therefore centred on a single 'general tax', which would triple the rates of the assessed taxes.[2]

The assessed taxes – those levies managed by the Board of Taxes together with the separate Land Tax – comprised a group which had been greatly enlarged in the past twenty years. In 1777 they were confined to a tax on windows: by 1792 inhabited houses, male servants, carriages, carts and stage coaches, carriage and saddle horses had widened the scope.[3] With increased wartime rates and some minor extensions, such a combination might be said to form a rough guide to the taxpayer's standard of life; and it was for this reason that Pitt fastened on it now. For the 'general tax', like its existing constituents, was to fall on expenditure: in that respect it did not depart from familiar practice. He had in fact thought of other possibilities: a heavy increase in the existing taxes and duties over a wide range; a tax imposed proportionately on all property – not, as currently, on inherited personal objects alone; and an income tax. But he rejected the first as likely to be excessively unpopular for its yield, and the other two as introducing 'a degree of inquisition which would be generally invidious'.[4] Any hint of such a threat always aroused lively mistrust, and he was anxious not to risk his hopes of unity at a time when he must make a substantial demand.

The proposal for the assessed taxes moreover had some important positive advantages. In the first place, since no *new* tax was included, collection could be by the existing machinery of the Taxes Office, overhauled in the eighties and recently enlarged, and the local, unpaid Commissioners of the Land Tax drawn very largely from the gentry and in particular the county JPs. Nothing further, in Pitt's view, needed to be done. He always attached importance to economy of administration, and this would leave a single large levy in the hands of a single board.[5] He also reckoned that it would raise much more than any other acceptable tax: he expected some £8 million gross, and allowing for exemptions and deductions a net £7 million. Such a sum would meet two-thirds of the charge for servicing and redeeming the loan which must still be raised for the coming

1. Stephen Dowell, *A History of Taxation and Taxes in England* . . ., II (1884), 209–12. Proposals for levies on canals and on parcels carried by stage coaches were defeated, and one on clocks and watches was later withdrawn. Cf. II, 517 for the annual need for a second budget from 1796.

2. Dowell, op.cit., 211, quoting Pitt's speech of 26 April 1797; speech of 24 November 1797 (*P.R., 3rd ser.*, IV, 273).

3. See Binney, *British Public Finance and Administration*, 67–73; and cf. I, 283 for the structure of the revenue boards. Since 1786 the Taxes Board had also managed some small items of Crown revenue.

4. Memorandum of 11 October; P.R.O. 30/8/273, ff. 27–8. See II, 522 for the fate of his earlier proposal to extend the limits of the existing tax on inherited objects.

5. Cf. I, Ch. X, section II, and 283–7, II, 521–2.

year.[1] Again moreover, it could do so more cheaply; for such a lesser dependence on borrowing would lower the rate of interest – if for instance the usual 3 per cent stock sold at par, each £1 million raised created £1 million of debt: if it sold at 50 (the kind of figure at which it stood in 1797) it created double the amount.[2] With this in mind, and in his pursuit of continued redemption of the whole Debt, Pitt thought indeed of continuing the tax for a period into peacetime: to the middle of 1800 if hostilities ended at the close of 1798, for a maximum of seven and a half years of peace if they did so by the close of 1801. In any case, the produce after its first year should be paid directly into the Sinking Fund, to help mop up future wartime loans and hasten the cancellation of the burden of the past.[3]

The 'new scheme' had a further merit in Pitt's eyes. For though he had to work through a tax on expenditure, he knew that a tax on incomes was in theory the most equitable method of tapping capacity to pay. Since however such an initiative 'might be imprudent if not dangerous', an assessment based on evidence of living standards was the best means to adopt. He tried indeed, in the circumstances, to claim the best of both worlds: 'Could there be a call . . . upon income more general, more effectual, or more comprehensive than that which he had proposed?'[4] This was debating language. But it gave him the ground on which to argue for a graduated scale in taxing on the increased rates.

For while the rates of the existing taxes were trebled, so that the result became known as the Triple Assessment,[5] the payments themselves were levied in proportion to the amounts due. Pitt proposed a sliding scale, for two distinct classes – those paying on the assessed taxes considered as necessities, and those paying on the 'luxury' taxes as well – from a rate in Class I of 50 per cent on a payment of below £1 to 300 per cent on £3 or

1. P. 100 above.

2. Richard Cooper, 'William Pitt, Taxation, and the Needs of War', *The Journal of British Studies*, Volume XXII, Number 1, 99.

3. Speech of 24 November 1797 (*P.R., 3rd ser.*, IV, 190); memorandum of 11 October (P.R.O. 30/8/273, ff. 33–4). The detailed forecast of effects from continued taxation in peacetime was circulated to some Ministers at least in a minute by Pitt of 25 October (*H.M.C., Dropmore*, III, 382–4). See also E.L. Hargreaves, *The National Debt* (1930), 109. Cf. p. 101, n4 above for the continued annual payments.

Such a proposal was in contrast to an idea considered probably at an earlier point, when Pitt contemplated 'Trebling assess'd Taxes for one year & no more & 30 pr Cent upon the assess'd Taxes aftwds' (nd; P.R.O. 30/8/282, f. 238).

4. Speech of 24 December 1797 (*P.R., 3rd ser.*, IV, 317, 325). Cf. I, 248–9 for the lines of thought as laid down in Adam Smith and followed now by Pitt on both the fiscal equitability of an incomes tax and its threat to individual liberty. The latter of course looked back to the poundage rate levied under Star Chamber and the Interregnum alike.

5. . . . 'all Assessed Taxes except on Houses & Windows to be trebled – Those on Houses and Windows &c to be encreased in different Gradations according to the Amount, rising to *Treble* Proportion on the highest' (undated paper in Pitt's hand, P.R.O. 30/8/197, f. 104). Cf. the draft of 23 September (loc. cit., f. 120), and a further draft paper, 'Sketch of Revne', nd, in Pitt's hand, in P.R.O. 30/8/282, ff. 331–2.

more, and in Class II from 300 per cent on £30 or less to 400 per cent on £50 or more.[1] Graduation of this kind was in one sense the product of familiar fiscal theory, that the choice and weight of levies should fall as far as possible on the better-off. But carried in this way into direct effect it was a notable experiment, for however taxes were designed to fall they had been generally imposed at flat rates; and as such it was liable to arouse fierce opposition. So in fact Pitt had found earlier, on the sole occasion on which he had tried it, when he introduced a sliding scale according to numbers in the tax on men servants in 1785 and withdrew it six years later after persistent complaints.[2] The critical state of the finances now, however, allowed him to speak out. The rates of payment were set so as to fall most heavily on 'those whose state of life rises to opulence'. Correspondingly, they would exempt large numbers – he thought two to three million – of 'the poorer classes'.[3] This was in truth the principle of a graduated income tax.

Indeed, such an alternative was itself introduced. There was a provision to opt for payment on income in lieu of the Triple Assessment, if the payer claimed that that assessment took more than ten per cent of his annual receipts: in other words, if the relation of his expenditure to income was disproportionate.[4] It was a voluntary choice; and the caution evident in any approach to such a sensitive subject was shown by the means suggested – a simple declaration of income to Commissioners appointed for the purpose. In no other instance however was 'optionality' intended. The basis of the tax was to be 'not future, but past assessment'.[5] Payment could thus not be avoided by sudden reductions on the items involved, though some 'abatements' – the provision for inadequate incomes, and a relief for certain shopkeepers and lodging house owners – were specified in the proposals which Pitt brought to the House.

The Aid and Contribution bill, as the more commonly known Triple Assessment was entitled, was 'a half-way house'.[6] It adhered to the well-worn practice of taxing expenditure. But it did so in a form that trespassed on the dangerous ground of an open tax on incomes, it was a graduated tax, and in greater degree than its predecessors it tried to avoid 'optionality'. In these respects it laid the foundations, as by its fate it

1. See Cooper, 'British Government Finance', Appendix II, 412–14.

2. Binney, op. cit., 69.

3. Speeches of 24 November, 4 December 1797 respectively (see *The Senator*, XIX, 184–5, 223. This is an instance where *P.R.* is less full). On 7 December Pitt was reported similarly of talking of 'the lower classes' (op. cit., 286). For use of such terms cf. II, 142–3.

4. See Cooper, loc. cit., Appendix II, 413–14. Exemption could be claimed by this choice for an annual income said to be under £60. The alternative appears in Pitt's undated papers in P.R.O. 30/8/197 and 282 (p. 99, n5 above).

5. Speech of 24 November 1797 (*P.R., 3rd ser.*, IV, 278–9). The point was not universally taken: 'We have, this very morning', wrote Fanny Burney the next month, 'decided upon parting with 4 of our new windows' (*The Journals and Letters of Fanny Burney*, IV, ed. Joyce Hemlow (1973), 49).

6. William Kennedy, *English Taxation 1640–1799 . . .* (1913), 169.

opened the way, for the central fiscal principle of the nineteenth and twentieth centuries. The preparation of the scheme was typical of Pitt's mind and habits. As George III once remarked (though the comment applied not only to his choice of cases), 'Mr Pitt was apt to put off laborious or disagreeable business to the last, but then, when forced to it, got through it with extraordinary rapidity'.[1] Parts of the package may have been earlier in his thoughts; but the package itself had to be put together, and this was done, while emerging from a spell of ill health, at concentrated speed. The product itself was of the kind which he always liked to have in his sights: a comprehensive treatment of interlocking causes yielding, one might hope, interlocking benefits – in this instance a relief on borrowing and a potent aid to debt redemption – the whole presented as a fresh development within the frame of a familiar approach.[2] Pitt was adept, and had grown more adept, at making a case for adjusting to circumstances. His pragmatism was aimed nonetheless, where possible, at a coherence which would shape them in turn.[3]

But a very real work of persuasion lay ahead. Higher taxes were always intensely unpopular; and the whiff of innovation moreover could not be ignored. *New System of Finance*, one pamphlet proclaimed, *as detailed in the Speech of the Rt. Honourable William Pitt, in the House of Commons on November, the 24th, 1797*.[4] That kind of title could arouse qualms. Would 'the Country Gentlemen . . ., the Inhabitants generally . . ., the Stock-holders' agree, to the methods, the sums and the length of time alike required? If so, thought Rose, closeted with Pitt, the nation could fight on for the next two years; if not, 'we must lie down & die, knowing we might have been saved'.[5] Parliament met on 20 November after the long recess, and Pitt explained the proposals on the 24th. They at once ran into serious trouble.[6] The Minister had an unaccustomed advantage at the start in the absence of the Opposition leaders, maintaining the secession from the Commons which had been announced in May. But Fox's constituents were so disturbed – and doubtless the misgivings in the House so evident – that he and Sheridan decided to make an exception in this promising case. He returned, on 7 December, to 'a great burst of applause' as he passed through the lobby, and 'a general sensation' in the Chamber

1. *Glenbervie*, I, 149; entry for 29 January 1801. Cf. I, 325 for earlier rather similar responses, not necessarily in disagreeable cases.
2. . . . 'if we are arrived at a moment which requires a change of system, it is some encouragement to look forward to benefits so far unknown' (24 November 1797; *P.R., 3rd ser.*, IV, 284).
3. Cf. I, 613.
4. Printed by R.H. Wesley, London, 1797.
5. To Pretyman, 26 September 1797 (Pretyman Ms 435/44). See p. 98, n2 above.
6. This paragraph is based on *P.R., 3rd ser.*, IV, 268–301, 316–77, 381–91, 410–61, 488–513, 517–20, 523–642; and draws on O'Brien, loc. cit., 401–2, and Cooper, loc. cit., 168–75, 415–18.

itself.[1] Three main lines of objection developed. Would the change of direction damage confidence in funding? Was it practicable? Were the burden and proportions of the tax fairly laid? Detail, as always with taxes, indeed proved all-important, and Pitt was forced to make significant amendments. Discussed from early in December, they were announced on the 18th. There would be exemption for shopkeepers letting lodgings, exemption for those paying less than £1 in assessed taxes, reduced rates in the lower brackets, higher rates at the top. Although these last fell quite heavily – Fox's nephew Lord Holland for instance had now to pay over £1,000 a year – the changes resulted in a large aggregate loss. Rose at the Treasury estimated that they would cost some £2 million. But it was better to settle for a gross of £6 million than fail in an attempt for a higher sum;[2] and so it proved when the revised bill passed on 4 January 1798.[3]

The reduction of revenue to a net £5 million[4] – later revised to £4½ million – had accordingly to be met in other ways, and one longer-term complement to the scheme, worked out earlier, was presented on 2 April 1798. This was for the sale of the Land Tax, the oldest of the levies by assessment, known and developed since the early years of the Restoration.[5] As with the Triple Assessment, the aim was to reduce the National Debt, in this case by commuting the tax into Government stock. A sale at just under twenty-three years' value, expected to bring in some

1. *The Annual Register for . . . 1798* (1800), History of Europe, 192. This passage is not in the earlier edition, nd (at History of Europe, 208). Both contain the statement about constituents' wishes, which Fox himself made in the debate. They were certainly not unusual in their reaction: 'I find *nobody, no not one*', remarked the retired Clerk of the Commons John Hatsell, 'that has Publick spirit enough to pay their money with alacrity, or even good-humour'. 'The fact is', he went on, 'that very few Persons indeed have sufficient *surplus* money to defray such a demand; &, with very many, it will be a *perfect impossibility*' (to his successor John Ley, Cranford, Wedny 13 [December 1797] (Ley Mss). Cf. *Diary of Farington*, III, 932, and the examples cited in Holland Rose, II, 329.

For Fox's secession see p. 42 above.

2. To Pretyman, 4 December 1797 (Pretyman Ms 435/44).

3. By 196 to 71. The Act, of 12 January 1798, was 38 Geo. III, c16. Pitt claimed that his own perseverance '*at all risks*' to see the bill through was, he believed, 'alone' responsible (to Earl of Mornington, 28 January 1798; Lord Rosebery, *Pitt* (1891), 205). Certainly he had debated hard and in many ways successfully, and doubtless brought pressure to bear. But the concessions had been significant, and as the King pointed out – not much presumably to the Minister's pleasure – they had not improved the bill (to Pitt, 5 January 1798; Stanhope, III, Appendix, x–xi).

4. See p. 102 above.

5. Cf. p. 102, n3 above. The proposition seems to have been in hand in the previous October and November (Auckland to Pitt, 1 October 1797, Stanhope Ms S5 01/5; 'Notes on Mr Pitt's Plan for the Sale of Land Tax 10th Nov.ʳ 1797', P.R.O. 30/8/278). It had been canvassed earlier still: the idea was mentioned in a Commons' debate at the end of June (Cooper, loc. cit., 182), and 'some such scheme had been proposed & disapproved' between the autumn of 1796 and that of 1797 (Nicholas Vansittart to Pitt, 30 March endorsed 1798, referring to one submitted by him in the former period; Stanhope Ms S5 06/59). There is an undated 'Memorandum on Redemption of the Land Tax' in Pitt's hand in Dacres Adams Mss, formerly P.R.O. 30/58/8, and other undated papers on the subject, one in his hand, are in P.R.O. 30/8/282.

£45 million, might redeem some £80 million of the 3 per cents, then standing at around 50. The plan rested on acceptance of the annual tax as a permanent levy, which in effect it had become; in that case the rate would be fixed at its current level of 4 shillings in the £.[1] If such a scheme were adopted, moreover, it would have the benefit of again easing the rates for borrowing. For another operation now, in a contrary direction, must be to raise a larger loan than had been forecast.

This of course was a blow. Pitt had hoped to reduce his call on the market for £22 million[2] by persuading the Bank of England to advance £4 million. But the Bank declined, and he had to rest content with £3 million on rather stiffer terms. Allowing for £7 million from the Triple Assessment, he would thus have been left with a loan of £12 million. But in a second budget in April, forced on him partly by the objections, he set the figure at £15 million. By then he had also revised his estimates for the expenses of the war, adding some £900,000 for the navy, £1,200,000 for the army and a small amount for the ordnance. He therefore thought it necessary, in addition, to levy some more in taxes, which he did by doubling the rates on salt, increasing that on teas, and introducing two new imposts, the 'convoy tax' (intended for one year only) on goods *ad valorem* carried in convoy, and one on armorial bearings, at graduated rates based on the classification for the assessed taxes.[3] These unwelcome increments were expected to produce some £760,000. They could not in themselves therefore go far towards filling the gap.

In the event, however, valuable relief was found in a further expedient. While the Triple Assessment was under attack, the Speaker, Addington, made a useful suggestion, for a Voluntary Contribution by 'persons of affluence' above their payments from the assessment itself.[4] Pitt adopted the proposal, which was included in the Act with provision for the sums to be paid into the Bank of England, nominally as an advance of obligatory payments but hopefully as an addition. The immediate response was as encouraging, at its level, as that to the Loyalty Loan of 1796: after a 'languid' few days, some £150,000 was received in London within a week.[5] Pitt came down as hard as he could on 'all those who are in marked Public Situations', above all on his immediate colleagues, and on the King. They were asked to pledge one fifth of their income computed in total '*on the largest scale*', although the highest rate under the Triple

1. W.R. Ward, *The English Land Tax in the Eighteenth Century* (1953), 135; Cooper, loc. cit., 181–4.

2. See p. 100 above.

3. Cooper, loc. cit., 189, 192–6, 389; Dowell, op. cit., 214–15. Notes by Pitt and Rose for the April budget are in Stanhope Ms S5 09/42.

4. Pitt's speech of 4 December 1797 (*P.H.*, XXXIII, col. 1089; not in *P.R.* or *The Senator*). He seems to have been consulted later on the detail of the arrangements, or perhaps on those for the taxes themselves (Addington to Pitt, 25 February 1798; Stanhope Ms S5 01/1).

5. Cooper, loc. cit., 177–8; Pitt to Mornington, 26 January 1798 (Rosebery, op. cit., 206–7).

Assessment was set at one tenth.[1] Not all paid up with 'alacrity, or even good-humour';[2] Grenville disliked a demand which, once agreed, was scarcely voluntary at all, and George III, not unreasonably pleading financial constraint – 'I am sorry to say the King of England is not so rich a man' – suggested that the Privy Purse should be repaid. But Pitt insisted; his colleagues complied, the King ended by giving one third of the Privy Purse, and he himself subscribed £2,000, to be paid in instalments over a year, from an official income already pledged in part to his bank.[3] The examples were widely followed, and not by the most prosperous alone. By mid-February £600,000 had come in, by late April some £1.3 million, and the final total was over £2 million. In his second budget Pitt reckoned on £1½ million. In that respect, unlike in some others, he put the figure too low.

For while these various measures were all adopted, while the sale of the Land Tax was voted in the end by a solid majority, and the annual loan negotiated on slightly better terms than had been feared,[4] the 'new system' itself could not claim success in the course of the year. In both its aspects – in the commutation of the Land Tax and in the produce from the Triple Assessment – it was to fall far short of the hopes. The country gentlemen proved largely unwilling to exchange their old levy for Government stock; and the lack of administrative rigour – contrary to opponents' fears – in settling assessments and incomes undermined the main scheme. Meanwhile events on the Continent and in Ireland called once more for higher expenditure.[5] Nonetheless, all was not black in the coming months. The change in monetary policy of the previous year was bearing fruit: the increase in bank notes and to some extent in coin, the revival of the Bank of England's discounts, were expanding credit again and giving fresh play to the economy.[6] Yields from duties were buoyant; and so, in his response, was Pitt: in October he cited 'the State of

1. See p. 104 above. Pitt to Camden, Private, 31 January (Camden Ms 0190A/1 (Maidstone)). He could be stern. Camden was told that he, and the eldest Grenville Buckingham, should 'regulate your Contributions by a very different Measure from that of any other Man in the Country', since their emoluments from their Tellerships of the Exchequer, benefiting from 'unprecedented' wartime expenses, were 'far beyond what on any average calculation could be in the Contemplation of either Grantor or Grantee'. Buckingham in fact paid in full; Camden, pleading the costs of his Lord Lieutenancy in Dublin, in part (loc. cit., 0190A/3, 0156A/25). For their common attitude to these sinecures see I, 177.
2. Cf. p. 106, n1 above.
3. Grenville to Buckingham, 2 February 1798 (Buckingham, II, 387); correspondence between Pitt and George III, 22–23 January 1798 (*L.C.G. III*, III, no. 1674 & n1; Pitt to Canning, nd, 'Secret, Wednesday, 5 pm' (Canning Ms 30, Leeds); Stanhope, III, Appendix, xi–xii); Pitt to Messrs Coutts, 19 January 1798 (copy in P.R.O. 30/8/195), and see pp. 75–6, above.
4. See *P.R., 3rd ser.*, V (1798), 492–525, 596–610, 616–30, VI (1798), 33–43, 131–40, 176–81, 212–22, 236–49 for the lengthy debates, which however ended in votes on the second and third readings of 153 to 38 and 135 to 33. The Act was 38 Geo. III, c60. P.R.O. 30/8/275, ff. 157–62 contains a memorandum by Pitt on the loan and associated measures.
5. Discussed in Chs. V, VI below.
6. See Ch. I, section I above.

Revenue' as a stimulant to better health.[1] But the next budget had then to be considered. His experiment had not gone well. And in the autumn he settled down to think again.

II

In the debates on the Triple Assessment much time was spent arguing the justice of the war. Opposition indeed, under Fox's renewed generalship, diverted some attention from relevant detail to topics congenial to himself. These however in point of fact now rebounded in favour of Government.[2] For however strongly sentiment was running against the tax proposals, it could be rallied in support of a struggle for which the proposals were required. The winter of 1797–8 saw a marked revival of the national will – more so in fact than some in Ministerialist circles appreciated or would have predicted,[3] and shown in the response to the Voluntary Contribution more clearly than in that to the compulsory levy. The abrupt and spurious end to the peace talks, Duncan's victory at Camperdown, the continuing threat of invasion from France, combined to concentrate the public's mind. There was widespread recognition, taking root from mid-October, that the struggle must be carried on; and it lost none of its vigour, or pride, from the knowledge that the country in effect stood alone. 'One of the great objects', Grenville remarked on the news of Camperdown, 'is the raising people's spirits'.[4] Within the next month, as Pitt found in the Commons, recent doubts were dying away. When he sat down after 'a most spirited speech' to rally opinion on 10 November, 'all the House rose to sing "Britons, strike home"', and the Member who had introduced a motion for peace seven months before followed immediately to express his support.[5]

The raising of people's spirits was not left unattended. One of the most copious channels of exhortation, by its nature, was the Church. The cord which bound together the two parts of the Establishment was never stronger, in the last quarter of the century, than at this time of beleaguerment and stress. Anglican defences, mobilised afresh in the

1. See p. 83 above.
2. See *P.R., 3rd ser.*, IV, debates of 24 November, 4, 5, 14 December in particular.
3. Eg William Huskisson to Dundas, 11 September 1797 (S.R.O., Melville Castle Muniments, GD 51/1/529/1); Wilberforce to Lord Muncaster, November 1797 (*Life of Wilberforce*, II, 243, 249); Cornwallis to Major-General Ross, 15, 17 December 1797 (*Correspondence of Charles, First Marquess Cornwallis*, ed. Charles Ross, II (1859), 327–8). Windham of course remained in despair; see *The Windham Papers*, II, 66, 68, and cf. pp. 54–5 above.
4. Grenville to Spencer, 13 October (*Private Papers of Spencer*, II, 196).
5. See Festing, *John Hookham Frere and his Friends*, 11 for the song; *P.R., 3rd ser.*, IV, 179–82, for the opening debate of the Session, on the Address; p. 41 above for Pollen's motion of 10 April. The independent Member James Martin, perhaps a more significant figure on both occasions, likewise signalled a change of heart.

debates on Toleration at the end of the eighties, and sustained since, were
again formidably deployed.[1] Earlier in the year Wilberforce had published his *Practical View*, an inquiry into the moral condition of Britain
which had an unexpectedly large sale. Contrasting, as the title proclaimed, *the Prevailing Religious system of Professed Christians, in the Higher and
Middle Classes . . . with Real Christianity*, it was a significant contribution to
the Evangelical drive for 'improvement of manners' and a reciprocal
acceptance from below. Not every Churchman welcomed what some saw
as a fanatical or Methodist book.[2] But general support across the range of
Anglicanism, largely in sermons, was at full flood. Pretyman at about this
time sought approval of one of his own from Pitt, an initiative which was
met by a characteristic response. The Minister suggested a different Text.

– I proposed 'Except these abide in the Spirit ye cannot be saved' – 'Oh
excellent . . . Then your sermon would be to prove that God, who
governs the World by his providence, never interposes for the preservation of men or nations without their own Exertions' . . . 'I really think
that with that Text it will be the best Sermon that ever was preached'.[3]

Government may have been prepared itself to trespass on such ground.
The prolific William Combe – hardly an orthodox source – was said to be
writing sermons as his 'staple employ',[4] and the Ministry certainly supplemented and instigated all forms of aid. 'Many able and excellent publications' appeared in the winter, together with paragraphs and letters in
newspapers, caricatures and pamphlets, to form a combined diet of independent and subsidised fare.[5] Most of it was familiar in tone, with perhaps
an increased emphasis on the value of monarchy and the virtues of the
monarch himself.[6] Most of it, too, was familiar in quality. But one effective
component was not, for the operations produced one minor classic, in
whose progress Pitt himself was involved. On 20 November 1797 the first
number of *The Anti-Jacobin* appeared.

1. Cf. II, Ch. III, section II, and 161–3.
2. See John Pollock, *Wilberforce* (1977), 153; and for the thrust of and reaction to
Evangelicalism within wider movements, II, 61, 162–3.
3. Pretyman to Mrs Pretyman, nd, endorsed 1797 (Pretyman Ms 435/5, published
largely in Ashbourne, op. cit., 345). She did not agree. Pitt's proposal was 'not a true
Christian argument' (to Pretyman, nd, loc. cit.); but then, as she observed more than once,
he lacked religious feeling – 'O that your friend would learn the *only* wisdom he is in want
of!' (to same, nd, endorsed 8 February 1801; loc. cit.).
4. *Diary of Farington*, III, 957, for 29 December 1797. The name given there is Coombes,
but it presumably refers to him (see II, 54 & n, and *D.N.B.*). Whether true or not, the tale
supports the impression in these months.
5. Auckland to Hugh Elliot, 12 February 1798 (*A.C.*, III, 387). For Government's earlier
mobilisation of media see I, 143–4, 605–8, II, 116, 194, 203n1, 230, 231n2.
6. For reflections on this see above all Linda Colley, *Britons, Forging the Nation 1707–1837*
(1992), ch. 5, particularly 204–17; also Frank O'Gorman in *Britain and The French Revolution,
1789–1815*, ed. H.T. Dickinson (1989), 29–30, and H.T. Dickinson op. cit., 113–14.

The idea was Canning's, canvassed a month before. It had then taken a rather different form. In conversation with Pitt at Walmer he discussed 'Measures to be taken for keeping the public Mind right upon all Subjects by the Press', and

> particularly a newspaper to be set up to which a certain Number of persons are to engage to contribute – & those persons to live together – to dine once a week for instance at Pitt's or elsewhere.

Names were suggested: Pitt himself, Canning, Ryder, Steele, Windham, Charles Long, Addington's brother Hiley and his brother-in-law Charles Bragge, Hawkesbury, Perceval, Hookham Frere, George Ellis. Grenville and Addington should assist occasionally. The proposal was well received, and Canning wrote to Ellis and Frere, and spoke to Long (the paymaster) and Windham – who however was 'not so sanguine as I could wish particularly as to the living together'. Long agreed to 'get the Paper set up, & to find a person to conduct it';[1] and arrangements went ahead over the next few weeks.

The editor of *The Anti-Jacobin, or Weekly Examiner* was William Gifford, a dependant of the Grosvenor family who had published two literary satires in the past few years.[2] But the real conductors were Canning and Frere, the associates of ten years before at Eton in that most memorable of schoolboy productions *The Microcosm*. They now carried their high spirits into this more substantial undertaking. The bulk of the paper, published weekly, consisted of comments on events and digs at Opposition; not much more distinguished, though sometimes more pointed, than others appearing elsewhere. But it was the verse that caught the eye: a journal which included 'The Friend of Humanity and the Knife Grinder', 'The Soldier's Friend', 'New Morality', could certainly claim 'to provide for the amusement, as well as information of our Readers'.[3] As intended – on the lines of an earlier model, the Whig *Rolliad* of the eighties[4] – it called on political colleagues, some of them in office and including Pitt. He almost certainly contributed one poem and possibly lines in another, as well as several pieces, mainly on finance, and to some extent a supervision of the contents as a whole. He spent 'above a fifth of one of the finest Mornings possible' on one 'Paper'. When he could not send another, because of illness, 'you will do wisely to prepare your *scurrilous leading Article*'. 'Some

1. Canning's diary, between 18 and 21 October 1797 (Canning Ms 29d). 'Conductor' was a term often used for manager and editor.

2. Ending his career as first editor of *The Quarterly Review*, he was thus associated with two notable journals. He is not to be confused – as he was at least once at the time – with another 'miscellaneous writer' John Gifford (John Richards Green), who edited a subsequent *Anti-Jacobin Magazine and Review*, and in due course wrote a three-volume Life of Pitt.

3. Introduction to No. 1. '. . . a new Paper which is to be full of sound reasoning, good principles, & good jokes' (Canning to Ellis, 19 October 1797; Canning Ms 62).

4. See I, 109n1.

Room must . . . be found for very inflammatory Comments . . . on *Horne Tooke* and *Fox*, and on The Duke of Norfolk'.[1] Amused but very much in earnest, he found time to scrutinise and help.

The paper came to an end on 9 July 1798. Exactly why is not clear; a rumour arose that Pitt was finding it embarrassing, but Canning himself may not have wished in fact to be known for too long as a weekly journalist.[2] Towards the end it was selling some 2,500 copies weekly, at a time when few dailies reached circulations of 3–4,000; and by its own computation this meant an immediate readership of 17,500, with a further 32,500 after copies had been lent.[3] These last figures were doubtless optimistic. But the venture may have succeeded in 'giving a wrench to public opinion', as its authors claimed in typical style. It certainly contributed to Canning's success in holding Pitt's ear.[4] It also gave a distinctive point and impetus to a broader trend.

The encouragement of support was followed by a discouragement of journalistic 'mischiefs'. In April 1798 Government introduced a bill to that end. The stamped paper required for newspapers was to be delivered to the proprietors and/or printer or to the publisher, on affidavit. The names of printer and publisher were to appear on each copy. A fine would be imposed on proprietors (to a maximum of two) and on printer and publisher if an unstamped newspaper was sent abroad, with a higher fine if that was to an enemy country. And any matter 'tending to excite hatred and contempt' of the King, Constitution and Government – the familiar phrase in a prosecution – which appeared under pretext of reporting from a foreign journal, would carry the liability of twelve months' imprisonment. The Act passed in June.[5] The objects as given were not unreasonable: to curtail a fraud on the revenue, to ascertain and state the names of those responsible for publication, to identify more precisely the persons subject to prosecution for libel, to block a gap made by war in the existing

1. Pitt to Canning, 6 February 1798, 'Saty 2 pm', 'Sat 9 pm' [both 1798] (Canning Ms 30; and see also same to same, 21 May 1798 and 'Friday 11 am' [1798], loc. cit.). He is supposed to have written the whole of the lines on Fox's bust in Catherine the Great's cabinet (see II, 39–40 and also William Dacres Adams to Earl Stanhope, 30 May 1861, in Stanhope Ms C 405/15), and ten lines of 'New Morality' (*Poetry of the Anti-Jacobin*, ed. L. Rice-Oxley (1924), 190). For one instance at any rate, conversely, of a restraining hand, see Canning's diary for 25 February 1798 (Canning Ms 29d).
   The copy of the journal in the British Library (c.40 1.2) has contemporary annotations, believed to be Canning's own, which give attributions to Pitt; see A.D. Harvey, *William Pitt The Younger 1759–1806, A Bibliography* (1989), 33–4.
2. At least according to Frere (see Marshall, op. cit., 64) – for the 'secret' of his role was of course soon out. He had stated in any case that the paper's life would be confined to one Parliamentary session.
3. No. XXXVI, 9 July 1798. Donald Read, *Press and People 1790–1850* . . . (1961), and Ian Christie, 'British Newspapers in the later Georgian Age' (ch. Fifteen, *Myth and Reality* . . . (1970), give an idea of circulations in parts of the provinces and in London.
4. See pp. 92–3 above.
5. 38 Geo. III, c78; the word 'Mischiefs' was in the title. The debates are in *P.R., 3rd ser.*, V, 576–96, VI, 279–81, 302–7, 386–94. Pitt was not present (see p. 81 above).

armoury.[1] They gave rise to two potential injustices, by penalising a proprietor or even an editor for matter inserted without his knowledge,[2] and
by including newsvendors in the definition of publishers. These however
were not primarily the grounds on which the statute was denounced, then
and later. Directed as it was at 'mischiefs', it was seen by political dissidents, and took its place in an historical tradition, as one weapon in a
fresh Ministerial offensive.

The charge of course was strictly correct – whatever connotation
should be placed on 'offensive'. The Act came at that moment as part of a
pattern. In a longer perspective it also formed part of another process, in
which newspapers, however regarded individually, whether in support or
for discouragement, were coming to demand rather more serious
consideration. For these years – the mid and later nineties – saw, it may be
argued, a noticeable development: the number of titles and in some
important instances the quality of the products rose. The former applied
to the provinces now more than London, which saw no such expansion –
in 1797 indeed, for the first time, the rest of the country supplied the
higher revenue from advertisement duty. Nor did an increase in stamp
duty that summer do more than temporarily depress circulations: a
measure, it has been widely held, designed by Government to that end. In
so far as this may have been so, political conflicted with financial advantage; but, as Pitt observed, the addition was unlikely to check advance
over the years.[3] This indeed was so. Numbers of papers printed in
London took two years to reach the former level; but they then increased
farther, and development in other directions was not affected meanwhile.
The first decade of the nineteenth century is often cited as a landmark in
the progress of journalism. Premonitory signs can be seen in the metropolis in the preceding decade.[4] To some extent this came from the forcing
ground of the war: the proportion of overseas news had often been large,
throughout much of the century; but higher demand now arose from a
struggle of exceptional severity and scale, requiring ampler coverage of
events and of Government itself. Movements and meetings of Ministers
were followed more closely than before, even as recently as in 1793–4; and
this applied particularly to Cabinet meetings, quite often with details of
attendance and duration and sometimes of subject – whether right or

1. The second object had indeed been law in Ireland since 1784, with the approval of
Grattan himself.

2. A matter recognised in the case of proprietors by the Whig Government in 1834.

3. Speech in the Commons of 14 June 1797; quoted in A. Aspinall, *Politics and the Press
c1780–1850* (1949), 18n5. The Act was 37 Geo. III, c90. Conflict of aim might perhaps be
deduced from Pitt's initial desire to raise advertisement duty as well – from which he
retreated – and also the introduction for the first time of a discount on the purchase of
larger amounts of stamped paper.

4. This is not to say that some provincial newspapers were not also showing improvements. But the developments there – the introduction of editorial articles for instance, and
the general effects of higher advertising revenue – may perhaps be attributed to slightly
earlier and later periods respectively.

wrong. There is even a hint here of official briefing:[1] an aspect in itself of a wider need, within the limits of continuing official distaste, to provide some kinds of factual information. Government's very efforts to extend its influence, by payments and proprietorship and selected favours, paid tribute indeed to the growing effect of the newspapers at large.[2] And the latter's advance was served also by a different process: by a clear improvement in the quality of the proprietors and/or editors themselves. A remarkable group within the leading dailies – James Perry, Daniel Stuart, John Heriot, with John Walter II emerging – represented mostly the rising generation and was starting to attract equally notable groups of contributors.[3] Coleridge from 1797 was a prominent literary star in a galaxy of regular or occasional writers who would soon contain Hazlitt and Southey, Wordsworth and Lamb, John and Thomas Campbell, Brougham and Thomas Moore. Most of these editors moreover had at least been entered at, though not all had then gone to, universities, and they moved in appropriate circles: Perry was brother-in-law to Porson, Daniel Stuart to James Mackintosh. They were not so far removed in ability and spirit, though they were in social recognition, from Canning himself on his brief excursion into the press.

Life on the stamped newspapers remained risky, as it was highly dangerous on the unstamped. The hazards for the former however were not excessive in 1798. Government indeed always found it hard, and impolitic, even in the sterner years that followed, to try to control them too closely, much as it would sometimes have liked to do so. All Ministries had to remember their professions of respect for the liberties of the press; compliance from their own dependants was not always complete;[4] and as one reads the more hostile journals one can scarcely call them gagged. *The Morning Chronicle*, *The Monthly Magazine* in London, *The Newcastle Chronicle*, *The Cambridge Intelligencer* in the provinces, are examples to the contrary.[5] But influence of course could take varied forms – withholding news and comment and official advertisements – and direct penalties always lay in the wings. Editors had to be careful, as they edged their way to a more substantial role. Perry of *The Morning Chronicle* was put in the Tower from March to June 1798 for a libel on the House of Lords, and Pitt in December had to defend *The Times* from a charge of misrepresenting

1. Though Opposition newspapers were not less diligent than Ministerialist – if anything perhaps more so – in such reports.

2. Cf. II, 116–18 for developments earlier in the nineties.

3. In April 1798 Perry was 42; but the other three were in their thirties, Stuart and Walter in their early thirties.

4. *The Times* was showing a growing impatience in 1798, and by 1800 Grenville could describe it as 'a paper which, under cover of a pretended support of Government, is in decided hostility to it' (*The History of The Times*, I (1935), 63). Cf. Chatham to Pitt in the same year on the 'little means . . . to keep printers in order' (I, 607).

5. The last however closed in 1803, probably from declining circulation with more than one cause; see Cookson, *The Friends of Peace*, 98, and 84–103 in general.

proceedings in the Commons.[1] Politicians by and large were sensitive, Ministers watchful, some intensely hostile.[2] For it was not only that, as earlier, journalists were still viewed largely with personal contempt; they were now suspect as a possible element in a potential nexus of disaffection.

The conditioning cause of this wider fear was the expectation of invasion from France. '. . . At no period in the History of this Country', said Pitt, 'invasion was ever so formidable', and the prospect had its civil as well as military effects. All possibilities had to be looked at in strengthening the defences; 'precautions applied to counteract the mischief of domestic foes, was equal to arming all the rest'. The Minister was speaking in the debate on renewed suspension of Habeas Corpus, passed through both Houses in a single day in April.[3] Two months later the annual Aliens Act was extended, with some added restrictions, to ensure that Government's powers were confirmed before the long summer recess.[4]

The powers were used; and action indeed was taken over a wider front, some of it not requiring legislative sanction. Fox himself felt the authorities' hand, if quite mildly. Since the summer of 1796 there had been stories that he was growing closer to the more extreme Parliamentary reformers – promoters of a cause towards which he had earlier proved ambivalent, and been distinctly cool at heart. The rumours above all of alliance with Horne Tooke, his opponent in Westminster elections, were strengthened by co-operation between the two wings in London politics as well as by Tooke's own conciliatory remarks.[5] In October 1797 Fox pledged himself more openly to a 'radical reform', 'an entire . . . change of system'; and attacks from both sources on the Assessed Taxes over the

1. *P.R., 3rd ser.*, V, 349–55, VII (1799), 440–1; *The Morning Chronicle*, 23, 26 March, 14 June 1798, *The Times*, 28 December 1798. The editor of *The Morning Post* found himself before a group of Ministers in March for his report on an arrest of suspected subversives (p. 117 below), where he was 'closely questioned' in particular by Pitt (3 March 1798).

2. Above all perhaps Windham; eg his remarks in the Commons in December 1798 (*P.R., 3rd ser.*, VII, 468–76); and see for his known position Jeremy Black, 'A Plan for the Regulation of the Press' sent him as a likely recipient in March 1799 (*Factotum* (B.L.), no. 36, 22–5). Pitt for his part was said in 1798, by an independent MP, to have shown 'much tenderness and delicacy' hitherto towards the newspapers (Sir William Pulteney, 4 April; *P.R., 3rd ser.*, V, 592); a better noun might have been forbearance.

3. See 38 Geo. III, c36, particularly clause 1; Pitt in the Commons, 20 April 1798 (*P.R., 3rd ser.*, VI, 22–3).

4. 38 Geo. III, c50. In the Commons' debate on Habeas Corpus the point at issue turned on the *duration* of the Act, Opposition contending for expiry on 1 November (when Parliament might not have reassembled), against the Ministry's successful choice of 1 February 1799 (*P.R., 3rd ser.*, VI, 20–7). For the limit of duration of the Acts cf. II, 395, 399.

5. See I, 64–6, 72, 76, 226, II, 76, 388n4 for Fox's feelings about Parliamentary reform; II, 75, 81n2 for Tooke's intervention at Westminster in 1790; J. Ann Hone, *For the Cause of Truth, Radicalism in London 1796–1821* (1982), 26–9, 32–4 for their recent relations and for City politics.

next three months seemed to point, now seriously, to the prospect of actual 'union'. In January 1798 Foxites and members of the very different London Corresponding Society combined in protests, and at the annual dinner for Fox's birthday on the 24th some of the latter and Tooke himself attended for the first time, making, according to Pitt, 'a Public Profession . . . of Reconciliation and Coalition'.[1]

This was the background to the celebrated incident, which took place at the dinner, of the Foxite Duke of Norfolk's toast to 'Our Sovereign's Health, the Majesty of the People'. Its substitution for the customary 'the Sovereignty of the People', and his earlier toast to Fox as 'a comparison with Washington', 'the application' of which he left to his audience, could be and were taken as seditious. A week later he was removed from his Lord Lieutenancy of the West Riding of Yorkshire and the colonelcy of his militia.[2] That of course caused something of a stir – and gave the Duke something of a shock. Greater interest was roused when Fox chose to repeat the phrase on 1 May at another Whig Club dinner. The Club in point of fact had not changed drastically: Fox also gave the traditional toast 'may the ancient Nobility of England ever think it their highest honour to support the Rights of the People'.[3] But the provocation could obviously not be ignored. Pitt, while happy enough to make capital earlier out of Tooke's rapprochement,[4] was not anxious now to take the matter to extremes. He saw a 'very great' objection to prosecution from 'the chance of acquittal and a triumph', though he was prepared to consider a pro-posal for an order to Fox to attend the Commons and, if avowing his words, to be reprimanded by the Speaker. If he thereafter offered

> a new insult (as he probably would at the next meeting of the Club) he might be sent to the Tower for the remainder of the session, which would assert the authority of the House, as much as expulsion, and save the inconvenience of a Westminster contest.[5]

Once more, as in 1791[6] and '97, and this time for obvious reasons, Pitt in fact preferred not to pursue his adversary too far. In the event Ministers

---

1. Pitt to Mornington [26 January 1798] (quoted in *L.C.G. III*, III, 18n1). See also Hone, op. cit., 37, 39. For the LCS see II, 106–8.

2. Posts given by virtue of the fact that much of his property lay in those parts. Pitt's first reaction was to call his speech one 'which even the Crown lawyers will hardly prove to be much short of Treason' (see n1 above). 'The Duke of Norfolk . . .', he wrote to Canning, 'must certainly be turned out of his Lieutenancy' ('Sat. 9 pm'; Canning Ms 30).

3. *The Morning Chronicle*, 2 May 1798. It was given every year. Cf. II, 108–9, 172–3 for the attitude.

4. Eg n. 1 to Mornington (above).

5. To Dundas, 5 May; quoted in *H of P*, III, 817. 'If he deserves it', however, 'the printer might be prosecuted with success'; the quotation of the same letter (now in the Clements Mss at the University of Michigan) given in Stanhope, III, 127–8 has the word 'disavows' for 'deserves'. Pitt also wrote to Grenville, sd, in much the same terms, and referring to the possible danger of making Fox 'a martyr' (*H.M.C., Dropmore*, IV (1905), 187).

6. See II, Ch. I, section IV.

advised removal from the Privy Council, and on the 9th the King 'ran his pen through Mr. Fox's name'.[1]

The personal challenge might thus be regarded as met. It was the more incumbent on Government to make this clear, if with limited impact, from the circumstances by May. For over the previous two months it had moved, more sternly, against men some of whom Fox knew, and for some of whom indeed he would shortly vouch in Court. The need to disown his respectability without inciting popular tumult was underlined in fact by a clutch of arrests and detentions or prosecutions. There had been something of the kind in Scotland in the previous November. But action in England – the herald in later tradition of the peak of 'Pitt's Reign of Terror'[2] – came from the end of February to May 1798. On 28 February five members of the leading Societies were taken up at Margate, trying to embark for France. Largely as a result of their evidence, arrests followed in Leicester and Manchester and in London where forty-seven members of the LCS were brought in from 18 to 20 April, some to be released in a few days, others rearrested under the suspension of Habeas Corpus[3] and some held for almost three years. In late May 'the Margate five' were brought to trial for high treason.

Government may well have felt sustained in these moves by the rallying of public sentiment as the nation waited for the French to arrive. 'The general zeal and spirit of the country', Pitt himself observed, 'is everything that we can wish'.[4] Broadly speaking, this certainly seems to have been so: the despair of radicals whose hopes had been reviving the year before testifies in itself to a deeply felt fact.

To defend the Bible in this year 1798 would cost a man his life.
The Beast and the Whore rule without control.[5]

1. *The Times*, 11 May 1798; Pitt to George III, 8 May 1798 (*L.C.G. III*, III, no. 1729).
Some years later, when Pitt was urging Fox's inclusion in a broad-based Cabinet and George III was said to have expressed his surprise, seeing that the latter had been struck off the Council when the former was Minister, Pitt was reported to have answered that he had not 'recommended' such a step, which gave Fox 'too much consequence' (Malmesbury's diary for 8 May 1804, repeating (sceptically) a story from Farquhar; *Diaries and Correspondence of Malmesbury*, IV (1844), 303).

2. It is hard to tell when this phrase was first used. It was later sometimes applied to the whole period since 1794, or even 1792. Francis Place however confined it to the years 1797 – 1800 – 1797 being inserted as an afterthought before 1798; B.L. Add. Ms 27808, ff. 110–11.

3. P. 115 above; this in fact was why the Act was rushed through, after consideration a fortnight earlier following discoveries in Manchester (see Pitt to Grenville, 7 April; *H.M.C., Dropmore*, IV, 167).

4. To Camden, 21 April 1798 (quoted in *L.C.G. III*, III, no. 1722, 49n1).

5. Blake, annotations to Bishop Watson's *An Apology for the Bible in a Series of Letters Addressed to Thomas Paine*, of that year.
Some other well known cases of current despondency, however, such as Coleridge's and Wordsworth's, are rather different, since their political commitments were beginning to change.

The sentiment was reflected through the closer political world. In the debate on Habeas Corpus, Sheridan, present for the occasion, opposed suspension but 'not . . . with much vehemence', and supported 'the necessity of exertion and unanimity in the present crisis'; while Tierney, now Opposition's regular leader in Fox's absence, supported the measure – to his later embarrassment.[1] In such circumstances, it has often been argued, Pitt could do pretty much as he liked, and decided to exploit the climate of opinion by deliberately exaggerating the dangers. Such a process – an added burden, one might think, at a very busy time – was not in fact necessarily so free of risk as seems to have been assumed. The familiar constraints on executive power did not all disappear amidst the deepening support; and indeed when the Margate five came to Court, all but one were acquitted on the evidence produced.

Government in point of fact was well aware of such a possibility. It had moved cautiously with Fox; and it brought this prosecution with misgivings. The Home Office knew that its statements in Court could be challenged as inconclusive. But it also knew that the men were traitors, involved in conspiracy, and it judged that the case was too important to ignore. The authorities indeed were now proceeding in general with much improved knowledge, enabling them to act while preventing them from disclosing their sources of information. Nonetheless, and as a result, scepticism was not removed, for after all how could one tell if the Ministry was right in a given case? Doubters and opponents could point to a reduction in the activities of radical movements, and in the degree of unrest since the Two Acts of 1795. Government appeared now to have gained the advantage in the endless see-saw with the Societies; and the acute dearth and inflation of that year had not been repeated.[2] Such signs of course could not be taken as conclusive, and the armed forces themselves had given the country a fright. But that had ended without a real confrontation, and popular sympathy had died away. Yet, given all these indications, Ministers were proclaiming potential danger, and using their powers amply, it could be said, on that excuse. Amid the deepening support for preventive precautions, specific instances could thus still raise doubts when it came to giving a verdict under the law.[3]

1. Pitt to George III, 20 April 1798 (*L.C.G. III*, III, no. 1722). See *P.R., 3rd ser.*, VI, 20–1 for Sheridan's speech, the tone of which may indeed be compared with the Foxites' on the last comparable occasion, in February 1795. As a Parliamentary tactician, the Minister was quite pleased. Sheridan's remarks, he commented, had 'certainly been quite useful'; had 'done him some Credit and not too much; and added to the Disgrace of his Friends' among the more unaccommodating Foxites (to Camden, nd; Camden MS 0190 A/5, Maidstone).

2. Cf. II, Ch. XII *passim*, and 615–16.

3. As in earlier years, evidence from the Courts themselves points both ways (cf. II, 156–7, 389–92, 396–8, 401), and a balance overall is hard to strike; there are examples in F.K. Prochaska, 'English State Trials in the 1790s: A Case Study' (*The Journal of British Studies*, XIII, Number 1, 64–7), and Clive Emsley, 'Repression, 'terror' and the rule of law in England during the decade of the French Revolution' (*E.H.R.*, C, no. 397, 811–19). In a

The Ministry's knowledge was not of course comprehensive, or always sure. It was based largely on reports from agents who had penetrated the Societies: a form of intelligence liable to distortion and sometimes self-interest. Nevertheless, when combined with intercepts by an active Post Office, it gave some answers that had been lacking in the early years of the war. For experience was now yielding results in what was developing into a system. The quality of the agents had risen, on aggregate, from a very low pitch; the Post Office was refining methods which it had employed throughout the century; and the management of domestic intelligence was in the hands of a network of officials working more competently and closely together in the departments concerned.[1] Francis Freeling in the Post Office, Richard Ford in the Bow Street police office and later the Alien Office, William Wickham in the Alien Office followed by Charles William Flint, John King at the Home Office, in touch with William Huskisson (formerly of the Alien Office) at the War Office and Evan Nepean (formerly of the Home and the War Offices) at the Admiralty, were the main figures in a confidential group whose conclusions were relayed Ministerially to Pitt by Dundas and, principally, by Portland as Home Secretary.[2] Much remains unknown; many records have vanished; but the centre of organisation may have come to lie increasingly in the Alien Office, given greater independence when the Aliens Act was renewed in 1798, and involved by its nature equally in foreign intelligence and now also subversion in Europe.[3] All these activities, obscure as they are, suggest one aspect of the development, apparent in other respects, of a more sophisticated conduct of the war. They mark an early phase moreover in the creation of an administrative tradition which seems to have lingered in corners of Whitehall through the nineteenth century into our own.

Knowledge of possible domestic danger was also now more precise because of developments in the centres of disaffection themselves. The

---

climate now much more generally favourable to Government's actions, one may repeat the importance of continuing significant restraints, intended or unintended (eg the precise impact of law on alleged seditious publications), which, among both magistrates and juries, could include strictly local influences.

1. William Wickham, once more in the Home Office (see II, 372–3), asserted later that it had absolute evidence, which however must remain secret, on the scope and sources of a conspiracy in England as well as Ireland (to Pitt, 19 January 1799; P.R.O. 30/8/189). Historians, while properly cautious, are more prepared than their predecessors to admit that the claim could have been good (see the treatment by Albert Goodwin, *The Friends of Liberty* (1979), 447–8, Hone, *For the Cause of Truth*, 55, Wells, *Insurrection*, ch. II, and 125–6).
Some light is also thrown on the subject in Kenneth Ellis, *The Post Office in the Eighteenth Century* (1958), and R.R. Nelson, *The Home Office, 1782–1801* (1969). Cf. II, 136–8 for earlier years.
2. The Duke was not in fact the last of his line to be involved in intelligence matters. Victor Cavendish-Bentinck, later ninth Duke, was chairman of the Joint Intelligence Committee in the War Cabinet Offices in the Second World War.
3. For the Act see II, 225 above; for the office's role, Elizabeth Sparrow, 'The Alien Office, 1792–1806', in *H.J.*, vol. 33, no. 2, particularly 361–7, 375–7 for domestic affairs.

decline in the Societies' overt activities, the greater caution of many of their members, weakened the moderate elements and drove the activists largely underground. Since nature abhors a vacuum, leadership concentrated on the more extreme, in a crop of bodies emerging more or less simultaneously out of the old. The United Scotsmen, the United Englishmen, the United Britons arose in 1797, attracting growing if uneven support in the following year. The limited numbers and familiar identities of those centrally involved had their advantages for the investigators: if one set of contacts could be exposed, the way to others was more easily open. But attention could also be narrowed by a less familiar fact. For the new bodies were all linked with and in some degree modelled on the Society of United Irishmen.

It was indeed this connexion that largely decided the Ministry to prosecute the men arrested at Margate. The authorities in Dublin and London had been watching an Irishman, Coigley (or O'Coigley), who was the focal point of the group; and the Irish dimension, visible in the naval mutinies[1] and seemingly pervasive now, was the Ministry's most serious cause for alarm. For if reinforcement of its powers and vigilance arose from the threat of French invasion, the situation in Ireland was itself a prime aspect of that threat. The dangers there had been rising inexorably over the past year, and from the web of information and rumour gathered in Dublin and from Europe there seemed every prospect of some form of French support. As they mounted their forces therefore against disaffection within the British Isles, Ministers were alerted particularly by developments across the Irish Sea.

III

That dimension was visible in another respect: indeed it was soon propelled to the centre of the stage. For in June 1798 the situation in Ireland was such that troops had to be despatched who were needed, or thought to be needed, for strategic defence at home.

Fears of invasion of England had been acute in the early months of the year, as the flat-bottomed boats were assembled from Antwerp to Cherbourg – and particularly when Bonaparte was known to have been placed in charge. Reaching a peak perhaps in the spring, they remained active into the summer, producing by far the most vigorous and widespread response so far. For this was recognised as an 'awful crisis', a prospect deemed to be as 'formidable' as that of any period 'in the History of this Country'.[2] Government set to work to deploy its plans and resources at a pace and, it hoped, on a scale to meet an urgent major threat.

1. Pp. 19–20 above.
2. Dundas to Spencer, attr. 29 January 1798 (*Private Papers of Spencer*, II, 240); Pitt on 20 April (p. 115 above).

The military and naval designs had been scrutinised in the late winter of
1797–8. They drew very largely on the latest appraisement, in 1796. But
under these sterner circumstances other wartime proposals were
reviewed, and indeed proposals earlier than that. Dundas set the historian
John Bruce to research preparations as far back as the time of the
Armada, and looked at some of the documents himself.[1] The results
repeated and brought up to date the traditional approach. Small naval
squadrons were placed in the Downs, at St Helens and Portland, with
divisions of gunboats there and farther west. A stronger squadron cruised
off the Scillies, the main blockading squadron watched Brest, and units
from the Mediterranean fleet kept an eye on Cadiz. The regular troops
were disposed preponderantly around London and in the eastern and
south-western military districts, with a substantial garrison and striking
force in the Channel Isles; the part-time forces, militia and voluntary, as
far as possible in the south and east. Arrangements were made, as on
earlier occasions, for 'driving the country' – removing livestock, crops and
transport. The outer seaward approach to London would be protected by
removing the buoys, as in the recent mutiny at the Nore.[2] Action however
should not be confined to passive defence. Pitt had observed earlier that
the navy should not simply wait to guard the coasts, and Dundas was keen
now to 'alarm' the enemy 'along their own'. There should be selective
raids from Holland to Biscay, and bombardments of assembly ports.
Some of these last in fact took place, and in the early summer a small
expedition was mounted to destroy the canal locks at Ostend, embarking
eventually some months later than planned.[3]

1. Discovering in the process the inadequacy of arrangements for keeping the public
papers. He congratulated himself on having taken a copy of one set of proposals sent him
by Pitt in 1793, and since lost, 'because unless I do so I am by no means certain I can ever
see it again' (to Spencer; *Private Papers of Spencer*, II, 239). Further papers of Pitt's that *have*
survived on the subject are in P.R.O. 30/8/245, and in general see *Private Papers of Spencer*,
II, Part V *passim*, and Dundas to Grenville, 10 August 1798 (*H.M.C., Dropmore*, IV, 278). For
reviews of defence in 1795–6 see II, 611–12, 635.

2. *Private Papers of Spencer*, II, 299–301, 303–5; P.R.O., W.O. 30/65, no. 7 for military
strengths and dispositions, February 1798. Cf. II, 261; p. 29 above. Pitt had thought earlier
that gunboats might be manned 'on the first Alarm, by Fishermen and any other seafaring
Persons who might be on the Spot' (to Camden, 24 August 1796; Camden Ms C123/11).
For 'driving the country' see eg Henry Motz to Pitt, nd but endorsed 28 February 1798
(P.R.O. 30/8/161).
There was some disagreement and cavil in the process. Cornwallis, Master General of
the Ordnance, was apparently kept in the dark by Dundas (to Major-General Ross, 14
April 1798; *Correspondence of . . . Cornwallis*, II, 334), and Spencer's 'Ideas', shown to the
Cabinet in February, were queried, to his annoyance, in April. As he complained to Pitt,
the navy, hearing nothing, had assumed that the plans were approved (*Private Papers of
Spencer*, II, 295–302). The Lord Privy Seal, Westmorland – for whose capacity Dundas had
profound contempt –, complained that the Cabinet should have been consulted in greater
detail throughout (Dundas to Pitt, 31 May 1798; John Rylands Library, University of
Manchester, English Ms 907).

3. See *Private Papers of Spencer*, II, 232–8, 285–6, 351–2; op. cit., 326–53; William Laird
Clowes *et al.*, *The Royal Navy, A History . . .*, IV (1899), 339–43.

Ministers expressed confidence as they set to work. Dundas in January welcomed the challenge given two months' grace, and Pitt looked forward to 'the option between burning their ships before they set out, or sinking them either on their passage or before their troops can land, or destroying them as soon as they have landed, or starving them and taking them prisoners afterwards'.[1] The spirit was broadly sustained as the alarm bred defiance.

> Sons, brothers, husbands, all
> . . . Stand forth! be men! repel an impious foe![2]

And many did stand forth. Not every one was swept into action. The War Office had looked on the public for some time as inclined to be soft, and complaints were now heard of a 'Commercial Nation' being slow to rally to the colours.[3] Nor was the regional response as evenly spread – or the reasons as predictable – as a first impression might suggest.[4] But certainly the spirit suddenly looked formidable. The various Volunteer formations were drilling, their ranks swollen by recruits. Political opponents served together; gentlemen, from the Prince of Wales downwards, called up retainers; the Senate at Cambridge gave its undergraduates leave of absence to bear arms; the Archbishops had to discourage clergy from enlisting part-time. Above all, there was a strong response from among those employed in industries and trades. 'The thoughts of every man', it was said in April, 'are now occupied about an invasion',[5] and newspapers and print makers made the most of the fact. Gillray published his *Consequences of a Successful French Invasion*, one print showing Pitt being whipped in St James's Street, and planned to illustrate the landings; Rowlandson followed later with his series of military exercises, and the uniforms of *The Loyal Volunteers of London and Environs*. The demonstration of zeal itself was hardly likely to prove adequate in practice: while the Volunteer corps had gained some experience over the past three to four years, arms and ammunition were short, the spirit was amateur and independent, many of the recruits were distinctly vague as to their duties. If Bonaparte's troops had come, on this first of the serious alarms, one must wonder how these willing but untrained defenders would have fared.

They were far however from being the only ones to stand forth, or be

---

1. Dundas to Grenville, 5 January 1798 (*H.M.C., Dropmore*, IV, 48); Pitt to Mornington, 26 January 1798 (Rosebery, *Pitt*, 206).
2. Coleridge, 'Fears in Solitude, Written in April 1798, During the Alarm of an Invasion': lines sounding his first retreat from the 'jacobinism' for which he had been kept under observation a few months earlier, in company with Thelwall, down in Somerset.
3. J.R. Western, 'The Recruitment of the Land Forces in Great Britain, 1793–99' (Ph.D. thesis, University of Edinburgh, 1953), 16; *The True Briton*, 28 March 1798.
4. See Linda Colley in *Britain from 1689 to 1815 An Imperial State at War*, ed. Lawrence Stone (1994), 168–79.
5. *The Morning Post*, 17 April 1798. See II, 401, 486–7 for the voluntary forces.

stood forth. Every effort was made to bring the regular formations up to strength, half the English militias were embodied in February and the rest in April, and those in Scotland were all in the field by autumn. Their numbers drew partly on measures taken quite recently. For despite the substantial efforts of 1794–5 manpower remained short, and in the autumn of 1796 Pitt tried again. He introduced a Quota Act to do for the army what was already being done for the navy, and a Supplementary Militia of 60,000 distinct from the existing force. A new body of Provincial Cavalry, set at 20,000, was also provided, to be raised by ballot on a levy of one horse in ten of those liable to tax. The Minister took care to sound Parliamentary opinion in meetings beforehand.[1] Even so, while the bills overcame misgivings, some of their drafting soon needed amendment; and the implementation was markedly less smooth. There were widespread if scattered riots against the supplementary militia in England, while 'Scotland', particularly the Lowlands, 'went stark mad'.[2] The worst demonstrations died down in time. But the targets could not be reached: despite a reduction in the establishment of the regular army in 1796 and '97, when commitments in Europe and available funds alike were low, the deficit persisted at about 50,000, while the militia's increased strength on paper was not matched on the ground. Discounting the Volunteers, there should have been some 255,000 men under arms in 1798. As far as the figures can be interpreted, there may in fact have been between 185,000 and 198,000; and of a regular force of 100–103,000, only some 44,000 at most were stationed in Britain and the Channel Islands in June.[3] The best-trained troops were badly stretched.[4] No strategic reserve could be built up. Recruitment seemed to have passed its peak. And perhaps most ominous, Government's attempts to gain more control and flexibility in the different formations were encountering the usual constraints.

Something could be done in this last sphere within the confines of Government itself. Early in the year Dundas was able to gain one enlargement of his own powers. When his Secretaryship of State for War had

1. J.R. Western, *The English Militia in the Eighteenth Century* . . . (1955), 221.

2. Gilbert Elliot's phrase, quoted in Western, 'Recruitment of the Land Forces', 172. See II, 485–9, 642–3 for the efforts of 1794–6.

3. It is hard to be sure of the figures, taken here to the nearest thousand. But cf. Fortescue, *History of the British Army*, IV-Part II, Appendices C and D with Piers Mackesy, *Statesmen at War, The Strategy of Overthrow 1798–1799* (1974), 93n14. The latter computes the militia at some 98,000 in June 1798, whereas Western in *The English Militia* . . ., 222 cites a figure of 82,000 effectives in February 1799. Other figures of the same period, similar but not identical, are given in Pitt's papers in P.R.O. 30/8/240, ff. 89–95v.

The rest – in fact the bulk – of the regular army was spread between the West Indian and Canadian colonies, the Cape of Good Hope, and India, with a small body in New South Wales and some troops in Portugal and Gibraltar.

4. So badly indeed that a request had been made to Russia in November to send some men – as could be demanded under the treaty of alliance of 1795 (see II, 550) - for the defence of the kingdom (Grenville to Whitworth, no. 30, Secret and Separate, 10 November 1797; P.R.O., F.O. 65/38). The Tsar responded by announcing that he would once more despatch a naval squadron for the North Sea (cf. p. 28 above).

been created in 1794 it did not include control of the part-time land forces: the militia, as the ancient common law force, remained under an existing Secretary of State – the Home Secretary, Portland – and the Volunteers, given statutory authority, were placed, not illogically, in the same hands. The position, unsatisfactory in the past few years, now seemed really dangerous, and Dundas exploded at great length to Pitt. The 'Confusion . . . and the Publick Responsibility' must be cleared up: either by abolishing his own office with 'the few Duties that now belong to it' or assigning to it all 'the Detail of the Defence of the Country . . . in co-operation with the Commander in Chief, and the Board of Admiralty'. He must be given 'the Correspondence . . . during the war' with the part-time forces and the Lords Lieutenant of the counties who raised and largely administered them and appointed the officers.[1] This specific change was accepted. Portland, the Home Secretary – not normally one, as a Whig leader, to see his influence curtailed – seems to have concurred in the 'awful crisis', and his role here passed to the Secretary for War.

This was a helpful readjustment, which speeded things up.[2] But there was much that it did not touch. Dundas had gained 'the Correspondence', but the actual scope of the Lords Lieutenant was not thereby narrowed; rather, they were directed to a new address. Their position, and that of the regimental colonels, was of real importance, for it affected not only the dispositions and recruitment of the part-time troops, but those, in consequence, of the regulars as well. When the army was short of men, flexibility was the key to management. But that was something which the system of dispersed authority had largely denied. The 'principle of multiple diffusion', designed to restrain the central executive,[3] anchored the militia and Volunteers largely in their own areas, and discouraged the transfer of men to the regular formations. Three initiatives by Government showed indeed the strength of the sentiment. In the autumn of 1797 the War Office examined the possibility of recruiting militiamen into the army, and in January 1798 an Act was passed to that end, with a ceiling of 10,000 men from the supplementary militia who might serve at home and in Europe.[4] Few Lords Lieutenant however would co-operate, and the plan failed. So did an attempt to empower Government to appoint officers to such commissions in the supplementary militia as the Lords Lieutenant had not themselves filled. At the same time the Ministry found itself embroiled with the militia colonels

---

1. Dundas to Pitt, 10 February 1798 (P.R.O. 30/8/157). The letter occupied nineteen sheets. And cf. same to Grenville, 12 February 1798 (*H.M.C., Dropmore*, IV, 79). For the arrangements in 1794 see II, 328–9, 412 14, 484, 487; and op. cit., 261n1 for the Commander-in-Chief.

2. It was indeed perhaps the most immediate result, for in practice the Home Secretary was acting very largely only as 'a clerical agency' in these matters (Nelson, *The Home Office, 1782–1801*, 141).

3. I, 312, and see II, 483–4.

4. 38 Geo. III, c17; the provisions extended to mid May by 38 Geo. III, c55.

over a proposal to combine their flank companies – the best in the battalions – with the regulars for training and possibly for action. A furious quarrel indeed developed, led by Grenville's elder brother Buckingham, to which Pitt and Dundas had to spare some badly needed time.[1] Ministers knew well enough that the answer lay in 'one general Combination of efficient Strength': in April in fact they called for returns of all men between the ages of fifteen and sixty.[2] But they knew equally well that Government was placed in 'a disagreeable state' in Parliament by 'any measure relating to militia';[3] and even in this crisis the old habits would not die.

All was not dark, however. If Ministers were often frustrated in 1798, they found ways thereafter towards improvements which by the end of the Revolutionary War were starting to produce a greater flexibility. A significant element in this progress was in fact provided by Buckingham himself, on the heels of his delaying action over the flank companies. For in the early summer he pioneered the way for militia formations to leave their areas, by volunteering his own regiment *en bloc* for service in Ireland. While such transfers had been made on a modest scale with Fencible troops since 1794,[4] this introduced a practice of a larger dimension, and gave Government ground on which it hastened to build. An Act in June legalised such service in Ireland to a figure of 12,000 men, for a period ending one month after the start of the next Parliamentary session; and this was duly extended at the end of the year, and again late in 1799.[5] There were improvements likewise in relations with the local authorities. A Defence Act in April gave Ministers specific powers in the event of invasion,[6] and drawing on their recent adverse experiences they took care to inform and consult those concerned. Details were printed and circulated to Lords Lieutenant and others such as colonels, mayors and magistrates – Pitt was one recipient, as Lord Warden of the Cinque Ports, in a series from Dundas –[7], meetings were held, advice was provided for organising voluntary efforts. Encouragement was given to finding more men for the Volunteer corps themselves from urban formations – a marked shift of emphasis, which would soon show some social effects.[8] And some months later a survey was ordered from each county of the numbers of Volunteers, to include – an interesting innovation – the percentages of those willing to serve only within their immediate locality, or within their

1. For this last see in particular *H.M.C., Dropmore*, IV, 169–70, 177–81, 223–4, 227; for all three proposals, Western, *The English Militia*, 224–32.
2. Dundas to Pitt, 10 February 1798 (P.R.O. 30/8/157); 38 Geo. III, c27, section 1.
3. Dundas to Grenville, 17 April 1798 (*H.M.C., Dropmore*, IV, 170).
4. See II, 488.
5. 38 Geo. III, c66; 39 Geo. III, c5; 39 & 40 Geo. III, c15.
6. 38 Geo. III, c27.
7. See P.R.O. 30/8/244.
8. Cf. J.E. Cookson, 'The English Volunteer Movement of the French Wars, 1793–1815: Some Contexts' (*H.J.*, Vol. 32, No. 4, particularly 879–85); and II, 401–2, 486–8.

county, or within the military district of which the county formed a part. Not every such return has survived, some are incomplete, some unreliable. But together they gave the central Government a far better picture of the realities than it had ever had before – a not unimpressive indication of the administrative advances which war was bringing in its train.[1] Official thought had been moving over the past two years. The pace quickened, and the direction to some extent altered, in the alarm of 1798, hastening the evolution of a system of domestic defence which in time would underpin the military effort as a whole.

The land forces were not alone in wanting more men at this time. The navy was in like case. In contrast to the army its establishment had been raised the year before, from 110,000 to 120,000, and this figure was repeated for 1798. But the effective strength as usual was lower, at a time when every ship was needed at sea and with as skilled a complement as could be supplied. The Quota Acts of 1795 and 1796, particularly the first, had made a real contribution to numbers; nor was the quality of the products as poor by and large as has often been held. First impressions in fact were quite favourable, though less so from the second Act. But few of the entrants had sea experience; too many boys and Irish were coming in; and the shock of the mutinies, and the still lingering scattered instances of unrest, made the Admiralty even more anxious now to find seamen on a larger scale.[2] One obvious if unpopular source lay to hand: the men protected, in an uneasy balance with naval needs, in the sea and river trades. In May 1798 Government decided to suspend all such exemptions for five months, except in the coastal coal trade for one month; and on the 25th Pitt, citing 'the present alarming situation of the country', asked the Commons to pass the necessary bill within the day. They did so, the Lords followed suit, and on the 26th it became law.[3]

The brief debate on this subject had a celebrated sequel. George Tierney, in his capacity as the Foxites' resident leader, objected to Pitt's demand. He did not necessarily deny the need for the measure; but he wanted it argued and demonstrated, and he condemned 'the precipitate manner' in which the Minister had come to the House. Referring clearly to the recent similar call to suspend Habeas Corpus within the day,

> he must view all the measures of Ministers as hostile to the liberty of the subject; and the present measure he must regard with peculiar

1. Pitt's copy of the assembled returns is in P.R.O. 30/8/244, and has been printed by Linda Colley in *Britons*, Appendix 3.

2. See II, 496–7; Christopher Oprey, 'Schemes for the Reform of Naval Recruitment, 1793–1815' (M.A. thesis, University of Liverpool, 1961), 127–81 and Appendix B; pp. 18–20 above.

3. Oprey, loc. cit., 37–59; *P.H.*, XXXIII (1818), col. 1460. The Act was 38 Geo. III, c34.

jealousy, as it went directly to rob them of the few remaining privileges they were still permitted to enjoy.[1]

Pitt responded angrily. He had given notice of the motion, and if the notice was brief that arose from circumstances on which Government alone could have the knowledge to judge. In such a case therefore, 'how can the hon. gentleman's opposition to it be accounted for, but from a desire to obstruct the defence of the country?' Tierney at once called him to order: the language was not Parliamentary; he appealed to the Speaker; and the Speaker asked Pitt to explain himself. The question had no effect.

> Mr. *Pitt* said, he was afraid the House must wait a long while before they heard such an explanation as was demanded of him, for he must adhere to his former declaration (which he again repeated). He knew that he had no right to impute motives to the language used by the honourable gentleman, however impossible it might be not to suspect motives; but he knew that he had a right to state such arguments as appeared to him conclusive against those adopted by the hon. gentleman, and whilst he would submit these to the judgment of the House, he must say, that he would neither retract from, nor farther explain, his former expression.[2]

The next day he received a call from Major-General George Walpole, acting as Tierney's second, with a challenge to a duel, which he accepted at once.[3]

Things then took their course. Pitt sent a note asking Tom Steele to be his second; but Steele was out of town, and Dudley Ryder agreed to act. The Minister asked the Speaker, as a friend, to come and see him – thereby making it harder for Addington to take steps to prevent the meeting. He made his will; and at about noon on 27 May walked with Ryder and Addington into Birdcage Walk, where he and Ryder entered a chaise and set off for Putney Heath, to the gibbet which stood on the hill leading down to Kingston Vale. The affair took place in a dell nearby, with pistols at twelve paces. Both men missed with the first shot, and Pitt fired in the air with his second. Neither was injured, and they went back to town well satisfied with themselves. Watchers had gathered on the skyline, including the Speaker, who had ridden to the

---

1. *P.H.*, XXXIII, col. 1461. This is to be preferred to the version in *P.R.*, *3rd ser.*, VI, 231, which however, unlike *P.H.*, contains a direct reference to the suspension of Habeas Corpus (for which see p. 115 above). Curiously, there is no report of the debate in *The Senator*, XXIII (nd).

2. *P.R.*, *3rd ser.*, VI, 232. This is followed virtually *verbatim* in *P.H.*, XXXIII, col. 1462.

3. See *H of P*, V, 472–3 for Walpole.

spot. He must have been as relieved as any one that nothing worse had occurred.[1]

On his return Pitt wrote to his mother and his brother and several of his friends. His antagonist, he declared to old Lady Chatham, had 'behaved with great propriety'; and indeed the two men thereafter viewed each other with greater tolerance. He was not displeased with the business, and carried it off calmly enough.[2] But not every one felt the same, and some were the more shaken because the affair took place on a Sunday – in fact on Whit Sunday. Wilberforce naturally was one of those, and he was quick to act. On the 30th he gave notice in the Commons of a motion condemning duelling. Pitt again took a high line: he must look on such a motion as 'one for my removal'. That, and advice from others, caused Wilberforce to withdraw, and the two friends were writing amicably again by the end of the week.[3] But if the Evangelicals' emphasis was their own, they were not alone in their concern. The political world was surprised and dismayed, as were Pitt's own colleagues; the King expressed strong disapproval; and similar sentiments were aired in newspapers and society at large.[4] The Minister was not the only target: Tierney was censured for going so far as to issue a challenge which could then not be avoided, and Addington attracted observations for letting the exchanges develop as they did.[5] But whatever roles were assigned to the other players, Pitt was the central figure in an episode for which he received the worst of the blame.

This was not entirely because duelling was seen as unacceptable in itself. It persisted as an element in the gentleman's code of honour. While it was attacked, as it had long been attacked, for brutality and immorality, and was perhaps viewed increasingly as anachronistic, it was still accepted

1. Stanhope, III, 130–1, and Holland Rose, II, 334–5, give the standard accounts. Those in the newspapers of the 28th, supplied officially (see Pitt to Canning, 'Monday 2 p.m.' (Canning Ms 30, Leeds); *L.C.G. III*, III, no. 1745; *The Times*, 29 May), were, Pitt stated, 'correct' (to Hester Countess of Chatham, 28 May 1798; Stanhope, op. cit., 132). There is an interesting longer account in *The Morning Post* of 2 June.

Steele's and Ryder's early friendships with Pitt are noted in I, 107, 108, 109n1. Pitt gave the pistols to Ryder as a memento, and they remain in his descendant's keeping.

2. Eg Stanhope, III, 131–2, for two of the letters. Pitt remarked to Camden, in another, that he believed he and Tierney 'parted better satisfied with each other than on any other occasion in our lives' (quoted in *L.C.G. III*, III, no. 1745, p. 68n1).

When the duel ended, he greeted Addington by inviting him to dinner. The next evening he celebrated his birthday with a company invited by Dundas.

3. The fullest accounts are in Stanhope, III, 133–4, and Robin Furneaux, *William Wilberforce* (1974), 183–5.

4. Eg – a few from many sources – George III to Pitt, 30 May (Stanhope, III, Appendix, xiv); Buckingham to Grenville, 29 May 1798 (*H.M.C., Dropmore*, IV, 222); Spencer to Dundas, 28 May 1798 (*Private Papers of Spencer*, II, 355).

5. On Tierney, Rose (who had not been in the House) to Pretyman, 6 June 1798 (Pretyman Ms 435/44); on Addington, Ziegler, op. cit., 82–3, and cf. *Diary of Farington*, III, 1034, and Mrs Pretyman Tomline's 'Notes' of October–November 1801 in Stanhope Ms S5 C41. The Speaker had certainly acted more firmly four years before, when he required Pitt to withdraw some personal remarks about Fox in the debate on the latter's motion to end the war (see *P.R.*, XXXVIII (1794), 366–8).

by many in the ranks of those socially eligible – and indeed socially aspiring – as inherent in an ethos which remained very strong.[1] In practice the results were shielded from the rigour of laws invoked over two centuries, and there was a general recognition that this was likely to be so. Much of the weight of the feeling against Pitt among traditionalist gentlemen themselves lay rather in the charge that he should not set his private against his public duty at such a time. That had long been the argument of rulers, anxious to bring personal quarrels within the orbit of the state. It was used now by George III,[2] and it was widely echoed, in quarters which did not necessarily condemn a challenge on grounds of morality and 'improvement'. The concern and disapproval, from whichever quarter, proved of limited effect. Duels in general may in fact have been on the increase in these decades, and prominent politicians certainly continued to indulge.[3] Fox and Shelburne had each 'been out', both of them shortly before Pitt entered Parliament; his disciples Canning and Castlereagh fought each other three years after he died, and Wellington (characteristically the last Prime Minister to do so) accepted a challenge twenty years later. It took a change in the concept of the gentleman and a major development of the forces of order to remove the duel as a permissible means of conducting one's affairs.

In this respect Pitt was indeed very much a private gentleman of his time: abundantly so indeed, given his full share of the family pride.[4] Wilberforce noted sadly, 'Strange the length to which he carries the point of honour',[5] and the Minister would perhaps have acted as he did at any point in his life. When he chose to do so, however, it was at a point of considerable strain. Public pressures had been and were severe, the prosecution at Margate had just virtually failed, and his health, uncertain in the past two years, was reflecting his problems.[6] He was indeed on the verge of the illness which alarmed his friends in the next two months; and it was one that kept him from attending the Commons for the rest of the session. The quarrel with Tierney marked in fact the last occasion on which he was seen there before Parliament rose on 29 June. Nonetheless, whatever the impact of his current state on his personal judgment, policy was not visibly affected. By the time indeed that he was forced to seek comparative rest, a strategic decision had been taken, in which he was centrally involved, which was to produce an outstanding victory with some far-reaching European effects.

1. This paragraph draws largely on Sir George Clark, *War and Society in the Seventeenth Century* (1958), ch. II, and J.C.D. Clark, *English Society 1688–1832* ... (1985), 109–18.

2. 'Public characters have no right to weigh alone what they owe to themselves; they must also consider what is due to their country' (to Pitt, 30 May; Stanhope, III, Appendix, xiv).

3. Including – not surprisingly – Irish radicals and reformers; see the list in J.C.D. Clark, op. cit., 114n255.

4. See I, 3 5.

5. *Life of Wilberforce*, II, 282.

6. Pp. 81, 118, above.

CHAPTER V

Reviving Hopes

I

In the summer of 1798 the situation in Britain might be viewed with rather greater assurance. The finances had been moved on to a changed footing – the old mould had been cracked, whether or not the yield would prove immediately adequate. Public support for Government had risen and the danger of subversion from invasion been reduced; and the military defences themselves were being overhauled. The country, it might be said, was emerging from the trough of the year before. Its ability to continue the war was markedly improved. But the further question remained. Britain had endured more than two years of strategic stalemate, and for the past eighteen months had been looking mainly to survival. If the war seemed less likely now to be lost outright, how was it to be won, or salvaged? What prospect was there, for all the expense, of a realistic improvement?

Was it possible, however, to move as yet to that point? Neither the state of Europe nor indeed the outlook for home defence could provide a sure guide. In the course of April there was a growing suspicion that the odds against a landing were lengthening,[1] and that the spirit of the nation was equal to the task. But 'the intended invasion'[2] might of course still come at some point in the summer; and the prospects in general moreover were becoming less easy to weigh. For in April and May assessments were complicated by a run of mounting events, to which the British response itself mounted as their course became confused.

The first signs, in the light of later developments, came at the start of April. On the 1st the Austrian Minister in London made an approach for a fresh alliance; on the 2nd the main French Mediterranean squadron

1. Cf. for example the opinions of two competent observers recently returned from the Continent: the newly ennobled Lord Minto, formerly Sir Gilbert Elliot (see II, 346–7, 643) in late April (quoted in Piers Mackesy, *Statesmen at War*, 18n14), and Mallet du Pan (see II, 313, 581) in May (Holland Rose, II, 338).

The Government itself went so far as to say in June that invasion might not come before the autumn or winter; though this was in order to seek a longer retention of the Russian North Sea squadron (p. 123, n4 above); Grenville to Whitworth, no. 13, 5 June 1798 (P.R.O., F.O. 65/40).

2. George III to Dundas, 12 April 1798 (*L.C.G. III*, III, no. 1715).

returned to Toulon from its station, held on and off since the autumn, in the Ionian Sea. These events, though simultaneous, were not directly connected. They represented separate developments. But together they raised possibilities, initially hard to pin down, which would soon make their impact on British action, and on British strategic thought.

Within the Continent itself much had changed over the past six months. In October 1797 – when the last British hopes from Lille disappeared – the Austrians signed the treaty of Campo Formio with Bonaparte which the Preliminaries of Leoben had introduced in April.[1] The peace terms, not broadcast in detail or indeed at all for some time, gave body to the earlier outlines in a context which he had rearranged meanwhile. As before, the Emperor was given Venice with part of its hinterland and the head of the Adriatic. But, to his surprise, the French took the Ionian Islands. He lost some Venetian territory, again unexpectedly, to the neighbouring new Cisalpine Republic, and some fiefs around Genoa to a new Ligurian Republic. As before, he surrendered his claim to the Austrian Netherlands, and acknowledged that of the French Republic in principle to extended frontiers. But he also now agreed to use his influence in a Congress of the Holy Roman Empire, of which he was the protector, to cede the lands west of the Rhine, in return for those of the Archbishopric of Strasbourg and (in lieu of the Netherlands) part of Bavaria;[2] and he complied with a demand to pull back his troops on the east bank of the river.

These arrangements, actual and potential, would make their mark on European attitudes. But they were not the only developments to have taken place. For, particularly while their detail remained uncertain, it was the growing pressures by France in other quarters, through aggressive interpretations of agreements and fomenting of disturbance, that were causing farther changes and rising unease. The tactics had been employed with Venice in the run-up to Campo Formio. They were equally evident elsewhere. Bonaparte had earlier borne down on the Papacy; the process was completed in February 1798, on the pretext of an incident, with the occupation of Rome and the creation of another Republic. By then moreover a worse occupation, as it seemed in England, had taken place. Exploiting signs of internal discontent, the Swiss Valtelline region was annexed to the emerging Cisalpine Republic in November 1797; and two months later French troops marched on Berne, the Swiss Confederacy was dissolved, and a Helvetic Republic set up. Geneva and Mulhouse were directly annexed, fines levied, arms and treasures removed. In Venice too this last process was actively under way: Veroneses and Titians, the bronze horses of St Mark's, made the journey to Paris, while the

---

1. See pp. 50–1, 56 above. The plain of Campo Formio lay outside the town of Udine, and at the time the treaty was often called by the latter name.
2. This last being a diminished survivor from an old and strong Austrian ambition; cf. I, 473, II, 198.

Austrians found they had lost their newly acquired ships and naval stores. Meanwhile the Germanic Congress, assembled at Rastadt from December 1797, pursued a despondent course amid the rival diplomacies of Austria and Prussia and the Austrians' troop withdrawal, accompanied by renewed French assaults on the Rhine. In March 1798 it confirmed the surrender of almost all the territories west of the river.

Passing judgment later on the period which these stratagems introduced, Pitt characterised it as finally proving that 'neither solemn professions, nor the general law of nations, nor the obligations of treaties . . . could restrain' the French 'unrelenting spirit' 'from the subversion of every state into which, either by force or fraud, their arms could penetrate'.[1] The verdict did not come from England, or from one in authority, alone. Nor was it only retrospective. Whatever the merits proclaimed from France's mission – the benefits, administrative, political, intellectual, which could emerge from a dawning age – the methods soon disgusted some of the finer spirits who had welcomed the dawn. Resistance from former supporters appeared in Switzerland and the Cisalpine Republic, the latter soon attracting a sterner treaty than that which had brought it into being. Small states throughout Europe sheltered as best they could in the harsher wind. The larger Powers tried uneasily to balance potential safeguards and gains.

Such was the setting in which the Austrians made their approach in London. It did not seem very likely to be immediately productive. The two Governments had kept in touch since Austria left the war; but there was no meeting of minds, and in fact both were feeling aggrieved.[2] The British resented (rather unreasonably) the manner of their ally's withdrawal; they were angry at being denied information on both the Preliminaries and the final treaty; and they suspected (rightly) that the terms would diminish Austria's protection of the Germanic Empire. These feelings gained a sharper point from a more intimate concern, over Austria's conduct of her financial obligations; and the resulting anger had not been assuaged – indeed it had been heightened – by some inconclusive soundings from Vienna to test the prospects of support if French pressures increased, while still avoiding too wide a commitment and contesting London's financial case. Relations suffered accordingly; in January 1798 the British Government even thought of recalling its envoy;[3] and on the eve of receiving the fresh message on 1 April, its own were no more intimate or indeed amicable than before.

The quarrel was to prove significant, souring the atmosphere in the next two years even more than earlier complaints over aid had done since

1. In the Commons, 3 February 1800 (*P.R., 3rd ser.*, X (1800), 321). A list of examples on which the case was based, made probably for this speech, is in Grenville's hand among Pitt's papers in P.R.O. 30/8/196.

2. This paragraph draws on Michael Duffy, 'British War Policy: the Austrian Alliance 1793–1801', 296–322. And see II, 627, 645–6, pp. 50–1 above.

3. Grenville to Morton Eden, nos. 1, 2, 16 January, 2 February 1798 (P.R.O., F.O. 7/51).

1794–5.[1] It arose out of the most recent loan, raised for Austria in 1797 following its larger predecessor two years before. There had been talks in 1796; but as usual they had been protracted, and meanwhile cash advances were sent, though with growing interruptions as Britain's own reserves declined.[2] These remittances, it was agreed, were to be repaid from the future loan: the Austrian Minister in London, Count Starhemberg, was in fact authorised to accept that stipulation, though not the terms of the loan itself, without recourse to Vienna. The sum to be raised on the London market seemed likely to be set at £3½ million, of which £1,620,000 was reckoned by Government to be already absorbed by the advances. But the prospect faded with the news of a possible Austrian armistice, and Pitt promptly took steps to secure the money needed for those latter payments. He prepared to raise a loan for the £1,620,000, and on 14 April 1797 – four days before the Preliminaries of Leoben were concluded[3] – Starhemberg was called on to sign his agreement to meet that amount. He did so by way of a Convention of the 16th, and the next day Pitt introduced a bill for a Parliamentary guarantee – as in 1795 – of the terms. It passed on the 24th. Meanwhile the Convention was sent to Vienna. Reaching there on the 27th it caused immediate consternation, and three weeks later ratification was refused.[4]

Deadlock followed. The British were amazed by the Austrians' reaction. Starhemberg had been given authority: how could it be withdrawn now? The Austrians for their part, tired of being lectured by a Power whose land force had at best been small, replete with their own complaints of treatment,[5] and naturally distressed as their resistance collapsed, were outraged by the haste of the process and protested at the terms, which they found more severe in the level of interest than those – bad enough, they claimed – of 1795. The British responded that the Austrians, as before, seemed unable to master technicalities, or to appreciate what had been done for them despite all the problems. Matters were not improved when Vienna defaulted on a payment of interest under the loan of 1795, and when a subsidy (not a loan) was suggested in one of the soundings for contingent future support.[6] The Foreign Secretary's temperament added its own flavour to the rejection of Austria's arguments. His lofty distaste, a

1. See II, Ch. X sections I, IV, Ch. XIII section III, Ch. XIV section I.

2. Op. cit., 595, 609, 627, 638 for discussions in 1796; pp. 51, 53 above for the position early in 1797.

3. See p. 51 above. And while a mission was on its way to encourage Austria and settle the terms for the larger loan (pp. 54–5 above).

4. Duffy, loc. cit., 295 and Appendix C discusses the figure of £1,620,000, rejecting an alternative suggested by John M. Sherwig in *Guineas and Gunpowder . . .* (1969), 91. The arrears in the remittances by then amounted to £530,000 (see Duffy, loc. cit., 296), representing defaults while the Austrians were still fighting (and see II, 627n3 for one British admission in private of their case). See pp. 41–2 above for Parliament.

5. Cf. for the Coalition's final year II, 627–9, 637–8.

6. Duffy, loc. cit., 298–300. The Austrians normally disliked the idea of a subsidy as against a loan, though they had proposed it once themselves in 1794 (see II, 363, 365).

familiar irritation in Europe, had been fully roused, and a personal cold and rigid anger breathed in the insistence that 'the full, complete and unqualified performance of this engagement is an absolute and indispensable condition of any idea of friendship, union or concert'.[1]

Well and good; and the dispute was not allowed to die. Nonetheless it could not be allowed entirely to suspend relations. The aim of British policy, at the very time at which Grenville was thinking of recalling his envoy,[2] ensured indeed that contact at least should be maintained. For in January 1798, responding to signs of heightened apprehension of France, the Government completed proposals for a Quadruple Alliance to embrace Russia, Prussia and Austria, making up 'the Four Great Powers, which alone can afford protection to their own dominions or to the rest of Europe'.[3] The scheme was far-reaching. Its prime purpose was to achieve a combination close enough to force both a 'Continental' and a 'Maritime' peace: to reach the balanced comprehensive terms which had eluded unilateral efforts. Two things were necessary for that to happen: properly concerted strategic plans and operational movements, and prior agreement between the partners on their interests and claims. Neither had been achieved in the First Coalition – lack of the second had damaged the first – and 'union' now must rest on a firmer, broader basis. But that union should not end with the signing of peace. It should be continued, to preserve its members' safety and that of Europe against any fresh 'encroachments'. The design in fact was extensive; and it was later to prove significant. The various elements were not new, nor in principle perhaps was the pattern itself. It had been adumbrated as far back as the more hopeful days of 1793–4, when a close and extensive 'concert', and even a peacetime system for territorial guarantees, had been put forward by Britain, then a Power that had only recently joined the war.[4] But much had happened since; the emphasis was now based on experience and it encompassed well digested needs; and against that background the proposals in 1798 may be allowed a difference and importance of their own. They had been germinating since the early winter; sparked off possibly by a suggestion from the veteran Duke of Brunswick, the most anglophil of the German rulers, who acted sometimes as a guide to Prussia's intentions and occasionally as an intermediary. If so, he deserves a mention in the

1. To Eden, nos. 51, 52, 24 November 1797 (P.R.O., F.O. 7/50); 'this point', he added, 'never will be departed from'. And cf. his remarks to same, no. 1 of 16 January, no. 4 of 13 March 1798 (F.O. 7/51), and to Starhemberg, 17 March 1798 (*H.M.C., Dropmore*, IV, 131). His mode of expression on occasions is mentioned in II, 365–6.
2. See p. 132 above. And if that was in fact a bluff it might surely have been called, or stalled.
3. Grenville to Whitworth [in St Petersburg], no. 3, Most Secret and Confidential, 14 January 1798 (P.R.O., F.O. 65/39). Cf. same to Elgin [in Berlin], Separate and Confidential, sd (F.O. 64/47).
4. See Peter Jupp, *Lord Grenville* (1985), 210. But I rather doubt myself if the latter proposal was more than a thought loosely thrown out, or did much to modify Grenville's initial intention to restrict agreements to the period of war (see II, 272).

formulation of a policy which Pitt and later Castlereagh would develop in the course of the next sixteen years. That pedigree in fact gives this occasion its greatest interest.[1] At the time it represented an acknowledgment that so far as Austria was concerned, and with whatever reservations, communication could not be reduced too far.

This indeed was underlined by the fact that Vienna would not be the main target of the initiative – on the contrary, only a brief indication was vouchsafed. The principal addressees rather were Russia and Prussia. A year before, the prospects in both would have seemed decidedly dim, and Prussia in particular hardly ripe for fresh cultivation.[2] But the position there was now thought to be improving, and in London the approach owed something moreover to the personal concern of the King. Interested in Brunswick's reports on the attitude of a new Prussian ruler, Frederick William III, who succeeded his father in November 1797 and was in gratifying touch with the Duke, George III was disposed to profit from his family ties[3] and Electoral knowledge, and suggested sending a personal agent who would sound out the ground. Pitt and Grenville agreed, taking care indeed to involve themselves in such a venture from the start, and the King duly despatched a certain André de Luc, a respectable Genevan philosopher and publicist who had caught the royal eye on a visit to England and been given a post in the Queen's household. One of those peripatetic *savants* who featured in the margins of eighteenth-century diplomacy, his 'very judicious though most *tedious*' reports encouraged the Ministers after a time to take the matter openly into their own hands. In January 1798 the British envoy in Berlin, hovering uneasily on the sidelines, was instructed to make an official approach.[4]

The decision was not unreasonable, in the case of either of the two Continental Powers. The death of the increasingly obstructive Frederick

1. It is hard to apportion responsibility exactly. But the earliest explicit mention of the most novel element in the proposals – for a continued alliance in peacetime – seems to be in a *Mémoire* by Brunswick of 5 December 1797, sent to London privately on the 12th (see *H.M.C., Dropmore*, IV, 27–9, particularly 28). His contribution, if such it was, does not figure in most British accounts; but it is noticed by Duffy, loc. cit., 341n1.

2. See pp. 4, 51–2 above; though also 53.

3. Brunswick being George III's brother-in-law, and father-in-law to the Prince of Wales.

4. The quotation is from George III to Pitt, 11 January 1798 (*L.C.G. III*, III, no. 1670; and see same to Grenville, 25 February 1798, no. 1689). Pitt's full participation, with Grenville, in handling the private talks is clear from op. cit., nos. 1639 and 1656 as well as 1689. De Luc's mission, which lasted from November 1797 to March–April 1798, may be followed in *H.M.C., Dropmore*, III and IV (including the latter's editorial introduction). Although it led, as such arrangements do, to some crossed lines, and to some resentment on the part of Elgin in Berlin, it seems to have been competently managed on the whole, and the Ministers, working closely with the King, checked any tendency towards a 'Secret du Roi' which might be applied in particular to his Hanoverian interests – de Luc, it may be noted, being sent under the title of a (freshly appointed) Professor at the Hanoverian university of Göttingen.

See I, 60 for old British links with Geneva.

William II of Prussia opened an opportunity, particularly as his son showed immediate signs of amity and resolve. He was making cordial noises to Russia and conciliatory gestures to Austria, and above all seemed ready to defend northern Germany if the French marched in. The climate in St Petersburg too was rather warmer than before. The Emperor Paul was noticeably civil to the British envoy, he was said to be using his good offices with Prussia and Austria to help settle their German quarrels, and to be growing increasingly disillusioned with France. Caution remained necessary. Direct requests from London were apt to be ignored, or even rejected as the recent appeal for troops showed at this very time.[1] There had been plenty of disappointments in the past, and the Tsar's own temperament was known to be unstable. Even so, when taken with the omens in Prussia, it seemed well worth while to stir the embers of growing alarm into fresh resistance to France.[2]

And so, in a frozen winter, the messengers set off to battle through northern Europe and endure the delays and miseries of Channel storms and German ice.[3] It was soon apparent that the obstacles to the proposals were severe. The key lay in Prussia, as George III stressed;[4] and while Frederick William III was sympathetic he was not proving as strong as forecast, and contrary influences – above all from the veteran Haugwitz, now the main British bugbear[5] – were potent. Some progress was visible: Prussia and Austria agreed to submit their German claims to Russian mediation. But Brunswick was drawing in his horns, and Paul, while amiable, remained immobile. In mid-March Grenville acknowledged a 'conclusive' lack of response from Berlin.[6] The concept of the Quadruple Alliance appeared to be dying or dead.

In that case, it would 'only remain . . . to promote a good understanding between the Powers': to try to achieve the less effective substitute of a second Coalition, reached probably, as the First had been, through a series of bilateral agreements.[7] The new Austrian approach in April could of course take its place in such a process. But its contents seemed scarcely attractive, or indeed to say anything new. They consisted in fact very largely of questions. In what way should each party give pledges against fear of a unilateral peace ('a point', Grenville commented acidly, 'which seems to interest us more than them')? What financial aid would be forthcoming in London? Would a fleet be sent back into the Mediterranean – a

1. P. 123, n4 above.

2. The despatches for the preparatory months are in P.R.O., F.O. 64/45–6, 65/38 respectively.

3. The delays indeed were such that Grenville at one point feared they might have affected the chance of success (to Elgin, no. 9, 13 March 1798; F.O. 64/47): another example of the impact on events of the pace of communications. Cf. II, 241, 555.

4. To Grenville, 2 April 1798 (*L.C.G. III*, III, no. 1704).

5. Cf. II, 626.

6. To Elgin, as in n3 above. The British position in this complicated period may be followed in F.O. 64/47–8, 65/39, 7/51.

7. Cf. II, Ch. VIII, sections I, II.

matter which appeared 'to be pressed with peculiar earnestness'? Would Britain declare itself able to continue the war in 1799? These queries and demands were not balanced by equivalent promises of action on Austria's part, and the Foreign Secretary's first impression was broadly dismissive. Pitt however was not so sure. While sharing his cousin's anger in the financial dispute, and placing no great trust in Vienna, he was not inclined to throw away any sign of a chance. 'I will not despair that it may lead to something worth trying'. 'We must endeavour to overcome the impossibilities', some of which indeed might not be impossible at all. We would certainly be able to carry the war into 1799; and he did not see 'much' difficulty in sending a fleet into the Mediterranean. No great hopes were held out in general, and he was not certain if the country would approve: he thought he saw in the awakened spirit a dislike of fresh commitments 'at our expense'.[1] At best, the possibilities should be pursued with deliberate care. But one of his assumptions was in fact to be tested without such delay. For not only did it seem that the return of a fleet was Austria's most pressing demand. Events were about to bring it to the forefront of British thought.

The Austrians' anxiety for a naval presence sprang from obvious causes. A British fleet could help reinsure their surviving position in northern Italy, threaten the enemy's flank if they re-entered the war, and, most immediately, support the kingdom of The Two Sicilies. The Bourbons at Naples were closely related by more than one tie to the Habsburgs, and their interests were being watched in Vienna with acute concern. Now that a French force was on the border with the Papal States,[2] they provided the last hope of maintaining a balance in southern Europe, and Naples as a base was highly important to any renewed southern front. The future of The Two Sicilies should therefore be of interest to Britain. By the same token it was of interest to France. Protection of the territories, necessary in itself, might thus also be a ready stimulant to the wider Anglo-Austrian agreement which was being sought.

However that might be, the call for a fleet succeeded in rousing attention in London as a prominent question which should be followed up. Once alerted to the prospect indeed, Pitt, Grenville and Dundas were well disposed, provided that the right strategic conditions could be met. To Grenville these meant a guarantee by The Two Sicilies of a British use of Naples, and an Austrian guarantee of support for The Two Sicilies if the French then attacked – thereby producing in itself one commitment from a quarter in which none had been forthcoming so far. Pitt was less precise –

1. Grenville to Pitt, 1 April 1798, and Minute of Conversation with Count Starhemberg sd (*H.M.C., Dropmore*, IV, 150–1, 153–4); Pitt to Grenville, sd and 7 April (op. cit., 152, 167). Cf. p. 52 above for Austria's earlier eagerness to see a British naval force in the Mediterranean.

2. P. 131 above.

'if a port can be secured, or even occasionally without it' –, and Dundas, fully occupied at this point with preparations against invasion, may not have considered conditions in detail.[1] But of course the Admiralty's view was central to a judgment; and the Admiralty was far from favouring the idea. In fact the Department was alarmed. The main Channel fleet was watching Brest, while a squadron lay in defence of southern Ireland. Others were blockading or lying in readiness from the Texel and the Downs to Cherbourg and Plymouth, and away to the south, completing the ring, St Vincent's fleet was watching off Cadiz. Allowing for the prospect of a Russian reinforcement in the North Sea, thirty-five ships of the line would be needed in home waters and a further thirty-five if St Vincent was to send a detachment into the Mediterranean while maintaining his station in the Atlantic. But only sixty-two of these seventy were to hand, the other eight must be brought into service, and that would mean finding a further 5,000 men. There was already a deficit of 1,000 in home waters. The suggested new commitment could therefore not be met.[2]

The verdict seems to have been accepted by the Foreign Secretary. On 7 April, writing half humorously to Spencer – in a tone reserved for a congenial equal – he lamented a response 'which I need not tell you, has very much spoiled all the dreams in which I was indulging myself of Austrian succour, of France driven within her ancient frontier, and of Europe saved'. However, he would have to prepare his answer to Austria accordingly.[3] But Pitt, while wishing a despatch to be drafted so as to focus discussion, sent the First Lord a list of questions and asked Grenville to call a Cabinet in the next few days.[4] Two Cabinets were in fact held, on the 11th and the 18th, in which Spencer's answer was tested by examination. This may have been the more stringent because the First Lord was often suspected of merely echoing professional opinion;[5] nevertheless in the

1. Grenville to Pitt, 1 April 1798; Pitt to Grenville, sd (*H.M.C., Dropmore*, IV, 151–2); Dundas to Spencer, Tuesday [17 April] (*Private Papers of Spencer*, II, 317). See pp. 132, 136–7 above for the lack of any specific Austrian commitment either in earlier approaches or in that of 1 April. I use the word 'fleet' here and in the following pages because it was used generally at the time. But 'squadron' would really denote better what at least the British had in mind.

2. Correspondence is published in *Private Papers of Spencer*, II, 433–41, and *H.M.C., Dropmore*, IV, 166–7. Additional material for the first is to be found in the Spencer papers in B.L., catalogued temporarily as Althorp Mss. The problems are summed up admirably in Mackesy, *Statesmen at War*, 16. For the Russian reinforcement see p. 123, n4 above.

3. *H.M.C., Dropmore*, IV, 166. I interpret his letter in this way, rather than as 'a cry of anguish' (Mackesy, op. cit., 16), because his hopes of Austria – and even The Two Sicilies – were still far from extravagant: apart from anything else, he was counting on Vienna first to meet his financial demand. He seems to me in fact to have been putting his familiar views on policy in a half-bantering tone which would be well understood. One may wonder if he would have written in such a way to Dundas.

4. To Grenville, sd (op. cit., 166–7). The questions, with Spencer's answers, are in *Private Papers of Spencer*, II, 435–7. See I, 309 for the Foreign Secretary's status in calling a Cabinet.

5. A disposition on which Dundas for one was explicit: to Spencer, attr. 29 January, and 5 May 1798 (op. cit., 240, 333).

upshot the Admirals gained a qualified victory. A fleet would be sent to Naples; but it would not leave England until early in June, and then subject to agreement from The Two Sicilies to supply 3,000 seamen for the period of the war, and from Austria for 1,000 likewise, so as in total to relieve the British shortage. The force furthermore might have to return if the French and Spaniards increased their strength in the Atlantic and the Channel. While some aid was thus on the cards it was scarcely the answer to the Austrians' prayer.

The naval proposal formed part of a wide review of the various questions from Vienna – themselves now supplemented by a flurry of further messages.[1] Specific as the plan was, it did not convey an extreme sense of urgency. Yet within the next ten days the picture was changed. On 28 April the Cabinet met again and decided to send a fleet through the Straits at once; the King approved warmly the next day; and on the 30th the orders were sent.[2] The Admiralty's objections, renewed since the earlier meetings,[3] were overcome. What had happened in that short interval so abruptly to transform the scene?

Possibly the decision would have been taken in any case. Pitt, unhappy with the Admiralty from the start, and perhaps reinforced by Dundas and the King, was said on the 26th to be a 'convert to measure about Mediterranean'.[4] But in any case the matter was about to be settled by some fresh news. For while the Cabinet had been talking there had been a sudden turn of events in Vienna. Resentment of the French, long simmering in the city, had produced a dramatic escalation. On the 27th the first report reached London of a riot a fortnight before, in which their embassy was sacked after the Ambassador, Bernadotte, had displayed the tricolour despite police warning. He demanded immediate compensation, and the dismissal of the authorities concerned including Thugut; and when both claims were refused he had left the capital on the 15th. War, it was thought, could be imminent. It must certainly not be discouraged

1. The despatch, dated 20 April 1798, was Grenville to Eden, no. 9 (P.R.O., F.O. 7/51). The relevant part of it was conveyed to Sir William Hamilton in Naples, no. 2, sd (F.O. 70/11). *H.M.C., Dropmore*, IV, 167–72 contains letters from Starhemberg on his further instructions. Windham's diary (*Diary*, 392–3) notes the Cabinet meetings of the 11th and 18th, and the latter is confirmed by a Cabinet Minute of that date (on an associated element of policy) in B.L. Add. Ms 59306 and by a copy of 'Head of a Despatch' and 'Further Instructions' to Eden, 'read at Cabinet on 18th April 1798' in B.L. Add. Ms 59061. See also Jupp, *Lord Grenville*, 217–18 and n36.

2. *Diary of Windham*, 394; correspondence of Grenville and George III, 28–9 April 1798 (*L.C.G. III*, III, no. 1725); Spencer to St Vincent, 29 April 1798 (*Private Papers of Spencer*, II, 437–41); Mackesy, op. cit., 21n23 for the Admiralty's orders.

3. See Spencer to Grenville, 26 April 1798 (*H.M.C., Dropmore*, IV, 178).

4. *Diary of Windham*, 394, for 26 April 1798. He could however have meant that Pitt was a 'convert' to the idea, despite the obstacles, without necessarily being prepared to force it through.

Dundas's strategic views, and sentiments, are discussed on p. 142 *et seq.* below; the King's on this point are clear from his letter to Grenville of 29 April, in n2 above: Mackesy (op. cit., 21) speculates indeed if it might not have been he who tilted the scales.

from London. The naval risk should therefore be accepted, for 'the appearance of a British squadron in the Mediterranean' had become 'a condition on which the fate of Europe may at this moment be stated to depend'.[1]

II

These were words on an elevated plane: designed in part perhaps to assuage the recipient of 'a plan . . . very different from what we have hitherto adopted'.[2] But allowing for that, they represented the Cabinet's view, and the decision was a bold one. St Vincent was given the choice of detaching a squadron while maintaining the blockade of Cadiz or of taking his whole fleet into the Mediterranean. But to assist his decision Ministers took a further step, despatching as a reinforcement eight ships of the line from the defence of Ireland, rather than waiting for that number from those not yet manned. This, as Spencer observed, should enable the Admiral both to stay in the Atlantic and to provide a strong detached force.[3] The weakening of the Channel fleet may have been made slightly easier by the news on that same day that Russia had agreed to send ships, as asked, to the North Sea; for while their likely efficiency was rated no higher than before, they would at least afford some numerical relief.[4] Nonetheless a real risk was being taken at a time when invasion could still not be ruled out – and of Ireland now perhaps more than of England.[5] Indeed the decision has no exact counterpart in British history: the closest perhaps, though centred on land rather than sea forces at moments when invasion seemed possible and the land defences were weak, might be said to lie in Marlborough's proposal and William III's order in 1690 to reinforce Ireland, and Churchill's in 1940 to send tanks to Egypt – and through the Mediterranean.[6] The decision of 1798 was to produce a great

1. Spencer to St Vincent, 29 April 1798 (*Private Papers of Spencer*, II, 438; and see p. 138, n1 above for 'squadron'). The reception and impact of the news can be followed in Eden to Grenville, no. 26, 14 April, Grenville to Eden, no. 13, 28 April 1798 (F.O. 7/51), Grenville to George III, 28 April 1798 (*L.C.G. III*, III, no. 1725).

The Foreign Secretary may have viewed the scene the more hopefully because he was told by Starhemberg on the 26th that Vienna was prepared after all to ratify the Loan Convention (*H.M.C., Dropmore*, IV, 178; see p. 133 above). That impression proved false.

2. *Private Papers of Spencer*, II, 437; to St Vincent, as in n1 above.

3. Spencer to St Vincent, 1 May 1798 (op. cit., 444–5). Cf. p. 138 above. This information was in fact sent with the instructions dated two days before (*Diary of Windham*, 395).

4. Whitworth's no. 17 of 6 April was received on 1 May (F.O. 65/39). See p. 28, n2 above. Grenville remarked later that this had been a factor in the decision (to Whitworth, no. 19, 29 August 1798; F.O. 65/40). Some diplomatic licence should doubtless be allowed; cf. Mackesy, op. cit., 2n27.

5. Pp. 115, 120 above.

6 The proposal in 1690 may in fact not have been Marlborough's initially, or at least his alone. But the fact that his descendant thought that it was, had its, no doubt minor, influence some 250 years later.

success. One has only to posit failure to see how easily such an outcome would have been attacked and retrospectively explained.[1]

The success itself however took a form different from the object that had been urgently raised. For the Mediterranean squadron was not bound directly for Naples. It was to watch Toulon, where the French force returned from the Adriatic,[2] joined with that already there, was assembling apparently to escort an expedition. First priority in fact was given to surveillance of the enemy's ports, now extended at the expense of capacity at home. The ships might represent a support for The Two Sicilies, a deterrent to further French coups, an added incentive to Austria – and so to others[3] – to take up arms again. All this might follow from their reintroduction to Europe's southern flank. Meanwhile however for the British the higher urgency of their role lay not in Italy but farther to the west.

The first question to be answered indeed now was the destination of the force in Toulon. News of its existence had been received for some weeks. Opinion in London was divided: the armament, though not the escort, was thought to be 'very extensive',[4] and while possibly intended for Naples more likely to be aimed at Portugal or Ireland. This was a view of the majority, in the Admiralty and among Ministers, as information on equipment and readiness pointed alternately east and west. As late as the end of May Pitt still plumped for Ireland, and he continued to do so when, the next day, he learned the news which would prove him wrong.[5]

For on 19 May the French sailed from Toulon, in weather that had scattered and damaged the small watching force which St Vincent had detached before his reinforcement arrived.[6] But the expedition did not pass Gibraltar; and its disappearance, unexpectedly prolonged, opened a new chapter, for both the short and the longer term.

As the days lengthened into weeks in fact with no further reliable news, speculation in London, and throughout Europe, increased. It did so the more keenly because Bonaparte was said to be on board. His movements for the past three months had been known well enough; but not his intentions, and the British Ministers were unaware of the well kept secret that invasion of England – not of Ireland – was postponed and that an expedition would be mounted against Egypt instead. Indications in point of fact were not lacking for an eastward movement of some kind: British envoys and consuls above all, particularly in Italy, were relaying signs and

---

1. No doubt, among historians, by Fortescue above all.

2. See p. 131 above.

3. Spencer to St Vincent, 29 April 1798 (*Private Papers of Spencer*, II, 440–1).

4. Same to same, sd (op. cit., 438).

5. Pitt to Mornington, 31 May 1798 (Mackesy, op. cit., 24); same to Grenville, nd but attr. 1–10 June and probably 1st or 2nd (*H.M.C., Dropmore*, IV, 229–30). And cf. Spencer to Admiral Peter Rainier, 30 May 1798 (*Private Papers of Spencer*, IV, ed. Rear Admiral H.W. Richmond (1924), 168).

6. The first reports, from the Paris press, reached London on 1–2 June (*The Times*, 5 June 1798; *Diary of Windham*, 397).

forecasts from early in the spring. But these were not all equally credible, many were hard to reconcile, and the most obvious dangers seemed still to point nearer home. Wide possibilities were canvassed. Sardinia, Leghorn, Naples, Malta; Corfu, the Aegean, the Black Sea; the Levant, Alexandria – all were mentioned, and some at least could not be dismissed. An attack on southern Russia – feared in St Petersburg – or on Constantinople was also not discounted. But to most quarters in Whitehall Egypt came very low on the list.[1]

Not however to all. One Cabinet Minister took that prospect seriously. Dundas had his own advisers and his own perspective, both rather different from his colleagues'; and as the signs pointing to an eastward destination multiplied in May, his fears for Egypt grew.[2] 'Did the instructions to Lord St. Vincent', he asked Spencer on 9 June, 'mention that Egypt might be in the contemplation of Bonaparte's expedition? It may be whimsical, but I cannot help having a fancy of my own on that subject'. The fancy indeed at that moment was distinctly his own; for so far from being a 'romantic plan', as a colleague was inclined to think, he saw in such a move 'a great and masterly stroke'.[3]

The reason did not lie in Egypt for the sake of its territory. In Dundas's view its occupation was rather 'the master key to all the commerce of the world';[4] and that by definition pointed east as well as west. It was in fact as a key to India that the country figured in his calculations; and anything affecting India roused his concern at once. He valued his post as Chairman of the Board of Control more highly than that of Secretary of State for War; he was profoundly interested in the business, and his political standing as master of Scotland was buttressed and extended by the

1. Spencer was particularly explicit about this on 1 May (to St Vincent; *Private Papers of Spencer*, II, 445), though four days later he was prepared to speculate on the Black Sea or the Levant, the latter of which, like Egypt, was within the Ottoman Empire (to Grenville; *H.M.C., Dropmore*, IV, 185). The Foreign Office files from various Courts contain the pointers, and Egypt was mentioned – the earliest of such forecasts possibly coming from Turin on 4 April, received on the 24th (Thomas Jackson to Grenville, no. 18; F.O. 67/26) and from Leghorn on 16 April, received on 23 May (consul John Udney to Grenville; F.O. 79/16). Captain Sidney Smith, in prison in Paris, had smuggled out a similar warning from a spy in January; but circumstances were different then.

2. Particularly perhaps when the confident report from Leghorn (n1 above) was received. It also contained the intelligence that Bonaparte would call first at Malta, which would surrender. Edward Ingram, *Commitment to Empire . . . 1797–1800* (1981), 43 lays much stress on the influence of this report. Another to the same effect, received in May from de Luc – now back in Brunswick; see p. 135 and n4 above (*H.M.C., Dropmore*, IV, 192–3) – could also have played its part.

3. Spencer to Rear Admiral Sir Hugh Christian, 17 June 1798 (*Private Papers of Spencer*, IV, 172); Dundas to Mornington [in India], 14 June 1798 (*Despatches, Minutes and Correspondence of the Marquess Wellesley . . .*, I, ed. R.B. Martin (1836), 350). And see also op. cit., 688–94.

4. To Spencer, 'Tuesday', almost certainly in mid April (*Private Papers of Spencer*, II, 317–18). The phrase (as Ingram, op. cit., 40 points out) derived from the knowledgeable British consul general in Cairo, George Baldwin, who was still acting as such, ignoring instructions to the contrary from London five years before; see I, 438–40.

Indian patronage it brought. Opinions and intelligence from East India House, and from his own experienced sources, always found a ready hearing and took up much of his time.[1] The defence of the subcontinent, the linchpin of our Eastern interests, had accordingly long bulked large in his mind: in 1787 he had reacted sharply to a possible loss of St Helena as a staging post, in 1791 he reflected on Russia as a possible future threat by land, from 1787 to 1796 he stressed the importance of the Cape of Good Hope, and he reiterated this as the pieces of his jigsaw seemed to be falling into place.[2] He was well aware that his colleagues had not shared, and did not share, his preoccupation: that they looked on the 'contingencies' he sketched as 'very remote'.[3] But to him those contingencies were assuming an even wider significance. They supported a view of policy which was beginning to form in his mind for the war as a whole.

Dundas has been uneasy for the past three years about the balance of strategy. Content earlier to employ resources simultaneously in and outside Europe, to argue a comprehensive case and eschew a choice which seemed both unnecessary and 'disagreeable', his growing impatience with Coalition warfare had been brought nearer to a point by the failure at Quiberon in 1795. He had confined himself then to certain indications: on the proper limits to the use of British troops in aiding royalist resistance in France; on the importance of success in the West Indies as the determinant of terms for peace.[4] Recent events had broadened his caution over too heavy a commitment to the Continent – whether military or, since the crisis at the Bank of England, financial. In 1798 the country's strength must be nurtured, primarily for home defence; 'Plans of great moment and splender' [*sic*] however could be conceived as circumstances allowed.[5] To Dundas, it was clear, these centred on distant operations, to gain bargaining points at the peace table and promote our trade. But the current regional emphasis as well as the priority could be adjusted. For the West Indies themselves could now scarcely command the same hopes as before.

Operations there in fact, as it proved with minor exceptions, were in their final phase of the war. A revised design at the end of 1796 had concentrated on the Spanish possessions – on Trinidad and then Porto Rico, with perhaps a separate expedition against Buenos Aires.[6] This last project, to be mounted from the Cape of Good Hope, was dropped early in 1797; but Trinidad was taken in February, and Porto Rico attacked in

1. See I, 132, 189–92 and Ch. XIV *passim* for background; Dundas to Pitt, 10 February 1798 (P.R.O. 30/8/157) for one example of a preference stated usually at moments of stress; Ingram, op. cit., 41–2 for some of his current advice.

2. I, 440 & n2; M.S. Anderson, *Britain's Discovery of Russia 1553–1815* (1958), 202–3 (for an interesting letter to the historian William Robertson); I, 426, II, 561–2, 612, 628 & n2; Dundas to Spencer as in p. 142, n4 above.

3. Ibid. And cf. II, 578.

4. See II, 269, 578, 589.

5. Dundas to Colonel Thomas Graham, 29 October 1797, cited in Mackesy, op. cit., 3; same to Pitt, 10 February 1798 (P.R.O. 30/8/157).

6. II, 634.

April. That attempt failed, and with it the campaign ended in the southern Caribbean: the commander, Abercromby, returned home in August, and a form of peace ensued. Meanwhile in the centre of the arc a holding operation was intended for St Domingue – the scene of so much effort, and the key to the rich British island of Jamaica. After varying fortunes however in 1797, negotiations were begun for an evacuation which was completed in October 1798; and, as conducted with the negro leader Toussaint l'Ouverture, these ended by providing a form of *status quo* over the next three years. Jamaica was safe, and the produce and trade of the British possessions in the West Indies continued to swell the home country's resources for war.[1] The losses and expense incurred for the region had arguably been justified. Nonetheless a succession of undertakings seemed at least temporarily to be exhausted, and the main theatres of the area were governed in practice by a kind of truce.

Little 'splendour' was thus in immediate prospect from further independent British operations in the West. The best hope in fact might lie in an alternative which would involve a normally unsympathetic Power. For in the first half of 1798 it seemed quite likely that the United States would go to war with France; and in that case Britain should take care to be associated. Anglo-American relations, though scarcely serene, had in fact improved since Jay's treaty of 1794. Conversely – and partly in consequence – Franco-American relations were acrimonious. A spark was lit in 1796 when the French envoy expressed his preference among the candidates in the Presidential election for Washington's successor. It was fanned when a new American envoy was refused acceptance in Paris, and became a flame when a negotiation for a comprehensive settlement of differences ended with the publication in the States of France's unacceptable terms. This last indeed caused uproar, and the new nation prepared for war. Arms were raised, privateers commissioned, warships laid down for the first time; Aliens Acts, a Naturalisation and a Sedition Act were passed. The Government in London was not slow to try to take advantage. British naval protection of American trade had been proposed as early as January 1797; in June 1798 a squadron was offered, to be manned partly by Americans to relieve the British shortage, accompanied by a wish for 'Concert and Cooperation' and a hint that the conquest of Louisiana and Florida would not come amiss.[2] This last had in fact been considered earlier and rejected as a purely British operation.[3] A more

1. Cf. I, 350–3. In 1798 itself Pitt estimated that the West Indies accounted directly for nearly 7 per cent of the national income and 8–10 per cent 'at a conservative estimate' if profits from West Indian investments were included (Michael Duffy, *Soldiers, Sugar, and Seapower* . . . (1987), 17n20). Jamaica was easily the richest of the British islands.

2. Grenville to Robert Liston [British Minister in Philadelphia], no. 2, 27 January 1797 (P.R.O., F.O. 5/18), no. 12, 8 June 1798 (F.O. 5/22). See II, 507–16 for earlier wartime relations and the Jay treaty; pp. 126, 138 above for the shortage of naval manpower.

3. In the so-called Chisholm plan, submitted through Liston and turned down in April 1797 (Grenville to Liston, no. 4, ? 7 April 1797; F.O. 5/18). The decision was repeated in June (Huskisson to Canning, 14 June 1797; F.O. 5/21).

hopeful opportunity on the mainland might now be envisaged from a possible ally. Similarly a chance might arise in the West Indies themselves, perhaps by joint action. Such dreams were gratifying; but their reality had still to be proved, and in any case that would depend on the formation of a fresh alliance. If there were to be 'plans of great moment' overseas, and the sources of wealth enlarged, there remained a need for solid achievements to be protected or gained elsewhere. Whatever therefore might develop in the Atlantic sphere, it was as necessary as ever to defend against a threat to the East.

Dundas's predilections were still not assembled systematically. He was more certain of what he disliked than of a detailed comprehensive replacement. It would take further experience of a policy he distrusted to make him formulate a full case; and then India would not in fact lie at its centre. At this stage his views – his sentiments – could rest largely on the absence of a European Coalition; and they offered no vision of foreseeable talks for peace or victory in its place. A Quadruple Alliance after all was designed to achieve the necessary *combination* of a 'Continental' and a 'Maritime' settlement.[1] Otherwise Britain must expect a long drawn-out stalemate while maritime pressure built up essentially on its own. Such a policy, or at least such a theme, had of course been argued for over a century. The finances themselves in this very period were being adjusted for a longer conflict. But not for voluntary acceptance of an indefinite span: Pitt himself had talked of two years;[2] and while he acknowledged the unpopularity of further loans or subsidies abroad, neither he nor the markets themselves would welcome a deliberate reliance on 'a remote and perhaps lingering war'.[3] That prospect – which of course might have to be faced – was not in fact advocated, at a time when former allies might be stirring again. But if Dundas's preference was unlikely to offer a suitable strategy at this point for Britain, it divined, or stumbled on, the thrust of a strategic initiative by France.

For Bonaparte in essence agreed, with a contrary conclusion. What Dundas saw as a source of Britain's strength he saw as a corresponding weakness if major elements could be damaged or removed. In the late summer of 1797 he was already looking, as an area commander, beyond peace with Venice to the eastern Mediterranean and farther afield. Possession (not merely use) of the Adriatic islands[4] would affect British influence and trade in south-east Europe, gains that could be reinforced if Malta was taken as well. It would also – and then at Turkey's expense – open another prospect; for 'the time is not far distant when we shall feel that, truly to destroy England, we must occupy Egypt'. There (as Dundas felt so strongly) lay a key to the approach to India, by the old Suez route

1. P. 134 above.
2. See p. 98 above.
3. To Grenville, 7 April 1798 (*H.M.C.*, *Dropmore*, IV, 167).
4. Cf. p. 131 above.

which could then outpace the Cape; and India was the focus of England's wealth and position in the East.[1] A threat to that complex would divert some of her attention from Europe; active encroachment could diminish the sinews of power itself.

Such thoughts were not wholly new: France had long had a trading presence in the Near East (including Egypt) and a base in India. Nor were the views developed, any more than were Dundas's, into a solid system now. Neither Bonaparte nor the Directory indeed favoured them on purely intellectual grounds. The former turned to them when he was convinced that immediate invasion of England was too hazardous, could see no quick opening to power in Paris, and was searching for some other road: the latter as a means of despatching a restless and dangerous soldier, and, like him, saw in the venture a use for resources – reckoned small at first – which would otherwise be locked up or inadequately employed. No long-term commitment was necessarily envisaged; the operation might be simply a step towards a future. But Dundas was right to prick up his ears: in some form and degree, and with unknown obstacles, the Near and Middle East and India itself were on France's list.

The proof, however, was delayed. For two months passed before the armament from Toulon was found. The watching warships which it had evaded, detached under Nelson by St Vincent, were strengthened as soon as reinforcements reached the latter's main fleet from Ireland. The search began on 9 June, turning to the east on the 15th, a decision confirmed when Nelson learned a week later that Malta had surrendered to the expedition. Deciding that Bonaparte must be at Corfu or Alexandria by this time, he crowded on sail 'in a fever' and made for the Egyptian coast. But there was no sign when he reached Alexandria on the 28th; the next week saw him ranging the Levant; he turned back to Sicily to water and store; and set off for Alexandria again. Once more the roads and port were empty, and he carried on once more to the east, to find the enemy's warships at last anchored in Aboukir bay. That was on 1 August. By the next morning almost all had been destroyed.

The frustration over those long weeks was extreme, for Nelson himself and equally at home. It was learned later that in point of fact he had missed the French twice by a few hours; once at Alexandria itself when he had, remarkably, outstripped them. The chase was a graphic instance of the uncertainties of sea warfare. It also underlined once more those raised by the pace of communications.[2] For even after the French were

1. And see eg his letters to Talleyrand of 16 August and 13 September 1797, in *Correspondance de Napoléon Ier . . .*, III (1859), 313–14, 391–2. In his copy of Volney's *Considération sur la Guerre Actuelle des Turcs* of 1788, he had written earlier 'Through Egypt we shall reach India, we shall re-establish the old route through Suez and cause the route by the Cape of Good Hope to be abandoned'.
2. Cf. p. 136, n3 above, and the earlier examples cited there.

discovered, reliable news of the result was not received in London until 26 September, and Nelson's despatch for a further six days.[1] Meanwhile only two hard facts emerged from a stream of rumour and varied reports: that Malta had surrendered to Bonaparte instantly, an event learned early in July, and that the expedition had landed at Alexandria at the end of June, which was thought probable in London from late August and confirmed early in the following month. While hopes were alternately raised and dashed by reports of a victorious battle at sea, the main trend of the news was therefore increasingly depressing. Ministers' anxieties rose as they awaited an outcome, and in September, when indeed he had won his battle, Nelson was coming in for blame.

Dundas naturally was the most disturbed. His temper had not been improved by the fact that, like Pitt though much less seriously, he had been ill at the turn of May and June.[2] His anger erupted when news of the landing in Egypt arrived. '. . . even a Brilliant Success of Nelson against the Fleet will not compensate to my feelings for the consequences of having made good the landing'; 'I must in Charity presume . . . he will be able to give a good reason for his leaving Alexandria after he had got there in so auspicious a manner'; 'The calamitous consequences . . . haunts me [*sic*] like a Spectre night & day, it is enough to drive me Mad . . .'; 'As to Sir Hor. Nelson, I hope he will have a pretty good story to tell at last'.[3] And if others for the most part felt less acutely, they too were cast down. How could Nelson have missed the enemy 'in a narrow Sea', wrote George Rose, later the Admiral's friend and champion; the consequence 'will be worse I fear, infinitely worse, than any of the Misfortunes . . . in this event-ful War'. 'I have seldom', confessed Spencer, 'experienced a more severe disappointment'. 'Alas!', Canning confided to his diary on hearing from Pitt that the squadron had probably sailed back to Sicily. 'The disappoint-ment . . . is indeed mortifying', wrote Pitt himself.[4]

1. Reports from the French newspapers however came in, and were widely credited, from the 20th.

2. His vehement letter of 31 May to Pitt (p. 121, n2 above) seems to me to show signs of the state of his health.

3. To Huskisson, 27 August, 16, 17, 23 September 1798 (B.L. Add. Ms 38735). He did add on the 17th, 'but we must not be too ready to censure him . . . till we know the exact state of the Intelligence which he received on his Arrival' [at Alexandria], a caution which Spencer echoed (to Dundas, 23 September 1798; *Private Papers of Spencer*, II, 469–70).

4. Rose to Pretyman, 12 September (Pretyman Ms 435/44); Spencer to St Vincent, 16 September; same to Dundas, 30 August (*Private Papers of Spencer*, II, 459, 455); Canning's diary for 8 September (Canning Ms 29d, Leeds); Pitt to Rose, 10 September 1798 (B.L. Add. Ms 42772). See also, eg, Hawkesbury to Liverpool, 1 September (B.L. Loan Ms 72, vol. 54), where Nelson is called 'Neilson', as he is in other of Hawkesbury's letters (12, 21, 25 July, 13 September) – a curious pointer to some people's pronunciation?

Pitt's hopes earlier may be followed in a series of letters to his mother – unusually fre-quent, as he learned of her intense interest – from mid July (P.R.O. 30/8/12), in one to Canning of 26 July (Canning Ms 30), and in the latter's diary for 25 July and 22 August (Canning Ms 29d).

Mortification in fact was, naturally, the predominant feeling: at the failure of a British squadron to impose its will. In so far as there was apprehension, it centred on a possible loss of trade and, more immediately, of British standing in the eyes of Turkey and Austria. No other Minister however shared Dundas's fears for India in the same degree.[1] Spencer, who granted the possibility, discounted its immediacy; while Grenville, to Dundas's resentment, refused to credit it at all. He had not believed in an attempt on Egypt until a very late stage, and he dismissed such a sequel, in fact such a concept in any form.

> If I am wrong [he addressed his colleague in the tone used sometimes with his allies] no one is more able to set me right than yourself; but do it, if you please, with a map in your hand, and with a calculation of distances . . .[2]

Nor was Pitt himself prepared to support too large a diversion of resources to the East. Despite Dundas's prompting he had proved cautious earlier, and when the news of the Nile was received he wrote off 'all' fears for India at once.[3] This was indeed the general reaction: Bonaparte was stranded, and his force might be left to wither on the bough. The Secretary for War nevertheless deployed such resources as he could find in the following months. His suspicions of trouble in the subcontinent, easily roused, had already been heightened by reports of exchanges between the old enemy Tipu[4] and the French in Mauritius, and by others from the north-west where the ruler of Afghanistan, Zeman Shah, seemed to be stirring. He continued therefore to press for reinforcements, from whatever quarter, and managed to extract six battalions in all from England, Portugal, Gibraltar and the Cape. Meanwhile a small naval presence was

1. Nelson himself in point of fact was inclined by this time to suspect that India was Bonaparte's aim.

2. 'Memo' by Spencer, 3 October 1798 (*Private Papers of Spencer*, IV, 184–6); Dundas to Huskisson, 27 August 1798 (B.L. Add. Ms 38735); same to Canning, 20 September 1798 (Canning Ms 77); Grenville to Dundas, 20 September 1798 (*H.M.C., Dropmore*, IV, 319). In Huskisson's exaggeration, the Foreign Secretary 'sees nothing beyond the Rhine' (to Dundas, 11 September 1798; S.R.O., G.D. 51/1/769/1).

Grenville's scorn was the sharper because he was commenting on information forwarded by Dundas purporting to suggest a possible attack from Afghanistan with *Russian* support – an idea heard before, in the Ochakov affair of 1791 (for which see II, Ch. I). In his reply the Secretary for War pointed out the relevance of such a move now to a 'conjunction with France' (28 September; op. cit., 326–7). He also remarked that he had no maps – of a probably unmapped part of the world.

The offending report was not in fact as absurd as the Foreign Secretary thought. Shortly before her death in November 1796 the Empress Catherine had launched an attack on Persia – called off by her successor – to open her 'Oriental Project' for the capture of key positions between Turkey and Tibet.

3. Pitt to Auckland, 4 October 1798 (*A.C.*, IV, 59); and see Ingram, op. cit., 80–1 for his caution.

4. See I, 443, 460.

found from the Cape for the Red Sea. By the turn of the year he had done what he could.

Dundas's congratulations on the Battle of the Nile were accordingly hedged by his continuing fears.[1] To most of the Cabinet, and the public at large, the victory brought unfettered relief.[2] The country plunged into celebrations, the more intense after the long wait, for a naval achievement without precedent in any of the wars with France. To have effectively wiped out the enemy, in daunting tactical conditions and without the loss of a single British ship, showed an audacity and skill, and a concept of command unmatched at Camperdown, St Vincent or the First of June. The navy returned with added lustre to the nation's pride and trust. Nelson was made a Baron, and given an annuity; he had also gained a charismatic image, and enduring fame.[3] Ministers allowed themselves briefly to rejoice. Pretyman, hastening to Downing Street after touring the illuminations, was present when Pitt came in via the Admiralty from Holwood, whither Rose had carried the news. The Minister was 'in the highest possible spirits', though with 'a little return of his bilious complaint'.

> ... the room is full – Mr Pitt, Long, & Master of the Rolls – ... Be assured that this is the finest & most glorious Event ever known ... Mr Pitt is confident that Buonaparte *must be destroyed*. O my Love what joy![4]

No doubt it was a convivial night: as an absent friend wrote from experience, 'I envy your quotations & potations when you received the news of the 1st of August'.[5]

The excitement was caused not only by the welcome boost to morale, and the justification, if unforeseen in its nature, of the risk taken at the

1. As Huskisson put it, unendearingly and particularly when one compares his tone to Dundas himself who was then in Scotland, 'He is upon velvet in the Mediterranean, mad at Alexandria, alarmed at Cairo, & in fact preparing to quit the Highlands . . ., *indulging* (before dinner I suppose) in "*retrospective Melancholy*"' (to Canning – whose own habitual tone he was doubtless trying to adopt –, 2 October 1798; Canning Ms 67).

In his relief at the victory Dundas was however led to 'hope' (briefly) that the French would not 'escape' from Egypt (to Huskisson, 6 October 1798, sent on to Pitt; P.R.O. 30/8/157).

2. Windham however shared some of Dundas's fears, and certainly did not underrate Bonaparte's chances. 'Fleets', he observed, 'may be destroyed, and the armies who came in them be successful' (to Canning, 17 October 1798; Canning Ms 34A).

3. As Pitt had to stress, dwelling on the latter, in a speech defending the grant of a barony rather than some higher rank, denied because there was no precedent in the case of a subordinate naval commander (speech in the Commons, 21 November 1798; *P.R., 3rd ser.*, VII, 65–6). The Minister's own thought at first seems to have been for a Viscountcy (Pretyman to Mrs Pretyman, nd but 3 October, Pretyman Ms 435/45; and see also Pitt to Spencer, 7 October 1798, in B.L. Add. Ms temp. Althorp G31), and there was in fact much public disappointment at a decision imposed by convention.

4. To Mrs Pretyman, nd, 'amost three' (Pretyman 435/45).

5. Mornington to Pitt, 17 November 1798 (Stanhope Ms S5 04/8).

end of April.[1] It arose also from the eager hope it raised in the wider sphere. For many of those concerned looked to great results from this display of British power. An 'event', the First Lord informed the King, 'which Earl Spencer flatters himself will produce the most important consequences'. '. . . if it electrifies Austria and Naples', the King replied, 'it may save Italy'. The 'stupendous victory', wrote Portland, 'may surpass in its effect and consequences the most . . . important event in our naval annals'. 'I cannot doubt', observed the Governor General from Bengal, 'that this success must awaken Europe'.[2]

III

In one quarter, so it seemed, the event had already done so. On 9 September the Turks declared war on France, and this moreover followed the agreed despatch of a Russian fleet through the Dardanelles. It had been a British interest since 1793 to damp down the two Powers' mutual hostility, one that was known to be actively encouraged by the French; and while in point of fact London's influence had been marginal in preserving peace in the Balkans, and the origin of these new developments preceded the outcome at the Nile, Nelson's achievement suddenly provided a fresh dimension. Initially it had been Bonaparte, as was becoming usual, who was responsible for a change of scene. The Porte, disturbed by a perceived threat, had already promised the British better naval facilities, and after his landing in Egypt the talks included an offer of alliance[3] – a sounding aimed also at a possible balance against excessive reliance on St Petersburg. Normally, such a negotiation would have been a leisurely process. But the ensuing naval battle gave it unwonted speed. The Turks resolved to take a line. Warships were assembled to accompany the Russians, in suspicious amity, to attack the Ionian Islands; an army would be mustered in Syria for operations against the French. The immediate prospects showed unwonted promise, in south-east Europe and the Near East. Old rivals were co-operating at sea; the enemy might be harried or at least placed under pressure in the Adriatic, and British influence in an extensive region enlarged at his expense. And there could be farther

1. P. 139 above.
2. Correspondence of Spencer and George III, 2–3 October 1798 – the King's view being echoed by the Lord Chancellor, Loughborough, [to Pitt] on 5 October (*H.M.C., Dropmore*, IV, 336); Portland to Pitt, 5 October 1798 (Dacres Adams Mss, formerly P.R.O. 30/58/2); *L.C.G. III*, III, no. 1844 & n3; Mornington to Grenville, 18 November 1798 (*H.M.C., Dropmore*, IV, 385). Cf. also for Liverpool's opinion Hawkesbury to Liverpool, 7 October 1798 (B.L. Loan Ms, vol. 54).
3. Spencer Smith [acting Minister in Constantinople] to Grenville, no. 18, 1 August 1798 (P.R.O., F.O. 78/19). The permission for passage of the Russian fleet overtook a planned British representation to that end (Grenville to Smith, no. 14, 14 September 1798; F.O. 78/20, and see also Spencer to Dundas, 30 August 1798, *Private Papers of Spencer*, II, 456).

effects: Russia and Austria, both stirring under the same stimulus, might be able to shift land forces hitherto held down by the Turkish presence. No wonder that Pitt exclaimed, when reports of Nelson's victory seemed to be confirmed from Constantinople, 'Vive la Marine Anglaise! Et Vive le Pacha Gezzar!'[1]

It remained to be seen meanwhile what might happen in more familiar quarters. Within the Mediterranean itself there were some favourable signs, all in fact antedating the victory and now the readier for exploitation. In the first place, Naples should be available for the fleet. The British demand on The Two Sicilies had received 'fair' assurances, but nothing more. That however was hardly surprising while an answer was awaited to the demand on Austria; and though the two Powers signed a treaty for support on 20 May against a French attack, it was not ratified in Vienna until 16 July, the document reaching Naples early in August.[2] Thereafter there was general confidence that the base could be used; and a month later there was another promising development. On 2 September the Maltese people rose against the French garrison, giving an opening which Nelson might seize when he had refitted from his victory, and which in fact part of his squadron was quick to supply with some small arms. The island of course could be a notable prize. Meanwhile plans were under way independently to secure a strongpoint in the western basin. Since the summer of 1797 there had been a force in Portugal of émigrés and British troops, sent at the Portuguese request to help defend against a Spanish threat.[3] The command had had a discouraging time, in the face of the Portuguese army's shortcomings and incessant demands for material and money from a Government in disarray, one which in fact seemed on the brink of making peace with France.[4] In the summer of 1798 the British element was raided for a small

---

1. To Windham, 26 September 1798 (B.L. Add. Ms 37844). The despatch from Constantinople (no. 24, of 22 August) reached London on the day of this letter (endorsement; F.O. 78/19). Together with one from Vienna received the same day, it conveyed the first reliable news; cf. p. 147 above.

The Pasha Gezzar (or Djezzar), 'a cruel, faithless old monster', was one of those formidable Balkan adventurers who established themselves in outlying regions of the Ottoman Empire: in his case in Syria. Combining, as he did periodically, the Sultan's interests with his own, he was said to be preparing a large if primitive army for a descent on Egypt. For a sketch of his character and career see *H.M.C., Dropmore*, V (1906), 482–3.

2. See pp. 137–8 above, and the despatches between London and Sir William Hamilton from April to August in P.R.O., F.O. 70/11.

3. For the decision late in 1796 see II, 634, where I give the mistaken impression that the troops were confined in the upshot to émigrés mustered in Britain.

4. See p. 64 above for the peace treaty concluded by its Minister in Paris, over which it then havered for several months, first denying responsibility, then proposing ratification but with certain clauses excluded, finally sending an envoy privately to London for consent to full ratification if necessary. In the event the French themselves disowned the treaty, counting on a fresh and less cluttered approach. The despatches from the British Minister in Lisbon, Robert Walpole, are in P.R.O., F.O. 63/24–8; those from the force commander in P.R.O., W.O. 1/218–20.

reinforcement for India.[1] But part of it was soon found a more encouraging role. Its commander, the capable and somewhat acerbic Major-General Charles Stuart, had come home in June for a spell. He returned in September with instructions to capture the island of Minorca, that incessantly contested base – taken, like Gibraltar, in the War of the Spanish Succession and held by the Peace of Utrecht, lost by Byng but returned at the Treaty of Paris following the Seven Years' War, lost again towards the end of the War of American Independence and kept by Spain at the Treaty of Versailles. Well placed to mask Toulon, to give notice of a sortie towards the Atlantic, and to nourish a fleet and troops for action from Spain to the Italian coast, it had, as its history suggested, long been viewed as of prime importance, a possession which 'England ought never to part with', giving 'the law to the Mediterranean in time of war and peace'.[2] Circumstances now might have somewhat diminished this pre-eminent role. But occupation remained desirable, and a serious effort was put in hand. St Vincent was ordered to arrange transports and supplies and an escort – and a naval commander who could act with Stuart –,[3] all of which he did with his usual grasp. When the news of the Nile was known, and the risk of French naval opposition reduced, there seemed a good chance of the island falling once more to British attack.

The southern flank of Europe might thus be opening up. But what about the rest of Europe itself? To judge by the reports, Nelson's victory had kindled a flame. Nevertheless Pitt's own immediate hopes were noticeably selective. While he expected Bonaparte's destruction, with possible implications in France, he was distinctly sceptical about the future in Austria and Italy. He was not impressed by the 'sanguine' views received from 'the King and the Keeper of his conscience';[4] on the contrary, he feared that the French, precisely because of their reverse, would hold out sufficient inducements to make Austria 'prolong its present wretched system'. This unusually sombre view may have owed something to Grenville's caution.[5] It certainly expressed the two men's opinion of Vienna's attitude since May.

For after the uncertain improvement in the spring, relations had again deteriorated. One minor incident further irritated Ministers in

1. P. 148 above: one regiment – less than originally intended, in view of the need to sustain Portugal's morale.

2. General James Stanhope (Pitt's great-uncle by marriage; see I, 68) in 1708.

3. . . . 'a niggard in his praise to the navy', as the Admiral observed from what he had been told, and indeed knew by experience (to Spencer, 6 December 1798; *Private Papers of Spencer*, II, 487. Cf. II, 347 for relations between the two services in Corsica in 1794–5, which had helped form the General's opinion). Dundas's instructions are dated 29 August; P.R.O., W.O. 6/20, ff. 96–103.

4. See p. 150 and n2 above.

5. Pitt to Grenville, 6 October; cf. Grenville to Rufus King [U.S. Minister in London], 4 October 1798 (*H.M.C., Dropmore*, IV, 337, 335). And see eg pp. 136–7, above.

mid summer. Having called for a British fleet, primarily for Naples, the Austrians announced in June that by the terms of Campo Formio they could not admit it to their Adriatic ports. A compromise was reached, for small numbers only; and the subsequent confirmation of the alliance with Naples was a better sign.[1] But the episode was not encouraging, and there were more substantial reasons for doubt. For weighing the odds in Europe once more, and the reply from London to his earlier overture, Thugut had drawn back from a decision in May while he manoeuvred for any concessions that would allow him after all to preserve peace with France. He even resigned the Foreign Ministry, briefly, to his colleague and rival Count Louis Cobenzl, though this was partly to provide a screen behind which he would be less exposed.[2] Talks lasting until early in July showed that the French would not oblige; but again it was not a promising augury for a whole-hearted alliance with Britain. Nor was there any real sign in the summer of a settlement of the Loan dispute, which continued to frustrate exchanges over prospective finance. Grenville and Pitt were confirmed in the belief that Austria was unlikely to commit herself, or, if she did so, to pay sufficiently serious attention to British interests. It was in this frame of mind that they accordingly rejected a further approach from Vienna to ratify the Loan Convention once arrangements were signed for further wartime support.[3]

The continuing financial dispute spilled over into a wider sphere. Austria's talks with France had been taking place alongside a four-Power conference, at Seltz in northern Germany, of herself, Prussia, Russia and Britain. Centring on Russia's offices with the two Germanic states, which were still engaged in diplomatic warfare at Rastadt,[4] it failed to settle those differences, or larger questions of policy and aims. By July it was clear that Prussia would stay neutral, and the British envoy Elgin was given home leave. Any immediate prospect of co-operation between Berlin and Vienna likewise seemed dead. But then there was an unexpected development. In mid August a proposal reached London which kept Ministers' declining hopes alive.

It came from St Petersburg. Little had happened since April to forward an Anglo-Russian alliance. The Tsar had agreed to leave his ships in the North Sea until the winter;[5] but his attention was focused on Prussia and Austria, and he was still on terms with the French. As so often, however,

1. Eden to Grenville, nos. 53, 56, 59 of 19 June, 4, 14 July 1798 (P.R.O., F.O. 7/52); and see p. 151 above.

2. Cobenzl had been the emissary and signatory at Campo Formio, for which see p. 131 above.

3. Eg Grenville to Count Simon Vorontsov [Russian Minister in London], 12 July 1798 (*H.M.C., Dropmore*, IV, 253); Dundas to Grenville, 19 August 1798 (op. cit., 284); Grenville to Whitworth, no. 19, 29 August 1798 (P.R.O., F.O. 65/40); same to Eden, no. 24 of 21 September 1798 (F.O. 7/53); Pitt to Grenville, 6 October 1798 (*H.M.C., Dropmore*, IV, 337–8). See also Duffy, 'British War Policy', 332–5.

4. P. 132 above.

5. See pp. 123, n4, 130, n1 above.

the Directory brought matters to a head themselves. For Bonaparte's seizure of Malta sparked off a sudden, unforeseen response. Russia had shown an interest in the Mediterranean over at least the past two decades, since Catherine the Great's 'Greek project' of 1780 had included bases in the Aegean to help foment Balkan unrest against the Turks. The annexation of the Crimea and the formation of the Black Sea fleet established a concentration of power which, even if not aimed immediately beyond those waters, must heighten an influence already felt from south-east Europe to the Levant. There had been signs also that the Empress would welcome a presence farther west: it was indeed recognition of this fact that had led the British in 1796 to offer Corsica as one inducement to closer cooperation. The bait was declined by the new Emperor, in reaction against his mother's policies. But, paradoxically, these were given a new twist by one of his personal obsessions.[1] The Knights of St John, long seated in Malta after their expulsions from the eastern Mediterranean, had already captured his imagination as a chivalric nursery of arms in which men of gentle birth could be trained to confront the ideological foe. He had earlier shown his interest in a surviving priory in Poland, and when at the end of July he learned of Malta's surrender – gained, ironically, by collusion of the Grand Master with the French – he took the Order formally under his protection. By so doing he was tacitly claiming a voice in the island's future.[2] More immediately, incensed by the news and by his failure at Seltz, for which he blamed Prussia, he decided to act on his own without more ado. A force of 16,000 men was ordered to Galicia in case Austria should call for support; another of 60,000 to aid the Turks if the French should cross the old Venetian border; and the Porte was approached for permission to allow the Black Sea fleet through the Straits.[3] Such moves, the British were told, meant that he was acting as an auxiliary ally. But he wished to become more completely involved. Vorontsov in London was instructed to propose a treaty of alliance on the lines which were being discussed when Catherine had died almost two years before.[4]

That treaty would have contained a subsidy, offered by the British at £1,500,000 in the first year and £1,200,000 thereafter, in return for a force of 60,000 men to act in Austria's support.[5] The proposal now was for the

1. II, 633, 644–5 for this episode and for Paul's temperament.
2. This fact was underlined moreover by an agreement with The Two Sicilies, added to a recent treaty of defensive alliance with them, which, recognising an ancient claim to their suzerainty over the island, associated them with Russia in a joint garrison and protectorate on behalf of the Knights when the French were expelled.
   The depth of Paul's feelings for the Order may still be seen in the name and decoration of the Hall of the Knights in his palace of Pavlovsk.
3. P. 150 above.
4. Whitworth to Grenville, no. 31, 24 July 1798 (F.O. 65/40): a discussion which had lapsed abruptly after Paul's accession (see II, 632–3, 644–5).
5. II, 632–3: the initial sum including an 'extraordinary' payment for arms and materials. A credit of £600,000 – or if necessary under pressure up to £1 million – would have been provided over and above the payments, to be repaid after the war.

same sum, for a force of the same size, which would be sent to the Rhine on Austria's entering the war. The despatch reached Grenville on 15 August, and was forwarded to Pitt at Walmer. The Minister found no difficulty in consenting to terms comparable with the earlier British version: in fact he saw no need to go up to town to consult. The Foreign Secretary however had assumed, not unnaturally, that the Cabinet would meet; and when it did so on the 18th, some implications began to emerge.[1]

No firm decisions seem to have been reached on the spot. But certain options at least were discussed.[2] For the Russian proposals, tempting as they were in the search for an ally, raised some awkward problems. As they stood, they depended on Austria re-entering the war. But if she did so, it might be only after gaining direct financial help from London as well as from Russia; that would mean her ratifying the Loan Convention; and even assuming such an outcome, could Britain afford both a fresh loan to Austria and a subsidy to the Tsar? Furthermore, suppose that Austria did not enter the war. Should the prospect of a new Anglo-Russian alliance be sacrificed to that non-event? Were there not other ways in which the troops could be used, more conducive to our own interests? It was on these linked questions, not easy to resolve, that discussion followed in the next few weeks.

The Cabinet's answer was determined quite soon, on 22 August. It was for 'Conditional acceptance of offer'.[3] Not every one was entirely clear,[4] after what must have been a complicated review. But a preference had in fact been found which satisfied the Ministers principally concerned. It had been much aided by a conversation between Dundas and Pitt, driving together to Wimbledon after the earlier meeting, which led the former to set down thoughts that, 'as usual, haunted' him 'in the . . . night'. Pitt's preoccupation was with finance. His earlier misgivings of political trouble if new support for Austria was proposed surfaced more insistently after the continuing disappointments. Parliament and the country might not 'adopt the idea cheerfully'; they might in fact be 'revolted' by it. In the same context, and applying to a public swayed usually by 'feelings' more than by 'reasoning', Dundas for his part queried the wisdom of a wide Continental commitment at all. Our wartime costs, already heavy, had been increased by the efforts for the Mediterranean; Austria had proved 'unfaithful' in the past and could do so again. He could not bring himself

1. Pitt to Grenville, 16 August 1798 (*H.M.C., Dropmore*, IV, 283); Hawkesbury to Liverpool, nd but endorsed 17 August (B.L. Loan Ms 72, vol. 54). Pitt proposed that the credit (p. 154, n 5 above) on this occasion should be at a rate of £50,000 a month for the duration of the treaty, again repayable after the war.

According to *The Morning Chronicle* of the 20th, Portland, Spencer, Grenville, Pitt and Dundas attended the Cabinet; but Windham for one was also there (*Diary*, 401–2).

2. See Mackesy, op. cit., 36n28 for a comparison of Windham's impression with that of Canning, who learned of the upshot – 'nothing decided' – shortly after the meeting.

3. Canning's diary, 22 August 1798 (Canning Ms 29d).

4. Certainly Windham was not (*Diary*, 401).

to give 'a cold negative' to Russia, which – echoing an old theme less in favour recently – he saw as 'the natural ally of Britain'. But if she could not produce a real promise of effective effort from Austria, he would like to 'subsidise an army of Russians for British purposes' – for an attack on Holland, or the recapture of Malta, or the defence of Switzerland, or 'the opening of markets in South America', or the capture of Brest.[1]

There were obvious inconsistencies in this argument, which itself might be said to mark a half-way stage in the progress of Dundas's thought.[2] But it addressed the immediate problem; and this time moreover in a way that the Foreign Secretary could share. For as the pattern in Europe constantly shifted, Grenville was momentarily drawn to an option less comprehensive than his avowed principal aim. He was also attracted to the suggestions of an attack on Holland and support for Switzerland, from both of which countries there were reports of discontent and plans for resistance.[3] The Cabinet was therefore able to agree on the lines it wished to follow. It saw no possibility of finding more for Europe than £2 million in all. Portugal had already been allotted £200,000, and £500,000 was now earmarked for Switzerland on the strength of the latest information. A sum of £1.2 million had been provisionally reserved in the spring for Austria if the Loan dispute was settled and she declared war. This, it was now agreed, should be transferred to Russia,[4] to be used as the Tsar had proposed provided that the Convention was ratified and he was properly informed of Austria's operational plans, stress being laid on their immediate importance for the rescue of Switzerland. Such an object was the British preference. But if agreement could not be attained British funds were otherwise to be used for that purpose, and would be offered instead in return for 50,000 Russian troops to be sent to England when Austria declared war on France, for an attack on Holland or some other operation. As soon as this programme was decided Grenville got in touch with Vorontsov – helping indeed to compose his despatch –, and the British despatch itself followed by the end of the month.[5]

Communications took their customary time. While Ministers waited in September for reliable news of Nelson, they waited also for the Tsar's

1. Dundas's expression of Pitt's views was relayed to Grenville on 19 August (*H.M.C., Dropmore*, IV, 284), together with his paper shown previously to Pitt. The latter, undated, was first attributed (op. cit., 433–5) to December, but subsequently corrected (see op. cit., xxvi). See II, 22, 10–11 for the theme of 'the natural ally', and for its tradition I, 504.

2. Cf. p. 143 above.

3. Dundas's paper referred to a 'note' by Grenville (*H.M.C., Dropmore*, IV, 435); and see Mackesy, op. cit., 36–7 for Holland, 73–5 for Switzerland.

4. The 'extraordinary' expenses (p. 154, n5 above) being set at £500,000 rather than the larger sum envisaged earlier.

5. The 'Heads' of the latter were read and minuted at the Cabinet of 22 August (B.L. Add. Ms 59306); see also Grenville's note of them for Vorontsov, dated 'August' (*H.M.C., Dropmore*, IV, 297–8). His co-operation in Vorontsov's despatch may be seen in their correspondence of the 24th–25th (op. cit., 285–6). The British despatch was Grenville to Whitworth no. 19, Most Secret, 29 August, and see also no. 20, sd (F.O. 65/40).

response. None had been received when the victory of the Nile was finally confirmed on 2 October; but two days later a despatch arrived from the British envoy in St Petersburg, Whitworth, announcing that his Austrian counterpart in London was being instructed from Vienna, to Paul's delight, to concede the 'just demand' on the Loan Convention. Unfortunately Whitworth was not always a reliable informant, and Vorontsov was informed otherwise on the same day. But Pitt at least was not much surprised to hear that so uncharacteristic a retreat had not in fact been ordered; and meanwhile he and Grenville prepared for another Cabinet to keep matters under review.[1]

As autumn opened, Ministers, though tired, were not displeased with their labours. The promise of the early summer seemed rather firmer now. England had not been invaded. The return to the Mediterranean, so apparently hazardous and then disappointing, had produced a triumph. Bonaparte was cut off from Europe, with an army which might wither away. Turkey had declared war on France, and others might soon join in – the United States, Russia more fully than before, perhaps even Austria and The Two Sicilies. An Alliance was once more on the cards, if not in the form that had been sought. And the position at home had improved notably over the year. 'Let us', Pitt said when Parliament met, 'do justice to ourselves'.[2] He was congratulating the Commons as the embodiment of a nation which, as Dundas told him, had 'settled itself into a calm determination' since the collapse of the peace talks at Lille.[3] Trade had picked up, as had confidence; Opposition was at a low ebb. A long slide, it seemed, had been arrested; a balance was being restored. And there was something else. Another, long threatening danger had been met. Insurrection in Ireland had been militarily crushed.

1. Whitworth to Grenville, no. 41, 12 September 1798, received 4 October (loc. cit.); Vorontsov to same, 4 October 1798 (*H.M.C., Dropmore*, IV, 334, and see also 336–7); Pitt to same, 6 October 1798 (op. cit., 337–8). Despatches to St Petersburg in August and September were taking five to six weeks to arrive.

See also Canning to Pitt, 8 October 1798 (Dacres Adams Mss, formerly P.R.O. 30/58/2). Whitworth did not gain in reputation; loc. cit., and correspondence between George III and Grenville, 5–11 October (*L.C.G. III*, III, nos. 1845, 1850, 1854). Cf. however p. 140, n1 above.

2. Speech of 1 December 1798. This is the version given in the earliest collected edition, *The Speeches of the Right Honourable William Pitt, in the House of Commons*, ed. W.S. Hathaway, III (1806), 327; which I very seldom choose. The wording in *P.R.*, VII, which is followed by *P.H.*, differs to some extent. But the phrasing of the passage here is so much in character that I have given it the benefit of the doubt.

3. Dundas to [Pitt], nd but 19 August (*H.M.C., Dropmore*, IV, 433).

CHAPTER VI

Ireland: Insurrection to Union

I

At the beginning of 1798 Pitt received a cheerless letter from his old friend Camden, whom he had sent to Dublin as Lord Lieutenant in 1795. The state of the island, he was told, was 'most alarming'. Of the part-time forces on whom so much turned, the Yeomanry (mostly landed and farming) was 'splitting into factions', while the militia was 'almost entirely catholick'. Unrest was widespread, magistrates themselves were being 'intimidated to the greatest degree', and there was 'no safety' now except to declare a general state of rebellion and impose powers amounting to martial law. Almost exactly two years earlier the mood in the Castle had been very different. Despite signs of disaffection serious enough to have produced an Insurrection Act, Camden was then still 'of opinion that this Country, may be governed with little trouble & great advantage to Great Britain by trifling concessions . . . in the way of trade & by a determination to support the Protestant interest'.[1] Such expressions of hope thereafter faded away.

In the light of what was to come, indeed, one may wonder how they could have been made. Nonetheless, on an immediate view they had not been wholly misplaced. The first year of Camden's incumbency saw a lowering of tension in important quarters, after the high excitement of his predecessor's brief spell.[2] By the end of 1795 Ministers were congratulating themselves that the call for admission of Catholics to the Dublin Parliament, which Fitzwilliam in their view had so incontinently pressed, had been restored to a proper setting. The Cabinet was not bent on denying the measure at all costs if circumstances seemed to dictate. But circumstances were all-important, and the issue needed very careful handling. Meanwhile, as Camden himself observed, the Protestant interest must be sustained, in whatever fashion; and the

---

1. Camden to Pitt, 30 March 1798, 4 April 1796 (P.R.O. 30/8/326). Volunteer formations on British lines, cavalry and infantry, were quite recent innovations, given statutory authority by 37 Geo. III c2 in the Irish series in November 1796.

See II, 439–40 for Camden's appointment in 1795. 'The Castle' in Dublin was often used as a term for the Administration.

2. For Earl Fitzwilliam's Lord Lieutenancy and the rest of this paragraph see II, Ch. XI, section IV.

perceived 'dispersal' of the 'clouds' could favour a more protracted approach.

The British Government had thus not been rushed: the pressure had been held. Nor had the Fitzwilliam affair really constituted a turning-point in Irish history, as was later claimed, though in its timing and symbolism it may have marked a watershed.[1] Camden's words in 1796 indeed might be said to have suited the middle eighties better than the middle nineties; and if that was so, it was because the episode itself had occurred at a time of change. Stemming on the one hand from the movement for reform whose traditional spokesmen remained the Parliamentary Whigs, and on the other from the Castle's own wish to engage propertied Catholics more firmly in the country's defence,[2] it embroiled social interests which were now being rivalled or bypassed by others to which the issue was of high concern, but in an altered frame of reference. For in both Catholic and Protestant spheres the emphasis was altering over the decade; and it was not the Catholics in fact who had made the running so far. The quest for greater independence from Britain, for ensuing Parliamentary reform, for removal of denominational civil disabilities, had hitherto come mainly from the Protestants. The campaign included some mutual co-operation: 'Romans' were admitted, illegally, to the Volunteer movement of the seventies and eighties, and Wolfe Tone himself, formally an Anglican, accompanied the foundation of the United Irishmen in 1791 with his pseudonymous *Argument on Behalf of the Catholics of Ireland.*[3] Many Dissenters in the north in particular – providing, as in England, a focus and thrust – were not at odds with Catholic groups, centred on the Dublin trading interest, which were moving away impatiently from an older, more gentlemanly Association. These developments, radical in nature, burgeoned in the final years of peace. They gained pace and a new dimension in the first three to four years of war.

For the effect of the French Revolution on the British 'empire' – a word sometimes applied informally, after the loss of the American colonies, to the British and Irish isles[4] – was nowhere more seductive and continuous than on the latter, in both the north and south. By 1796 the United Irishmen had progressed from sympathy and some contacts with Paris to hopes of a landing and a rising to follow. A catalyst in this transition – a factor which seemed to give new substance to the hopes – was however not predominantly of the earlier type. In the first phase of the war, 'it was', as

1. Op. cit., 438, drawing on R.B. McDowell's comment.
2. And notably therefore in 1793; op. cit., 82, 221–2, 424–5.
3. II, 220; and see I, 50–1 for the Irish Volunteer movement.
4. Eg in Portland and Fitzwilliam's correspondence in 1795; see II, 432–3. The usage was not uncommon: cf. Burke to Windham, 20 October 1794 (*The Correspondence of Edmund Burke* . . ., VIII, ed. R.B. McDowell (1969), 51). It has its bearing on the concept – disputed then and since – of Ireland as a colony analogous to the white transatlantic possessions; cf. I, 370n2.

it had been in the initial movement for reform, 'within the protestant community, rather than among the discontented catholic majority, that revolutionary nationalism developed';[1] but in 1795 this process was over-taken by another. Elements in the Catholic populace had shown their growing potential in the early nineties. A new phenomenon indeed, a secret society known as the Defenders – an early example in what was to be a long unhappy line – had emerged by then to protect the property and interests whose debasement had aroused hatred, though passive for the most part, since the land settlement of the seventeenth century. Undenominational in principle, and drawing its members mainly from the towns, it nonetheless became identified with clashes between Catholic peasants and Protestant militants – with the extremist Napper Fleet, Peep O' Day Boys and the rest. The trouble was uneasily contained. But a deep-ening recession, experienced above all in the linen trade, falling on a work-force moving easily between small-scale industry and the countryside, and felt the more suddenly after a period of exceptional prosperity,[2] helped spark off a wave of violence unknown in extent since the Tory and Rapparee excesses almost a century before. Starting in Armagh and spreading fast, the attacks provoked equally savage counteraction, facing the Castle indeed with a loss of control over both sides. The threat was met; the risings were subdued; an Indemnity Act in 1796 rang down the curtain on the methods, and a draconian Insurrection Act was passed to cover the future.[3] But this last was now held to be the more necessary from a contingent danger, as 'Defenderism' took a more subversive tone and the United Irishmen were known to be strengthening their links with France.

In the course of 1796, therefore, different strands of discontent were being knit together. Ironically, the process in point of fact held the seeds of fatal mutual conflict, for the 'Armagh outrages', hailed as a spur by the largely Protestant exponents of a general challenge, did much to destroy the non-sectarian hopes bequeathed by a less violent time. Catholic law-lessness indeed was followed at once by an ominous counter: the first Orange lodges came into being, and in 1797 the Grand Lodge itself. But in the shortest term the direction of events was clear. A stream of revolution-ary nationalist aspirations was gathering breadth and speed, and flowing towards a sea on which the French might appear. In 1796 Wolfe Tone, as the authorities suspected, persuaded the French to prepare an invasion; and its failure in December[4] only intensified further plans.

---

1. Marianne Elliott, *Partners in Revolution* . . . (1982), 3. The sentence, applying to the longer period, continues 'spasmodically and took off' in the last two decades of the century'.

2. Cf. II, 220. For the endemic feature of underemployment in the pre-industrial British economy as a whole, and its effect on labour practices, cf. II, 98–9.

3. 36 Geo. III, cs 2, 20 in the Irish series; and by 37 Geo. III, c1, later in the year, Habeas Corpus was suspended.

4. P. 5 above.

Shaken by the threat of the landing, coming on top of the unrest, the Dublin Government kept up pressure on London for troops and for funds. The latter indeed was the most urgent problem early in 1797. The Irish finances had been deteriorating, and the pace had now accelerated to the point where there was a lack of cash to meet immediate demands and a new loan was needed to sustain credit. Military expenditure had greatly increased, and must increase further. But there seemed to be no hope of raising the supplies within Ireland; and the concurrent crisis in London scarcely promised quick relief. Camden, as one of Pitt's circle of friends and his personal appointment, supplemented the Lord Lieutenant's despatches to the Home Office with private letters to Downing Street. But he could not be accommodated for a while. Pitt had to refuse remittances of cash – even when it was sent later, 'every coin will be an Object of the utmost Jealousy and Solicitude'[1] – and so far from supporting credit he was calling in February for partial repayment of the Irish debts. He did his best as soon as he could: by March arrangements were in train for a loan on the London market, and while coin remained short and the finances were still embarrassed in the summer, the worst was over in May.[2]

The need for regular troops was likewise held by Dublin to be critical. For the prospect of a French invasion had fuelled savage risings in Ulster – though not in the south – which the Irish Government was engaged in stamping out. It claimed to have only 14,000 men 'collected' and to require 5,000 infantry, since service in the militia was deeply unpopular – as riots in fact had shown – and the recently embodied Volunteers were disunited.[3] The call was far from welcome in England, with the need to put home defence in order, and after the large expedition to the West Indies of 1795 and the aid for Portugal in 1796.[4] Two regular and two Fencible regiments of cavalry moreover had been sent to Ireland the year before. In the event no further regular formations could in fact be spared; nonetheless another two regiments of Fencible cavalry were found in March, with two more again and two of Fencible infantry in May and June. Early in the following year the returns of forces in Ireland showed some 7,200 regulars, 3,800 fencibles, 25,000 militia, and 40,000 yeomanry. But the augmented numbers in themselves did not meet the circumstances. Some of the troops were unreliable, much of the quality was very poor, and thanks to the continued policy of distributing men in packets

1. To Camden, Private, 23 March 1797 (P.R.O. 30/8/325).

2. Camden's personal appeals may be followed in P.R.O. 30/8/326 with one in Dacres Adams Mss, formerly P.R.O. 30/58/2, and in Camden MS U840 O156A; Pitt's response in letters to him and to the Bank of England, February–May 1797, in P.R.O. 30/8/195, in a Note and a Memorandum of March in P.R.O. 30/8/196, ff. 233–40v, and a letter to Camden of 23 March as in n1 above. Senior figures in the Castle also wrote and/or talked to the Minister in this period: the Chief Secretary Thomas Pelham, the Chancellor of the Exchequer Sir John Parnell, the Civil Under Secretary Edward Cooke. Cf. Ch. I, section I above for the situation in England.

3. Camden to Pitt, 10 February 1797 (P.R.O. 30/8/326).

4. Pp. 123, 121, II, 566–7, 596–7 above.

where unrest threatened, the Irish authorities still reckoned that they were sadly short of 'concentrated' force.[1]

In 1797 the Castle therefore felt itself under siege. This did not mean that it despaired of short-term success. Reports in plenty were received in London which gave cause for alarm. But others still gave hope that the position could be held. Discontent was rife; seditious plans were hatching; the French, it was thought, would try again. On the other hand the authorities' intelligence was not to be despised, from time to time they reckoned they had the upper hand of unrest, and not least there were serious uncertainties among the revolutionaries themselves. Senior officials, and Camden, did not wholly despond.[2] But they were at best in a highly delicate situation, facing on the one hand a strong if uneven tide of unrest both Catholic and Protestant, and on the other a relentless pressure from sections within the Protestant interest for outright approval of anti-Catholic tactics which the authorities themselves disliked. Nor could they seriously consider anything but the immediate future. The horizons were narrowing: it was a matter of working from month to month. This was not the time for initiatives which could be taken as concessions. For the foreseeable future the Administration was simply dug in.

Its state of mind was not improved by a sense of lack of support from London, where all too often indeed complacency seemed to reign. Camden, it was true, was liable to appear easily dispirited: he had not wanted to go to Dublin, and in the autumn of 1797 he asked to come home.[3] But it was hardly reassuring to be told that his Insurrection Act shocked 'the fine feelings of British legislators', or that Ministers did not fear an invasion of Ireland after Bantry Bay.[4] Portland indeed – once himself a Lord Lieutenant – was not greatly impressed by the Castle's apprehensions; nor did Pitt himself provide much comfort for some time. As so often, he was a poor correspondent.[5] More to the point, he showed scant interest: as Camden reminded him, he had 'candidly acknowledged' in private in the spring of 1795 that Ireland occupied 'little of

1. See Fortescue, op. cit., IV–Part I, 518–19, 568–9. R.B. McDowell, *Ireland in the Age of Imperialism and Revolution 1760–1801* (1979), 612–13 gives the numbers cited here as nominally available by the monthly returns. By comparison, the military establishment voted by the Irish Parliament for 1796 was 19,012 regulars and Fencibles and 22,698 Irish militia; for 1797, 37,667, 22,698, and an unnumbered force of yeomanry; for 1798, 39,620, 26,634, and 37, 359 respectively (Fortescue, op. cit., IV–Part II, Appendix C).

2. Eg Camden's letters to Pitt of 1 January, 1 June (though see also n3 below), 10 October 1797 (P.R.O. 30/8/326), as well as, more frequently, to Portland in P.R.O., H.O. 100/69. The correspondence of Thomas Pelham, in the vital post of Chief Secretary, gives an impression of the variety and fluctuation of views (B.L. Add. Ms 33103).

3. To Pitt, 10 October 1797 (P.R.O. 30/8/326). In the summer he begged the Minister if possible to make a 'tolerable' peace with France (1 June, loc. cit.).

4. Same to same, 4 April 1796, 10 January 1797 (loc. cit.). Portland had been dismayed and surprised by the need for the Act's severity 'in a country enjoying the same form of government as this' (16 March 1796; P.R.O., H.O. 100/62).

5. Camden to Pitt, 7 May 1796 (P.R.O. 30/8/326). The disparity in the number of their respective letters may be seen from the sources cited in p. 161, n2 above.

[his] thoughts',[1] and matters did not seem to change much in the next two years. It had not always been so. He had invested youthful enthusiasm and some political capital in an effort to settle basic problems in 1785. But failure left its mark: his distaste for Irish politics was reinforced in the Regency crisis, he allowed himself to follow advice in the inadequate Relief Acts of 1792 and '93 which he had first wished to be of greater scope, and if in 1794 he supported the campaign to found a seminary for the Catholic priesthood – which led to the establishment of Maynooth – he refused to reconsider commercial policy while the war continued, and in 1795 was talking of 'the unlucky subject of Ireland'.[2] The Fitzwilliam affair confirmed a rooted impatience, and he greeted its demise with relief. While he moved perforce in 1797 to stem a financial haemorrhage, he was still reluctant to apply himself closely to the island's affairs.

In the early months of 1798, however, the Minister found that he could no longer evade the need. Events on both sides of the Irish Channel demanded growing attention. The impact of Irish sedition on Britain, first suspected seriously in the naval mutinies, was placed fairly before Ministers in the following spring.[3] The Margate arrests threw light on the connexion – with severe effects on the English elements themselves; they also forced a hastening of preparations within Ireland for a general rising in conjunction with the French. There was enough evidence moreover for the British Government now to take these latter reports seriously, for a good deal was known, partly from the consulate in Hamburg, a well known entrepot of agents and spies, and partly from the Castle's own sources within the United Irishmen, providing intelligence that was far from comprehensive but a source of confusion to that body in turn. As the signs mounted of impending trouble – at the least of widespread unrest – the authorities in London and Dublin forged closer links.

There was a further propellant, through an untoward incident which caused them both some trouble. The virtual state of war in Ulster in 1797 – involving martial law for the province – raised the need for a more effective Commander-in-Chief. Two obvious choices from England, Sir Charles Grey and Cornwallis, declined; but one suitable candidate came to hand in Sir Ralph Abercromby, the captor of Trinidad who had lately returned from the Caribbean. In the view of Dundas (a distant relation) he was indeed 'one of the best if not on the whole the very best officer in

1. Ibid.
2. II, 430. See also I, Ch. VIII, section II, and p. 663; II, 219–22, 424–5, 438. Holland Rose, II, 343–4 argues Pitt's personal involvement in a proposal for Maynooth in 1794–5 which was favoured by both the Irish and the British Governments as a potential institutional alternative to heterogeneous hostile influences.
3. Pp. 19–20, 120 above.

the King's Service'.[1] Accepting unenthusiastically, he was soon repelled by what he found: the 'abuses of all kinds', and not least among the military, could 'scarcely be believed or enumerated'.[2] The gentry, to whom the part-time forces should look, were deservedly hated by the peasantry, while the regular formations, too widely scattered, were too often out of hand. Nor was the Commander-in-Chief's own status easily determined in relation to that of Lord Lieutenant, responsible directly even if perhaps 'nominally' for the forces.[3] After a few months of increasing frustration the General accordingly decided on shock treatment, issuing an Order of the Day in February 1798 for a return to discipline on the part of an army 'in a state of licentiousness which must render it formidable to every one but the enemy'. He also drew attention to 'the standing orders of the Kingdom', whereby the presence of a magistrate was needed to permit action by troops in support of the civil authority, unless they themselves had already been attacked.[4]

The difficulties in this last situation were of course not new; they were in fact the subject of wide debate. But such a statement was a curious error, for a Proclamation to the contrary, of May 1797, still remained in force. Abercromby thus could be and was accused of challenging his Government; while his wholesale condemnation of the forces brought a storm about his head. It also annoyed the British Government, for it came at a peculiarly unfortunate moment. Only a week earlier there had been an important debate in the House of Lords in Dublin, moved by Lord Moira – an Irish as well as a British peer – to attack the methods by which the Castle's repressive policies were carried out. As a distinguished soldier, who in 1797 had twice raised the matter in the British Upper Chamber, and a British politician of some note, he commanded attention. But there was something more: as a friend and close adviser of the heir to the throne, he had been urged by the Prince on Pitt in that same year as the ideal man to take over as Lord Lieutenant. The proposal was rebuffed.[5] But if the episode was not widely known, at least as yet, Moira's speeches gained strength from the connexion; and against this political background Abercromby could be suspected of political intent. The Protestant hawks in Dublin fell upon the controversy, and it naturally fuelled interest in

1. To Camden, Very Private, 2 October 1797 (Camden Ms C106/5). Cornwallis, rather less flatteringly, had called him the best of a 'melancholy list' for the West Indies in 1795 (II, 567). See also p. 375 below, and II, 491 for Abercromby; II, 322n7, 325, 356–7, 491, 542, and p. 27 above for Grey. Cornwallis himself, Master General of the Ordnance and a Cabinet Minister (II, 428, 492), was often thought of when the going was hard in any quarter (cf. I, 453, II, 330–1, 341–2, 364–5, 374).

2. James Lord Dunfermline, *Lieutenant-General Sir Ralph Abercromby KB 1793–1801, A Memoir by his Son* (1861), 114.

3. The quotation is from Camden to Pitt, 26 March 1798 (P.R.O. 30/8/326).

4. The text was widely published. It may be found in full in Dunfermline, op. cit., 93–4.

5. The best account of this episode, in February 1797, is in *Correspondence of George Prince of Wales . . .*, ed. Aspinall, III, 313–28. See pp. 43–5 above for Moira as a politician in England in the same year.

England. Ministers themselves were astonished and upset, and the sequel followed soon. Portland sent Camden a strong letter of complaint; a formidable group in the Castle closed in; and the Lord Lieutenant, at first sympathetic to the General and content to let the matter pass, but unable to withstand the pressures, left the latter little choice but to resign.[1] The affair would soon be overtaken by greater events. But it was not insignificant. It confirmed a balance of power within the Irish Government to which Camden was reluctantly bowing, and cast a fiercer light on the disarray governing the prospects for military conduct as 'the unlucky subject of Ireland' moved towards the centre of the stage.[2]

II

For as Abercromby wound up his command, and his successor took over, there was a run of dramatic developments. In March 1798 the Irish Government swooped on suspected dissidents as the British was doing at home. On the 12th it arrested all but three of the Dublin committee of the United Irishmen, following with further members of the Society in the next few days. The leading places were soon refilled. But two months later, on 19 and 20 May, one of the three survivors – the tragic Lord Edward Fitzgerald, soon to become a figure of legend – and two of the replacements were seized in turn, and in the latter's papers a draft was found of a call for a national rising. On virtually the eve, as it proved, of an insurrection the authorities thus had evidence that it was in the wind.[3]

These moves and preparations might convey a sense of clear direction coming as a climax to well assembled plans. Things however are seldom so tidy, not least in Ireland, and in point of fact the quickened pace followed months of 'remarkable indecisiveness on the part of the government and the United Irishmen alike'.[4] Both contained elements reluctant to be pushed too fast to extremes: in the Castle, Camden and some of his officials, bound to the Protestant interest but anxious for restraint; in the Society, those who feared a move in advance of French support. For the revolutionaries faced the two linked problems so often inherent in wartime risings: how accurately could they gauge their own strength, in

---

1. Portland's and Camden's correspondence on the affair is in P.R.O., H.O. 100/75; Camden's and Pitt's in P.R.O. 30/8/325–6. Pitt took a calmer view than the Home Secretary, but felt obliged to let Abercromby come home. Camden's own attitude, as so often happens on such occasions, was more hostile to the General by the end than at the start.

2. From the early months of the year one can indeed see that last topic occupying a progressively larger amount of space for instance in the London newspapers.

3. The more gratifyingly so, in a way, because papers found in the March arrests had revealed very little.

4. Marianne Elliott, op. cit., 193.

relation to the prospects for help from outside? Dare they hazard the first without sound knowledge of the scale and timing of the second; or might independent action suffice, or itself bring in the prospective aid? These uncertainties, which had beset the United Irishmen's counsels since Bantry Bay, divided the main executive as some now proclaimed that the hour was at hand.

It was in fact hard for the leadership to be sure where it stood. Some estimates of domestic numbers and performance were certainly extravagant; and the crucial answer to French intentions remained as elusive as it had long been. Despite high hopes in 1797, there were signs that the Directory had learned caution from experience: a further attempt from Brest was at a discount, and while preparations were put in hand at the Texel these centred so largely on the initiative of the commander – the young General Hoche, retained since the previous attempt – that the likelihood fluctuated with his own fortunes and declined when he now, prematurely, died. Camperdown in any case removed expectations from that quarter.[1] Irish hopes however revived in the winter as invasion, of some kind, gained priority in Paris.[2] The Society's representatives pleaded with the Directory, and Bonaparte himself; intimations – assurances, as it seemed to ready listeners – were vouchsafed, and messages home (probably from the unreliable Napper Tandy) suggested April as the month. Such news brought the uncertainties and divisions in the central committee to a point; for it came at a time when support in the countryside seemed to be growing in response to growing Protestant – largely Orange – aggression, and the proponents of immediate action were eager to catch the tide. The arrests in March intensified the tension, and effectively settled the issue. Lord Edward and the leading replacements were of that party, and as the weeks went by without the French they pursued their plans as best they could. Harried and hunted, some ill suited to the task, they could not impose cohesion. But in the week which ended with their arrests, a date was settled for the opening blow. Columns of insurgents would march on Dublin in the next few days, and on 23 May the Castle would be attacked.

'The great rebellion' of 1798 was thus set on foot in haste and confusion. It bore that stamp throughout its brief life. The Irish Government, it was true, was surprised by the timing: the Castle's confidence had lately been growing, and the Lord Lieutenant indeed had just reported 'no apprehension of insurrection or even tumult'.[3] The opening plan however, in a sense justifying the judgment, went badly wrong. No rising took place within the capital, the combined assault emerged as

1. Cf. p. 28 above. See II, 641 for Hoche in 1796. He had become suspect for a time in 1797 after involvement in the complicated politics of Paris; but while his credit rose again with Fructidor (see p. 65 above), he had in fact himself lost confidence in a serious invasion before he died in September.

2. See p. 120 above.

3. Camden to Portland, 21 May 1798 (H.O. 100/76).

scattered clashes, and the authorities' greatest worry in the first few days was perhaps the threat of excessive reaction. Loyalists looked ominously set on unlimited revenge. But if the revolutionaries' plans could not achieve their aim, there remained a mass of men determined to fight; and lit by fervour or simple hopes of betterment, the flame burned in the Catholic provinces. It was by no means universal: while there was trouble in the west and extreme south, the heart of the risings was confined, beyond the Leinster plain near Dublin, to Wicklow and above all Wexford, and the main concentration there was defeated in the second half of June. Meanwhile however the lesser threats spread beyond the Catholic ranks: despite uncertainties and divisions, the Protestant dissidents rose afresh in eastern Ulster.[1] But their effort too proved useless: the operations again were quickly and ruthlessly crushed; and though some fighting continued, particularly in the Wicklow hills, the Irish Government soon knew that the immediate spectre of a national rebellion was dead.[2]

The military measures had therefore sufficed. The earlier jeremiads might have seemed unwarranted: even the largely Catholic militia had played its part.[3] Things might have been different if the revolutionaries' expectations of themselves had not proved unreal, and if there had been a French invasion at the same time. Nor, doubtful of the quality of its own forces – not least of their capacity to act while observing restraint – were the Irish Government's apprehensions unjustified. In the event not all was black when the insurrection came and had to be suppressed: the story was not one of unrelieved cruelty. But there were most certainly savage excesses, and these were all the more glaring to losers ready to query all methods, justifiable or not. The rising left a disastrous legacy to haunt later generations: martyrs to fuel the cause and adorn the potent self-sustaining tale.

> Who fears to speak of Ninety-Eight
> Who blushes at the name? . . .
>
> They rose in dark and evil days
> To right their native land;
> They kindled here a living blaze
> That nothing shall withstand.
> Alas! that Might can vanquish Right –
> *They* fell, and pass'd away;

1. Cf. pp. 159–60 above.
2. Camden was confident in fact by the middle of June (to Portland, 16 June 1798; H.O. 100/77). Admittedly he had a personal point to make by then (see p. 168 below); but later alarms proved indeed not to be on the same scale.
3. Cf. p. 161 above.

But true men, like you, men,
Are plenty here to-day.[1]

The experience naturally made an immediate impact on the Government in London as well. What was wanting was better trained troops and an effective command, capable both of imposing order and also, in the aftermath, confronting excessive 'friendly' political pressures. Pitt himself was aware of both needs. In the last days of May Camden was calling for a further 10,000 men, and the Ministry felt, particularly since the French might still come, it must agree. The Home Secretary promised 3,000; but Pitt was already arranging for 5,000, and in the next few days this was increased to 8,000.[2] The formations were to be provided from regulars, Fencibles, and also the militia for which service in Ireland was given statutory authority.[3] At the same time, however, the Minister tried to lay down two conditions. The troops were to be returned as soon as possible, for upon that might depend 'all chance of Vigorous Operations during the War'; and '(even more important)' they must be used 'only for Purposes consistent with your own Principles & Feelings', and Camden was to 'resist . . . the Intemperance of [his] Friends' as much as the efforts of the enemy.[4]

These injunctions, as it turned out, were the last to be addressed to Camden himself. In the past few months he had repeated his desire, for personal reasons, to come home; more important, he had coupled it with the need for the Lord Lieutenant to be 'a Military Man'. The imbroglio over Abercromby brought the matter to a head: the structure of government in his view was not designed for the current problems, and once he could pause for breath in the rebellion he returned to the charge. Some '*most efficient* Military Man' should replace him, and 'the properest' would be Cornwallis.[5] Faced by these repeated pleas, Pitt came to the same

1. Published in 1843; quoted in Elliott, op. cit., 368–9. And one can travel farther:

> How could you dream they'd listen
> That had an ear alone
> For those new comrades they have found
> Lord Edward and Wolfe Tone
> (Yeats, 'Sixteen Dead Men', on the 1916 Rising).

2. Camden-Portland correspondence, H.O. 100/77; Camden to Pitt, 7 June 1798 (P.R.O. 30/8/326); Pitt to Camden, 2 June 1798 (P.R.O. 30/8/325).

3. See p. 125 above; and Western, *The English Militia in the Eighteenth Century*, 265–7, but also 431–2, for discipline. The plans for the regulars, including a force from the Guards, are summarised in *L.C.G. III*, III, nos. 1748, 1751–2.

4. 2 June 1798 (n2 above). Camden had confessed a few days before that his 'friends' were almost out of his control (to Pitt, nd, P.R.O. 30/8/326; and see also same to same, 31 May 1798, Dacres Adams Mss, formerly P.R.O. 30/58/2).

The condition applying to the troops was met to some extent. There were the familiar muddles in getting them all quickly to the spot; but formations then came and went throughout the summer, thereby providing a reinforcement or reserve, if a shifting one, for the regulars stationed in Britain and available for operations elsewhere.

5. Camden to Pitt, 10 February, 26 March, 8 June 1798 (P.R.O. 30/8/326). He had also clearly been thinking of his political prospects when Pitt made a minor Ministerial change

conclusion. He had been doubtful earlier: Camden must stay until the repercussions from Abercromby died down, and since the co-operation of the gentry was essential to any commander that must mean achieving a policy 'more Political than Military'. Despite his frequent dependence on Cornwallis, moreover, the Minister questioned his fitness for this particular post. But in the second week of June he proclaimed himself 'convinced'. He talked to the General, who agreed to go at once – rather disconcerting Camden, who was now 'somewhat hurt at the very great speed' with which he was taken at his word; and on 20 June the Marquess landed to take up his post.[1]

He had therefore been in Ireland for some time when the French at length arrived. They did so at Killala Bay, in the far west of Sligo, on 22 August. Events had complicated the Directory's decision, taken finally in June, to support the rising: arrangements made in principle had to be reviewed, plans put into detailed effect, finance found and forces gathered in a period of distraction elsewhere.[2] Three expeditions were designed, from Dunkirk, Rochefort and Brest, with Wolfe Tone and his brothers and Napper Tandy divided between them. It was the second of these, under an incompetent General Humbert, that reached the west in August, with just over 1,000 men. After an initial success[3] it was quickly subdued, surrendering on 8 September. Meanwhile Napper Tandy had sailed from Dunkirk with a handful of Irish exiles, landing in Donegal on 16 September and re-embarking farcically on the 17th. That same day the force from Brest sailed at last, escorted by a squadron. It never reached its destination of Ulster, the escort being brought to battle off the north-east coast, when Tone was captured and sent to Dublin, where he died following a suicide attempt.[4]

The Government had been fortunate, in the French misapprehension of the state of Ireland – as marked as earlier Irish expectations of France – and in the shortcomings of their eventual efforts. For there was certainly an intention in Paris in the summer to mount an invasion, particularly towards the close when success was seen as antidote to the crushing defeat at the Nile. Dutch and Spanish co-operation was sought, substantial forces were allotted on paper, arms provided to rouse the Irish people themselves once more. But the authorities' own resolve also played its part

---

in February (for which see p. 410, n1 below); see Chatham to Camden, 7 March 1798 (Camden Ms U840 C102/5).

1. Pitt to Camden, 31 March, 11 June 1798 (Camden Mss U840 O190A/4, 7); Camden to Pitt, 16 June 1798 and nd, endorsed as received 19 June (P.R.O. 30/8/326). And see p. 167, n2 above.

2. For which see pp. 220–1 below. Elliott, op. cit., ch. Seven, gives a good account of background and events for this paragraph.

3. When the local militia lived up to earlier suspicions of their loyalty by running away.

4. A final expedition in mid October, to the west coast, was driven off at sea.

in the outcome. Cornwallis moved firmly against Humbert, with forces which he had been regrouping, and aware that he might expect further militia regiments from England. He had indeed been impressing himself on the scene since his arrival, bringing his authority to bear on military dispositions and as far as possible on discipline. In pursuit of the latter he supported where he could the due processes of law, so widely ignored though not wholly superseded, while trying simultaneously to improve the atmosphere with offers of amnesty to rebels and deserters through proclamations which were given statutory force.[1] And in taking these measures he began to tackle the political pressures which Camden had experienced, the 'friends' whom the latter had failed to subdue. Buttressed by his dual powers, and impressed by the need to set the pace, he set to work with the knowledge that he enjoyed the personal support of Pitt, himself now seized of the need for a policy to bring Ireland into closer control.

III

Such a policy must aim to endure: temporary expedients would not suffice. The instrument was already in the front of Pitt's mind. On 28 May, the day after receiving news of the rising, he inquired of Camden 'Cannot Crushing the Rebellion be followed by an Act appointing Commissioners to treat for an Union?' We must, he repeated to another friend, 'follow up' suppression 'by immediate steps for a union'; and at the beginning of June he had 'a great deal of discussion' on the subject with Grenville.[2] The steps should clearly be made over ground prepared carefully on all sides. Cornwallis's own immediate moves, aimed it might be hoped at a passing situation, would not relate in such a context to the shortest term alone.[3]

The idea was not particularly surprising. It had cropped up at times since the fourteenth century, and once, under the Commonwealth, Irish MPs had even sat at Westminster. In Queen Anne's reign proposals had been canvassed, and in one instance made from Dublin itself; and the suggestion had been revived more recently in England, by politicians and by others including Adam Smith. More recently still, the current had set in a different direction: in the early 1780s a liberalisation of trade for Ireland was followed by virtually complete judicial and legislative independence. But these last concessions, made under the pressures of discontent and setbacks in war, had not raised great hopes in London at the

---

1. 38 Geo. III, c55 in the Irish series.
2. Pitt to Camden, 28 May 1798 (announcing his duel with Tierney earlier in the day; Camden Ms U840 O190A/6); same to Mornington, 31 May 1798 (Rosebery, *Pitt*, 210); same to Grenville, 1–10 June (*H.M.C., Dropmore*, IV, 229–30); same to Auckland, 4 June (*A.C.*, IV, 2).
3. A connexion may be deduced from Pitt to Camden, 11 June 1798; Camden Ms U840 O190A/7.

time, and successive Ministries were soon complaining that the measures were failing to achieve the balance, sought by their own advocates, of 'distinctness' with 'inseparable annexation' to Britain.[1]

Pitt had seen something of the problems as Shelburne's young Chancellor of the Exchequer. When his turn came, in 1785, he approached them by the different route of his prospective commercial settlement. If a comprehensive arrangement could be reached of trading interests and financial obligations, that in his view could

> find some line according to which the Parliaments of the two countries may exercise the rights of legislation, without clashing with each other on the one hand, or, on the other, being encumbered by the necessity of actual and positive concert on every point of common concern.

Such a result could indeed achieve 'a permanent and tranquil system', by – as he had earlier put it – 'making England and Ireland *one country in effect*, though for local concerns under distinct Legislatures'.[2] It would not in fact create a constitutional union; rather it would render one unnecessary, after the extension of legislative independence only three years before.

The failure of Pitt's scheme was likely to turn his thoughts, when he indulged them,[3] towards union itself. The subject surfaced in the period of the Catholic Relief Acts in the early nineties, and he then claimed that it had 'long been in my mind'.[4] He was not hopeful that it could be accomplished – though prepared apparently for discreet soundings – and it lay dormant in the next few years. But it must have been stirring as the situation worsened in 1798, and when or by the time that the crisis broke he decided to pursue an object which a crisis could now be held to demand. He was quickly on the trail. Camden replied with his own thoughts in some detail, probably shortly before he left; Grenville, acquainted with Irish problems as a brother and Chief Secretary to a former Lord Lieutenant, also responded with 'a paper'; and the King, who approved the idea, and Cornwallis were told when the latter was appointed.[5] From these indications, the initiative was Pitt's and he meant at least to look hard at the case.

---

1. See I, 195–7. The phrases were Grattan's.
2. Op. cit., Ch. VIII, section II, and for the first two quotations, of September 1785, p. 199, for the last, Pitt to Rutland, 6 January 1785 (*Correspondence between The Right Honble. William Pitt and Charles Duke of Rutland . . . 1781–1787* (1890), 58).
3. Cf. pp. 162–3 above.
4. To the Earl of Westmorland [Lord Lieutenant], 18 November 1792; quoted in Holland Rose, II, 390.
5. Camden's memorandum, nd but not before 31 May 1798 when he acknowledged Pitt's first letter (Dacres Adams Mss, formerly P.R.O. 30/58/2; and see p. 170, n3 above) and placed with another letter to Pitt endorsed as received 19 June, is in P.R.O. 30/8/326 and printed in Holland Rose, *Pitt and Napoleon*, 335–8. He sailed for England on 22 June. Grenville's paper is mentioned in *A.C.*, IV, 2 (p. 170, n2 above), but I have not found it, though possibly it may be his undated 'Note', in Dacres Adams Mss, formerly P.R.O. 30/58/8,

As so often when seized of a question, he was brisk and hopeful at the start. He thought that he and Grenville could 'see daylight in almost everything' barring 'trade and revenue' – the old stumbling blocks of 1785.[1] In June and to some extent still in July he was recuperating from illness, the Parliamentary session was winding up to be followed by dispersal in the long recess, and the rebellion in any case had not come to an end. In August however he was becoming impatient. The pace of the work was hastened. He was soon 'very sanguine' once more, and by the end of September the ideas were taking shape.[2]

Legislation would of course be for the Irish as well as the British Parliament. The process thus far had centred on England, where Pitt was working closely with Grenville and Auckland – also a former Chief Secretary – and with Dundas and Canning, Portland and Camden in greater or lesser degree, while the powerful Lord Chancellor, the Earl of Clare, and the old ally John Beresford were canvassed privately and informally in Ireland itself.[3] Once the outlines were drawn, and as the embers of the rebellion faded with the French failure, the amount of consultation with Dublin rapidly increased; officials and some prominent politicians began to visit London, and from October the Lord Lieutenant and the Chief Secretary were more closely drawn in. The latter was then new to the post, though not entirely to the duties. He was Robert Stewart, Viscount Castlereagh: the first appearance in office of an illustrious name. In point of fact he had deputised since March for the absentee

---

f. 98, on the sketch of an Act which itself is possibly the memorandum printed (from the Pretyman Mss) in Holland Rose, *Pitt and Napoleon*, 338–41. See I, 195 for his earlier spell in Ireland, and Jupp, *Lord Grenville*, 265 for Buckingham's concern now. George III's approval may be seen in his letters to Pitt of 11 and 13 June 1798, in Stanhope, III, Appendix, xv–xvi and *Pitt and Napoleon*, 243 respectively. Cornwallis referred on 20 July to 'the great point of Ultimate Settlement' (to Pitt; P.R.O. 30/8/327); surely a reflection of Pitt's thoughts as relayed to Camden at the time of the General's appointment (p. 169 above).

1. To Auckland, 4 June (*A.C.*, IV, 2).

2. The quotation is from Canning's diary for 20 August (Canning Ms 29d). Ten days earlier, Hawkesbury, calling at Walmer [see p. 91 above], found him 'decidedly bent on an Union with Ireland' (to Liverpool, 10 August 1798; B.L. Loan Ms 72, vol. 54). See also G.C. Bolton, *The Passing of the Irish Act of Union . . .* (1966), 62.

3. Dundas joins Grenville in August in *H.M.C., Dropmore*, IV; Auckland's substantial contribution from June may be seen in *A.C.*, IV, B.L. Add. Ms 34454, and *The Correspondence of the Right Hon. John Beresford . . .*, ed. the Right Hon. William Beresford, II (1854). See my I, 207–8 for his experience of Ireland. Canning is glimpsed, in late July and August, in Canning Ms 29d. Clare and Beresford – whose 'notes' on trade and finance Pitt characteristically mislaid at one point (*A.C.*, IV, 42, and cf. p. 121, n1 above), and for whom see I, 201, 211–12, II, 421, 430, 439 – seem to have been consulted largely through Auckland. Exactly how far Portland and Camden on his return were drawn in I do not know. The former, from his position as Home Secretary, must have been involved to some extent before October, as must the latter, who joined the Cabinet without portfolio in June, and seems certainly to have been in touch from September (eg Camden to Pitt, 11 September 1798; P.R.O. 30/8/119), and see his letters to Castlereagh (for whom below) in *Memoirs and Correspondence of Viscount Castlereagh . . .*, ed. by His Brother, Charles Vane, Marquess of Londonderry, I (1848), 391, 412, 448–50; and also op. cit., 345).

holder of the post, Thomas Pelham, forced to leave by a recurrence of illness which in the autumn obliged him to give up.[1] Placed in acting charge by Camden, who was his maternal uncle, his competence secured his continuation under Cornwallis; and if Pelham's experience and judgment and weight with Ministers were shortly to be missed, his replacement gained steadily in reputation, not least with Pitt.[2]

In tackling so considerable a matter there was a useful precedent. Pitt's first move, with Grenville and Auckland, was to look at the Union with Scotland of 1707.[3] That event indeed had stimulated thought at the time on both sides of the Irish Sea,[4] and the Act yielded some valuable guidance now. Its influence was evident in the articles and proposals which were assembled in draft in November and given effect by the end of the year. The kingdoms would be joined in a United Kingdom of Great Britain and Ireland. The Parliament of Great Britain would become the Parliament of the United Kingdom, Irish representatives being added to the British in the numbers of 32 peers, spiritual and temporal – the latter, over and above peers holding British titles also, to be elected by their fellows for life and not, like the Scottish, for a single Parliament – and of not more than 100 Members to the Commons. The Established Churches of England and Ireland would be united in composition, and members of both Houses in the enlarged Parliament would take the existing denominational oaths, though this was specifically subject to any change which that body might make. Freedom of trade would be secured within the enlarged economic unit, but Great Britain and Ireland would continue each to service its own debt.[5]

1. Cf. p. 162, n2 above, and for Pelham in general see II, 406–7, 439, 594 & n4. His loss was thought at the time, and indeed was, serious, for he was held in high respect by both the British and Irish Governments: when Pitt in June 1798 persuaded him to go back, which then proved impossible, the King went so far as to observe that the Minister had thereby 'saved Ireland' (13 June, Holland Rose, *Pitt and Napoleon*, 243, and see also his letter of the 11th, in Stanhope, III, Appendix, xvi). Pelham's illness was at its height through the spring, and he hoped to follow business thereafter. He was certainly kept in touch in the summer and autumn (see correspondence in B.L. Add. Mss 33105–6 and a paper in 33119, ff. 169–75). But his health prevented much application: he was said even during a temporary recovery in the later summer to be 'still afraid of engaging too deeply in business', and in October to be easily tired (see *Correspondence of Castlereagh*, I, 378, 412).

2. The appointment dated from November 1798. The post had been offered first to Thomas Grenville (see II, 407, 419, and p. 36, n3 above), who declined it for at least the second time (II, 422).

3. Pitt to Auckland, 4 June (*A.C.*, IV, 2). He and Portland also instructed the historian John Bruce (see p. 121 above) to search the records 'both here and in Scotland' (Dundas to Grenville, 10 August; *H.M.C., Dropmore*, IV, 278).

4. See p. 170 above.

5. The 'heads of a Treaty' were sent to Dublin on 12 November, and followed on the 25th by some more specific 'suggestions and observations' (Portland to Cornwallis, Secret and Confidential and Secret respectively, H.O. 100/79). A copy of the first is in Pitt's papers in P.R.O. 30/8/327, and the text is printed in, *inter alia, H.M.C., Dropmore*, IV, 397–400; that of the second, in part in *Correspondence of Cornwallis*, II, 452–3, and more fully in *Correspondence of Castlereagh*, II (1848), 19–23. Some adjustments and additions of detail were incorporated in December.

Some of these provisions encapsulated differences of opinion already resolved; others, not surprisingly, left matter for future settlement. In most cases detail was still needed to fill principles now mainly reached. Should, for instance, the Crown retain its normal power to create fresh Irish peerages, when Irish peers would be able to sit in the House of Lords? How best to reconcile a strictly limited number of representatives in the Commons with representation of a larger number of existing Irish constituencies? Exactly how could equal trade regulations and duties within an inherited complex, itself raising intricate questions, be fairly combined with unequal contributions to a national debt? These last difficulties, which had seemed the most threatening from experience in the past, proved in fact not impossible to adjust once a comparative study was made of imports, exports and expenditure, the proportions of servicing debt were fixed correspondingly for the next twenty years, and some reduced tariffs retained for a similar maximum period to ease the impact of domestic competition.[1] But if economic problems loomed large in the minds of their earlier Ministerial victims, it was constitutional implications that soon demanded the severest thought. The British determination in particular to restrict the number of Irish MPs at Westminster raised issues, of practice and theory, which caused much concern. It would not be simple to reduce 300 politicians – the current size of the Irish Commons – to 100. One early idea was rejected, to retain a legislature in Dublin for certain local questions,[2] consisting of MPs who would be left over from a ballot for representation in the 'United' House. Instead, however, it was proposed that all 32 Irish counties and 8 or 10 of the boroughs should return one Member (Dublin and Cork perhaps two each), while the remaining 108 boroughs should be divided in two groups and each send a Member to alternate Parliaments.[3] That would have the advantage moreover or reducing the figure of 100 possibly to 96: a further illustration of the British resolve not to be swamped by the new entrants.[4]

1. Bolton, op. cit., 90.

2. Cf. Pitt in 1785 (p. 171 above). The idea may have been advocated now by Grenville (McDowell, op. cit., 680). Cf. I, 370n2 for an inherited 'colonial' aspect to the principle, and p. 159, n4 above.

3. There is an undated memorandum on such lines in Pitt's hand in the file for 1800 in the Dacres Adams Mss, formerly P.R.O. 30/58/3, which may refer rather to this earlier period.

4. As one British politician put it, 'I do not think any of our country gentlemen would venture into parliament if they were to meet 100 Paddies' (Lord Sheffield to Auckland, 13 November 1798; Bolton, op. cit., 86). There was also the fear that the Crown would benefit from a new version of the Ministerial (Dundas's) 'Scotch pack' (ibid). This last in any case could also apply to the Irish peers (cf. I, 622–3).

Pitt himself was satisfied with the figure of 100 (Canning to Windham, 23 October 1798; B.L. Add. Ms 37844); and Lord Hobart, a former Chief Secretary in Ireland (see II, 221), submitted schemes in October, the second of which, for 100 Members, he claimed conformed in number to Pitt's ideas (to Pitt, 27 October 1798; Dacres Adams Mss, formerly P.R.O. 30/58/2). Portland would have preferred fewer (to Cornwallis, Secret, 25 November 1798; H.O. 100/79).

It also reflected certain other presuppositions: the need to give proper weight to the counties in relation to the boroughs, and more generally not to risk the danger offered by any change in Ireland of introducing through that medium a fresh concept of Parliamentary reform.[1] The political arrangements propounded at the start of the campaign for Union showed that what might apply to one country could be judged inapplicable to the other.

The force of such a maxim was shown at the same time in a more far-reaching question. For might not the chance be seized at such a juncture, when the Constitution would be formally remodelled, to grant Irish Roman Catholics admission to Parliament and to the higher Irish offices? That would crown the most recent reliefs conceded in the Acts of '92 and '93. It would remove a cause of discontent, reducing an incitement to disaffection among sections of the middle and upper orders disposed in general to be loyal. And in an altered context the demerits should not be so marked: what affected, in theory, a large element in Ireland would have less impact in a United Kingdom.[2] Moral arguments in themselves, long canvassed, could be held to point either way. But those of expediency had so far pronounced against, and it was they that were weighed again now.

There was some prospect at first that the scales might be tilted in favour of such a measure: that civil emancipation might be included in an Act of Union itself. Camden had recommended it on leaving Dublin; Cornwallis's sympathies for the Catholics were well known; so were Dundas's; and Grenville, once hostile to such relief, had become better disposed.[3] Pitt seems to have made some favourable noises at the start.[4]

1. A principle made clear alike by the Old Whig Portland in response to a scheme proposed from the Castle (Bolton, op. cit., 87), by Grenville (to Buckingham, 5 November 1798; Buckingham, II, 413), and by Auckland (B.L. Add. Ms 33119, ff. 169–75).

2. Pitt had made this point indeed in 1792 (to Westmorland, 18 November; Holland Rose, II, 390). The calculation of current proportions was Roman Catholics to Protestants in Ireland 3:1, in a United Kingdom 3:14.

3. See p. 171 above for Camden's memorandum, of which paras. 4 and 9 were relevant (Holland Rose, *Pitt and Napoleon*, 336–7). He and Pitt were well aware of Cornwallis's 'inclination to the Catholics' (Camden to Pitt, 6 June 1798, and see Pitt to Camden, 31 March, in P.R.O. 30/8/326 and Camden MsU840 O190A/4 respectively); and the same knowledge affected attitudes in Dublin after the Lord Lieutenant's arrival. Dundas's sympathy had been noted several years before (eg Burke to Thomas Hussey, endorsed as received 28 November 1795; *Correspondence of Burke*, VIII, 352), and his championship of civil emancipation now emerged clearly in a letter to Pitt, written from internal evidence at about this time and probably in May (nd, P.R.O. 30/8/157). See also Cyril Matheson, *The Life of Henry Dundas . . .* (1933), 257–9. Grenville, earlier opposed, had been attracted to the idea in the past year, though he was changing his mind again when confronted by insurrection (*Diary of Windham*, 368, for 16 June 1797; Buckingham, II, 411–12).

4. On an undated paper headed 'Plan of Union' – which was possibly by Pelham among whose papers it lies or (at least in part) by Edward Cooke (see p. 161, n2 above), and received comments possibly from Camden and certainly from Pitt and from Auckland – Pitt wanted the admission of Catholics to 'all offices [under Government] civil and

Whether the case would stand up to determined opposition remained to be seen. One sure obstacle in England would lie in the King himself, who had already made his view clear. Expressing his support for Union at the time of Cornwallis's appointment – he 'must not lose the present moment of terror for frightening the supporters of the Castle' into that step – but obviously with the Marquess's sympathies in mind, he stated bluntly that 'no further indulgences must be granted to the Roman Catholics, as no country can be governed where there is more than one established religion'.[1] This put the matter in a nutshell, and the strength of his feeling was well known. It had surfaced in the Fitzwilliam affair three years before, and Dundas remarked now – possibly even before the monarch wrote – on his 'Prejudice . . . on that whole Subject', 'agitated' and 'inflamed' as it was by emotion.[2] Pitt had not taken the eruption too seriously in 1795. But with the object of Union in mind now, which should not be hazarded, he was anxious not to risk losing supporters for that cause in Ireland itself. It was in fact Cornwallis who first gave him pause. Though the Castle contained a party in favour – the Lord Lieutenant and Castlereagh and the Under Secretary in the Military Department, William Elliot[3] – some powerful figures were strongly opposed, most prominently John Foster, the Speaker, who disapproved of Union as well, and – of more instant importance – Lord Clare, who however was that measure's weighty advocate. Cornwallis was indeed soon surprised by the uncertain prospects for 'the great point' of relief, and although still convinced that by rights it should be included, he acknowledged the difficulties with a plea that denial, if it came, should not appear 'irrevocable'.[4] Hoping to influence a decision, which he knew in October was being prepared, he asked Pitt to see Elliot, who was going to London and could state his thoughts.

---

military', and added 'why are Corporation Officers to be exclusively Protestant when those of the State may be Catholics?' ('Notes by Mr Pitt', in B.L. Add. Ms 33119, ff. 169–75). The contents would seem to point to an early stage in the process; in the summer rather than the autumn of 1798. Cf. I, 200 for his approach in 1784.

It may not have been entirely without significance that *The Times*, with its Ministerialist connexions, declared on 29 June that it had 'no doubt' of Emancipation being 'granted to Ireland whenever the rebellion is at an end, though still under certain restrictions'.

1. To Pitt, 13 June 1798 (Holland Rose, *Pitt and Napoleon*, 243). He had written the same two days before as something that 'Lord Cornwallis must clearly understand' (to same, 11 June 1798; Stanhope, III, Appendix, xvi. See p. 171, n5 above.)

2. II, 432; Dundas to Pitt as in p. 175, n3 above. He was 'positive that there is somebody about him [the King]', though 'I know not who', doing 'much mischief by agitating his Mind and inflaming his Prejudices on that topick'. Prescient words.

3. Elliot was more important than his official title might suggest. Capable, and enjoying his superiors' confidence, he was brought into this matter largely because his colleague for the Civil Department, Edward Cooke, was against Emancipation at the start.

4. Cornwallis to Pitt, 20 July, same to Major-General Ross, 30 September, same to Pitt, 8, 17 October 1798 (*Correspondence of Cornwallis*, II, 365, 415–16, 418–19); same to Pitt, 23, 27 September (Dacres Adams Mss, formerly P.R.O. 30/58/2), and cf. same to Portland, 16 September 1798 (*Correspondence*, II, 405), and to Pelham, 16 October 1798 (B.L. Add. Ms 33106).

Earl Camden, *by Lawrence*   Marquess Cornwallis, *by William Beechey*

Viscount Castlereagh, *by Lawrence*

The Irish House of Commons

It was too late. Earlier in that month Lord Clare crossed the Irish Sea, bent on pursuing the case for Union and resisting that for Emancipation. Recognised on all sides as a crucial figure whose support for the first was essential, he was resolutely convinced that the second should not be tried. His visit, lasting a month, was successful: Ministers were persuaded to drop the idea of instant relief.[1] This did not mean that 'future consideration of the Catholic claims' was restricted. Cornwallis took comfort that at least the draft heads of a treaty contained no statement of exclusion; and the article on the Parliamentary oath in fact left the matter inferentially open.[2] But the important point was resolved. Pitt, after much consideration, was now 'inclined most strongly' to Union 'on a Protestant basis'; and 'the leaning of the opinion of the Cabinet' had likewise settled against any other immediate move.[3]

The decision affected two other possibilities. It removed the need to consider treatment of the Irish Dissenters, who might otherwise have been placed – and no doubt vociferously – in an invidious position. The King had already expressed his predictable dislike of any civil relief for them;[4] it could now safely be left for later consideration. And the same applied to a question complementary to these main issues. There had earlier been thought of providing endowments from the state for both the Catholic church and the Dissenting congregations; this idea too was now reserved, privately, for further reflection.[5] So too was an accompanying possibility, this time for the Established Church of Ireland itself: for a commutation – naturally with compensation – of Anglican tithes. The background here, however, was wider, for this

---

1. His stand may have been reinforced by others also present at this time, who however, to differing extents, did not share his enthusiasm for Union itself: by John Beresford, who was only moderately in favour of the latter, and Sir John Parnell (p. 161, n2 above), who was against.

Civil emancipation will be called Emancipation henceforth for convenience.

2. See p. 173 above.

3. See Camden to Castlereagh, endorsed 11 October 1798, and Elliot (also in London now) to same, 24, 27 October 1798, for Pitt's attitude, and the last for developments in general (*Correspondence of Castlereagh*, I, 391, 404, 412); also Canning to Windham, 23 October 1798 (B.L. Add. Ms 37844). Clare himself (unlike Elliot; see *Life and Letters of Sir Gilbert Elliot*, III, 28) seems to have thought Pitt 'decided' against Emancipation as early as 16 October (to Castlereagh of that date; *Correspondence of Castlereagh*, I, 393). Dundas remained throughout strongly in favour of 'a Union on the broadest basis' (William Elliot's phrase on 9 November; loc. cit., 431). Jupp (*Lord Grenville*, 271) places Windham, Spencer and Portland 'almost certainly' in that camp; but the evidence seems to me less conclusive. For Cornwallis's acquiescence see his letter to Major-General Ross of 15 November 1798 (*Correspondence of Cornwallis*, II, 433–4), and also Castlereagh to Camden, Private, 22 October (P.R.O. 30/8/326).

4. George III to Pitt, 13 June 1798 (Holland Rose, *Pitt and Napoleon*, 243).

5. Bolton, op. cit., 90. It was in fact raised again by Castlereagh two months later, but without success (see George III to Pitt, 24 January 1799, Stanhope, III, Appendix, xviii; 'Minute of Cabinet', 2 February [almost certainly 1799], Dacres Adams Mss, formerly P.R.O. 30/58/8, f. 115). Further discussion of the whole package took place in the late summer of 1800; but by then it related to treatment after Union (see Jupp, op. cit., 274–5).

measure was considered with one for England as well, in a context in which the two Establishments would be united.[1] Pitt was certainly considering a plan for England in September, when his sale of the Land Tax had become law; and the sequence was not in fact an unnatural one for him to envisage. He had looked at the situation once before, to no avail; and an unusually favourable chance seemed now to be provided by the combination of change in taxation and the prospect of ecclesiastical fusion. Tithe reform would help further simplify the revenue system in Britain and gratify Catholics and Dissenters in Ireland. He pursued the prospect at home beyond the end of the year, again finally without success; meanwhile the Irish element, like its fellow measures, was temporarily laid on one side.[2]

In November and December the draft proposals accordingly took final shape. They did not do so without some signs of hesitation in London. The conversations with the Irish visitors, and impressions gathered from Dublin direct, had muted the inner circle's earlier show of optimism.[3] Whatever view Ministers might take of policy, they were now aware of the likely obstacles; and their uncertainty was heightened by fresh arrivals of doubters and opponents – Speaker Foster above all.[4] But a persuasive advocate was also at hand, for Portland had asked if Castlereagh could come over, and in the next few weeks the new Chief Secretary was able to help stiffen Ministers' resolve. He was also able to modify the suggestions for Irish representation in the Commons, and with these last improvements matters were brought to the point. On 21 December 1798 the Cabinet approved the principle of Union, together with the shape of the proposals and the arrangements for presenting them to the two Parliaments.[5]

1. See p. 173 above.

2. See notes in Pitt's hand, 30 July 1798 (Stanhope Ms U1590 S5 09/43); Pitt to Pretyman (consulted now as he had been a few years before), 9 September, 24 October 1798 (Pretyman Ms T 108/42, the second printed partly in Ashbourne, op. cit., 340), and also Pretyman to Mrs Pretyman, nd but probably 2 December 1798 (loc. cit., 503: 2); Portland to Pitt, 5 October 1798 (Dacres Adams Mss, formerly P.R.O. 30/58/2); Archbishop of Canterbury to same, 14 December 1798 (Stanhope Ms U1590 S5 06/15); Canning's diary for 15, 17 June 1799 (Canning Ms 29d). Details of the scheme, specifically noted as following on the approval for sale of the Land Tax (for which see pp. 106–7 above) are given in a paper, nd but of this period, in P.R.O. 30/8/310: there are two copies, at ff. 97–115 and 122–39, the second of which is fully annotated by Pitt. The connexion in principle with that sale, for England, is also to be seen in Auckland to John Beresford, 15 April 1798 (*Correspondence of Beresford*, II, 55). Cf. II, 84–5, 469n5 for Pitt's thoughts earlier about commutation, and n1 above for the proposal to unite the two Anglican Churches.

3. Pp. 176–7 above.

4. See p. 176 above for Foster; also in general Elliot to Castlereagh, 4, 23 November 1798 (*Correspondence of Castlereagh*, I, 426, II, 9).

5. See Portland to Cornwallis, 24 December 1798 (*Correspondence of Cornwallis*, II, 53–60). The date of the Cabinet meeting appears in a copy of the Minute printed in Ashbourne, op. cit., 285.

IV

In considering how best to introduce the measure, Pitt and his advisers had again rested on the precedent of the Act with Scotland, when Commissioners from both Kingdoms were appointed by the Crown to introduce a bill for a treaty.[1] For this purpose it would be necessary first to declare the proposed contents, and to secure the consent of the two Parliaments. These steps were taken in January 1799: after publication of the draft proposals early in the month, the King's Speech was read and debated in Dublin on the 22nd, and a King's Message read at Westminster on the following day.[2]

Despite their misgivings in October and November, Ministers in London were reassured on the whole by Castlereagh's confident forecast of success. Pitt and Portland indeed were said to be growing 'sanguine' again even before he arrived.[3] There were less optimistic estimates however,[4] and for Ireland with good reason. For in fact the exercise was launched there with some significant disadvantages. It was not helpful that the Castle itself was divided over Emancipation, to an extent that led one Under Secretary to think of resigning.[5] But there were more extensive drawbacks. Such soundings as had been taken were meant to be private; but Dublin was always riddled with leaks, rumour had been circulating as early as July, and the flow of senior figures to London from the autumn brought speculation to a head. By November the prospect of Union was the talk of the town.[6] There had thus been ample time for people to argue without reliable knowledge – never a good combination – and the effects could be compounded in this instance by inadequate contact with London. For while gossip was flourishing in Ireland, proper consultation was lacking both there and in England until very late in the day. Some leading figures in Dublin were sent questions, and the Castle gauged opinion as best it could. But it was not until Cornwallis was empowered in November to open the business officially that there was any real prospect

1. And cf. p. 173 above. Pelham was now proposed as one of them (Portland to Pelham, 28 November 1798; B.L. Add. Ms 33106).

2. The slightly different procedure, designed to result in simultaneous presentation, was necessitated by different dates for the opening of the respective sessions. Since the British would precede the Irish by more than a month, the King's Speech for the former would not mention the Union, and an adjournment would ensure that debate in the latter was not forestalled.

3. Elliot to Castlereagh, 27 November 1798 (*Correspondence of Castlereagh*, II, 28).

4. Including the King's: '. . . that it [the measure] will not be obtained on either side of water [*sic*] with the ease Mr. Pitt expects, I should fear will prove but too true' (to Pitt, 17 November 1798; Stanhope, III, Appendix, xvii).

5. Elliot to Castlereagh, 23 November 1798 (*Correspondence of Castlereagh*, II, 10); and see also *Life and Letters of Sir Gilbert Elliot*, III, 27, 30.

6. Bolton, op. cit., 69–70. The earliest public reference in England which I have found, in the form of a newspaper report, is on 20 September in *The Morning Chronicle*; followed on 13 October elsewhere, including (with its habitual air of authority) *The Times*.

of testing what might be in store.[1] Nor did British Ministers in point of fact receive much assistance from that quarter. The Lord Lieutenant was occupied of course in the summer as a General by events on the ground; but there was more reason to complain in the autumn that he did not communicate as he should.[2] He was a man of great experience and reputation and good sense; but he was a soldier who respected his orders, he had been told that confidentiality was the order of the day, and he was accustomed more to rule and command than take the views of local politicians whom he mostly disliked.[3] He despatched officials to London from the end of September;[4] but their authority was limited, and could provide no proper substitute for himself. The only person who could do that was Castlereagh; but he was not Chief Secretary until November,[5] and in any case was largely unknown. In the early autumn, when decisions were hardening, Ministers were thus operating from an unsure base.

The inadequacy however was not Dublin's alone. Pitt was not well served by the system there; but at the same time he did not try to impose his authority on it, or indeed consistently on the process at home. He liked usually to work through a small circle once he took up a subject; but he was usually careful then to involve himself also with the relevant Departments. In this instance however he seems to have left Portland alone, as Home Secretary, to a large extent: to have refrained in fact from stepping on ground within the province of a Secretary of State.[6] Nor did he take matters firmly in hand in his own efforts. He was resolved to speed a measure 'which can never be so well accomplished as now'; in October he was said to be 'eager and anxious to the greatest degree'; Ireland was 'the subject on which he contemplates most and is the most uneasy'.[7] But perhaps for that very reason – while he remained uncertain which course to adopt – he seems to have delayed bringing his personal influence and powers of persuasion to bear. Elliot for instance thought that he should

---

1. Eg Camden to Castlereagh, 16 November 1798 (*Correspondence of Castlereagh*, II, 448).

2. Eg Pitt to Grenville, 6 August 1798 (*H.M.C., Dropmore*, IV, 275); Grenville to Buckingham, 5 November 1798 (Buckingham, II 412); Camden to Castlereagh, 16 November 1798 (*Correspondence of Castlereagh*, I, 449). The Grenvilles, thanks largely to Buckingham, were on bad terms with Cornwallis at the time.

Cornwallis's own view of procedure is shown in his letters to Pitt of 1 November and to Portland of the 27th (*Correspondence of Cornwallis*, II, 427, 448).

3. Cf. p. 169 above for Pitt's reservations in this instance about a respected figure on whom he often liked to call.

4. P. 176 above.

5. Pp. 172–3 above.

6. Eg Camden, complaining of Cornwallis's lack of communication, remarked that Pitt 'certainly does not take upon himself any part of that duty . . . It has always been customary for the Secretary of State to be informed of every event by the Lord Lieutenant' (to Castlereagh, 16 November 1798; *Correspondence of Castlereagh*, I, 449). Cf. I, 309–11 for the position of the First Lord of the Treasury vis-à-vis the Secretaries of State, and 324–5 for Pitt's administrative habits.

7. Pitt to Grenville, 6 August 1798 (*H.M.C., Dropmore*, IV, 275); Camden to Castlereagh, endorsed 11 October 1798 (*Correspondence of Castlereagh*, I, 391).

have tackled Parnell – who might have given way – much sooner, and it was on Portland's initiative that Castlereagh was sent for late in the year.[1] Of course, as always, there was other important business; but not in point of fact to an exceptional extent. Ireland was now receiving his high priority, and his health at this point was not a serious impediment. It might perhaps be argued, from the vantage of the future, that a loss of grip here was a portent: of a slackening of Pitt's grasp soon to be suspected increasingly in other areas of policy.[2] In so far however as such a process became evident, it was not evident yet: this was indeed a year in which in many ways he had been showing a feeling for the way ahead.[3] The intention to go for Union, whatever the preparatory shortcomings, was itself a decisive act. One may rather hazard the impression that Ireland was casting its own familiar shadow: that when he tried at intervals to master the question, he never felt at home.

These contingent misfortunes bore significantly on the problems of substance. The proponents of Union were sure of the merits of their case: whether or not Emancipation should be added, there were high gains to be claimed. Most immediately, the measure would strengthen defence of a vulnerable flank in a struggle in which the margin of safety was increasingly small.[4] Ireland was peculiarly open to French influence and threat; but the executive there was faced with an unreliable Parliament capable of being highly awkward, even to the point of cutting military supplies.[5] Legislative unity would bring administrative benefits, achieving a more effective management of combined resources. And such a promise pointed to others of wider and enduring import, and of greatest relative advantage to Ireland herself. For wherever one looked, Union was the key. Pitt took care to put it in the clearest terms.[6]

> I say that Ireland is subject to great and deplorable evils, which have a deep root, for they lie in the situation of the country itself – in the present character, manners and habits of its inhabitants – in their want of intelligence or, in other words, their ignorance – in the unavoidable

1. Elliot to Castlereagh, 28 November 1798 (op. cit., II, 29), and see p. 177, n1 above for Parnell; p. 178 above for Castlereagh's visit.

2. To be discussed particularly in Chs. VIII, XV below.

3. In the financial measures of the spring and summer, the cultivation of the swing in public opinion, the decision to re-enter the Mediterranean, the search for a revived and more solid Alliance.

4. The King's Message to the British Parliament recommending consideration of a Union did so in fact specifically in reference to the enemy's intention of separating the two countries (23 January 1799; *P.R., 3rd ser.*, VII (1799), 577). The point of course was politically a tactical one (cf. George III himself, and Pitt, on pp. 176, 180 above); but it was none the less valid for that.

5. As Grenville warned the Lords (see McDowell, op. cit., 686).

6. Speech of 23 January 1799 in the Commons (*P.H., XXXIV* (1819), cols. 247–8). I have quoted from this version in cols. 242–54, rather than from *P.R.* (*3rd ser.*, VII), because it is the fuller and seems to me to strike a more authentic note.

separation between certain classes – in the state of property – in its religious distinctions – in the rancour which bigotry engenders and superstition rears and cherishes.

Such problems could not 'be cured in a moment'. But could we not 'adopt some plan which may lead to that cure in the course of time?' One beckoned, pointing in every aspect to a shift of responsibility.

> An imperial legislature standing aloof from local party connexion, sufficiently removed from the influence of contending factions . . . That is the thing that is wanted for Ireland.

And its place must be 'Certainly . . . in England', for 'I say also, that much of the evil which Ireland now labours under, arises unavoidably from the condition of the Parliament of that country'.

This was an unequivocal statement. Some two years earlier he had spoken differently. We had granted independence to an Irish Parliament in 1782: could we then say that that Assembly was 'not qualified to act for the good of the people of Ireland?'[1] In 1799 it seemed that we could: the arrangement had 'been found incompetent to the blessings it was intended to convey'.[2] The argument was also comprehensive. It embraced 'the understanding of the people of Ireland', the improvement of their industry and trade by less illiberal treatment, their better absorption in fact in the blessings of the British polity. The same might perhaps apply moreover to the sectarian question, but in that case later; for if it was tackled now Emancipation would surely not pass through an Irish Parliament, or, in a context confined to Ireland, succeed in 'annihilating religious animosity'.[3] Union again was required first. In short, it was essential for all these purposes. 'I say it is upon this, and this only, that the happiness of the people of that country depends'.[4]

Pitt never expressed more forcefully than in this instance the primacy accorded to Parliament's role, the capacity of the Constitution to set the scene – to provide the climate – for social and economic ends,[5] the superiority assumed for things British over things Irish, and – with a personal emphasis – the contempt in which Irish politics were held. It was indeed an expression of faith. But many in Ireland pledged their faith differently. For them, their Parliament was the guarantor of their degree of independence: certainly a 'distinctness' that stood in balance with an 'inseparable annexation to Great Britain',[6] but one that by definition excluded

1. Speech of 23 March 1797 (op. cit., XXXIII (1818), col. 161).
2. 23 January 1799 (op. cit., XXXIV, col. 249).
3. Speech of 11 February 1799 (*P.R., 3rd ser.*, VIII (1799), 8).
4. Speech of 23 January (*P.H..*, XXXIV, col. 249).
5. Themselves attainable, and limited, always precisely by its recognition and adjustment of natural economic laws; cf. II, 154–5.
6. Cf. p. 171 above.

Union itself. 'God and Nature . . . never intended Ireland to be a province'; her legislature should be 'distinct, national, resident'.[1] It was this belief, which could be held with passion, that lay at the heart of the resistance to the British case; an element stronger even than the sectarian, or commercial or financial fears, or doubts about the exact extent and nature of a changed representation. 'We must stand or fall together', Pitt declared.[2] Opponents of Union would not necessarily disagree: rather, they drew a contrary conclusion as to means. The Parliament in Dublin, as currently constituted, was central to their concept of identity. That fact was critical in defining responses in detail to specific proposals as the individual combinations of principle and self-interest might dictate.

When the new year dawned, Ministers in London rated the chances of success quite high. So did a range of opinion in Dublin on which perforce they drew. But confidence there in some informed quarters was less firm than could have been wished, and in point of fact signs of strong recalcitrance had been mounting in the past month. The atmosphere in Irish political circles had soured since Cornwallis arrived; his taciturnity and lack of attention to those accustomed to a ready hearing, his comparative leniency to rebels, his known predilection for Catholic relief, soon raised him a host of enemies in and around the Castle and within the Protestant interest at large. Temperamental impediments played their part. It might not matter too much that the Lord Lieutenant was not on speaking terms with Buckingham, one of his predecessors, the senior Grenville and now in the country with his militia regiment:[3] that intensely touchy nobleman was an irritant rather than a danger. It was more serious that personal antipathy could deepen the difference on policy with the influential Speaker, Foster, that supporters had not been rallied fully and waverers closely cajoled.[4] The Castle in fact was ill prepared for such cultivation: both Cornwallis and Castlereagh conspicuously lacked the touch. Perhaps things might have gone somewhat better if Pelham could have been there. As it was, while the young Chief Secretary set to work from December with, he thought, some success, politicians of various sizes had not been effectively wooed.

In this limbo of uncertainty, with many members of both Houses waiting on developments, strong and vocal pressures were forming from outside. The lawyers and then the merchants of Dublin, in well attended meetings, passed anti-Unionist resolutions, the former by a large majority, the latter *nem. con.* Provincial opinions were harder to come by, and the

---

1. For quotations and argument see Bolton, op. cit., 79–80; McDowell, op. cit., 688.
2. Speech of 23 January 1799 (*P.H.*, XXXIV, col. 250).
3. P. 125 above; and cf. I, 43 for his position as the eldest brother.
4. John Foster, normally one of the strongest props of the Administration, had long been widely respected in an impressive career – as a practical agriculturalist, an expert on economic subjects, a Chancellor of the Exchequer, a Parliamentary manager.

capital continued to make the running: a flush of pamphlets appeared, some selling in large numbers, and newspapers were set to work. The Castle tried to strike back and demonstrate its firmness: one of the barristers' leaders was deprived of his legal patent of precedence and dismissed from the Yeomanry, and Cornwallis dismissed the Chancellor of the Exchequer, Parnell, who had finally decided to oppose.[1] But amid the signs of hostility the forecasts were still of success. On the eve of the new session Castlereagh estimated a majority of about seventy.[2]

The Lord Lieutenant opened Parliament on the afternoon of 22 January 1799. His Speech did not specify a bill for Union as such. It expressed the hope that 'the Parliaments in both Kingdoms' would 'provide the most effectual means of maintaining and improving a connexion essential to their common security, and of consolidating, as far as possible into one firm and lasting fabrick, the strength, the power, and the resources of the British Empire.'[3] The debate on the Address in the Commons lasted until the following noon, centring on an amendment to provide for the maintenance of 'a resident and independent legislature, such as it was recognized by the British Legislature in 1782'.[4] It was an occasion full of drama; of high oratory, anger and excitement – 'you would have thought', one Member remarked, 'that you were in a Polish diet.'[5] When the vote was taken in an exhausted House, the amendment was defeated by 106 to 105.[6]

Such a victory was a defeat. As John Beresford remarked, 'with a majority of one, it was impossible to proceed'.[7] Castlereagh announced at once that he would not press a measure while the House felt as it did. But the Administration was not allowed to leave it at that. Following the vote on the amendment, the offending clause in the Address itself was pressed to a division, and opposed successfully by 107 to 105. The next day the anti-Unionists moved for its deletion, carrying the vote by 109 to 104. This was outright defeat for the Castle – a phenomenon unknown since the Regency crisis ten years before.[8] Dublin was illuminated that night, and Lord Chancellor Clare's unlit windows were broken.

On 23 January the Parliamentary session resumed at Westminster, and

1. Both in mid January 1799; see *L.C.G. III*, III, no. 1904 for William Saurin – who eight years later became Attorney General of Ireland – and Bolton, op. cit., 103 for Parnell. The Castle however refrained from taking steps against four senior officials, two of whom in point of fact very soon resigned.

2. Bolton, op. cit., ch. VI and particularly 104–5 for that and other estimates in the first three weeks of January; and see *A.C.*, IV, 75–8.

3. Bolton, op. cit., 105. The mover of the Address in reply was indeed careful to stress that the Speech did not demand or the proposed Address involve a pledge for a specific measure (op. cit., 106).

4. See op. cit., 107.

5. *Correspondence of Beresford*, II, 194.

6. Two amendments in the Lords were meanwhile easily defeated.

7. To Auckland, 24 January 1799 (*Correspondence of Beresford*, II, 195).

8. See I, 663. Division numbers exclude the tellers.

the debate on the Address considered the King's Message on Ireland.[1] Opposition's attack was entrusted, appropriately, to Sheridan; his orations then and on the 31st, acknowledged to be brilliant, had to contend with Pitt's replies, the second of which in particular was held to be as great a speech as he had ever made.[2] The result in any case was not in doubt: Sheridan's amendment on the Address did not reach a division, and the vote on the 31st for considering the Message further was carried by 140 to 15. The majorities held in debates in February – 141 to 25, 149 to 24; and these moderate numbers in fact reflected the limits of interest. While the debates contained long and thoughtful and sometimes forceful contributions, there was never any serious question but that in England the measure would pass.[3]

The continuation of these debates was significant not only for their contents. It demonstrated Pitt's resolve not to drop the matter on the Castle's defeat. 'Be they [those proceedings] what they may', he wrote, 'they can only make it more necessary to open fully and state decidedly our plan'.[4] He did precisely that, and, assured of convincing support, proceeded to the point in April of securing consent to detailed Resolutions for an Act once the Irish Parliament had likewise approved.[5] His spirit in fact was roused. He was not going to be blocked by a rebuff in Dublin, and he encouraged every means of seeing the business through.

The struggle was accordingly resumed in Ireland. Both sides mustered their arguments and forces. As the months went by the anti-Unionists became increasingly hard pressed. Their very diversity indeed,

---

1. See p. 179 and n2 above.

2. Eg for the 31st Auckland to Beresford, 2 February – it 'surpassed . . . perhaps, even any former exhibition of parliamentary eloquence' (*A.C.*, IV, 87); *The True Briton* and *The Morning Post*, sd. Sheridan and Pitt were both reported, most unusually, *verbatim*, and according to Buckingham the effect produced by the Minister on Dublin itself was 'beyond all expectation' (to Grenville, 8 February 1799; *H.M.C., Dropmore*, IV, 469). Old Lady Chatham, down at Burton Pynsent, received glowing reports (see Pitt to Hester Lady Chatham, 9 February 1799; P.R.O. 30/8/12); cf. Vorontsov to Grenville, 1 February (*H.M.C., Dropmore*, IV, 461). The delivery may have been less impressive than the content: according to a listener who had not heard Pitt before, 'there was gout in it' (see *Correspondence of Beresford*, II, 207); and indeed on the 23rd his voice was said to have broken after ten minutes, becoming 'shrill, hoarse, and irregular', which he corrected by speaking lower to regain 'a more firm and stronger sound' (*The Morning Post*, 24 January 1799; and see also *Life and Letters of Sir Gilbert Elliot*, II, 48).

Some undated brief notes for a speech on Ireland may be found in the Dacres Adams Mss, formerly P.R.O. 30/58/8 at ff. 112–14.

3. See *P.R., 3rd ser.*, VII, 577–743, VIII, 1–4, 42–111, 187–95; *P.H.*, XXXIV, cols. 208–515.

4. To Grenville, 28 January (*H.M.C., Dropmore*, IV, 458). And cf. Rose to Pretyman, sd (Pretyman Ms 435/44).

5. See *P.R., 3rd ser.*, VIII, 482–542, 544; *P.H.*, XXXIV, cols. 657–988. This procedure replaced the earlier suggestion of a treaty to be prepared by Commissioners in accordance with the Parliaments' proposals (pp. 170, 179 above).

A Cabinet was held, after the Commons' debates in January, at which the main lines of Ministerial agreement on policy were confirmed (Minute, nd but endorsed 2 February; Dacres Adams Mss, formerly P.R.O. 30/58/8, f. 115).

so impressive in the opening debates, placed their continuing effectiveness at growing risk. The issue had brought together some unaccustomed allies: strong anti-Catholic Protestants found themselves acting with the Grattan Whigs. It was also fed by arguments which could tactically be mustered together but in their essence were mutually opposed. Some anti-Unionists supported the commercial proposals but held – not unreasonably – that those did not require Union. Others by contrast saw a threat to an indigenous system that was providing its own distinct benefits. They pointed to a decade and more of healthy exports, agricultural and industrial, which might now be upset by excessive competition; and such a change could heighten the undesirable case for a single kingdom by destroying the framework for continuing 'distinctness'. This last approach struck a strong chord; for one must remember that if Ireland was poorer than England, if her backwardness in parts was deeper, and there were underlying difficulties which later developments would expose, the economy in aggregate was nonetheless buoyant, and seemed capable of recovering from the recent sharp depression which – as in England in 1795 – fused economic troubles with political unrest.[1] This was not the scene, to be so vividly imprinted in due course, of the still distant post-war and Famine years. While rebellion and external danger could confirm the Unionist side in its arguments, they did not convince opponents of the need to abandon, within the 'inseparable annexation' to Britain, responsibility for the discussion and legislation of their own affairs.[2]

The various lines of opposition could be confronted alike on financial, economic and strategic grounds. A more strictly political weakness was exemplified in other ways. For while the controversy was a genuine controversy, invoking real principles and evoking real passions, the outcome was assisted by less elevated means. It was of course normal, on either side of the Irish Sea, for Government to use its resources to gain its way: there was the less disinclination to do so, in this weighty issue, because Irish politicians were held in London to be venal by British standards. As early as November 1798 Pitt had mentioned the prospect of a reward – a peerage and sinecure – for Foster if he became more amenable; after the failure in January he was said to be prepared to wait until 'people' came 'a little to their Senses, . . . with the Assistance of a little *quiet* Coercion if it should be necessary'.[3] Cornwallis and Castlereagh entered on the

---

1. P. 160 above, by comparison with Pitt's argument on p. 182. For England in 1795 see II, Ch. XII.

2. Eg Clare, nd but the second half of 1798: 'I have long been of opinion that nothing short of [Union] can save this country' (quoted in Ashbourne, op. cit., 266); for anti-Unionist emphasis on the 'common interest' of the two distinct countries see quotation in R.B. McDowell, *Irish Public Opinion 1750–1800* (1944), 254–5.

3. Pitt to Cornwallis, 17 November 1798 (*Correspondence of Cornwallis*, II, 440); Rose to Pretyman, 28 January 1799 (Pretyman Ms 435/44). The Cabinet on 21 December 1798 stated that 'the conduct of individuals on this subject [Union] will be considered as the test of the disposition to support the King's Government' (Ashbourne, op. cit., 285).

process, the former with distaste – 'an occupation . . . of the most unpleasant nature, negotiating and jobbing with the most corrupt people under
heaven' – the latter with a steely and contemptuous sense of duty 'to buy
out and secure to the Crown for ever the fee-simple of Irish corruption'.[1]
The efforts were attacked at the time and later as the channel by which the
measure was carried; and indeed Castlereagh himself remarked on 'what
has been promised, and by what means the Union has been secured'.[2]
Grattan was fond of saying that only seven at most of the Castle's
supporters had not been bribed by the end; and the tradition endured.

> How did they pass the Union?
> By perjury and fraud;
> By slaves who sold their land for gold
> As Judas sold his God.
> . . . And thus was passed the Union
> By Pitt and Castlereagh . . .[3]

Historians more recently have chipped away at – some virtually dismissed – this charge. Corruption does not exist in a void. It has its
meaning in relation to what it distorts: in this instance the patronage
system which was the cement of public life. The methods employed in this
case were a combination of appointments and pensions, peerage creations and promotions, financial compensation for proprietors of
Parliamentary boroughs which the Castle wished to secure or, later, see
suppressed. They were undertaken on the scale necessary: £1½ million
was spent on the eventual abolition of boroughs; Cornwallis's successor
found his patronage mortgaged in unusual degree; in the six months from
July 1800 to January 1801 thirteen new Irish peerages, four Irish promotions, and four British peerages for Irish peers were granted directly in
connexion with the passage of the measure.[4] These last figures were
exceptional in that they were not related to a general election, and they
exceeded the highest known then – eighteen Irish creations and four promotions in 1776, fifteen such creations twenty years later. They were such

1. Cornwallis to Ross, 8 June 1799 (*Correspondence of Cornwallis*, III (1859), 102);
Castlereagh to Edward Cooke (see p. 161, n2 above), 21 June 1800 (*Correspondence of
Castlereagh*, III (1849), 335).
2. Referring specifically to peerages; to Cooke as in n1 above.
3. Quoted respectively in H.M. Hyde, *The Rise of Castlereagh* (1933), 365, and Bolton, op.
cit., 51. Lecky himself, in his great *History of England in the Eighteenth Century*, V (1892), ch.
XIII, subscribed to a more measured expression of the tradition.
4. I put it like this on my reading of others' more expert interpretations of evidence.
There were in fact 45 creations and promotions in all in the Irish peerage in those months.
But some were granted, in the familiar way, to Englishmen whom it was not intended to
admit to the British House of Lords, and others were not connected directly, or others
again predominantly, with this occasion. My figures have been drawn from *GEC*, III,
Appendix H, *L.C.G. III*, III, no. 2315, and Bolton, op. cit., chs. IV–V, particularly 101, 153,
205.

indeed that British Ministers had belated qualms over what had been promised.[1] These various forms of persuasion might therefore seem to support the old charge.

A closer look helps set the various parts of the package in context. Vacant places, and pensions, went to Unionist supporters, not 'converted' opponents:[2] a practice familiar and normal in itself. The offence here indeed, as claimed by a subsequent Administration, was that posts were filled and treated in such a way that it limited its own freedom of action. Compensation to borough owners was likewise tolerable in principle: it was or could be held to be in aid of a reforming as well as a tactical exercise[3] – an analogous proposal indeed had figured in Pitt's own bill of 1785 for Parliamentary reform[4] –, and to be a permissible instrument in a situation in which political, like other kinds of property, was widely seen as a marketable investment. The peerages for their part did not go to avowed early opponents – few of whom indeed changed their minds throughout[5] – but, as was usual, to friendly or uncommitted patrons and Members for services rendered. Such practices therefore, it has been argued, were perfectly defensible. Their scale may have been distasteful, but in principle they did not transgress accepted norms.

The line is a shadowy one. In the first place the number of waverers was large – there were 82 abstentions in the decisive debate in January 1799 – leaving a notably extensive area for manoeuvre.[6] And the norms themselves moreover were not rigid or static. Some appointments, to take one area, were subject to legal regulations; but the latter in themselves did not deny competing interests, and in the whole wide range of influence acceptance turned on interpretation. Patronage, 'not itself by definition corrupt' – in fact the only 'way of doing things' – was moved by 'an ethos';[7] and Irish practices were agreed to be traditionally laxer than English, within the parameters broadly common to both. Bearing this in mind, it may be hard to maintain that Cornwallis and Castlereagh broke

1. Portland attempted in fact at the last minute to quash some of the Lord Lieutenant's recommendations, which he feared the King would dislike. But he soon had to comply almost entirely (see Bolton, op. cit., 206–7).

In the first of these earlier elections, a few of the creations again did not relate directly to the convenient occasion itself.

2. Nor, apart from Parnell, who was a Minister, were hostile office-holders in the Castle dismissed (p. 184, n1 above): unlike the experiences of the Fitzwilliam affair in 1795 and, more marginally, the Regency crisis in 1789. Cf. I, 179 & n1 for views of wholesale dismissals in England.

3. Cf. Castlereagh's remark on p. 187 above.

4. See I, 226–7; in that instance it was the electors in the boroughs concerned who would have been compensated.

5. Bolton has calculated that only twelve of those who voted against Union in 1799 voted for it finally in 1800 (op. cit., 169).

6. Nor am I so sure, despite Bolton, op. cit., 181, that Secret Service money – of which he seems to disapprove – was not used in some form as well. See Portland to Pitt, 11 April 1800 (Dacres Adams Mss, formerly P.R.O. 30/58/3).

7. See J.M. Bourne, *Patronage and Society in Nineteenth-Century England* (1986), 8.

the conventions. We might well say rather that in the terms of place and time they strained them to the limits.

But what in the end did the effort amount to? However one views the operations, did they in fact achieve the object by themselves? For this after all was the crux of the charge: that the exercise was not only illegitimate, but decided an outcome that might otherwise not have been attained. Again, a closer look suggests that the position was not so simple: that the passing of the Union resulted rather from a combination of factors.[1] Even fully deployed indeed, the Castle's resources were not overwhelming; nor were Irish politicians wholly amenable on their own customary premisses. Their very reputation for venality rested on their cheerful assumption of a bargain; and on such an issue the bargaining did not necessarily ignore the feelings in the districts from which they came. In the campaign for Union both sides constantly took pains to appeal to the country: through the press and literature – the Castle for its part acted as a sponsor, and on the other side of the water Pitt himself was said to have approved a treatise –[2], and perhaps more to the point, in eliciting addresses, resolutions and petitions which should not always themselves be entirely dismissed. Much of course was a charade. After a generally slow start, Government and its supporters went to work: meetings were held throughout the country, the Lord Lieutenant toured Ulster and the south, and by the autumn of 1799 the tide was on the turn. By the end of the year an Under Secretary could claim that in petitions 'we have a fine superiority of surface'.[3] Nonetheless the expressions of opinion were by no means always induced or imposed, and they would seem to have exerted their own influence in turn. Ireland, like England, was a patchwork of interests, very largely given local flavour within a polity less highly integrated than that of England itself.[4] When they are examined, it appears superficial to isolate corruption or exaggerate its strength. If Parliamentarians were under exceptional pressures from the Castle in this exceptional matter, it was likewise one in which they could not wholly ignore their countrymen's views.

As it mobilised support, there were two broad regions in which Government had to tread vigorously but carefully. Much of its eventual success came from the Catholic areas of the south and west. By the end of 1799 in fact this seemed likely to be so, for the ecclesiastical authorities there and a sizeable part of the Papist gentry – not an insignificant body – had settled decidedly in the Unionist camp. One of the encouragements – though by no means the only one, for their Unionism was linked with

1. Cf. Bolton, op. cit., 119, and chs. IV–V *passim*.
2. By Sylvester Douglas, a former Chief Secretary in Ireland (see II, 407, 473); *Life and Letters of Sir Gilbert Elliot*, III, 29. See in general Bolton, op. cit., 76–7, and McDowell, *Irish Public Opinion*, ch. XIII and 287–91.
3. Edward Cooke to Auckland, 6 December 1799 (B.L. Add. Ms 34455).
4. Cf. II, 100.

fear of 'French influence' – was the feeling that the measure could bring Emancipation in its wake; and certainly the rumoured predilections of Cornwallis and a party in the Castle, and Pitt's words in the Westminster debates, were unlikely to discourage such hopes.[1] Ministers in London were kept well aware of the region's importance in the campaign; and the knowledge had its effect on the sensitive problem that remained unresolved. The expediency which had earlier led them in one direction now pointed them in another:[2] how far could they go in holding out prospects of final relief? They trod the tightrope as delicately, but they hoped firmly, as the pressures dictated and allowed. In February 1799 they learned of plans by the Irish Opposition to move such a measure.

> I should hope, [wrote Portland] . . . that it will not be found impossible to satisfy every reasonable Roman Catholic and man of property of that persuasion that such an attempt could not be made in the present circumstances without the most imminent danger . . .

but also

> that a Union is as indispensably necessary for the purpose of affording them a reasonable probability of being admitted to a full participation of rights in common with the Protestants, as it is to remove and quiet those apprehensions which are at present entertained of them on account of the superiority of their numbers.[3]

That did not seem to have much effect, and in so far as broad categories could be drawn, the Catholics in general seemed to be neutral over the next few months. But when many seemed to be veering towards the Union in the latter part of the year, the Castle became anxious to clarify its position. Cornwallis himself would have liked to be able to hold out a definite assurance: he doubted if the measure would pass without Catholic support, and the Cabinet, apparently at several meetings, 'mooted' the possibility of 'pledging' itself to relief.[4] This, it has been stated, was in August and September,[5] and the Lord Lieutenant

1. See pp. 175, 181–2 above.
2. Cf. pp. 175–7 above.
3. To Cornwallis, 3 February 1799 (quoted in Bolton, op. cit., 154). At the Cabinet meeting the day before (p. 185, n5 above), it was decided to give 'no different pledge on the subject of Union from that already given by Lord Castlereagh'. Meanwhile 'the Catholic Question' would be 'opposed'.
4. According at any rate to Camden's account, nd but at least two years later from memory (Camden Mss U840 O127).
5. The dating is Jupp's (*Lord Grenville*, 275, citing Windham's diary), and the talks also included revived consideration of state endowments for the Catholics and the Dissenters (see p. 177 above), which had been given evasive treatment at the meeting in February (n3 above).

approached Ministers again through a visit by Castlereagh which began in the latter month. At some time in his prolonged stay through the autumn, and probably in November, the Chief Secretary attended a Cabinet meeting or meetings at which the knotty question was again discussed. By a unanimous decision of those present, as he himself recalled, the Lord Lieutenant was then authorised to state

> that the opinion of the Cabinet was favourable to the principle of the Measure, that some doubts were entertained as to the possibility of admitting Catholics into some of the *Higher Offices*, and that Ministers anticipated considerable repugnance to the Measure in many Quarters, and particularly in the *Highest*; but that, as far as the sentiments of the Cabinet were concerned, His Excellency need not hesitate in calling forth the Catholic Support in whatever degree he found it practicable to obtain it.

This was for guidance: 'it was not thought expedient at that time to give any direct assurance to the Catholics'; 'but . . . should circumstances so far alter as to induce His Excellency to consider such an explanation necessary, he was at liberty to state the grounds on which his opinion was formed for the consideration of the Cabinet.'[1] Cornwallis accepted the judgment when Castlereagh returned. 'I have no doubt', he wrote, 'of the wisdom of . . . avoiding all engagements until the business shall be completed'.[2]

---

1. Castlereagh to Pitt, 1 January 1801 (P.R.O. 30/8/327; published in *Correspondence of Castlereagh*, IV (1849), 8–12). A letter in similar terms from Castlereagh to Cornwallis, of 9 February 1801, is also in P.R.O. 30/8/327.

The Chief Secretary mentioned one meeting; Camden, writing on the same event in categorical terms though also not before 1801 (see p. 190, n4 above), mentions two, both of which Castlereagh was said to have attended. The accounts however are identical in substance, and Camden, like Castlereagh, ascribes the decision to 'all the King's Servants' present.

It is hard to pin down the date. Castlereagh was in England from the first half of September until early in December. It has sometimes been stated that the meeting took place at or just before the start of the Parliamentary session, which began on 24 September; and one was indeed reported for the 23rd, at which the King's Speech was said to have been read. But according to Camden there were two meetings on successive days in November, at which the formula was reached. A report in *The Times* of 18 November refers to two 'Cabinet Councils' on the 16th and 17th (the latter being a Sunday), the former mentioned specifically as being – though not exclusively – on Irish affairs. But there was a spate of, allegedly, Cabinet meetings throughout the autumn.

Ireland was certainly occupying attention in one way and another over these months. Castlereagh was not the only visitor. Clare, Edward Cooke, and John Beresford among others were in England, seeing Pitt and some attending a meeting held under Auckland's auspices.

2. To Portland, 9 December 1799 (*Correspondence of Cornwallis*, III, 149). He qualified his compliance however with the proviso that 'nothing' else in that time should have led the Catholics 'to alter the present impression' (Castlereagh to Pitt, 11 December 1799; Dacres Adams Mss, formerly P.R.O. 30/58/2).

There was one likely reason for Ministers to have decided as they did, besides the wish to conciliate a vote. As a former Chief Secretary observed to Pitt a little later, the Fitzwilliam affair had been bedevilled largely by misunderstanding, and it would be only prudent, particularly since 'expectations . . . seem now to be indulged', to apprise the Lord Lieutenant privately of 'your real sentiments' while avoiding 'a public or . . . official declaration'.[1] Matters in point of fact had been taken beyond that: 'the Cabinet' had expressed a 'unanimous' sentiment.[2] Ministers took care to guard their flank, and to preserve their immediate position. Some at least must have been content that they had gone this far.

The process of inducement, in all these ways, went on throughout 1799.[3] The Castle was leaving no doubt that it meant business: one prominent boroughmonger was even removed from his military and civil posts.[4] Its morale had recovered by the spring with a run of majorities in Parliament on a range of questions, and when the next session opened on 15 January 1800 it secured a victory in the Commons on an amendment to the Address.[5] The temperature rose for a time again. The battle of petitions revived, anti-Unionist funds were raised afresh, handbills proliferated on the walls of Dublin. On 5 February there was a debate on a Message recommending Union, which Government won in the Commons by 158 to

1. Lord Hobart [see II, 221–2 above] to Pitt, 2 November 1799 (P.R.O. 30/8/328). Five months earlier he had married Eleanor Eden (see Ch. III, section I above).

2. Castlereagh had also used that phrase in an earlier letter on the subject (to Pitt, 11 December 1799, as in p. 191, n2 above).
But who was there? I have found no record of attendance for the dates suggested. In view of his later behaviour (Ch. XV below) it would be interesting to know if the Lord Chancellor, Loughborough, was present. If the meeting took place on 23 September (see p. 191, n1 above) it is possible that he was not, though he was reported as leaving Weymouth, where he had been with the King, the day before. There is silence too for the meetings in November. Camden later noted in his account that no Minute was taken then: not that a Minute would seem to have been at all appropriate in such a case – see I, 629 for customary procedure. But the confidentiality which he was obviously stressing would have been the greater if Loughborough had been absent, and unable to pass on the result to George III.

3. It may have been in this year that regular confidential meetings began to take place between British and Irish Privy Councillors, possibly four from each kingdom with Pitt and Portland in addition, to 'settle' the articles for Union. Evidence, as was apparently intended, is hard to come by; according to Sylvester Douglas – who was not himself involved, but as a fairly recent Chief Secretary in Ireland may have known something of what was going on – Pitt refused to allow Minutes to be recorded of the 'proceedings', or the meetings to be regarded as those of 'a committee of council' (*Glenbervie*, I, 337, 391–2).

4. '. . . that proud Leviathan, Lord Downshire'. Long courted, by Pitt among others, and abstaining from an early vote, he moved into opposition late in 1799 and early in 1800 led his militia regiment in a hostile petition. He was reckoned to control eight Commons' seats.

5. On the morning of the 16th by 138 votes to 96, after 'one of the fiercest [debates] ever heard in a legislative assembly' (Lecky, *History of England in the Eighteenth Century*, V, 346).

115.[1] Even so, the majority was less than forecast, and the fight went on in the next two months.[2] But after a motion for a dissolution of Parliament was lost on 13 March by 150 to 104, the anti-Unionists saw clearly the writing on the wall. The steam appeared by then to have gone out of the renewed public demonstrations, and the Castle moved to the final attack. Castlereagh carried a series of resolutions and introductory bills to the main measure, culminating in May in the bill for Union itself. It passed through the Commons on 7 June, and through the Lords six days later, and on 1 August the two Irish Houses assembled in their Palladian edifice to hear the Lord Lieutenant give the Royal Assent which closed the session and their own life.[3]

The opponents had secured some gains on the way. Protection on some textiles was extended, by progressive reductions within the period allowed earlier,[4] and the peerage was assured of continuing creations by settling its upper limit at the numbers extant when the Union became law.[5] These concessions suggested once more that the Castle could not simply bull-doze its way through. So too did the final form of the arrangements for the Commons' representation at Westminster. After much thought and bargaining, it was settled that the 100 Members should represent 66 con-stituencies: two each for 32 counties, two each for the boroughs of Dublin and Cork, one each for 31 boroughs, and one for the University of Dublin. Compensation for amalgamated boroughs, set at two-thirds the value of their computed interest, would reduce the numbers immediately to 105, with the remaining reduction to come from further purchase. Negotiations were close and laborious, but in April 1800 it was agreed that the surviving constituencies would be selected according to size of populations, themselves to be calculated from the tax (basically the hearth money) returns.

In the spring all seemed clear for the British Government likewise to press ahead. It did so in April, without excessive trouble. The debates, from early in that month to early May, were sometimes long, and

---

1. The majority in the Lords being 75 to 26. The Irish Speech from the Throne had again (cf. p. 184 above) not itself mentioned the subject of Union, the idea being that it would be introduced three weeks later. But the Address was then opposed in the Commons by an amendment on the same lines as the year before.

The Commons' division on 5 February was the largest ever recorded.

2. Castlereagh had expected a majority of 80 on one debate in January (to Pitt, 16 January 1800; P.R.O. 30/8/327). Cornwallis confessed even at the end of March that much of the support remained unwilling (to Pitt, 31 March 1800, and see also 7 April; Dacres Adams Mss, formerly P.R.O. 30/58/3).

3. The majorities in the Commons varied with the question: they did not fall below 40, and in the closing stages on the main bill were in the upper 50s and lower 60s.

The Act of Union was 40 Geo. III, c23 in the Irish series.

4. See p. 186 above. Castlereagh was forced to admit the need to give way here (to Pitt, 20 February 1800; P.R.O. 30/8/327).

5. This was a matter which Cornwallis himself was particularly anxious to settle (to Pitt, 7 April 1800; Dacres Adams Mss, formerly P.R.O. 30/58/3).

progressively more detailed; but they did not pose a challenge. The majorities were substantial, Opposition managing only once to avoid crushing defeats.[1] On 2 July the bill received the Royal Assent.[2]

The Act for the Union of Great Britain and Ireland was to come into force on 1 January 1801. Preparations now went ahead. The royal style had to be altered, with new Seals, Great and Privy, altered documents and a new flag – the Union Jack as we know it, reflecting the determination to change as little as possible and thereby abandoning the last pretensions to aesthetic design, greeted the century over which it would preside.[3] The two Houses at Westminster had themselves to be adapted. James Wyatt, as Surveyor General of the Office of Works, found extra space for the Commons by cutting into the walls of St Stephen's Chapel and providing a further row for Members on either side. He also fitted up the Court of Requests – the old Little Hall of the Norman Palace, a space now used residually for some legal processes – as a Chamber for the Lords.[4] There was indeed some uneasiness about the physical effects on business: the retired Clerk of the Commons, John Hatsell, expected an awkward increase and a lack of committee rooms. A certain interest stirred in London as the date for the event approached. 'On the 31st of December next', the public was solemnly informed, 'the whole existing fabric of our Government dissolves'.[5] The King and Queen inspected the altered Chambers;[6] the new session was announced for 22 January; and on that day 'the Imperial Parliament' met.[7] It did so however only to swear in new Members and elect a Speaker, for the King's Speech was suddenly postponed. And when that was read eleven days later, a changed Ministry as well as legislature, itself thrown up from the course of the Union, was about to start its life.

1. And that was on a commercial question, when it achieved a minority of 58 against 133. Other figures were 30 (to 286), 34 (to 176), 28 (to 208). See *P.R., 3rd ser.*, XI (1800), 159–72, 216–17, 247–58, 261–305, 311–22, 339–426, 430–82, 485–520, 523–34, 537–68, 586–9, *P.H.*, XXXV (1819), cols. 25–6, 37–198, for the debates. Pitt's speeches on 21 April purport in *P.R.* to be given verbatim.

2. 40 Geo. III, c67.

3. As happened a hundred years later, there was in point of fact a dispute as to when the new century began. One newspaper for instance greeted 1800, correctly, as the last year of the eighteenth century (*The Morning Chronicle*, 1 January).

4. Cf. I, 27.

5. *The Morning Chronicle*, 6 November 1800.

6. Op. cit., 11 November. They were said to be particularly pleased by 'the beef-steak kitchen and establishment of Mr. BELLAMY', which was adjacent to the Court of Requests (see I, 27).

7. So termed in the Proclamation of 8 November 1800 for its assembly.

Part Two

CHAPTER VII

The Opening of the Second Coalition

I

T he turn of the year in 1798–9 might be termed a time of preparation in London. The attempt at union with Ireland (as it turned
out, the first) was about to be launched. The search for a second
Allied Coalition was actively under way. And Pitt, working on his budget
for a seventh year of war, was assembling the case for a major step in his
recently altered system of taxation.[1]

These varied efforts did not lack boldness. They could not be called the
products of unforced purpose, as some of Pitt's peacetime reforms had
been. They responded to harsh pressures. But they were constructive in
themselves. In the Irish issue, Ministers compromised on Catholic
Emancipation; but 'the great point' of union itself[2] was grasped and
would be vigorously carried through. The new scheme of wartime taxation had had to respect political limits; but it marked a change of principle, and Pitt was now prepared to take the method farther. And if the
Government was frustrated in its aim of a Grand Alliance, in which
members' claims were agreed in advance and guaranteed for the future, it
was pursuing once more a nexus of firmly related connexions on which
reviving British hopes of a strategic offensive might rest.[3]

That pursuit was proving tortuous. For the conditions were mixed.
Fresh French aggressions, proclaimed specifically in the service of revolution, were rousing fears and resentments, the latter now emboldened
perhaps by Nelson's victory, which might bring former European partners
together. But whether either factor – the seizures or the ideology – would
suffice as a catalyst was not as certain as many in England, rejoicing at the
victory, assumed.[4] The greater Continental Powers did not act on anti-
revolutionary sentiments alone, or at times predominantly; and while the
movements of French armies always spelt danger, the prime scourge
Bonaparte was stranded overseas. In that respect indeed the battle of the
Nile was scarcely a stimulant in western capitals, moved as they were by

---

1. For which see Chs. VI section III, V section III, p. 109 above.
2. P. 171, n5 above.
3. See pp. 134–5 above.
4. Cf. pp. 131–2, 150 above.

197

postulates of territory and status which might be subsumed but would not disappear. French ambitions themselves were an integral feature of a traditional European pattern; and if their latest form was revolutionary the geographical aims were as familiar as were the equally tenacious interests of other states. The relationships of Austria and Prussia, of Russia and her various neighbours, the repercussions on the smaller entities in an historically intricate map, were not refashioned simply or equally by a common fear.

These facts of life were exemplified in the last quarter of 1798. None of the major European Powers, watching the French and one another, felt free to follow a consistent policy; nor was any of them consistently anxious to establish too close a connexion with Britain, a Power which might yield financial aid but within a framework distinct from theirs. The reading of the national interest in London was likewise producing its uncertainties, in which hopes and reservations were as yet markedly unresolved. And these were now underlined by the latest turn in the fluctuating talks, for the Russian proposal of a new bilateral alliance received in August 1798 pointed a range of possibilities in a shifting scene.[1] On the one hand the Tsar, now personally involved, seemed better placed than the British themselves to bring a wider combination into being from a position which they as yet lacked. For the linchpin of an effective European campaign was, as always. Austria; and Austria, not unnaturally cautious after 1797 and on frosty terms with London over the Loan Convention, was more likely to respond to inducements which he was prepared to supply. He was already mediating between Vienna and Berlin in their Germanic disputes; his offer now to employ a British subsidy partly in Austria's support held out a hope of action which was otherwise in doubt. The prospect was enticing. On the other hand it suggested enticements elsewhere. For might there not in fact be an alternative to be conjured from the Russian approach? The overture itself could hardly be declined – even Dundas, sceptical of a renewed European alliance, did not go so far.[2] But could the overall cost in fact be accepted, and what might follow in practice if Vienna agreed to the initial plan? Russia was asking for $£1^1/_2$ million for the future. But this sum was already reserved for Austria herself if the Loan dispute was settled, and a further total of $£700,000$ was earmarked for Portugal and Switzerland. We could not go much beyond $£2$ million in all – that would be financially and politically hazardous; and Austria would be unlikely to accept a subsidy received meanwhile through the Russians as meeting her independent needs. It was an unpalatable problem. Pitt and Grenville already had their apprehensions about a fresh loan for Vienna: they could not pretend that

1. The rest of this and the next paragraph follows pp. 152–7 above. A repetition is perhaps permissible here to introduce a period of continual permutations.

2. See pp. 155–6 above; and cf. his readiness to offer Corsica, or other baits, to the Empress Catherine in 1796 (II, 609, 633, 635–6).

paying the piper had always produced the right tune. To ask the Bank of England and the House of Commons now to underwrite an expansion of commitments, and one which would include Austria, would be asking a great deal.[1]

There were awkward implications, therefore, to set against the attractions of gaining a Russian force in western Europe and establishing some elements of a Coalition. But again, to take the matter a step farther, what would happen if Austria declined? Might a Russian alliance then be adjusted to operations directly of use to ourselves? We could supply a list, headed probably by Holland; and might not such an outcome even prove to be something which we 'very much preferred'?[2] Nonetheless, whatever happened we must try to make sure of the Tsar. The response, late in August, was accordingly to give his proposal our preference and, so long as he brought Austria strictly to the point on operational plans, to transfer to him the sum reserved provisionally for her. At the same time we posed our alternative in case he should fail – which would not be surprising – and in that event would be glad to set forth a detailed choice. Early in October, when Nelson's news had come in, Pitt and Grenville were not unduly anxious. Disgruntled with Austria – Grenville in particular – and highly sceptical of Prussia, they saw in the Russian initiative a solution in whichever form it might take. Their aim remained the same: pressure on France in Europe was the key to an acceptable peace, simultaneously 'continental' and 'maritime', within an acceptable time.[3] The likeliest way to achieve this, moreover, remained a broad, well concerted effort: 'the advantages of a real bona fide co-operation with Austria and Russia for a fresh campaign on the Continent are almost beyond calculation'.[4] But if that road was closed at least for the present – if Vienna did not fully respond – another might be taken which could lead, if less directly, towards the same goal. Such was the position as seen in London when prospects appeared to open. It was to take some unforeseen turns over the next few months.

1. See II, 524–5, 617–21 for the Bank of England in 1795–6.

2. Grenville to Whitworth, 29 August 1798 (P.R.O., F.O. 65/40).
This was not the first time in point of fact that the idea of an Anglo-Russian treaty had been linked with some kind of Allied action for Holland. The connexion had been made in the War of the Austrian Succession in 1746–8.

3. Cf. p. 134 above.

4. Minute, 'Read and Approved' in Cabinet for 'Heads of a Despatch' to St Petersburg, 22 August 1798 (B.L. Add. Ms 59306). This ultimate perception needs to be held in mind; for while Pitt and Grenville were irritated by Austria, and doubtful of her real intentions, I do not believe that those sentiments had hardened into *policy*, as some of their remarks might suggest (see the interesting argument, covering the autumn and winter, in Paul W. Schroeder, 'The Collapse of the Second Coalition'; *The Journal of Modern History*, Volume 59, No. 2, particularly 261–6). The 'advantages' were still seen as real: the question whether they were properly attainable could not be answered yet.

The first surprise indeed was on its way. The Tsar had been acting from a highly individual mixture of temperament and reasons of state: to counter a growing French threat to his version of Russia's eastern expansionist policy – an interest which for once, though with its own emphasis, overrode his dislike of his mother's example; for the satisfaction, now emerging fast from an earlier state of withdrawal, of appearing as the mediator – the arbiter? – of a comprehensive alliance; from idealism for a Europe to be purged of the levelling atheism of France.[1] Impelled along his path with characteristic force, his relationships were changing: disappointed by his old favourite Prussia, he was turning towards the rival Power. The approach to Britain was centred in fact on a rising sympathy with Austria; and the ambivalent response from London was not at all to his taste. It was the less so for the explanation he was given of the British view on the Loan Convention, which was represented as the sole obstacle to Austria's entry into the war.[2] Angered by this check to his design, Paul accordingly changed tack. He would not accept his own British subsidy 'until the more pressing Necessities of the Court of Vienna shall be provided for'; action on his proposal must therefore be 'postponed'.[3] Further indications seemed to confirm that the subsidy, even if accepted, would not be taken as meeting those needs in itself; the upper limit of a total of some £2 million in aid might therefore have to be breached. Such an extension, Ministers in London decided, was not to be risked. On 2 November the Russians were informed that we had gone as far as we could: if they wished us to support both Powers in one package, we could not oblige.[4]

This looked like the end of that particular road, at least for the time being. Military proposals vanished with the refusal of the subsidy: no major ally was thus available only a few weeks after the prospects had seemed to improve. The blow was severe – 'total disappointment', wrote Grenville[5] – and in part, paradoxically, for financial reasons; for among the 'advantages . . . almost beyond calculation' of a 'real' Russo-Austrian effort had been the thought that the subsidy 'might save ten times that sum which would otherwise be destined to a lingering defensive, and

1. Cf. II, 644; p. 154 above.
2. This came from Cobenzl, who was thoroughly distrusted in London – and not by the British alone: both Starhemberg and Vorontsov – 'ce vil Scapin politique . . . [qui] a trompé mon Empereur' – were equally angry (*H.M.C.*, *Dropmore*, IV, 352–9).
   Briefly Foreign Minister in Vienna (see p. 153 above) but then dispossessed by his predecessor Thugut, he had been sent off to Prussia and then Russia, where he could be out of his rival's way for a time.
3. Whitworth to Grenville, no. 43, 25 September 1798; received 19 October (P.R.O., F.O. 65/40). Not content with having recently reported that Austria *would* ratify the Convention (pp. 133, 157 above), the envoy was now 'given to understand' that she would shortly show herself 'satisfied' with the subsidy given to Russia for her support. Whitworth's perceptions were not acute.
4. Grenville to Whitworth, no. 35, 2 November 1798 (F.O. 65/41).
5. Ibid.

strictly naval, war'.[1] The wording, in a Cabinet Minute drawn by Grenville, could have been aimed at Dundas: it could certainly apply to the ready suspicions of Parliament and public. But now the possibility of just such a war had to be taken seriously again. 'I am not very sanguine of anything', wrote Pitt, 'but our . . . continuing to fight well our own battle; and Europe must probably be left for some time longer to its fate'.[2]

The verdict rested on a dual assumption. Austria would not commit herself; but neither would the other candidate Prussia, which would wait for Austria to act.[3] It was a reasonable judgment. But even as it was being made, Prussia was in fact showing signs of stirring once more.

From hard-earned experience, no one in London was prepared to put it higher than that. Nevertheless, new soundings were taking a decidedly tempting form. For as well as supplying a force on the Rhine, the Prussians now proposed an invasion of Holland, to be combined with Dutch guerrillas and British naval support. The information, from talks between Haugwitz and the Russian envoy in Berlin, together with a paper from the Duke of Brunswick, reached London through Vorontsov. It struck a chord which vibrated farther when a despatch arrived from Vienna, inquiring if Britain would support a Swiss force if – or when – France attacked the Grisons, the last independent canton outside the Helvetic League.[4] These interesting communications were received on 2 and 10 November respectively.[5] Speculative as the prospects were, the Government decided to follow them up. The scenario was changing again. Our two favoured targets were coming into focus: risings in Holland and Switzerland, to be joined by action in each case from the relevant German Power.[6] From such foundations an Alliance might come into being. A Cabinet was summoned, and on the 16th a fresh trial was approved.[7]

Its object this time was comprehensive – an echo from the start of the year.[8] Now that both Prussia and Austria might rejoin the war it was possible, and desirable, to revive the idea of 'a general co-operation'. And if co-operation was to be real, there must be 'one general and digested system'; a return to the concept of prior agreement on both military and diplomatic aims. That now meant putting some flesh on the bones of

---

1 Minute 'Read and Approved' in Cabinet for heads of a despatch, 22 August 1798 (B.L. Add. Ms 59306). The use of 'advantages' in the plural would seem to counter suspicion that the 'calculation' was limited to finance.

2. To Grenville, 29 October (*H.M.C., Dropmore*, IV, 355). Cf. II, 624.

3. See also Grenville to Vorontsov, 2 November 1798 (*H.M.C., Dropmore*, IV, 358).

4. See p. 132 above; and 134–5 for Brunswick.

5. *H.M.C., Dropmore*, IV, 346–8, 350–1, 358–9 for receipt of the Prussians' overture; a hint however was available on 29 October, in Benjamin Garlicke [chargé d'affaires in Berlin] to Grenville, no. 28, Secret and Confidential, 19 October 1798 (P.R.O., F.O. 64/51). The despatch from Vienna, Eden to Grenville, no. 95, Secret, 27 October 1798, was received on 10 November (F.O. 7/53).

6. See p. 156 above.

7. Minute of 16 November 1798 (B.L. Add. Ms 59306).

8. P. 134 above.

principle; something that had not been feasible when the concept itself was first proposed. And that in turn should be done by sending our thoughts at once to St Petersburg and, by special envoy, to Berlin followed by Vienna.[1]

Grenville and Pitt did not look far for the envoy. He was to be Thomas Grenville, the second of the Foreign Secretary's brothers. It was not the first time of course that he had been mentioned for a post: in the past few years he had declined on three occasions to go to Ireland as Chief Secretary, he had gone on a mission to Austria, and his name had come up earlier in connexion with the India Board. This was not simply a case of the Grenvilles, as so often, looking after their own, though it was certainly that.[2] Tom Grenville was respected for his qualities, some of which his brothers lacked. He had a good brain and good judgment, wide experience of politics, and with greater charm and wit was far the most popular of the three. What he lacked was personal ambition, 'the careerist's temperament':[3] all in all, he was in fact well suited to this kind of task.

The framework of the British proposals was broadly the same as before. A quadrilateral treaty should be signed, now 'immediately', to achieve a 'continental' peace, negotiated and guaranteed for the future by the signatories in combination. It would be accompanied by a 'maritime' peace between ourselves and France, which we would negotiate simultaneously on our own. Certain provisions and guidelines were laid down. The central principle was clear: France must be reduced to 'within her ancient limits'. But some exceptions were allowed: the *status quo ante* need not be followed in every respect. Savoy and the Rhineland territories should be handed back; but Venice with its mainland regions, and the Low Countries, would not, and while the French Directory must be removed, as a regime devoted to aggression, the return of the Bourbons was not a necessity.[4] Surveying the several parties' roles and likely demands, we assumed that Russia had no territorial claims on the mainland of western Europe; neither did we, nor on Malta or the Ionian Islands.[5] Territorial

1. Grenville to Whitworth, no. 36, Most Secret, 16 November 1798 (F.O. 65/41).

2. The reputation was well earned, and it endured. When the family's sun had set, Lord Rosebery, versed in Whig tradition, was driven to describe its history as 'the annals of the hive' (*Chatham, His Early Life and Connections* (1910), 135). The process of accumulation may be followed in *GEC* under Buckingham, Buckingham of Chandos, Temple, and Temple of Stowe. Tom Grenville's own sense of accumulation was focused, more sympathetically, on his library; for his public position see II, 188–9 and 189n2, 410, 422, p. 173, n2 above.

3. Mackesy, op. cit., 52.

4. Cf. II, Ch. IX, 371–2, 440, 575–6, 581–4, 599–602 for the British, and Pitt's own, attitude on this last question. There was also a noticeable silence on Nice (as distinct from Savoy) and on some other territories lost by Sardinia; cf. op. cit., 628–9, and ibid and 647–8 in general.

5. Which however did not stop Grenville from suggesting that the Tsar, whose ships were now operating with the Turks in the eastern Mediterranean (p. 150 above), might like to hand over Corfu, if captured, in recognition that it was the battle of the Nile which had opened such opportunities (to Whitworth, 30 March 1799; *H.M.C., Dropmore*, IV, 513).

questions could therefore be related to Austrian and Prussian interests. The former in our view should lie in Italy; the Emperor could keep his Venetian gains and recover his losses in Lombardy, and any further ambitions should be directed likewise south of the Alps, where he would not be in rivalry with Prussia. Prussia's own claims, however, were not known, and she should be invited to declare them. But while we would welcome her military intervention in Holland we doubted that she would wish to stay there; and it was to be hoped that her ambitions would not threaten the survival of the Holy Roman Empire. On this extensive view, the most obvious vacuum lay in north-west Europe. There was no longer any need to consider the Austrians' old plan to exchange their Netherlands for Bavaria – we had always opposed it, but in any case it had been settled in principle at Campo Formio[1] –, and we were hinting clearly that we did not want Prussia in the Dutch territories. Our preference therefore would be to see the Low Countries, so important to our safety, united in one state, with the Prince of Orange restored as Stadtholder in Holland.

The survey, sent initially to Russia as the most likely catalyst,[2] amounted with minor omissions to a blueprint for western Europe. As such, it took its place in the process that ended with the wars. Its immediate elements, military and financial, were set forth more particularly to Thomas Grenville, destined for Berlin.[3] We looked to Prussia and Austria to combine if possible in the Rhineland, and at any rate each to stand guard; Austria in addition should operate in Italy and in concert with Swiss forces in Switzerland, while Prussia should move into Holland in co-operation with the Dutch. Our own operational contribution would lie by sea in the Mediterranean, to help defend Naples and to assist the Austrian campaign farther north. British troops might play a part in Holland; but while the effect might be important, their numbers could not be so large as 'with propriety to become a subject of stipulation', and the matter could be discussed separately with Prussia. Financial arrangements with the two Powers would be eased by the fact that Russia had declined a subsidy; we could therefore allocate £2 million equally between them, on conditions in each case. Austria must ratify the Loan Convention of 1797 – still a firm prerequisite. She must then agree to apply half her portion to raising and helping maintain Swiss resistance, and to supply forces for 'an eventual plan' of operations in Germany. Prussia for her part must apply £500,000 to resistance in Holland,[4] and provide troops for a plan of German operations. An alternative scheme, however, should be held in reserve if one of the two Powers would not take up arms. In that case the

1. P. 131 above.

2. Grenville to Whitworth, no. 36, Most Secret, 16 November 1798 (P.R.O., F.O. 65/41).

3. Grenville to Thomas Grenville, nos. 1–3, nd but between 13 and 15 December 1798 (F.O. 64/52). The dating derives from the latter's papers in box 307 of the Stowe Mss, Huntington Library, San Marino, California.

4. Thomas Grenville was authorised also to advance up to £15,000 for direct use by the exiled Dutch representatives in Germany.

other might receive the whole £2 million, for action in Switzerland or Holland respectively, or £1 million if Russia decided to act as a full ally to either[1] and, after all, reapply to London for funds. In that case too our own position might be realigned: we might wish to 'reserve' our engagement not to make a unilateral peace, and consequently our proposals for territorial settlement.

The package is instructive as an indication of preferences and intended pressures which would affect the atmosphere and to some extent the course of later events. It failed however to forward them, let alone produce a result. The approaches to both Prussia and Austria were prejudiced by mischance; and the balance of expectations, now swinging to the former, was once more to be reversed.

For the mission to Berlin encountered a setback at the start. Fog and east winds held up Tom Grenville for some days in mid December, and on reaching the mouth of the Elbe he was forced to turn home because of ice. At the end of the year he was back in London; and there he had to stay for another month while the hard weather held and the mails piled up at Hamburg, the main collecting point for despatches from the Continent. When at last they arrived, moreover, it was to reveal a changed situation which caused his instructions to be largely recast. For the accumulation of news was both encouraging and distressing: a mixed bag from St Petersburg, an uncovenanted setback far to the south.[2]

The prospect of aid to The Two Sicilies if the French attacked had led the British to re-enter the Mediterranean, as the best incentive to contact with Austria, which was pledged to protect her ally.[3] It now seemed increasingly likely that an assault was preparing from the direction of the Papal States; and Nelson was in Naples with part of his force after the Nile.[4] The combination, at first sight promising, was in fact unfortunate. Nelson's driving impulses were heightened at this time by strain compounded by exhilaration, a recently 'splitting' head wound from the battle,[5] and perhaps the dawning of exposure to Emma. Persuaded – like others before him – of the potential of Neapolitan troops and their current commander General Mack, once the Austrians' chief of staff in the Low Countries,[6] he

1. Having of course hitherto destined this element of the British subsidy for Austria alone (pp. 154–5, 156 above).
2. It was indeed an accumulation; 'I wish', exclaimed Pitt to Auckland, then Postmaster General (see p. 260 below), 'you as Post Master could have deferred the arrival of the 9 Mails with which we have been overwhelmed last night and this morning' (19 January 1799; B.L. Add. Ms 46519). Two more had come in just before he wrote.
3. Pp. 137–40 above.
4. P. 151 above.
5. 'My head is splitting – splitting – splitting'; to St Vincent, 1 September 1798 (see Carola Oman, *Nelson* (1947), 307). The 'headache' was still present several months later (Tom Pocock, *Horatio Nelson* (1987), 197).
6. Cf. II, 279, 306 for the first, 329, 339 for the second.

threw the full weight of his influence behind a plan, already in discussion, for an offensive strike before the French themselves could move. '. . . every person', he had already written to Pitt, seemed to see 'the propriety of an immediate war', and nothing would be wanting on his own part 'to destroy the French and to save Italy'.[1] The design, based on an estimate of numerical superiority and the anticipated Austrian support, was for a drive on Rome with a simultaneous seaborne landing at Leghorn, for which he had offered British escort. Operations began on 17 November, and at first went well. The troops were landed successfully at Leghorn, and the main force reached Rome. But that was the peak. The French regrouped, on 9 December the Neapolitans were routed, there was a collapse, and a fortnight later Nelson evacuated the royal family. The Mediterranean fleet had lost the facilities of a major, well placed port. Its freedom of manoeuvre was lessened by the greater need to watch Sicily, where the King and government were now based. A potential asset, maritime and even military given careful handling, was turned at once into a liability.

That was not all. While The Two Sicilies' treaty with Austria was being ratified in the summer, talks for a similar treaty with Britain, projected earlier, were pursued in London. They reached a hopeful stage early in October, though the Foreign Secretary then warned Naples of the danger of breaking with France unless the support from Vienna was assured.[2] When news of the offensive was received – as usual indirectly and perhaps unreliably – it was however greeted with relief. For whether the venture succeeded or failed was taken as 'much' less important than the fact that an ally of Austria's was at war. Austria herself, it was accepted, must then be engaged;[3] and once that happened the wider consequences could follow. But when the ice in northern Germany eased in January, Ministers had a shock. For they then learned from the despatches that Austria had refused to help Naples, since the recent treaty was defensive, Naples was the attacker, and moreover without consultation. The only talks there indeed had been between the Court and the British authorities, Hamilton and Nelson; Britain was held responsible, and with the object of luring Austria into the war.[4] The charge was rejected: the warning of October was on record.[5] But so far from bringing about the result which Ministers

1. 4 October 1798 (P.R.O. 30/8/163). While this was not the only letter that Nelson wrote to Pitt, it is the only survivor in the collections of the Minister's papers.

In considering the impact of Emma Hamilton, with the accompanying novel experience of adulation from a foreign Court, one has to bear in mind that the Admiral's advice was first given early in his interrupted stay at Naples, before either had taken real effect.

2. Pp. 151, 152–3 above; P.R.O., F.O. 70/11 *passim* from 20 April; Grenville to Hamilton, no. 6, 3 October 1798 (loc. cit.). That despatch however also declared that Britain was willing to support The Two Sicilies whatever the latter might decide.

3. Grenville to Thomas Grenville, 19 December 1798 (*H.M.C., Dropmore*, IV, 419).

4. See Duffy, 'British War Policy', 347–8, which adds to the accounts by Holland Rose, in *Napoleonic Studies* (1904), 353–4, and *The Cambridge History of British Foreign Policy*, I, 287–9. The despatches reached London on 19 January.

5. Above.

anticipated, the ill starred venture in fact served only to reinforce Vienna's distrust.

The outlook for the second part of Grenville's mission thus looked less promising. It was threatened further by an occurrence at St Petersburg relayed in the same crop of mails. The British Minister, Whitworth, was not a brilliant diplomat. He had in fact already raised doubts in London, most recently by his impression of Austria's stance on the loan dispute.[1] His position was certainly far from easy, against a constantly shifting background and the presence of an unbalanced autocrat with whom, to his credit, he managed to keep on good terms. Nonetheless he would have been well advised to be cautious when Cobenzl hove in sight: as it was, anxious to conciliate the Tsar, he let himself be led into talks from which he emerged in December with a draft Convention for a new Austrian loan. He could scarcely have chosen a more inflammatory issue, or as it happened a worse time, for instructions were waiting at that moment to be sent him to steer clear of Cobenzl on that old issue.[2] Ministers and the King were furious – the more so as they seem to have thought that Whitworth had actually signed a provisional agreement.[3] The Cabinet disavowed 'the whole negotiation' and confirmed Grenville's wish to recall the envoy, Pitt's friend Bathurst being earmarked for the post.[4] Only a plea from Vorontsov, who feared the effect of a vacuum at a critical time, enabled Whitworth to survive; to receive in due course a peerage and the Paris Embassy.[5]

These diverse events therefore went far to alter Tom Grenville's instructions. A third, more cheerful possibility added to the need. For while the unfortunate Whitworth was incurring his superiors' wrath, he was also pressing their latest proposal for a Russian alliance. A not unpromising

1. P. 200, n3 above. In the negotiation of 1796 with the Empress Catherine he had been rebuked for exceeding his instructions on the terms for a subsidy.

2. Whitworth to Grenville, nos. 54, 55 of 4, 13 December 1798, endorsed as received 19 January 1799; Grenville to Whitworth, no. 42, 15 December 1798 (P.R.O., F.O. 65/41).

See p. 200, n2 above for London's view of Cobenzl. His proposal was for a loan of £3.6 million, to be raised in London on the terms of Britain's domestic loan for 1799 and with a Parliamentary guarantee (a familiar formula by now). Part of this should be assigned to pay off the debt of 1796–7, but by a separate and secret article that would be written off at a peace brought about by Allied operations in which Austria had been effectively involved. Britain would advance £600,000 to Austria when she declared war. The Loan Convention of 1797 would be ratified following Britain's acceptance of the new Convention. Other, separate, articles covered terms for an alliance: a pledge, together with Russia, not to make peace unilaterally, and a guarantee by Britain to support the Austrians in Italy by maintaing a fleet in the Mediterranean superior to the French.

3. See both Grenville and George III on 19 January (*L.C.G. III*, III, no. 1908 on p. 181).

4. Op. cit., pp. 182–3; Grenville to Bathurst, 20, 21 January 1799 (B.L. Loan Ms 57, vol. 2). There is no notice of this meeting in Grenville's file of 'Cabinet Minutes' (B.L. Add. Ms 59306), despite the interesting statement of his normal practice in a later letter to Windham which is printed in *L.C.G. III*, III, no. 1918 on p. 183n1.

5. *H.M.C., Dropmore*, IV, 448–9 for Vorontsov on 22 January; Grenville to Whitworth, no. 1, 25 January 1799 (F.O. 65/42).

start (if he had read it correctly) was followed by silence. But on Christmas eve he saw the Tsar in person, and all suddenly changed. Paul had just learned that the King of Naples had marched against the French. Fired, it seemed, by what he saw as a chivalrous regal enterprise, he decided to enter the war himself immediately as a principal. Eight thousand troops, from the Danube region, would be sent to Naples's aid; he would renew his request for a British subsidy, and make some strategic proposals relating to Malta and to Holland.[1]

This report was received with the rest of that voluminous package of mails.[2] It added its own complications to resuscitated hopes. A Russian subsidy would mean that funds would be short in total for Prussia and Austria.[3] Tom Grenville was therefore to concentrate his efforts on Berlin. In return for an army to attack Holland, in concert it was hoped with a Russian force, Prussia would receive £800,000 (£1 million if necessary), some of which might go at her discretion to raising Dutch resistance. Austria however would get nothing. She had let down Naples and been extremely rude. She still refused to service her debt, and the terms for a further loan were unrealistic. And if she did enter the war, which seemed as doubtful as ever, it would probably be only when others had done so, yielding possible benefits for herself from their operations.[4]

The assessment, once again, seemed not unreasonable. It proved once again to be wrong. Tom Grenville's mission continued in its course of bad luck. Setting off for a second time on 28 January 1799, he was wrecked by ice off the Elbe, and the gallant bibliophile[5] – scrambling across the floes, half drowned once more on the treacherous sands, preserving his papers throughout, finally pushing through the frozen plains – was able to reach Berlin only on 17 February. By then a Provisional Anglo-Russian Convention had been signed in St Petersburg, for 45,000 troops in return

1. Whitworth to Grenville, nos. 57–9, 12–24 December 1798 (F.O. 65/41). See p. 203 and n2 above for the British approach of 16 November.
 The troops for Naples had been intended for Turkey, under the recent *rapprochement* (for which see p. 154 above); but the Porte was now holding them up. Russia had in point of fact just signed a treaty of limited aid with The Two Sicilies, for the defence of Sicily itself (29 November 1798; see *The Consolidated Treaty Series*, ed. Clive Parry, 54 (1969), 325–31).
 Sherwig (*Guineas and Gunpowder*, 111) seems to ascribe the Tsar's decision to satisfaction with the outcome of Whitworth's talks with Cobenzl. The run of events – and perhaps the fact that the outcome was provisional – makes this unlikely. Paul seems to have resolved quite suddenly to come in, he then moved fast, and in fact in a mood of *revulsion* from Austria when he learned – as he did very quickly – that she would not support Naples.

2. See p. 204 above.

3. Cf. pp. 154–5, 203–4 above.

4. Grenville to Thomas Grenville, no. 2, 25 January 1799 (F.O. 64/53). The Cabinet of 20 January (see p. 206 and n4 above), which discussed the mission as well as Whitworth's performance, stated that £1 million would be furnished to Prussia. In his no. 3 to Whitworth, sd, the Foreign Secretary argued that City financiers were unlikely on experience, and should not be forced, to lend to Austria at the same rate as to the British Government.

5. P. 202, n2 above.

for a subsidy of £900,000 a year, with a further payment of £225,000 for their 'preparation' and one of £75,000 when they crossed the border, plus a monthly credit of £37,500 which would be cancelled at the peace. Russia for her part would do her best to bring Prussia into the war, and in that event would send the subsidised force to act in combination in Holland, Prussia receiving as reward in due course the non-ecclesiastical territories conquered by France on the eastern bank of the Rhine.[1] These terms could not yet be taken for granted. The treaty had to be ratified, and the Tsar stressed that their acceptance depended on Prussia's agreement and accession.[2] Nor could he himself be fully relied upon: he could change his mind all too easily – alter the troops' destination, or delay them, or even find a pretext for backing out.

The Convention's contents were not known in London until early in March.[3] But the prospect suggested that all might still turn on Tom Grenville's success; and it was distinctly worrying to learn that the atmosphere on his arrival had cooled. The Prussians were experiencing Russia's pressure; but they were reluctant to commit themselves, and instead of discussing territorial claims and operational plans for Holland the envoy was faced with suggestions for money to support a 'vigorous defence'. Early in March these turned into a proposal for a tripartite pact to protect northern Germany; and while the possibility was held out of a subsequent change to an offensive, that soon receded under questioning, problems were raised in every direction, and it seemed as clear as anything could be in Berlin that, at least for the time being, Prussia was going to remain neutral.[4]

Meanwhile however, in a last twist of fortune, the Austrians were heading on an opposite course. Once again indeed they appeared to be on the brink of war. The proximate cause this time lay with Russia – with the troop movements set in motion in the late summer of 1798, and again to aid Naples in more recent months. As those forces deployed, the French

1. The Convention was signed on 29 December 1798 (New Style). The text is published in *Consolidated Treaty Series*, 54, 381–8.
    There was also agreement on a separate item which was to come into prominence later. The Tsar's concern for Malta was acknowledged by an undertaking similar to one which he had made recently in his treaty with The Two Sicilies (p. 207, n1 above): that on the expulsion of the French from the island it would be garrisoned and a protectorate established on behalf of the Knights by the three Powers in combination.
    2. Paul to Vorontsov, 30 December 1798 (*H.M.C., Dropmore*, IV, 427–30, particularly 428).
    3. Whitworth to Grenville, no. 1, 2 January 1799; received 6 March (P.R.O., F.O. 65/42). They were circulated to Cabinet Ministers at once, Pitt, Dundas and Loughborough agreeing with an endorsement by ? Spencer (initialled obscurely, on Grenville's copy) that 'Ratification cannot be too . . . speedy' (– March 1799; B.L. Add. Ms 59306). It followed in St Petersburg on 25 April (NS).
    4. Thomas Grenville to Grenville, nos. 2–5, 28 February–16 March 1799, received between 12 and 23 March (F.O. 64/53), and cf. *H.M.C., Dropmore*, IV, 481–2, 485–91. '. . . vigorous defence', he observed privately, 'are two fine words that not understanding myself I do not presume to explain to you' (to Spencer, 28 February 1798; B.L. Add. Ms temp. Althorp G27).

Lord Grenville. *Sculp. Joseph Nollekens*

Henry Dundas, Viscount Melville, *by Lawrence*

became increasingly anxious, and when protests were unavailing they despatched two armies across the Rhine on 1 March. Austrian troops moved in turn, while Thugut sent a message to London proposing that the 45,000 subsidised Russians (of whom of course he had learned) should march for Switzerland, where they would be supported by operations from the Archduke Charles. This was a suggestion which now might well be to the British taste. But it had not reached Ministers when on the 16th they gathered that Austria was in fact at war.[1]

So the war of the Second Coalition began. The Coalition itself did not yet exist. France was encountering renewed opposition, as some new alliances showed: Russia with Turkey; Britain with Turkey; Austria, Russia, Britain with The Two Sicilies.[2] But all these were bilateral, and with differing limits; far more important, the four main intended partners were not bound on unifying terms. Austria was allied with Russia, and Russia had an unratified Convention with Britain; but Austria and Britain had no new treaty, and Prussia was still neutral. Of the earlier British wartime agreements, only those with Portugal in 1793 and with Russia in 1793 and '95 were still fully in effect.[3] Looking back over all that had passed since the start of 1798, it was a disappointing result.

Nor was it particularly reassuring for the future. The obstacles to a comprehensive quadrilateral concert had been rooted in divergent interests which would now be carried into the narrower alignments. The British had argued that proper control of strategy and operations was likely to need prior agreement on specified national claims. That had not been reached, and failure in its turn exacerbated the differences which underlay respective attitudes to the war. As in fact the diplomatic upset of 1791 – the Ochakov affair – pointed sources of discord that would help destroy the First Coalition,[4] so the tortuous tale of the long nugatory diplomatic prelude explains much of what was to happen to the Second.

For the differences ran deep. They impinged directly on operations. And in this instance, without the pressing preoccupations in eastern Europe which had helped check earlier campaigns,[5] the focus was squarely on the west. None of this was highly exceptional: all wartime alliances are subject to differences, liable – not least in a period inheriting a concept of limited

1. Eden to Grenville, no. 18, 6 March 1799 (F.O. 7/54); Grenville to George III, 12, 16 March 1799 (*L.C.G. III*, III, nos. 1936, 1938). Austria had declared, or formally accepted, war on the 12th.

2. See p. 150 above for Turkey, 205 for Naples. The British negotiation for an alliance with the former ended in a treaty on 5 January 1799; the Convention of 1793 with the latter (see II, 279) was converted into a treaty on 1 December 1798 (*Consolidated Treaty Series* 54, 391–4, 333–8 respectively).

3. II, Ch. VIII, section II, and op. cit., 337, 550, 557. The commercial Convention with Russia of 1793 was renewed in 1797.

4. See II, 540, and in general op. cit., Ch. I, sections I–III.

5. Op. cit., Ch. XI, section I, and 540, 586, 632.

warfare – to bear on strategic and operational aims. The trouble in this case was that the problems centred on the vital element; for the focal contribution lay with Austria: determined or reluctant, she held the key.[1] The Austrian army was still held to be the best on the Continent, other perhaps than the French; Austria could save the strategic strongpoint of Switzerland, and from her sector on the Rhine provide the launching pad for the most promising line of entry into France, through Franche Comté to the Lyonnais.[2] Her interests however were far from those of either Russia or Britain. As Pitt and Grenville did not tire of telling, she took up arms only when forced, to preserve her security and her primacy within the Holy Roman Empire. French conquests in northern Italy and Germany, with the latter's added bearing on Prussian ambitions, threatened the bulwarks of the Emperor's power and prestige. He was prepared to fight hard to this end: to admit a reliance on Russia, and to raise forces larger even than those in the First Coalition. That did not mean that Austria lacked ambitions: they had not been removed, or indeed diminished, by her misfortunes in 1796–7. She did not despair of her troops or her generals – with reason, when only Bonaparte had proved irresistible; she was ready (as at Rastadt, in bringing the Congress to cede the left bank of the Rhine) to place her own interests above those of the Empire with which they were linked; and was also in fact reconsidering her views on the Austrian Netherlands, whose repossession might yield a counter worth holding at the peace.[3] Her aims were not slight. But in certain circumstances she could hold them as a subject for negotiation with France,[4] and they now postulated a strategy which itself could diverge from those held by either of her partners. The Austrians wished to expel the enemy from Italy and Germany. But they were not necessarily prepared thereafter – and this bore on the shape of their opening designs – to drive deep into French territory to replace the Republic itself.

In short, Austria subscribed to a limited strategy. Russia's position by comparison was open. Less subject to the imperatives governing so much of western Europe, her policy continued to respond to the Tsar's ideals alongside the state's diplomatic aims. In the light of his crusading fire and the consequent strength of the 'European party', there were some substantial overlaps in the mix. Paul – unlike his mother as so often – was not necessarily committed to restoring the Bourbons.[5] But he was resolved to

---

1. For what follows cf. Mackesy, op. cit., 66–70 and, with a critical emphasis, Schroeder, 'The Collapse of the Second Coalition', 244–52, 259–66.

2. See II, 282 for Switzerland, 579–81, 584–6 for Franche Comté and Lyons. Pitt's remarks in 1795, op. cit., 588, directed to the current situation, could be applied with necessary changes now.

3. P. 132 above for Rastadt; and see p. 213 below for the Netherlands. Cf. T.C.W. Blanning, *The Origins of the French Revolutionary Wars* (1986), ch. 6, particularly 176, 178, 195, 197.

4. Cf. pp. 152–3 above.

5. Whitworth to Grenville, no. 31, 24 July 1798 (F.O. 65/40).

suppress the Republic as it stood, and that forcible impulse buttressed his national interests in south-east Europe and now the Mediterranean, as well as the arguments for exploiting the sharp rivalries between the two main Germanic Powers. They also coincided once more with the case for favouring Prussia, now that Austria in his view had abandoned Naples.[1] He was in fact disposed to discipline Vienna: to keep it up to the military mark. And such an approach broadly suited British interests, as the best insurance against the likely failure of 'a real . . . co-operation with Austria and Russia for a fresh campaign'[2] which itself was central to the Government's hopes.

For, turning to the third of the horses in what might yet become a troika, British policy was at once far-reaching in intent and, to Europeans, tangential in practice. After the uncertainties of recent years it was looking to a victory, within measurable time, which would ensure territorial containment of France and the destruction of her regime. This, it has been termed, was a 'strategy of overthrow';[3] Britain's own contribution however would be maritime and financial with only restricted military aid. Such a combination required, more than ever, a substantial complement; and if the implications could be questioned in London as weighted unduly in favour of the Continent, on the Continent itself the balance could be viewed as tilting the other way. The British, it was held in Vienna, would again be fighting to the last Austrian grenadier; worse, they would employ the power of the purse to try to dictate how he should be used. The mutual resentments endured. Meanwhile Russia's role had still to be tested – her influence on Vienna, the true nature of her preferences, the steadfastness of her resolve. When the campaigning season suddenly opened, with no detailed prior consultation, the outlook for an Allied 'digested system'[4] was thus distinctly unsure.

II

British Ministers themselves were certainly sceptical. They placed little faith in Austria, and wondered at the start even if she would stay the course.[5] In the latter respect however they had a pleasant surprise over the next three months. By the end of March 1799 the Archduke Charles was forcing the French back to the Rhine, they were likewise retreating in Lombardy, and the good news continued. In the extreme south the enemy, now exposed, withdrew from Naples and Rome, leaving a few scattered garrisons and suffering a heavy defeat as he reached the northern plain; and by then, too, Lombardy and much of Piedmont had been regained,

1. Cf. pp. 207–8 above.
2. P. 199 above.
3. The title of Mackesy, op. cit.; see p. 123, n3 above.
4. P. 201 above.
5. Mackesy, op. cit., 82–3.

and a sizeable army was available for fresh operations. For in the opening weeks the Austrians in Italy were joined by two Russian forces, from the one ordered earlier to Galicia and the other designed more recently for Naples.[1] Under the veteran Marshal Suvorov, placed in overall command on the spot, the Allies entered Milan late in April and Turin late in May. Meanwhile the Archduke Charles with part of his force turned to the northern Swiss frontier, beyond which, after a pause of some weeks, he advanced into the country in May, while a corps in the south-east, having entered the Grisons, was overrunning the French forward positions. In mid June the Austrians were in Zurich, on the lake of Lucerne, and the St Gotthard. Northern Italy was largely cleared, Bonaparte's republics crumbled, and the Helvetic League seemed about to follow suit.[2]

This run of events was greeted with, sometimes rather puzzled, elation in London.[3] It was perhaps hard to credit such unaccustomed success. But in June Pitt could hope for 'further progress in the little that remains to be done in Switzerland and Italy'.[4] What might follow from that happy state remained largely unresolved.

For these gratifying gains on the ground were not matched by strategic agreements in the capitals. One warning signal had been hoisted almost at once. Thugut's request for the Russians in Switzerland, with the Archduke Charles acting in support, was accepted in London and the Tsar informed at once.[5] But when the Austrian commander approached the frontier he was ordered from Vienna to halt until the Swiss themselves were fighting and the Russians arrived. As Thugut explained to a colleague, there was no point in weakening an army unduly in operations which others were now going to undertake.[6] Nor was the instruction modified, as it was eventually, without a fresh change of plan. For as soon as Vienna could rest assured that the subsidised Russians would not be used to support Prussia, a proposal was sent to London for them to be deployed on the Middle Rhine. They could then assault the belt of fortresses shielding the Palatinate, opening the road to Luxembourg and the options beyond.[7] The suggestion however did not impress. The Russians, ill equipped for western siege warfare, would face a network of strong defences, while the chance of concentration farther south would be lost.

1. Pp. 154, 207 above.
2. See p. 131 above.
3. Malmesbury to Thomas Grenville, 19 April 1799 (B.L. Add. Ms 41855); Spencer to same, 23 April 1799 (B.L. Add. Ms 41854). The Foreign Secretary, however, could still not bring himself to trust that Austria would continue (to Morton Eden, no. 15, 17 May 1799, P.R.O., F.O. 7/55; same to Lord Minto [for whom see p. 239 below], no. 1, [29] June 1799, F.O. 7/56).
4. To Auckland, 22 June (*A.C.*, IV, 98).
5. Grenville to Eden, no. 6, 29 March 1799 (F.O. 7/54); same to Whitworth, no. 14, 27 March 1799 (F.O. 65/42); see p. 209 above.
6. Duffy, loc. cit., 349–50. It was hoped that some German troops in British pay would also take part.
7. Eden to Grenville, no. 34, 24 April 1799 (F.O. 7/54).

The Foreign Secretary indeed made it clear that he had learned from the First Coalition: 'nothing would be more repugnant', he had already commented, '. . . than to re-establish that system of cordon, which by attempting to provide for every part exposes the whole'.[1] The Cabinet swiftly rejected Thugut's plan, and the Austrians were duly informed.[2]

The episode was not insignificant; for the arguments on either side were not military alone. The Austrians' proposal may have contained a precautionary interest, revived by knowledge of others' thoughts on Holland,[3] in reviving their own rights in the Low Countries, for which they would wish to keep their main army intact; they were certainly anxious, despite their initial request for Switzerland and the timely aid in Italy, to keep the substantial Russian army carefully under watch. Where it should be placed, however, posed awkward questions. One problem was already arising in Piedmont, where Suvorov proclaimed the restoration of the King – a policy by no means necessarily to Austria's taste;[4] and opinion in Vienna was swinging to and fro on how best to contain an ally who could be militarily helpful but might forge his own links across the Alps. Thugut felt obliged, on receiving the British rejoinder, to return in part to the original design, and a detachment of the Archduke's troops moved belatedly on Zürich. But he also proposed that the Allies in the cantons should act separately from one another;[5] and, paradoxically as it might seem, the same idea was favoured briefly in London. For while the British Government was anxious, for diplomatic as well as military reasons, to keep the Russians away from the Middle Rhine, where they might be dragged into 'the whole chaos of Prussian and Austrian politics',[6] it also wished to guard against their enticement into Austrian purposes in Switzerland, and in particular to avoid British money going thereby to the Austrians themselves. Doubts of Vienna remained acute: the Loan Convention had still not been ratified, and events in the past few months had deepened the sense of mistrust. There was no question of regaining the 'former footing of cordiality and confidence, or even of re-establishing any contact', let alone – in contrast to the year before – of discussing war aims.[7] Grenville and Thugut in fact were agreed on one thing at any

1. Same to Whitworth, no. 16, 16 April 1799 (F.O. 65/42). Mackesy, op. cit., 79 points out that the Minute to Vorontsov which is misdated editorially February–March 1799 in *H.M.C., Dropmore*, IV, 484–5 is in fact a summary of this despatch.

2. Minute of 7 May 1799 (B.L. Add. Ms 59306). Although long preceded by Whitworth's relaying of the news in his no. 15 of 26 March (F.O. 65/42) which was received on 16 April, Eden's despatch from Vienna, conveying the proposal at first hand, arrived only on 5 May (endorsement in F.O. 7/54).

3. See eg pp. 203–4 above.

4. Cf. II, 540, 606, 647.

5. Eden to Grenville, no. 58, Most Secret, 23 May 1799 (F.O. 7/55).

6. Grenville to Whitworth as in n1 above.

7. Same to Eden, no. 8, 16 April 1799; and see nos. 6 and 10 of 29 March and 26 April (F.O. 7/54), and, on the use of the subsidy, same to Whitworth, no. 11, 15 March, no. 22, Most Secret, 3 May 1799 (F.O. 65/42).

rate: if there was to be a marriage it would be one strictly of convenience. The Foreign Secretary did not pursue the idea of trying to guide the Russians' movements in Switzerland.[1] But conjoint Allied action there had a distinctly limited appeal.

This was an odd state of affairs. The British had embraced the concept of a second Coalition. Their hopes must turn largely on the prospects for a Continental campaign. One of the favoured arenas at this stage lay in Switzerland, for which funds were being provided. But none of those should go, even obliquely, to one of the two main parties involved. It was hard for London to avoid the obvious fact that Austria was of vital importance; Grenville indeed claimed that 'the smallest Grounds for Difference' should not be allowed to 'interfere with the great work of directing the whole Resources and Energy of Europe' against France. But having said that, it did 'not become' Britain to 'press directly' for an Austrian alliance;[2] and this last sentiment was not weakened over the next few months.

The continuing distrust fostered the Government's persistent interest in operations elsewhere which might form a complement or, if events dictated, an alternative to those in train. It also affected opinion as to their shape and timing. For the obvious target, to the British, remained Holland;[3] and if that was achieved, a door might be opened to the Belgic Provinces, the former Austrian Netherlands. It would have been strange if such a possibility – quickly suspected – did not stimulate thought in Vienna; for circumstances could alter cases, and now indeed might hold out prospects of change. The provinces had been lost to France in 1792, and the loss confirmed by treaty in 1797.[4] But the latter was nullified by renewed war, as the former might yet be, and whether the Emperor would wish to reinsure his ambition of exchanging his Netherlands for Bavaria, or perhaps conversely to reinstate himself, it would obviously help if they were first reconquered, and if possible with his own participation. Whether or not such a concern affected the Austrians' plans for the Russians in the spring, it did not take long to surface. Meanwhile the British were forming their own ideas;[5] and it was the British who were in the better position to set the pace.

The allocation of the subsidised Russians to Switzerland obviously ruled out their use against Holland, a proposal which the Tsar moreover

1. Mackesy, op. cit., 83.
2. Grenville to Whitworth, no. 14, 27 March 1799 (F.O. 65/42).
3. See pp. 203–4 above. The Dutch United Provinces, observed Grenville at the start, were 'precisely the object most interesting to Great Britain' (to Thomas Grenville, 27 March 1799; quoted Mackesy, op. cit., 89).
4. P. 203 above.
5. Ibid; 213 above.

had rejected earlier with the subsidy itself.[1] His very commitment to full partnership however, and Tom Grenville's anticipated presence in Berlin, kept alive hopes, if dim at first, that something might still be done. Prussia's response in March and early April seemed to put paid to her assistance.[2] But some interesting developments in other quarters gave greater encouragement. Intelligence from the Low Countries themselves was now thought to be full of promise: the French were said to be pulling out troops towards the upper Rhine; Dutch patriots were stirring; new conscription laws produced discontent in the Belgic Provinces, where the puppet Batavian government was in growing trouble. Reports suggested furthermore that a restored Prince of Orange might be accepted throughout the region. The exiled Orangeists, in Berlin and London, were given instructions and funds. Plans to support and act with a rising were studied more precisely.[3] And such a prospect might again be envisaged; for if Prussia would not oblige, there was a rather more favourable outlook in Russia herself. The Tsar indeed, swinging once more, was losing patience with his resuscitated favourite.[4] Late in March he made threatening gestures, reinforcing his army on the frontier and sending the Baltic fleet along the Prussian coast. Whitworth was even told that if Prussia remained neutral Russia would declare war on her;[5] and the effect, once grasped, was evident in Berlin. As April wore on Tom Grenville heard more of the advantages of action, and on the 28th Haugwitz proposed a Convention with Britain by which, in return for £1 million subsidy, 60,000 Prussians would be made available from mid June and in place by mid July, when they could take part if required in operations to free Holland.[6]

So the wheel appeared to be coming full circle; though again with the familiar embarrassment that finance would have to be found in such case for two partners instead of one.[7] That problem in fact was posed at once, for Tom Grenville's news arrived on 6 May, three days after a despatch

1. For which see p. 200 above.
2. P. 208 above.
3. Mackesy, op. cit., 90–2. Correspondence between the Foreign Office and leading Orangeists in P.R.O., F.O. 38/4 gives a vivid if incomplete picture; so too does that with Thomas Grenville in F.O. 64/53, and privately between him and his brother in *H.M.C., Dropmore*, V and Stowe Mss, Huntington, boxes 309–10. The latter source has been combed so extensively by Mackesy that I shall cite references hereafter from his work.
4. Cf. p. 200 above.
5. Whitworth to Grenville, no. 17, 29 March 1799 (F.O. 65/42).
6. Thomas Grenville to Grenville, no. 23, 28 April 1799 (F.O. 64/53); and see also his no. 21 of 24 April. Haugwitz put this in preparatory form, ostensibly at least as something he had not yet placed before his King.

The £1 million would be augmented by a payment of £200,000 for mobilisation. The troops would be available until the end of the year. The military engagement carried the proviso that it did not necessarily bind Prussia to enter Holland: circumstances – a French threat to Prussian soil at the one extreme or a sudden Anglo-French peace treaty at the other – might dictate different measures.
7. Cf. pp. 201, 203–4, 207–8 above.

had been sent from London to St Petersburg proposing Russian troops for the same purpose.[1] The request was for a force of between 20,000 and 45,000 men, to be transported by sea (up to 20,000 in British vessels) either to England or direct to deployment in Holstein. Detailed information would follow soon, by hand of one or more emissaries. But utmost secrecy must be preserved: neither the Prussians nor the Austrians must learn anything yet.

The design – for such it now was – had naturally to embrace varied considerations. The possibility and strength of a British contribution – earlier adumbrated[2] – had to be weighed against a choice of targets in western and southern Europe. The likelihood of internal assistance, and the diplomatic implications, must be assessed in each case,[3] while the resources themselves must be carefully scrutinised. For it seemed unlikely at this point that more than one major assault could be mounted from Britain; as Dundas observed, while home defence might now be adequate there remained a 'want' of offensive force.[4] Landings in western France could claim their adherents, and were being actively canvassed; the Mediterranean had its attractions – to clear Egypt and Malta, strengthen Sicily, harry Italy, perhaps even land in southern France. But the former had an unhappy history, and the latter would be bedevilled by transport and time.[5] These were negative arguments for Holland. They had to be added to the positive merits: an area thought to be ripe for insurrection, important to the safety of England, potentially open to British influence, close to the home ports with a short haul for shipping, and accessible, as was essential, to support from powerful allies. Of course there were potential problems: while Prussia would be militarily welcome, her ambitions must be kept in check; Austria's assistance, which might be pressed, was not desirable on any ground. Holland moreover was geographically marginal to the main directions of thrust. But that in itself could be turned to advantage: Allied occupation would pose a flexible threat – to Luxembourg and the central Rhine, or to the Belgic Provinces and (a developing argument) thereafter to northern France.[6] Such reasoning placed the operation, now seen increasingly in a grand strategic context, together with the liberation of Switzerland at the top of the British list.

1. Endorsement of receipt on Thomas Grenville's no. 23; Grenville to Whitworth, no. 21, Most Secret, 3 May 1799 (F.O. 65/42).

2. P. 203 above.

3. Eg, in the instance currently favoured, Danish consent would have to be obtained if troops were to be transported through the Baltic.

4. To Cornwallis, March 1799 (*Correspondence of Cornwallis*, III, 79). See pp. 123 and n3, 125 above for figures.

5. Possibilities in the Mediterranean had further to be balanced with commitments to Portugal, for which see p. 151 above. A letter from Camden to Pitt of 6 April 1799 (P.R.O. 30/8/119) suggests that southern France was an option not to be ruled out at this point.

6. Grenville to Whitworth, no. 24, 7 May 1799 (F.O. 65/42) for the first effect.

As spring gave way to summer, Ministers were in a robust mood. Their nerve indeed was tested while the proposal to Russia was being prepared. Command of the Channel and the Western Approaches, and assurance in the safety of Ireland, were necessary conditions for committing transports and troops to Holland. At the end of April however they learned that the Brest fleet had slipped out undetected, and were faced by the familiar conundrum of its destination.[1] Was it Ireland? Or the Mediterranean? Or the West Indies? Or the Cape and India? Would there be diversions? And would the fleet pick up the Spaniards at Cadiz? The Admiralty, faced as so often with inadequate evidence, plumped for the Mediterranean; Ministers were divided, and some changed their minds with the trickle of reports. Windham from the start agreed with the sailors. Spencer and Grenville opted for Ireland, Grenville initially holding out the alternative of Portugal. Pitt and Dundas – the latter predictably perhaps[2] – at first favoured the Mediterranean, but Pitt at least inclined towards Ireland in the course of the next two weeks. The Admiralty proved to be right: the French were bound for the Mediterranean. But while their escape pointed the problems of the Atlantic blockade as currently practised, and their arrival in the south, perhaps threatening a reinforcement of Egypt, was to raise others for a badly stretched command, it was noticeable that the Ministers were not unduly shaken. They made their dispositions, in the main for Ireland, hoping for the best but with basic confidence, and plans for Holland were not interrupted while the enemy's fleet was hidden at sea.[3] British Admirals covering southern Europe would soon be faced by some hard choices. Their masters' initial response to danger reflected a faith now crowned by the Nile.

The Prussian offer for Holland – for so it was taken – coming on top of the despatch to Russia, led to an immediate Cabinet which was followed at once by fresh instructions. The Foreign Secretary worked through the night of 7–8 May, drafting a treaty for 60,000 men which required a previous summons from Berlin to the French to leave the Dutch United Provinces within the next two months. If such a force was obtained, however, there would be no need for 45,000 Russians: 20,000 should

1. This was three days before the despatch on Holland was sent to Russia (p. 216 and n1 above). The Cabinet may have approved that decision itself on 25 April, though it is hard to tell (*Diary of Windham*, 408).

2. Cf. p. 142 above.

3. The episode is discussed by Mackesy, op. cit., 97–101, and by Ingram, *Commitment to Empire*, 262–4. See also Rodger, *The War of the Second Coalition*, 97 104, for a critical view of events at sea. *Private Papers of Spencer*, III, Part II, and *H.M.C., Dropmore*, V give a good idea of Ministerial opinions to which the relevant ms collections add nothing significant, though there is one interesting account of the Sea Lords' thought in William Marsden [Second Secretary of the Admiralty] to Spencer, 9 May (B.L. Add. Ms temp. Althorp G210). Pitt's concern for Ireland may be reflected in a query for Dundas, placed first among many for a general review of military dispositions on strengths in the island (11 May 1799, P.R.O. 30/8/240, f. 89).

suffice, and a fresh despatch was sent off to St Petersburg. It included the news that a naval Captain, Home Popham, would be on his way immediately to discuss and assist the combined transportation plans.[1]

With this last initiative matters in fact moved towards a new stage. The emphasis on secrecy, conveyed to Whitworth, proved wise,[2] for Prussia once more was showing signs of fading out. Haugwitz had covered his flank well;[3] the King, so Tom Grenville was told, first reacted to his Minister's proposal by preferring to put 230,000 men into the field – for whom no doubt he would wish to be paid – and then, on 13 May before the British despatch of the 7th had arrived, announced that Prussia would have to remain neutral. 'God help them', exclaimed the infuriated envoy, 'for I believe they are past the help of man'.[4] His prayer, as it happened, was not needed yet; for the Tsar was reverting to his earlier mood, and turning again from menaces to conciliation. He now offered for joint operations with Prussia the troops whom he had stationed near her border as a threat, and no sooner did Tom Grenville send his latest news than he was told that this offer might well be accepted.[5] Long weeks of frustration lay ahead, as hopes waveringly rose and fell. But the British had decided, at least momentarily, not to count on Berlin; Whitworth was instructed to ask once more for 45,000 Russians;[6] and with that renewed request operational detail came to the fore.

---

1. 'Minute read and approved at the Cabinet', 7 May 1799 (B.L. Add. Ms 59306) – in which possible financial adjustments were noted; Grenville to Thomas Grenville, nos. 19, 20 of 7 May (F.O. 64/54), and 8 May 1799 (*H.M.C., Dropmore*, V, 45); same to Whitworth, no. 24, 7 May 1799 (F.O. 65/42).

2. P. 216 above.

3. See p. 215, n6; and also p. 136 above.

4. Thomas Grenville to Grenville, nos. 24, 27 of 5, 13 May 1799 (F.O. 64/54); same to Spencer, 12, 13 May 1799 (B.L. Add. Ms temp. Althorp G33).

5. Same to Grenville, nos. 31, 32 of 21, 27 May 1799 (F.O. 64/54). For his private thoughts see *H.M.C., Dropmore*, V, 67–70. Cf. p. 215 above for the Tsar.

6. Grenville to Whitworth, no. 29, 25 May 1799 (F.O. 65/42). Tom Grenville's news, of 13 May (n4 above), was received on the 22nd.

CHAPTER VIII

Fate of a Grand Design

I

The conduct of the war in 1799 in London indicates certain themes. Not least of these, running like a thread through the design for a grand offensive, was the role assigned to national insurrection. A pattern of thought may be discerned for the various theatres affected, first visible, as hostilities opened, in Switzerland. For the emphasis laid on operations there derived partly from forecasts of aid from, and in turn heightened the pressure for aid to the Swiss themselves.[1] Both elements were necessary. The spirited revolts of 1798 gave promise of success when Allied troops should arrive. But that proviso was held to be essential, for British policy looked not so much to risings which would pave the way for support as to a campaign from outside which would signal the time.[2] Some money and organisation had already been supplied by the Minister in Berne, William Wickham,[3] and after he left by his subordinate James Talbot. The level now rose in the spring and early summer. Wickham was sent back, to the northern border, as political representative, and two soldiers – Colonels John Ramsay and Robert Craufurd (or Crauford) – were attached to the Russian and Austrian forces respectively.[4] The planned subsidy had to be reduced from £500,000 to £300,000, as greater demands increased.[5] But there was no doubting the Government's purpose. The clearance of Switzerland was a cardinal aim.[6]

1. For which see pp. 132, 207–9, 212–14 above.
2. Eg Grenville to James Talbot [former chargé d'affaires in Berne, and now in Augsburg on a 'mission of observation'], nos. 1, 3, of 25 January, 15 March 1799 (P.R.O., F.O. 74/23).
3. For whom see II, 372–3.
4. Ramsay, who was appointed in June, had some experience of liaison on the Continent, having been sent on a mission to the German Prince of Waldeck in the summer of 1798 to plan for mercenary service. Craufurd, appointed in March in place of Talbot, was a member of a gifted family who later achieved fame in the Peninsular War (see II, 585n1).
5. See Grenville's figures for the Cabinet, 7 May 1799 (B.L. Add. Ms 59306), repeated in notes by Pitt nd but slightly later in the year (P.R.O. 30/8/197, f. 102). Cf. pp. 156, 203–4 above for the higher figure.
6. '. . . the success of the whole and every part of this war depends on pushing the campaign with vigour in Swisserland'; Grenville to Thomas Grenville, 3 June 1799 (*H.M.C., Dropmore*, V, 79).

A similar pattern was visible for Holland: encouragement of latent resistance which could aid Allied operations themselves marking the necessary moment to rise. Buoyed up by agents' reports, and above all by those from his brother in Berlin, the Foreign Secretary did not hesitate to urge the argument on the Russians. Early in May he could even speculate that 15,000 of their troops 'would do the business';[1] certainly his confidence, combined with the reading of the Alliance's prospects elsewhere, carried the day with the Cabinet in the late spring. In point of fact the assessment discounted some less satisfactory elements. The French were certainly unpopular – though not in every quarter; but would the liberators be actively welcomed when they came? The Dutch had gained a reputation in London for passivity in moments of crisis;[2] when the call to action sounded, how many would commit themselves? Furthermore, as so often when resistance movements have to be associated with exiles, there were simmering political problems to be sorted out. The United Provinces contained sharp disunities; the Orangeists were by no means fully representative, and there were differences of opinion among the Orangeists themselves.[3] Nor were the prospects simplified when the Belgic Provinces were considered. But such uncertainties were largely disregarded as the tide of fortune rose, and if some Ministers had reservations – Windham, as always, would have preferred all available support to be reserved for France, and Dundas later voiced his doubts with a vigour which suggested earlier growth – these do not seem to have been strongly pressed at the time. Grenville was the responsible expert, 'in the daily habit of receiving the intelligence, and of combining it, and drawing . . . conclusions from it';[4] and the conclusions were allowed to stand.

Such hopes, for two distinct regions, amounted to an element in strategic thought which had perforce been absent, or insignificant, before. Discontent in occupied countries could now be brought into the reckoning in ways that had hardly been possible until 1798. That year saw demonstrations or risings in the Ionian Islands, parts of Italy, and Luxembourg, as well as in the Belgic Provinces and Switzerland themselves. The conditions for support varied. Unrest might be fuelled by money, or money and supplies, or either plus advice: Switzerland was currently the most promising target for such treatment. Or, where British interests were more prominent, and possibly aid with British troops was envisaged, some involvement in domestic politics might be accepted – or grasped. This could apply to the Low Countries, where there were choices, explicit or implicit, to be weighed in reconciling policies for the future with current military needs. But whatever form the assistance, and

1. To Thomas Grenville, 3 May 1799 (op. cit., 38).
2. See II, 253 & n4, 263, 273.
3. See Simon Schama, *Patriots and Liberators, Revolution in the Netherlands 1780–1813* (1977), chs. 8, 9 for the background after the French occupation in 1795.
4. As Dundas himself still acknowledged after his doubts had surfaced (to Grenville, 31 July 1799; *H.M.C., Dropmore*, V, 215).

demands, might take, there was an expectation in London – which in some cases became a high one – of reciprocal aid from insurgency itself.

Such a concept was new in effect as applied to occupied states in Europe. In another aspect however it was familiar enough. There was a history of attempts by now to profit from discontent within France; a history more-over that was far from being a closed book. The contents admittedly were not encouraging. Landings at Toulon and above all at Quiberon, covert support in the regions and in Paris, had shown the hazards and limitations attached to efforts of whichever kind. The argument was inconclusive: had we done too little, or too much? Would a higher priority have yielded higher results – the case identified particularly with Windham, seeking to concentrate the bulk of military resources on the royalists' cause? Would it have been wiser to have set stricter limits, as Dundas came to think; pro-viding funds and some supervision, some arms and supplies, but no British troops?[1] With the revival of an Allied partnership the debate revived on familiar lines. We were now contributing once more to a Continental campaign. How far could and should we encourage insurrec-tion in France: what role should it play in the main operations, and our policy for the future, and should we commit our own forces to it – perhaps in preference to other objects?

Intelligence, as so often, was hard to assess. The royalists' cause, the focus of resistance despite their interminable disputes, had taken several turns in the past eighteen months.[2] In the spring and summer of 1797 it had reached something of a peak, with the second round of elections to the Assembly in Paris and the Directory's obvious weakness. The doors then no longer seemed firmly closed to constitutional change; and it was possible to encourage hopes of a close working agreement between moderate and 'Court' royalists, and increasingly between the former and conservative republicans. But then came Fructidor in September, and the chance of political challenge was lost. For the time being at least, it was back to the old channels of subversion; and the subversive organisations themselves were also now hard pressed. The Paris Agency was destroyed; provincial activists lay low; the prospects looked bleak in an atmosphere of mingled apathy and fear. Nonetheless they revived in 1798. An agency in exile – the Swabian Agency – emerged to claim powers of co-ordination. A Secret Royal Council was formed in Paris to advise Louis XVIII.[3] Regional organisations reappeared, particularly in the south-west. By the

1. See II, Ch. IX, *passim*, 368–73, Ch. XV, sections III, IV, 610.

2. Cf. II, Ch. IX, pp. 368–73, Ch. XIV, section III, 581–7.

3. But not his brother in England, the Comte d'Artois, whose judgment he did not trust. Typically, there was no liaison with the latter's council, which may not indeed have even known of the Paris Council's existence.

For agencies outside France see Elizabeth Sparrow, 'The Swiss and Swabian Agencies' in *H.J.*, vol. 35, no. 4, 861–84.

time that the Austrians and Russians were engaged from Germany to Italy, royalists were once more planning a rising, against the day that the Allies drew near.

Their activities did not lack British support. At first it was not well directed. Wickham's successor Talbot, impressed by the discontent both outside and inside France, seems to have held out hopes before the Coalition ever came into being, and certainly encouraged some hazardous plans over the turn of the year. His reward for approving premature action was Grenville's disavowal and his own recall.[1] But the departure from considered policy only underlined the interest in the policy itself. Talbot's failure soon led to Wickham being sent out again.[2] For with the wave of Allied successes, prospects in France became of more immediate concern.

There were two distinct areas to cover: the east and south, which would relate to military advances from the upper Rhine, Switzerland and Italy; and the north and north-west, the old target of direct British aid. The lines of information, responsibility and means of assistance followed correspondingly. Wickham, given broad discretion and financial resources, explored the first region, keeping also in touch with the Swabian Agency which had claims to supervision there, and with the army of exiled royalists under Condé long designed by the British for invasion from the Rhine.[3] The second lay, as before, within the purview of the exiles in London combined with the Government's own intelligence and contacts, and with policy resting under its control. The chief link in this sphere of information was Windham, recognised by his colleagues as such;[4] and now that offensives were again on the cards he updated his familiar argument.

... whatever Coalitions may be formed in Europe, unless the parties shall learn to take for their allies the Royalists in France, meaning by

---

1. For Talbot see p. 219 above. His activities in 1798 are followed closely in Sparrow, loc. cit. Over the turn of the year he was in touch with plans for a *coup de main* in Paris which would include the assassination of the Directors, and approved a number of selected risings in the spring to complement unrest in the Belgic Provinces (to Grenville, no. 31, 25 November 1798 (F.O. 74/22), no. 1, 2 January 1799 (F.O. 74/23)). The former idea met with a hasty repudiation of responsibility from London – '*wholly abhorrent*' to '*the character of a civilized nation*' and '*the Laws and rights of civilized War*' (Grenville's no. 2, 25 January 1799; loc. cit.) – and rebukes of his involvement with the latter ended in his relief by Craufurd (see loc. cit., Grenville's nos. 1, sd, and 3 and 4 of 15 March). Mrs Sparrow however sets all this in context ('Swiss and Swabian Agencies', 879–80), and Talbot was allowed to go as chargé d'affaires to Sweden.

2. P. 219 above.

3. Grenville's Instructions to Wickham, in Separate and Secret with no. 1, 6 June 1799 (F.O. 74/24). See II, 371–2, 582–8, for Condé.

For some thought of a landing from the Mediterranean to support an 'insurrection' in the south see letters to Pitt from Camden, 6 April 1799 (P.R.O. 30/8/119) and, of less importance, from Sir Nathaniel Wraxall [for whom see I, 604], 4 March 1799 (P.R.O. 30/8/192).

4. See Grenville to Windham, 22 February 1798 (*H.M.C., Dropmore*, IV, 100).

that, in a larger sense, all that are willing to combine against a Jacobin Government, the present monstrous system will never be overturned, nor Europe restored to peace and safety. A radical cure for the disorder can, in my opinion, never be effected but in France itself.[1]

This of course was a political quite as much as a military argument. But as operations developed in the summer the emphasis fell on the latter case.

That was almost bound to be so; and – while Windham would have thought the statement in effect pointless – the combination found a readier hearing in the quarters that really mattered than either of its elements had done in the past two years. The moment seemed perhaps indeed to be approaching on which British hopes had risen last in 1795: the attention given to French affairs accordingly moved into a higher gear. Pitt, bruised by past lessons, proved cautious; but he was convinced once again, as now was Grenville, that the enemy was near to exhaustion, and felt the more disposed to admit the value of action if it was brought within a larger design. Grenville himself, uncharacteristically, grew more enthusiastic.[2] Already sympathetic, it would seem, to the idea that France's rescue must include 'civil war', he was now fired by his growing belief in the role of insurrection in general, and in this instance as a propellant towards the necessary conditions for the future. And Dundas too, disagreeing with Windham over an involvement of British troops, had long agreed – all the more – that the French would have to fight for their own salvation.[3] Such approaches were far from carrying consent for Windham's specific demands: they did not guarantee hard commitments from a set of options. They reflected indeed divergencies and shades of emphasis within a wider context. But they did not dissent from the proposition that the royalist resistance could play a worthwhile part, at the right time, in an Allied campaign.

But when would be the right time? And – once more – could British troops be used? As the summer wore on, some relief was expected from the old constriction of inadequate strength.[4] For, continuing its efforts of the previous year, Government was preparing a revised scheme to recruit from the militia for voluntary service in Europe. Working fast and hard in this delicate area, it secured an Act in mid July which promised – and in

1. To Grenville, 17 May 1799 (*H.M.C., Dropmore*, V, 207–8). And cf. other similar urgings at this time from him on 2 and 8 May (B.L. Add. Ms 37846).

The argument of course was directed to the Directory's impact on Europe: domestically it was by no means a Jacobin government, whatever had happened at Fructidor. In 1798–9 in fact some Jacobins were in uneasy contact with royalists against it.

2. Cf. I, 132–3.

3. See Mackesy, op. cit., 72 for the current belief in French exhaustion; Pitt's persistent conviction can be seen retrospectively over the turn of the year, in notes for a speech in P.R.O. 30/8/197 (f. 316) and in the speech itself (*P.R., 3rd ser.*, X (1800), 301). For Grenville's opinion on 'civil war', as given by Windham, in October 1797, see *Diary of Windham*, 379. For Dundas in 1796 see his letter to Windham of 31 March, in B.L. Add. Ms 37876.

4. Cf. p. 216 above.

fact procured more than – 10–15,000 men to that end.[1] These might be available from mid August. But there were other, and overriding, factors still to be weighed. Both Pitt and Grenville were extremely anxious that risings should not take place prematurely, and to Windham's despair they would not afford 'assistance or countenance' in advance – a policy which he claimed on the contrary could help impose guidance and restraint.[2] Above all however there was the commitment to invade Holland, long desired and now in active contemplation. From June onwards the main resources were being gathered for that design; and, again to his disgust, Windham was told that in fact it would suit his own purpose best. Given the presumption of revolt in the Low Countries, and the expected Allied pressure farther south, it should not take long to clear the region and enable the British to enter France if apposite, in line, it must be hoped, with a general offensive. That would be the time for the risings; the one success could lead to the other; and the priority must go to Holland, crucial to our policy in so many ways.[3]

It was against this background for the main British effort, and their hopes of the Allies' plans, that Ministers discussed the various means of support. They naturally received suggestions, from assorted Frenchmen and some of their own colleagues.[4] On the Continent, Wickham, augmented by Pichegru[5] sent earlier to Hamburg and now to the Archduke Charles, was hard at work picking up old contacts and trying to recruit a Swiss regiment for émigré command. Meanwhile a substantial contribution could at least be discussed for north-west France itself. Almost all the resistance leaders who had earlier fled to London were back in the region,

1. See p. 125 above for 1798. The process, spearheaded of course by Dundas, involved extensive consultation in and outside Cabinet. It can be followed in Western, *The Militia in the Eighteenth Century*, 227–32. The Act was 39 Geo. III, c106, which produced altogether some 15,700 men. The key lay in reducing the militia establishment so as to favour voluntary transfer to the regular army, with inducements, for a limited period. A further Act in October, 39 & 40 Geo. III, c1, imposing a further reduction, produced an additional 10,400 men.

2. Windham to Grenville, 13 June; same to Pitt, 16, 24 July 1799 (*The Windham Papers*, II, 98, 102–4). He himself was likewise opposed to premature revolt (to Grenville, as above; entry for 1 September 1799, *Diary of Windham*, 413). His contention was rather that the only way to stop it was by 'acquiring' an 'ascendancy' over the movements, which involved helping and influencing their preparations while simultaneously making our own – for 'a Force to be raised . . . when operations in France are actually begun, must come too late' (to Pitt, 24 July as above, 106).

3. Windham's reaction was clear: 'If we succeed in France, Holland falls, of course [ie, in its course]; but not *vice versa*' (to Pitt, 24 July; *The Windham Papers*, II, 105–6). See also *Diary of Windham*, 411; and same to Grenville, 10 August 1799 (*H.M.C., Dropmore*, V, 271–2, 307). Grenville continued to develop the argument, on 26 August 1799 and 5 September (B.L. Add. Ms 37896; *H.M.C., Dropmore*, V, 360), pointing out in particular the connexion with the Russian alliance.

4. Eg two notable surviving memoranda, from the Comte de Coigny to Pitt (1 August; P.R.O. 30/8/335) and from Huskisson at the War Department (3 June; B.L. Add. Ms 38764).

5. See II, 586, 610 above.

and grants amounting to some £28,000 had been made in the first four months of the year.[1] Money and supplies continued to be provided, though they were not increased; but in the third quarter the level of attention rose. There may have been some thought in August, perhaps not significant, of preparing an émigré force for a landing; d'Artois was brought south from his debtor's sanctuary in Holyrood, though with another aim in view.[2] In the next few weeks, however, a more ambitious idea emerged.

It sprang from events at sea. The French fleet, which had picked up the Spanish in its southward cruise three months before, was known in July to be heading north with it again. Would the Combined Fleets attempt to threaten the Channel, and the preparations for Holland? If so, as Spencer remarked, 'we shall be in a scrape'.[3] On 13 August however they entered Brest; the threat was removed; and even while a royalist expedition assembled for a potential assault Dundas – from whom the suggestion stemmed[4] – Pitt and, after hestitation, Grenville canvassed the feasibility of a British attack on the naval base. The assumptions reflected persisting hopes. British troops might be brought back from Holland if that undertaking 'should terminate speedily'; the French armies would be tied up on the Rhine 'if the Allies continue to push their operations';[5] and in such circumstances, which would have included successful risings in the Low Countries, use might also be made in October of an insurrection in Brittany and Normandy. If and when this chance came, it must be grasped quickly. A sudden Ministerial correspondence ensued. It was indeed a somewhat curious interchange, in which Grenville and Windham found their roles temporarily reversed. For the Foreign Secretary, earlier lukewarm, now suddenly saw the project in a wider setting: not only, as Dundas and Pitt envisaged, as the means to damage the enemy fleets, but beyond that to combine with the resistance in a threat, at whatever point, which would compel the French to divert large forces from the main Allied fronts.[6] He wished accordingly to arm and organise a more cohesive royalist force, increasing the level of supplies and providing advice against the coming day or, given the growing

1. According to Windham's report of 7 May 1799 (cited in Norman Frank Richards, 'British Policy and the Problem of Monarchy in France, 1789–1802', 395; Ph.D. thesis, University of London, 1955 – not 1954 as stated in II, 659).

2. See II, 577n3 for Holyrood. Correspondence on where to house him if he remained in this country, in *H.M.C., Dropmore*, V, 305, 316, might possibly suggest such a plan. But see p. 237 below for a more pressing reason for the visit.

3. *Private Papers of Spencer*, III, 13. See p. 217 above for the cruise.

4. To Spencer, 11 August 1799 (op. cit., 162).

5. Pitt to Sir Charles Grey [see p. 163 above], who was intended for the command, 23 August 1799 (Holland Rose, II, 381). There is a long 'Memo' of the 22nd in the Minister's hand, with detailed questions on a major assault, in Stanhope Ms U1590 S5 09/53. His interest seems to have been aroused initially by Dundas (*Papers of Spencer*, III, 111–12).

6. See Mackesy, op. cit., 221–2. Dundas later explicitly disassociated himself from Grenville's enlarged views (to Grenville, 20 October 1799; *H.M.C., Dropmore*, V, 493–4).

lateness of the season, the need to survive until the spring. His impetus, deriving from his overall view of events which might be reaching a climax, also pointed the importance he was attaching in general to internal pressures. His colleagues in this instance, however, were not greatly impressed. Dundas, his hands full enough already, did not pay much attention. Windham, having failed to secure a comparable policy in advance, demurred at this now impracticable speed. And Pitt likewise, despite or more likely because of his interest in a British assault, gave the proposal a distinctly cool response. 'I can hardly state my opinion satisfactorily until I learn more exactly the amount of the expense'. If that was kept strictly under review, such a royalist force would be 'more than worth the money'. But 'If it is not raised, no harm will be done. And it certainly cannot be raised in so short a time as to interfere with our grand scheme for that quarter, supposing we can realize it this autumn'.[1] From an opposite starting point the Minister agreed with the Secretary at War. The combination tipped the scales against a project which in any case was soon overtaken by events.

For neither externally nor internally did the right conditions in fact exist. Within France itself it proved impossible, as Windham had foretold in arguing for autonomous control, to direct and co-ordinate resistance movements from outside.[2] This was indeed soon proved in the region which now came immediately under review. Wickham and the Swabian Agency were unable seriously to influence matters in the south, where a coherent organisation under the latter's aegis[3] was more evident on paper than on the ground. Plans were made for a rising to take place in mid August. But the results could not be synchronised, and in the two main areas, of Toulouse and Bordeaux, action was respectively too early and too late. Initial successes were soon halted, and the affair was over by the end of the month. The example then spread to the north-west itself, and the *chouans*[4] began to muster in September; of their own volition, however, and not on lines which the British could guide. Attacking early in October, they too made some immediate gains. But only briefly, and the thrusts faltered against mounting force. Allied troops did not arrive, and aid was confined to arms from England assembled hurriedly but belatedly in November.[5] By the end of the year the revolt was ended. Its dying embers flickered in a scene very different from that in which the fire had been laid.

---

1. Dundas to Grenville, 10 September (*H.M.C., Dropmore*, V, 383–4); Grenville to Windham, 2, 5 September (op. cit., 346–7, 360); Windham to Grenville, 4, 6 September (B.L. Add. Ms 37846); Pitt to Grenville, 10 September 1799 (*H.M.C., Dropmore*, V, 380).

2. Apart from anything else, effective guidance on the spot was heavily hampered by the prevalent limits on communications both locally and with England.

3. See p. 222 above.

4. The northern peasants of the resistance; see II, 568.

5. Correspondence between Windham and Pitt, in Holland Rose, *Pitt and Napoleon*, 287–8; and see Piers Mackesy, *War Without Victory, The Downfall of Pitt 1799–1802* (1984), 33.

The degree – the very nature – of British involvement with the concept of French insurrection brought once more into prominence the question of the political future. The role of resistance was explicitly supposed to hinge on the progress of Allied operations; and the final target of those operations, to the British, was Paris itself.[1] Strictly speaking, this aim was not new. There had been dreams of a 'march on Paris' in 1794.[2] But they had then been shared, in fact induced, by Austria, were indulged only briefly, and had not been revived. In 1798 the purpose of an Alliance was defined in London as 'France reduced to within her ancient limits'.[3] That however was a matter for the peace table, a territorial *consequence* of victory; and victory itself would now be deemed incomplete, indeed of no lasting value, without the suppression – the destruction – of the present French regime at source. There was no real prospect otherwise of a durable peace. An insatiable appetite required surgery; Europe must be rid of an unlimited threat. It was an unfamiliar order of demand – a striking indication, it might be said, of the effect of a Revolutionary enemy – and not least because it was placed at the centre of a military design.

That last fact thrust an old issue inescapably to the fore. Whatever the pace of operations – whether victory might come in 1799 or in 1800 – the prospect revived questions affecting the exiled monarchy. What role should the Princes play? And what of Louis XVIII himself? If a royalist insurrection was to be drawn closely into Allied plans, did the British Government favour – was it committed to – the Bourbons' restoration?

Both Pitt and Grenville found themselves obliged to refer to the subject in public. It figured, as it was almost bound to do, in debates on the conduct of the war.[4] Both took the same careful line, in response very largely to Foxite suspicions; they confined themselves to repeating the policy expressed in earlier statements. Some of the repetitions were indeed notable: historic passages from Pitt on British war aims, acclaimed at the time and quoted down the years. They were also tactically adroit, an example of the debater's skill in turning defence into successful attack.

> With respect to that which appears so much to embarrass certain gentlemen [the deliverance of Europe] I will not say particularly what it is. . . . it is assumed by the hon. gentleman, that we are not content

1. Eg Grenville's Instructions to Lord Mulgrave [for which see pp. 240, 241 n6 below], 7 August 1799; *H.M.C., Dropmore*, V, 255.
2. See II, 329–30. The phrase became associated with Hawkesbury [for whom see p. 91 above], who had used it then with youthful confidence and after things went wrong in Flanders had to endure its repetition, in newspapers, from Opposition, and even from his own associates (eg *H.M.C., Dropmore*, V, 9), for the rest of the war.
3. P. 202 above.
4. On the subsidy to Russia; on 7 June in the Commons, 11 June in the Lords. See *P.R.*, *3rd ser.*, VIII (1799), 652–73, 687–99. The version in *The Senator*, XXIII (nd) resembles that of *P.R.*; that of *P.H.*, in XXXIV, cols. 1043–8, 1050–2, like W.S. Hathaway's collection of *The Speeches of the Right Honorable William Pitt . . .*, III (1806), 412–24, is somewhat, and in places quite significantly, reduced.

with wishing to drive France within her ancient limits; that, on the contrary, we seek to overthrow the Government of France; and he would make us say, that we never will treat with it as a Republic. Now I neither meant any thing like this, nor expressed myself so as to lead to such inferences. Whatever I may in the abstract think of the kind of government called a Republic, whatever may be its fitness to the nation where it prevails, there may be times when it would not be dangerous to exist in its vicinity. But while the spirit of France remains what at present it is, its government despotic, vindictive, unjust, with a temper unchanged, a character unchanged, if its power to do wrong at all remains, there does not exist any security for this country or Europe. In my view of security, every object of ambition and aggrandizement is abolished. Our simple object is security, just security,[1] with a little mixture of indemnification. These are the legitimate objects of war at all times . . .

He has supposed[2] that I said, we persevere in the war, . . . to impose a government on another country, and to restore monarchy to France. I never once uttered any such intention. What I said was, that the France which now exists, affords no promise of security against aggression and injustice in peace, and is destitute of all justice and integrity in war. . . . He will still persist . . . in saying, that we have an intention to wage war against opinion. It is not so. We are not in arms against the opinions of the closet, nor the speculations of the school. We are at war with armed opinions . . . Whilst the principles avowed by France, and acted upon so wildly, held their legitimate place, confined to the circles of a few ingenious and learned men, whilst these men continued to occupy those heights which vulgar minds could not mount, whilst they continued to occupy themselves with abstract inquiries concerning the laws of matter or the progress of mind, it was pleasing to regard them with respect . . . Whilst these principles were confined in that way, . . . we saw nothing in them to alarm, nothing to terrify; but their appearance in arms changed their character. We will not leave the monster to prowl the world unopposed. He must cease to annoy the abode of peaceful men.

And he went farther.

Whilst Republican France continues what it is, then I make war against Republican France; but if I should see any chance of the return of a Government that did not threaten to endanger the existence of other Governments, far be it from me to breath [*sic*] hostility to it.

1. Meaning of course a security based on justice.
2. Referring to a speech by Tierney [for whom see pp. 126–7 above]; see *P.R., 3rd ser.,* VIII, 663–6.

Grenville said the same in the Lords; in his case indeed to a different demand, from an Old rather than a New Whig, Fitzwilliam,[1] for deliverance 'not only' from 'the tyranny of the French republic, but from the *French Republic itself*'.[2]

> No man would . . . deny that the existence of the present Government of France was incompatible with the security of the other Governments of Europe. It was against this Government, acting on its present principles, . . . that he would wage war. . . . Yet if ever the government changed in such a manner as to make it safe to treat with it, favoured by proper circumstances, he would enter upon the work of peace without any regard to the name of its government.[3]

Those who saw the need for our efforts in the war 'must' in fact 'see the necessity of not coming to any specific declaration'.

> For one, he would avow his object. He wanted security; . . . a security resting on the tried good faith and justice of a well tempered government. . . . Much had been said of a crusade against France, and of a war waged for the extermination of opinion. Such declamation very little deserved to be seriously commented upon. If used reproachfully then he would say that the word *crusade* was improperly introduced; for the truth was, it was a coalition of powers gloriously in arms to defend all just and legal governments, and the rights of every people, against the madness, the wickedness, the oppression, the tyranny, and the injustice of the French Directory.

All this was consistent with the Ministry's approach since 1793, when Hood had mistakenly received possession of Toulon in the name of Louis XVII.[4] There had been three intervening episodes which, it might be claimed, suggested complications. Hopes in 1795, not dissimilar from now, had brought us closer to the exiled monarch – unofficially given the style of King for the first time – than had been thought desirable before. On the other hand we had twice treated for peace with the Republican government, in 1796 and again in 1797.[5] Both Burkeans and Foxites might therefore reasonably ask for some further clarification. Pitt and Grenville would have replied that their formula covered and in fact emphasised the preferred flexibility. We had stipulated certain provisions for the future if we were to work with Louis XVIII. Our two approaches to the Directory were made when the omens for a more proper French foreign policy seemed

1. Cf. II, 417.
2. *P.R., 3rd ser.*, VIII, 689.
3. Op. cit., 695–6.
4. II, 309–12, 320.
5. Op. cit., 581–4, Ch. XV, particularly sections II–IV; Ch. II, sections III, IV above.

brighter – and when, as Pitt a little later admitted, he feared that our threatened finances could have soon stopped us from waging war at all.[1] But we
had given no pledge to any one; we had not compromised our own interests;
our different moves showed – with impartial failure indeed – the middle
course we pursued. Our position remained both consistent and open to
yield advantage as it might offer. We demanded, as we had done in the
opening year, 'some legitimate and stable government . . . capable of maintaining with other Powers the accustomed relations of Union and Peace.'[2]

The drafting of that statement however had drawn a comment at the
time from Pitt. Could there not be, he had asked, 'a more pointed
recommendation of monarchical government with proper limitations?'
After all, it was in practice 'the only force from which we expect any
good';[3] and despite all the frustrations since, this perforce remained the
case. He had never held a high opinion of the Bourbons, and he did not
do so now. Louis XVIII's stubbornness – or his Court's – was exasper-
ating, and d'Artois' relations with the moderates scarcely less so. He had
not changed his views of the old monarchy's ambitions in Europe, which
he had watched in peacetime. But at least it was a form of government
broadly respectful of accepted conventions, and looking to the future it
would in any case be occupied for 'a considerable interval' in trying to
restore an 'exhausted and impoverished state'.[4] Grenville for his part
made his feelings clear in private. 'Europe can never be really restored to
tranquillity but by the restoration of monarchy in France'.[5] This again
was not the result of any inborn respect for the old regime, or of a liking
for the Princes themselves: on the contrary, he was contemptuous of the
first[6] and had too much experience of the second. He was no Bourbon-
lover, like Windham. He was simply and unyieldingly a hater of
'Jacobinism' – a term he used to describe the spirit of all stages of the
Revolution so far. Less volatile than Pitt, rather less concentrated on the
supreme importance of finance, and less prepared to make significant
concessions in pursuit of peace,[7] he was now ready to go to lengths he had
not countenanced before. In his sudden enthusiasm for the attack on Brest
for which he saw wider consequences, he was even willing to take the
French fleet in the name of Louis XVIII.[8] Shades of Toulon! But all must

1. Speech in the Commons of 3 February 1800 (*P.R., 3rd ser.*, X, 343–4).
2. Declaration of 29 October 1793 (II, 311). And cf. Pitt's statement of 17 June, op. cit., 303.
3. To Grenville, nd but 5 October 1793; op. cit., 312.
4. Since it would not be able to 'extort from its ruined inhabitants . . ., in peace,' the exactions open only to a 'system of robbery and confiscation' like the present (3 February 1800; n1 above).
5. To Mulgrave, 5 August 1799 (*H.M.C., Dropmore*, V, 243). Other similar expressions can be found in his letters to his brother Tom during the year.
6. As late as 1795 he was prepared to repeat the traditional defence of the events of 1789 as springing from 'a government in itself bad'; see II, 456.
7. I, 132–3; II, 629–30, 647–8; pp. 55, 57–60 above.
8. Mackesy, *Strategy of Overthrow*, 222, citing a letter to Thomas Grenville of 27 August.

now be adjusted to the overriding need to seize every means of expunging the 'root and origin' of wickedness.[1]

This guiding impulse did not disappear with the collapse of the royalist risings. How it would have operated given their greater success, it is hard to tell. The Government's support was spread, as earlier, over 'ultras' and 'moderates' alike: to strict legitimists, and to constitutionalists such as Pichegru and his surviving circle. Hard problems would have lain ahead if the summer's hopes had been realised, and choices been forced on a sponsoring Power.[2] As it was, the monarchist cause taken as an entity was to remain an integral element of the British plans.

II

It was in statements of policy arising from Parliamentary debates that Pitt's place in the conduct of the war may be traced most sharply in 1799. Away from that arena, the moulding and pursuit of the Ministry's strategy can be followed more clearly through the Foreign Secretary's eyes. For particularly perhaps in the first, formative stage of the Coalition's plans, Grenville was not only conducting diplomacy but shaping military ideas. One has indeed the strong impression that his was the driving force behind the efforts to implement a policy which he, more than any of his colleagues, had designed. As always, one has to be careful. The Foreign Office of course was the Department centrally involved and its files tell a continuous story. Ministers for their part as usual did as much, or more, by talking as by letters, and this was particularly true of periods when Parliament was in session. And Grenville's personal correspondence, above all his intimate disclosures to his brother Tom, may naturally be weighted in his own direction. Nonetheless one senses a commitment combined with a confidence which is unambiguous. If he was the necessary channel of communication within the Alliance, he appears also in his own right as the instigator of the contents. He certainly identified himself entirely with them, for success or failure. At one point he adjured Pitt to persist on the course which would bring 'credit and reputation to myself, and lasting benefit to the country'.[3]

Given Grenville's prominence in this whole matter, what in fact of Pitt himself? Was it the case that the Foreign Secretary was assuming 'an increasingly dominant role in the Cabinet' at a time when the Minister was wearying of the war and its control?[4] How far can either proposition be deduced? Are the two men's positions to be seen in terms of a seesaw? And are we witnessing in 1799 the start of a decline in grasp which in 1800 would become the 'downfall' of Pitt?[5]

1. Grenville to Thomas Grenville, 16 July 1799 (*H.M.C., Dropmore*, V, 147).
2. Cf. II, 320.
3. 2 August 1799 (Dacres Adams Mss, formerly P.R.O. 30/58/2).
4. Jupp, *Lord Grenville*, 224.
5. See the subtitle to Piers Mackesy's *War Without Victory* (p. 226, n5 above).

Some facts can be cited in support. From the winter of 1798–9 the Minister was busy on the successive stages of his latest, and large, financial plans. This was demanding in time, and in technical and political effort.[1] His health moreover, while not endangered as it had been recently, was still not good; in April he was said to be indisposed and depressed.[2] Against such a background, the complications of a fresh system of alliances may well have fallen the more easily into Grenville's hands. And Grenville himself was in a sterner mood. His uneasiness had been growing for some time: he had been disturbed by Pitt's handling of the Spithead mutiny, and, much more important to him, of the negotiations at Lille.[3] Now that new opportunities offered he was determined not to be bypassed but to see that the Ministry followed a consistent forceful course.

A strong Secretary of State – and Grenville's resolve and vigour were at a peak – could draw on reserves of institutional power in a structure of diffused powers.[4] It was indeed the availability of such ready means of aggression or defence that gave personal relationships their distinctive flavour. Pitt had achieved an ascendancy over the years which pervaded the system – on the system's own terms, which were equally real. His authority was tested and revealed most sharply of course at moments of disagreement;[5] but it was the product of accumulation in less dramatic ways. This must be borne in mind in trying to assess its extent in this instance; for the two colleagues in point of fact were genuinely agreed here on their aims. Pitt was always apt to be attracted to a giant design – to a policy which satisfied a range of interlocking objects[6] – and this was one which could be taken as meeting precisely such a requirement. He subscribed to the basic policy of a Coalition as fully as Grenville: imbued with a foreboding sense of time, of the strong desirability of victory within two to three years, he had not followed Dundas's broad if still undeveloped alternative.[7] He certainly shared Grenville's disgust with the Austrians over the Loan Convention and, if perhaps less vehemently, his general distrust of their intentions. He was quite ready – as his record suggested – to woo the Prussians if it seemed worth while. He favoured an attack on Holland, as a desirable element in a Russian alliance and the main British contribution to the land campaign, carrying also valuable maritime and diplomatic effects. It is hard to be categorical given the inadequacy of his own papers and correspondence.[8] But that drawback is nothing new; it applies, often equally, to other periods; and if the evidence is incomplete it

1. To be discussed in Ch. IX below.
2. P. 82 above.
3. Pp. 29, n3, 230 above.
4. Cf. I, 169–71, 309–11.
5. With Grenville himself for example in 1795; see II, 548–55.
6. Cf. II, 9 at the time of Ochakov.
7. Pp. 142–5, 148, and for his own financial expectations 98 above.
8. Cf. xii above.

does not seem to me to suggest that he simply accepted what his cousin proposed, or held views which were simply overborne.[1]

Timing as always is all-important. The war itself changed in the following year, and Pitt's position then was to be seen in circumstances which were not those of 1799. An arguable line of progression did not in fact run entirely straight. Grenville of course did not always have his way in the early phase itself; one instance has been cited in September, when his unusual impulsiveness – running to a willingness to alter his own plans – was checked in part at least by the lack of Pitt's support.[2] For one must not lose sight of that factor. Pitt's backing remained a necessary element in framing and pursuing an effective design – as indeed was later to be proved in reverse. The letter in fact in which the Foreign Secretary linked his own responsibility with the national advantage[3] contained an impassioned plea to the Minister not to let him down. In 1799 Grenville was the protagonist and main executant of a policy which, with Pitt's positive agreement, was dominant in Cabinet.[4] Pitt himself was dominant as Minister, against the background of affairs at large and while the shape of the war still offered a coherent policy to which he could bend his mind.

III

Parliament rose on 11 July and reassembled on 24 September: an unusually early date, as the King's Speech observed, brought about by favourable developments demanding legislation to free more militiamen for service overseas and provide further financial supplies. The Speech itself was full of confidence.[5] 'In the short interval since the close of the last Session, our situation and prospects have . . . improved beyond the most sanguine expectation'; and in one quarter, of most direct interest, there was particular room for promise. 'There is, I trust, every reason to expect that the effort which I am making for the deliverance of the United Provinces will prove successful'. These buoyant phrases proved in the event to be the epitaph of the summer's hopes.

The hopes had indeed been high. For France now really seemed ripe for defeat. Tired and increasingly divided at home, increasingly unpopular abroad, her armies were becoming increasingly hard pressed. If the pace of Allied operations slowed down in Switzerland, there were further successes in Italy:[6] the last isolated strongpoints in the north capitulated in

---

1. A relationship which does justice to both men emerges, as an example, in Pitt's letters to Grenville in June and July 1799, in *H.M.C., Dropmore*, V, 78, 149, 152–3.
2. Pp. 225–6 above for the proposed sudden expansion of aid to the French royalists.
3. See p. 231 and n3 above.
4. Cf. pp. 35–8 above.
5. *P.R., 3rd ser.*, X, 2. There is a fair copy in Pitt's files in P.R.O. 30/8/234. Cf. p. 224, n1 above for the second militia bill of the year.
6. See pp. 212–13 above.

July, and a French debouchment from the mountains ended in defeat at Novi in mid August. The Tsar moreover had decided by then to send Suvorov through the Alps, reinforcing the Allies around Zürich for a combined attack.[1] Meanwhile the plans were preparing for the Anglo-Russian assault on Holland, with an insurrection in the Low Countries, to be followed possibly by risings in France.

At the same time, the very height of the expectations posed them on a knife-edge. For the British design rested more closely than ever before – even than in 1794[2] – on common acceptance of complementary roles in a military offensive. As such it postulated intense diplomatic effort within a Coalition lacking agreement on diplomatic, and hence military, aims.[3] When the irresolution of a neutral Prussia was added, the compound was complete.

> . . . international relations [it has been remarked] . . . are, by definition, the relations of independent wills, each one regarded by its subjects as embodying the highest and most general good which is practically conceivable . . . This is why diplomatic history, more than any other kind of history, is 'one damned thing after another' . . .[4]

The sequence is notably evident in 1799.

From June to August the effects fell directly on the preparations for Holland. Calculations for shipping, manpower, geography had to be reconciled as far as possible with those of a political future for the Low Countries which involved strategic consequences, and balanced for some weeks in the light, or murk, of the Prussians' intentions.[5] In the early stages the plans turned naturally on technical feasibilities. Dundas set to work to find troops; at first on quite a modest scale, 'borrowing' from the Channel Islands and Ireland, the latter now better placed again to fulfil its familiar role.[6] But the main problem soon proved to be shipping, to transport a British force of some 10–15,000 and a larger Russian army – its size still uncertain – either altogether or in part.[7] As so often in seaborne assaults, the difficulties grew with the demands; and indeed the early assumptions had been grossly optimistic. Vessels, to be taken largely from trade, were harder to come by than Ministers had thought; the Admiralty was unwilling to lend extra seamen; a great design was hinging on

1. Whitworth to Grenville, no. 52, 9 July 1799, received 31st (P.R.O., F.O. 65/43). The Marshal received his orders on 27 August.
2. II, Ch. X, sections I, II.
3. Cf. pp. 209–11 above.
4. Richard Pares, 'Human Nature in Politics', repr. in *The Historian's Business and Other Essays* (1961), 38.
5. The following three paragraphs lean heavily on Mackesy's account in *Strategy of Overthrow*, ch. 8.
6. Cf. II, 305, 343, 358, 597, 634.
7. Pp. 216–18 above.

marginal figures.[1] The obstacles were overcome, not least in St Petersburg where the resourceful Captain Home Popham, sent to work out arrangements,[2] persuaded the Tsar to find some ships of his own. By the second half of June his needs were met: transport for 10,000 men in British hulls and 8,000 in Russian, with a handsome subvention to keep the Russian Admiralty up to scratch.

The final answer could not have been found if the size of that force had not been settled by then. The numbers requested most recently proved, again, to be optimistic. The Tsar made it clear that he would not supply 45,000 men as the British were hoping: he wished to hold some among the troops reserved for whichever policy he adopted with Prussia.[3] The limit would be 26,000; and he was soon relieved of part of that, for his neighbour Sweden, now increasingly unhappy with her familiar benevolent stance towards France,[4] offered in May to join him in the Coalition with 8,000 troops financed by herself. Accepting them at once, Paul reduced his contribution to 17,000. This news, which disturbed Whitworth and Popham, was received at first quite calmly in London, where the prospect of an accession to the Alliance was marred only by the fact that the Tsar was thought to have 'blabbed' to Stockholm the secret of the men's destination.[5] The arrangement however became rather less popular when his final terms for the British subsidy were presented and found to include a secret provision for Sweden as well. At the end of June matters therefore stood thus: Russia would provide some 17,000 men, the Swedes prospectively 8,000, and Britain 8,000 or 13,000 depending on the event. Britain would also supply all the horses needed, to save Russian shipping, and pay Russia (separately from the commitment to Sweden) £88,000 for mobilisation, £44,000 a month while her troops were retained, and £19,600 a month for their transport.[6]

Plans for the invasion itself were under way while the size of the force was being determined. One set indeed had been drawn up earlier by the Duke of Brunswick,[7] for a purely British effort; another was now completed in outline by Grenville working with an elderly General de Stamfort, a useful European contact with the Dutch Orangeists and Prussians,[8] who

1. One may cite the not dissimilar experience – given much more expert assessment – in the marginal but perennial shortage of assault shipping in the Second World War.

2. P. 218 above.

3. See pp. 215, 218 above.

4. II, 277, 505–7, 551, 609.

5. Grenville to Thomas Grenville, 1 July 799 (*H.M.C., Dropmore*, V, 115), referring to the information in Whitworth's no. 34 of 13 June, received on the 30th (F.O. 65/42).

6. The French text of the Convention, of 22 June 1799, is in *Consolidated Treaty Series*, 54, 493–504. It was the need for the Commons to approve this subsidy that led in part to Parliament's recall as early as September (p. 233 above).

7. Kept closely in touch as always for efforts with Prussia; cf. p. 135 above.

8. He had long been in the service of one or the other, including periods as military tutor to their princes, and was involved in the talks with Berlin early in 1798 (for which see pp. 135–6 above). He was usually called Stamford in the British correspondence.

agreed to go to St Petersburg late in May. But this was quickly overtaken by Popham, never short of ideas or loath to air them, and using his 'dashing spirit', as Grenville called it, to press them on the Tsar.[1] In mid June he produced a result, managing to 'tempt the Emperor into a quick decision' and to impose his own specific scheme.[2]

These were curious ways in which to introduce an important undertaking. The Grenville-de Stamfort plan of April–May concentrated the British part of the assault on the island of Walcheren – a name of ill omen – at the southern mouth of the Scheldt. A commander was then appointed for that task: Sir Ralph Abercromby, currently commanding in Scotland after his Irish imbroglio; and he was soon busily engaged in preparations with Dundas.[3] But he was the field commander. There seems to be no record of military advice being taken at a higher level in London while the design was first being shaped.[4] Grenville, de Stamfort, Popham form an odd trio to present ideas on operations; only one of them was a soldier, and he not in British service. Popham's proposal moreover, absent as he was from the seat of government, proved to be out of line with Grenville's intentions. For whereas the Foreign Secretary envisaged a Russian landing in the far north-east of Holland by the river Ems, which would lead to a concentrated advance towards the British based on Zeeland, he advocated a three-fold assault, by Russians (divided in three sections) on the north-east, by Russians again on the northern Scheldt, and by the British on Walcheren. Such an emphasis on the western provinces had its attractions. But it might well need a complement in strength from the north, and in Popham's plan that was weakened and in fact endangered. For not only were the landings themselves dispersed, but the scheme, at least as presented, seemed to cater specifically only for the

1. Grenville to Thomas Grenville, 26 June 1799 (*H.M.C., Dropmore*, V, 105). See Mackesy, op. cit., 108 for a précis of Popham's unusual naval career. He is remembered best as the author – or perhaps perfecter – of the revised signal code which formed the basis of a system for the fleet in use to this day. Characteristically, he had it printed privately, circulated it himself, and produced his own further revisions until it was adopted officially in due course.

2. Mackesy, op. cit., 114–15. He had in fact submitted an earlier version of this to Grenville as long ago as the previous autumn, when he was involved in the clandestine correspondence with part of the Dutch resistance.

3. See P.R.O., W.O. 1/179, 6/25 *passim*; pp. 163–5 above for his experience in Ireland.

4. Cf. Mackesy, op. cit., 136. It is hard to know indeed exactly where the advice would have been sought at this point, for Cornwallis, the habitual and natural source, was in Ireland. Chatham, a Major-General (who indeed would soon himself be operationally involved), was available as a member of Cabinet; but his military reputation was scarcely impressive. Richmond of course had long since been removed from the centre (II, 428). General David Dundas was a possibility, and so was the Duke of York (both of them, like Chatham, soon in fact to be operationally involved). But the former seems to have been available mainly for measures of administration, training and defence, and Ministers were rather wary of the Duke after 1794–5 (see II, 489n5, 490, 491n3, 635 for Dundas; II, 364, 374–5, 428, 491 for York). The lack of opportunity for a serious offensive in Europe over the past three years may have left its mark on the structure of consultation.

opening phase and to ignore penetration inland. This last movement, however, lay in Grenville's eyes at the heart of the operations, for it enabled the Dutch people to rise with the assurance of Allied support. Although the zealous naval Captain had known something earlier of the preparations for an insurrection, he had thus failed to seize its importance in an integrated design.[1]

His proposals were also lacking in a larger dimension; unable to take wider considerations into proper account. For even while the talks were proceeding in St Petersburg the landings in Holland were on the point of becoming affected by calculations in Vienna and Berlin. Hitherto these had provided a background – an incentive – for the concept itself. Now they would impinge directly on acceptance of the detailed plan.

Early in June Grenville and Pitt addressed themselves to the prospects for the main fronts over the rest of the year's campaign. They did so on the understanding, recently secured, that the Austrians would use the Russians in Switzerland and not on the Middle Rhine; that part of the Archduke Charles's army would operate likewise in Switzerland; and that the rest (the larger part) would cover southern Germany and also lend direct support by pressure on the defences around Belfort, lying between the Vosges and the Jura, and continue into the Belfort Gap itself.[2] Both men were seized of the importance of such commitments. Pitt made it clear at that point that the Russians' main strength should not be reduced on any account: the subsidised force of 45,000 should be kept 'unimpaired', but we must be content if necessary with 20,000 allotted to Holland.[3] Even so however it seemed doubtful if the former would suffice for the next stage of our overall design. For that remained constant: a massive thrust through Franche-Comté to Lyons, where the standard of insurrection could be raised for either the autumn or the following spring. To this end it would be desirable for a Bourbon to be on hand, and since freedom of policy for the future would be prejudiced by the presence of Louis XVIII himself, d'Artois should be chosen to raise the banner in his name.[4] The central advance could now be accompanied on the right by the Archduke's operations, and on the left, thanks to the successes in Italy, by an attack from Austrians and Sardinians (the latter in possession once again of Piedmont) through the Alps into Savoy. The Italian victories

1. See Mackesy, op. cit., 115–18; and p. 236, n2 above.

2. Cf. pp. 210, 212–13 above; Eden to Grenville, no. 58, Most Secret, 23 May 1799, received 4 June (P.R.O., F.O. 7/55).

3. To Grenville, 3 June 1799 (*H.M.C., Dropmore*, V, 78); and see p. 219, n6 above for Grenville's own opinion on the same day. Cf. also p. 235 above for such a background in London to the opening response to a Swedish involvement.

4. Grenville to Eden, no. 17, Most Secret, 8 June 1799 (F.O. 7/55). Possibly at the head of a Swiss force. This was in fact the project for which the Prince was brought from Holyrood two months later (p. 225, n2 above).

moreover could remedy the comparative weakness in Switzerland. For once Piedmont was wholly cleared – which was expected to happen very soon – what should be done with Suvorov's troops? Why not send them north through the mountains to reinforce their fellow countrymen? On 8 June this suggestion was despatched to the Tsar.[1]

The British were thus now proposing that the Russians should be the instrument for the Allies' main drive deep into France. Suvorov's appearance would bring their force in Switzerland, it was thought, to 65,000 men: a formidable concentration, and there could well be accessions.[2] The prospect was seen as holding strong advantages from our point of view. In Grenville's eyes an army controlled by Russia would not be 'thwarted or checked . . . by the contracted policy of Vienna', in operations which did not directly support Austria's aims.[3] It would bring a renowned commander to the centre of affairs. And whatever the degrees of difference in their answers for the future in France, it would align the two major Powers most anxious to see the Directory expunged.[4] Given the frequent essential disingenuity in statements of Anglo-Austrian relations, the arrangement might indeed have been argued further to hold advantages for Austria herself. For while it postulated action on the southern flank which would revive Sardinia's mainland status, it would remove the General who, to Austria's dismay, had called for the imminent return of the King;[5] it would relieve Austria of any need to consult Russia's preferences in northern Italy; and by reinforcing the Russians in Switzerland would conserve Austrian strength north of the Alps.

Although these considerations do not seem in point of fact to have been advanced from London at this point, they would be unlikely to escape Vienna's notice. They had however to be assessed with others. Thugut, while not aware of the suggestion to the Tsar that Suvorov should be sent north, himself proposed a certain strengthening of the Russians in Switzerland. But he did so with a fresh statement of plans for Italy and for the Archduke Charles, the latter of which in particular ran entirely counter to the British hopes.[6] He disagreed that Piedmont could be

---

1. Grenville to Whitworth, no. 41, sd. The despatch is not in the Foreign Office file F.O. 65/43; and the Embassy's own archives in the P.R.O. (F.O. 181) start only in 1801. Nor is there a copy in the relevant letter book in Grenville's own papers, B.L. Add. Ms 59195. But Mackesy found one in Thomas Grenville's, in the Stowe collection at the Huntington Library at San Marino, California (op. cit., 85n44).

2. It was hoped that there would be some 20,000 'resolute' Swiss in addition. Over the next few weeks it also seemed possible that 6,000 men could be procured from Württemberg for Russian use, on a British subsidy and, it was hoped, despite the principality's links with Austria.

3. To Whitworth, no. 46, 26 June (F.O. 65/43).

4. Cf. pp. 210–11 above for the Russian approach, with a reservation on the Bourbons.

5. Cf. p. 213 above.

6. Eden to Grenville, no. 75, Most Secret, 26 June 1799, received 10 July. The latter's despatch of 8 June (p. 237, n4 above) had reached Vienna on the 23rd (F.O. 7/55).

cleared quickly and Savoy penetrated in the current campaign: Austrian troops should instead enter Provence in the extreme south, east of the river Var.[1] Furthermore, of much greater importance to Pitt's and Grenville's strategy, he had 'changed his ideas' for the Archduke himself. That army, instead of attacking Belfort, should turn towards Mainz and lay it under siege. Such a move would help operations in Switzerland by drawing off large French forces; the fortress might well fall before the winter; and the Austrians could then advance on the Low Countries in the spring, regaining the Austrian Netherlands, a project presumably favoured by Britain[2] and one that would be greatly helped if a British 'diversion' could be mounted in Holland. In this context, the Russians, with some Swiss, should penetrate into France, and d'Artois could join them when the Allies had reached an understanding on the objects of the war.

These statements were received with anger in London. Nor was that surprising, for they not only reversed the latest intimations; they hoisted the Government with its own petard. The British proposal for the central front in fact became hopelessly vulnerable unless Austria agreed to an advance which did nothing directly to forward her own ends. It was foolish to maintain, as Grenville did, that the Russians' operations in France could not be 'checked' by Vienna: they required the support of the Austrian army on their right. If the bulk of that was removed two hundred miles to the north, their impetus, even their safety, was seriously at risk. He himself in particular had rested the plan partly on distrust of Vienna. It was galling to find his predictions being borne out at the plan's expense.

The Foreign Secretary indeed was reluctant to think that the move on Mainz could be carried out. The Archduke's army, as it stood, would probably not be strong enough. Nonetheless his disgust was extreme. 'If he [Thugut] were paid to thwart all our measures, . . . he could not do it more effectually.'[3] And the reasons seemed clear. With northern Italy secure, Austria was looking to the Low Countries 'as the next object of scramble', and 'our forward move . . . as a diversion' by which she could also 'cut and carve' on the left bank of the Rhine.[4] He was broadly right. The Austrians, like other Powers, were nurturing their interests: in Italy, in Germany, and now in their erstwhile Netherlands. Six days after Grenville wrote these words, the Emperor announced his resumption of the rights in those provinces which he had ceded at Campo Formio.

What was to be done about Thugut's response? One step had already been taken to strengthen our voice in Vienna itself. Eden, long thought inadequate and a victim now of Grenville's frustration,[5] was given notice of recall in June and replaced by Lord Minto, the former Gilbert Elliot:

1. Which debouched at Nice; and no mention was made of Sardinian troops.
2. See pp. 203, 214 above.
3. To Thomas Grenville, 16 July 1799 (*H.M.C., Dropmore*, V, 147).
4. To Lord Minto [for whom see below], no. 3, Most Secret, 26 July 1799 (F.O. 7/56).
5. See II, 343n4, 367n6, 594n4 for earlier doubts of his capacity. Some recent requests from him to come home were now gratified.

perhaps the most impressive of that group of Scots who were always on tap for preferment.[1] But the main hope was to take the Austrians' statements simply as proposals, to stress the need for the Archduke's close support, and, under pressure, disclose more of our own plans. These were the lines of the answer sent in mid July.[2] Thugut had made one helpful suggestion for British officers to be sent to the Archduke's headquarters, and the offer was at once taken up: Lord Mulgrave,[3] it was said, would leave in the next few days. The Austrians were also now informed officially that an expedition to Holland was in train; and 'a full explanation' of 'our general object' would follow very soon.

The message did not do the trick. Eden's final meetings with Thugut yielded some uncertain hopes.[4] The Russians, including Suvorov's troops if sent, should enter Franche Comté; and a force of 40,000 Austrians and subsidised Germans (the latter preferred in London to serve under Russian command)[5] 'might' also undertake 'some expedition into France' from the upper Rhine. In the south, the Austrians would aim at striking in due course at the Dauphiné – an area of operations less remote than southern Provence.[6] But no guarantee was given that the force on the upper Rhine would concentrate on Belfort; and above all, the plan to direct the Archduke to Mainz had been 'determined'. That moreover had an unwelcome consequence: Mulgrave should not be sent to Austrian headquarters, but to Vienna instead. None of this could relieve the fears that concentration of effort would be lost, and that military considerations were being sacrificed to diplomatic ends.

Matters did not improve in the next few weeks. On the contrary, they grew worse. This was not solely because of the decision on Mainz, which Minto confirmed, though now mitigated – or cloaked – by a further statement on the upper Rhine. The vague assurance of support there, it was true, was converted into a promise of action against Belfort, 'at the proper season', by 30,000 Austrians with the German additions when the latter should arrive. But the phrase could cover an indefinite period,[7] and its

---

1. For some of whom in, usually secondary, diplomatic posts see op. cit., 8 & n2. Sylvester Douglas (op. cit., 405n7, 407) also springs to mind. For Minto's own career see II, 176n3, 310, 346, 403–6. He was appointed in this instance however after two other choices had declined: one unidentified, the other the perennially courted Thomas Pelham (see op. cit., 594n4 and p. 173, n1 above). He reached Vienna on 1 August, the day on which the Emperor made his announcement about the Netherlands.

2. Grenville to Eden [now created Lord Henley], no. 20, 16 July 1799 (F.O. 7/55).

3. See p. 90 above.

4. Eden to Grenville, no. 97, Most Secret and Confidential, 3 August 1799, received 16th (F.O. 7/55).

5. P. 238, n2 above.

6. See pp. 238–9 above.

7. Minto to Grenville, no. 2, 9 August 1799 (F.O. 7/56). He doubted if the Germans would in fact be available for the current campaign – and a pencilled annotation, made presumably in the Foreign Office, survives against the phrase respecting Belfort, construing that as meaning 'next year'.

significance was overshadowed in any case by other news concerning Switzerland itself. Early in August the first battalions of Russians arrived there at last from their long march. On the 9th, Minto was told that the Archduke's force around Zürich would accordingly be withdrawn at once.[1] Figures were supplied, for the Allies and the enemy, to prove that the new arrivals could cope. But these proved inaccurate: Swiss recruitment was disappointing; the Russians' own strength was shown to be less on the ground than on paper[2]; and in any case a transfer of command and positions was bound at the least to be awkward. Other announcements were equally discouraging. Mulgrave's mission was now said to be unnecessary, since the plans for the remainder of the year's campaign were 'settled'.[3] Conversations on Piedmont produced the impression that Austria was determined to keep it, and perhaps the twin possession of Sardinia as well. She was unwilling to accept British pressure for the Württemberg contingent to operate under the Russians. And her policy for France seemed to rest on 'a stronger inclination to divide [the country] and perpetuate the distractions . . . than to reestablish either monarchy or any other steady government'. In particular, Thugut discounted the claims of the royalists' strength.[4] All in all, the successive despatches amounted to a cheerless report.

This drift of worrying news, coming in through the high summer,[5] had to be balanced with other uncertainties on the thin line between hope and disappointment. As the months went by, it seemed increasingly possible that the final stage of victory would have to be postponed until the following spring.[6] But that itself might be prejudiced unless the deep lodgement in France had been well established before winter set in. There was nothing that the British could do about this in the last resort: their weapons were restricted to persuasion and inducements. But the latter could be deployed in relation to their own sphere of responsibility. Their action against Holland was both affected by and could affect the Austrians' plans.

1. Ibid; received on the 26th.
2. It was suspected while *en route* to muster 30–35,000, of the supposed 45,000. On arrival the strength proved to be 29,000.
3. Despatch as in p. 240, n7 above. This was not exactly eased by the remark that his assistance would be welcome in discussing plans for the next year. As it happened, he had left England already.
4. Minto to Grenville, nos. 3, 6, 8 of 10, 13, 17 August 1799, the last received on 2 September (F.O. 7/56). He thought however that while Thugut seemed to be 'considerably behind the rest of Europe' in these remarks on France, he might be brought to agree to a declaration for a restored monarchy – a further indication, if any were needed, of Grenville's own views.
5. From 10 July to 2 September; pp. 238 and n6–41 above.
6. This in fact seems to have been taken fully into account by August, to judge (taking one example) from Mulgrave to Grenville, 2 August 1799, and his Instructions of the 7th (*H.M.C., Dropmore*, V, 227, 255).

It was a matter of timing; and that could turn on the fate of the talks with Prussia, which seemed to have taken a turn for the better at the end of May. The Tsar's offer of troops, while reducing the force he would provide in concert with Britain, led the government in Berlin to keep Thomas Grenville's mission alive. Ministers in London had judged it wise to discount success.[1] But after some weeks of familiar frustration, the outlook looked promising in July. Early in that month Haugwitz presented a sketch of articles for a Convention: a 'plain unequivocal declaration', as the envoy saw it, to co-operate in freeing 'Holland and the neighbouring Provinces' in return for £1 million for 60,000 men to cover the whole of the campaign. Prussia would open hostilities after the Russians had begun to blockade Mainz: a demand based on the Tsar's generalised offer of troops. Tom Grenville felt encouraged, and his hopes rose higher in the next few days when Haugwitz accepted his objections to the terms of the subsidy and to a specific operational condition. Prussia instead would now come in when the Tsar's troops moved towards a junction on the Rhine, and would take a subsidy paid by the month according to the size of her force at the time. In a further talk, the envoy went so far as to hint at the prospect of the British expedition – already rumoured in Berlin – which he suggested might encourage the Prussians' earlier entry into the war. They might indeed even find it unnecessary then to invade the Low Countries, acting instead, on their subsidy, on the lower or middle Rhine. This again met with a favourable response, from the King as well as the Minister, and it seemed really on the cards that an agreement might be signed very soon.[2]

The information reached London in stages, on 17 and 19 July, a week after Ministers learned of the Austrians' intention to move on Mainz.[3] Pitt and Grenville were pleased, though now, paradoxically, with reservations brought about by the course of recent events. For our own expedition, they agreed, was almost ready. We expected rapid success to follow. What, Grenville asked, would we then be paying Prussia to do for the rest of the campaign? And what, both wondered uneasily, would she claim in reward? The phrase 'Holland and the Netherlands', as Pitt paraphrased it, covered all parts of the Low Countries.[4] We were not anxious for her to stay in Holland itself any longer than was needed;[5] what was to be done if she moved into the Austrian Netherlands as well? For this posed a further and very significant complication. Although Austria's behaviour was thankless, we could hardly hand over her former provinces to a rival who

1. See pp. 215, 218 above.
2. Thomas Grenville to Grenville, nos. 48, 50 of 7, 11 July (F.O. 64/55); same to same, 8, 12 July (twice) 1799 (*H.M.C., Dropmore*, V, 135–9). A prospective Russian move on Mainz would not of course suit Austria now; but this did not figure in the intimations to Eden in Vienna.
3. Pp. 238–9 above.
4. In point of fact the phrase did not specify the Netherlands, but rather 'pays limotrophes' to Holland; cf. above.
5. Cf. p. 203 above.

had been neutral while she herself was at war. Furthermore – a question now of immediate import – might not a hint, or even promise, be given of their return in due course if Vienna dropped the idea of Mainz? As Grenville observed, an arrangement with Prussia was thus 'not without its difficulties' on the lines suggested. And these, as Pitt observed, related to our own intentions after Holland was won. For, more than ever, we would wish now to move into the whole of the Low Countries: whatever Austria might decide on the future of the main fronts, we should be present in Flanders the better to offer our bait. At the same time, the very fact that speed was daily becoming more crucial made a Convention with Prussia directed primarily at Holland more urgent even than before.[1]

The problem was taken to a Cabinet on the 20th, and the result sent to Thomas Grenville three days later. While we were 'afraid of being involved blindfold in the Prussian politics', particularly for the Netherlands, we 'much wish', his brother wrote privately, 'to get the . . . [military] declaration'.[2] We therefore accepted Berlin's proposals, with one notable exception: the phrase 'pays limotrophes' taken in immediate conjunction with Holland.[3] This could cause 'uneasiness' in St Petersburg as well as London, and some alteration was required. With that proviso however we trusted that the formal signing could follow at once, accompanied by Prussia's call on France to withdraw from the United Provinces. At the same time, while not holding up any action there that might ensue, we would want to negotiate further over terms for a subsidy paid as a sequel or alternative for other operations on the lower or middle Rhine.[4]

But whatever might have happened when this broadly favourable message reached Berlin, it proved to be out of date before it was sent. For, yet again, the Prussians had had fresh thoughts. On 21 July Haugwitz told Tom Grenville that his Court would not go ahead with the Convention. Rather than threaten France to evacuate Holland, it was opening a negotiation for a peaceful withdrawal.[5] There were signs, he said, that this could be achieved. If it failed, however, Prussia would be ready to act with the Allies.

1. Pitt to Grenville, 16, 18 July; Grenville to Thomas Grenville, 19 July 1799 (*H.M.C., Dropmore*, V, 149–50, 152–3, 159–61). We have Pitt's views in writing on this occasion because the Foreign Secretary was spending the summer largely at home at Dropmore.

2. See Windham's diary of 20 July (*Diary of Windham*, 411) for the Cabinet meeting, on which no Minute survives in Grenville's papers in B.L. Add. Ms 59306; Grenville to Thomas Grenville (from Dropmore again), 23 July 1799 (*H.M.C., Dropmore*, V, 177). By a slightly later letter, Dundas was clearly in favour of acquiring this Prussian co-operation as soon as possible (to Grenville, 29 July 1799; op. cit., 206).

3. See p. 242, n4 above.

4. Grenville to Thomas Grenville, no. 34, 24 July 1799 (F.O. 64/55). It was, as he remarked, a 'voluminous despatch'.

For the call on France see p. 217 above.

5. Thomas Grenville to Grenville, no. 57, 22 July 1799 (F.O. 64/55). In a despatch of the 18th, no. 55, he had already detected disturbing signs. The decision was formally confirmed on the 24th; same to same, no. 59, 25 July 1799, received 7 August (loc. cit.).

The bombshell landed in London on the 31st. Pitt was in Kent with Dundas, hastening the last preparations for the expedition. He learned of it on 1 August. It led, he wrote to Grenville, to 'so much *new* consideration' when there was 'not a minute to be lost' that he begged the Foreign Secretary to leave Dropmore for Walmer at once.[1] For this was indeed an upset. Operational plans had proceeded in June and July without reliance on Prussia; but, as so often, the problems had been mounting elsewhere, to a point in fact recently where the potential value of that aid had mounted equally fast. Now it was summarily almost definitely removed. And that was not the only blow. On the same day it was learned in London that the Swedish force was almost certainly withdrawn.[2]

If this was really so – for despite gloomy reports, talks between Stockholm and St Petersburg continued – it meant that the Russians' contribution for Holland was reduced to less than 20,000 men.[3] Not only therefore would the plans for their landings be altered: the change would affect the latest British plans for the exploitation of their own assault. It would indeed go far to confirm a fact which had become increasingly obvious: the conjunct operation, in its successive stages, would be predominantly a British affair.

That prospect had not been so clear two months before. In May the British contribution had been announced as either 8 or 13,000 men.[4] But the efforts already under way then to supply a greater pool of 'offensive force' came to fruition in July with the passing of Dundas's new Militia Act.[5] This did nothing to increase the strength of the initial landings, which in any case was settled by the limits of transport. But it did provide on paper an extra 10–15,000 men who could be used if required to follow up. In point of numbers therefore we might now talk, at best, of some 25,000 infantry, together with 3,000 cavalry earmarked in the original plans. And we not only stood in that case on an equality with the Russians and Swedes, or a superiority to the Russians; we were developing a more definite design for the Low Countries as a whole, and we were in charge of the military and political plans for revolt.

These were building up in the summer. Intelligence was still far from firm, though taken as encouraging by and large. There was no guarantee,

---

1. 1 August (*H.M.C., Dropmore*, V, 217).

2. Whitworth to Grenville, no. 53, 9 July, received 31st (F.O. 65/43). See p. 235 above. There was no effective direct communication with the Swedes themselves over their offer to Russia, in part at least because they were currently embroiled with London over British claims of maritime belligerent rights (cf. II, 503–7). But an emissary – William Gartshore, a rather unsatisfactory Scot, foisted on Dundas and doubling as his private secretary in the Secretary of State's office and as a MP – was sent to Stockholm to discuss arrangements. He decided at once that nothing could be done (to Grenville, 8 August 1799; *H.M.C., Dropmore*, V, 259), and meanwhile the Russians were taken aback by the extent of Sweden's financial demands, after her initial apparent generosity (p. 235 above; and cf. II, 9).

3. Ibid.

4. Ibid.

5. Pp. 223–4 above.

despite promising soundings, of initial hopes that the Dutch fleet would be delivered when the British appeared, and military commanders for the most part were distinctly anglophobe. But sympathy for the Allies was said now to be evident in the forces, and widespread enough in the country to warrant serious preparations. It remained hard to tell how effective those would prove: caution and political differences – ascending, among the Orangeists themselves, as far as the Stadtholder and his heir – had to be weighed against undoubted resentment of the French.[1] The Foreign Office was inundated with papers of varying quality, mostly from exiles in London and Berlin, and Grenville's confidence, so pronounced earlier, wavered as the moment approached. Nor were others as optimistic as he; Dundas indeed became so uncertain of the 'Dutch coming forward' that he doubted if Holland could be conquered quickly, or the Austrian Netherlands occupied without Prussian co-operation.[2] Nevertheless, the Foreign Secretary persisted in his hopes, and Dutch (and Belgian) resistance remained embedded in the Allies' design.[3]

Planning for the landings did not go smoothly. On the contrary it was beset by uncertainties in a timetable first extended and now uncomfortably short. The appointment of a commander brought a proposal for a radical change, scrapping Popham's arrangements as approved by the Tsar.[4] In place of three separate assaults – or of two as envisaged by Grenville and de Stamfort – Abercromby wanted one, concentrated on the estuary of the Maas. This should include in the opening wave a first contingent of Russians brought to England for the purpose – which however would mean in Ministers' view that the expedition could not be under way until the third week of August. The advantages were seen as those of concentration at a critical point; threatening the enemy's rear in the northern provinces, giving a defensive flank on the river Waal in the south, and opening the way to the country's richest region and administrative centre.[5] Grenville and Pitt agreed that Popham's plan would not

1. Nor was the Stadtholder himself, resident at Hampton Court, of much use: lethargic as ever (cf. I, 521), he was determined only to oppose the more active policies of the Hereditary Prince. 'You . . . ask what the Stadtholder is doing', Grenville wrote at one point to his brother Tom, 'why, he is fast asleep, snoring, and not even dreaming of doing anything' (26 June 1799; *H.M.C., Dropmore*, V, 105). Cf. p. 220 above, and see in general Mackesy, op. cit., ch. 9 and Schama, op. cit., 391–2.

2. To Grenville, 29, 31 July 1799 (*H.M.C., Dropmore*, V, 206, 215). Auckland, a former Minister at The Hague, doubted even more.

3. The state of his feelings in mid July is reflected in a despatch for Russia. The initial expectation of success had turned 'in a great degree on the probability of internal risings'. With the means now for a more powerful assault we need not depend on that 'precarious effect'. But the resulting plan had 'the advantage of having its front towards the enemy covered by a Country in insurrection' (to Whitworth, no. 55, Most Secret, 15 July 1799; F.O. 65/43).

4. Pp. 235–7 above.

5. Abercromby's 'Note' of 6 July 1799 (*H.M.C., Dropmore*, V, 123–5). While the plan did not rely on action or a threat, even passive, from Prussia, it was worked out against that possibility at least. The targets would be one or more islands to the north of Walcheren, itself (p. 236 above) now dropped from the plan.

do. But they returned to the idea of two assaults and drew up separate memoranda on that basis in the next few days, allowing for the greater available British strength.[1] Both envisaged two main waves of landings: in Pitt's case of 12,000 British early in August, supported some three weeks later by 8,000 Russians and a further 13–18,000 British; and of 10,000 Russians and 8,000 Swedes in the north in September, joined by some British cavalry and an artillery train. Some 50,000 men might thus be involved, raising fresh questions for shipping; and, if Abercromby's plan in particular was adopted, the Russians must obviously be approached at once. Time was becoming of the essence. And this was pointed sharply in the same few days. For it was on 10 July, while the two Ministers were preparing their Minutes, that they learned of the Austrians' intention to send the Archduke to besiege Mainz.[2]

That news probably tipped the scales. They may well have been in the balance already from Grenville's well-founded liking for 'operations *en masse* preferably to demonstrations'.[3] Abercromby's plan was accepted, at a further meeting, with one notable exception: the British force would sail on its own without waiting for the Russians, as soon as the wind allowed after 1 August,[4] to be joined in Holland by a first Russian contingent probably not long after the 20th. That in turn would be followed, or accompanied, by the second British force; the second contingent of Russians and Swedes would follow late in September; and a smaller 'diversion' by some 3,000 British, to be reinforced possibly by some Russians, would meanwhile seize the northern island of Ameland, from which to supply insurgents east of the Zuider Zee. These proposals were sent to St Petersburg at once; if indeed they could be called proposals, for the Russians were told that we intended to proceed with our own programme, and took it to be 'improbable' that they for their part would refuse.[5]

The despatch in fact announced that we would be acting 'without delay'. But if that was Pitt's and Grenville's decree, it did not appear so easy to others. There were still shipping problems to be worked out for a remodelled operation; plans for the assembly of larger forces and the raising of militia; inquiries, with Dutch assistance, on the approaches and defences of new landing points; final contacts with the Orangeists; increased preparations in Flanders. There were further lists to be made, charts to be studied, fresh intelligence to be scanned, detail altered and adjusted against a date now only a fortnight or so away. Of course many

---

1. Grenville's 'Minute' of 10 July, Pitt's of the 13th (op. cit., 130–4).

2. Pp. 238 and n6, 240 above.

3. To Thomas Grenville, 16 July 1799 (*H.M.C., Dropmore*, V, 146). He gave this in fact as his reason, adverting to the Austrian news apparently separately in the course of the letter. On the evidence already adduced, however, one may take leave to hold both factors in view.

Cf. p. 213 above for his views on concentration of force.

4. Cf. p. 244 above.

5. Same to Whitworth, no. 55, Most Secret, 15 July 1799 (F.O. 65/43).

such shortcomings were familiar in major seaborne assaults – they always are – and the system in the Revolutionary War was subject to compelling constraints. But with such a deadline, and the complication of a distant partner, any administrative system would have been hard pressed. It was hardly surprising that a good deal was missing at the end of the month. Transports were short – according to Abercromby, by a third. So, as usual, were effective strengths – according to him, by a quarter. There were not enough warships in place, particularly to carry the craft needed for landing. There were not enough arms, and not enough waggons.[1] Worse, some of the vital information on the defences had not arrived from Holland, and there was thus no true means of telling if our first contingent could suffice on its own. Abercromby had never wanted to land without the Russians. He accordingly asked for the British embarkation to be delayed.

This proposal roused Grenville, the more sharply when Dundas, though not himself supporting the General's plea, began to question the Foreign Secretary's continued assumption of success. Such qualms were brushed aside from the pleasaunces of Dropmore.[2] But Pitt's letter of 1 August on the news from Prussia, with its talk of *'new* consideration',[3] was another matter, and it sparked off an anguished appeal. Grenville would not come to a meeting at Walmer, as asked, to witness 'the disappointment of all the hopes I have been cherishing'. It was essential to launch the assault at once. The 'laziness of Clerks and Staff Officers' had caused enough trouble already; all the more necessary, particularly in 'the present political situation', to accept that time counted more than 'insufficiency of force'. This was a matter beyond the sphere of the military commander; it was one affecting the future of Europe itself. While he did not feel that he could contribute to the administrative efforts, he begged the Minister not to let the 'blessed project' slip.[4]

The 'remonstrance', as Pitt called it, evoked a reassuring and sooth-ing response. Grenville was told that his fears were unnecessary. 'All military difficulties are completely overruled, and every step will be instantly taken for the immediate embarkation of the troops'. The remaining transports were expected in the next few days.[5] Pitt and

---

1. See Mackesy, op. cit., 161–2, and for shipping a few days later, 167. The *quality* of the first echelon was however said to be unusually good; that of the second, largely from the militia, much less so. From descriptions of the latter's arrival in camp, indeed, it was a Rowlandsonian scene.

2. See p. 244 above. Correspondence 29–31 July, in *H.M.C., Dropmore*, V, 206–16, and see also Grenville's letter of 30 July in B.L. Add. Ms 40101. Cf. p. 245 above for Dundas's doubts now of success without Prussia's co-operation.

3. P. 244 above.

4. 2 August 1799 (Dacres Adams Mss, formerly P.R.O. 30/58/2). He had already written the day before, on similar lines though in less passionate terms (Holland Rose, *Pitt and Napoleon*, 262–3, giving part of a letter in P.R.O. 30/8/140); and he did so again, refer-ring specifically to Prussia, six days later (8 August; B.L. Add. Ms 40101).

5. Pitt to Grenville, 2, 3 August (*H.M.C., Dropmore*, V, 224–5, 232). The first of these letters elicited a more contented acknowledgment (2 August 1799; *Pitt and Napoleon*, 263).

Dundas, now based at Walmer, were indeed hard at work, with the soldiers and sailors on the spot, with the military Departments, with Spencer at the Admiralty.[1] The pace had certainly quickened. But the intelligence from Holland was still lacking, and Abercromby really should not sail until it came in. At last it did so; but it was inadequate, leaving continued doubts as to where precisely to disembark. Dundas had again heard from Grenville on the perils of delay: he now sought his opinion, by way of riposte, on this last unsolved problem. The Foreign Secretary however declined to be drawn at this stage on an operational point. He was more concerned about any postponement that might discourage the Orangeists, and – a fresh twist in the story – might enable the Prussians, now seen as spoilers rather than helpers, to march into Holland themselves after making a deal with the French. It would be dreadful to be forestalled. The expedition must leave at once.[2] And so it did, after a final readjustment of plan: on 10 August Abercromby was given a last-minute addendum to his final orders which gave him latitude over where to land. The two Ministers down at Walmer were now in high spirits, Pitt as so often ready and Dundas allowing himself to hope. The ships were due to sail on the 13th, and Pitt rose early that morning to cruise about the convoy and wish it godspeed. Having seen it 'completely off', he left at once for London.[3] The project hatched for so long had moved from paper to a force at sea.

IV

One part of the grand design was thus about to be put to the test. The fate of the rest meanwhile remained in the balance on the central front. So far as was known in mid August, the Archduke's main army had not actually moved north; and to balance that uncertainty, something at any rate had been achieved. The news of the Tsar's agreement to send Suvorov through the Alps came on the same day, refreshingly, as those of the blow in Berlin and the disappointing outlook in Stockholm.[4] The Russian armies would thereby be concentrated in Switzerland; and the

1. Who was not always happy, by the time things were over, with the way in which his two colleagues were ordering the navy about (*Private Papers of Spencer*, III, 157–60).
Perhaps it was at about this time that Pitt acquired the copy of the *North Sea Pilot* which was among his books at his death ('Catalogue of the Library at Walmer Castle late Belonging to the Right Honble. Wm. Pitt taken 12 Feby, 1806'; Pretyman Ms 562:21).
2. Grenville to Dundas, 5 August (B.L. Add. Ms 40101); Dundas to Grenville, 6 August (*H.M.C., Dropmore*, V, 246–7); Grenville to Dundas, 7 August (B.L. Add. Ms 40101); same to same, 9 August 1799 (*H.M.C., Dropmore*, V, 269–70).
3. *The Diary of Sir John Moore*, ed. J.F. Maurice, I (1904), 340 (a former subordinate of Abercromby's in Ireland and now commanding a brigade in the expedition, he dined with Pitt and Dundas on the 11th); Dundas to Spencer, 11, 12 August (*Private Papers of Spencer*, III, 162, 111); Pitt to Grenville, 13 August 1799 (*H.M.C., Dropmore*, V, 278).
4. See pp. 234, 238, 243–4 above.

Austrians' latest decision, to withdraw from that theatre, had not yet been received.[1]

There might therefore still be all to play for. And there was one possible card to play. In the last half of July Grenville mulled over the idea of guaranteeing possession of the Belgic Provinces to Austria, in return for 'co-operation afforded for the attack on France'. The question was probably discussed in a Cabinet held on the 20th or slightly later; but, as the King then remarked, any such promise made it the more necessary to be 'quite certain' of occupying the territory ourselves before someone else arrived. That could apply to the Prussians; it applied clearly to the Austrians themselves, for such a position would allow us to talk to Vienna in 'the only style' that would be understood.[2]

The new line of approach appeared the more probable from a suggested withdrawal on an old issue. Grenville was apparently prepared to drop his insistence on ratification of the Loan Convention. If this was really so, a page had been usefully turned.[3] But in any case a further spur was applied at the beginning of August; as soon as Prussia withdrew from the talks, Pitt advised that the Emperor should be 'distinctly' offered 'the guarantee . . . at the peace'.[4] A possibly fatal pause, however, ensued. For as Grenville saw it, such a step should be taken only if the proposal was included in 'an extensive consideration of measures and objects for the prosecution and ultimate termination of the war'.[5] In other words, Austria must meet our wishes: we could then reciprocate. As a result nothing was said to Vienna throughout the month.

Whether an offer of the provinces would have made any difference one cannot guess. It might have become embarrassed by a complication from

1. See p. 241 above.
There was the prospect moreover of some additional if marginal strength. The Tsar had earlier sent Condé's army of exiles, for whose pay he was now responsible (cf. II, 584–5), from its lodgement in Poland (p. 222 above) to Switzerland: a move which in fact raised some embarrassment when he stated clearly, and maintained until the British refused to budge, that he preferred Condé himself – not unnaturally – to d'Artois as the Bourbon representative in an invasion of France (p. 237, n4 above; and cf. II, 371–2). Now it seemed likely that some German troops would also be engaged. The negotiations for 6,000 Württembergers, to be employed on British terms in return for a subsidy (p. 238, n2 above), ended successfully in August; and Bavaria too was offering a force, possibly of 10,000 men, to operate likewise with the Russians if we would meet the bill. In point of fact the value of these reinforcements was doubtful: numbers were uncertain, quality was said to be poor. But at any rate they suggested that the smaller German states retained confidence in the Allies. See P.R.O., F.O. 65/43, 82/2, 9/18 covering July to September for Russia, Wurttemberg and Bavaria respectively.

2. Grenville to Dundas, 27 July 1799 (*H.M.C., Dropmore*, V, 199). But he had 'nearly' reached a decision on his idea on the 19th (to Thomas Grenville, op. cit., 160; and cf. pp. 242–3 above), when he wrote of 'further discussion in Cabinet', perhaps on the 20th. On the 27th he referred to a talk with the King on 'Wednesday', which probably meant the 24th.

3. Same to Eden [Henley], no. 20, 16 July 1799 (F.O. 7/55). Cf. pp. 133–4 above.

4. To Grenville, 2 August 1799 (*H.M.C., Dropmore*, V, 224). He was staying that day near the main assembly camp in Kent.

5. To Mulgrave, Private, 3 August 1799 (op. cit., 234–5).

a different quarter. For towards the end of July the Tsar, increasingly suspicious of Austria's conduct in Switzerland, announced that he proposed
to hold an Allied conference in St Petersburg on war aims. The news
reached Vienna before London – in the latter case late in August – and it
may have been responsible for a suggestion from Thugut of a full bilateral
'explanation' with Britain.[1] In any case a guarantee which postponed
possession until the peace cut across Austria's obvious wish to stake a
physical claim soon. Perhaps a declaration of intent, in some direction,
would have been worth while; Pitt himself was soon to show that he
thought so. As it was, such a possibility was quickly rendered out of date.

As Minto's run of despatches came in, through the second half of
August into early September,[2] the Foreign Secretary's reaction indeed
pointed quite the other way. If Austria persisted with the plan for Mainz
she must bear the consequences: no military co-operation or financial
support (which, Thugut might have replied, had not been noticeable yet),
no further talks, and even the withdrawal of Minto himself. Unless some
better answer was received he was indeed to leave Vienna. We could continue to fight the war on our own lines. For, as Grenville stressed when he
showed his despatch in rough draft to Pitt, the Minister 'must see that
every part of the plan you had flattered yourself with when we talked
together in Downing Street, has (as far as it depended on . . . Austria)
fallen to the ground before it began to be executed'.[3] The message was
duly sent. Nonetheless Pitt still wished to persevere. For his mind was
ranging as circumstances moved. If Austria showed no sign of meeting us,
we would be well advised (as Grenville thought also) to bring Flanders and
Holland together, as earlier envisaged, in one new state. This would probably – or certainly – need Russia's support, perhaps at the Tsar's conference; and an alternative offer to Austria would then be an acceptance –
even an extension – of her pretensions in Piedmont, finding some
recompense for Sardinia elsewhere. In fact he was prepared to favour

1. Whitworth to Grenville, no. 58, 28 July 1799, received 21 August (F.O. 65/43). For the
proposal's reception in Vienna and the possible consequence see Minto to same, no. 8,
Most Secret, 17 August 1799 (F.O. 7/56).

2. P. 240, n1 above.

3. 28 August (Dacres Adams Mss, formerly P.R.O. 30/58/2) – a not untypical example,
one might think, of a member of Cabinet taking the precaution of reminding a Prime
Minister of his involvement in the member's own favoured policy; same to Minto, no. 5, 31
August 1799 (loc. cit.). For good measure he also returned in his despatch to the subject of
the Loan Convention. His disgust was repeated a few days later as the catalogue of 'scan-
dalous' behaviour built up (same to same, no. 7, Most Secret, 4 September; loc. cit.), and
was made clear to Russia (same to Vorontsov, 3, 4 September (*H.M.C., Dropmore*, V, 355,
357)), same to Whitworth, no. 79, 6 September 1799 (F.O. 65/44). See also his letter to
Windham of 2 September (*H.M.C., Dropmore*, V, 347).

In point of fact, Grenville might have admitted one element in the design which had so
far 'fallen to the ground' thanks in part at least to British mistakes. Craufurd [see p. 219
above] had quarrelled with the Swiss, and failure to recruit levies as had been hoped could
be laid to some extent at his door (eg Wickham to Grenville, Most Private and
Confidential, 2 September 1799; *H.M.C., Dropmore*, V, 348–9).

'*any* arrangement of Italy which Austria desires, and Russia can be brought to approve'. Nor was he dissuaded by Grenville's reluctance to make such a concession in the south. Austria, he wrote on 13 September, 'should hold the key of Italy', and the Tsar be brought to agree to a united Netherlands, preferably under the House of Orange.[1] We should therefore, by implication, not go to extremes at once – though clearly he did not disapprove of a threat. Others too tried to calm Grenville. Vorontsov, while concerned about Austrian ambitions, wrote in moderating terms, and Dundas, at Walmer once more, 'entirely' agreed with Pitt. It began to look as if the Foreign Secretary must keep the lines open to Vienna.[2]

And then on 14 September the Government learned that the Archduke had started to withdraw from Switzerland. Any ideas for the near future were at once given up. In his 'rage and despair' Grenville could see only 'the most mournful future' for Europe, and Pitt for his part felt that his recent proposals were 'at present quite out of the question'. He still did not abandon hope: perhaps Prussia might yet be induced to join ourselves and Russia; more likely it would be a matter of carrying on with Russia alone. We might soon be making our attempt on Brest to destroy the Combined Fleets;[3] and thereafter we could look 'with security to a limited and defensive war'. That need not rule out a blow against Spain from the Mediterranean, perhaps aided by the Russians, while the two partners held Holland in strength. It was a resilient response. But the fact could not be blinked that such measures fell 'wretchedly short of the prospects which seemed so lately to be within our reach'.[4]

One thing in any case seemed almost certain. The Russians around Zürich would now be exposed, at least until Suvorov's army arrived. And so it proved. The Austrians, as it happened, soon began to change their minds. The Archduke, reluctant but obedient, had been withdrawing fast; at the beginning of September his forces were still poised to threaten Belfort, but on the 5th he set out for the north. Moving swiftly down the Rhine, he forced the French once more to cross the river, and after taking Mannheim on the 16th continued towards Mainz. Meanwhile however his Government was becoming anxious: he was shortly ordered to return, and Thugut furthermore told Minto that some 10,000 Austrians would then remain in Switzerland – though this was apparently only to guard

1. Pitt to Grenville, 10, 13 September (*H.M.C., Dropmore*, V, 379–80, 396–7). He had indeed wanted Thomas Grenville to leave Berlin – which itself had been arranged – for St Petersburg to aid such talks. The Foreign Secretary's reluctance emerges in a letter to Pitt of the 12th (P.R.O. 30/8/140).
Cf. p. 203 above for the thoughts on a united Low Countries.
2. Vorontsov to Grenville, 9 September; Pitt to same, 13 September 1799, on Dundas's 'entire' agreement (*H.M.C., Dropmore*, V, 377, 397). In point of fact there was possibly a hint that Grenville was cooling down even by the 6th (to Mulgrave: op. cit., 368).
3. Pp. 225–6 above.
4. Grenville to Vorontsov, 14 September; Pitt to Grenville, 15 September 1799 (*H.M.C., Dropmore*, V, 400, 404).

the routes to the south.[1] But it was too late. The French moved first, on 25 September. By nightfall on the 26th the Russians at Zürich were routed. On the 27th Suvorov emerged near the Lake of Lucerne after a month's hard march, only now to confront destruction in his turn. Plunging back into the mountains, he fought his way circuitously towards Lake Constance, where he joined the remnants of his fellow countrymen. It was a legendary performance, through the autumn snows; but only half his troops survived, he lost all his artillery, and if the Russians were at last combined they were also out of action. Switzerland was firmly in the enemy's hands once more; and until it was reconquered no advance could safely be made into south-east France.

V

On 27 August, a month before Suvorov emerged briefly from the Alps, British troops landed at the Helder, some eighty miles north of the Maas estuary on which so much ink had been spilt.[2] Date and place were in the hands of the commander once the convoy had sailed:[3] a prolonged North Sea gale decided the first, forcing the ships to beat off the coast for ten days, and last-minute intelligence persuaded Abercromby to switch the point of attack. The approaches to the islands off the Maas were even more difficult than he had thought, now that it was certain that the French could not be diverted immediately by a Prussian threat.[4] A landing on the mainland seemed preferable; the Helder, while posing its own problems for assault, offered a defensible bridgehead and a port for men and sup-plies; and it could promise a further bonus if earlier persuasion had paved the way, for the harbour was the base of the main Dutch fleet.[5] The attack was successful – a great relief on an open coast in the aftermath of a storm – and the bonus was secured. On 30 August the Dutch fleet surrendered with twenty-five warships.

This opening raised spirits in London.[6] The Tower guns were fired, there were the usual illuminations, mail coaches were hung with Orange colours. Duncan's work at Camperdown had been completed: a naval threat was

---

1. Minto to Grenville, no. 20, 14 September 1799, received 27th (F.O. 7/56). And see no. 21, loc. cit., a week later.

Thugut later claimed that the Austrian force originally from eastern Switzerland (see p. 212 above) had been expected to suffice in support of the Russians. He may have been sincere; but if so, that military advice had been full of risk.

2. Section III above.

3. P. 248 above.

4. Cf. pp. 243–4, 245 above.

5. P. 245 above.

6. And not only there. Down in Kent Pitt and Dundas attended a *feu de joie* on Canterbury race course in honour of the landing, where after the militia's celebrations 'It was not thought prudent to attempt a march past' (quoted in Richard Glover, *Peninsular Preparation . . .* (1963), 228).

removed; and the first wave of the army was safely ashore. Hopes ran high. The second British wave was gathering for embarkation, under the command of the Duke of York, with Pitt's brother Chatham, a soldier by origin, in charge of a brigade.[1] On 1 September Abercromby began his advance to secure the bridgehead, and six days later the first Russian transports arrived in Yarmouth roads. All was 'bustle and hurry' on the Kent coast, where Pitt was back at Walmer, entertaining York who had arrived with 'his retinue . . . in the highest style and magnificence', talking to the Generals in the nearby ports, watching the efforts to put the horses aboard.[2] The wind was delaying departure. But the altered programme was not badly adrift. The design in its final form seemed to be in train.

There was indeed more than one indication of confidence at this point. Not the least was the idea of the attack on Brest, burgeoning even before York sailed.[3] For that would have to be on a scale which would mean switching forces from Holland within a very short time, before winter set in. How the details could have been worked out it is hard to see. But either the French would have had to be beaten, or at least driven back and held mainly by the Russians; or the Allies would have had to rest in favourable circumstances on a line which could be held until the spring. This last in fact briefly became Grenville's thesis; and while it drew on his sudden zeal for the resistance in France, it rested perforce on a belief that matters in Holland would be safely advanced. For even if the Allies had to wait until the spring to complete their victory – and he was obliged in September, from the lateness of the season, in any case to think on such lines – he was expecting not only the military but the political position in the Low Countries to allow of a British presence established and awaiting the final step.[4]

That in fact was already clear. For Grenville had earlier privately disclosed his thoughts. Forecasting victory, he was intent on securing 'a permanence' of influence at The Hague. In good Grenvillean style that indeed could also forward the family's own interest, for he had his brother

1. Cf. p. 236, n4 above. The Duke had been selected in July as prospective commander of the combined forces of the expedition, which gratified his father. The choice also, as it turned out, met a proposal then received from the Tsar that the appointment should go to the senior General present – whom Russia was able to provide – unless outranked by a royal prince.

2. *The Morning Chronicle*, 5, 7 September; *The Morning Post*, sds and 11 September; *The Times* (from which the quotations are taken), 5–7, 9, 10 September 1799. The Duke, though not the retinue, was lodged with the Minister at the Castle.

3. Pp. 225–6 above.

4. As early as 15 July he had indeed declared in a despatch to Russia (no. 55, Most Secret, F.O. 65/43; see p. 246, n5 above) that there seemed 'little reason to doubt' that the Allies would be possessed by the winter of 'the whole of the Dutch province north of the Waal'. This may however have been said in order to preserve a strictly British interest in the territories beyond, as a phrase immediately following in fact strongly suggests. More seriously, he had to compose a 'Note', probably for use in Cabinet, on 28 September – by which time operations were in a state of uncertain balance (p. 255 below) – calculating the forces likely to be available to the Coalition for the coming year (B.L. Add. Ms 39306).

Tom in mind for the post.[1] Prussia's change of heart brought the issue to a point. Tom was told to leave Berlin as soon as he liked, and join the Hereditary Prince of Orange (the Stadtholder's heir, hitherto resident in Berlin) near the Dutch border. He did so, on 1 September,[2] with a twofold brief: to keep in close touch with the Orangeists preparing the rising, and to attend on a provisional government set up by the Stadtholder, occupying the Embassy in due course to direct 'that shapeless mass which we must . . . reduce into a form of efficient and permanent utility to ourselves'. This was a task for 'now or never', to abolish a 'dead weight' on our affairs – when it had not shifted to hostility – over the past hundred years.[3]

An ambitious vision, extending influence into dominance, particularly when it might embrace the future of the Belgic Provinces as well.[4] Its strength was reflected in a further proposal, to send over the Foreign Secretary in person for a month or six weeks to carry any necessary 'changes' into effect. This was apparently suggested by Pitt and Dundas at the end of August – if Grenville had not dropped the hint himself. Of course 'things' might arise in the interval to affect the intention. But otherwise, he announced, 'I must certainly practice as I preach'.[5]

Things did arise. The encouraging military start in Holland was not sustained. Abercromby advanced a few miles to a line of defences protecting his base; but there he halted, with what seemed in London to be undue caution. It was certainly natural for Ministers to be concerned. But

1. Grenville to Thomas Grenville, 30 July 1799 (*H.M.C., Dropmore*, V, 212–13). The prospect was clouded at one point when he felt himself bound to consider Malmesbury, the hero of 1787–88 in The Hague (see I, Ch. XVII, section II); but a fortunate spell of illness in that quarter left the way clear. For good measure, Tom would apparently be 'Ambassador', in a post hitherto rating a Minister.

2. Same to same, no. 40, 9 August; Thomas Grenville to Grenville, no. 69, 1 September 1799 (F.O. 64/55), and sd, Private (*H.M.C., Dropmore*, V, 342). See p. 251 and n1 above for Pitt's short-lived idea of sending him to the Tsar's projected conference in St Petersburg.

3. A dubious return, one might think, for the, naturally self-interested, involvement of Dutch finance in British stocks over that period, at least down to the American War. Grenville to Thomas Grenville, no. 40, 9 August (n2 above; same to same, 31 July 1799 (*H.M.C., Dropmore*, V, 213). Something of what he really felt may have been revealed in a further letter, of 5 September, in which he referred to Tom's position at The Hague as the King's '*Viceroy*' (Mackesy, op. cit., 129).

4. Cf. p. 243 above. On 4 September Grenville was talking of inciting a rising in those provinces 'now' (to Dundas; *H.M.C., Dropmore*, V, 356). Of course such an event, together with the desirable aim of bringing the Austrian Netherlands into the Dutch orbit, might have been prejudiced if resources had been transferred to France as he was simultaneously suggesting.

5. To Canning, whom he invited to come as 'Secretary to the Embassy' to look after business forwarded by the Foreign Office – where Canning had been an Under Secretary (p. 59 above); 1 September 1799 (Canning Ms 63, Leeds). The dating of the proposal, said to have been made before Pitt and Dundas 'left town', may be established from *The Times* through the last days of August and particularly on the 31st. The idea was still in the air a fortnight later; indeed it had been brought to a point at which the King had to be informed. He thought little of it (to Grenville, 13 September 1799; *L.C.G. III*, III, no. 2034).

they had underestimated the enemy's potential; he was quick to rally and, it soon became clear, must be dislodged in strength. Allied reinforcements were coming in fast: both York and the Russians were at hand; and by 18 September the Commander-in-Chief could count on some 30,000 men.[1] He attacked the next day, and suffered a setback. But the French thought it prudent to withdraw a few miles, and on 2 October he tried again. The result was indecisive, though it gained some farther ground, and so was a further effort four days later. This time however the Allied Generals decided that the end had come. They had lost some 8–9,000 men, the sick list was growing, supplies were running short, and the navy could not promise adequate communications in autumn in the North Sea. On 8 October the troops were back on the line of a month before.

These were anxious weeks for Ministers, the more so as news was spasmodic and uncertain. It was in fact the frequent silences that worried them most. Anything was seized on to nourish expectations, and there were moments of genuine optimism; with Grenville until the end of September, with Dundas for another week at least. There was even talk early in October of giving Abercromby a peerage.[2] Pitt himself, for once keeping his mother in touch – with information about Chatham – appeared, and probably was, buoyed up if tense.[3] But in mid October, when rumours began to come in of the Russians' disaster in Switzerland, it was also learned that the commanders in Holland had decided 'to bring away our Army as soon as We can'.[4]

By then York was in fact about to start negotiating an armistice, which was embodied in a local Convention on the 18th. In return for the freeing of 8,000 French and Dutch prisoners of war in England, for which he vouched personally, the expedition could evacuate Holland unmolested within a period ending on 30 November. The terms, taken on his own responsibility, of course could be, and were, attacked. But his action proved fortunate, since the weather was breaking and conditions for a

1. On 2 September Pitt made a list of troops available, allowing for 18,000 Russians (P.R.O. 30/8/197, f. 158v).

2. See for this period correspondence between Dundas and George III, 10–11 October 1799 (*L.C.G. III*, no. 2054); also Dundas to George III, 7 October (op. cit., no. 2051). Grenville – to Wickham, 29 September 1799 (*H.M.C., Dropmore*, V, 434) – was still hopeful, though Ministers were then 'in an uproar' at the lack of information from the army (same to Thomas Grenville, sd; op. cit., 431).

3. Pitt to Hester Countess of Chatham, 24 September, 8, 12 October 1799 (P.R.O. 30/8/12), the last published in Stanhope, III, 198. He also wrote regularly to his sister-in-law (P.R.O. 30/8/101). For his more usual epistolatory habits with his mother see eg II, 547.

4. Pitt to Countess of Chatham, 14 October 1799 (P.R.O. 30/8/101).
The first reports of the Russians' defeat, from French newspapers, seem to have reached London by 12 October (see *The Morning Chronicle* of that date, and cf. *The Morning Post* of the 14th). Reliable news from a British source was received on the 16th (Wickham to Grenville, no. 30, Most Confidential, 30 September, received 16 October 1799; P.R.O., F.O. 74/24, printed, without the endorsement of reception, in *Correspondence of Wickham*, II, 223–34).

different future – for a contested withdrawal or a winter's stay – would have been dire indeed. As it was, the men and guns and even most of the horses, comprising 'England's . . . only army',[1] were taken off unscathed, the last contingent as the time expired.

That at least was a great relief. Without it, the Ministry could have been in trouble.[2] York's conduct earned official support, and not only in public.[3] Now the reckoning had to be cast. It could show some mitigations. The Dutch fleet had been disposed of, and though the enemy was not diverted by Allied pressure elsewhere to the extent that had been hoped, he at least had had to pull out some troops from Flanders and the Rhine to the Austrians' advantage on the latter front.[4] Nor was the British army's performance as inadequate as would be claimed. It had been operating in terrain that was difficult for attack, with an ill disciplined if brave ally, against forces which could call if necessary on sizeable reserves. Abercromby and York had not been brilliant; but they had not been inept – Abercromby in fact, though his heart had not been in this operation, was a shrewd and competent commander. But arguments salvaged from failure seldom carry much conviction at the time; and the venture had certainly failed. After the fine words of the King's Speech;[5] after all the months of complicated planning, of assiduous effort to find fresh manpower, the rising wear and tear on the Ministers concerned, their army, with three of the most prominent British Generals available,[6] had been permitted to quit the field by consent of the enemy in a matter of weeks. It was a humiliation; the worst military setback yet.[7]

For the operations themselves were not the only fiasco. So too was the expected insurrection by the Dutch themselves. The doubts of Dundas

1. Chatham's phrase; to Pitt, 19 October 1799 (P.R.O. 30/8/122). Cf. another military Cabinet Minister in 1793; II, 267.

2. In Chatham's view indeed it would have been 'overset' (to Pitt as in n1 above) – an unlikely outcome in point of fact.

3. Grenville, unlike his colleagues, questioned the Duke's right to have committed his Government; but he did not persist (correspondence with Dundas in *H.M.C., Dropmore*, V, 502–4). Pitt for his part found it possible 'under the present Circumstances' to 'rejoice' in 'the Arrangement' (to Huskisson, 21 October 1799; B.L. Add. Ms 38735).

4. Cf. p. 251 above for a possible impact on the Austrians' operations; and Mackesy points to the fact (op. cit., 312) that a French attack on Swabia was crippled by the diversion of troops. The point however could be carried too far: Dundas earned some ridicule in the Commons when he claimed that the assault on Holland had contributed to the enemy's defeat at Novi in Italy (see p. 234 above) – a battle fought two weeks before the first landing.

5. Delivered, as it happened, five days after York's first setback; see p. 233 above.

6. York, the Commander-in-Chief at the Horse Guards; Abercromby, a former Commander-in-Chief in the West Indies and then General commanding the army in Ireland; Sir David Dundas, formerly commanding the troops in the Mediterranean, now Quartermaster General at the War Office and acting in Holland as Chief of Staff to York (cf. II, 428, 491; op. cit., 492, 499; II, 316, 347, 635 respectively).

7. Pitt himself, trying to put as good a face on it as he could, had to admit that it was 'certainly no small Disappointment to be coming away by Compromise' (to Countess of Chatham, 21 October 1799; P.R.O. 30/8/101).

and others were fully borne out.[1] One set of preparations bore fruit: when the British appeared at the Helder there were sympathetic mutinies in the fleet which aided its surrender and easy removal. But by way of contrast scarcely a dog barked inland: a call from the Hereditary Prince for an uprising was ignored. There were a few scattered affrays at first, and a small incursion near Arnhem by Dutch émigrés, all easily put down. But nothing followed, and the National Guard of militia supported the French. In their own narrow area the Allied troops found at best a muted welcome, and more often indifference stretching to a hostile response. People wanted to be let alone. Abercromby put his finger on the point: 'the Hereditary Prince has been deceived in thinking he had more friends than enemies in this country. If we can advance, everyone will be on our side, but there are few who are willing to risk anything'.[2] The landings in point of fact lay in a region which was not Orangeist territory; and beyond that, the dilemma was revealed which can always threaten such schemes. As Wellington once remarked later, it is 'a fearful responsibility' to give the signal to rise. The Ministry had been wise to insist that outside support must be in sight. The trouble was that in this instance such support had originally been calculated, and ensuing policy based, on exaggerated expectations of the reciprocal aid. The equation was false: the reports of exiles and agents proved grossly optimistic. And the dual failure in Holland removed any chance of risings in the Belgic Provinces, for which preparations had recently been stepped up.[3] Some hopes were still entertained until late in September, at least by Grenville himself; but early in October they were fading away.[4] With their effective disappearance a final link was severed within the most extensive design, embracing Allied assaults and offensives, a pattern of complementary insurrections, the extension of British diplomatic interest, yet conceived in London in the course of the war.

1. See pp. 220, 245 above.

2. See Schama, *Patriots and Liberators*, 393–5; Mackesy, op. cit., 207–8, 248–9. By 'country', the General was referring to his immediate part of it.

3. See p. 254, n4 above. Money, arms and direction were to be provided, the last in the form of a British military adviser. Unfortunately, the first choice, sent to the frontier early in August, proved useless, and had to be replaced after discussion between Pitt and Dundas by the more competent Major-General Thomas Maitland, who two years before had conducted the negotiations with Toussaint l'Ouverture in the West Indies (p. 144 above). See P.R.O., W.O. 1/408 *passim*, *H.M.C., Dropmore*, V, index on 545.

4. Grenville to Thomas Grenville, 26 September; same to Sir James Craufurd [Minister in Hamburg], 9 October 1799 (*H.M.C., Dropmore*, V, 423, 467).

CHAPTER IX

An Order under Pressure: The Financial Treatment

I

'All modern Wars are a Contention of Purse'.[1] So a century's experience for Britain at any rate seemed to suggest, and a new Coalition would certainly mean some fresh financial commitments. There would be no treaties of alliance, no control of insurrections, without remittances and subsidies or loans. Government could look to some possible relief: Austria was not in line for immediate support, and loans – of which the Imperial Loans had formed the largest element in foreign aid – fell directly on the London market and not on the Exchequer. Nonetheless those private risks had to be guaranteed by the public;[2] other outgoings were met by the Treasury; and a major Continental campaign might mean more money for the British army as well. Such burdens were welcome in a sense, for they underwrote the preferred answer to a war which might otherwise drag on with indefinite expense.[3] Nor indeed on recent experience were they decisive – given an upper limit[4] – in any balance between acceptable and unacceptable levels of cost. In 1798 it had been possible to allocate a mere £200,000 to 'foreign States', and a like sum, as in 1797, to British land forces 'abroad'.[5] But even in those circumstances, net expenditure on the armed forces stood higher in both years than any previous wartime year.[6] When Pitt

1. Dundas to Pitt, 9 July 1794; see II, 412, and also op. cit., 530 for Pitt's implicit concurrence.
2. Op. cit., 363–5, 519–20, 557, and 377 for the Parliamentary guarantee. The very fact moreover that Austria would be denied aid until she agreed to the terms for settling her default on the last loan (pp. 200–3 above) meant that if and when fresh support was provided it was likely to be by direct Governmental subsidy.
3. P. 4 above. They could in fact represent 'true economy' (Pitt on 7 June 1799; *P.R.*, *3rd ser.*, VII (1799), 657).
4. See p. 98 above.
5. P.K. O'Brien, 'Government Revenue, 1793–1815' (see p. 100, n1 above), 531 table 37. And cf. p. 100 above.
6. Mitchell and Deane, op. cit., ch. XIV, table 2. A sizeable element of naval debt funded then but contracted earlier has to be allowed for in 1797; even so, the rest of net expenditure stood at a peak in that year, and at only a modest reduction from it in 1798 (some £29,433, allowing for the additional funding of almost £11,596, and £28,715 million respectively). The highest comparable figure previously was £24,782 million (allowing for a funding of £1,491 million of earlier naval debt) in 1795.

came to consider his budget for 1799, he had thus to reckon that whatever happened such expenses were unlikely to fall.

If therefore the annual deficit and the swelling volume of the National Debt were to be reduced, more money must be raised by taxes to set against the frightening dependence on domestic loans. The annual charges on debt, funded and unfunded, had risen from some £10,470 to some £16,029 million in the past four years – by over 50 per cent, to a figure which accounted for almost a third of the Government's total net expenditure.[1] It was with the object of raising a greater proportion of the supplies 'within the year' that the Triple Assessment was proposed towards the close of 1797.[2] Once the Act, as amended, had passed early in 1798 Pitt kept a close eye on its operations.

By the end of the summer he had reason to be heartened by the aggregate returns of revenue.[3] But these of course derived largely from Customs and Excise, reflecting an emergence from the recent depression;[4] and while higher rates on the assessed taxes naturally resulted in a higher yield, that was by no means as great as had been forecast. The Minister's opening calculation had been for a net £7 million on the Assessment and complementary measures. But the House of Commons had imposed changes to the former which cut the estimated total to £5 million, he himself lowered that to £4¹/₂ million, and although there was an unexpected bonus from the Voluntary Contribution – brought in to help fill the gap – the Assessment itself probably produced some £2 to £3 million in the event.[5] At the end of the day the Treasury remained more than £1 million down on Pitt's first hopes, the shortfall would have been much worse without a relief not initially designed, and the main scheme had to be pronounced a failure as it stood.

This last indeed soon became clear. The original bill, according to one well qualified observer, was 'deprived of all its principles, & much of its efficiency' by the Commons' alterations.[6] That however was not the only trouble. The amendments were responsible for the first lower estimates of

1. Of £47,422 million; ibid. In the same period the nominal amount of the funded National Debt itself also increased by a half, from £247.9 to £378.6 million (op. cit., table 5).

2. Pp. 101–2 above.

3. Eg Pitt to Pretyman, 24 October 1798 (Ashbourne, *Pitt: Some Chapters of His Life and Times*, 340).

4. See Mitchell and Deane, op. cit, ch. XI, table 1; Ashton *Economic Fluctuations*, 171–3; p. 108 above. Cf. Rose to Pretyman, 12 September 1798: 'Our Revenue and Commerce are going on famously' (Pretyman Ms 435:44), and Pitt on 7 June 1799 (*P.R., 3rd ser.*, VII, 683–4).

5. Cf. O'Brien, loc. cit., 402, and Cooper, loc. cit., 200 with Mitchell and Deane, op. cit., ch. XIV, table 1, the latter giving a figure for Land and Assessed Taxes, sources generically distinct but under common administration. The unaltered Land Tax yielded just under £2 million. See pp. 104, 106–8 above for measures planned in complement to the Triple Assessment, and for the unplanned Voluntary Contribution.

6. Auckland to Lord Sheffield, 23 January endorsed 1798 (B.L. Add. Ms 45729).

yield; but the difference between Pitt's initial forecast and the figure eventually obtained was attributable very largely to the fact that there were
'numerous and notorious evasions'. The liberty to opt for declared
income instead of past payments of taxable expenditure had made 'defal-
cations' all too easy.[1] Meanwhile the costs of war, actual and envisaged,
continued to rise: the first from the extended measures of defence, which
led to a now customary supplementary budget; the second from the
prospect of subsidies to bring about the Allied Coalition.[2] At some point
probably in the later summer or early autumn of 1798 Pitt was therefore
considering replacing the Triple Assessment by an outright Income Tax.[3]

Work then went ahead. The idea of course, as often with taxation, was
not new in principle. The oldest surviving annual levy, the Land Tax,
included an element of income through rents; Pitt himself had considered the practicability of a comprehensive tax on either property or
income in 1797; and he was acquainted with broad suggestions ranging
from Auckland in 1796 to Shelburne in 1782, when he himself had first sat
in the Treasury. A proposal indeed could be found as far back as 1628, and
Charles I's Ship Money and Tudor subsidies pointed to a simpler end.[4]
The difference lay, as again so often, in the will to carry an idea into effect.
The Minister followed familiar lines of consultation: with a handful of
colleagues and officials – Auckland (now Joint Postmaster General) and
Rose and Fordyce at least – and with figures outside. According to
Nicholas Vansittart, a backbench MP and future Chancellor of the
Exchequer, he gained approval – but in how much detail? – from 'the
principal moneyed men' in the City.[5] His hopes of Parliamentary success

1. Pitt in the Commons, 3 December 1798 (*P.R.*, *3rd ser.*, VII, 98). For the option see
p. 104 above.

2. Pitt's speech of 25 April 1798 (*P.R.*, *3rd ser.*, VI, 58–60) for the first. Cf. II, 517 for
second budgets; p. 235 above for prospective subsidies.

3. It seems impossible to specify a date. In a letter undated but (from its references to the
Minister's reviving health, to Ireland, and to the redemption of tithes) written probably
between mid June and mid October and possibly (from Pitt's movements) in late July or
very early in August, Pretyman mentions a conversation at Holwood which also included a
'new Finance Bill for a tenth of income in place of the Assessed Taxes' (to Mrs Pretyman;
Pretyman Ms 435:45). Undoubtedly the Minister had got as far as 'Heads of a Plan' in
September (P.R.O. 30/8/279, ff. 88–100, and by 31 October he had made extensive notes
as background for a bill (loc. cit., ff. 104–5v). Rumours of an impending scheme appeared
in the London newspapers during that time (eg *The Morning Chronicle* of 10 October, *The
Times* of the 14th, *The True Briton* of the 17th), and in November it was being widely discussed (see *Diary of Colchester*, I, 162).

4. See p. 102 above for Pitt in 1797, and I, Ch. IV for his Chancellorship under
Shelburne; Ward, *The English Land Tax*, 2 for examples. Professor Patrick O'Brien has
reminded me of Tudor and Stuart origins.

5. For Auckland and Rose see papers in P.R.O. 30/8/279; for Fordyce, a letter to Pitt of
1 December 1798 in P.R.O. 30/8/136; for Vansittart, a reminiscence of 11 August 1845,
quoted in Pellew's *Life* of Addington, II, 198. The knowledgeable MP Charles Abbot (see
n3 above) mentioned approval at the time from the City in a speech of 31 December 1798
(*P.R.*, *3rd ser.*, VII, 486–7), and reports of meetings with the Minister appeared in the
London newspapers in November. One of the more notable 'moneyed men' who supplied

rested on the impression that the necessity of such a measure appeared 'to be so strongly felt, . . . both among the landed and the Commercial Interest, that there would probably now be a general disposition to admit Provisions which would have been very objectionable under other Circumstances, and before the Subject had been so fully considered'. The basis of the plan 'for the ensuing Year' should still however be the Assessment, on which experience could offer a guide; but so framed that proof of income could be obtained more satisfactorily.[1] This last problem figured quite prominently among Pitt's provisional list of questions and suggestions, among them the appointment and powers of Commissioners, those of an 'Inspector' for referral of disputes, denial of compulsory powers for the examination of evidence in cases of 'surcharge', secrecy of returns and their examination, a special method of assessment in London (and possibly in Jersey), publication or otherwise of the 'Sums finally assessed'.[2] The aim was a yield which 'would not fall short' of £8 million, and which in Pitt's view was in fact 'likely' to be £10 million.[3]

On 3 December 1798 Pitt introduced his proposals in a budget speech of some two and a half hours, and next day leave was given to bring in a bill.[4] The provisions were inevitably lengthy – 124 clauses – and in places complicated; but the tenor was clear. The Triple Assessment was replaced. Its precedent was adopted in a sliding scale of payment: exemption on incomes below £60 a year, graduated levels from one twentieth to one tenth on those between £60 and £200, and one tenth on those above

---

comments on the scheme was Samuel Bosanquet, a former Governor of the Bank of England (papers in P.R.O. 30/8/279). The Solicitor General, John Mitford, who was already involved with legal questions affecting recent financial ideas, was also soon drawn in (see his letters to Pitt, 31 August, 7 September, and for the tax 26 December 1798; P.R.O. 30/8/170).

1. Paper in Pitt's hand, nd and unfortunately incomplete, misplaced among his diplomatic files in 'Spain, miscellaneous papers, and dispatches and letters' (P.R.O. 30/8/341, ff. 37–8v).

2. Paper in Pitt's hand, 31 October 1798 (see p. 260, n3 above). There were fourteen numbered and five unnumbered items in the list. 'Surcharge' presumably referred to payments in the higher graduated rates of tax (for which see below). Pitt was paying a good deal of attention – as he had been for the past two years – to the unsolved problems of assessing property in London (see papers in P.R.O. 30/8/280–1).

3. P.R.O. 30/8/341, f. 37v for the first figure; speech of 3 December 1798 [below] for the second.

According to Pretyman, in a letter written clearly towards the end of this year, the Minister calculated a yield of 'about twelve Millions, but he means to take it for nine Millions' (to Mrs Pretyman, nd, from Downing Street; Pretyman Ms 503:2).

4. *P.R., 3rd. ser.*, VII, 94–118, 133. According to the émigré Mallet du Pan (see II, 313, 581), who was in the gallery, the speech was 'a complete course in political economy' (quoted in Rosebery's *Pitt*, 153), and to an equally impressed if more prosaic supporter it bore the Minister's 'best style' (*Diary of Colchester*, I, 164). This was despite a bad cold (see *L.C.G. III*, III, no. 1885).

There is an account of the speech in George Rose's papers (B.L. Add. Ms 42772, ff. 204–28), taken from shorthand notes by a 'Mr Ramsey'.

£200.[1] Sources of income were assembled under four heads (themselves divided into five schedules), the two main branches being divided into landed property on the one hand and personal property, interest on money, trade or profession, offices, pensions and the like on the other. All would be taxed on the same basis, and enjoy the same deductions – particularly complicated in the case of houses and land.

The produce – together with that of the recent and continuing convoy tax[2] – would be applied in an order of priority: first to the costs of the year up to a limit of £10 million, secondly to the interest on loans charged on war taxes, thirdly to the purchase of stock to redeem the Funded Debt up to an amount equalling those loans. Much of course would turn on the methods of collection: the yield from the Assessment had been a fiscal problem largely because it was an administrative problem. But, as foreshadowed, the answer here was muted once more. The taxpayer would still not be required to supply a detailed return in the first instance: he would provide a statement of the aggregate sum 'which he means to pay'. That would be considered by the Commissioners and if necessary the Surveyors (the offices inherited respectively from the Land Tax and the Taxes Office), and the former would have powers then to require an itemised schedule. Taken throughout, the detail of the bill, as Pitt had laid down, derived largely from the Assessment.[3] The new, and historically important elements lay in the open shift of principle from expenditure to income, the latter moreover within the scope of a single tax;[4] and to a lesser immediate extent, but adumbrating later developments, in the taxpayer's obligation of greater disclosure at a second stage.

These were not matters of small substance. When the tax was first publicly rumoured, the idea was described as 'a daring innovation in English finance'.[5] The provisions had now to be accepted, and Pitt was taking few chances; he sought his object strictly in politically permissible terms. The limits he chose were soon seen to be too strict; and to later generations he seemed to have been unnecessarily timid for a Minister so powerfully placed. But that was not how the case appeared to men at the time. Compared with his experience on the Triple Assessment and the sale of the Land Tax, Pitt carried the new measure quickly and with apparent ease: the lowest majority in its passage was in a division of 183 to 17, and the bill became law five weeks to the day after it was introduced.[6] This apparently smooth achievement however emerged from less tractable realities. The swift passage owed a good deal to the earlier lengthy

1. In their final form the provisions were contained in 39 Geo. III, c13. Cf. pp. 103–4 above for the precedent of a sliding scale.
2. See p. 107 above.
3. Pp. 104, 108 above.
4. Cf. Binney, *British Public Revenue and Administration 1774–1792*, 73 on this last point.
5. *The Morning Chronicle*, 3 November 1798.
6. The respective dates were 5 December 1798, 9 January 1799. Minor amending Acts (39 Geo. III, cs 22, 42) were passed on 21 March and 10 May respectively.

discussions which had introduced the House to the issues involved, and it rested firmly on a recognised failure to meet a now generally acknowledged need. In the last resort, the tax commanded patriotic wartime assent. But that did not mean that some of its features were accepted without deep alarm. Above all, the investigative powers held at the discretion of Commissioners and Surveyors aroused a sense of outrage which did not recede. The invasion of liberty, the prying by the Crown into the personal affairs of the subject, was establishing, in Pitt's own recent words, an 'inquisition which would be generally invidious'.[1] It was something, the City's Court of Common Council formally resolved, 'unknown in this Country'. It would subvert the Constitution, declared one MP who supported the need for the tax.[2] Such cries of course were often heard – were common coin – in response to change. But in this instance the suspicion and resentment ran deep. Half a century's experience indeed would prove the fact. The Income Tax was repealed at the first opportunity after the war ended, and in a quite exceptional step Parliament ordered the Commissioners' records to be destroyed.[3] So extraordinary a fiat revealed the depth of feeling concentrated on that aspect of a levy bound to be unpopular in its direction and range. Nor was that the last expression of a vivid sense of threat. Reintroduced under another name when war broke out once more, the tax was again repealed within a year of peace, against the Government's resistance and to 'loud cheering . . . for several minutes'. Not until 1842 could it be revived, by Peel, in conditions irrelevant to Pitt's wartime purpose; to be retained thereafter into our own day,

---

The division followed the debate of 14 December 1798 on the motion for considering the bill in committee. *P.R., 3rd ser.*, VII gives the figures as 183 to 23; *P.H.*, XXXIV as 183 to 17 (not including the Tellers), which is generally preferred. Three divisions recorded on other stages give figures of 116–3, 123–9, 93–2 (*P.R., 3rd ser.*, VII, 279, 303, 497).

The minority on 14 December nonetheless included one leading City figure: Francis Baring, an erstwhile confidant of Pitt's (see I, 242, 244, 458).

1. Memorandum of 11 October 1797, on the possibility of a tax on income or property; pp. 101, n4, 102 above.

2. Resolution of the Court of Common Council, 19 December 1798, sent to Pitt (P.R.O. 30/8/279, ff. 115–16); Thomas (Tyrwhitt) Jones on 27 December 1798 (*P.R., 3rd ser.*, VII, 448). Jones admittedly was not of great account.

3. The only parallel to this in English history is the Act to abolish Charles I's Ship Money (17 Car. I, c14, of 1641), which included 'the vacating of all records and process concerning the same'.

In this later instance the records were to be cut into small pieces and conveyed to a paper factory where, under 'the eyes of one of the Commissioners, they were to be committed to the mash tub. The Commissioner was to stay in the paper mill until the contents of the tub were reduced to pulp' (Arthur Hope-Jones, *Income Tax in the Napoleonic Wars* (1939), 1; and see William Frend, *The Principles of Taxation* (1804), 3). Parliament however had forgotten that duplicates were sent, like parish returns under the Land Tax, to the King's Remembrancer in the Court of Exchequer; and these escaped, to lie neglected with their evidence for over a hundred and thirty years.

The tax was repealed in May 1802 (42 Geo. III, c42), the peace treaty of Amiens having been signed in March, and the Preliminaries in October 1801.

despite Disraeli's hopes in the fifties for its eventual disappearance and a plan for abolition by Gladstone in 1874.[1]

Such a climate of opinion could not be ignored, and Pitt did not intend to do so. He took care to stress his respect for familiar norms. The Commissioners would be of the traditional order; 'independent of all . . . influence' by 'their situation and rank in life'.[2] The judgments would be their responsibility, and the paid officials, Surveyors and Inspectors, would be strictly responsible to them. Nor indeed was this defence wholly, though it was largely, forced; he himself was not unsympathetic to the suspicions with which he was faced. The landed gentry lay at the centre of Government's whole range of measures to protect society and, as it was claimed, traditional liberties from attack. And the Minister had another reason for calling on familiar services once more. Anxious as he had been, and remained, to improve and strengthen the professional Taxes Office, he was always intensely averse to any avoidable rise in costs. His career had been devoted, with some success, to combining efficient with cheap administration, and one advantage of the Triple Assessment had been continuity and economy of management.[3] The same instruments, recently augmented, could be applied to the new task. He was not striving for a radical enlargement of powers to overload them.

He had less sympathy for other objections. He dismissed charges of inconsistency in changing his attitude to the funded debt.[4] They could be referred to his full explanation of the previous year. He argued equally against forecasts that the tax would damage the economy, weakening the very sinews of wealth on which he was depending for swifter relief. The nation's means remained 'ample and extensive', and he did not change his mind: 'there was nothing gloomy in the finances of the country', he repeated in the following months.[5] Nor was he prepared to concede that the levy bore unfairly on certain sources of payment. He denied that it favoured 'permanent' (unearned) against 'precarious' or 'hazardous' (earned) income, or conversely that it would hit at investment in the Funds.[6] The whole point was that all would contribute 'in proportion to

1. J.H. Clapham, *An Economic History of Modern Britain*, I (1939), 329.

2. Speech of 3 December 1798 (*P.R., 3rd ser.*, VII, 99–100). Cf. I, 284. The nominations for the Income Tax Commissioners outside London would in fact be submitted to the Grand Jury of the county by the Commissioners of the Land Tax, while in London Commissioners would be elected by Directors of the large Corporations (East India and South Sea Companies, Royal Exchange) and the Bank of England. Surveyors would not be permitted to attend the latter's meetings.

3. See pp. 102–3 above; I, Ch. XI, sections I, II for his peacetime achievements and their limits.

4. 'I hear and see that the Chancellor of the Exchequer of 1798 censures, . . . unmercifully, the Chancellor of the Exchequer of 1796' (George Tierney, 3 December 1798; *P.R., 3rd ser.*, VII, 123). See p. 101 above.

5. Speech of 7 June 1799 (op. cit., 684).

6. Speech of 14 December 1798 (op. cit., 267–76, or a rather fuller version in *P.H.*, XXXIV, cols. 98–109).

their means' whatever the 'quality'; the graduation of the scale in point of fact would therefore leave 'the nature of society' as it was.[1] What was being called for was a subscription, to be found most equitably in this way, towards a 'public defence' which was necessary for all.

The fiscal principle was thus soon settled. Attention continued to focus on detail, and – the subject itself of principle – the process of assessment. This last introduced a distinction of which there was no specific mention in Pitt's early thoughts. He had envisaged that London might require its own treatment. It was soon apparent that some separate provision was demanded by the mercantile community at large. Income from trade was accordingly assigned to a body of Commercial Commissioners, who were enjoined to keep their books 'private', and to whom statements of payment could be 'sealed up'.[2] The Minister also found himself pressed further on the Surveyors' powers, the limits of which he underlined;[3] and he accepted a range of minor amendments by the end of the year.[4]

The immediate result of the change was disappointing. Pitt's second bite at the cherry was no more rewarding than the first had been in 1798. He himself reduced his expectations in the summer to a yield of £7.3 million, and in the following winter to £6.2 million.[5] Once again it is hard to establish a reliable figure in the event. But the Exchequer *collected* some £2.7 million from 5 April 1799 – when the tax came into effect – to 5 January 1800, and the best later calculation of the final net produce for the year reached the surprisingly low sum of £1,671,000 out of an aggregate of £6,446,000 from 'Land and Assessed Taxes'.[6] Nothing significant, if

1. And thus, he went on, would preserve a 'social state' which 'It would be a presumptuous attempt to derange' (*P.R., 3rd ser.*, VII, 106–9). Cf. his remarks again on 31 December (op. cit., 498). Prominent speeches in opposition came from Sir John Sinclair on 3 and 14 December (op. cit., 135–6, 230–43) and Tierney on 3, 17, 31 December (op. cit., 115–25, 291–4, 490–5); and see Abbot's *Diary*, I, 165–6.

2. 39 Geo. III, c13, arts. 108, 97.

3. *P.R., 3rd ser.*, VII, 269–7.

4. They may be followed in the first and final prints of the bill, and in Pitt's copy of the first as amended in P.R.O. 30/8/235, ff. 267–92. The published debates are vague; see *P.R., 3rd ser.*, VII, 313–14, 497, 499. *P.H.*, XXXIV confines itself to stating that 'a variety of amendments and modifications, were after long and desultory conversations, agreed to' (col. 131).

5. Speeches of 7 June 1799, 24 February 1800 (*P.R., 3rd ser.*, VII, 678; X (1800), 695). Cf. pp. 102, 106–7, and cf. 261 above.

6. Figures from *House of Commons Sessional Papers 1868–9*, XXXV, Part I; for the second see Mitchell and Deane, op. cit., ch. XIV, table 1, with note *a* – to be compared with op. cit., table 16, which gives a slightly different figure. It is however 'extraordinarily difficult to construct an authoritatively consistent series of either gross or net assessments' for the period of the wars. A helpful Note on the perplexities may be found in Phyllis Deane and W.A. Cole, *British Economic Growth 1688–1959* . . . (1962), Appendix II, from which this quotation is taken.

By 39 Geo. III, c22 (see p. 262, n6 above) in March, the operation of the Triple Assessment had been extended to 5 April 1799.

anything, would therefore seem to have been gained in the tax's opening year, a period moreover in which there was a noticeable increase in the net total revenue.[1] The trouble lay largely, as before, in the ease of evasion. Pitt soon ordered the Taxes Office to report on the working of the Act, particularly in respect of commercial returns, which seemed to cause the greatest problems from the start.[2] Based on the findings, he introduced a bill in April 1800 to help remedy some of the defects.[3] It was a distinctly more radical document than the original measure. The taxpayer would now be obliged to itemise his income, 'divided and distinguished' in amended schedules, and likewise his claims for deductions, specifying the names and addresses of creditors and others concerned. He would not be allowed to aggregate the items: that would fall to the Commissioners in making their assessment of the net payment.[4] The degree of secrecy allowed in particular to commercial returns would be abolished. So too indeed would the separate existence of the Commercial Commissioners themselves.

The bill did not reach the statute book. It evoked such hostility that it was withdrawn and a milder one introduced.[5] The most objectionable features disappeared; and the defeat was underlined. For while the schedules and some procedures were altered, particularly where they had borne too easily on farmers' returns, the Commons, so far from complying with the Minister's wishes, forced the retention of the Commercial Commissioners

1. Total net income 1798, £26,946,000; 1799, £31,783,000 (Mitchell and Deane, same table).

2. Treasury Minute of 26 July 1799 (P.R.O., T. 29/74). Results may be seen among Pitt's papers in P.R.O. 30/8/282, which culminated in a comprehensive report from the Taxes Office on 25 April 1800 (copy in P.R.O. 30/8/279, ff. 280–306). He followed the early returns closely by districts (see loc. cit., *passim*).

3. A copy of the bill (and it may be the only one), of 4 April 1800, survives in Pitt's papers (P.R.O. 30/8/249). A. Farnsworth, *Addington Author of the Modern Income Tax* (1951), 26–8 summarises the most important of the contents. A fragment of a paper in Pitt's files (P.R.O. 30/8/196, ff. 27-v) may relate to the preparations.

4. Cf. pp. 262–3 above.

5. According to Tierney, it was 'brought into the House in silence [ie without proper notice] and taken away in the same manner' (5 June 1800; *P.H.*, XXXV (1819), col. 332). But its fate can be followed best in *P.R.*, *3rd ser.*, XI and XII (1800). The Ministry slipped up in its procedure, omitting to specify deductions allowed in the existing Act and thus being deemed to be introducing a 'new tax'. On 17 April the Speaker therefore advocated withdrawal for eight days, in a lively debate in which George Rose, the Secretary of the Treasury responsible, admitted 'inadvertency'. When he moved – on 19 May – to introduce a revised measure, Tierney noted that 'the Chancellor of the Exchequer was prudent in his silence'; and while Pitt took over on the 23rd, he took care to say that its predecessor had been 'presented to him by persons of experience' (5 June 1800; op. cit., XII, 70). The episode, according to one knowledgeable observer, was discreditable: 'It is extraordinary that . . . This Business should have appeared in so crude and imperfect a State' (Hawkesbury to Liverpool, nd but endorsed 19 April 1800; B.L. Loan Ms 72, vol. 54).

Although the report from the Taxes Office (n2 above) was sent to Pitt shortly after the bill was introduced, the inclusion of the 'strongest' of its recommendations, the abolition of the Commercial Commissioners outside London, suggests that its contents were already known.

and intensified the secrecy of commercial returns.[1] Following on the humiliating withdrawal, this spelt danger for further attempts. Pitt had also been persuaded by professional advice to add substantially to the number of Surveyors: 99 officers to a current establishment of 213, of whom 36 had in fact been chosen though none as yet appointed.[2] But this process – potentially a notable departure from his persistent aim of cheap collection – seems thereafter to have largely faded away.[3] It was clearly no time to be forcing the pace; he may, as in the past, have been discouraged by the experience of failure;[4] and no more proposals for reform or amendment reached Parliament before the tax was repealed.

The restricted system thus carried on for another two years. Pitt's estimate of yield for 1801–2 was for £6 million, and there were signs, amid the restrictions, that matters were starting to improve. A comprehensive change in accounting practice adds a fresh uncertainty to chronological comparison; but a net produce of perhaps £4.5 million for 1800–1 was followed by a *gross* figure in the following year of some £5.3 million from 'Property and Income Tax'. 'Land and Assessed Taxes', now distinguished from them on the same revised basis, accounted at that time for some £4.6 million.[5] Nonetheless, when the gross figure for the new impost is reduced to a broad estimate of net produce, the latter was not approaching the Minister's early forecast of £9–10 million or equalling his latest of some £3–4 million less. He himself observed that his 'mistaken . . . calculation' showed the problems of a 'new subject'.[6] In the

1. . . . 'the Income of every . . . Person [making a return to them] shall be cognizable only by such Commercial Commissioners' (39 & 40 Geo. III, c49, art. 2). This went farther than the provisions for secrecy applied to all Commissioners in earlier Acts (cf. 39 Geo. III, c13, arts. 96, 97, 106, 108,; 39 Geo. III, c42, art. 8). The new bill was passed, by 114 to 24 – a higher minority than any attained, as recorded, on the Income Tax itself (p. 262 above) – on 5 June, and became law on the 20th.

2. 'Account of the Actual and Estimated Expence of collecting the Tax on Income, for the Years 1799 and 1800', laid on the table of the House of Commons, 5 June 1800 (*P.R., 3rd ser.*, XII, 50–2). A substantial addition was one of the recommendations in the report from the Taxes Office of 25 April; against which cf. p. 264 above.

3. See Hope-Jones, op. cit., 59.

4. Cf. eg I, 215–16, II, 475.

5. There are slight variations between O'Brien and Cooper for 1800–1 and again 1801–2 (ending 5 January in all cases): £4.8 and £4.5 million respectively for the first year (O'Brien after deducting £0.5 million coming in from the continuing Voluntary Aid and Contribution), £6 and £5.8 million for the second (O'Brien, loc. cit., 422 table 10; Cooper, loc. cit., 218, but see also 222). Mitchell and Deane give some £4.5 and – under 'Property and Income Tax' – £5.8 million respectively (op. cit., ch. XIV, table 1, note *a*, table 3, but see also op. cit., table 16). Other figures are given by Stephen Dowell, *A History of Taxation and Taxes . . .*, III (2nd edn., 1888), 95: 'nearly' £6.25 million for 1800–1, £5.6 million for 1801–2; by Farnsworth (op. cit., 22, 25), £5.8 and £5.3 million respectively; by Hope-Jones (op. cit., 23) for 1801–2: £5.6 million. The change-over in Government's published accounting took place in 1801–2; for the effects see Mitchell and Deane, op. cit., 382. Cf. for the difficulties throughout, p. 265, n6 above.

6. Budget speech, 18 February 1801 (*P.R., 3rd ser.*, XIV (1801), 197). He could have added, political as well as technical.

longer run the Income Tax, administratively improved, would produce quite different figures before the wars were done. As so often with an historic innovation, the significant benefits were delayed.

II

Whatever the limitations to Pitt's efforts over the last three years of the century, taxation as a whole, with some increased rates and broad if uneven commercial expansion, was bringing in a much larger revenue than had been seen before. A mean of some £30 million for 1798–1800 was very different from one of just under £20 million for 1793–7.[1] The gap however persisted against a mean annual expenditure of some £48½ million for 1798–1800, compared with some £37¾ million for 1793–7;[2] and some £17–19 million must thus still be found. While less had to be borrowed proportionately against increased outgoings, the sum itself, on such figures, remained much the same.

Pitt had first planned to seek a loan of £14 million in 1799, which he ended by increasing to £15.5 million. The figure for 1800 was £18.5 million, and after thinking at first of £19 million for 1801 he ended with the much larger target of £25.5 million.[3] He was able to extract some benefits on both sides of the ledger. One of the greatest problems in forecasting wartime national expenditure lay in the freedom of the naval and military Departments – one embedded in the constitutional balance – to estimate, borrow and, largely, spend without detailed Treasury supervision.[4] He had managed to curtail this independence somewhat in 1796–7, by a fresh funding of Navy bills and a proposal to reform the system for repayment, and by inducing the Paymaster General of the Forces to submit the army Estimates to Parliament in a form that covered costs which might arise in the year, instead of applying later for moneys already spent. This combination of financial and administrative pressures produced a useful result. Neither the army nor the navy incurred such expenditure for the rest of the war, and if Navy bills were still widely issued to meet the flow of demands inherent in sea service, the costs did not exceed those of 1796, and the sale of army and ordnance debentures (the bills' equivalents) remained stable in volume and low in relation to the total outgoings

1. Let alone from a tax yield of under £13.8 million for the peak year of the last war, of American Independence (1782; Mitchell and Deane, op. cit., ch. XIV, table 1).
2. Op. cit., tables 1–4.
3. See Cooper, loc. cit., 219, 221, 225, and Appendix I, 388–95. The levels of borrowing were also of course affected by past deficiencies in estimating both revenue and expenditure, the former itself being affected by the economic climate, which for 1799–1801 is discussed in section III of this Chapter.
4. Cf. I, 311–12 (where the partial exception of the Ordnance is noted); II, 482, 494, 517.

involved.[1] Enforced virtue brought spending on contingencies rather more closely within the Commons' view,[2] and the Minister had applied a rather closer discipline to an awkward area of the 'floating' debt.[3]

In the other column, Pitt managed for a time to secure more favourable rates of interest for his loans; and from 1800 a source of modest but continuing relief for several years. The rates had stood at above 5½ per cent on the successive occasions since late in 1796, rising to 6.3 in April 1797, declining to 5.7 at the end of 1798. In his second budget of June 1799 the figure was 5.4, and in February 1800 it was 4.9, before rising a year later, in what was effectively the last wartime exercise, to 5.7.[4] The amount to be borrowed on the market moreover was eased after 1799 by an expedient with the Bank of England for the medium term. Its charter would come up for renewal in twelve years' time, and in December Pitt pledged its continuation then for twenty-one years in return for an immediate annual loan of £3 million free of interest for six years.[5] The agreement was welcome – not the less so when compared with the Bank's attitude a few years before[6] – covering as it did an unusually lengthy span. It was also opportunistic, secured by a presumably unrepeatable manoeuvre: a palliative which underlined the problems facing policy itself.

These indeed were becoming increasingly evident. Pitt maintained a similar emphasis in servicing the loans for 1799 and 1800. As always, taxes

1. O'Brien, loc. cit., 125–6, 497–8, tables 16, 17, 20; and cf. II, 517–18. The sums involved in 'expenditure without Estimate' had been far from inconsiderable: for 1795, army £3.5 million, navy £4.7 million; 1796, £3.8, £16.6 million respectively. In 1797 they were army £1.4 million, navy nil, and in 1798–1801 nil for both. Similar expenditure by the Ordnance was reduced from £1.1 million in 1795 to £0.6 million in 1796, £0.2 million annually for 1797–9, and £0.1 million annually for 1800–1.

For the funding of navy bills see II, 518, 619 (and I, 259–60 for an earlier funding); Mitchell and Deane, op. cit., ch. XIV, table 2, note *c*. In future the Treasurer of the Navy was to repay his unfunded bills with a marketable asset bearing 5 per cent interest and repayable after ninety days.

2. Cf. Pitt's remarks in 1796 on the limits in practice to Parliament's 'command of a retrospective authority' over money spent (II, 517n2).

3. As defined in I, 258.

4. O'Brien, loc. cit., 499–500 table 18, to the nearest decimal (slightly different figures are given in William Newmarch, the traditional Victorian authority, *On the Loans Raised by Mr. Pitt during the First French War, 1793–1801* (1855), 40). Pitt drew attention more than once to the connexion between this achievement and the role of the new form of taxation in improving Government's credit (see Cooper, loc. cit., 228). Cf. II, 617 & n5 for rates in late 1795 and the spring of 1796.

The operation of February 1801 was followed by another in November, at 4.75 per cent; but the Preliminaries to a peace treaty had been signed by then (Chapter XVII below).

5. The whole would be repaid in 1806, or part earlier at Government's choice when 3 per cent Consols stood at 80 or above, in which case interest *would* be paid, on the residue, at 5 per cent for the remaining period. The Bank agreed in January 1800, and the Commons confirmed in February. Part of the correspondence may be found in P.R.O. 30/8/195, 276; Pitt had made notes on the charter in October 1799 (P.R.O. 30/8/276, f. 187).

6. Cf. II, 524–5, 617–20 for 1795–6, and p. 107 above for 1798.

were intended 'not . . . to pay for the war but to support the funding system which would pay for the war'.[1] The difference now was that the burden was placed heavily on the Income Tax, and that the proportion was designed to slow the pace significantly in the pressure on the Sinking Fund. In 1799 the Minister first charged £9½ of his intended funded borrowing of £14 million on the new impost, and then £11 of the final £15½ million; in 1800, £13½ of his £18½ million. This policy left the need to find a further £316,000 in 1799 to service the remaining £4½ million for the Sinking Fund itself, which was to be raised by adjusting various revenues from sugar and by a tax on banknotes of the lower denominations; and some £313,500 for the remaining £5 million in 1800, found by increased duties on some teas and on spirits.[2] He thought of following the same line for 1801 in providing for the loan of £19 million; but by the time of the budget he decided against. The Income Tax for the year would be saddled only with the debt already charged to it since its inception, and that charged to the Triple Assessment in 1798; the servicing and redemption of the current loan would be placed entirely on the 'permanent' taxes.[3] To meet the large bill, of £1,785,000, a host of fresh levies was imposed in the old style: higher duties or taxes on paper, tea and horses; higher stamp duties on a range of bills and notes and documents; higher customs duties on imported sugar, raisins, pepper, and timber.[4]

This was a sad turn. Pitt's 'double purpose' was proving unrealistic. The yield from the Income Tax could not simultaneously meet its quota of

1. II, 522, quoting Cooper, loc. cit., 89.

2. Pitt's memorandum of 2 June 1799 (P.R.O. 30/8/197, ff. 129–31); speeches of 7 June 1799, 24 February 1800 (*The Senator*, XXIII (nd), 1652; *P.R., 3rd ser.*, X, 699–700). He had not specified earlier for the first of these years because he borrowed only £3 of the £14 million before April, hoping for conditions which would produce more favourable terms. The duties for 1800 became law by 39 & 40 Geo. III, c23; those for 1799 were included in 39 Geo. III, c13.

3. The alternatives are set out clearly in a memorandum by Pitt of 14 December 1800 (P.R.O. 30/8/197, ff. 122–5) – and some notes in his hand in P.R.O. 30/8/196, ff. 333–4v may also refer; the decision was given in his speech of 18 February 1801 (*P.R., 3rd ser.*, XIV, 191). The past debt so specified amounted to £56 million.

A few weeks later the Minister defended his record. Since the beginning of the war he had provided an extra £4 million a year from the 'permanent' taxes and now almost £5 million from the taxes appropriated to the Sinking Fund [in effect the income tax]; a sum of £9 million, which was within £10 million of 'the total amount of the interest of all the sums borrowed during the nine years [of] the war'. Therefore, he is said to have claimed, it 'cannot for a moment be disputed' 'that the expenditure of the present has been very considerably less than in all other former wars' (speech of 25 March 1801; op. cit., 621). This argument, legitimate in its own terms, omitted some other figures: the amount added in those nine years to the capital of the funded debt, and the amount of current short-term unfunded debt (for which see p. 272 below).

The passage clearly drew on the calculations (which Pitt would have approved and may have assisted) in George Rose's *A Brief Examination into the Increase of the Revenue, Commerce and Manufactures of Great Britain, from 1792 to 1799* (1799), 16 – and on the statement, on p. 17, that they contained 'few points subject to the smallest doubt'.

4. 41 Geo. III, cs 8, 9, 10, 28.

the year's costs and service its quota of the year's remaining deficit so as to relieve the accumulated national Debt.[1] He was obliged to admit as much, and the necessary consequence that persistence could lead the wartime levy soon to 'partake of the quality of a perpetual Tax'. Rather, therefore, than mortgage it more deeply while the war lasted, greater recourse must be had once more to the Sinking Fund.[2]

Fresh calculations were therefore made. Before the innovations of 1798–9 the Minister had considered the possibility of discharging the funded debt within fifty-six years, some 22 per cent of the total being redeemed by or in 1808.[3] Further estimates to the same date followed in 1799, requiring taxes 'on present Plan . . . a little above 2 000.000' for eight years of war, with a further eight years for every additional wartime year thereafter.[4] The change of plan early in 1801, coming shortly before a change of Ministry and the end of the war itself, gave no opening for fresh forecasts then. They awaited his attention under different circumstances the next year. But he had by no means lost sight of the goal. By whatever methods, and however long it took, the National Debt was to be paid off; and if the Income Tax could not play its anticipated part, other taxes must be raised to service and redeem the 'terminable annuities'.[5] He had hoped to circumvent – Opposition called it 'abandon' – the funding system in its full extent by a more heroic wartime effort[6] in the Gladstonian sense. That seemed to have failed, at any rate for the time being, and he returned, well knowing the implications of operating from a deficit, to a programme devised by him in the days of surplus. There appeared indeed to be no better way, paradoxically, of attaining an object that must now be receding; one which kept up the price of stocks through the purchases for redemption, and sustained Government's solvency, at home and abroad. Arguments heard in the middle nineties, and one above all, still held their force. It was all too easy to recall the fears of bankruptcy at the end of the last war; a steady commitment to the Sinking Fund, if on a more massive scale than Pitt had lately hoped, remained the strongest bulwark against their repetition, 'a source of comfort to ourselves and our allies'.[7]

There was however another means of mitigating the Fund's headlong growth, at least as an interim measure so as to strike a balance. If taxes

1. Cf. pp. 101–3 above.
2. Memorandum of 14 December 1800 (p. 270, n3 above); speech of 18 February 1801 (*P.R.*, *3rd ser.*, XIV, 197, which may be compared with and supplemented here by *The Senator*, *2nd ser.*, I (nd), 228–9).
3. Pitt's undated memorandum of April 1796, in P.R.O. 30/8/275, ff. 138v-40v (there is a copy, nd and not in his hand, in P.R.O. 30/8/197, ff. 51-2v); and see loc. cit., f. 219.
4. Paper in Pitt's hand, nd, P.R.O. 30/8/197, ff. 139v-40; and see also loc. cit., ff. 224-5v, 4 April 1799.
5. See II, 527.
6. The charge, voiced by Tierney, was made in June 1800 (see Cooper, loc. cit., 228). Cf. I, 249.
7. Cf. II, 527–8 for the arguments in conditions of rising deficit; I, 157–8 for the old vivid fears.

could not be raised in its relief or support beyond a certain point, unfunded borrowing might take part of the increased strain. Certainly its volume rose sharply in this period, and if the earlier restraint on the Service departments reduced the effect in those quarters, they were not in any case responsible for the bulk of short-term debt. That total rose from £19.3 million in 1797 and £20.3 in 1798 to £23.2 in 1799, £29.3 in 1800, and no less than £37.9 in 1801 – by almost double in fact in four years. And of this the Treasury's unfunded Exchequer bills accounted for £13.2 million in 1797 and £26.1 in 1801: for almost 60 and just over 70 per cent respectively.[1] Some of the issues, in both Exchequer and Navy bills, were sold to redeem others that had matured. But there was undoubtedly a relaxation from the earlier approach, which was particularly noticeable as the prospects for peace appeared to improve in the final year. The practice gave scope, though that was not fully exploited, for bargains on fresh issues at points of redemption, and when the market discounted bills while it awaited the terms for new funded loans.[2] Funding itself, as Pitt could claim, stood behind the financing of current supply. Nevertheless, Government's release of this amount of 'floating' borrowing was disobliging to a Chancellor who had counted on a surfeit of paper to lead to the collapse of France.[3]

III

The enlarged provision of short-term credit by way of official negotiable instruments thus stemmed in part from the shortfall persisting despite increased taxation. It also reflected easier acceptance of an increased circulation of money by way of non-Governmental issues from the banks. The years around the turn of the century saw more of their own paper changing hands than ever before. It was not therefore surprising that it also saw the opening of a debate on currency which would reach a first peak in the celebrated Bullion Report of 1810. There had been adumbrations, before and after the Bank Suspension of 1797.[4] But a spate of publications, starting with the banker Walter Boyd and influencing a series of Parliamentary debates, now marked a seminal phase in a discussion of growing range and depth. Finding classical expression in Henry Thornton's *An Enquiry into the Nature and Effects of the Paper Credit of Great*

1. O'Brien, loc. cit., 495 table 16. The figures for 1798–1800 were £13.4, 14.3, 20.4 million – thus higher annually after 1797 than those for the budgetary loans; those for navy bills from 1797 to 1800, £4.2, 6.4, 5.6, 6.0, 8.7 million, and see pp. 268–9 above for the restraint on their costs.
2. Loc. cit., 139–43 for an account of the process, including sales of issues to redeem some of their predecessors, and 507–8 table 21. Cf. II, 518 for Pitt in 1795–6.
3. Eg II, 541, 558.
4. See eg II, 620–1 for Walter Boyd in 1796, and pp. 10, 12 above for Sir Francis Baring's *Observations on the Establishment of the Bank of England* in 1797, and Pitt in the same year.

Britain, of 1802,[1] the process indeed formed the introduction to monetary and banking theory as it has developed in the Western world down to 1914 and in some respects beyond.

The discussion might well not have come as it did at this point without a change in circumstances. Pitt's action in lifting the statutory requirement of convertibility on the Bank of England[2] had proved a distinct success. Recovery of confidence, hesitant at first particularly in the provinces, was sustained, and within a year the early doubts were largely removed. By then it was possible to claim that an 'event [the Bank Stoppage] . . . which it was supposed would involve the Kingdom in general bankruptcy and intire ruin, was the crisis which gave the happy turn, and . . . dismissed all the horrors and fears'.[3] But monetary policy, to adopt a later term, is not self-sustaining, and in this case it proved suited to conditions whose advance it augmented but could not guarantee. The revival of the nation's economy, gathering way by the end of 1797, persisted through 1798 and well into 1799. Rises in output across much of industry, and a buoyant overseas trade, supported favourable rates of exchange with Europe, as measured in the principal exchange now at Hamburg; the most favourable in fact since 1793.[4] In the course of 1799, however, the recovery was shaken. Expansion continued in significant areas: in coalmining, shipbuilding, certain textiles, while in housebuilding, a sensitive indicator, a long depression closed in the following year.[5] There was indeed a boom in some important activities. But the summer and autumn saw two setbacks with origins beyond domestic control. In April and May 1799 there were signs of a financial crisis in Hamburg, which were followed by a wave of bankruptcies. The discount rate there appreciated, funds were attracted from London, sterling fell and the British

1. Developed from his evidence to the Commons' Select Committee on Finance in 1797. It was republished in 1939 with an introduction by, appropriately, F.A. von Hayek. See II, 639n2 and p. 85 above for his acquaintance with Pitt. Boyd's pamphlet, of 1801, was *A Letter to the Right Honourable William Pitt on the Stoppage of Issues in Specie of the Bank of England*. It provoked an immediate response from Baring, *Observations on the Publications of Walter Boyd, Esq., M.P.* (1801). Other notable publications from that year to 1803, out of a larger clutch of lesser material, came from William Morgan (for whom see I, 263–4, II, 526), J.C. Herries – a name of later note –, and Lord King.

2. Ie the obligation to pay current coin to the value of its note on demand; see p. 9 above. In principle therefore this limited the value of such notes in circulation to that of the Bank's bullion reserve.

3. *A Letter to the Proprietors of the Bank of England . . . by a Proprietor of Bank Stock* (July 1798), quoted in J.K. Horsefield, 'The Duties of a Banker, II, The Effects of Inconvertibility', in *Papers in English Monetary History*, ed. T.S. Ashton and R.S. Sayers (1953), 19.

4. Norman J. Silberling, 'British Financial Experience of 1790–1830' (*The Review of Economic Statistics*, I, Tables 7, 8). Hamburg convincingly replaced Amsterdam for much of Europe from 1795.

5. Cf. for this last, II, 443. See Mitchell and Deane, op. cit., chs. IV tables 1, 2, VII tables 5, 10, IX table I for brick production; Ashton, *Economic Fluctuations in England 1700–1800*, chs. 3, 4. The limitations of recorded figures must of course be borne in mind throughout.

exchange rate moved quickly into the red.[1] Of much greater visible effect throughout the country, after an unusually good run in the previous two years,[2] was a catastrophically bad harvest from August to October. Prices of certain cereals, above all wheat, began to rise; and they continued to do so dramatically through 1800, when a second bad harvest took the process into 1801. While other commodities, domestic and imported, did not show a comparable pattern, the effect was such that the index in aggregate rose by some 50 per cent in two years.[3]

It was thus in a bout of savage inflation that the currency question was systematically broached. And of course not only systematically. A 'flood of paper' was attacked emotionally as fuelling the fall in the value of money and a deepeningly adverse rate of exchange.[4] The charge in point of fact was overplayed, as the earlier praise had been. There was certainly a significant rise in the circulation of Bank of England notes in 1799 and 1800; in the first year by some 30 per cent on that of two years before, in the latter by some 48 per cent on 1799. Notes from country banks moreover, likewise issuing more freely though under ultimate check from Threadneedle Street, must also, if without less detailed knowledge, be taken into account. At the same time, the volume of Bank of England notes at the time of the Suspension had been at its lowest since 1788, and the figure early in 1799 approximated to that in 1795. The total circulation therefore would not seem to have been excessive for a level of economic improvement which continued to need support while food prices rose.[5]

1. Silberling, as in p. 273, n4 above; Ashton, op. cit., 135. The crisis in Hamburg arose largely from over-speculation in West Indian produce. London's rate of exchange with Hamburg fell from +3.9 in 1798 to –4.4 in 1799.

2. Cf. p. 40 above.

3. Figures yield their customary shortcomings. Mitchell and Deane, op. cit., ch. XVI, tables 1–2 reproduce the classic calculations of Schumpeter and of Gayer, Rostow and Schwartz, with a preference for the latter trio as explained on pp. 465–6. While the picture in each case is broadly the same for cereals (as defined by Schumpeter), there are interesting differences for other domestic commodities and for imports – a factor concealed in fact in an index of comparison by Deane and W.A. Cole, in *British Economic Growth 1688–1959*, table 23, between the price of wheat and that of a combination of other consumer articles. Cf. moreover Wells, op. cit., Appendices, Figures 3–4, 7–12 for (sometimes marked) regional variations in the prices of wheat, barley and oats. See also Mitchell and Deane, op. cit., ch. XVI, tables 9, 10, 14 for wheat and bread in London, 7 and 8 for coal in the London area, 11 and 13 for some raw cotton imports and raw wool.

4. From – 4.4 with Hamburg in 1799 (n1 above) to – 12.9 in 1800.

5. Henry Thornton's brother Samuel, then Governor of the Bank of England, remarked indeed that the volume of bank notes circulating in 1797–8 did not exceed the average annual issue in 1790–2 (Commons' debate of 27 November 1800; *P.R., 3rd ser.*, XIV, 303). On the same occasion Pitt is reported (unusually in *oratio directo* – perhaps a degree more trustworthy) as stating, more rashly, that the increase since the Bank Suspension was 'very inconsiderable' (op. cit., 301). Cf. Silberling, loc. cit., Table 11 and Chart 5.

See Mitchell and Deane, op. cit., ch. XV, table 2; Frank W. Fetter, *Development of British Monetary Orthodoxy 1797–1875* (1965), 28; Horsefield, op. cit. (p. 273, n3 above), 15; J.H. Clapham, *The Bank of England*, II (1944), 5; L.S. Pressnell, *Country Banking in the Industrial Revolution*, 160.

The causes of deterioration lay initially elsewhere. But that said, the level of the money supply could, again, augment a process, and if accusations were sometimes off target the danger in principle was not necessarily so.

The intricacies of the problems, tackled now at deeper levels but with restricted data, were perforce imperfectly assembled or assessed. Historians indeed can still debate the interaction of forces; Pitt's comments for his part seem to have been notably cautious and sparse. He had earlier recognised a connexion in broad terms between prices and the balance of trade, and been inclined to rely on a self-regulating relationship between the volume of commercial activity and the volume and velocity of notes.[1] He still appeared to do so now, and to place his faith in the important difference between a system of paper circulation promulgated on the one hand directly by Government and on the other by instruments emanating from a private if central Bank.[2] He 'allowed' that an excessive issue of paper produced a depreciation, though not that a depreciation had 'any real effect' on a rate of exchange. But he remained unwilling to commit himself in general: on one occasion he spoke 'in the hearing of many who have better judgments than I have, especially on the subject of paper money', and clearly he would have agreed with Auckland, who had been in touch with him on such matters, that the subject was one 'in general very ill understood'.[3] The course of Government policy showed in any case that he was not ready to change; nor indeed were his successors – five years after his death Ministers, headed by his disciple Spencer Perceval,[4] strongly resisted an attempt to force the Bank of England to resume cash payments. Neither he nor they were prepared in fact to risk a loss of confidence in the paper pound, or to return to the former direct restraint on economic activity. Whether or not he himself would have argued the case, as they did, in terms of principle, he rested it tacitly in wartime conditions on pragmatic grounds.

Money supply, provision of credit, taxation and debt management were interlinked, and soon increasingly seen to be so as economic thought developed. That process took place, over several decades, in a framework provided in the setting of the late 1790s by the Chancellor of the Exchequer. The climate of the time was unpropitious: one in which

1. Cf. p. 12 above.
2. Cf. p. 10 above.
3. Pitt's speeches, 21 March 1805, referring to the rate of exchange with Ireland (*P.D.*, IV (1812), col. 70), 27 November 1800 (*P.R., 3rd ser.*, XIV, 300); Auckland's speech, 30 March 1801, referring to 'paper credit' (*P.R., 3rd ser.*, XV (1801), 9 – a version perhaps preferable to *P.H.*).

This caution did not mean that he was ignorant of the arguments. He possessed a copy of Thornton's *Enquiry*; and also a copy of Malthus's anonymous *Essay on the Principle of Population* – perhaps in the greatly altered second edition of 1803 where a monetary cause for rising food prices was tentatively suggested (Pretyman Ms 562:21).

4. For whom see p. 91 above.

expedients had to be tried and adjusted against the war's rising demands, political constraints, and a necessarily uncertain state of the art. It was not surprising that some proved disappointing in the immediate term. Nonetheless Pitt's response were not timid in conception, or lacking in recognition of relations between the parts; and while they failed to meet all the pressures under which they were produced, they proved of lasting value over long and anxious years. A system of tax revenue had been introduced which provided a fresh means of tapping the economy, and thus a 'vital interest' for Government in the level and distribution of wealth.[1] Economic improvement could be facilitated by an enlarged circulation of paper and coin, the latter particularly to meet the more modest needs.[2] The yield from higher taxes eased, though it could not meet, the growing strain on war finance, relieving, under varying arrangements, the heavy dependence on the Sinking Fund and aiding the terms on which the annual loans were raised. In this last respect it moderated the inflationary tendencies inherent in borrowing, while the income tax itself, in so far as it was an enforced means of saving, also acted as an anti-inflationary element. The Treasury's tactics with the money market could have been improved in some ways: by opening the loans more often to genuine competition;[3] by better timing of some operations; in particular by more flexible handling of unfunded bills, selling when bonds declined and funding when they rose again,[4] possibly even in stocks of higher denomination. But 'in general', it has been concluded, 'those who managed the debt should be commended rather than criticised';[5] and their transactions held them in close and constant contact with the Bank of England, affecting and affected by its own policies for credit. The Minister's reading of the combination remained broadly set for the rest of his life; and its conclusions endured. With some temporary departures, and some modifications to the structures of taxes and the Sinking Fund, his main lines of approach endured until peace was finally won.

1. O'Brien, loc. cit., 485. And for what follows here see loc. cit., 223–9, 482–6.
2. Cf. pp. 267–9, 12–13 above.
3. Cf. II, 522.
4. As was in fact done on a larger scale after Pitt's death. Cf. For the advantages and difficulties in placing 4 and 5 per cent stocks rather than the usual 3 per cents see I, 259–60, 262–3, p. 272 above.
5. O'Brien, loc. cit., 484. And cf. his article in *Review, A Journal of the Fernand Braudel Center* . . ., vol. XII, Number III, 381: 'Pitt's policies liberalized credit, depressed real interest rates, and contained the accumulation of public debt by squeezing current consumption' [the last through his taxation].

CHAPTER X

An Order under Pressure: Dearth and Unrest

I

On 10 August 1799, while Pitt and Dundas were completing their efforts at Walmer for the attack on Holland,[1] *The Times* reported heavy rains through much of the country and anxiety for the harvest. It was the start of a disaster in which a sodden autumn was to be followed by an icy winter, a late spring in 1800, and then, after a fine mid summer, more heavy rains in August and a second failure of corn. The cumulative effects would produce the worst food crisis in a decade of peculiar misfortune;[2] exceeding even those of the last great dearth in 1794–6, witnessing the now exceptional occurrence of serious food riots in London itself, and more generally hitting living standards harder in many working homes than at any point perhaps in the last two and a half centuries. To old Lord Liverpool at the Committee of Trade, nearing the end of his long experience, it seemed indeed that the pressures could 'shake the Foundations of the Government of Great Britain'.[3]

The crisis must be placed in chronological perspective. Taking 1701 as par, it has been reckoned that the price of cereals in aggregate may have increased from 148 in 1798 to 160 in 1799, 212 in 1800, and 228 in 1801. By the same measurement it then fell abruptly, to 174 in 1802 and 156 in 1803, before rising again by degrees to 212 in 1809, then falling slightly for a further two years and soaring once more, to a fresh peak of 237–243, in 1812–13. Thereafter it declined steeply until it reached a level of 125 (virtually that of 1792) in 1822.[4] In the eye of time, the experience of 1799–1801 was thus comparatively brief, was overtaken swiftly, and could

---

1. See p. 248 above.
2. Cf. II, 444–4.
3. Roger Wells, *Wretched Faces, Famine in Wartime England 1793–1801* (1988), 1, using sources on prices and wages particularly since the 1550s as cited op. cit., 340n1; 37–8, and Appendices 5, 7. Cf. my II, Ch. XII for 1795–6; op. cit., 92 & n3, 454, 467 for the general avoidance of food riots in London. Liverpool's warning, characteristically sombre but not to be dismissed, was given to Dundas, with whom he tended to be on more sympathetic terms than with Pitt himself (see eg op. cit., 513–14, 529); 11 October 1800 (B.L. Add. Ms 38311).
4. Schumpeter-Gilboy Price Indices, in Mitchell and Deane, *Abstract of British Historical Statistics*, ch. XVI table 1, and cf. Wells, op. cit., figures 3–4, 7–8, 11–12, for 1799–1801. The cereals covered by the former are barley, beans, oats, peas, rye, wheat, with flour.

revive as steeply to recede swiftly again. On the other side of the account, it is hazardous to try to measure as a unitary element relevant levels of wages within and through a comparable period. That ground, fought over by economic historians and econometricians, is strewn with mines set off by variations in areas and occupations and by serious limitations in evidence. One must, furthermore, again balance the medium with the very short term. Allowing for the fact that in some cases money wages could rise appreciably but also then fall, it would seem that in aggregate over a generation payments kept pace at the least with broad levels of food prices. They do not seem however to have risen rapidly in flexible response to the latter's sudden leaps; and one may therefore conclude that in the crisis over the turn of the century large numbers of men suffered a temporarily crippling fall in real wages, induced in particular by the cost of wheat.[1] In the end, the picture is one of uneven but widespread and very real hardship imposed quite suddenly on the more normal regional standards of living, and also quite quickly removed.

While the proportions were exceptional, such a pattern was familiar. As always, the onset of trouble was characterised by speed; appearing as a force of nature, with effects often more easily heightened than controlled by human response. In 1799 the outlook had not looked promising since a cold dry spring, which was widely followed by frosts in the summer. The possibilities were not ignored: Ministers – at least Liverpool himself – kept a wary eye on the position after the lesson of 1794–5, including the prospects in Europe and North America. At the same time, attention at this juncture was fastened closely on other events, the most urgent of which moreover could detract from one form of potential relief. The expedition for Holland was absorbing shipping, and continued to do so for much of the autumn: an uncovenanted complication if foreign grain was to be brought in. Some weeks in any case were needed to accept the fact and extent of *national* shortage, for certain kinds of help at least would demand more than local treatment. Various expedients could be drawn on; but not all might be relevant at once, and experience furthermore suggested that some were debatable in principle and some likely to prove awkward to apply.

One precaution had been taken before the rains descended. Government was given temporary powers in July to stop export of corn at its discretion and admit imports free of duty.[2] No mention was made of

---

1. See Note on Sources to this Ch. for my authorities on this perennially debated subject of the standard of living in the late eighteenth and early nineteenth centuries.

2. By 39 Geo. III, c87 of 12 July 1799, putting in motion once more a process followed in the crisis of 1795–6 which had lapsed after a last repetition late in 1797 (38 Geo. III, c10). A stipulated period always imposed the need for extension.

Liverpool was quick to propose bringing the measure into effect (to Pitt, 27 August 1799; P.R.O. 30/8/152). But that waited for another month until the King and Ministers were in London again, after the long recess, to sanction an Order in Council on 25 September (see ibid and note on P.R.O. 30/8/291, f. 14). It came into force on 16 October (P.R.O., P.C. 2/153).

the harvest when Parliament met early and briefly in September;[1] but in mid October the first steps were taken – an embargo on the making of 'low wines' and spirits from all grains in Scotland until 1 March 1800 and from wheat in England until 20 September, and the reduction until June of duties on spirits distilled from molasses or sugar.[2] These harbingers heralded a spate of enactments from February to July 1800: no fewer than seventeen bearing directly on a crisis of mounting growth.

Their nature and range pointed lines of action drawn largely from experience of the last model. In making its choices Government deliberately excluded others from a combination which was intended to follow a pragmatic course but one contained by acknowledged doctrine. Each element in fact, as Pitt saw it, reinforced the other.[3] Acknowledging the need for continuing inquiry and discussion,

> I do not hesitate at the same time to declare, that, to go beyond the remedy which is plain, practical, sanctioned by the soundest principles, and confirmed by the surest experience, must ever be a dangerous course: – it is unsafe in the attempt; it is unworthy of a Statesman in the design – to abandon the system which practice has explained and experience has confirmed, for the visionary advantages of a crude, untried theory. It is no less unsafe, no less unworthy of the active politician, to adhere to any theory, however just in its general principle, which excludes from its view those particular details, those unexpected situations, which must render the scheme of the philosophic politician in the closet inapplicable to the actual circumstances of human affairs.

'But', he continued, alluding to much that by then was going on around him, 'if it be unwise to be guided solely by speculative systems of political economy, surely it is something worse to draw theories of regulation from clamour and alarm'.[4]

These somewhat Polonius-like generalisations had a specific base. The 'soundest principles' remained those conceived as governing the springs of the economy. '. . . in times of peculiar scarcity and distress' it was the more necessary to have 'duly considered the causes from which the prosperity of the country had arisen' and 'well understood the foundation on which it stood'. The final progenitors of any relief were 'the freedom

---

1. To free militiamen for overseas service and grant fresh financial supplies for the war (pp. 233 above).

2. 39 Geo. III, cs 7 and 8, 12 October 1799; the former extended by c21, the latter by c61. By c8, in addition, duties on imported starch (a substance containing coarse grain) were lowered and methods of collection improved. Cf. II, 469 for some similar measures in 1795.

3. Speech of 11 November 1800 (*P.R., 3rd ser.*, XIII (1801), 47–8; given the double inverted commas indicating *oratio directa* which reporters sometimes used).

4. And cf. an earlier remark: 'It was . . . always inexpedient to frame a general law to remedy a particular evil' (speech of 11 February 1800; op. cit., X, 416).

of trade, and the application of industry and capital'.[1] Subject to and supported by law, they must prove the best, because enduring, recourse.

Such an approach did not rule out intervention. Rather, it determined the latter's forms. By the end of July 1800 these could be seen as falling under four heads: imports of grain, to be encouraged while powers were retained to prohibit exports; reduction of consumption, voluntarily under guidance together with some regulation; substitutes, some imposed, some to be promoted, for food and certain products using grains; special allowances, carefully defined, as a part of poor relief. Further legislative measures followed, heightened by the second bad corn crop, until a kinder harvest in 1801 led to their expiry or progressive repeal.

The most immediate source of help, in a country no longer self-sufficient and increasingly favouring a wheaten loaf,[2] lay in larger imports – of various grains but of wheat above all. Pitt's methods here in the earlier crisis had landed him in trouble.[3] A bold, in fact unprecedented campaign of purchase overseas by Government direct, offsetting total reliance on the private trade, had then ended in acrimony and some financial and political embarrassment. The intricacies of commercial transactions, and merchants' calls for compensation when stocks were released onto earlier, private consignments bought more expensively – and, they claimed, with official encouragement – raised novel problems in an exercise which showed Ministerial concern but whose scale in any case decreed only a marginal impact. The Minister had been personally involved, with Liverpool and scarcely to the liking of all his colleagues, and the consequences deterred him from a fresh attempt. The Commons, and also much expert advice, had pronounced firmly against the experiment. He therefore abandoned its repetition now, going out of his way indeed to stress the point, and returned wholly to the system of bounties as the familiar prime mover of 'an easy, expeditious, and effectual mode of obtaining supply'.[4] This did not however rule out very active official

1. 11 November 1800; p. 279, n3 above.

2. The year 1791 proving to be the last in English history in which the nation did not have to rely for its bread in part on foreign supplies (I, 92n5). See II, 444 and n1 for the growing preference for wheat over barley or rye, at least – but notably – in the Midlands and south.

3. See II, 464–7.

4. Cf. his account on 11 November 1800 (*P.R., 3rd ser.*, XIII, 46). He wrote a paper for the Committee of Trade on 22 October, the detail of which however he then found too complicated 'to be easily understood, or executed' by those affected, and accordingly followed with two others suggesting a choice of phrasing (Rose to Dudley Ryder [Vice President], 22, 23 October 1800; Harrowby Mss, vol. XXXIV, at Sandon Hall, Staffordshire). Rose earlier commented on the fact that the Minister's 'declaration in Parliament' prevented him from importing 'at the expense or risk of the public' (to Wilberforce, nd but from the context in 1799, and according to Wells (op. cit., 379) in November; *Private Papers of Wilberforce*, 86–7).

support for the private purchases. Any effort to bring in supplies was encouraged. 'We have several adventurers', the Under Secretary at the Home Office advised Pitt, who were going to try their hand at imports from Flanders 'by connivance'; agents were found in the distant and hazardous Morea who, given armed escort, would venture inland.[1] The Mediterranean indeed was a useful adjunct to the main source of North America, and the results overall were certainly impressive. Where 313,793 quarters of wheat and its flour were imported in 1795, 879,000 in 1796, and 463,185 in 1799 itself, the amount in 1800 was no less than 1,264,520, and this was followed by 1,424,765 in 1801.[2] In May 1800 there were said to be some three hundred 'corn ships' in the Thames, and in January 1801 some seven hundred among the forest of masts below London Bridge.[3]

While these operations were returned entirely to the private sector, Pitt took care in addition to foster and influence their practices. Merchants at the start were confused, and some disposed to panic. Rates of exchange were uncertain, particularly with North America, sellers' prices thought to be aggravated by the reports of shortage, and Prussia, usually a ready source, also had a shortage and imposed a ban. In these circumstances, Government gave such encouragement as it could. Licences were issued to overcome some wartime restrictions, including trade with the enemy. Some facilities were given to support transactions through the rates of exchange. Above all the Minister favoured a new method – 'a new principle', in Rose's words[4] – for settling the bounties themselves, by a guaranteed price for wheat and rice imported from certain regions by a given date. Instead of a sum paid according to quantity, as in 1795–6, this would operate equally on all shipments bought at less than the figure set by statute for the area concerned – 90 shillings a quarter for the Mediterranean and North America, 80 shillings for the Baltic.[5] Such a policy was designed as and proved to be a useful inducement to trade.

It did nothing however to reduce prices. Rather indeed it could heighten the level of the platform on which profits would then be imposed. So much in fact seemed obvious to one well placed opponent who detested

1. J. King to Pitt, 9 October 1800 (P.R.O. 30/8/308), and see also a letter to him on 13 January 1801 from the Privy Council, following a meeting which the Minister attended (P.R.O., P.C. 2/153). I am obliged to Dr Colm McNamara for information on procurement in the Peloponnese.

2. Dropping to 647,663 and 373,725 in the two following years (Donald Grove Barnes, *A History of the English Corn Laws from 1660–1846* (1930), Appendix C). This of course does not take account of imports of other grains; at least one table listing all kinds was sent by Thomas Irving at the Custom House (for whom see I, 324) to Pitt, covering September 1800 to April 1801 (P.R.O. 30/8/291).

3. Wells, op. cit., 197, 201.

4. To Wilberforce, as in p. 280, n4 above.

5. 39 & 40 Geo. III, c29, of 4 April 1800. This was followed on 1 May by c35 and on 20 June by c53, extending the treatment to oats and rye respectively; all until 1 October. The detailed provisions were close to Pitt's 'principle', apart from inclusion of the Baltic which Ministers had not wished in view of Prussia's position.

the whole approach, particularly coming from the man with whom he had studied Adam Smith in their youth. To Grenville, 'the whole system on which we are indeed now acting' was in fact 'impious and heretical'. Prices of provisions, he reminded Pitt, could never be lowered '*by contrivance*'; 'like every other article of commerce, if left to themselves, [they] will and must find their level'. One could not and should not buck the market, increasing the evil one sought to remedy. It was a sad day when his cousin was 'lured' by Liverpool 'into all the mazes of the old system'.[1] He might indeed have argued in this instance that the pupil was outdoing his new teacher; for Liverpool, as it happened, was not wholly enamoured of all aspects of the scheme. Dealing continually with the corn factors, he could detect their manoeuvres on the openings now provided; and while he was induced by large imports in 1800 to favour extending the Act beyond its date,[2] he was not prepared to concede any more. He found however in the early autumn that this was precisely what Pitt wanted. The Minister had been disturbed by complaints from the merchants in London of low margins in the face of difficulties – of mediocre quality sometimes of shipments, problems of congestion in the river. He was anxious therefore to adjust the bounties farther, and make the necessary administrative arrangements: the former should be calculated on actual sale prices measured against the average of the regional source, itself reckoned as a percentage of the average British market price; the latter would require inspectors to confirm and issue certificates of sale. The question was argued indecisively at the Committee of Trade and then taken to Cabinet, where Liverpool, in poor health, failed to attend the critical meeting.[3] Not unnaturally he lost, and Pitt's preferences were carried into law.[4] The episode showed the Minister's resolve to safeguard imports at any cost. Nor was this surprising, for he now rated the 'growing dangers' from 'the scarcity' more 'formidable' even than 'the question of peace or war'.[5]

Foreign supplies could produce wheat; economies and alternatives could help limit consumption. Longer-term agricultural improvements could

1. To Pitt, 24 October 1800 (Stanhope, III, 248); and cf. I, 359 & n2. See also same to Auckland, 20 October 1800 (*A.C.*, IV, 111–12).

2. See p. 278, n2 above.

3. Wells, op. cit., 199–200 discusses the affair. The relevant Cabinet meeting seems to have been on 25 October, and it may have been with this in mind that Pitt asked Rose to bring a monthly account of 'corn and flour' imports in 1800 to Woodley (see p. 82 above), where he was staying with Addington (25 October 1800; B.L. Add. Ms 42772). It was not the first time that Liverpool had endangered his case by not attending a Cabinet; cf. II, 514 for an occasion on which however the absence was deliberate.

4. By 41 Geo. III (GB), c10, of 15 December 1800, including a wider range of foodstuffs than its predecessors. See *P.R., 3rd ser.*, XIII, 46 for Pitt's defence of the proposals on 11 November.

5. To Addington, 8 October 1800 (Stanhope, III, 244). Some lists of grain imports for 1799 and 1800–1 remain among his papers in P.R.O. 30/8/291.

be only of limited help. Every one was agreed in principle on the need for their stimulation, and early in 1801 an earlier statute was amended to encourage a larger acreage of tillage and the growth of potatoes.[1] It was hard to tell how much effect that could have at once; and Pitt himself indeed had not been active in furthering the work of the Board of Agriculture which he had set up a few years before. He was in touch with the Secretary, Arthur Young – Young saw to that –, and was 'inclined to think favourably' of the Board's idea of a general Enclosure Act to obviate the need for a private bill in every case. But that was a passing remark, which was not followed up.[2] His interest was focused on more immediate measures. At the height of the crisis he maintained that he had 'all along' tried to foster the use of substitutes,[3] and one early step was in fact taken in that direction, following private examples and proposals which had engaged public interest. The dearth of 1795–6 had seen the development and provision of soup kitchens using coarse meat and veg-etables, an experiment continued thereafter as a social measure in some towns and landed estates. Members of the Government themselves now took up the idea, and towards the end of December 1799 it was advocated officially in a circular from the Home Office.[4] It did not stand alone. Substitutes and economies were twin aspects of a single policy, and the circular contained a request for information on the prospects of enforcing earlier restrictions, specified by statute, on the quality of wheaten bread.[5] Partly as a result, an Act was passed in February 1800 forbidding the sale of bread which had been baked for less than twenty-four hours – a measure reckoned to lower consumption in London alone by a tenth.[6]

This legislation concealed serious difficulties. A more effective attack had in fact been contemplated.[7] The earlier statutes had

1. 41 Geo. III (UK), c20. A few months before, Pitt had mentioned to Grenville, 'you remember we talked of tythes [see pp. 177–8 above] and of other measures of permanent encouragement to tillage' (23 October 1800; *H.M.C., Dropmore*, VI, 357).

2. The quotation is from his speech of 11 November 1800 (*P.R., 3rd ser.*, XIII, 76). He had, he said, consulted 'many persons' about the future in general. For his relations with the Board, or rather its progenitor Sinclair, and his passivity when the latter introduced a general enclosure bill in 1796, see II, 468–9.

3. Speech of 12 November 1800 (*P.R., 3rd ser.*, XIII, 84).

4. See Wells, op. cit., 214–15. George Rose was among those who were now 'making the experiment', on his Hampshire properties (to Wilberforce as in p. 280, n4 above, 88). Pitt himself received advice (eg from the 'improver' Lord Sheffield, 18 December 1799; P.R.O. 30/8/177). The circular, to the Lords Lieutenant, was dated 20 December; a voluntary 'engagement' to reduce consumption of food and articles containing wheat, as had been promulgated in 1795 (see II, 470–1), was drafted in addition but not included. The earlier efforts were promoted largely by the Society for Bettering the Conditions of the Poor, using a design from the fertile hand of Count Rumford.

5. The operative measure had been 13 Geo. III, c43 of 1773. This, with other statutes, was repeated in 1791 by the comprehensive 31 Geo. III, c30. Cf. II, 444.

6. 39 & 40 Geo. III, c18, extended beyond its date of expiry by 41 Geo. III (GB), c17 in December.

7. This and the following paragraph draw on Wells, op. cit., 205–18. See also II, 470.

enabled magistrates to allow the sale of wheaten bread of coarser quality than that covered by the assize – the ancient system which in theory governed quantity, quality and price. The assize itself moreover catered for the prices of mixed loaves. But there were two serious drawbacks. The enactments did not apply to London without the voluntary assent of the Court of Aldermen; nor to the ratio prescribed between the price of wheat and that of flour. In 1795 they had been tested and found wanting: the City, by the narrowest of margins, blocked their operation, and magistrates throughout the country varied greatly in response. The problems indeed were considerable. As the Law Officers had found, the language of the Acts appeared 'obscure' in trying to cover the spectrum of needs, and local particularities frequently combined with commercial interests to defeat the intention. When the new crisis arose, however, one circumstance seemed more propitious. A shift of balance on the City's aldermanic court favoured possible action, and some neighbouring counties were on the verge of applying the Acts. Government therefore reckoned it could move, and a bill was drafted to amend the assize and extend it to London. It soon ran into trouble. Some of the most sensitive contents were leaked; the House of Commons, or its committee, was said to prefer the voluntary principle; and that rumour infuriated magistrates who had decided on compulsion. The bill was quickly dropped, and with it the attempt to bring the capital into line.

It was a depressing warning. But Ministers, and Pitt it seems in particular, were not prepared to give up. After some months of preparation they decided to embody the experience of two concerns which had lain outside the regular channels of the trade. The Albion Mills in London from 1786 to 1791, and the Birmingham Flour and Bread Company since 1796, had operated as co-operatives, buying in bulk, establishing a more stable ratio between wheat and flour prices, and – it was claimed by their opponents, through inferior quality – undercutting the more orthodox millers and bakers.[1] Information was sought from the latter as soon as the preferred legislation was withdrawn;[2] Liverpool set to work and became convinced that an Act could be framed for the metropolis; and while he then appears to have fallen out of the process Pitt caused a measure to be introduced in June 1800 to incorporate on a temporary basis 'the London Company for the Manufacture of Flour, Meal and Bread', which would confine itself to wheaten products and be required to submit its accounts to Parliament. The passage of the bill was hard fought, if in rather thin Houses. Some

1. There were other examples: a mill club for instance in Mansfield in the 1770s, sick clubs in Sheffield in 1795, a union of Friendly Societies in Manchester emerging at this time (Wells, op. cit., 326–7). Co-operatives may also have developed in the naval dockyards – certainly one did so at Portsmouth (see Ian R. Christie, *Stress and Stability in Late Eighteenth-Century Britain* (1984), 123).

2. See P.R.O., P.C. 2/153 for meetings on 25 February and 10 March 1800, at which the relevant Ministers were present.

Ministerial supporters – one was Spencer Perceval[1] – voted with Opposition, prompted by fears of a massive threat to commercial freedom and variety. The second reading in the Commons passed well enough, by 55 votes to 27; but leave to bring in the third was allowed by only 48 to 44 (it then passed by 35 to 17), and the measure scraped through the Lords by a single vote.[2] Meanwhile another bill passed more quickly, enabling the Lord Mayor to decide flour and bread prices of his own volition, independently of the assize. The two Acts were on the statute book in July.[3] To that extent, on paper at least, the problem of London was eased.

These were not inconsiderable efforts, in which Pitt was exercising guidance and support in a variety of ways. He did not grace the meetings of the Committee of Trade at which much of the detail was considered – Liverpool indeed complained of the lack of attendance by members of the parent Privy Council. But he was present fairly regularly at the Council itself when shortage was on the agenda; he was in touch directly with some of the interested parties; and he took a lead in the Commons' debates.[4] If the efforts were real, however, implementation was not simple, and when the second bad corn harvest was piled on the first it was clear that more was required. The position now was serious enough for

1. See p. 91 above.

2. Which, it might be claimed, was Liverpool's own. He had come to the House from his sickbed, roused it seems because Pitt, acting on his own, had passed the conduct of the unpopular bill in the Commons to the old man's son Hawkesbury. Liverpool himself was adamant that he had known nothing about the step in advance (to Sir Joseph Banks, 25 September 1800; B.L. Add. Ms 38311). There had indeed been disagreement within the Government itself over the legitimacy of a scheme which, it was estimated, might capture ten per cent of the metropolitan market or even exert something like a monopoly. Grenville in particular, who feared the latter, had been strongly opposed, but lost against Pitt's 'express desire', as Liverpool put it, that the bill be brought in (see Jupp, *Lord Grenville*, 281 & n62). It is against this background of disquiet, inside and outside the Ministry, that one must judge Pitt's handling of the matter; was it in fact casual, or tactically adroit? The unfortunate Hawkesbury complained of being 'Abandoned . . ., with three or four exceptions, by every Person in Office', and entrusted 'Personally' with 'the whole Responsibility of the Measure'. Not unnaturally he felt aggrieved (to Pitt, 5 July 1800; Dacres Adams Mss, formerly P.R.O. 30/58/3). But the controversial bill passed the House, on that basis, without direct Ministerial commitment.

The temporary nature of the ensuing Act, 39 & 40 Geo. III, c97, was defined by a provision that the Company could be suspended or dissolved on six months' notice by Order in Council. The debates in June and July can be followed best in *P.R.*, *3rd ser.*, XII, 118–24, 251–72 (with the majority for consenting to the third reading given in *P.H.*, XXXV, col. 461), 576–89 for the Commons, 390–2, 427–49, 566–9 for the Lords.

3. The second was 39 & 40 Geo. III, c74. Two others, permitting sugar to be used in brewing beer, and tightening the regulations for buying and selling hops (39 & 40 Geo. III, cs 62, 81) became law in the last four weeks of the session. It was also enacted (by c71) that bread baked for less than twenty-four hours (see p. 283 above) could be sold to troops on the march – a tribute to the prosecutions brought for illegal sale under the recent statute c18.

4. For his attendances at the Committee of Trade and the Privy Council between August 1799 and March 1801 see P.R.O., B.T. 5/11–12 and P.C. 2/153 respectively. He was present at only two of the former's relevant meetings in that time.

Parliament to be summoned sooner than intended,[1] and a crop of bills followed at once. Earlier statutes were extended, amended or explained, and bounties on imports improved. Salt for curing fish was freed from duty, encouragement given for the latter's consumption, and fishermen were protected from the naval press. Powers were given to stop export of – in the words of the preamble – 'any Sort of Provisions or Victuals whatever, or any Articles used as Food for Man'. Barley for malting which was damaged in the harvest could be kept for a shorter time than normally allowed. And bread baked 'solely' from fine flour was forbidden, with legal regulations set for the admixture or alternative use of lower quality wheat.[2] This last, the so-called Brown Bread Act, proved the most controversial of the measures; and not least because it accompanied one for 'the better Provision for the Maintenance of the Poor'.

For the two areas of aid were naturally closely linked. They had been so in the last crisis, guidance had again been given for both in the past year, and in this legislation the lines of approach met. The full title of the Act indeed was explicit: it was 'for the Maintenance of the Poor, and for diminishing the Consumption of Corn, by directing the Manner of applying Parish Relief'.[3] The treatment was grounded on earlier practice. It eschewed possible alternatives; and the reasoning behind the preference was reasserted firmly by Pitt.

The Poor Laws had been left alone since the Minister himself had made his brief attempt at reform in 1796–7.[4] The occasion left its mark. He did not lose his concern when a fresh need arose; he consulted, and received and kept papers.[5] But Government itself did not move at first, and his own approach lay now within the parameters as they stood. In March 1800 he spoke in support of a backbencher's bill requiring the parish to provide for certain 'casual' residents who did not have legal 'abode'. The proposal had strict limits. It was designed to help wage earners, so placed, who could not meet the price of bread; it did not apply to the old or infirm or unemployed. In Pitt's own view indeed it did not go far enough; nonetheless he was careful to emphasise the bill's temporary nature, its coherence with the general pattern of settlement, and its

1. See Pitt on 1 April 1801 (*P.R., 3rd ser.*, XV, 40). The session opened on 11 November.

2. Measures of extension &c in November–December 1800 were 41 Geo. III (GB), cs 1, 3, 4, 5, 10, 17, 19, 20; the others as specified above, cs 21; 2; 6; 16. The last in practice extended earlier measures, but was not limited to that, and in fact repealed an extant statute, 36 Geo. III, c22.

3. 41 Geo. III (GB), c12, passed on 22 December 1800 with the usual setting of a time limit – in this case 6 November 1801, and thence until the end of six weeks after the beginning of the next session (cf. p. 278, n2 above).

4. See II, 471–6.

5. Of which perhaps the most valuable survivor came from Patrick Colquhoun, the metropolitan magistrate (see II, 196) who was turning his attention increasingly to the connexions between crime and indigence. See P.R.O. 30/8/308.

reinforcement of the orthodox distinction between the deserving and the undeserving poor. He then had to watch its defeat after a hopeful start.[1] A minor amendment, Ministerial this time, to the working of 'Gilbert's Act' of 1782, where that distinction was enshrined, did nothing to disturb principle.[2] And neither did the further, more important new Governmental measure itself.[3] For the 'manner of applying' the relief was to be wholly through substitute foodstuffs, and the basic alternative of increasing wages, canvassed once more, was ruled out of court. Pitt reaffirmed the position he had taken in the winter of 1795–6, when Samuel Whitbread had brought in a bill for the latter purpose. Remaining sympathetic – as Whitbread himself had acknowledged – to a benevolent intention, he did not this time formally oppose.[4] But the remedy was false; 'it was impossible', he said later, 'the rate of wages could be made to correspond with a sudden and temporary rise in the price of provisions. Such a system, if carried into effect, would have the most pernicious effect'. More money in the pockets of the poor would in fact only contribute to *raising* prices.[5] Far better to confine 'all parochial relief' to a range of substitutes. The real question was, should this be done at discretion or by compulsion?[6]

He himself, one has the feeling, inclined strongly towards compulsion. He remembered all too well 'the unfortunate experience we have had of the efficacy' of urging substitutes for voluntary acceptance; though he was of course well aware – and had plenty of reminders, not least from the Foxites – that a forced diet could be highly unpopular, and endangered by local refusal to act.[7] Nonetheless he was convinced that the composition of

1. Again in thin Houses, by 23 to 30, after passing the second reading by 21 to 19 (see *P.R.*, *3rd ser.*, XI, 43, 53–6, 146–51, 179–84). The promoter was William Baker, the active knight of the shire for Hertfordshire and an epitome of the broadly pro-Ministerial, one time broadly Foxite, fundamentally independent Member (cf. I, 30–5, 38–9): the account of him in *H of C*, III, 114–16 portrays an almost archetypal response to many of the issues of these years.

The Minister also spoke in support of another backbencher's bill which failed in the same session, for an increase in the parish poor rates in London. The promoter was William Mainwaring, county Member for Middlesex (*P.R.*, *3rd ser.*, XII, 204–7, 226–9, 375).

2. 41 Geo. III (GB), c9. See II, 448, and 447–9 for background.

3. Speech of 11 February 1800 (*P.R.*, *3rd ser.*, X, 465).

4. See Cf. II, 471.

5. Speeches of 12 November, 9 December 1800 (op. cit., XIII, 84, 427). On the former occasion he is said to have added that the method 'would destroy at once the organization of society'.

Once more Grenville did not agree on principle; he found an outright increase in wages preferable to 'alms' (to J. King [p. 119 above], 25 October 1800 (P.R.O. 30/8/308)). And see his letter to Pitt of the 24th (Dacres Adams Mss, formerly P.R.O. 30/58/3, from which the relevant passage is omitted in Stanhope, III, 247–50). His elder brother Buckingham's letter, cited there, is likewise in Dacres Adams Mss, 14–15 October 1800.

6. Speeches of 12 November, 4 December (*P.R.*, *3rd ser.*, XIII, 84, 388). He may have varied his words in the course of the former, talking also of 'as much as possible of the relief'.

7. Speech of 11 November (op. cit., 46). Fox's reaction was heated: 'this abominable . . . compulsive adoption of a new sort of food' (to Grey, 1 December 1800; *Memorials and Correspondence of Charles James Fox*, III, 316–17). He followed Whitbread in advocating higher wages, and cf. II, 446 for his stance in 1795.

the wheaten loaf itself could no longer be left, as a Commons' committee put it, to 'Measures of Permission and Recommendation'.[1] The Brown Bread Act therefore was compulsory,[2] the Poor Relief Act by contrast was not; rather, it was an enabling – a recommendatory – measure.

The distinction made little difference. The Brown Bread Act was ignored. 'Brown George', as the loaf was known, proved no more popular than an earlier version introduced voluntarily in 1795, when the poor themselves had proved depressingly reluctant to abandon the staple loaf.[3] Reappearing now in compulsory form, the expedient was rejected; to such an extent indeed that the statute was repealed within two months.[4] The Poor Relief Act by comparison was a partial success; sometimes ignored, often hard to implement, but nonetheless giving a lead. Soup kitchens spread, substitutes were introduced, including some novelties – both rice and fish now reached parts they had not reached before. The pattern indeed over the whole spectrum of supply showed the familiar variations. Ministers could cite ports crowded with corn ships, inland transportation assisted by Government,[5] economies of use whether by legislation or guidance. They could acknowledge, as in the previous crisis, very real efforts throughout society, to succour the poor in the parishes and to aid the efforts of the state. The instances were legion; so too were others of opposition or neglect. It was an uphill task, administrative and political, to limit physical shortages, and while it was tackled with growing energy success could be only partial. Nor could it be gained in a way which satisfied the great accompanying dilemma. Food might be made available, to mitigate the impact of famine. That did not remove the most conspicuous feature of the crisis – and, because conspicuous, widely seen as the cause: the lack of control over the price of wheat.

For this was the problem to which Government found no acceptable answer. Not every foodstuff was equally affected. The two other bread

1. Speech of 11 November 1800 (*P.R., 3rd ser.*, XIII, 47); Fourth Report of the Select Committee on the Price of Corn (*House of Commons Sessional Papers of the Eighteenth Century*, ed. Sheila Lambert, Vol. 131 (1975), 392).

2. 41 Geo. III (GB), c16 (p. 286, n2 above).

3. More prominently – or surprisingly – in fact than many of their betters. But then 'it was easier to induce some voluntary denial in those least affected than in those closer to the margin and jealous of their preferences and needs' (II, 471).

4. It was first suspended for some six weeks on 9 February 1801, and repealed in its entirety on the 24th; 41 Geo. III (UK), cs 1, 2. Cf. p. 286, n3 above.

5. As Pitt stressed, in asserting the need for this: 'the exertions of private charity must always be limited; and there are no individuals in the interior . . . who could send to the Forth for herrings, or to seaports for rice, to accommodate the poor of their district' (11 December 1800; *P.R., 3rd ser.*, XIII, 448, in *oratio directa*).

He may in point of fact have exerted himself personally over rice; at any rate he was urged by his neighbour Auckland [see pp. 69–70 above] to send three or four barrels a week, with some sugar, to Holwood for the poor (to Pitt, 26 November 1800; Dacres Adams Mss, formerly P.R.O. 30/58/3).

grains, barley and oats, by and large showed much more modest rises, and prices of wheat themselves were not uniform throughout the land.[1] A national statistic was an imprecise guide; as indeed national failure was an imprecise term. The latter in fact could be challenged after the harvest of 1799 even while 'the trumpet of approaching famine' was 'heard from the Orkneys to the Land's End'.[2] The Ministry elected to rest on evidence from what it claimed to be more soundly based quarters.[3] But it would have agreed without hesitation that prices responded to supply and demand. That indeed was the nub of the official case, the basis of the Government's stance. For if intervention became permissible on certain lines for supply itself, it was excluded for prices beyond the flexible but often ineffectual settlements of the assize.

Some steps could be taken. Despite the fears voiced, competition was heightened in the capital by the London Company. The assize of bread itself was set aside in the City by the complementary Act. Local authorities were urged to enforce existing regulations by which prices could take account of lower quality.[4] The law could be brought to bear on merchants and others who broke the law as it stood. None of these measures, however, was put forward as detracting from the central principle:

> trade, industry and barter would find their own level, and be impeded by regulations which violated their natural operation, and deranged their proper effect.[5]

Rather in fact they could be held to support it. The assize, although the child of earlier doctrine, necessarily responded to market operations, and competition was the latter's guarantee and restraint. This last indeed was the crux of the question, and it applied fully to domestic agricultural produce. For here 'The interest of the inland dealer, and that of the great body of the people, how opposite soever they may at first appear, are, even in years of the greatest scarcity, exactly the same'.[6]

1. See eg Wells, op. cit., Appendices, 445–7. And cf. pp. 286–7 above for wages.

2. Speech of the Earl of Darnley in the Lords, 20, 27 February 1800 (*P.R., 3rd ser.*, X, 722, and see also 654–5, 711–22). He lived in Kent.

He was by no means alone in his contention; and a reading of newspapers and private diaries and correspondence shows the very real difficulty of accurate central assessment.

3. Largely in the corn trade – which could be and was accused of self-interest. Pitt himself may also have been influenced by Arthur Young (see the latter to him on 28 November 1799, in P.R.O. 30/8/193) – who, though so often scornful of others, was not in fact always a sure guide. Such qualifications however are far from invalidating the seriousness of the crisis.

4. Pp. 282–6 above.

5. Pitt on 12 February 1796; quoted in II, 447, and argued then with particular reference to the price of bread.

6. Adam Smith, *Wealth of Nations*, bk IV, ch. V, ed. Edwin Cannan, II (1904), 25. It should be noted that the great work was written during and shortly after the massive food riots of the later sixties (for which see II, 92).

But was this in fact true? Whatever the earlier circumstances, could the confident verdict survive years such as these? Not every one in authority, let alone elsewhere, was now convinced. Within the Ministry there were those, like Grenville and also Portland in a key position as Home Secretary, whose belief was not shaken;[1] but there were others who were not so adamant, like Dundas,[2] or were opposed. Liverpool himself, a central figure here, was of the last school. In 'Times of Distress', he commented, 'the Seller' became 'Master of the Market', and it would be absurd to rest one's confidence in Adam Smith, who 'has pushed his Principles to an extravagant Length, and, in some respects, has erred'.[3] The 'Principles of Commerce', he had already remarked, 'must to a certain degree be different when they are applied to the Necessaries of Life'.[4] What, however, were the dimensions of 'a certain degree'? For there were two allied questions to be answered. If the shortage was real, as Government accepted, how could prices be restrained effectively without distortion, and real hardship to farmers as well? And if the shortage, while evident, was not as deep or extensive as claimed, could general regulations which might hinder extortion be imposed without hindering proper trade, and also the risk of raising consumption to a point at which the shortage would in truth be severe?

These arguments, if often self-interested, were not to be lightly dismissed. Defenders of the natural price mechanism stressed the importance of natural encouragement. Deter farmers and merchants – particularly the importers – by denying proper profit, and you took away the incentive to bring relief. Moreover, how were general impositions of prices going to work? The assize was a clumsy device, widely disregarded. To balance the hardships and misery of the poor with the needs of the suppliers, official constraints were much less suited than were the proper movements of economic forces to bring as speedy, effective and just results as one could hope to reach.

So argued a score of pamphlets, and columns in newspapers, and spokesmen in Parliament. Pitt himself, as we have seen, was not prepared to disagree. Having settled on 'the soundest principles' it would be most unwise 'to draw theories of regulation from clamour and alarm'. He took his stand rather on investigation of abuses of existing law, and where one was proved 'the remedy will be canvassed on its own merits'. If the

1. For Portland cf. II, 446. Unlike Grenville however, though both put their trust in competition, he was one of only two Cabinet Ministers – the other being Loughborough – to support Liverpool in the business of the London Bread Company in the Lords (Liverpool to Banks, 25 September 1800, B.L. Add. Ms 38311; see p. 285, n2 above).

2. Cf. I, 132, 457 for his 'liberal' principles; but he had shown earlier than Pitt that he did not shrink from some aspects of intervention (II, 154), and he clearly had some sympathy for Liverpool's point of view. See p. 277, n2 above.

3. To Sir Joseph Banks, 25 September 1800; same to Dundas, 11 October 1800 (B.L. Add. Ms 38311). In the latter instance he added that, even if the economist was right, 'it is absolutely impossible to convince the common People, who suffer so greatly'.

4. To Lord Sheffield, 30 July 1800 (loc. cit).

principles indeed were to be followed by their proper consequences, the path must necessarily be kept as clear as possible. Freedom of trade should not be threatened by inaction; frauds, individual or collusive, should be punished. Even so, in the last resort 'partial evils' must be left to 'pass' if punishment meant resorting to 'oppressive general regulations'.[1]

In taking this position the Minister was also not disposed to pronounce on the cause – or causes – of inflation. He was content to say that there were 'many opinions'. Some people, not least politicians, were blaming the war – a judgment taken seriously now by historians on the longer-term process as a whole, but which he rejected for the narrower problem of short-term movements of the prices of wheat.[2] His attitude in the crisis was conditioned at least partly indeed by a self-confessed and general lack of information; and though he remarked at one point that 'a knowledge of the precise deficit' of stocks was not required 'for the practical remedies proposed',[3] such ignorance was serious in assessing how far the scarcity was, as many charged, 'artificial'. He certainly could not discover all the facts he would have liked; when he tried, as he had done in 1795, to establish regular returns of corn by area, he was told once more that the method was questionable, and could give rise moreover now to 'mischievous' arguments.[4] The only statistical advance – though it would prove a major one – to emerge in the course of the dearth, lay in the other half of the equation of supply and demand: on 31 December 1800 the Act empowering the first national census of population was passed.[5] Meanwhile Government had to do its best within the constraints, administrative and conceptual, which were imposed on knowledge and approach by the weapons to hand.[6]

Against this background, Pitt strove to keep his feet in a growing storm. Public clamour over prices rose to a fresh pitch as the second corn harvest failed: if there was a flood of publications supporting market freedom, there were also plenty to castigate its results. Abuses by forestallers,

1. Speeches of 11, 26 November 1800 (*P.R.*, *3rd ser.*, XIII, particularly 48, 239, 244; and cf. pp. 279–80, 289 above).
2. Citing successive rises and falls under wartime conditions – in 1797 indeed to levels 'perhaps too low for the profit of the farmer' (11 November; op. cit., 49–50).
3. Sd; op. cit., 51.
4. Loughborough to Pitt, 13 October 1800 (Dacres Adams Mss, formerly P.R.O. 30/58/3). The Lord Chancellor distrusted the potential accuracy of the accounts; and the probable inaccuracies could 'give an Alarm of there being a Pretention to fix a limit of Price'. In 1795 a main objection had lain in the high-handedness of such an inquisition (II, 467).
5. 41 Geo. III (GB), c15. An event, it might be thought, of apt symbolism as the eighteenth century gave way to the nineteenth. For an indication of Pitt's role in effecting the measure see *Colchester*, I, 209–13.
6. Cf. II, 154–5: 'Governments disposed of clumsy weapons, and liberal [economic] doctrine rationalised a situation which it may have accentuated but did not create'. 'I even doubt', wrote Pitt for example on one occasion, 'if [,] controverting [as he did] the principle of raising wages, fixing them by law or by magistrates can be made practicable' (to Grenville, 23 October 1800; *H.M.C., Dropmore*, VI, 357).

engrossers and regrators, familiar for centuries, gathered pace once more. And, as in the last crisis, an immediate voice of redress was heard. The Courts had taken close interest in claims against these offences in 1794–6, and the Lord Chief Justice, Kenyon,[1] in particular had advised grand juries to be vigilant. He took the field again now, to an extent indeed that provoked politicians and produced a royal warning, while the Home Secretary rebuked local authorities who hindered merchants' operations. Taken as extremes, their repeated pronouncements represented opposed policies. But policies themselves in the upshot were seldom taken to extremes, and Pitt for his part was trying to steer a way through a maze of opinions and interests: amid magistrates exceeding their legal powers in the extent of their 'benevolence',[2] between colleagues who disagreed in relating practical means to doctrinal ends. He did not share Grenville's 'almost mathematical certainty' of infallible Smithian truth,[3] and the conviction, common to Old and New Whigs, of the evils of any form of intervention. He had moved in fact some way since 1792.[4] But he also differed from Liverpool, who wished to apply intervention to prices as well as supplies. He was not unsympathetic: he had earlier been prepared to accuse merchants of illicit combination, and he was genuinely anxious – perhaps the more so since Joe Smith had shown him misery on the ground, and he had looked into the complex of parochial practices for himself[5] – to do what he could to bring relief to the poor. But he was determined to stick to his last; to seek pragmatically effective answers within a corpus of thought and experience which was 'equally removed from extremes'.[6] At the end of the day he was relying on the expectation that the dearth, like all dearths, would pass, and prices return to more bearable levels. The foundations of economic principle must therefore

1. See Wells, op. cit., 86–7, 238–42. Cf. *H.M.C., Kenyon Mss* (1894), 554–5.

2. Out of 'an amiable and humane sympathy', perhaps 'so general as not to require any legislative interference' – a significant admission (speech of 12 November 1800; *P.R., 3rd ser.*, XIII, 85). See II, 61 for 'benevolence'.

3. Grenville to Pitt, 24 October 1800 (Dacres Adams Mss, formerly P.R.O. 30/58/3).

4. Cf. II, 154.

5. Op. cit., 467, 471–4.

6. 12 November 1800 (*P.R., 3rd ser.*, XIII, 48). Liverpool's distrust of the merchants emerges clearly from his correspondence of that autumn (B.L. Add. Ms 38311). He was not prepared however to ascribe more than a small proportion of the distress to them (loc. cit., to Banks, 25 September, to Dundas, 9 October).

The developing, though not complete, convergence in intellectual approach between the two Ministers (see also p. 282 above) did not mean or stem from any greater personal intimacy. Liverpool, always awkward in personal relationships (see I, 331) and not the less so as he grew older, remained essentially wary of a younger and likewise often awkward colleague whose political origins and tone differed from his and from whom he was liable to receive disobliging treatment (eg p. 285, n2 above). Pitt continued to look on Liverpool as a necessary fact of life; highly useful, ponderous and didactic and altogether something of a bore. 'I am obliged', he wrote as the scale of the shortage began to sink in, 'to set out for Addiscombe [Liverpool's house; I, 105], to hear a Lecture upon Corn' (to Canning, 10 December 1799, Canning Ms 30; and cf. I, 331n2).

not be undermined: despite appearances, they were the best available for the occasion, and they must certainly not be seen to have been jeopardised in its course.

Such a strategy – for in its definitions it cannot be designated simply a compromise – gave hope of a broad political consensus. It could thereby promote the tactic Pitt chose, as he had done less prominently in 1795. He set out to associate Parliament directly with Ministerial measures, and the pace was quickened in 1800 after the second bad harvest occurred. All expedients should now be reviewed. Let a Select Committee investigate them: that was the best way to ascertain and survey, and secure authoritative collective opinion. He was explicit on this, and in the event the later measures largely followed the Committee's reports.[1] It was a sensible course to proclaim and where possible to adopt; to share responsibility which he could influence for an approach which he could approve. For there was a further, important consideration, a linked benefit to be gained. Close Parliamentary involvement could buttress Government's response not only to shortage, but also, by reflection, to the ensuing shocks of unrest.

II

'After all, the question of peace or war is not in itself half so formidable as that of the scarcity with which it is necessarily combined, and for the evils and growing dangers of which I see no adequate remedy'.[2] When Pitt wrote these words it was at a particularly low moment, for in September 1800 a wave of troubles began suddenly to spread. Riots were reported from Yorkshire, Lancashire and Derbyshire, from the Midlands and Oxfordshire, in pockets of the south and east, even the West Country where the corn harvest had not been so badly hit. Above all there was a surge in London on a scale which revived some memories of the Gordon Riots and of the mob violence in the dearth of 1768.[3] It was an alarming phenomenon, and Pitt himself moreover was ill – 'not the better for brooding during the confinement' he was forced to keep.[4] That did not prevent him from rallying with proposals for further relief.[5] But the unusually sombre tone showed the dismay at a state of affairs in which the threat was immediate while the only real answer lay in time.

1. Of which there were six, submitted to the House in November and December 1800 (*House of Commons Sessional Papers* . . ., ed. Lambert, Vol. 131, 341–438). Good examples of Pitt's emphasis on the Committee's role may be found in *P.R., 3rd ser.*, XIII, 49, 85.

2. Pitt to Addington, 8 October 1800 (see p. 282 above). The particular question affecting peace or war is discussed on pp. 381–90 below.

Cf. Canning too on 'a scarcity of grain this winter, which may put spirits into both Jacobins and Opposition' (to Lord Mornington in India, 20 October 1800; quoted in Mackesy, *War Without Victory*, 6).

3. For which see I, 22, II, 92 respectively.

4. To Addington as in n2 above. Cf. p. 82 above.

5. To same, 9 October 1800 (Stanhope, III, 244–6).

In some respects the picture might not have seemed as black as it had done five years before. Taking food riots on the same criteria of measurement, the numbers could be said to have been less at the peak in 1800 than at the peak in 1795.[1] Nor in fact had the year been particularly troubled by violence hitherto – Pitt's own windows this time indeed had remained intact in Downing Street, and for that matter the King's coach was not attacked on its way to the opening of Parliament.[2] The physical means of countering violence moreover were rather ampler than before. The size of the regular army and the militia had been increased; the state of the war imposed, and that of Ireland now allowed more easily, a concentration of force at home; more barracks favoured more rapid deployment; the Volunteers had grown in numbers and, it seemed, settled down.[3] The Ministry had more resources, and was more ready to use them: experience from the earlier crisis had been absorbed. And in fact, when it came to the point, the defences held. The riots fell away in November, as did another, lesser upsurge in April and May the next year. In the capital itself, the mob was quelled within four days. The fears, undoubtedly vivid, in the early autumn of 1800 might thus appear excessive at first sight.

There were other factors, however, to account for their sudden effect. The success of the military as a policing force had certain inherent limits; nor indeed in these circumstances could it be taken wholly for granted. Magistrates were often slow to call for troops, and troops still often slow to arrive;[4] and soldiers' loyalty had to be watched when confronted with hardship among their fellow subjects. The regulars by and large were thought to be reliable – though the assumption had been dented in 1797. But they now contained more militiamen, and in the dearth of 1795 the militia had been known to sympathise with rioters and in fact to riot themselves.[5] There were anxious days again now, and all the more so,

1. See John Bohstedt, *Riots and Community Politics in England and Wales 1790–1810* (1983), 17–19, figs. 1–3. His definition of riot is 'an incident in which a crowd of fifty or more people acted in hostile fashion to damage or seize property, to attack persons physically, or to coerce individuals to perform or desist from some immediate action' (op. cit., 4).
The outbreaks in September–October 1800 occurred, as it happened, just after the only fall in the average price of wheat since August 1799. But the decline was brief – a matter of weeks – and the relationship between prices and unrest was not always as simple as the graphs might suggest; cf. on a broader canvas II, 94–5.
2. See II, 454–5 for those demonstrations in 1795.
The King *was* shot at in May 1800; but the assailant, James Hadfield, was found to be insane. Pitt for his part was said to have been subject to a threat of 'pistolling' in March, by, of all people, his relation Lord Camelford. But Camelford – who may in any case have been acting a part imposed on him by activities abroad for the Alien Office (p. 119 above) – was notoriously wild and at times seemed distinctly odd.
3. See II, 126, 195, 328–9, 401–2, 406–8, and pp. 122–6, 166–7, 169–70 above. The regulars at home were even supplemented in 1800 from the British force in Portugal (p. 151 above), where calls on the contrary for its enlargement had recently been heard (Mackesy, *War Without Victory*, 182).
4. Cf. II, 126, 132–3.
5. Op. cit., 451; p. 123 above.

surprisingly, as some of the apprehensions were roused by the Volunteers.[1] And while failure was avoided, success itself was relative. Troops could suppress a riot, but not the practice – the principle – of rioting, emanating from deep wells of habit within a society whose physical civil defences remained uncomfortably slight.[2]

Against such a background the dangers were seen as both actual and potential. A second catastrophic corn harvest was a wearing blow.[3] One year's shortage was bad enough; two in succession on this scale were appalling. And the focus of much of the unrest in this instance posed a particularly ominous prospect. The fact that the crisis revolved so prominently around the question of prices – more so even than in 1795[4] – provoked deep and widely held suspicions of farmers and merchants causing artificial scarcity. It was indeed this that pointed Lord Liverpool's warning of a threat to 'the Foundation of . . . Government':

> there will be Insurrections of a very serious nature, and . . . different Bodies of Yeomanry may possibly fight each other . . . those of the Cities and great manufacturing Towns, who are adverse to the Farmers will fight those of the Country, who will be disposed to defend them.[5]

Such an antagonism in fact was a cause for worry which troops could not remove and might themselves reflect. Nor, given the Ministry's – Pitt's – resolve against intervention in this area of the markets' activities, except where breaches of the law might be proved, could the suspicions be dispelled or reduced by the official response. Families suffering, and those who saw them, were not always consoled by assurances that costs were responding to natural demand, and would as naturally decline in due course. Other forms of help became the more necessary, whether from Government itself in the area of supply or from a range of local and private support.

This last was forthcoming, unevenly, in various ways. In the middle term the pattern of rising wages, differentiated by place and occupation, helped to mitigate some at least of the strains. Parishes met higher costs of parish relief according to their choices of method.[6] Gifts in money or kind

1. See Wells, op. cit., 268–73 for this disturbing development (see Colley, op. cit., 312–18). It may have owed something to the growing urbanisation of many of the corps (see p. 294, n4 above).

These considerations may have been borne in mind when the Government decided in November to recall the regulars stationed in Portugal (p. 294, n3 above), now needed at least temporarily for 'the preservation of tranquillity . . . under the present scarcity' and for the continued security of Ireland (Grenville to Charles Arbuthnot [chargé d'affaires in Lisbon], 19 November 1800; P.R.O., F.O. 63/34).

2. A discussion of this extensive subject may be found in II, Chs. IV–V, particularly in sections I–II of the former and I of the latter.

3. Though the barley and to some extent the oats harvests were better than in 1799.

4. Cf. p. 277 above.

5. To Dundas, 11 October 1800; see loc. cit and n3 above.

6. See II, 447–50.

were made, by individuals and – a developing process – associations. The pure light of economic doctrine, diffused in the prism of Governmental measures, was further refracted in this denser air. Driven by mixtures of alarm and benevolence, by self-interest, officiousness and charity of heart, there was a notable movement, from gentry and clergy and parish communities, urban institutions and self-help societies, to stem the worst effects of a calamity which central policies themselves could not fully meet.

Such applications of relief, however, were not invariably welcomed by Government, as Pitt's remark on magistrates' charity made clear.[1] They could appear critical of its conduct; and it was not in that respect alone that Ministers could feel some unease. For relief was one part of a response which had also to deal with unrest over prices and shortage; and in that respect the attitudes of natural allies were not always certain in a pluralistic state. Government itself in point of fact was not always draconian in its dealings with food riots. The army disliked using troops on that duty more than was strictly needed, and officers on the spot could show restraint in their turn.[2] And the Home Office for its part normally observed the strict letter of the law: it called on the military directly where the Crown had direct jurisdiction (in the royal dockyards for instance), but not where the civil authority was vested elsewhere at a remove. This is not to attribute to the Ministry a general leniency it would not have approved. These were certainly not the times in its view for such an approach. Its treatment of the problems of shortage has been characterised as one of 'Cavalry and Soup Kitchens',[3] and in 1800–1 the first were as notably in evidence as the second. One difference now indeed from the earlier crisis of 1795–6 was the volume of instructions from Whitehall to authorities, military and civil, to *prepare* diligently and adequately for trouble. The commanders were urged to remain on instant warning from the magistrates, the magistrates not to hestitate in summoning the troops. Portland's missives were profuse in the most anxious months, and they had their effect. Nonetheless they did not invariably meet with a wholehearted response. Particularly where riots could be assigned unmistakably to shortage, both magistrates and judges could display their independence; as had occurred not infrequently before and would remain a feature of the scene. The strong sense of local identities, manifested sometimes in 'community politics',[4] the sense of the law, expressed sometimes surprisingly both among juries and on the Bench, the survival of a political diversity not always prepared to give the Ministry a ready hand, could provide checks and balances which had by no means vanished from – rather, which could accompany – support for the state against sedition

1. P. 292 and n2 above.
2. Cf. II, 126.
3. Title of ch. 4 in Bohstedt, op. cit. And cf. II, 464.
4. See the title of Bohstedt's book, p. 294, n1 above.

itself.[1] 'England was a country both highly integrated and minutely differentiated',[2] and the fact was in evidence once again in both respects. Some authorities acted in ways that Ministers saw as misguided or disruptive; many others on the contrary sometimes went farther than the Home Office would have liked. The pattern was not uniform, or entirely consonant with the guiding design. One gains the impression of a diversified society often vigorously aroused, hardened under its pressures but still not cast in too rigid a mould.

III

The reactions to disturbances aroused by dearth held a certain place in the conception of order which, if not wholly distinct from, was not necessarily the same as those aroused by other causes. The distinction however cannot be too exactly defined, since more than one ingredient could be present; and Government in these years was not prepared in fact to take food riots in isolation. As in 1795, it was alert to signs of influence from what it saw as more sinister elements.[3] And one possible source, which itself had lately been receiving attention, was seen to lie in bodies producing 'combinations' of working men.

There was nothing new in point of fact about these, or for that matter about strikes themselves. Nor had either been viewed historically as an excessive threat. Both had been evident throughout the century, and one form of such associations indeed had quite recently been accorded Governmental protection. The Act of 1793 regulating friendly and benefit societies, brought in by Rose from the Treasury, recognised a fact of life long existing and widely spread.[4] The provisions were unusual in that they embraced the country as a whole, and by and large were supportive: other statutes – ten since the 1720s, including Ireland – were directed to specified areas and types of labour, and were aimed at forbidding combinations 'in restraint of trade'.[5] Such prevention rested on the old common law against conspiracy. But in practice the measures were seldom pressed hard, and indeed they were often ignored. Masters and men – each in varying degrees, and the latter in particular, combining among themselves– became accustomed to processes of negotiation, in which the

1. See II, 127, 149–50, 156–7 for 1795–6, pp. 109–26 above for 1798.
2. II, 100.
3. Cf. II, 451–3.
4. In the mid 1790s, for instance, Nottingham had 51 such societies with a total of some 2,000 paid-up members, while the small town of Lancaster had eighteen with only a slightly lower number (Christie, *Stress and Stability in Late Eighteenth-Century Britain*, 128). The Act was 33 Geo. III, c54; see II, 93.
5. I take this figure from Dr John Rule, who has pointed out to me that, considering legislation directly covering and confined to those forms of association, the figure of forty-odd statutes for that same period, which is sometimes cited, is wrong. Some Acts however might have been seen as relevant where they referred to or bore on such activity.

men in fact appear quite often to have been the more skilled. Initiatives from below were not strange, or challenged systematically, and when the courts were involved they were sometimes used to offer mediation.[1] In some degree, too, a similar attitude could be seen applied to strikes. Violence of course could call for suppression, as the records of the Home Office show. Other instances reveal more even-handed treatment. The response could naturally vary with the causes: from caution or fear, sometimes from the local authorities' indifference or even sympathy. The background was far from uniform, over decades of largely particularised pressures in which the capacity for organisation was developing lower down the scale.[2]

The pace however had been growing, with the economy itself. It attracted comment as the century wore on, and sooner or later some further legislative reaction was doubtless on the cards. By the later nineties a 'general disease' could be perceived which demanded a 'general remedy'.[3] But when the occasion came, it seems to have been suggested by an example of the older kind. In April 1799 a bill was introduced by a private Member to prevent combinations among the millwrights of London and the neighbouring districts. It went through its stages, passed in the Commons, and was sent up in June to the Lords. But there it was allowed to drop; for by then the 'general remedy' was under debate, and if that was accepted it would overtake the particular instance.[4]

The suggestion for such treatment came from Wilberforce when the millwrights' bill was brought in. Whether he was acting for Government from his position as a backbencher is not clear.[5] At all events he spoke; and on 17 June a bill 'to prevent unlawful Combinations of Workmen' was read for the first time – six days after the lesser measure had passed the House. A fortnight later it passed in

1. There were more formal instances of arrangements for mediation in some of the statutes themselves: in those concerning the Spitalfield weavers and the London tailors.

2. For the fear of influence spread by mobility as a factor in this process see I, 130.

3. Wilberforce in the Commons on 9 April 1799 (*P.R., 3rd ser.*, VIII, 323).
A special form of combination in support of higher wages was moreover provided in the naval mutinies of 1797 – 'a protracted episode of wage-bargaining' which raised its own different problems but also influenced attitudes over a wider area (John Stevenson, 'Popular Radicalism and Popular Protest' in *Britain and the French Revolution, 1789–1815*, ed. H.T. Dickinson (1989), 76).

4. The process can be followed in *P.R., 3rd ser.*, VIII, 323–4, 687, and op. cit., IX, 562, and otherwise in *H.C.J.*, 54 (nd) for 5, 9 April, 10, 20 May, 5, 9, 10 June, and *H.L.J.*, XLII (nd) for 1 July 1799. The bill was moved by Sir John Anderson, an active Member for the City who had been Lord Mayor for 1797–8. Its connexion with the 'general' bill was specifically attested by Pitt (see p. 299 below).

5. He may at least, and more likely, have spoken with its knowledge, since despite a partial withdrawal from social life at this time and his reduced intimacy with Pitt (*Life of Wilberforce*, II, 352; and see p. 89 above), he was seeing a certain amount of the Minister in his renewed campaign for the slave trade (see e.g. pp. 428–9 below), and they also discussed the question of sedition (*Life*, II, 335).

its turn, eight days later it went through the Lords, and it received the royal assent on 12 July.[1]

The Act cancelled current contracts and agreements, written or unwritten, reached by unlawful concerted pressure from workmen. Men alleged in future to be acting in this way were to be taken before one or more magistrates within three months of the offence, and if convicted should serve up to two months' hard labour in a local institution. Men contributing money to combinations were to be fined. Appeal in any instance lay to the Quarter Sessions. Magistrates' current powers against combinations by masters would remain as before.[2]

The statute, with its modifying sequel, has long been notorious, inscribed with little question from the early nineteenth century in the litany condemning Pitt's 'Reign of Terror' and, in due course, class warfare. In recent years the perspective has been opened to change; and whatever one's judgment on the contents of the Acts, one may suggest that they did not figure, to supporters or opponents, so prominently at the time. The passage of the first measure seems indeed to have aroused remarkably little interest: the two main contemporary collections of Parliamentary debates pay it scant attention; only one Opposition Member is recorded as speaking on the sole occasion covered in the Commons and one on the sole occasion covered in the Lords, and the latter complained that the subject was not such as to attract much atten-dance.[3] Pitt himself seems to have been vague. In giving notice of an intention 'to provide a remedy to an evil of very considerable magnitude', he could not 'state particularly' the nature of the bill other than it would be 'modelled in some respects' on that for 'the Paper Manufacturers'; and a year later he clearly showed – if he did not in fact confess – that he could not recall its details.[4] The subject indeed seems to have lacked appeal not

1. 39 Geo. III, c81. The notice of a motion in the Commons may be found in *P.R., 3rd ser.*, IX, 65–6, and the same occasion, with Pitt's speech prefacing it, in *The Senator*, XXIII (nd), 1716. The third reading of the bill in the Lords is likewise briefly reported on p. 562 of the former, and in somewhat more detail in pp. 1857–61 of the latter. Otherwise there is no mention of the debates in either source, and none at all in the retrospective *P.H.*, XXXIV. The progress of the measure may be identified from *H.C.J.*, 54: 17–19, 21–5, 27–8 June, 1 July; and *H.L.J.*, XLII: 1–2, 4–5, 8–9 July 1799.

2. These last powers, according to Foxite Whigs, being applied with notable rarity (see *P.R., 3rd ser.*, IX, 66, 562).

3. Lord Holland on 9 July. Benjamin Hobhouse opposed the first reading in the Commons, and the emerging radical hopeful Sir Francis Burdett had apparently tried to defer the passing of the millwrights' bill (*P.R., 3rd ser.*, IX, 66).

4. Speeches of 17 June 1799 – all the more surprising as the first reading was taken on the same day –, 30 June 1800 (*The Senator*, XXIII, 1716; *P.R., 3rd ser.*, XII, 220). According to the latter, he acknowledged that 'The particular provisions of the bill he could not pretend at present to recollect'; according to *The Senator*, XXVI (nd), 1710 for the same debate, Sheridan remarked that 'it was very evident that the Right Honourable Gentleman was totally ignorant of its provisions'. There seems even to have been some doubt by then as to who – the Minister or someone else – had introduced the bill.

By 'the Paper Manufacturers' Pitt must have meant the millwrights (p. 298 above).

only to the peers of 1799. When the Act's successor, incorporating much of itself, was done away with in the 1820s, the Prime Minister of the day, a survivor of Pitt's Ministry, was not aware at first what the replacement would contain.[1]

The lack of precise attention – the almost casual treatment – was responsible at least in good part for the amendments which soon followed the measure of 1799. In the early summer of 1800 a wave of workmen's petitions reached Parliament, and leave was sought to bring in a fresh bill. Pitt opposed this, but was ready to accept modifications reached after 'temperate discussion': proven inequities 'ought certainly to be removed'; ' "he wished that everything might be done consistent with a principle of mercy and lenity to the parties, and of justice and safety to the public" '.[2] His preferred procedure was dropped in the next few weeks since a consolidated enactment seemed the best answer, and a new bill, repealing the previous Act but repeating most of its provisions, duly passed both Houses, becoming law on 29 July.[3] The Minister appears to have taken a hand in reaching amendments on which there seems to have been a respectable amount of common ground.[4] A main cause of grievance, shared at least to some extent by masters and men, lay in the absence of specific provision for arbitration. This was remedied: each side could nominate an arbitrator, and if a settlement was not reached in three days – unless an extension was agreed – the case would go to a magistrate for judgment. At the same time, two or more magistrates (instead of one or more)[5] were now required to attend a prosecution; and reference to masters' combinations was made more distinct. The purpose was to

1. This was Liverpool, the second Earl who had been Hawkesbury under Pitt. He said later that he would have opposed the new bill – the important Act of 1825, introduced by his colleagues Peel and Huskisson with Thomas Wallace – if he had known its contents (see A. Aspinall, *The Early English Trade Unions* . . . (1949), xxvii).

2. Speech of 30 June 1800, the first quotation taken from the report in *P.R., 3rd ser.*, XII, 220, the second from *The Senator*, XXVI, 1707 where it is given the interesting double inverted commas (p. 279, n3 above).

3. 39 & 40 Geo. III, c106. Once again the debates are not given in *P.H.* (XXXV). *P.R., 3rd ser.*, XII, 110–11, 218–24, 459–61, 590 follows the preliminaries, the discussion on the motion, the passage of the third reading in the Commons, and the brief debate in the Lords; *The Senator*, XXVI, 1609, 1671, 1698, 1703–12, 1854, 1902, 1969–72, 2039–40 also fastens on those occasions as well as noting some of the intervening stages recorded in *H.C.J.*, 55 (nd).

The bill was moved by Colonel Isaac Gascoyne, the broadly independent Member for Liverpool, with the Foxite Lord Mayor of London Harvey Combe, and Sheridan in support. Brought late in the session, there was little time for scrutiny in the Lords, where however it was said to have 'received a very ample discussion' in the Commons (Liverpool on 8 July; *P.R., 3rd ser.*, XII, 590, and cf. *The Senator*, XXVI, 2040). Even so, the figures in the only division I have found recorded for the Lower House (on the third reading) – 31 to 14 (*P.R., 3rd ser.*, XII, 461) – hardly support an impression of broad interest.

4. It is not uninteresting for instance to find Rose from the Treasury taking over the moving of the third reading of a bill introduced in a spirit of criticism by a private Member (see *The Senator*, XXVI, 1712, 1854, 1902, 1969).

5. See p. 299 above.

achieve a more equitable treatment while not removing the procedures for saving 'time, trouble and expense'.[1]

The useful if limited improvements, and Pitt's own role, found some approval at least. 'The Managing Committee for the Journeymen of this Country' – an interesting title, though the connotation is hard to establish[2] – wrote to thank him

> most cordially, and to pray that prosperity may abide with you, for the very liberal and Manly support you were pleased to give a Bill for the repeal of an Act . . . by which *We* were greatly grieved – . . .
>
> We beg Rt. Hon. Sir, you will excuse the stile of this Letter, which comes from the heartfelt Gratitude of Us, and those we have the pleasure of Representing[3]

This rather touching document – reminiscent in tone of some of the earlier popular reforming Societies'[4] – might indeed be thought to reflect an impression held more strongly in Parliament itself: that in one aspect at any rate the two successive Acts represented a not untypical order of legislation, that of the 'improving' and rationalising kind.[5] Taken in combination they were designed to clear up, at least largely, an untidy string of enactments covering part of a common problem, in order to forward arbitration and mitigate delay.[6] But of course there were other inducements for Government to take such a step. The measures gained in desirability as a potentially stronger weapon against enforced pressure on the wages' market when the latter was under exceptional strain.[7] In seeking to save 'time, trouble and expense' they could assist masters when talks broke down, providing for and speeding legal processes when the men's position might otherwise gain strength.[8] Nor was the purpose, once

1. Pitt on 30 June (*P.R., 3rd ser.*, XII, 222).

2. It may have referred to those trades contained in the petitions which led to the Act. If so it still covered extensive ground, including London, Liverpool, Manchester, Derby and Bristol. Alternatively, 'Country' could have referred to a region, rather as MPs, particularly the County Members, were still sometimes said to represent their 'Countries' (cf. I, 31).

3. Nd; thirteen signatories headed by Thos. Mollison (P.R.O. 30/8/148). The Minister's conduct was contrasted with that of the Lord Chancellor, Loughborough.

4. Cf. II, 107.

5. It may be worth noting for instance that at the time of the first Act the Commons were looking at the whole complicated and tedious subject of expiring and expired laws, at the instigation of that dedicated 'improver' of Parliamentary procedures, the future Speaker Charles Abbot; see p. 477 below.

6. I insert the qualification because a separate Act 'for settling disputes in the cotton manufactures of England' (39 & 40 Geo. III, c90, of 28 July 1800) was passed at the same time as the second general Combinations Act, and in fact almost certainly influenced the latter's provisions for arbitration.

7. See p. 298 above.

8. In the speech from which the quotation is taken (n1 above), Pitt referred in point of fact specifically to the benefits for workmen. But this was a debating point, against Sheridan, and the balance may be thought to have stood often the other way.

addressed, only administrative and economic. Despite Parliament's rather relaxed attitude – the haphazard origin of the first statute, the rather surprising absence of interest, the extent of agreement to its successor when flaws were pointed out – the measures took their place in a political context: one in which combinations of labour could not be taken so quietly on their own. Some overlap had long been conjectured – as far back as the sixties – between food riots and occupational strikes: that could be suspected more strongly, and seemed more alarming, now. And the suspicions could stretch farther: not only towards the influence of workers, already experienced in union, on their behaviour under hardship and unrest, but also into the covert area, hard to assess, of sedition itself. Labour relations in trades and industries were seen in fact as standing at one of the meeting points in a nexus of connexions which must be watched with care.

In the event the Acts seem to have made little direct difference. Not much more notice was taken of them than had been taken of earlier laws. The experiences in different trades of course continued to vary – as did the economic fortunes of the trades themselves: variety is as potent a factor here as in the local incidence of unrest itself.[1] But within such parameters a lengthy process was not halted. Masters and men acting collectively continued to test out each other in talks; if arbitration was perhaps encouraged, strikes did not die away; workmen's associations continued to function and their experience was not lost. Nor were the results always precisely as feared. The persistence of the 'combinations' did not strengthen the practice of rioting for food: rather the former tended to replace the latter, as a weapon more suited to a changing world. The 'overlap' existed,[2] but its proportions were shifting: organised industrial action came to the fore as the incidence of older forms began to decline. By 1800 indeed the associations themselves were calling on their members to refrain from riot – another reminder of some of the early calls from the popular reforming groups.[3] In so far as an effect can be assigned to the Acts it lay however in an impression; and one that proved more important than any result specifically ascertained. For if the strictly political content may not have been pre-eminent in their origins or aims,[4] its legacy was pervasive in both the short and the longer term. It was of course seized on by active 'Jacobins', and beyond their ranks may soon have encouraged more disaffected sentiment than it deterred; and it hung thereafter like a cloud over developments on whose course the arrangements themselves failed very

1. Cf. II, 92–9.
2. The phrase is John Stevenson's, in *Popular Disturbances in England 1700–1800* (1979), 112.
3. Cf. II, III, 453–4.
4. The definition could of course depend on who was framing the arrangements. Thus the Solicitor General, objecting to one clause in the second bill as originally introduced (see pp. 299–300 and n3 above), did so partly because of its 'political' nature (Sir William Grant on 22 July 1800; *The Senator*, XXVI, 1972).

largely to impinge. The measures may not have merited all the blame they have received. But one can scarcely wonder that it should have stuck.

IV

The timing underlines the reason. The Combinations Act of 1799 was introduced on 17 June and became law on 12 July. An Act 'for the more effectual Suppression of Societies established for Seditious and Treasonable Purposes; and for better preventing Treasonable and Seditious Practices' was introduced on 19 April and became law likewise on 12 July.[1] This latter measure followed and was accompanied by others, offensive or defensive according to taste: the extension (for the second time) of the expiring statute of 1797 against incitement to mutiny; the renewal, twice, of the suspension of Habeas Corpus, as usual with a time limit, and providing in the second instance for the dispersal among various gaols of detainees and prisoners charged with treasonable practices, including Irish sent to Britain for security; and an Act, sought by a private Member, to ensure that forfeiture of property for high treason remained fully in force.[2]

The particular inclusion of Irishmen in a British Act indicates the background to this crop of statutes. For the Irish dimension, visible since the naval mutinies, was now a part of the British scene. The arrest of the conspirators from the sister kingdom, with their colleagues, in 1798 had

---

1. The latter was 39 Geo. III, c79.

2. These Acts were respectively 39 Geo. III, c4, of 19 December 1798 (the complementary measure of 1797, against administering unlawful oaths (p. 29, n1 above), had had no time limit); c15, renewed on 9 January 1799 until 21 May and again by c44 on 20 May until 1 March 1800, the latter with added powers confirming action taken in March and April following two King's messages respecting Irish prisoners to be held in Britain (for which see *P.H.*, XXXIV, cols. 56–7); c93, of 12 July 1799, on a motion brought in May by Charles Abbot, alert as usual to statutory definitions, to repeal those parts of earlier statutes which confined forfeiture to Jacobites.

There was a backbench attempt, again in May, to secure an Act for the suppression of Sunday newspapers (moved in the Commons by Viscount Belgrave – a supporter and acquaintance of Pitt's with whom the Minister later fell out, and who after developing Belgravia ended his days as first Marquess of Westminster). While this formed part primarily of the campaign for the reformation of manners associated with Wilberforce and the Evangelicals, Sunday newspapers were held to be notably 'jacobinical'. The bill however failed on the second reading.

One other potential measure, which came to a point in the following spring, was projected in these months: to empower magistrates to withhold a licence to preach. A bill including such a provision was indeed drafted in the event which Pitt, influenced at least in part by Pretyman, intended to support. He seems to have been given pause by Wilberforce, who was shocked both by the likely effect on respectable Dissenting and Evangelical ministers and also by the depth of Pitt's dislike now of both. His own influence in such matters had waned, as he recognised; but the bill was laid aside for the moment, and as it proved altogether (see *Life of Wilberforce*, II, 335–6, 360–5, and also Rose to Pretyman, 28 March 1800, Pretyman Ms 435/44).

led to the discoveries in England itself.[1] Those in turn led to the setting up, in January 1799, of a Commons' Committee of Secrecy to examine the current state and past course of sedition. Its report was received in March; debate and a bill soon followed in the Commons; a similar report was submitted to the Lords by their own Committee in May; and the Act of July was the result of these events.[2]

The emphasis of the measure thus fell directly, as the title proclaimed, on the Societies. They were the natural focus of the Commons' Committee's report, and while the wave of arrests might be presumed to have dealt a blow, the existence and growth of such bodies shocked MPs and peers. The new organisations on this side of the Irish Sea – United (or True) Britons, United Scotsmen, United Englishmen[3] – modelled on and apparently closely in touch with the United Irishmen themselves, were an ominous addition to the now veteran and fading London Corresponding Society, and might even be prototypes for other groupings, nascent or unknown. The size of the membership was not clear: one MP cited a figure, apparently in circulation, of 80,000 'Jacobins' as much too high.[4] But whatever the numbers, it was the activities and the geographical spread that caused alarm. The taking of oaths – now a common practice –, the stress laid on persuasion to mutiny, the alleged proliferation of branches, seemed dangerous signs. The Act 'utterly' suppressed and prohibited the main bodies by name, and all others in which oaths were administered unlawfully and members' identities were not registered. It tightened the earlier restrictions on arrangements for lectures and on reading publications in places where payment was taken – a move to render more difficult such exercises as Thelwall's programmes. And it extended the provisions of a year before for keeping track of those engaged in publishing and printing, particularly of newspapers. Type founders, press makers and printers would now have to obtain certificates to follow their trades, and the last would have to keep a copy of their products which must show the name and address of their employer.[5]

The reports of the Secret Committees, and the Act itself, marking the peak of 'the climax' to 'Pitt's policy of repression',[6] have often been seen

1. See pp. 117, 120 above.

2. The report of the Commons' Committee may be found in *House of Commons Sessional Papers . . .*, Volume 121 (1975), no. 4919, and, *inter alia* – and misdated 1797 in the list of contents – in *P.H.*, XXXIV, cols. 579–656; that of the Lords' Committee – less important for the sequence of events – in the latter, cols. 1000–6 (again misdated). For the Commons' debates, leading to the introduction of the bill in April, see *P.R., 3rd ser.*, VIII, 456–82, 546–9, 557, 560.

3. The first largely overtaken by the last, a development which caused some confusion to Government then and later. Cf. p. 117 above.

4. Thomas Tyrwhitt Jones (not a reliable source), in the debate of 25 June 1799 (*P.R., 3rd ser.*, IX, 64).

5. Cf. II, 456 for lectures in 1795; pp. 112–13, 114–15 above for publications in 1798. But see also p. 303, n2 above.

6. See Emsley, 'Repression, "terror" and the rule of law . . .' (see p. 118, n3 above), 816.

as particularly alarmist. Certainly the language of the Commons' opening finding was high, and the momentum was sustained.

> The most effectual engine [for the intention throughout the war to overturn law and government], has been the institution of political societies, of a nature and description before unknown in any country . . . A continued intercourse and concert has been maintained from their first origin to the present moment; sometimes between the leading societies themselves, sometimes between their leading members; and a frequent communication has been kept up with the government of France.[1]

This determination to trace a consistent line of Francophil revolution from the older to the new Societies was taken after the committee of the LCS at its final meeting had considered arming against a French invasion.[2] The Parliamentary findings have further seemed suspect because the authors declined to reveal their sources. Government indeed added to the Committees' caution by persisting in its own policy of partial secrecy – Pitt was urged not to appear in evidence because of the danger of inadvertent disclosures[3] – and the quality of information of course lies at the heart of the matter. Deductions must turn on one's own judgment. But discounting the Committees' confident resolve to interpret the past wholly in terms of the present, the formal detail revealed by the seizures of material was bound to intensify their fears. There could be no doubt that a network of bodies was in being, in varying degrees of mutual contact, and declaredly revolutionary in aim. The Societies emerging in the last two years, like some elements in the LCS, were out to overturn the system, and by all available means. To that extent, the conclusions were far from absurd.[4] The question remained, how significant were these facts?

In the Commons' Committee's own words, its reports were meant to be 'the most effective engine' for alerting the country; that indeed had been the Ministry's intention in seeking to have it set up. The Act for its part was designed to identify and plug certain loopholes in the law. Surveying legislation already on the statute book, the existing range might be thought to have sufficed. But in point of fact application to the Courts had proved a fallible course. This was not as surprising as it might seem at first sight: the ample, sometimes draconian powers of statute in all criminal matters were exercised in – had to find their way through – the 'caution'

1. *P.H.*, XXXIV, col. 580. For the dramatic preceding paragraph see p. 31 above.
2. See Clive Emsley, *British Society and the French Wars 1793–1815* (1979), 69; and cf. Wells, *Insurrection*, 127. This was almost certainly not the desire of all present, but in a heated discussion it may well have been that of the majority.
3. William Wickham (see p. 119 above) to Pitt, 19 January 1799 (P.R.O. 30/8/189).
4. There has been renewed discussion on the evidence in the past two decades. I have leaned in particular on Hone, *For the Cause of Truth*, ch. 2 and Wells, *Insurrection*, ch. 2.

or 'lottery' of the process of trial.[1] Their very severity indeed had been leading to some reaction: 'Judges and juries were certainly as savage on occasions as the law decreed; but they were becoming, rather more frequently, as evasive as it allowed.'[2] Sedition, with its extreme of high treason, was an exceptionally serious matter, to be taken perhaps on a level of its own; but the normal requirements of judgment were not thereby to be dismissed. The published collection of *State Trials* is incomplete; but it is an instructive guide. Prosecutions for seditious libel had fallen off noticeably since the incidence of failures in the early and middle nineties, while those for treason and conspiracy – where definition was more precise, but proof sometimes impeded by the secrecy of the sources – also fell short of the desired results. Well known cases such as those of William Stone and Robert Crossfield in 1796, and perhaps still more prominently of Coigley's co-defendants in 1798, were reminders of the hazards for the Crown; when William Wakefield was brought to the dock in a celebrated instance in the latter year, it was with misgivings in the Home Office, and while he and two others were convicted and sentenced one other was released in the final trial. The weapons at Government's disposal weighted the odds, once in Court, rather in its favour; but not dependably so, and statutory reinforcements did not come amiss.[3]

The impact of the measure took its place in a campaign already under way. The London Corresponding Society finally disappeared as an entity with a broad popular membership, and the recent Societies, like its own survivors, went more deeply underground. Government's powers of detention had earlier removed a sizeable crop of activists,[4] and the rest were conscious of immediate pressures and threat. The disruption was not without some disadvantage to the authorities themselves; for when the best intelligence came largely from penetration of the movements, there was likely to be a point at which survivors' caution could make that harder to achieve. The quality of reports and intercepts had risen in aggregate over recent years; but much would still remain in darkness or difficult to assess. Conspiracy and its alleged detection alike tend to be self-renewing. The Ministry had had a success with the revelations produced by the

1. The descriptions are those respectively of the reforming magistrate Patrick Colquhoun and the reforming barrister Samuel Romilly; for an interesting commentary see Norman Gash, 'A Glaswegian Criminologist: Patrick Colquhoun, 1745–1820', in *Pillars of Government and Other Essays . . .* (1986), 139–52.

2. II, 127.

3. See the *Complete Collection of State Trials*, XXII–XXVII (1817–20) for the years 1792 to 1800, which may be supplemented for some leading cases by the articles by Prochaska and by Emsley cited in p. 118, n3 above, and for other less important, provincial cases by Appendix B of Clive Emsley's 'An aspect of Pitt's "Terror": prosecutions for sedition during the 1790s', in *Social History*, 6, no. 2, 179–84.

4. According to one list for the Privy Council, 47 persons were 'apprehended . . . for Treasonable Practices' in 1798: according to another at the end of that year, 89 were arrested under the suspension of Habeas Corpus (Emsley, loc. cit., 816).

Margate arrests. It continued to harass the now proscribed groups; but without so clear-cut a result.

For the years 1800–1, the former particularly from the autumn, remained full of unrest: a situation made for revolutionaries and radicals who had recently been hard hit. Activists were bound, despite the pressures, to try to fan the discontent, and take advantage of those falling on Government in its turn.[1] The authorities were convinced of 'Jacobin' incitement in the Midlands and north-west, and equally suspicious as they watched a spate of handbills in the London food riots. Their response was vigorous, with further measures of 'Cavalry and Soup Kitchens';[2] and troops held the immediate situation in check. But the reiterated calls for united protest, the news retailed in one region of troubles in others, tales of infiltration of the army and Volunteers,[3] all roused fears of an organised grand design. That alarm was exaggerated: such preparations scarcely lay within the activists' scope. It was not unreasonable however to acknowledge the men themselves as influences and agents. And if one shifted one's focus from unrest over food to political disaffection, a further nexus could be evisaged taking revolutionaries at the centre and stretching on the one hand into the problems of dearth and labour relations and on the other to assorted efforts, in Parliament and outside, for the protection of domestic liberties, and an end to the war, and Parliamentary reform.

This last banner had been raised in Parliament itself since May 1797, when Charles Grey's motion had disconcerted Ministers by the size of the supporting vote.[4] But that had been a demonstration, taking advantage of a critical time, with no hope of actual success; the subject was not one to be addressed persistently by such means; and there was no attempt to stage a further such occasion now. The issue continued rather to be sustained within a pattern of causes centred on the containment of executive power and supported, not always in combination and with marked differences over method, across a spectrum of opinion, lay and clerical, ranging from extreme radicals to respectable men not all to be described as Dissenters or Whigs.[5] Their alliances, seldom close and liable to fluctuate according to the issue, had been weakened in the moral and political demands of recent years. But now there were some signs of revival. The

1. What follows draws in particular on Wells, op. cit., chs. 9, 10.
2. Cf. p. 296 above.
3. See pp. 294–5 above.
4. Pp. 42–3 above.
5. The possible consequences in the secular sphere were noticeably bound with those in the denominational, where there had long been evident a 'correlation between support for electoral reform and for attempts', in the eyes of both Church and State, 'to subvert the Anglican establishment' (J.C.D. Clark, *Revolution and Rebellion* . . . (1986), 161n119). This last was now something which might appear to demand more effective containment; hence for instance the consideration of a bill to allow magistrates to withhold licences to preach (p. 303, n2 above).

familiar figures of Wyvill and Cartwright were stirring, each in his own way: the former to reconstitute a county movement for a limited Parliamentary reform, based in the old style on his native Yorkshire, which should now follow the removal of his former ally Pitt; the latter for a campaign of mass petitioning for universal male suffrage, which would include urban associations particularly in London and the north.[1] Both men approached Fox in hopes of strengthening and extending the Parliamentary Opposition. And while there was little evidence in that quarter of effective activity – the latest suspensions of Habeas Corpus, the Societies' bill itself, were weakly opposed[2] – a new focus of attention was coming into sight, and forging his own links with radical discontent. The young figure of Sir Francis Burdett, less hampered in his operations and indeed already suspect among the more orthodox New Whigs,[3] was embarrassing Government and bringing a fresh force into the popular politics of the metropolis. In the City itself, the majority of the Livery, at war persistently with the Court of Aldermen, succeeded with the Common Council in electing a sympathetic populist as Lord Mayor in 1799,[4] and there were busy efforts in favour of reform and preparations for the next general election. All such symptoms of a mood of discontent, distinct as they were and with their own particularities, might seem nonetheless to be threatening a convergence of approach – perhaps a programme – which could accommodate the diffused, overlapping groupings among 'the Friends of Liberty' and 'the Friends of Peace'.[5] They also marked, appropriately enough over the turn of the century, a meeting point of past traditions and the forces which would bear them into the future.

All these activities were perfectly legal. They embraced men of independent means. They were also now looked on with suspicion for links with others which lay or might lie beyond the law.[6] The authorities could point to some contacts. Thus Fox, Sheridan and Grey had talked to the Irish conspirator O'Connor before his arrest with Coigley, and Foxites spoke in defence of his character at the trial. Cartwright was known to be in touch with men in Lancashire and Yorkshire who, at least to start with, had gone underground. Burdett's correspondence with the United Irishmen had earlier brought him within range of prosecution, and his metropolitan connexions caused him to be watched. Meanwhile the extremists themselves managed to survive in their twilit spheres, and a hard core to keep in touch with the revolutionaries in Ireland – this after

---

1. Cf. I, 66–71; 70n1, 105, 109.
2. And cf. p. 115 above for 1798.
3. He was not a member of either the Whig or the Fox Club.
4. See p. 300, n3 above.
5. Broadly generic titles which were applied sometimes by those involved to themselves; and taken, very usefully, as descriptive reference points by Albert Goodwin and by J.E. Cookson in the titles of their respective books (pp. 119, n1 and 40, n4 above).
6. And it was, for example, in order to discourage men of property that forfeiture for treason was brought up to date (see p. 303 and n2 above).

all was approaching the preparatory period of the Emmet and Despard conspiracies. The Seditious Societies were proscribed, many of their leading members were in gaol, working men's associations and clubs wary and uncertain. But the Ministry still had grave misgivings: the apprehensions remained. Early in 1801 Pitt was reading fresh evidence soon to be referred to a further Commons' Committee.[1]

The 'peak' period of 'Pitt's Terror' in fact imposed a peak of anxieties on Government as well as of pressures on the seditionists themselves. It reproduced at a higher intensity the mix of factors, not all of them supportive, which had affected the course of repression from 1792. For in the conditions of Britain and of Ireland in the late eighteenth century, these provided in a sense a mirror image of the polities in which they were contained. The treatment in Ireland stood on its own, as had forcibly struck English Ministers even before the insurrection; and Scotland had its particular circumstances, not to mention its own law.[2] England's case was likewise distinctive, in the executive's strengths and constraints. The statutory powers were wide: one might indeed say that by now there was little they could not be held to cover,[3] so long as a charge could be made to stick. At the same time, as has been argued, that last was by no means always easy; and the result was that in practice the legislation was applied with some care. Some two hundred prosecutions for sedition, in all its legal forms, have been counted for the 1790s in England and Wales.[4] That was a much smaller number than had been brought when the regime had last been thought to be in danger, in the Jacobite emergencies of 1715–16 and 1745–6.[5] Nor were the sentences always as severe: Jacobite printers publishing a seditious pamphlet could find themselves facing a capital charge for treason; one man in fact had been hanged, in 1719. English Jacobin printers faced prison – and not transportation as in Scotland – and if convicted were rarely sentenced to more than two years.[6] Taking England by

---

1. Paper from Pitt's secretary, W. Dacres Adams (Dacres Adams Mss, formerly P.R.O. 30/58/8); *H.C.J.*, 56, 259 for 1 April 1801. The information again centred on Ireland, raising once more the question of the Irish connexion.

2. See p. 162 and n4 above for the first; II, 217–19, 389–90 for the second.

3. And cf. indeed II, 457.

4. See Clive Emsley, 'An aspect of Pitt's "Terror"', 155–84.
This can only be an approximation; some instances will have escaped. Two prosecutions for treason (a different charge from sedition) in 1800 are listed in *State Trials*; but one was in Ireland, and the other was of the lunatic Hadfield (see p. 294, n2 above) – whose attack however roused some popular applause.

5. Which were in fact quite largely responsible for the powers inherited by Governments in succeeding decades, and in some respects then reduced; see II, 121.

6. Emsley, 'Repression, "terror" and the rule of law', 522; and see also his list of provincial trials and judgments in 'An aspect of Pitt's "Terror"', Appendix B, 179–84. Some of the smaller cases at Quarter Sessions attracted very light sentences – fines, or only a few weeks in gaol – and some were dismissed when drunkenness was proved. But see p. 312, n1 below for the length of detention possible for prisoners awaiting delayed trial.

itself, one notices indeed a curious phenomenon: there were fewer prosecutions for treasonable and seditious practices in the higher Courts, as listed in the *State Trials*, in 1796–1800 than in 1792–5. While the laws in fact were being extended, the number of such cases decreased.[1] There are always spheres of life in which the available legislation is not thoroughly implemented; at first sight one would not have expected that to apply to this sphere at this time.

It is necessary also to note the limits to the contents of the Acts: the requirements that had to be met, and what was omitted as well as what was said. Almost all the new legislation had its time limits, and renewal had to be approved;[2] and while one may presume that in general Government could rely on its majorities –

> He saw a certain minister
> (A minister to his mind)
> Go up into a certain House
> With a majority behind –[3]

that could not always be taken for granted on detail when cases had to be made afresh. Carelessness itself could land the authorities in an awkward scrape, as Ministers found in 1800 when they neglected to check the date on which Habeas Corpus should be further suspended;[4] and other features may be noted. The ancient constitutional right of petitioning was protected;[5] and proved a valuable outlet. Owners of premises in which lectures could be given or publications read for payment had to clear themselves with the magistrates; but taverns and the like were normally exempted for the normal habits of the day, as were places of education and learning. Associations such as Friendly Societies were exempted from the prohibitions on Seditious Societies, provided they complied with the regulations governing their own affairs. Such limits to the area of 'terror' could mean careful drafting in the measures themselves – a fact which emerges not infrequently in the Parliamentary debates, and the neglect of which, again, could lead to trouble.[6] And the need for such care in turn bore witness, within a policy of acknowledged repression, to an effort, continually proclaimed and at any

---

1. One has of course to repeat the caveat on p. 309, n4 above. But it would not seem to alter the conclusion.

Pitt himself alluded to the limits of the law's operations, arising from an acknowledgment by Sheridan at the end of 1800 that there had been few charges under the recent renewals of the suspension of Habeas Corpus. That was 'a proof of the lenity used' (speech of 11 December 1800; *P.R., 3rd ser.*, XIII, 436). A debating point of course, and an easy one to make when the fact was taken strictly by itself. But cf. Emsley 'An aspect of Pitt's "Terror" ', *passim*, for a more valid demonstration of the argument.

2. See II, 456, and p. 115, n4 above.
3. Coleridge, 'The Devil's Thoughts', 1799.
4. Which meant that prisoners held for trial on any form of sedition should be released.
5. Cf. II, 456.
6. As in the instance of the first Combinations Act (pp. 299–300 above).

rate borne in mind, to preserve familiar liberties in an acceptable sense. As so often in such situations, in fact, both sides claimed that principle for their own: the authors of the laws arguing the need for curtailment in order to protect the essence, the transgressors, or victims, condemning a summary removal of precious rights. Pitt himself illustrated the maxim in specific instances: for example in his support of the second Combinations bill, and in the Societies' bill itself where he stipulated that existing members should not be open to prospective penalties – 'many weak-minded individuals' had doubtless been 'drawn into . . . snares': 'it will, I trust, be sufficient . . . to provide against future guilt'.[1] His approach in general indeed was that of so many liberal-minded statesmen confronted by a threat, as they see it, to the system they are pledged to sustain. He was 'at war with armed opinions', in England as well as in France: with those who were out to force 'opinions', which should seek to find their effects in persuasion, by fomenting subversion[2] or even by arms themselves. If he ever really made the kind of remarks about Tom Paine which his niece Hester Stanhope attributed to him, they were a revealing expression of his stance.

> Mr. Pitt used to say that Tom Paine was quite in the right, but then he would add, "What was I to do? . . . It would be very well, to be sure, if every body had sense enough to act as they ought; but as things are, . . . we should have a bloody revolution" . . .[3]

And he was not in office to let that succeed.

The line was not easy to draw precisely. In so far as it was drawn, it was in the light of practical experience of attitudes as well as the teachings of 'abstract inquiries' in 'the closet'.[4] The two influences of course were not distinct: together they interpreted – in the end formed – the Constitution, and Government's use of laws which it claimed conformed to while protecting that 'beautiful Combination' was conditioned largely by the degree of acceptance it might expect.[5] It was a less edifying reflection of

---

1. Speech of 19 April 1799 (*P.R., 3rd ser.*, VIII, 458).
2. . . . ' "the peculiar character of Jacobinism . . ., its peculiar object is, to avail itself of every cause of discontent to operate upon the sufferings, the prejudices, the passions, or the errors of every man in the country" ' (speech of 11 December 1800; op. cit., XIII, 437–8). The report here uses the double quotation marks referred to in p. 279, n3 above.
3. See II, 80n4. Any such conversations – and Hester Stanhope is a notably unreliable witness – would have taken place between the autumn of 1803 and the end of 1805. Cf. pp. 227–9 above for the same distinction as applied in 1798 to France.
4. To use Pitt's phrase in the latter instance.
5. Thus it could have been rash for instance to try to overturn Fox's Libel Act of 1792, which Pitt had supported (II, 81), and which proved so helpful to defendants on occasions. And see Emsley, 'An aspect of Pitt's "Terror" ', Appendix A, 176–8, for a list of instances in which the Home Office or the Law Officers recommended provincial magistrates not to prosecute: of 54 cases cited there for possible trial, the Department wished 37 to be dropped and advised on checking on another 7 before proceeding.
For the phrase describing the Constitution see I, 45.

this fact that the authorities resorted to practices which bypassed or might hope to counter the procedures: filing evidence *ex officio* on information received, which avoided an initial hearing by a jury and enabled defendants to be held in gaol pending a trial that could be long delayed;[1] packing juries themselves when that seemed feasible, though even then without always gaining the verdict. But this last device, used intermittently and perhaps declining,[2] leads one beyond the Courts and the statutes themselves. For repression was not of course a matter only of prosecutions. It was in the air in the country as a whole.

To what extent this was so, in the peak period as others, one cannot really say; or exactly how far support for Government positively aided Ministers' efforts. Attitudes which may have been basically persistent were always liable to surface fluctuations, as indeed were the fortunes of subversion itself.[3] The mood, or moods, of much of the nation, reaching probably well down into the social scale,[4] contained in all their variety feelings both of resolution and alarm, of distaste for extremes and, at least by 1800, a growing desire for an acceptable peace. From such an amalgam there were many who endorsed the Parliamentary measures, whether strongly or reluctantly; and also many who, as always, did

> not care to know . . .
> Nor ask what doubtful act allows
> Our freedom in this English house

The public support of course owed its share to the Ministry's own efforts – in sponsoring and encouraging pamphlets and caricatures, subsidising and influencing newspapers[5] –, while a host of others rallied of their own volition. Pitt in person, now seen in sterner guise, was widely if sometimes grudgingly viewed as a necessary guardian of order and of society itself. And in such a setting the social and economic weapons were brandished

1. This odious practice of filing *ex officio* information – not, it must be said, employed often in the nineties – had been known earlier, in the Jacobite period and even in an instance in 1770, when it was said to be almost as bad as the proceedings of Star Chamber (Emsley, 'Repression, "terror" and the rule of law', 819). It had the further advantage of laying the costs on the defendants.

Confinement until trial could last many months; in the case of the later notorious Colonel Despard for over two years.

2. Cf. II, 390.

3. Thus Pitt could assert at the end of 1800 that there was less sedition than had been seen 'for many years' – though he stressed 'seen' (11 December; *P.R., 3rd ser.*, XII, 437) –, two months after he feared growing dangers from the wave of outbursts over bread, in which extremists were strongly suspected of being at work.

4. See II, Ch. V, section IV.

5. Cf. pp. 109–12 above for achievements, and limits; and Pitt's remark at the end of 1800 on the difficulties of 'Keeping printers in order' (I, 607).

On the other hand, one should note the disappearance of metropolitan debating societies by the end of the decade; see Mary Thale, 'London Debating Societies in the 1790s' (*H.J.*, 32, no. 1).

as they had been, often unpleasantly, in recent years: by landowners and masters, in local government, in the universities and the professions. The Dissenter, the freethinker, any one expressing what might now be taken as radical views, could come under suspicion, or the pretext could serve private ends. It was indeed the uncertainties thus engendered that could make the pressures often so effective: that could close down or emasculate some newspapers, and induce many men and women to keep their thoughts to themselves. One could not be sure: it might well need courage to carry on even if that was possible. And if the authorities might deem a prosecution unwise, the threat of one was not.

Again caution is necessary in trying to detect the tone and the effects of the 'terror' in general. Sturdy limitations still survived amidst a wide abhorrence of revolution. If *The Manchester Herald* and *The Sheffield Register* disappeared, for instance, and *The Sheffield Iris* was tamed, some other obnoxious provincial journals were not – *The Cambridge Intelligencer* springs to mind – and the London newspapers, sometimes treading delicately, were nonetheless on the eve of an advance. There were fewer Church and King riots now than there had been earlier in the war; nor does there seem to have been an attempt to revive or support Loyal Associations on the pattern of 1792, before war had been declared.[1] Familiar restraints, across the country, were not wholly swept aside: there were countering forces, shown most clearly where hardship was concerned but not confined to that, whose patriotism need not be questioned but which might not give the Ministry automatic support. Social ties, forming a frame for the 'vertical' structures in many rural areas, could still throw a protective cloak over protests in which radical influence might be alleged. So too could political sentiment in places where Pitt was not acclaimed – within East Anglia for instance; a lack of enthusiasm, running sometimes among the upper and the middling orders, which could have its effect when added to the inherent limits of administration. For the state of the civil resources remained perhaps the greatest constraint of all, when troops would not always be called on and the parish officer was the guardian of the peace. London was rather better served than before, with an improved magistracy and the Bow Street runners;[2] but even so, only by comparison with the provinces. It was one thing to pass legislation, quite another to see it implemented: particularly to impose anything approaching a national treatment for what was taken now to be a national threat. In the last resort, the military presence must operate within a sufficient consensus that violent subversion must not be allowed to succeed. To that extent Pitt could claim that 'If the mass of the people were disloyal, the measures of

1. One must remember, however, that riots of any kind, ostensibly favourable or not, had long been suspect; see II, 103–4, 134n3. In the case of the Loyal Associations, for which see op. cit., 229–33, perhaps the unfortunate experience of the founder John Reeves in 1795–6 (op. cit., 258) was something of a deterrent.

2. The latter apparently being also available, in sparse numbers, for action outside the capital; see II, 123.

Parliament . . . would be ineffectual', which events, despite disappointments, were showing was not the case.[1]

Such a combination of factors was familiar, from 1795 and indeed from
the beginning of the troubles in 1792.[2] The dimension of the problem had
grown from that earlier time beyond anything that Ministers could have
foreseen, and there had been developments some of which would henceforth grow in significance. Pitt was becoming worried from the end of
1799, and as he and Liverpool showed, in the autumn of 1800 the
Government was really alarmed.[3] The reports flowing in from all over the
country, particularly at the latter point with the forbidding conjuncture of
riots and the rising tide of petitions for peace, raised fears which perhaps
were not sharper but may have been deeper than those of 1795–6. That
experience indeed was bound to have left its mark on a more prolonged
crisis. The question is whether the signs of revived discontent around the
turn of the century suggest a degree of change so great that it was really
one of kind; or whether they amounted rather to an extreme instance of a
familiar phenomenon, a frightening but passing example of the unrest
endemic in a shortage of bread. Was this in fact another, though major,
specimen of a traditional threat? Or might the cords of the state really be
loosened to a point at which they could not be renewed?

Some developments could be cited in either direction when assessing
the immediate outlook. Government, as has been argued, could reflect
that its varied weaponry had improved. The greater dangers moreover
brought their counter effects. Insurrection in Ireland had heightened the
senses, and the public was also alert to the thought of a French invasion
which might spark off risings in Britain itself. The established order, at
different levels, felt more closely besieged, while the popular movements
for reform were split increasingly by the more revolutionary elements.
These were sources of comfort for authority. At the same time they contained seeds of doubt. If there were widespread fears of revolution, there
was also some disgruntlement among men of property: a very real dislike,
even fear, of a form of taxation which invaded individual rights, and
impatience, born largely of the cost, with the lack of success in the war.
And at the other end of the scale, while there were more soldiers – many
of them part-time – in evidence, what might happen if they showed signs
of sympathy with popular radical unrest? Ministers were alive to both
types of threat. No one could forget the origins, aristocratic and bour-
geois, of the Revolution that turned into a real Terror, and the memory
lent its force to the watch on the reviving signs of 'reform from above'.

1. Speech of 11 December 1800 (*P.R., 3rd ser.*, XIII, 438).
2. This paragraph and the next pay a final return to the scene of II, Chs. IV and V and
the summary there on 170–1.
3. Pp. 278–9, 280–1, 282–5, 293 and 277 above.

The watch on the armed forces for its part drew on more direct experience: of some of the militia in '95, of the Guards and, far worse, the naval mutinies in '97.[1] Now, following the fears of invasion in 1798, a greater degree of reliance had perforce to be placed on the urban elements in the auxiliary forces, in a period of great social strains.[2] And beyond these possible weaknesses within the elements of support themselves, there lay the challenge posed by the growth, now more instantly perceived, of the capacity for organisation within the lower orders, shown most specifically in the day to day handling of their wage negotiations. There were competent men well down the social ladder, with links arising from common activities which could be extended and exploited in times of stress. That was not the whole story of course: such activities were not necessarily subversive – they can indeed be viewed as an element making for stability – and the impression itself did not inform the Combinations Acts as strongly as has often been assumed.[3] But the anxiety was not surprising when those 'hitherto . . . beyond the political pale'[4] were showing themselves increasingly adept at protecting and advancing their concerns.

The dilemma also gives rise to the reflection that more than one timescale might be borne in mind in trying to assess the balance of danger as it was currently viewed. One may well trace to the years around the turn of the century an impetus in the process of working men's growing consciousness of association – after all, one is entering the anteroom of trade unionism in its historical form. But by the same early token, while such a development would become of great importance, its nascent impact at this point was not necessarily so: we may allow a need here for distinction between the medium and the immediate term. The discussion will always continue. But my own conclusion abides that if the scale of the threat to an order was altered, the fundamental nature of its elements remained much the same as in the past decade. Under greater pressures the opposing sides were divided rather more sharply than before, though bridges had by no means fallen in. Radical leadership had shifted towards extremes, and become more conspiratorial; but its difficulties in any case were still largely those which had beset the moderates in recent years. It still looked out on a nation in which popular unrest was related to specific causes, often localised and liable to decline as fast as they might arise. The lower orders, viewed perhaps increasingly as an entity in a period of strain, were by no means unified; in fact they were still subject to strong internal as well as external constraints. Many people, perhaps most, remained unaccustomed to the idea of seeking their remedy for grievances in a wholesale attack on the system they knew. They still moved instinctively within the familiar norms, particularly when the alternative

---

1. II, 451; Ch. I, section III above. For the earlier complacency over the French example cf. II, 146–7.
2. Cf. pp. 123, 295n1 above.
3. See for this argument Christie, *Stress and Stability*, ch. V; pp. 299–300 above.
4. See II, 107.

was associated with France. Meanwhile their superiors were still not in the yielding mood – many among them decidedly not, while virtually all, in their diversity, were determined in the last resort to uphold the Constitution as that was broadly understood. And unless that final resolve was eroded from within, or – perhaps aided by such a process – the armed forces themselves deserted the Crown, revolution from below stood no real chance. These were overriding facts. As discontent and disturbance continued, it was the business of Government to attend to them, and show its own resolve.

That was not lacking, in varied directions. The *bienpensants* were discouraged or harried, often without good reason. Considerable efforts were made to mitigate hardship from dearth. Soldiers and sailors held, and were held, broadly true to their allegiance: the French were fought at sea; troops could be deployed, even in the West Indies for which desertion was highest, to execute strategy or, despite some worries, deter riot at home. Revolutionary conspiracies, with their Irish links, were pursued and contained. The measures and expedients, taken by men now hardened to sterner times, had still to acknowledge – could not ignore – the character of the system whose limits they were straining; and the practices themselves did not form a tightly connected whole. 'There was much governance with consent, much governance without consent, and some localised safety valves without governance at all'.[1] Naturally enough, it was largely a case of responding to events piecemeal. But the responses somehow sufficed; the established order survived. The achievement was not a small one. Drawing on the strengths of the society which sustained it, 'the English ruling class, often in spite of itself, and even more regularly owing to itself, proved to be the world's premier successful example of its genre'.[2]

---

1. Wells, *Wretched Faces*, 325: an admirably balanced and proportioned verdict.
2. Ibid. My own demurrer to so definite a concept of 'class' in this period may be found in II, 142–4.

CHAPTER XI

Strategy in Limbo

I

The domestic pressures of these grim years, mounting from the autumn of 1799, had their mounting effects on attitudes to the war. Among the lower orders, cries for peace were heard once more with those for relief. Among their betters, deeply suspicious of the new tax which they felt they must accept, resentment was growing with a new force at the ever rising cost of the struggle. The need to carry on the fight was still broadly allowed by those who paid. But the old dislike of European entanglements became stronger with the disappointments, while naval predominance fed the attraction of the old 'blue-water' alternative – or aim.[1] If we could not have a satisfactory peace, let us direct our own kind of war. When the Russians were broken in Switzerland, and the Austrians failed to exploit recent gains, and a British expedition to Holland had to be brought out almost at once, the Ministry, so buoyed up with expectations a few months before, was barely given the benefit of the strategic doubt.[2]

Nor was the Ministry itself free of this last sentiment. It was indeed entering on an increasingly uneasy span. Over the next year the old inner circle would be under growing mutual strain. But when the Dutch enterprise collapsed the scene was still too confused, and the prospects were still too open, for firm conclusions to be drawn. In the first place, the domestic discontents did not register fully at once; the impact was less marked towards the end of 1799 than towards the end of 1800. And peering into the immediate future, Government was not prepared to jettison a Continental concept, pursued for almost two years, which should not lightly be let drop. Such a response was not very surprising: it is not a simple matter to abandon a strategy many of whose pieces are still in play. For after all the Austrians remained in the field, with large forces which had had some success. Russia could restock in the west if the right targets and inducements could be offered. British resources, material, financial and, within their constraints, in manpower, were gathered and in some respects remodelled for the task in hand. And what of the enemy? The

---

1. For which see II, 347–8.
2. See Ch. VIII, *passim* and section V in particular.

French were still held to be in sore straits. If Allied disunity had once again let them off the hook in recent months, and the planned internal risings had erupted in the south too soon, the Directory was discredited, the *chouans* of the Vendée were in arms, and the country as a whole was in a state of discontent.[1] Might not royalist resistance, admittedly ill organised, yet be aided and if necessary revived to accompany offensives in the spring, diverse but complementary, in which British troops could take an integral if limited part? Victory, at least its prologue, had recently appeared within grasp. The game, it could be held in London on the eve of winter, was not played out.

The possible dangers in this line of thought were obvious enough. They had all been exposed before and might well be exposed again. But no other course, it could equally be held, would subscribe so directly to a timely outcome – for time seemed likely to be of the essence – which only combined Allied action could bring. The decision was defensible. The drawbacks however were soon evident, generating a confusion quite as intense as that experienced recently in the desperate efforts to salvage earlier hopes.

The first steps towards a plan were discussed at a run of Cabinet meetings in the latter half of October 1799; on the 18th, 23rd and 26th. The first was provided with a paper from the Foreign Secretary, written in late September when operations in Holland seemed still to be in the balance. Assuming nonetheless that the war would now continue into the following year,[2] it proposed that the Tsar should be offered a subsidy towards the costs of 90 or 100,000 men in 1800, the bulk of whom, under Suvorov, should establish a 'seat of operations' in France. We should further subsidise some 25,000 or perhaps 45,000 Germans (particularly Bavarians) and Swiss, as well as royalists in both the north and south of France.[3] This intention was outlined, as it happened, at the moment of disaster which engulfed Suvorov himself in Switzerland.[4] But in the event that did not discourage the line of thought, for the Russians' fate was held, and rightly, to be due to the Austrians' behaviour in removing their own troops. In any case a move would be welcome which would give the former a greater independence of the latter, and 'Such an Army as this' should provide such a result.[5] Developed further in a second Note, read at the Cabinet of 23 October, the idea was placed in an extended perspective: 'without making us principals in the Land War, [it] would nevertheless very materially assist the Austrians, and preserve our own pecuniary resources more

1. See pp. 223–6 above.
2. Cf. pp. 253, 258 above.
3. 'Note' by Grenville, 29 September 1799, in his record of Cabinet proceedings (B.L. Add. Ms 59306). The phrase quoted was said to reflect Suvorov's own 'expectation'. The number of Germans and Swiss was given differently in two different parts of the Note.
4. P. 252 above. And which, unknown when the paper was written, had been learned just before the meeting (p. 255, n4 above).
5. Grenville's Note, loc. cit., n3 above.

entire to support a longer contest, if it should become necessary.'[1] Such merits were advanced, obviously, to meet unresolved doubts.

For the possible shape of the operations themselves was forming by then in Grenville's mind. There might be two armies, one to invade northern France by sea, the other to regain Switzerland and act against eastern France. These tasks would together require 160–180,000 men, of whom he thought 40,000 might be British; and the transport for invasion, to be 'concerted', would presumably fall mainly on the British as well.[2] Commitments of that kind, whatever the disclaimer, looked suspiciously like those of a 'principal in the Land War'; and so in fact the trend of the Foreign Secretary's approach appeared to the Secretary of State for War. Dundas began to query his colleague's view before the troops from Holland reached home. The two Ministers had some ground in common. Both remained in favour of an assault on Brest; but in Dundas's case purely to destroy or damage the enemy's fleets, and not to join the French rising inland.[3] Both were highly sceptical of the current quality of the Russian army – a doubt soon increased when the Russians from Holland were quartered temporarily in England and the Channel Isands; but Dundas was less willing to count on a timely improvement.[4] He was in a quandary; feeling a strain which had been growing over at least the past eighteen months, unhappy in his post,[5] and at the prospect of renewed reliance on a frustrating Coalition. But his disquiet seems to have been

1. 'Note Respecting Russian Subsidies *etc.* Read at the Cabinet Oct. 23d 1799' (B.L. Add. Ms 59306).

There is an undated paper in Pitt's hand in Dacres Adams Mss, formerly P.R.O. 30/58/8, which may relate further to the calculations at this point. Referring as it does to estimates of Russian numbers and the accompanying expense to Britain from 1 January 1800, it would seem to have been composed in the later part of 1799. But I find it hard to say exactly when, and the paper may well have been simply an aide-mémoire for the Minister's own consideration and use.

2. 'Note' read 23 October (B.L. Add. Ms 59306).

3. Cf. pp. 225-6 above.

4. To ? Pitt, 24 October 1799 (*H.M.C., Dropmore*, V, 498–9), though he did not rule it out for the coming year (to Grenville, 20 October 1799; op. cit., 493). The impression made by the returning Russians on those who saw them was indeed marked. 'Squalid and disgusting', 'really not human', with officers who seemed 'to care much less for them than we do for our sheep'. These remarks, echoing others from an amazed public in the seaport towns, came from authorities who could make authoritative comparisons with British troops; from Sir Charles Grey, the General commanding in the south-east (see pp. 121, 163 above), and from Huskisson at the War Office reporting his experience to Dundas (Mackesy, *War Without Victory*, 53-5). They fell on Ministers already worried by similar reports from Switzerland and Germany (see *H.M.C., Dropmore*, V, 498), let alone from Holland itself.

5. See e.g. pp. 121, n2, 124, 143, 147 above for a state of mind observable by May 1798, which may perhaps have been affected by some decline in health from early in 1797. The strain was heightened now by a clash with the King over a matter of military administration, involving an appointment for Granville Leveson Gower (see p. 59, n3 above) in a battalion of Volunteers, which caused much ill feeling on both sides, not composed by an unsuccessful attempt at a settlement by Pitt (see Cyril Matheson, *The Life of Henry Dundas, First Viscount Melville* . . . (1933), 275-6; *L.C.G. III*, III, nos. 2067-8, 2070, 2074, 2079).

expressed more openly between than in the meetings of 'our large Cabinet';[1] and no other focus of opposition emerged. Windham was disgruntled with the conduct of strategy; but he could not decide on the latest proposition, and ended by giving 'a hesitating assent'.[2] And Pitt, canvassed on all sides, was prepared to favour a renewed involvement, perhaps even over two campaigns, although 'our best comfort is that if it fails us, we can return to our defensive system with unbroken spirits and resources, and trust to our own anchors to ride out the storm.'[3]

The agreement thus gained, in places grudgingly or without high enthusiasm, was aimed, once again, at an extended concept. For if the Russians were to lie, in British eyes, at the centre of the strategy for 1800, that implied a pattern, in which military and diplomatic interests must so far as possible be reconciled. Its prospective shape was mapped out at the meeting on 26 October. The Tsar should be offered a subsidy in return for a force of 80 or 90,000 men (over and above the Bavarians, for whom we would pay). He should be asked to negotiate with Vienna for military 'cooperation', which might be 'facilitated' by British concurrence in arrangements for Italy and the Austrian Netherlands – specifically for a transfer of the Sardinian territory of Piedmont, Sardinia being compensated elsewhere in the peninsula, while the future of the Netherlands would be settled as was best subservient to this plan.[4] These proposals were elaborated, in operational, diplomatic and financial detail, in a series of despatches to St Petersburg on 1 November.[5]

This was returning, and with a vengeance, to the recent idea of entrusting the main assault on eastern France to the Russians instead of the Austrians. Whitworth was told in fact that the plan in its entirety could enable the Tsar and ourselves to act together on our own, though it would gain force if Austria would play her part.[6] Reliance on Russia to such an extent was indeed a major risk, over and above that presented by doubts of

1. As Grenville called it, to Dundas himself (*H.M.C., Dropmore*, V, 487). He was quite right as to the size. The numbers had risen from seven at the end of 1783 and eight in 1784 to thirteen and then twelve in 1794, reduced to eleven in 1795 and ten in 1796, and standing at eleven from 1798 (see *English Historical Documents*, XI, table of Lists of Cabinets at end).

2. *Diary of Windham*, 416, for 26 October 1799. And see his letter to Minto of the 29th (*The Windham Papers*, II, 132–5).

3. To Mornington, 6 November; quoted in Mackesy, op. cit., 25. This, it might be noted, was written despite the disappointing indications of revenue from the Income Tax, and before the Minister's unsuccessful attempt to improve the scheme (pp. 265–7 above).

4. 'Minute of Cabinet', 26 October 1799 (*L.C.G. III*, III, no. 2072. Grenville's copy is in B.L. Add. Ms 59306). For Austria's ambitions in Piedmont see pp. 213, 238–9, 241 above.

5. Grenville to Whitworth, nos. 87–9, all Most Secret, 1 November 1799 (P.R.O., F.O. 65/45). It was suggested there that Sardinia might be rewarded with Tuscany, while the Habsburg Grand Duke of Tuscany (for the past half century the Emperor's eldest son) might be given the Austrian Netherlands, for whose most recent series of 'dispositions' see pp. 249, 253–4 above.

6. Grenville to Whitworth, no. 87 as in previous note. Cf. pp. 237–8 above. The same emphasis was revealed to Mulgrave, whose mission to the Austrians, constantly subjected to shifting plans (cf. pp. 240–1 above), was now wrapped in gloom. He was therefore

the quality of her troops. She might still be portrayed as a natural ally whose main interests need not conflict with ours; but that very remoteness – infiltrated now in any case by Mediterranean ambitions[1] – and the presence of an unpredictable ruler, posed their own daunting problems. Despite periods of sudden wooing from London moreover, her contribution in the past seven years had emerged in practice as of secondary rather than independent value. Useful as she could be to help influence the Baltic states and support our definition of neutral trade,[2] her commitment by land was apt to be sought when other allies were recalcitrant or failing: as an encouragement or discipline for Berlin and Vienna, and a card to be led when our hand was otherwise weak. This applied above all in the case of Vienna, for Austria remained ideally the pivot on which the British conception of a Continental strategy turned. In essence then, Russia was of auxiliary or alternative importance; scarcely a Power on which primarily to depend.

This was an inconvenient fact, endemic in both the First and the Second Coalitions. Its prospective testing on this occasion, however, was brought to a stop by a simpler deterrent. For no sooner had the despatches gone than the dawning suspicions of Russian effectiveness were dramatically heightened by evidence on the ground. On 2 November a crop of reports, coming as so often in a single batch, was received from Germany on the state of Suvorov's forces and Suvorov himself. They made depressing reading. The army, or what was left of it after Zürich and the retreat through the mountains, was little better than a rabble, needing time and massive reform to be fit for a further campaign. The men were badly fed and badly paid, they rioted and looted on the march, the junior officers neglected them and the senior were unfit to command. Suvorov's own entourage was dreadful – 'treacherous', 'ignorant', 'brutal', 'shag all over' – and he himself was impossible to make out. Vigorous and lucid at one moment, apparently senile at another, was he really as weird as he seemed, or a 'cunning mountebank'? These impressions, sent urgently and strongly, were taken very seriously; for not only did they confirm those now arising at home but they emanated from Wickham, long the trusted confidant of Grenville and a man whose views always carried weight.[3]

---

instructed to head for Suvorov's headquarters to lay these ideas before him and offer his own services on the staff (Grenville to Mulgrave, no. 8, 1 November 1799, P.R.O., F.O. 74/27; and see same to same, Private, 29 October 1799, *H.M.C., Dropmore*, V, 504–5).

1. Pp. 150, 154, 207 above.

2. See II, 275–7, 504–7.

3. 'Your letters have been throughout the whole my chief guide and direction, and they have, in this last instance, prevented my falling into a very great error' (Grenville to Wickham, 30 November 1799; *H.M.C., Dropmore*, VI, 52). The relevant 'letters' were Wickham to Grenville, nos. 35–40, 11–18 October, received 2 November 1799 (P.R.O., F.O. 74/25, printed, without the endorsement of receipt and no. 39 unnumbered, in *Correspondence of Wickham*, II, between 256 and 292), 19 October 1799, and [October] (*H.M.C., Dropmore*, V, 484–6, 508). He had sent a preliminary, less decisive warning on 7 October (to Grenville, private, no endorsement of date of receipt; F.O. 74/25).

Furthermore, set in this framework was one piece of hard news. The Marshal dismissed any notion of acting in the near future with Bavarian troops: he wanted Austrians, or no one at all.[1] The Foreign Secretary took all this to a Cabinet on 7 November, which accepted – with Dundas's subsequent agreement after absence for most of the meeting – that the earlier intention could not stand as it was. This of course meant that Austria must be brought more clearly into view. Her troops were necessary for the next campaign; her opinions must therefore be canvassed on the shape of 'the combined efforts of the Allies'. If the result proved acceptable to London it should be conveyed to Suvorov by a British hand, before, one might hope, being recommended jointly to St Petersburg. At the same time the Austrians must be made entirely aware that any agreement must rest on their provision of a 'large' force with adequate supplies. If those conditions were refused, we would urge the Tsar to end all military cooperation with Vienna, while we for our part would cut off all financial aid.[2]

So the brief attempt to escape from the old Austrian constraint seemed to be jeopardised. Instructions to Minto in Vienna were sent in the next few days.[3] By then however they were able to include the diplomatic proposals entrusted to the Russians, thanks to reports from himself which were received at this very point.[4] For once more at a low point in Anglo-Austrian relations a glimmer of light unexpectedly emerged. Thugut, on whom Grenville had been pouring the vials of his wrath, suddenly appeared more forthcoming – perhaps because Vienna now saw itself successfully disengaged for what remained of the year's campaign from an operational prospect it had cordially disliked.[5] Towards the end of October he had outlined his thoughts.[6] Austria was willing to see the Netherlands joined to Holland – as the British (in theory secretly) had been considering – if the old issue of the Austrian loan was eased, as he saw it, by the debt being charged on them.[7] The Emperor intended to resume control of the Milanese in Italy and to acquire part, though not all, of Piedmont, Sardinia being compensated from the territories of the Francophil former republic of Genoa. He insisted on remaining in The

1. Same to same, no. 37 with enclosure, 17 October 1799. This was confirmed by his no. 41 of the 31st, which however was received only on 19 November (loc. cit.). See p. 249, n1 above for the Bavarians.

2. Cabinet Minute, 7 November 1799 (*L.C.G. III*, III, no. 2080, Grenville's copy being in B.L. Add. Ms 59306); Dundas to Grenville, 8 November 1799 (*H.M.C., Dropmore*, VI, 12).

3. Draft of Grenville to Minto, no. 13, 8 November 1799 (P.R.O., F.O. 7/57), sent after clearance with the King on the 10th (*L.C.G. III*, III, no. 2080). For Minto see p. 239 above.

4. 'Last night', according to Grenville on the 8th (to Minto as in previous note); probably after the Cabinet meeting.

5. Cf. p. 210 above.

6. Minto to Grenville, nos. 37, 38, of 20, 22 October 1799 (F.O. 7/57). They arrived in a batch comprising nos. 35–38.

7. This had indeed been one of Austria's provisions in the discussions for the Loan Convention in 1798 (for which see pp. 132–4 above).

Three Legations historically incorporated in the Papal States – their northern territories of Romagna, Bologna and Ferrara –, consolidating his own position in partial return for leaving the Low Countries. But while these statements were made with 'less moderation' than the rest, and the temperature rose when the Loan Convention was discussed,[1] the tone in general was conciliatory; and the reply from London in the new despatch, not unnaturally in the circumstances, was careful to meet it at least part of the way. We preferred to remain non-committal on the future of the Low Countries; but we would support Austria's aim in Piedmont (as Pitt had recently urged on a reluctant Grenville) and the consequential arrangements. Diplomatic interests however could not be divorced from military prospects. It was essential that Austria should provide a staff for Suvorov and his army, and we wished to see 25–30,000 of her troops 'permanently attached' to a Russian force of 80–90,000 men. The response showed a new tact in leaving the initiative on operational plans to Vienna. Meanwhile a copy was sent to St Petersburg, with an estimate that 50–60,000 Russians would be needed to augment Suvorov, some of whom, it was suggested, might be found from those recently in Holland.[2]

These days saw a detectable bustle and stir about the Foreign Office. No fewer than eight couriers, *The Times* announced on 12 November, had left for St Petersburg, Vienna and Berlin during the past week, and the object was shrouded in 'profound secrecy'. If the messengers' frequency declined somewhat thereafter, the momentum did not,[3] for as fresh news came in from Russia plans had once more to be changed.

When the British approached the Tsar on 1 November they did so in the belief, derived from Whitworth, that he was determined to act offensively and disposed to closer contact with London; the more so from his shock at the way in which the Austrians, in his view, had let him down. At the same time, his professed acknowledgment of the continuing need for the Coalition was thought firm enough to deter him from seeking to weaken them in turn.[4] But as October went by, his mood in point of fact had changed. The early discouragement in Holland left its mark; his zeal gave way to depression, and be became less attracted to a future with Britain, while his anger with Austria, held in check earlier, now threatened extremes. On the 27th the blow fell. He decided to recall Suvorov and the army, and withdraw all further co-operation with Vienna. The news

1. Thugut intimated that the Emperor would acknowledge the debt in a private letter to George III, and would ratify the Convention publicly on the day after he made peace. Minto did not think that good enough.

2. Grenville to Minto, no. 12, 8 November (loc. cit.); same to Whitworth, no. 93, 10 November 1799 (F.O. 65/45). For Piedmont see p. 320 above.

3. It is noticeable indeed that the Foreign Secretary swapped despatches with Whitworth over these months in virtually equal numbers; a highly unusual state of affairs when reports from missions, even in wartime, were usually well in excess of instructions from London. And cf. for peacetime I, 514.

4. Whitworth to Grenville, nos. 91, 92, 27 September, 6 October; both received 27 October 1799 (F.O. 65/44).

reached London on 19 November.[1] It overtook Grenville's latest thoughts, set down at length on that very day in the light of the recent shift of emphasis. As far as operations went, these were familiar in part. We and the Russians might again attack Holland, since the French were now embroiled in their own internal rising; or we might together aid that insurrection, keeping it alive into the spring.[2] Such proposals however were now not enough in themselves. Austria, it seemed, was essential to a decisive result in western Europe, and if Paul were really to act as he said before Thugut could respond to our overture there must be a high risk that she would make a unilateral peace. We had indeed just warned St Petersburg that a French peace offensive was possible, taking advantage, as in the past, of the divisions between the Allies.[3] It was therefore of the utmost importance that a calmer temper prevail, which even now might allow a Russian force, doubtless reduced – perhaps to 30,000 – to remain in Germany or return to Switzerland with the Archduke Charles.[4] Nevertheless that could not suffice in itself from so massive a source. There would be strength to spare, even if flawed in quality,[5] over and above the Russians in Britain. We would expect to benefit from that; and we could in fact specify a use, as Ministers began to review more closely the options available to ourselves.

For the evacuation from Holland raised the question of how to employ the British army, assuming that a further Allied campaign would be mounted in the coming year. There were three main possible areas for offensive operations: the Low Countries again, northern France, and the western and central Mediterranean. On paper, there might be strength enough for two of these prospects together. Numbers were as yet imprecise: Grenville was thinking of 60,000 not counting the contingent already in Portugal, while Dundas envisaged some 80,000 available in all.[6] As the plans developed, he settled on approximately that total – 62,500 British infantry with 15,000 cavalry 'if necessary' and 2,000 artillery, to which might be added 10 or 15,000 sailors and marines if there was a 'Great Expedition'. These figures would require a further large indentation on the auxiliary forces. Together by now with some 8,000 émigrés, French and Dutch, in Britain

1. Same to same, nos. 96, 97, both of 22 October, no. 100, 27 October; all received 19 November 1799 (loc. cit.).
2. Grenville to Whitworth, no. 98, 19 November 1799 (F.O. 65/45). These operational proposals are extracted from a *tour d'horizon* of 64 pages.
3. Same to same, no. 95, Most Secret, sd (loc. cit.).
4. Same to same, no. 101, 23 November 1799 (loc. cit.).
5. As Pitt noted to Grenville at this point (21 November; *H.M.C., Dropmore*, VI, 35).
6. Mackesy, op. cit., 26. In the second half of October, however, Dundas had talked of 50,000 infantry and 15,000 cavalry by the following May (to Grenville, 20 October 1799; *H.M.C., Dropmore*, V, 493). In the first half of November Grenville also mentioned 100,000; but that probably included the Russians in Britain as well as British troops. See pp. 151–2 above for the force in Portugal.

and including the French committed to Portugal, they amounted to a disposable total of some 87,500 men.[1]

If such calculations were realistic, there would therefore be scope for a British initiative as part of a Continental strategy in 1800. Despite Pitt's allusion to the possible need for two more such campaigns, eyes were really fixed on one if we were not to move thereafter to an independent form of warfare; and with that in mind thoughts were concentrating as a first priority on what was initially seen as 'an immense effort' in northwest France.[2] Its precise role, and thus shape, might be affected by the efforts of our allies elsewhere, expected or perforce assumed to take place though as yet entirely unforeseeable. But the pattern was also hard to envisage exactly on its own account, in the context of the uncertain current conditions in Brittany and the administrative problems which in part they posed. The *chouans'* rising focused continuing attention on the idea of an assault on Brest, thrust to the fore in the excitement of the late summer.[3] There was now little prospect of mounting an immediate raid, as Dundas had hoped: 'one splendid attempt, at one stroke, to annihilate the naval power of France and Spain', and confined to that.[4] But as autumn gave way to winter interest moved more closely to the spring, when the operation might become the 'immense effort' which, in association with the resistance, would lead to the engagement of powerful French forces as the main British stroke. Pitt himself entered fully into the plans, consulting the prospective commander General Grey, listening to royalist proposals, some borne by d'Artois, trying out ideas on Windham and Spencer as well as on Grenville and Dundas. Difficulties were soon apparent, as in his view were the opportunities. When the experts got to work, the usual depressing comments emerged. The estimates of available strength had now to be placed under detailed scrutiny, and while Dundas was prepared to endorse them he was made fully aware that time was needed to produce a properly effective force. Training was necessary for regiments augmented so heavily by militia. Transport was not easy, if indeed possible, to supply. Shipping for 60,000 troops would take some 200,000 tons over and above the naval transport service, out of a merchant total of some $1^1/_2$ million tons in a period of buoyant trade. Grey and his staff moreover were increasingly doubtful if a force of 60,000 would be enough; their faith in insurgence was limited, and when their

1. 'Expected Disposable Force – Dec. 20th, 1799' (copy in P.R.O. 30/8/197, ff. 108v-10). That this paper, not in his hand, was by Dundas is clear from the ms in his papers at Duke University, North Carolina (see Mackesy, op. cit., 55). No fewer than 21,000 of the infantry were expected from the auxiliary forces, to make up the usual shortfalls in the regular regiments (cf. pp. 123, 125, 223–4 above): 5,000 from militia in England, 10,000 from militia in Ireland, 6,000 from Fencibles who had already volunteered for service overseas.

2. A phrase of Pitt's; and see Grenville to Wickham, 30 November 1799 (*H.M.C., Dropmore*, VI, 52–3).

3. See pp. 225–6 above.

4. A phrase of October (to Grenville, 20 October 1799; *H.M.C., Dropmore*, V, 493).

own geographical intelligence seemed unreliable – as so often[1] – they became reluctant to countenance fewer than 80,000 men. That would mean yet more shipping, which the War Office despaired of finding. It therefore looked as if a lesser nearby base must be first secured and reinforced. Belleisle off Quiberon Bay – a name of ill omen[2] – was mentioned, and the royalist exiles suggested the peninsula of Rhuis on the bay's eastern arm. But incessant convoys to either, according to the Admiralty, would lay a strain on naval protection which could weaken the security of Ireland and the Channel itself. Pitt investigated the choices, and ordered a survey of others: Huskisson, deputising for Dundas in the latter's customary Christmas visit to Scotland, was told to confer with Grey and St Vincent, who was now back from his Mediterranean command.[3] The Minister was not dissuaded by the navy's objections, or the military's doubts of the royalists: the latter a very reasonable reaction, which he had shared in the past[4] but now thought must be held in perspective while France seemed to be growing ever more disturbed. His typical eagerness at a fresh prospect was tempered in this instance by greater caution – perhaps a result, at least in part, of a warning from Dundas.[5] But the enthusiasm survived, and in the course of December he took matters largely into his own hands. At the turn of the year the issue was still wide open, within a broad consensus that a major seaborne attack should be made at some point.[6]

Meanwhile what else could be done with any spare British resources? Holland had been mentioned; but the idea of a British involvement was quickly dropped.[7] The other possibility lay farther afield, on the southern flank of Europe, where the small force established in Minorca might be reinforced.[8] Such a theatre of operations might offer significant advantages: a heightening of pressure on Spain; a prospect of support, as in

1. Cf. II, 288, 318–19, 576–7; pp. 247, 252 above. On this occasion the Channel fleet, after eight years of blockade of Brest, was unable to furnish adequate information on the approaches or the shore defences, while the General had to work on papers produced in the American War of Independence (see Mackesy, op. cit., 61).

2. Cf. II, 574–9.

3. For which see pp. 140, 152 above.

4. Cf. pp. 223–4, 226 above.

5. Who was in Scotland at the time. 'I perfectly trust in the assurances you give to me, that you will not permit the eagerness or the sanguineness of your temper to carry you beyond the result which an accurate investigation of the subject actually presents to you. Others may refrain from saying so with equal candour . . .' (4 January 1800; Eng. Ms 907, John Rylands Library, Manchester).

6. 'I have been chiefly employed for the last Week in the discussion of very extensive Projects founded on the Accounts and the Solicitations received from Britanny' (*sic*); Pitt to Canning, 24 December 1799 (Canning Ms 30, Leeds). There is a mass of material on this phase of the planning, for which see Note to this Ch. on Sources. A good summary of the professional issues is contained in Mackesy, op. cit., 52, 55–64.

7. See pp. 319–20, 323–4 above. I have not found any further reference in these weeks to *British* participation in such an attack.

8. P. 152 above.

1794–6, for an Austrian drive into southern France; and above all the chance of enlisting Russian aid, whether or not Suvorov's army was recalled from Germany in full.

There were many unknown factors to consider before such an aim could be achieved. Whatever might be done in the Mediterranean must depend to some extent on the decision for Brittany: supplies of men, equipment and transport must be measured against priorities in the north. Nor was it a simple matter to gauge the Tsar's state of mind from impressions which varied with almost every crop of reports. Nor again for that matter would the Austrians' new mood necessarily mean much. No final outcome could be predicted in any of these respects. There was however one point on which near certainty reigned in London: while a Russian contribution was sought, no one wished to repeat the experience of acting in union with a Russian force. The commanders from Holland, Dundas, Huskisson, all were equally adverse, and Pitt, impressed by 'the deep prejudices which seem to have taken root in our service', accepted that Russians in close contact might be 'rather an incumbrance than an aid'. That appeared to rule them out from a combined descent on France. It also meant that they should complement, not form a part of a British offensive force in the Mediterranean.[1] But that did not lessen the desirability of their presence, without which such a British force might well lack substance for a significant contribution. As things stood, or could be conjectured, the latter's numbers seemed unlikely to exceed 10,000.[2] On strictly military, let alone wider grounds, we would therefore welcome 'auxiliary' strength.[3]

How great then should that be, and from what quarter should it be drawn? In the mists of uncertainty, choices were amply supplied. If the Tsar relented at least in part,[4] and left some 30,000 men with the Austrians, the residue (not very numerous by the latest estimates) might be marched to Leghorn to be augmented by a further contingent bringing the total to some 20,000. That addition might be found in the 15,000-odd Russians from Holland now quartered in Britain, who themselves might be replaced by 15–20,000 brought in their own shipping from the Baltic, to be deployed, perhaps with a contingent of Dutch exiles, against Holland in the spring. This laborious policy was aimed of

1. Pitt to Grenville, 21 November; Dundas to ? Pitt, 24 November 1799 (*H.M.C., Dropmore*, VI, 35, 39). Dundas, it is true, did not dismiss the possibility of accustoming the Russians from Holland to 'the habits and intercourse of British soldiers'. But he was clearly unenthusiastic.

2. That figure is mentioned by both Dundas (24 November as above) and Grenville (no. 102 to Whitworth, 22 – or perhaps 23 – November 1799; F.O. 65/45). But it seems to have been a maximum. Dundas also talked, at the same time, of 4,000; and Mackesy (op. cit., 35) concludes that 'about 5,000 British troops from the garrison could be spared for offensive operations'. Further reinforcements, from Portugal or home, did not enter the calculations seriously at this stage.

3. Pitt's phrase ('auxiliaries'); to Grenville as in n1 above.

4. Pp. 323–4 above.

course at the old concept of a triple offensive, with the Low Countries and Brittany tying down French forces while the Austrians (and perhaps some Russians) attacked France from the east. The same result however might be brought about differently if the Tsar adhered to his recent decision, for in that case his main army might be marched as a whole to the Italian coast, while the Russians in Britain could be prepared directly for the assault on Holland. Nothing then need come from the Baltic. There was moreover a further form of aid which would be helpful in the south. If Russia would provide 6–8,000 men in addition for garrisoning duties, present and to come, they would release more British troops for an active role. Such support might be sent from the Crimea, in Russian shipping which should then remain.[1] Likely operational targets, the Cabinet was told, were Majorca, Malta, Toulon, and Cartagena, and the Allied forces should be placed under British overall command. The proposals were completed for St Petersburg in the last week of November.[2] Marking an advance in British offers to Russia of a presence in the central Mediterranean,[3] their precise outcome would turn largely on the chances, which had already helped shape the invitation, of rescuing a major tripartite military and diplomatic design.

That effort was now well under way. It was intensified by the knowledge that Tsar Paul might be casting his eyes elsewhere. His moods, and his policies, were seldom confined to one object, and the announcement of a withdrawal of co-operation with Vienna had been accompanied by advice, somewhat startling, for London. At some point Britain would have to reach a negotiated peace, and this could best be achieved on the basis of France's reduction to her pre-war frontiers and the union of the Austrian Netherlands with Holland, while Prussia was conciliated by some accessions on the Rhine, and Britain itself rewarded with its conquests in the West and East Indies. Meanwhile Austria should be disciplined and her ambitions restrained, and that could best be done by a fresh alliance of Britain and Russia with Prussia, the lead towards which should be taken by

1. Mackesy (op. cit., 35) gives a précis of this series of conjectures.

2. Grenville to Whitworth, nos. 102, 106, 22, 30 November 1799 (F.O. 65/45); memorandum of 28 November by Dundas, presented to the Cabinet (copies in B.L. Add. Ms 59306 from Grenville's file of Cabinet Minutes and B.L. Add. Ms 38759 in Huskisson's papers. Whitworth was sent the contents with Grenville's no. 102).

The despatches however did not leave until mid December. Together with some others, from 19 November onwards, they were entrusted to Captain Home Popham, the naval expert on transport and associated plans who had played a prominent part in the Russian preparations for Holland in the summer (pp. 235–7 above), and had now volunteered and been encouraged to return to influence the Tsar. He was held up in the event by contrary winds.

3. See II, 633, 635 for Corsica in 1795; pp. 151 above for the possibility of Malta in 1798; and 318–20 more recently for offensive operations.

Britain in Berlin.[1] This information only added to the urgency of establishing arrangements with Vienna, which might perhaps help turn away
Paul's 'passion'[2] and at any rate forestall or evade the task of having to talk
to Prussia once more. For there was no wish in London at this time to take
any step in Berlin, which the special envoy Thomas Grenville had lately
left in an atmosphere of mutual chill. The Prussians, it was true, might yet
be militarily useful in any further operations in Holland; but that would
raise awkward diplomatic questions,[3] and in the larger European context
their involvement was much less attractive than that of the Austrians
themselves. So, basically, it had always been: 'to whom' in essence, if
conditions permitted, 'could we turn but to the Emperor?'[4] And the fact
was underlined moreover at this point, after the many frustrations, by a
sudden, almost desperate surge of interest in his potential military
strength. For in the same reports that condemned the Russian forces,
Wickham drew attention to an Austrian revival: the bearing and spirit of
the troops had risen over the past two years, and so had the calibre of
staffwork, to a level indeed which now outweighed shortcomings still to be
seen higher up the scale.[5] These observations found their mark. Whatever
the defects of Vienna's policy, the Austrian army was regaining a favour it
had never wholly lost. And now that there were some friendlier signals
from Thugut, quite possibly misleading but observable and transmitted at
a critical time, we had best proceed on our existing path.

The prospects furthermore seemed not unhopeful as the year drew
towards its close. In December Minto reported that the Austrians
appeared really anxious to concert plans. Their intentions in respect of
the Russians were shaken by their own experience of Suvorov's army.[6] But
they professed themselves ready to assist from Italy any Anglo-Russian
moves against southern France and, from a base in Mainz,[7] any renewed

1. Paul to Vorontsov, 15 October [OS, 25 October NS], enclosed in Vorontsov to
Grenville, 19 November 1799 (*H.M.C., Dropmore*, VI, 32–4). Vorontsov's private comment
was, 'On n'agit chez nous que par passion et violence.' In Britain itself the term 'East
Indies' was often used to cover the Far East (see I, 423).

2. N1 above.

3. Pp. 241–3, 253–4 above.

4. Pitt in February 1795 (II, 559); and see pp. 250–1 above.

5. To Grenville, no. 42, 31 October 1799; received 19 November (F.O. 74/25). He also
repeated Suvorov's high opinion of the Austrians, for which cf. p. 322 above (no. 37, 17
October, loc. cit.; cf. *Correspondence of Wickham*, II, 320, 274). The effect of the reports may
be gauged by Ministers' ensuing confidence in their ally through operations which were to
end in disaster.

6. . . . 'a sort of pestilence or visitation which is more dreaded than the enemy' (Minto
to Grenville, no. 43, 1 December 1799, received on the 17th; P.R.O., F.O. 7/57). At the same
time, they were prepared to place a corps of 10–15,000 under their own strict command.
Nine days later however they seemed to have changed their mind (same to same, no. 47, 10
December, received 27 January 1800; loc. cit.).

7. See pp. 239–40, 248–9, 251 above. When the Archduke Charles had turned round
towards Switzerland again in October, the French staged a limited recrossing of the Rhine
to the south of the city.

operations in Holland. They still wished to retain control in Piedmont while the war lasted, though they seemed prepared to allow self-government provided that the King himself did not return. They also demanded an engagement that Britain would not make a separate peace, or treat separately for a general peace – shades of 1796 – or with any neutral Power (obviously Prussia in particular) on the Coalition's affairs.[1] Some of these requirements were not accepted as they stood; Grenville still disliked the Emperor's claim on Piedmont, which with some of Austria's other Italian ambitions gave 'considerable ground for distrust'; and we could not deny ourselves the freedom of possible talks with neutrals, which it would be pointless to veto in advance. But Ministers were distinctly heartened by the tone of the military statements, and agreed to make no unilateral, or treat unilaterally for a general, peace. This rejoinder was ready to be sent – bitter weather permitting – on Christmas Eve.[2] Had further messengers from Vienna reached London in the harsh conditions, the Government might have been even better pleased. For by the middle of the month Minto was able to send distinctly encouraging news. The Austrians' operations would be divided between Italy with 100,000 men and Switzerland and the Rhine with another 100,000 plus 25–30,000 from German states; and a preponderance of the force north of the Alps would be assigned to Switzerland, of which the British would presumably approve – 85,000 men as against 40,000 for the renewed advance on Mainz.[3] Those movements might be followed by an attack (possibly limited, Minto thought) from the Swiss base in eastern France; but the main thrust would come farther south, to Savoy and Nice and into Provence or the Dauphiné. Such a strategy was by no means to be dismissed under current circumstances; and there were some contingent, diplomatic reasons for cautious hope. For a compromise was indicated now over Piedmont: the territory might be wholly restored to Sardinia, provided as before that the King did not return in wartime and his troops served under Austrian command. Furthermore, there was 'a positive promise' to ratify the Loan Convention, though London should shoulder the charges for the loan itself.[4] In return for such a package, Austria would

---

1. Minto to Grenville, nos. 43, 44, 1 December 1799; both received on the 17th (F.O. 7/57). See II, 626–7, 636–7, 645–6, 649 for Britain's behaviour in the autumn of 1796.

2. Grenville to Minto, nos. 18, 19 both Most Secret of 24 December 1799 (F.O. 7/57). The icy weather and some consequential arrangements were the subject of an unnumbered Separate and Secret of the same date.

The Foreign Secretary's distrust of Austrian policy in Italy was fanned by reports from the British envoys in Sardinia and now also in Tuscany, where Thugut was suspected of wishing to see British influence in Florence reduced (Thomas Jackson to Grenville, 7 September–13 November 1799; P.R.O., F.O. 67/28 *passim*; William Wyndham to same, unnumbered, 14 November, received 8 December 1799, F.O. 79/17).

3. For which see p. 251 above.

4. Cf. the earlier different suggestion on pp. 322–3 above. Minto had in fact already opened this last possibility on his own initiative, to apply for the duration of the war. Thugut replied that the expenses should remain a British responsibility until finally discharged.

need fresh help to the tune of £1.6 million – shortly raised to £2.4 million to include the German troops – with an immediate advance in bullion or coin.[1] These most reent despatches finally reached England, once more in a batch, towards the end of January.[2] But they reinforced a promise more faintly discernible several weeks before.

News from St Petersburg remained more ambiguous, in so far as any was received, for in fact not all the despatches could get through. The latest information, received early in December, held out little hope of rapprochement with Vienna, and that prospect was now virtually discounted, as it was by the Austrians themselves.[3] The British proposals therefore hardened on those already sketched for such a case, advancing for good measure the date for an attack on Holland so as to achieve greater surprise.[4] And when further despatches from Whitworth came in – mostly on the same day as the latest batch from Minto[5] – they suggested that, in so far as the issue lay with London, this might be the best course to pursue. For while the Tsar seemed no more disposed than before to change his attitude towards Austria, he still appeared ready to persist in the war. He was talking after all – almost inevitably – of closer contact with Prussia.[6] He had just completed talks for improved relations with Sweden by signing a fresh alliance – news which led Grenville, almost equally inevitably, to ask if the Swedes might declare war on France.[7] He had recently strengthened his connexion with Bavaria – primarily to embarrass Austria in the German Empire – and (now inconveniently) had

1. Britain had been required earlier to subsidise the Germans; the Austrians then decided (see p. 249, n1 above), in order to stymie Russia, to pay the troops direct, recouping from London. Before this proposal was received, Grenville had in fact undertaken to meet the cost of 10–12,000 men under Austrian command (no. 19 to Minto as on p. 330, n2 above).

Austria was also claiming some £40,000 for supplies issued to Condé's army of exiles in 1795-7, when that force was being subsidised by Britain (see pp. 222, 249, n2 above); Duffy 'War Policy', 388n1.

2. Minto to Grenville, nos. 47, 48, both of 10 December, 49 of 13 December; all received 27 January 1800 (F.O. 7/57).

3. Whitworth to same, nos. 105, 106, of '11' (really 13), 17 November, both received 6 December 1799 (F.O. 65/45); Minto to same, nos. 40, 43, 12 November, 1 December, received 28 November, 17 December 1799 (F.O. 7/57). See also p. 329 above for the Austrians' disinclination to act with the Russian forces.

4. Grenville to Whitworth, nos. 108, 114, 116 of 13, 17, 22 December 1799 (F.O. 65/45). Cf. p. 328 above for the 'alternative' case. The date now suggested for the Dutch operation was March.

5. Whitworth to Grenville, nos. 107, unnumbered (but 108), 109, 111-15 (114 being wrongly numbered; he was getting in a muddle), 28 November-31 December 1799; the first seven received 27 January, the eighth 6 February 1800 (loc. cit.). See n2 above.

6. Pp. 200, 208, 211, 215 above.

7. To Whitworth, no. 115, 20 December 1799 (loc. cit.). That would of course stop her trade as a neutral with the enemy. It would not necessarily involve her accession to the Coalition.

See p. 244, n2 above for Britain's own poor relations with Sweden earlier in the year. Their continuing stagnation may be followed in P.R.O., F.O. 73/27.

hired troops there as Britain had earlier hoped.[1] Not all these symptoms were related exclusively to the same cause. But they might be taken together as indications of continued involvement. If so, Russia might be expected not to reduce the contacts with ourselves. Even allowing for the impact of temperament, Paul would otherwise be cutting off his nose to spite his face.

So at any rate the reading might be taken at a delicate point. The prospects for the Coalition were finely balanced at the end of the year. All might still be upset; or, less palatable to the sceptics, might end in reluctant agreements leading to half-measures destined to fail. No one could yet guess. But by the same token this did not seem to be the time to falter or hold back. The alliances were strained; but they were still in being, and the British plans were developing, in principle at least, to accommodate the late disappointment.[2] The enemy too had his own weaknesses, which under pressure might yet prove mortal: Italy was almost wholly lost, Switzerland could follow, even perhaps Holland, and if the risings on French soil had not succeeded they showed the reality of discontent. British involvement in a Continental strategy appeared to be at least worth one more try. So it could be argued in London when an unusual event occurred.

II

On the evening of 31 December a messenger disturbed Grenville at Dropmore with a packet from London which the Foreign Secretary hastened to send on the last few miles to Windsor. Together with a covering letter to himself from his counterpart Talleyrand, it contained a letter from Bonaparte to the King.[3]

The missive was an overture for peace. Bearing in mind that it would almost certainly be published, in the manner of both sides on analogous occasions increasingly over recent years, the contents were admirably phrased.[4] Were there 'no means of coming to an understanding' after seven years of war? How could 'the two most enlightened nations of Europe' sacrifice the benefits of peace to 'ideas of vain greatness'? Such sentiments could not 'be foreign' to a King 'who reigns over a free nation,

---

1. Robert Walrond [envoy in Munich] to Grenville, nos. 30 and enclosure to 31 of 17, 23–4 November, received 4, 13 December 1799 (P.R.O., F.O. 9/18). See pp. 249, n2, 322 above for the troops.

2. See p. 324 above.

3. Grenville to George III, 31 December 1799, 7.15 pm (*L.C.G. III*, III, no. 2095).

4. Cf. for earlier occasions II, 310–11, 607, 649n5. For the translated text on this occasion see *The New Annual Register for . . . 1800* (1801), 56; also, *P.H.*, XXXIV, cols. 1197–8. The letter was signed 'Buonaparte'; a spelling, legally correct, which he had abandoned for common purposes some three years before (p. 50, n2 above). There is a copy of the untranslated text in Pitt's papers, P.R.O. 30/8/101.

and with the sole view of rendering it happy'. War would exhaust both their countries in the end, while 'the fate of all civilized nations' was 'attached' to its termination. It was an appeal, couched largely in a tone breathing the vanished spirit of ten years before,[1] which could attract much liberal and some commercial sympathy at a well chosen point.

A peace offering of some kind was not unexpected, as the Foreign Office had suggested to Russia and Austria.[2] The form however took Ministers by surprise. Bonaparte addressed the King as an equal; he ignored the accepted diplomatic channels and practices of western Europe; and he was acting without the hints and preliminaries, usually confidential and sometimes indirect, hitherto experienced by other allies when the French were testing the temperature.[3] His approach on the contrary was declared outright to be 'disengaged' from such methods, which were better suited to weak than to strong states. The whole mode of proceeding appeared extraordinary; a communication to a Head of State which in itself was out of order had been brought over by 'a common courier' without request for a passport,[4] in a vessel which was thereby not admitted but now lay off Dover awaiting a reply. Such a way of behaving offended against established usage. But that was not the reason for the response the letter received.

For the Ministers chiefly involved had already made up their minds in principle about an approach for peace which they had assumed might come soon. They did so in the light, or murk, of the latest twist of fortune in Paris which had raised Bonaparte suddenly to this height. For the turning-point in his life was now complete. On 13 October he had landed in Provence, leaving his army behind, from his Egyptian campaign.[5] On 9 November the coup of Brumaire saw the end of the Directory, and its replacement by the Consulate in which he was named the third of three. The following weeks witnessed his formal elevation to provisional First Consul, the drafting of a Constitution at first apparently in harness with the constitutionalist survivor Sieyès, and stern operations in the Vendée by which the insurgents were ground down. It proved to be the opening of an era. But it was far from giving that impression at the time. On the contrary, while the seeming confusion posed a range of questions for the future, their very indeterminacy shaped the answer in the immediate term. Two broad possibilities could be canvassed in London. Either, as Grenville maintained, this military adventurer was a typical product of the Revolution; the latest figure to come to the top of an endlessly

1. Cf. II, 46. Pitt himself thought it was in 'very civil' language (to Dundas, 31 December 1799; Stanhope, III, 207).
2. P. 324 above.
3. A hint had in fact been received on the 25th, the day on which the letter was dated in Paris. But that was all.
4. Cf. II, 627–8, 636. The account was Pitt's (to Chatham, 1 January 1800; P.R.O. 30/8/101).
5. For the start of which see p. 147 above.

unstable succession, whose advent did nothing to alter, and indeed pointed, the aggression inherent in the Jacobin threat. Or, as Canning argued privately on different lines from his former chief,[1] this was the latest and most significant stage in an inevitable process, signalling in one form or another the prospective transformation of a failing republic into a monarchy restored from within France itself.[2] He spoke better than he knew, though not at all in the sense he had in mind. But his argument stirred Pitt to set down his own thoughts at unusual length, in a letter of interest not only for current but for future events.

The occasion arose from a private talk or talks in November, perhaps at Holwood, in which Canning had clearly become alarmed that the Minister might contemplate the possibility of peace talks if current developments seemed to offer signs of hope. He himself was certain on the contrary that events should be left to work themselves out until they were eclipsed in the destined beneficial end. Pitt settled down to explain his position.[3] He thought that there was 'a reasonable Prospect of making a decisive Impression' on France 'in *One or Two* Campaigns more',[4] with a balance of strength on the Allies' side against waning 'Exertion' (though he would still not underestimate that) from a nation whose resources appeared to be exhausted and whose public opinion had now suffered a further 'Shock'. If however we should be 'abandoned' by the Continental Powers to a 'defensive War by ourselves', we still had the means for an indefinite time '*never* to think of Peace with a *Revolutionary Jacobin*

1. Canning had moved in March from his Under Secretaryship at the Foreign Office (p. 59 above) into a better paid Commissionership on the Board of Control for India.

2. 'Do you apprehend that there is any man in this Country [Grenville presumably excepted], do you believe even that there is any man in France, to whom the first idea suggested by this latter Revolution was any other than the Restoration of the Monarchy? Is it not plain that events are in full march towards that point?' (to Pitt, 28 November 1799, P.R.O. 30/8/120; printed in part in Holland Rose, *Pitt and Napoleon*, 319–20). On this reading, the interval would be filled either by Bonaparte's fall to 'the violent party', which would produce a revival of Jacobinism itself now destined to fail; or by the consolidation of Bonaparte's or Sieyès' authority which, whoever was the victor, could prove only a half-way house. While he agreed with Grenville that the General was an adventurer who would take all possible steps to preserve his power, he thus did not agree that Jacobinism could be expunged solely by outright defeat at the Allies' hands.

3. Pitt to Canning, 3 December 1799 (Canning Ms 30, Leeds). The letter runs to $17^1/_2$ pp.
The exact circumstances of the exchange are uncertain, and not all the correspondence seems to have survived. If Canning kept his diary in this period it has disappeared; as also, it would seem, have some letters to which others, surviving, refer. Pitt had written to him in late November (in one communication not found, and probably relating to Canning's immediate political prospects) and promised a 'second part' on the scene in France and its implications which, typically, did not follow. In its absence, Canning then despatched a long 'second part' of his own, perhaps again following on a screed about his personal position, which was exercising him at this time. Its relevant portion ended, 'For God's sake, no treaty, but with Monarchy' (P.R.O. 30/8/120 as in n2 above). It was probably to this document that Pitt replied now.

4. Cf. pp. 325, and 324 and n6, above.

Government'. He agreed with Canning that, as far as could be seen, the new event in France was 'a great Step to Monarchy', and that 'probably Nothing but premature Peace on our Part' could 'check or much retard the Progress to its Restoration, – Probably not even another *Jacobin* Revolution' which in his view would lead to a civil war. He found it hard to envisage either Bonaparte's survival as a military usurper relying on force in the absence of popular sympathy, or the maintenance of his authority in 'any mixed or moderate Plan of Government', such as his fellow Consul Sieyès was said to be preparing on 'the Model of the American'. Embarrassed as they were in their resources, and narrowly based politically, the Consuls would most likely suffer their displacement by monarchy at once or quite soon, in the latter instance after an intermediate change; and indeed, aware of their impossible position, they might themselves seek to parley for its restoration, to avoid 'the Perspective of a Voyage to Cayenne'.[1]

These were 'probable' eventualities. At the same time, 'Opposite Chances' were not out of the question. It was not 'absolutely impossible' that Bonaparte would establish himself as a military despot strong enough to subdue the Jacobins and also 'in a great degree' extinguish the royalists' hopes. And if that happened, it could have effects on the prospects for peace. For if the General then thought, as he might, that it could be 'really his Interest both to make Peace and to maintain it', and were to offer 'honorable and Advantageous Terms', Pitt could 'not see . . . on what Grounds We could justify to ourselves a refusal to Treat, and much the less how We could expect to be supported by Public Opinion'. Canning had stated his objection to negotiating at once. But in such circumstances we would be doing so with an 'established Despotism . . . *long since tried.*' 'The only doubt would then be what is *a sufficient Trial*; but this relates not to the Principle but to its application'. It was impossible to '*define* beforehand the Point at which one's own Judgment would be convinced'; and whenever that might be it was pretty clear that 'the Public Opinion would run before it'. He had also however to take into account 'the still more improbable but yet not *impossible* Supposition, that Bonaparte will succeed in establishing some moderate Form of Government, either the American for example or any other', and in maintaining it despite both Jacobins and royalists. He put this as 'an Extreme Case'. Nonetheless, 'No Man can pretend that there would be any Thing in the Form or essential Principles of such a Government, which would make Treaty with it unsafe'. Judgment, again, would then turn on the likelihood of its endurance.

At this point in his explanation Pitt had to leave the solitude of Holwood, where he was writing, for London. Attendance at St James's

---

1. The overseas penal settlement: the French New South Wales. The phrase may possibly have been picked up from Grenville, who had used it a few days before (to Wickham, 30 November 1799; *H.M.C., Dropmore*, VI, 53).

and an early dinner prevented him from pursuing the subject further; the press of business was as usual closing in. Moreover – he continued from Downing Street – he had just seen the latest newspapers from Paris, in one of which there was 'a Plan of a Constitution, containing a Collection of ridiculous and refined Extravagance, and promising a degree of Weakness and Confusion, almost beyond the most sanguine Expectations'.[1] Such an 'Abortion' scarcely promised stability. And he also had news of an armistice in Britanny, in which the royalists seemed to have been treated on 'rather more than a Footing of Equality'. Altogether, perhaps the Consuls might end our 'Perplexities' by 'abdication' soon. Whatever happened in the near future, however, his own approach was clear. 'We ought never to treat with a *Jacobin* Government; but . . . We ought on no Account to commit ourselves by any declaration that the Restoration of Royalty is the Sine Quâ Non Condition of Peace'.

This conspectus throws light on Pitt's patterns of thought – and on his propensity to snatch at the latest piece of news. His reasoning, given unconcealed to this particular confidant but soon to be repeated in essence to others,[2] was broadly in line with his past course and held implications for what might come. It did not however raise a doubt immediately, as he and Canning agreed with relief.[3] Indeed, on his reading, there was no reason to take up Bonaparte's initiative at once; the future, close or distant, could be left for the moment to look after itself. That view was echoed by those of his colleagues who were available for consultation; and if they seem to have allowed that the door need not be shut to possible talks with a republic under changing circumstances, it may well have been with the comfortable feeling that these were unlikely to arise soon.[4] The form of the letter to the King confirmed Grenville in his view that Jacobinism was and would remain 'unshaken'; there was no hint of Pitt's own acknowledgment of a 'very civil' tone.[5] And while the absent Dundas had earlier taken leave to doubt the Foreign Secretary's assessment, that did not stop him too from now subscribing 'heartily' to the consensus on the issue itself.[6]

1. And cf. Pitt to Grenville, 22 December 1799 (*H.M.C., Dropmore*, VI, 84–5).

2. Verbally to Grenville on the day before Bonaparte's letter was received, and to Spencer and Windham, as it happened, on the day itself; and further by letter to Dundas and to Chatham (Stanhope, III, 207 for the former, P.R.O. 30/8/101, 1 January 1800, for the latter).

3. Canning to Pitt, Private, 7 December 1799 (P.R.O. 30/8/120); Pitt to Canning, 10 December 1799 (Canning Ms 30).

4. See Stanhope, III, 207 for a statement of Pitt's advice, which Grenville and Windham at least must have taken contentedly in their stride (cf. Windham to Pitt, 18 November 1799; *The Windham Papers*, II, 143–4). The other Ministers to hand were Spencer and Camden (Jupp, *Lord Grenville*, 240n2).

5. For which see p. 333, n1 above. The King himself, not unexpectedly, was equally disgusted (to Grenville, 1 January 1800; *L.C.G. III*, III, no. 2095).

6. To Pitt, 4 January 1800 (Eng. Ms 907, John Rylands Library, Manchester). It was in fact Dundas's speculation of a change in France that had led Grenville to state his own vigorous view (letters of 24, 25 November respectively; *H.M.C., Dropmore*, VI, 38, 47).

For whatever their judgments on the newcomer's circumstances and political stance, Ministers were all agreed that he should not be met half way. France was in no state to offer 'any solid certainty to be derived from negotiation';[1] Bonaparte himself might not last long; and if he did, who could forecast his real intentions? His record in Italy was one of agreements broken in letter or spirit, and aggressions mounted by him or his subordinates on incidents all too easily aroused. Tuscany, Sardinia, Parma, Modena, Rome, Venice: all had seen treaties overturned or infringed and pretexts illegitimately seized.[2] And when one turned to the republican French Governments themselves, whatever their titles and composition, the dismal list extended to much of western Europe.[3] Quite apart from violations and infringements, there was the

> Impossibility of treating with Rev^y. Govt.
> from its Principles – its Perfidy
> from its Want of Stability – and
> from each new Gov^t. breaking off Negotn^s.
> or Treaties begun by the former. –
> (List of Treaties broken off by the same
> Govt. which formed them (. . . America
>   Prussia
>   & Naples & Tuscany
> do. by the Succeeding Gov^t. . . . Lisle
>   Portugal
>   Vienna
> List of Changes of Government . . .

It could certainly not be assumed that this 'Rev^y. System' had now 'ceased finally'; and that being so, it was not hard to determine 'Whether Circumstances require accepting an insecure Compromise'. For neither the enemy's situation nor that of the Coalition suggested an affirmative reply. On the contrary, it could be held, both pointed the other way. If one assessed the 'Permanency of Bonaparte' one could cite

> Grounds of Hatred against
> him in France (Royalists – Republicans – Moderés
> Nature of his Military Power – Seeds of disunion in the Constitution
> (Its Contradictory Quality)
> Jealousies . . .

1. Pitt to Dundas, 31 December 1799 (Stanhope, III, 207); and cf. same to Chatham, 1 January 1800 (P.R.O. 30/8/101).

2. These instances are taken from a memorandum in Pitt's papers (P.R.O. 30/8/195, ff. 111–15) in Grenville's hand, written probably in preparation for a Parliamentary debate which followed soon (p. 342 below).

3. The excerpts that follow come from comprehensive notes in Pitt's hand, probably for the same occasion as in n2 above. They are in P.R.O. 30/8/197, ff. 317v-18, with another copy loc. cit., ff. 268v-9v in a different hand.

And turning to the prospects of the Alliance, and more particularly comparing Britain's with those of France, some heartening indications could be discerned.

> our Army & Navy – (Dutch Fleet)
> Distractions in France (Royalists not instigated from hence)
> Diminution of French Armies
> & Want of military Supplies
> State of Finances –
> Bankruptcies (That since Bonaparte's Gov^t.) – Impossibility of violent Means.
> Future Taxes
> Probable Comparative Situation at the End of another Campaign. –

It was in fact possible to point (particularly, one might say, for debating purposes) to

Difference from State when We Negotiated
[in 1796 and 1797][1]

This comparison with France moreover could draw some adventitious strength, within the Cabinet if not in public, from the surprisingly favourable state of the current British exchanges with Vienna.[2] For if Bonaparte could look in part to the disunity within the Alliances, he could not count thereby on the expectation that Austria would leave the war. Particularly after her shattering experience in 1796–7, there was of course always that possibility, heightened when Britain proved especially demanding or managed to cause offence. Thugut had a harder row to hoe than he was often given credit for in London. But whatever bargain he felt bound, and was ready enough, to drive with his ally, he was apparently not proposing to countenance a separate peace, and had indeed required an assurance that Britain would not seek one on her own;[3] and his policy was said at this point to be in the ascendant. So Bonaparte in fact found – or was able to confirm – directly, for he had written to the Emperor as well as George III, and in due course would receive a similar if milder rebuff. That could not be known yet in England; but the prospects suggested by Austria's amiability might be taken, if cautiously, as tending to reinforce a conclusion already reached. Ministers had no intention of accepting the French overture, and the courier off Dover need not wait long for his reply.

---

1. See p. 256 above for the Dutch fleet, and 226 for the unfortunate spontaneity of the royalist risings. The 'impossibility of violent means' refers probably to enforcement of further exactions.

2. Minto's hopeful despatches nos. 43, 44 had reached London on 17 December, and the responses were dated the 24th (pp. 329–30 and ns 1, 2 above).

3. P. 330 above.

The decision therefore was reached quickly, at a sparsely attended Cabinet on 2 January 1800, two days after Bonaparte's letter had arrived.[1] The King had been advised of the likely outcome when Grenville forwarded the letter itself,[2] and it only remained to draft the reply. That however was not a formality: it would need some care. The Allied Governments must be borne in mind; and, in this instance of equal importance, so must public opinion in France and in England itself. For Bonaparte's document, when published,[3] would certainly make an impression, which would have to be countered if support for the war at home was to be properly maintained. Dundas, up in Scotland, put his finger on the spot. Unless we could make our own 'impressions' soon by the forthcoming offensive,

> we shall not be able to persuade the country with an honourable and advantageous Peace (as they will suppose) in their hands to continue the war upon a Speculation which many will think not within our province, and which still more will be disposed to think not at all within our reach but by an expenditure of money and blood, and even with that expenditure doubtful in the issue. I don't pretend to decide when these feelings will begin to operate, or how soon they may force themselves upon our line of conduct, but I think I see with clearness that they will sooner or later press upon us according to circumstances.[4]

Pitt himself, to judge by some of his phrases, was well aware of the same probability;[5] there was an undoubted desire in England for peace, again starting to be heard more widely after the failure in Holland and the bad harvest. The British public accordingly needed fresh assurance that, despite ample resources, Ministers were not blindly committed to a war of indefinite length, but rather required proper grounds for confidence from France on which they could consider negotiations for peace. That must mean the abandonment of revolutionary aggression. And that in turn meant evidence, which events or time alone could provide, of a verifiable change of 'system' in Paris: of acceptable behaviour abroad springing from a frame of moderation at home. Such a message moreover must be made clear across the Channel as at home, as both a requirement and a reassurance to a nation which itself by all appearances seemed to be reaching such a goal. In an exchange that would include a good measure of propaganda, the French people as well as the British must be taken fully into account.

1. Pitt to Chatham, 1 January 1800 (P.R.O. 30/8/101); Windham's *Diary* for that date (421). Those present were the Ministers noted on p. 336, n4 above. Windham had met Pitt and Canning at the Foreign Office the day before (*Diary*, ibid).
2. See p. 332, n3 above.
3. See p. 332 above.
4. To Pitt, 4 January 1800 (crossing Pitt's to him of 31 December; p. 336 and n2 above); Eng. Ms 907, John Rylands Library.
5. Cf. p. 335 above.

The resulting document was aimed at these various needs. The audience, at home and in Europe, was reminded of the fruits of the Revolution: the Low Countries and Switzerland overrun, Germany ravaged, Italy – now largely rescued – exposed to 'rapine and anarchy'; public treaties regularly broken, private 'stability' removed. Only a return to 'better principles' could end Britain's resistance to such deeds; it was not enough to offer 'general professions of pacific dispositions'. So much for Bonaparte's overture. And in stating their own position, Ministers agreed to a step, in the light of the circumstances, which they had not taken specifically hitherto. For the state of affairs in France – perhaps even the First Consul's own calculations[1] – now seemed ripe for a pronouncement at a critical point. The Government accordingly declared that it favoured a return of monarchy as 'the best and most natural pledge' of a return to conditions in which talks for peace could begin 'at once'. This was 'desirable'. Nevertheless, while openly avowed, it was not the 'exclusive' means to the necessary end. The former position was restated in sequel. We did not claim to prescribe a decision which must lie with France herself; we looked 'only' to security for ourselves, our allies and 'the general safety of Europe'.[2]

The draft of the text was considered by the Cabinet at its meeting on 2 January, and again the next day. The King was not slow to give his approval, and – agreeably to his own wishes – the paper was communicated to Parliament and to all Continental courts.[3] Both Grenville and Pitt were content with the substance. It should encourage royalists and less committed moderates, stating a definite preference for one path towards peace talks while retaining a freedom of manoeuvre; it avoided any possibility of charges of bad faith from Austria or Russia; it expressed resolution without barring a readiness to treat at a proper time. From potentially divergent starting points, as seen before and would be seen again, the two men's views thus converged on the immediate response from a Government speaking as one.

1. Cf. pp. 333–6 above. And see Mackesy, op. cit., 36 & n8 for an attempt to elucidate these calculations by sending an agent to Paris at the beginning of December 1799. He did not find out anything of significance.

2. *The New Annual Register for 1800*, 57–8. It must of course be remembered that the Ministry had in mind a Constitutionalist, not an absolute, monarchy (cf. II, 582); and, while perhaps not prescribing the form directly, would doubtless have tried to bring influence to bear in the event of a restoration.

3. Grenville to George III, 31 December 1799, 2 January 1800, George III to Grenville, 1, 3 January 1800 (*L.C.G. III*, III, nos. 2095, 2097). According to Rosebery however (*Pitt*, 143), the King 'could not stomach' the paper, and wrote on it "In my opinion much too strong, but I suppose it must go". I do not know his grounds for this statement. To Grenville himself George III wrote before the second Cabinet, 'I never read a paper which so exactly contained the sentiments of my heart . . ., and I cannot see the shaddow of reason for altering any expression it contains'. For the dating of the Cabinet's consideration see also Grenville to Buckingham, 3 January 1800 (Buckingham, III, 4), Windham's diary for 2 and 3 January (*Diary*, 421; B.L. Add. Ms 37924 respectively).

There was bound to be questioning beyond such circles. The open preference for monarchy was not to everyone's taste, not only among the diffused ranks of 'Friends of Peace' but also others, of different persuasion, who saw a threat to public unity in a specific statement.[1] That however was of less consequence than the *tone* of the reply, which aroused immediate and widespread offence. In some degree the language may have been affected by the fact that Bonaparte's letter was addressed to the King, so that the royal reaction carried extra personal weight. Certainly his disgust with 'the Corsican tyrant' did not discourage an acerbic flavour.[2] But that in any case was not unlikely when the main author was Grenville; his colleagues and the Allies could cite their own experiences,[3] and in an instance such as this the enemy would scarcely be spared. Bonaparte indeed was not granted a direct answer: the Foreign Secretary replied, and then to Talleyrand, there being 'no reason to depart from those forms which have long been established in Europe'. Pitt for his part was unhappy about this; he would have preferred an introductory paragraph as between Foreign Ministers, the rest following as 'a note or declaration in the King's name'. But his advice, though given quite strongly, was ignored;[4] and the prelude set the style. The language, self-righteous, lofty and in places contemptuous, was indeed highly inapposite to the purpose. It was hardly likely to attract French moderates; it gave Bonaparte an opening for a skilful rejoinder;[5] and it did not enthuse all moderates at home, or perhaps all in the Administration itself.[6]

1. Eg Thomas Grenville to Spencer, 5 January 1800 (B.L. Add. Ms temp. Althorp G38). In hoping that the answer would not jeopardise 'the prudent regard which the Government has hitherto wisely shewn in not pressing beyond that line where publick opinion went with them', he trusted that 'you have not, now more than at other times, put forward the re-establishment of Monarchy in France as the condition of peace'. He clearly feared his brother's inclination; but at least Pitt made certain of the qualification to a statement whose line he was then ready and willing to approve.

See p. 308 above for 'Friends of Peace'.

2. To Grenville, 1 January 1800 (*L.C.G. III*, III, no. 2095). Cf. pp. 333, 336, n5 above.

3. Cf. pp. 133–4, 148 above.

4. It 'would be a great improvement'. 'I am clear it would be much for the better'. '. . . the paper will be in a simpler and more dignified form, and fitter for publication as a manifesto' (to Grenville, 3 January 1800; *H.M.C., Dropmore*, VI, 96). The Minister probably did not help his case by explaining that his proposal had been suggested by Canning, whose relations with his former principal were ambiguous (see pp. 59–61 above). But the Foreign Secretary could afford in any case to stand firm on a matter of protocol in which he must have known he could count on the King.

5. Talleyrand to Grenville, 14 January 1800; which drew a final reply from Grenville on the 20th (*P.H.*, XXXIV, cols. 1200–4).

6. Certainly not George Rose, if his restrospective statement is to be believed (to Pretyman, 25 June 1800; Pretyman Ms 435/44). Others who may have felt likewise were Canning (n4 above) and Cornwallis in Ireland (to Major-General Ross, 3 July 1800; *Correspondence of Cornwallis*, III, 270), though the comments were made in different circumstances later. Speaker Addington, not of course within the Ministry though very much in touch, was however certainly unenthusiastic at the time (see Mackesy, op. cit., 50). Grenville himself perhaps had the language partly in mind in forecasting that the paper would 'alarm some weak friends' (to Buckingham, 3 January 1800; Buckingham, III, 4).

Without such language in fact the message might have achieved its object more fully. Nonetheless, despite such qualms the substance passed muster by and large. Wilberforce, highly doubtful himself, was probably right when he noted, 'All people disapproving of Grenville's uncivil answer, though in general approving of rejection of overture'.[1] His own strong reservations were eased after talking to Pitt, sufficiently at least for him to support Government in the ensuing Commons' debate. And it was Pitt who had the greatest effect when that time came.[2] His speech, of great length – it occupies 53 columns in the most commonly cited report – and composed on the lines and largely in the order of the extensive notes in his papers, was widely held to be one of his most impressive and was certainly fully prepared.[3] The climax drew on Cicero.

> Cur igitur pacem nolo? Quia infida est,
> quia periculosa, quia esse non potest.[4]

A splendid summing up. Nonetheless Members would have noted – and if they had not, Fox soon reminded them[5] – that it followed a passage which went farther than the reply to Bonaparte itself. For Pitt paused in his main flow of historical review and current perspective to indicate possible scenarios in which a negotiation might take place. These would certainly include one in which French policy was 'guided by different maxims'. But they might also have to allow for another in which the Allied forces failed to 'call forth such a spirit in France, as to make it probable that the act of the country itself will destroy the system now prevailing'; or again for one where 'the danger, the difficulty, the risk of continuing the contest, should increase, while the hope of complete ultimate success should be diminished'. At present, he stressed, the probabilities on the contrary pointed 'one way'. We had strong reasons to rely on Allied co-operation; the French themselves seemed disposed to resist the 'new tyranny'; and if we found we could not achieve 'complete success' as we now hoped, a

1. *Life of Wilberforce*, II, 359. For his doubts, and those of others, see op. cit., 354–8. The City however – the 'most important' quarter in one Minister's view – seems to have been more heartily in favour, and the stocks rose (Duke of Portland to Castlereagh, 11 January 1800; Portland Ms PwV, vol. 111; Nottingham University).

2. On 3 February 1800; there was a debate in the Lords on 28 January (*P.H.*, XXXIV, cols. 1242–1397, 1204–41 respectively). The collected contemporary accounts are in *P.R.*, *3rd ser.*, X (1800), 265–386, 213–60, and *The Senator*, XXIV (nd), 315–94, 253–309 respectively. The last is abbreviated and has other differences from its rival, and *P.H.* draws completely on *P.R.* in this instance. I quote from it however because its coverage is the best for the debate as a whole, in its report of contributions from others which are cited below.

3. *P.H.*, XXXIV, cols. 1301–53. The papers in P.R.O. 30/8/197, ff. 317v-18 (p. 337, n4 above) refer to material in documents which are not themselves in the file.

4. *P.H.*, XXXIV, col. 1349. The quotation is from the *Philippics*, VII, 3. 'Why then do I refuse peace? Because it is deceptive, because it is dangerous, because it cannot be'. In its report of the 'great debate', the Foxite *Morning Post* observed that 'Mr. PITT built up his periods, as usual, in all the stately order of rhetorical architecture' (6 February 1800).

5. In his winding-up speech which followed Pitt's; see *P.H.*, XXXIV, col. 1384.

'continuance of the contest' would still make our position 'comparatively better' rather than 'comparatively worse'. He had explained why there was nothing to be gained by accepting an overture for peace from such a quarter at this point. Nor, given our resources, should we be 'discouraged too soon'.

> ... but, on the other hand, considering the importance of not impairing and exhausting the radical strength of the country, there are limits beyond which we ought not to persist, and we can determine only by estimating and comparing fairly, from time to time, the degree of security to be obtained by treaty, and the risk and disadvantage of continuing the contest.[1]

This was covering every eventuality, and in public, with a vengeance. It went beyond the other speeches from the Government benches, and addressed situations not sketched in the context of Pitt's letter to Canning.[2] Not surprisingly, it was injected only briefly into his main line of argument; confined to a supplementary comment, presumably for the benefit of 'some weak friends'.[3] As such it may have served its purpose and contributed to the desired result. At all events Government gained a majority of 265 to 64, in which a full vote from regular Opposition was not swollen by Ministerial secessions or, with perhaps one exception, unexpectedly by habitual independents.[4]

The statement of policy was thus directed firmly to the moment itself. It was challenged forcefully by Fox with a question that has been echoed ever since, not least by some of Pitt's most devoted biographers. Why not at least put Bonaparte's overture to the test? If he proved to be sincere, something might come of it; if not, he would have been tried and exposed.[5] The

1. Op. cit., cols. 1343–4.
2. See Dundas and Canning in the debate itself; op. cit., cols. 1242–53, 1261–85. According to the former, there was 'no remedy but the overthrow of such a government [the Consulate], or its weakness and inability to disturb the tranquillity of other states'. The latter effectually ignored the question; 'It was sufficient for the vote of that night, if government should be allowed to have acted right under the actual circumstances of the case'. *P.R., 3rd ser.*, X, 282–7, and *The Senator*, XXIV, 336–44, give only abbreviated versions of this last speech. Grenville in the Lords on 28 January (*P.H.*, XXXIV, cols. 1204–22) had nothing to say, as one might expect, about Pitt's less optimistic eventualities. See p. 335 above for Pitt's letter to Canning of 3 December 1799.
3. Grenville's phrase in p. 341, n6 above. Did Pitt have Wilberforce in particular in mind?
4. A comparison of a list of the minority in *P.H.*, XXXIV, col. 1397 with the relevant entries of Members in *H of P*, III–V *passim* will, I trust, substantiate this assessment. The possibly unexpected exception was Sir William Pulteney, the veteran well known independent, who claimed, in a following debate, that the public wanted peace.
   The majority in the Lords was 92 to 6, one of the minority being Pitt's cousin and Grenville's brother-in-law Camelford (cf. p. 294, n2 above).
5. *P.H.*, XXXIV, cols. 1353–97. Cf. Rosebery, *Pitt*, 142–6, and Holland Rose, II, 384, 568.

new Consul might in fact have welcomed a peace at this point which would have given him relief at home and burnished his image as the soldier who turned his sword into a ploughshare. But that did not in itself meet the Government's argument that a negotiation would have been dangerous, and likely in fact to do much more harm than good. It would cause embarrassment or worse with Austria, which had been given provisional assurance that we would not parley on our own; and while of course we could follow by asking her to agree to a joint negotiation, that would hardly look good just as we were seeking concerted plans for the coming campaign. The Government was indeed to some extent committed to a rejection of the overture. But in any case it did not propose to do anything that might shore up the revolutionary system at a juncture when it might well collapse of its own accord. To negotiate with Bonaparte might well be to let him off the hook: to give him a chance to procrastinate while he embarked on a programme of propaganda which would help reinforce his position and divide his foes at home and abroad. Nor was this necessarily a fanciful argument, as his record suggested – and the next fifteen years would show. For if, as he claimed later, Bonaparte was forced at this time to persist in waging war, it was his attitude to peace that would always bolster his opponents' case. Offers, treaties, in his hands were counters with which to win the game. Pitt was not therefore deflected from his central theme, as indeed he made clear when the debate was resumed, which it was in effect only a fortnight later.[1] Fox himself was not present then – he had returned to his policy of absence[2] – but Tierney challenged the Minister to drop his '*ifs* and *buts*' and state his object in one sentence. The answer, in its turn, has echoed down the years.

> The hon. gentleman . . . defies me to state, in one sentence, what is the object of the war. I know not whether I can do it in one sentence; but in one word, I can tell him that it is Security. But it is also more than this: it is Security against a danger, the greatest that ever threatened the world. It is Security against a danger which never existed in any past period of society.[3]

Resting on that foundation, he was resolved in fact to await events which he could hope to assist. It had now to be seen if the assistance would be

---

1. 17 February 1800, on the issue of fresh financial aid for Austria (*P.R.*, 3rd ser., X, 559–94). This account is fuller than that in *P.H.*, XXXIV, cols. 1438–58, and Pitt's speech is accorded the double quotation marks meant to denote *oratio directa*.

2. See pp. 42, 105–6 above.

3. *P.R.*, *3rd ser.*, X, 567–8. He went on, in good debating style, to counter with a list of 'ifs and buts' of his own. 'The restoration of the French Monarchy, . . . I consider as a most desirable object, because I think that it would afford the strongest and the best security . . . *But* this object may not be attainable: and *if* it be not . . ., we must be satisfied with the best security which we can find independent of it. Peace is most desirable . . .; *but* negotiation could be attended with greater evils than . . . benefits. And *if* this is found to be the case . . . then I say, that it is prudent of us, not to negotiate at the present moment' (op. cit., 570).

effective; if the military 'impressions' could be mounted as expected, and could be made good.

III

In the opening weeks of the new year there was simultaneously good and bad news. The former arrived late in January with the belated reception of Minto's despatches of some six weeks before, bearing Thugut's outline of Austrian plans and his 'positive promise' to ratify the Loan Convention.[1] This last had a clinching effect. On 13 February a royal message was delivered to Parliament requesting provisional advances for Austria, and consent was easily gained in the next few days.[2] With his old bugbear apparently removed, Grenville felt more free to expand. 'We are now to begin a new score with our Austrian friends', he replied – adding 'and we must hope the best'.[3] He agreed to service the loan for 1797 for at least three years or the duration of the war, whichever was the longer, charging the debt on whatever Government was settled on the Austrian Netherlands at the peace. Meanwhile a fresh loan would be raised for £1.6 million on the same terms as the British domestic loan for the year, with a further £800,000 provided for Austria to hire German troops plus £200,000 for hire of Piedmontese once agreement was reached on that territory, while £2–300,000 would be advanced in specie when a Convention had been signed to pledge joint continuation of the war. Compared with past terms for assistance, these were on the generous side.[4]

The accompanying proposals and demands, for their part, showed forbearance. Grenville was indeed trying hard to see that 'nothing' was 'omitted' for 'the success of the Common cause'.[5] It was hard to define plans to aid Austria in the Mediterranean – that must turn on the extent of her own, and Russian, co-operation.[6] But we certainly hoped to provide a useful force. We were content to leave Austria's strategy to her own volition,

1. P. 330 above.
2. See p. 344, n1 above for the Commons' debate, where Government's majority was 162 to 19 on the 17th. The Lords had assented by 28 to 3 on the 14th. Pitt was asking for £500,000 to be available at once, in advance of a treaty which was still to be settled in detail.
3. To Minto, 13 February 1800 (*H.M.C., Dropmore*, VI, 124, misprinted 121).
4. Same to same, nos. 2, 4 of 8, 14 February 1800 (P.R.O., F.O. 7/58). Some sums were almost certainly put to the Cabinet on 9 February (Grenville's list of 'Subsidies *etc.* for 1800'; B.L. Add. Ms 59306). Duffy, in a summary in 'War Policy', 392–3, notes terms on the former date for the loan itself which were soon seen to be technically too generous at British expense. Cf. p. 322 above for Thugut's recent demands, pp. 318, 330 for the German mercenaries, p. 51, n2 for the terms in 1797, and II, 520, 552, 557 for those in 1795.
5. To Minto, 13 February 1800 (*H.M.C., Dropmore*, VI, 125).
6. This repeated an earlier statement, which had hinted moreover at the possibility of a direct Austrian contribution in that theatre if none could be obtained from Russia (Grenville to Minto, no. 19, Most Secret, 24 December 1799; F.O. 7/57).

but we trusted that the Archduke Charles would be given a free hand in the conduct of operations. Otherwise the usual provision was required for agreement not to make a unilateral peace – always by now given leading priority on either side; Austria must specify (perhaps by a secret article in a Convention or treaty) that she would not let the Austrian Netherlands fall to France at the peace; if she acquired Venice, Genoa and Leghorn, she must conclude a commercial treaty covering British interests there; and indeed a comprehensive commercial treaty should be agreed before anything else.[1] Altogether, the Foreign Office thought, such returns would be worth while in exchange for the proposed financial and operational support.

The pace from London was sustained, within its limits, over the next two months. Minto pressed on with the talks in Vienna, while Wickham, allowed ample discretion, raised German mercenaries for Austria's use: 20,000 by treaty with Bavaria in March, 7,000 from Würtemberg, 3,300 from Mainz, 6,500 to 8,000 from Swabia in April. Condé's émigrés (despite their Russian connexion now) and the Swiss in British pay were placed in addition at the Emperor's disposal.[2] These auxiliaries amounted in number to a significant force. Grenville himself continued to observe discretion; he took care to keep Vienna informed of British diplomatic moves elsewhere, and offered no official comment when the Archduke Charles – London's favourite general despite his frequent advocacy of peace, but in worsening health and an opponent of Thugut – was removed from his command in March.[3] This restraint was strengthened by the major qualification to expectations of success: the uneasy and persistent feeling that Austria remained open to feelers from France. The Emperor's reply to Bonaparte was thought to invite or at least not preclude further correspondence, and when Talleyrand tried a fresh opening in February, with the 'bait' of Italy as expected, Minto was not kept in touch for a fortnight and the refusal itself from Vienna was delayed for a month.[4] The Government's suspicion may well have been excessive; Thugut himself, thanks to continuing bad weather, had to wait until April for confirmation from Grenville that Britain would enter into a reciprocal agreement not to make a unilateral peace.[5] His position indeed was not

1. Grenville to Minto as in p. 345, n5 above.
2. See Wickham's despatches April–August 1800 (P.R.O., F.O. 74/31); Duffy, loc. cit., 395; Sherwig, *Guineas and Gunpowder*, 131; and cf. pp. 249, n1; 219, 238, n2 above for Condé and the Swiss respectively.
3. For his personal feelings see his Private letter to Minto of 28 March (*Life and Letters of . . . Elliot*, III, 105).
4. Minto to Grenville, 23 February (op. cit., 139), and nos. 6, 9 of 14, 22 February, no. 9, 24 March 1800 (F.O. 7/58). For the 'bait' of Italy see Grenville to Wickham, 11 February 1800 (*H.M.C., Dropmore*, VI, 123). The fear was never far from the Foreign Secretary's mind; eg to Minto, 28 March 1800 (*Life and Letters of . . . Elliot*, III, 105–6).
5. Grenville's 'Points for the Cabinet', and Cabinet Minute, 24 March 1800; Grenville to George III, with the Minute, sd (*L.C.G. III*, III, no. 2120). Cf. pp. 136, 330, 345 above for past exchanges on this subject. The ensuing despatch, no. 10, was dated the next day (F.O. 7/58).

fully understood; he had to guard his flank at Court, and he was not going to be careless of Austria's interests by undue haste. At heart, as events were to show, he was resolved to continue in the war if he could.[1] Nonetheless the doubts in London were understandable. The ratification of the Loan Convention in Vienna, promised on 10 December, was not despatched until 29 January, and to Ministers' surprise their package of February was coldly received. A direct supply of £1.6 million, they were informed, was inadequate; £2 million was essential, and furthermore no mention had been made of the claim for past payments to Condé. Nor had there been any reference to Austria's retention of The Three Legations. The Emperor would not countenance peace terms which alluded to the restoration of 'the King of France', though he would concur in requiring a government which would afford security. And intentions for Piedmont, the British found, were uncertain; their own proposals seemed to count for little, and Thugut, influenced it seemed by the likelihood of Russian – and Prussian – objections, was now considering an alternative territorial arrangement.[2] The talks continued in the face of shifting demands. But on 1 May 1800 Minto was able to send a Project for a Convention for one year. Austria was to receive £2 million direct, paid in three instalments and repayable after the war. She would require Britain's support at the peace for her retention of the eastern regions of Piedmont, of Genoa, the Legations and some other Papal territory, Lucca (a new proposition) and the Valtelline – this last presumably to link the Milanese with the Tyrol. Britain would be given trading advantages in Italy: most favoured nation status by a commercial treaty, while Genoa would be declared a free port.[3]

It was far from certain that this would be the end of the matter. The British Government was unusually anxious, in a case including trade and finance, for a binding conclusion;[4] but some of the articles were still not to Thugut's liking, and further changes would in fact soon be urged. Nonetheless the Project was despatched in propitious circumstances. The contents were deemed satisfactory enough in Vienna to influence a rejection of a new French offer for peace talks. More potently, the Austrian offensive had opened in Italy in the first half of April, and the initial stage was proving a success.

1. See Roider, *Baron Thugut*, 334–5; Duffy, 'War Policy', 405–7.
2. Minto to Grenville, nos. 4, 16 of 29 January, 10 April 1800 (F.O. 7/58). Cf. p. 210 above for Austria's reservations about political involvement in France.
3. Same to same, no. 20, received 14 May 1800 (loc. cit.). See I, 379n3 for the meaning of 'most favoured nation'.
4. See eg Grenville to Minto, no. 19, Most Secret, 17 May; same to Wickham, 20 May 1800 (F.O. 7/58; *H.M.C., Dropmore*, VI, 232–3 respectively).
Cf. I, Ch. XVI, section II for the close and patient attention paid to detail in commercial negotiations.

While hopes of Austria were thus sustained, those of Russia flickered as the mails were spasmodically received. For 'Jack Frost and the frozen Elbe' continued to hamper policy until well into March.[1] The news at first remained depressing. Enraged by an incident with the Austrians in the reduction of a lingering French coastal outpost, the Tsar capped his withdrawal from Germany by similar notice for some few remaining contingents in Italy. And while he repeated his professions of continued effort in the Allied cause, their effect began to seem doubtful as 'the necessity for vigorous measures . . . is lost in that of watching over the ambition of Austria' at large.[2] It seemed doubtful moreover if Austria in her turn would allow any Russians to march through her lines to reinforce the British in the Mediterranean.[3] By then however plans were being readjusted once more in London. Assuming (correctly) that a refusal was on the cards, all ideas were abandoned of 'employing' Russian troops in the southern theatre. On the other hand, Vorontsov had been informed that a new commander was coming to the Russians in Britain, with a design for a landing on the west coast of France between Bordeaux and Rochelle by a force which might be increased to 25,000 men.[4] If this proved to be so, it would add to the pressure exerted by the British on Brittany, and make more British troops themselves available for the Mediterranean. A total of 15,000 might in fact then be sent there, bringing the force to some 20,000 and making good the presumed loss of the Russian contribution. These possibilities added new questions to old. How would the Russians for France be supplied and transported, and how might that affect transport for the British reinforcements for the south? How closely should we co-operate with this new, distinct expedition? How would the Russians' relations with French royalists be settled and controlled – with the émigré regiments in Britain which might be placed at the commander's disposal, and with the internal resistance? Much and varied detail would have to be tackled, in the light of our own dispositions. But meanwhile one contributory fact became clear from the

1. The phrase was Minto's; to Lady Minto, 23 March 1800 (*Life and Letters of . . . Elliot*, III, 114). Cf. Grenville on the 4th: 'This frost is cruel . . . of course all our plans (or nearly all) are at a stand' (to Wickham; *H.M.C., Dropmore*, VI, 151).

2. Whitworth to Grenville, no. 10 [*sic*; he had despatched a no. 10 five days before], 4 February 1800, received 22 March. And see his nos. 1, 3–5, 7 of 3–21 January (F.O. 65/46).

Trouble had arisen at the port of Ancona when the besieging Austrian force refused to allow the commander of a Russian naval squadron (see pp. 150–1, but also 137) to be associated with the capitulation or to seize some French ships. The episode proved to be important because the Tsar concluded that his ally was suspicious of his intentions in the Adriatic and neighbouring Dalmatia.

3. For which see pp. 327–8 above.

4. Grenville to Whitworth, nos. 3, Most Secret, and 4, both of 8 February 1800 (F.O. 65/46); Vorontsov to Grenville, 27 January 1800, enclosing Paul to Vorontsov, 2/13 December 1799 (loc. cit); *H.M.C., Dropmore*, VI, 108–10. Whitworth mentioned the possible increase to 25,000 in his no. 5, 14 January 1800 (F.O. 65/46).

In acknowledging the likely disappearance of any direct Russian involvement in Italy, the British raised the possibility of using Condé's army instead.

despatches. The Tsar was not going to allow his troops in Britain to be used against Holland.[1]

A preliminary study of some of the problems was made at the turn of February and March, after the new commander arrived. He was in point of fact himself an émigré, the Comte de Viomenisl, recommended to the Tsar by the veteran Dumouriez in the latter's indefatigable efforts to destroy the Revolution he had served at the start.[2] A lengthy paper was prepared after a conference with Pitt, Grenville, Dundas and Vorontsov.[3] But answers of course must remain provisional until policy was affirmed in St Petersburg, and there was no guarantee of the outcome there. It became known all too soon. For even as Vorontsov was reporting back, the tide was ebbing fast. The battle for the monarch's ear, fought in this instance around an autocrat of high instability, was reaching its latest peak. Dumouriez's own influence was under attack; Paul's feeling of resentment since Holland was still fierce, reflected in the tone of his instructions for the prospective assault on western France;[4] and the British envoy himself had forfeited much of his earlier goodwill, partly from private indiscretions but also from having to stress the need to stay on terms with Vienna. The Tsar moreover appeared now to be virtually insane. No one could predict how he might move at any point. The situation in any case was fluid; neutral Prussia had emerged once more as an alternative to Austria, and the French were known to be active in a widening diplomatic campaign. The blow fell before March was out. Vorontsov was instructed that the Russian force in Britain was to return home, and after growing signs of displeasure the Tsar demanded Whitworth's recall.[5] There was not a final break. Business was continued. But no Russian troops were now forthcoming for either north-west or southern Europe; and Condé's army was disbanded for good measure. The upshot was clear. In considering a Continental western strategy, Russia could be ruled out effectively for the rest of the year.

1. Whitworth to Grenville, no. 11, 11 February 1800, received 22 March (loc. cit.).

2. See II, 197, 284.

3. It is printed in *H.M.C., Dropmore*, VI, 153–6, in response to one from Viomenisl, op. cit., 146–9. See also op. cit., 151–2, 158–9; Vorontsov to Grenville, 24 February 1800, Grenville to Whitworth, nos. 7, 9 of 4, 14 March 1800 (all in F.O. 65/46).

4. The Russian troops were to be strictly under their own commanders, and the Duke of York, foisted on them as overall commander in Holland (p. 253 and n1 above), was not to be in charge of any kind of conjunct force (*H.M.C., Dropmore*, VI, 109).

5. Grenville to George III, 31 March 1800 (*L.C.G. III*, III, no. 2123). The information came to hand on the 29th (see later in this note). Whitworth, writing on the 14th and repeating on the 25th, suspected that the decision to recall the troops, not communicated to him initially, had been sent to Vorontsov 'some time ago' (to Grenville no. 20, F.O. 65/46, and enclosure to no. 32, 19 May 1800, F.O. 65/47). His impressions and experience of this critical period may be followed in his nos. 13, 16–21 to Grenville, 6 March–2 April 1800 (F.O. 65/46); his recall, communicated to him on 2 April, had in fact been intimated as early as February (Paul to Vorontsov, 1 February (O.S.), received 29 March (loc. cit.)). Cf. p. 206 above for his earlier comparative personal success with the Tsar, which declined when he unwisely took a mistress who was involved with the party out of favour at Court.

But what of Britain's own contribution, more directly under Government's control? The 'immense effort' foreseen in the late autumn[1] was shrinking fast in the new year. The plan for the outright attack on Brest was already losing ground to a prior occupation of an island or coastal point; probably of Belleisle, off Quiberon, possibly of a strip within that bay.[2] Now that smaller project, suggested by émigrés and never very promising, was ruled out. Belleisle remained Pitt's last recourse, though without high hopes of the sequel, in preference to larger and cloudier ideas. A reconnaissance was set on foot in mid January.[3] But the only result was a further shrinkage of acceptable effort: a recommendation to seize the islets of Houat and Hedic – an even more dismal reminder of 1795 – as a preliminary to the preliminary capture of the larger island.[4] When this depressing report was swiftly followed by the royalists' final collapse in the Vendée, little remained of the strategy as presented at the start. Some hopes remained of Viomenisl's intervention farther south.[5] But these vanished with the knowledge at the end of March that the Tsar was withdrawing the necessary troops.

By then indeed it seemed that Ministers had virtually abandoned large ambitions for western France. Any plans for co-operation in a Biscay assault had perforce been tentative; and in fact one benefit from a Russian operation there was seen as a means of strengthening the British force in Minorca.[6] For that option had been rising in favour, and not only because of the difficulties elsewhere. While insurgency was fizzling out in the Vendée, William Wickham was at his old work of organising it in eastern and southern France. He was laying plans, of which he had his hopes, for the Vosges, the Dauphiné, Lyon, and the coast of Provence; and if these were to bear fruit, in an area lying athwart communications with Italy, they should be aided by arms at least and supplies from the Mediterranean fleet. More potently however they might also offer a possible sphere for British intervention, as the risings in the north-west had seemed likely to do. When the Government, always responsive to Wickham, learned of Austrian

1. See p. 325 above.
2. P. 326 above.
3. Mackesy, op. cit., 66–7; Pitt to Dundas, 11 January 1800 (Stanhope, III, 208–9). Grey and St Vincent (see p. 326 above) were not prepared in the event to advise on any specific operation farther afield, either on the Spanish Atlantic coast or (a rather unenthusiastic speculation of Pitt's) in the area of the Somme to the Seine so as to threaten Paris itself. Grey in particular remained deeply sceptical of direct involvement with the royalists – 'It is Rotten Ground, And Mr Pitt and Mr Dundas must not entangle themselves with it' (to Huskisson, 9 January 1800; B.L. Add. Ms 38736).
4. Mackesy, op. cit., 81–2. Cf. II, 576 for 1795. The reconnaissance was carried out under Thomas Maitland, whom we have met in the West Indies and briefly in Flanders (pp. 144, 257, n3 above), now a Major-General and brought more closely into the orbit of these successive plans.
5. See p. 349 above.
6. Cf. pp. 327–8 above.

intentions in January, the attractions of the southern theatre became the more highly marked.[1]

On 22 February a decision was taken. The Cabinet agreed to send to Minorca 'a body of British troops to co-operate with the Austrians or the Royalists in the South of France'.[2] The reinforcement was to consist of 'at least' 15,000 men; and General Stuart, returning at once to his command from a stay in England, was to consult with Wickham and the Austrians in the course of an overland route.[3] The preparations were put in train, and by mid March the Admiralty and the Ordnance had found the resources for a first convoy to transport a third of the force. But as the demands of a more substantial expedition came under more detailed review, the military authorities began to raise doubts, reinforcing the growing unease which their Secretary of State himself felt over large-scale contested seaborne assaults. And there was an even more critical weakness, all too often neglected by the makers of policy, on which George III remarked at once when he received the Cabinet's Minute. 'I trust', he warned – and it was not for the first time – 'attention will be had to the real state of our forces, not to falacious [*sic*] states on paper'.[4] The implications were in fact spelt out by his son as Commander-in-Chief, in a detailed paper stressing the consequences for home defence and Ireland and the regions beyond Europe.[5] Circulated to Ministers, it placed the case in a perspective with which, as a body, they were not regularly supplied,[6] and some of them at least began to have second thoughts. Windham and then, more sharply, Chatham – both with good claims for concern – called for a further meeting, and that took place on 21 March.[7] York's 'numbers' were debated; but nothing was 'professed' to be settled. In the end the despatch of the first convoy seems to have been approved, while arrangements were 'suspended' for a second and third.[8]

---

1. Wickham's plans may be followed in F.O. 74/25, 28; and see also his *Correspondence*, II, 355–7. For his influence in London see p. 321 and n3 above, and also Grenville to Wickham, 8 February 1800 (*H.M.C., Dropmore*, VI, 120). A possible hint of Austrian co-operation had been received as early as 1 December 1799 (Minto to Grenville, no. 43; see p. 329, n6 above); and see pp. 345–6 above for January 1800.

2. These were George III's words, on 22 February, replying to a Cabinet Minute relayed by Dundas which itself seems not to have survived. The date and hour of the King's letter, and one from the Duke of York, also to Dundas, on 28 February, suggest strongly that the meeting was on the 22nd; see *L.C.G. III*, III, nos. 2112, 2113.

3. York to Dundas, 28 February, ibid; Mackesy, op. cit., 75. See p. 152 above for an earlier visit by Stuart to England.

4. To Dundas, 22 February 1800, as in n2 above.

5. York to same, 28 February 1800, as in n3 above.

6. The paper was addressed to the Secretary of State, 'for His Majesty's information'. But York sent it out 'in circulation' (*Diary of Windham*, 422, for 19 March); on whose instructions or initiative I do not know.

7. See op. cit., 422, for 21 March for himself and Chatham; Pitt to Grenville, nd but 20 March (*H.M.C., Dropmore*, VI, 170), for the Minister's response. Windham of course was Secretary at War, Chatham a Major-General.

8. *Diary of Windham*, 422.

The deferment was intended to be only for the moment, and momentarily this proved to be so. The circumstances were undeniably difficult, when the Russians had still to pronounce on the fate of their troops in England, and the Austrians to specify more exactly how Britain could best assist their campaign. The prospect, however, of some easing in the latter case at least became providentially evident, for a despatch was received from Vienna on the 22nd in which Thugut, displaying 'impatience' to know the British plans for the Mediterranean, hinted that Russian troops might be allowed to march to Genoa after all if their means of supply were under British control.[1] This undoubtedly affected and may have swayed opinion in London, and on the 26th the Cabinet, summoned afresh, 'settled' the expedition. The remaining 10,000 men were to be embarked with their supplies, and Stuart himself was to leave as soon as he could.[2]

So matters, it might seem, were back where they had been before a brief interruption. But it soon became clear that Austrian and Russian determinants had not yet run their course. In the next few days it was known that the Tsar was going to remove his force from England, and thereby any chance or need to co-operate with his Biscay operation.[3] This development might be held, according to taste, to reinforce or to detract from the Mediterranean option. Over the following fortnight however there came much more disturbing news. Thugut's correspondence with Talleyrand, following the tone and date of the Austrian reply to Bonaparte, was already causing some perturbation, which was not allayed by Minto's assurance that he had at last been shown what was going on.[4] It was now suddenly deepened by what appeared to be an ominous change of mood. Thugut was disinclined to answer when asked if Austria, instead of Russia, would co-operate with the British and the royalists in southern France; and he protested strongly at the ways in which British diplomats were countering Austria's interests in 'all the Courts of Europe'. Perhaps these were ploys to gain extra funds, and easier acceptance of his wishes for Piedmont; and the first in any case reflected the Allies' divergencies in their intentions for France herself.[5] But

1. Minto to Grenville, no. 7, 23 February 1800, received 22 March (P.R.O., F.O. 7/58).

2. Since this could be regarded as simply repeating an earlier decision, it seems unlikely that a fresh Minute on the subject was composed, although Windham (cf. p. 351 above) gave notice that he would 'enter a minute of dissent' – a most unusual proceeding if in fact he did so; cf. II, 555. A letter to ? Portland of 31 March (B.L. Add. Ms 37845) sets out his case. Windham's *Diary*, 422, for 26 and 27 March, and Jupp, *Lord Grenville*, 250 (giving the final settlement as falling on the 27th, where Windham regards that as merely confirming the result of the day before), specify the date; Grenville's Private letter to Minto of the 28th (*H.M.C., Dropmore*, VI, 186) suggests the effect of the Austrians' influence.

3. See p. 349 above.

4. See p. 346 above; Minto to Grenville, no. 9, 9 March 1800, received on the 22nd (F.O. 7/58). Grenville's no. 12, probably of 14 March (loc. cit.), disclosed his dissatisfaction with the reply to Bonaparte.

5. Minto to Grenville, nos. 13, 14 of 23, 24 March 1800, received 8 April (F.O. 7/58). Minto suspected a ploy in the first instance, and instanced St Petersburg, Berlin, Florence and Turin in the second.

perhaps he was returning to something uncomfortably like his old stance. There was moreover a fresh complication, for it appeared by a report from Wickham that the Austrians had allowed their strength in Germany to become dangerously low.[1] In concentrating on Italy – initially to British satisfaction – their numbers for the Rhine had fallen to a broad equality with the French, at a time when Bonaparte was known to be assembling in addition a central army of reserve. Vienna's main demand on London was shifting accordingly. Diversions in areas familiar from the last campaign were coming into favour once more.

All this was thoroughly disquieting for an expedition soon about to sail as part of a concentration around France's southern flank. It fuelled Grenville's reviving scepticism of the real extent of Austria's will-power.[2] More to the point, it could not but intensify Dundas's rising apprehensions, which indeed had already reached a point where they could no longer be contained. Increasingly unhappy at the drift of events and the planning process itself, the Secretary for War now decided to challenge the whole cast of strategic thought. Even before the new reports reached him to support him in his opinion, he circulated a long paper to his colleagues at the end of March.[3]

IV

Dundas's memorandum is one of distinct interest and importance, on several counts: as a culmination of the doubts which he had been experiencing over the past five years; in the form of his particular answer, and its place in a longer perspective; in his method, leading to his subsequent tactics, of trying to reconcile an open change of emphasis with the still inescapable commitments of the policy he opposed. The second aspect, which lay at the heart of the case, will be discussed in a wider context later.[4] The immediate effect of the document was to open a further period of indecision, initially in what turned out to be a significant time, and to expose the bitterest disagreement on strategy within the inner circle in the course of the war.

The argument was based on two propositions: first, as Dundas wrote to Spencer at the Admiralty, that we had long 'calculated beyond our means'

1. The message, dated 29 March, was received 4 April 1800 (F.O. 74/28). Cf. p. 330 above for the prospective Austrian strengths earlier notified to Britain.

2. For which see eg Grenville to Minto, Private, 28 March 1800 (*H.M.C., Dropmore*, VI, 186).

3. 'Memorandom for the Consideration of His Majesty's Ministers', 31 March 1800. Pitt's copy, with a few marginalia by himself and Grenville, is in P.R.O. 30/8/243, ff. 88–107. A letter from Dundas to Chatham, whom he clearly regarded as a possible supporter, shows his rising worry and discontent a week before (22 March 1800; copy in B.L. Add. Ms 40102).

4. In Ch. XII, section V below.

in aiming at 'extensive operations' in areas where the enemy could count on considerable strength; and secondly that we were addicted to the habit of 'taking up only one point at a time' when 'we ought to take the whole under our view'.[1] That 'whole' could not be confined to the Continent. It embraced the balance of considerations 'essential to the permanent Interests of Great Britain, whatever may be the ultimate result of the present extraordinary Convulsion in Europe'. Those interests, it was 'obvious', were founded on the nation's resources derived from a world-wide commerce and indissolubly united with naval power. We should accordingly look always to our overseas markets, and extend them where possible in an age of upheaval induced not only by the immediate changes of war. There were limits likely to be set in future in Europe, North America and even in India. But one region of the globe offered a fresh and exciting prospect. 'The South American Market . . . of late has pressed itself on my Consideration with unremitting Force'. Its extent could be 'unbounded'; Spain's hold on her Empire was visibly weakening; and given our strength at sea, and the chance to deliver a coup de grâce, a diversion of military effort there could secure our position. That, Dundas hastened to add, should not involve 'extensive Conquest, or the Acquisition of Colonial Dominion' – experience farther north remained a cautionary memory even when applied to a very different case.[2] Any influence or intervention in 'forms of government' which might come our way with Spain's demise should follow strictly from 'the habits of Commercial Intercourse'. But we should recognise that the time had now come to seize our opportunity, for the position in Europe was showing ever more clearly that 'we cannot take a direct part in the Military Operations . . ., and can only act indirectly and collaterally with our Continental Allies'.

If that was accepted, it followed that we could have military resources to spare. Dundas proposed four points of attack designed to secure points of entry to a 'gradual' but 'permanent' pattern of trade: New Orleans, the Plate and the Orinoco on the Atlantic seaboard, and Concepción in Chile on the Pacific. At the same time it would be desirable to capture Tenerife in the Canaries, to service communications with our 'distant Possessions in every Part of the World'. He was of course well aware that this robust exposition of a blue-water strategy[3] could not 'expect . . . full Approbation' at a moment of intensive planning for the forthcoming Allied campaign; and the forces required were tailored to allow for a concept of 'collateral' action there. Twelve to fifteen thousand men should suffice for the first three South American operations, with an expedition from India and the Cape – the numbers not given – for the fourth, and some of the troops for the former would be West Indian native

1. 31 March 1800; *Private Correspondence of Spencer*, III, 324–5.
2. Cf. I, 159, 406, 420.
3. Cf. II, 347–8; pp. 143–5 above.

354

levies.[1] But what of the rest; and what about Tenerife? Here Dundas moved onto delicate ground. He was not going to risk outright rejection by directly opposing the full quota destined for the Mediterranean. Rather, he stressed the accepted uncertainties relating to that expedition, and proposed that if its size proved excessive a part could be sent to the Canaries, its residue proceeding thence when its work was done, perhaps via Jamaica, to attack New Orleans. He was clearly hoping that no more than 5,000 of the 15,000 need remain in European waters; and if the whole reinforcement turned out to be superfluous a further 3–4,000 could be sent, via Trinidad,[2] to the Orinoco, leaving a shortage of 4,000 or less for the Plate, to be supplied from England direct. This was virtually ruling out a British involvement in the southern Continental front. Turning closer to home, he suggested that 9,000 men should be used to capture Belleisle, with perhaps 5,000 forming a garrison; and – the latest twist in a now familiar story – that a separate force of 5,000 should attack Walcheren in Holland, supported by a Dutch émigré force. Dundas reckoned on some 23,600 British infantry in England available for foreign service by early June. Allowing 9,600 for Ireland and some minor necessaries, that would meet his favoured requirements (particularly on his lowest forecast for the Mediterranean) while catering for the diversions which Austria might want in north-west Europe, themselves perhaps exploitable farther from the surplus in Belleisle.[3]

Such a set of proposals, by one of the principal executants of war policy,[4] could not but heighten the uncertainty of the debate. The Cabinet met once more, on 5 April, and while no change resulted the uneasiness and sense of suspended judgment was underlined. Camden now advised Pitt to cancel the Mediterranean expedition, and Dundas, still ostensibly playing for time, brought the Minister to agree reluctantly that the bulk of the force, not yet embarked, should be held until Stuart reported on his meeting with Wickham.[5] The receipt of Minto's

1. One element of this design, an attack on Buenos Aires and the Plate, was familiar from 1796 (see II, 634). But it had then been raised in a different context, and was soon dropped (p. 143 above).

2. See ibid.

3. Figures to the nearest hundred for the total and for Ireland. A fortnight later he gave further details in a long explanation to the sympathetic Chatham (12 April 1800; and see p. 353, n3 above).

A statement of the numbers in Britain on 2 April apart from those earmarked for the Mediterranean, in Grenville's papers (*H.M.C., Dropmore*, VI, 188–9), suggests on the one hand that these calculations were optimistic but on the other that 10,000 additional men would become available in the summer as some drafts were due home from overseas and some formations returned from Ireland.

4. Cf. II, 531–2.

5. For which see p. 351 above. *Diary of Windham*, 423; unsigned paper, placed under Camden and misdated 6 April 1799, in Pitt's files (P.R.O. 30/8/119); Dundas to Grenville, 9 April 1800 (*H.M.C., Dropmore*, VI, 193), referring to a conversation on 'Tuesday', which was the 7th. He had also managed to induce Grenville to hold his latest despatches for Wickham and possibly for Minto (ibid; and see same to same, 10 April 1800, op. cit., 194).

despatches on the 8th[1] encouraged him to plunge for his real aim. On the 15th he urged Pitt to abandon the convoys for 10,000 men, leaving only the first 5,000 to proceed to Minorca. Grenville for his part was not prepared finally to oppose this recommendation. The general mood may well have been setting in its favour; Dundas was departmentally responsible;[2] he himself was depressed by Thugut's behaviour, and also dismayed by the successive postponements and some doubts now raised about certain supplies which it had been assumed the Austrians would provide. The Cabinet was summoned again, and on 19 April agreed to act as the Secretary for War wished.[3]

That conclusion however was not reached without an angry exchange with Grenville. For while the Foreign Secretary did not dig in, he was far from approving the administrative preparations or – ignoring the wider setting – Dundas's alternative European plan. He had warned earlier of the need to settle supplies with the Austrians,[4] and he claimed now to have no fear of their response so long as they remained in the war. He dismissed the strength proposed for Belleisle and Walcheren as grossly exaggerated, and in any case would prefer an assault on Bordeaux, where there was a royalist movement still in being despite the fiasco in 1799.[5] But above all he wanted action in some form or other soon.

> Do this [Belleisle and Walcheren], or anything else that you prefer, but for God's sake, for your own honour, and for the cause in which we are engaged, do not let us, after having by immense exertions collected a fine army, leave it unemployed, gaping after messengers from Genoa, Augsburg, and Vienna, till the moment for acting is irrecoverably past by.[6]

It was an extreme example of the Grenvillean style. Not unnaturally, it roused the recipient. Dundas replied at once, rebutting the criticism of his measures; but if he thought that was the end of the matter he was mistaken. Grenville wrote back, sarcastically, to ask for replies 'on paper' to some specific questions, since his colleague's plan, if rightly understood,

1. P. 352 and n5 above.
2. See Grenville to Pitt, 11 April 1800 (P.R.O. 30/8/140) – a fact which Dundas himself would be able to exploit (see p. 367 below).
3. *H.M.C., Dropmore*, VI, 197, 194; *Diary of Windham*, 423.
4. Mackesy, op. cit., 93 & n44.
5. For which see p. 226 above.
6. To Dundas, 10 April 1800 (partly printed in Holland Rose, *Pitt and Napoleon*, 266–8). The tone became even more contemptuous in the unprinted paragraphs that followed (see P.R.O. 30/8/140), and the call for action itself can hardly have pleased a man who seven weeks before had 'become truly uneasy' at 'the backwardness ... with regard to the chance of acting offensively in any quarter of the world' and was trying to establish the latest state of resources with the Admiralty and with York (see Dundas to Spencer, 1 March 1800; *Private Papers of Spencer*, III, 323).

was 'utterly impracticable'. Dundas responded with spirit, declining to do any such thing, and both Secretaries thereupon sent the letters to Pitt, Grenville expressing surprise that Dundas was apparently offended, Dundas wishing that Grenville 'would exercise his genius for two Months in executing as well as planning'.[1] With that, the tension seems to have somewhat subsided. Dundas had his way, Grenville complied, and their continuing correspondence, while still in disagreement, reverted more closely to its normal tone.[2]

Nonetheless, Dundas in particular was badly upset. Grenville, as on one earlier occasion, preferred to write rather than to meet,[3] and his manner, though carried here to its height, was not unfamiliar. He was exasperated, particularly since the messengers were waiting to carry his despatches announcing the disposition of forces for the imminent campaign. But his colleague was in worse state. For robust as he was, of long political experience, accustomed to the weight of high responsibilities, Dundas was now finding the burden almost insupportable. He seems indeed to have been – he certainly thought himself – near the end of his tether. In the midst of the discussions in April, he tried to set a date for resignation from the post he had never wanted, and from that of Treasurer of the Navy as well.[4] The beginning of October seemed to him suitable, when the campaign in the Mediterranean should be 'over' or at any rate solidly established, and with that in mind he pressed the matter hard.[5] Pitt however was obdurate, as always on this subject; so far in fact from obliging, he elicited a 'promise' that his colleague would not leave before the end of the war. And the promise was confirmed soon after, in a mournful account from Dundas of his wife's feelings and her final despairing acceptance of what he had done. He would stay. He only begged to be released if Pitt saw an earlier opening 'with your own perfect approbation'.[6]

1. Dundas to Grenville, 10 April 1800 (*H.M.C., Dropmore*, VI, 194); Grenville to Dundas, 11 April 1800 (Holland Rose, op. cit., 268–9); Dundas to Grenville, unsigned but in his hand, sd (P.R.O. 30/8/140); Grenville to Pitt, sd (Holland Rose, op. cit., 269–70); Dundas to same, sd (P.R.O. 30/8/157). Dundas seems to have sent all the correspondence, via Huskisson; Grenville to have enclosed Dundas's letters.

2. Grenville to Dundas, 15, 17 April (B.L. Add. Ms 40101), 23 April 1800 (*H.M.C., Dropmore*, VI, 200); Dundas to Grenville, 16 April (B.L. Add. Ms 40101), 20 April 1800 (*H.M.C., Dropmore*, VI, 199).

3. Cf. pp. 247 above.

4. See II, 411–13; I, 131. Under the added influence of his disagreement at the time with the King (p. 319, n5 above), he had indeed tried briefly to be 'relieved of . . . the War Department' in December 1799 (*L.C.G. III*, III, no. 2087 and n1).

5. To Pitt, 8, 10 April 1800, referring to a conversation on the 8th (B.L. Add. Ms 40102). In the sometimes imprecise way that irritated Grenville, he wrote (on the 10th) 'when the campaign, or at least its preparations, are over'.

6. Same to same, 14 April 1800 (P.R.O. 30/8/157). The letter is a sad one to read. Lady Jane Dundas had broken down at the news. She saw him properly only twice a year, for 'a fortnight' at Walmer (see p. 88 above) and a month when they went north for Christmas; his spirits and temper were badly 'affected' by the ever increasing weight of business; and, as he confessed, he had 'lost the talent of sound Sleep'.

The plea was heartfelt; the submission to duty and friendship complete.

V

The whole episode had been revealing: in bringing to a point and into the open Dundas's strategic preferences; in thereby forcing to the surface a growing sense of strain, intellectual but also temperamental, between himself and Grenville; in underlining once more his deep loyalty – both respectful and protective – to Pitt. It was also more widely significant, giving a damaging blow to the unity, preserved in essentials hitherto, of the triumvirate which had been running this testing war for seven years. It may indeed have marked a new phase in that set of relationships. But at least, one might have presumed, a final verdict had been reached on the immediate future,[1] and after two frustrating months that had come just in time.

The presumption would have been wrong. There were shifts in policy still to come, culminating in June in two changes of mind and an upset of the second within the space of two weeks. The cause remained the same: a dependence on Continental developments which then governed decisions on British operations whether co-operative in the south or with independent forces in the north. For one must bear in mind that the two possibilities were not mutually distinct, and remember, as one follows the Ministry's attempts to come to terms with the former, that the latter were designed to absorb at least equal strength, and now rather more. With the cancellation of the bulk of the Mediterranean expedition, the assault on Brittany should become the Allies' main second front.[2]

One would scarcely however have divined this intention from the pace of the ensuing efforts. In April and May the preparations for north-west France were not conspicuous for their speed. The all too familiar delays arose, postponing the attack to early June: a landing on Houat and Hedic, to be followed by the capture of Belleisle, to be followed at some point by a reinforced landing on the mainland itself. As the weeks passed, Pitt became despondent. No one seemed able to stir the military: the transports were short of landing craft, the troops, of varying quality, not fully ready in England and Ireland. When part of the Brest fleet compounded the anxiety by escaping to sea late in May, possibly to head for the

---

L.C.G. III, III, 343n5 summarises the arrangements of offices envisaged, with their financial consequences, if Dundas retained only the salaried post of President of the Board of Control for India (see I, 464) and acquired the post for life of Lord Privy Seal of Scotland, which had just become vacant.

1. Dundas himself indeed was at work on detailed strengths for Europe as early as 12 April (to Chatham, Secret; P.R.O. 30/8/368).
2. Cf. p. 355. An operation moreover to be supplemented possibly by Dundas's proposed smaller attack on Holland, ibid.

Mediterranean, he thought of reverting to the earlier abandoned plans. The design for Brittany was 'so wretchedly backward', the 'exertions . . . so languid', that he doubted if anything could be done there 'to influence the fate of the campaign'.[1] But the ships returned to port, the first British battalions at last got under way, Houat was occupied, and on 15 June the commanders, Maitland[2] and the naval captain Pellew, decided to strike on the 19th with some 4,200 men at Belleisle. This resolve was immediately followed by an Atlantic storm. The operation had to be cancelled, and was then put off further in answer to intelligence from the French resistance that the garrison was stronger than had been foreseen. The information proved to be wrong, as Maitland himself in fact had suspected. But he was not prepared to take a risk that Ministers might well not support,[3] and the assault force, which had been embarked, settled on Houat once more. A further two and a half months had passed since the Cabinet opted for the northern diversion. The first attempt had failed; but worse, by that time its original purpose was largely removed.

The whole pattern of a relevant strategy indeed was by then unravelling. For another event had fallen meanwhile on this sequence of confusion and mischance. Every aspect of British planning now seemed to be going awry; and in the spring the remains of the Mediterranean expedition suffered a change of commander, for late in April Stuart resigned. Never easy as a colleague or subordinate, and probably in declining health, he was already embroiled in disputes over supplies and staff. Those difficulties were resolved; but when he received his orders for the reduced force, he refused to accept them in one important respect. His objects had always included the possible capture of Malta, still under blockade since the aftermath of the battle of the Nile,[4] and with the alteration of priorities this was now placed high on the list. It had to be borne in mind however that the Tsar had an interest, acknowledged by the Allies, in the Order of the Knights, and had been assured that they would be restored, under his protection, at some point when the French were expelled. Dundas himself had once been far from averse to a Russian presence in the central basin. But now somewhat disturbed, as were his colleagues, by naval activities in the Ionian Sea, and suspicious of Paul's intentions, he wanted the island firmly secured. It should be occupied solely by Stuart's troops. To Grenville however this was not a question worth the risk of further alienating an uncertain but still desirable

1. To Grenville, 1 June 1800 (*H.M.C., Dropmore*, VI, 242). Grenville's own reaction to the sortie (to Minto, 3 June; op. cit., 243) shows the extent of the alarm.

2. See p. 350, n4 above.

3. In his defence, he was commanding a force of very mixed quality, and knew furthermore that Ministers had been much impressed by a *chouan* leader, Georges Cadoudal, known as 'General Georges', who had escaped to London, was now back in the area, and relayed the information. In all the circumstances, Maitland was in fact (as Pellew recognised) in a difficult position.

4. See pp. 151 above.

ally,[1] and Stuart was accordingly instructed to admit a Russian garrison if one was sent in due course. He declined to accept the order, and had perforce to be superseded. His successor was Abercromby, summoned to an overseas command once more, with the seizure of Malta named as his first object. He set sail in mid May; but, unlucky as ever, was promptly forced to put back by a gale.[2] While he was heading south after the delay, decisive events were taking place.

For Bonaparte was on the move. It had been known since the early spring that he was assembling an army of reserve at Dijon, though whether he could command in person, as First Consul, was not clear. The Austrians were confident that the French force would not be strong enough to upset their operations from Germany and Switzerland, the area which Wickham likewise thought would be the scene (as was in fact first intended) of the main attack. It was on this premiss that he urged a British concentration on north-west Europe.[3] But a month later, while he clung to his forecast, he reversed his plea. By then indeed the French campaign had opened, and in fact, as he expected, on the German front, where their forces on the upper Rhine had pushed the Austrians into Bavaria. This seemed to reinforce the estimate that their army of reserve would be deployed to attack the rear. But if so, Wickham now suspected, the move might be aimed at communications with Italy, cutting off the Austrian army in the south, so important to Allied success and a French insurrection, from immediate reinforcements and indeed from its base. Help therefore might well be needed, to augment Austrian strength and intensify a threat in turn to southern France. Britain, he stressed, should send all possible aid to the Mediterranean.[4]

This message was received on 19 May. It came too late, in Pitt's and Dundas's view, to rearrange the current dispositions; Abercromby was allowed an extra two battalions and that was all.[5] But as news continued to

1. See Dundas to Grenville, 29 March, 10 April 1800 (*H.M.C., Dropmore*, VI, 187, 199); Grenville to Dundas, 9, 15 April 1800 (B.L. Add. Ms 40101). Cf. pp. 328 and n3, 348–9 above for Dundas's attitude earlier to a Russian presence in the central Mediterranean, and 348, n2 above for developments farther east. His thoughts for Malta on the eve of the Cabinet's agreement to reduce the expedition emerge in his letter to Chatham of 12 April 1800 (for which see p. 355, n3 above), and one to Grenville of the 16th (B.L. Add. Ms 40101).

2. Cf. II, 597. As Grenville, who was no admirer of the General, remarked, 'If I were a seaman, with half the superstition that belongs to them, I should certainly throw him overboard as a second Jonas' (to Wickham, 20 May 1800; *H.M.C., Dropmore*, VI, 233).

3. Cf. pp. 321, 325 above.

4. Wickham to Grenville, 8 May (F.O. 74/30); same to same, Most Confidential, sd (*H.M.C., Dropmore*, VI, 213). Minto, the other source of information, was almost wholly occupied in April with the arrangements for financial support and in reading Thugut's diplomatic intentions.

5. See Pitt to Grenville, 19 May, Dundas to same, 20 May 1800 (*H.M.C., Dropmore*, VI, 232, 236). 'I don't think', the latter wrote, 'our friend Wickham always recollects that it is not so easy to move an army as it is to write a despatch'.

come in, the prospect became more ominous. The Austrians, whose campaign in Italy had opened promisingly in April,[1] remained largely unmoved by the reverses farther north. Nor were they greatly perturbed by uncertain reports of the movements of the army of reserve. No more was heard immediately from Wickham, and Minto's despatches from Vienna echoed the complacency.[2] Towards the end of May, however, it seemed that the enemy was crossing the Alps in force; the Austrian General Melas in Italy was warned a week later, information reached London at the beginning of June, and the fact, though not all the detail, was soon confirmed. Bonaparte, in person, was indeed on his way, to be supplemented by strong elements from the German front. The Austrians had been fooled: Italy was the real target, and its former conqueror was fast approaching the Lombard plain. There was still little gloom in Vienna; rather, confidence in the outcome. But British intentions were once more thrown into disarray. Dundas in particular took fright. The chief opponent of the Mediterranean expedition now suddenly reversed his views. By 8 June he was calling for the despatch of 'not less' than an extra 4,000 'effective and good men', and on the 10th, after consulting Pitt, he circulated a paper to the Cabinet. The additional strength would give Abercromby some 10,000 men in all, to reinforce Minorca and assist the Austrians; and the King should be advised that such a force ought to be immediately approved.[3] His colleagues eventually agreed in principle apart from Windham, who argued that the troops would arrive too late;[4] and when it was learned that Maitland had cancelled his assault on Belleisle, the Secretary for War, with Pitt's approval, ordered him to sail at once for the Mediterranean with his transports and his own 4,000 troops.

This last was a bold move. The King had not yet even been informed.[5] And it soon turned out that he did not agree. It would be wise, he objected, to wait at least a few days until there was clearer information on

1. P. 347 above.

2. See P.R.O., F.O. 7/58, *passim* for May.

3. Dundas to Grenville, 8 June 1800 (*H.M.C., Dropmore*, VI, 246); 'Memo', 10 June 1800 (B.L. Add. Ms 40102). Pitt himself had still been wavering after the French ships returned to Brest (pp. 358–9 above); 'rather inclined . . . to a certain extent' towards the Mediterranean, but not enough to decide at once (to Grenville, 2 June 1800; *H.M.C., Dropmore*, VI, 242). The more definite news would seem now to have moved him.

4. Windham's 'Note put in circulation', 11 June 1800 (B.L. Add. Ms 37879; and see also his diary for that day and 16 June in 37924). He had already complained that he was not being kept properly informed of current dealings with the royalists (to Pitt, 5 June 1800; Dacres Adams Mss, formerly P.R.O. 30/58/3).

Some of the Cabinet were worried – according to Dundas, unnecessarily – about the implications for shipping (see Dundas to George III, 16 June 1800; *L.C.G. III*, III, no. 2171).

5. Mackesy, op. cit., 111. And, for good measure, Abercromby was instructed at the same time to apply all his 10,000 men to aiding the Austrians, in whatever manner might emerge.

The sudden switch to Maitland's decidedly patchy force was hardly likely, one must note, to provide the 'effective and good' contingent which had been in view (cf. p. 359, n3 above).

Italy before deciding to send so substantial a force.[1] The Cabinet of course had to be told of this opinion; and to heighten the awkwardness there had been no Minute from its recent meeting with which to bolster Dundas. On the 19th it withdrew its consent, in a Minute this time which ran counter to what he, and Pitt, had proposed.[2] Instead, Maitland was to have a further 6,000 men and the necessary equipment to besiege Belleisle, after which a force of some 20,000 should be assembled there (taking almost all the regular army from Ireland), 'to support the royalists or to distract the operations and attention of the enemy'. The expedition against Holland was also confirmed. This seemed therefore to be the final answer to the problem of how, as the Minute put it, 'in the present critical situation . . . on the Continent to place the whole of the disposable force of this Kingdom . . . to produce an effect'. Even so, at such a late juncture, the tale was not yet told. Dundas's order to sail for the Mediterranean reached Maitland on 22 June. Since the transports were to hand, he embarked the troops under a subordinate officer and they left at once. The King and the Cabinet had been overset in part by unusually swift communications and action. Abercromby was in train after all to receive a further 4,000 men, and southern operations with Austria might still be alive.

But the departure came too late for its purpose. Bonaparte had crossed the Great St Bernard Pass late in May, and was down the Val d'Aosta with 30,000 men before the end of the month. Moving with his usual speed he entered Milan on 2 June, whence he turned south-west to confront the Austrians. The two armies met on the 14th at Marengo, a hamlet near Alessandria. The battle opened badly for the French, taken tactically by surprise, and indeed Melas prematurely announced a victory to Vienna. But, saved by the skin of his teeth on one of the most critical days of his life, it was the First Consul who emerged to report victory to Paris. Next day an armistice was signed. The Austrians were to evacuate Piedmont, Liguria and Lombardy west of the river Mincio, and withdraw their garrisons from Tuscany and Ancona. Their strategy for Italy was destroyed at least for the immediate future; and who could tell if in fact they would remain in the war? One thing seemed sure in London, when the news arrived on 24 June. There was no room now for co-operation with Abercromby's troops. Austria was on the defensive, confined in effect to Germany and Switzerland, and British strategy must bow to the fact.

1. See Mackesy, op. cit., 112 & n40 for George III to Dundas, 17 June 1800.
2. There are copies in B.L. Add. Mss 59306 (Grenville) and 40102 (Dundas), and it is printed from the latter in *L.C.G. III*, III, p. 363n2.

CHAPTER XII

The Coalition in Collapse

I

The report of Marengo came as a bitter blow. It was hard in the first place not to reflect that things might have been different if the British reinforcements had been sent south in time. One could argue the blame for that; Grenville placed it retrospectively on the Austrians.[1] But in any case, what was likely to happen now? The reaction in London on the morrow was to expect Austria to make peace. Pitt himself as usual put a brave face on misfortune, and it was indeed hard to gauge the odds: Minto could give no clear idea, though he thought that a negotiation might come before the end of the campaigning season, while Wickham maintained that the Emperor's 'real strength' remained untouched.[2] Grenville's expectations however were low, and his colleagues seem to have shared them; at any rate the Cabinet's initial response, while resolved to adhere 'steadfastly' to full co-operation, was to provide for that equally in any Austrian peace talks, which should then be 'general', if the co-peration could no longer be obtained in war. The intention at this point, it should be noted – the word 'general' itself – were directed to this specific situation. An Austrian armistice was perforce accepted, and that might have to extend to her withdrawal from the war. There was no need at such a moment for further implications to be fully considered, or in such an event for them to be spelt out. The precautionary step was a reasonable one in order to protect British interests. At the same time, if sent to Minto in Vienna as was intended, the message might encourage the peace party there; and George III, who fastened on that point, was distinctly upset, particularly when the exact extent of the defeat was not yet clear. Nevertheless his Ministers, to his displeasure, persisted.[3] Meanwhile they had to review their plans on the basis that the Alliance would fight on, and the Coalition itself continue to exist.

1. To Minto, 19 August 1800 (*H.M.C., Dropmore*, VI, 300). He had in mind Thugut's delays in agreeing to the treaty of alliance (see pp. 347, 352–3 above).
2. Minto to Grenville, 28 June 1800; Wickham to same, sd (op. cit., 257–8). Pitt bore the news, according to Rose, 'with Fortitude' – 'my Feelings for him personally', the devoted official went on, 'contributed very greatly to weigh me down on first hearing' (to Pretyman, 25 June 1800; Pretyman Ms 435/44).
3. Cabinet Minute, 26 June 1800 (B.L. Add. Ms 59306); correspondence of Grenville and George III, 27, 28 June 1800 (*L.C.G. III*, III, no. 2181); Grenville to Minto, no. 24, 27

One decision, founded on this latter hope, could be taken at once. Abercromby was specifically ordered to adhere to the 'original' understanding that Russia could garrison Malta after the island fell; and the Cabinet minuted moreover that Vorontsov should be so informed.[1] Dundas's concern for seapower was kept firmly in its place; the Foreign Secretary was guarding carefully all remaining links with the Tsar.

The largest immediate question however was that of the treaty, or Convention, with Austria herself. The two sides had been drawing closer through the usual bargaining over the past two months, and by mid June they seemed near the verge of agreement on finance and, in secret articles, the arrangements for Italy. Time was drawing uncomfortably short, for Ministers hoped that Parliament would rise after the Act of Union with Ireland was passed, hopefully at about the end of the month, and Grenville was urging Minto to bring Thugut to the point if Vienna was to gain ratification and start receiving its new funds.[2] The shadow of Marengo now hung over the completion of the task. What should be done about the articles on Italy, 'most of them become of little consequence' at least in the short term?[3] And would the financial provisions attract significantly greater opposition or doubts? In the event, the haste reinforced Austria's advantages. Minto gave up two contentious stipulations, for the Netherlands and a general commercial treaty, allowed those for Italy to stand, and on his own responsibility signed the Convention on 23 June. The document reached London on 12 July, was placed before the Commons on the 15th, ratified by the King on the 17th, and passed

---

June (P.R.O., F.O. 7/59), and Private and Secret, sd (*H.M.C., Dropmore*, VI, 256). The wording in the Minute was for a 'general peace only' and the intention was apparently to exclude 'an armistice' by Britain meanwhile (see Windham's *Diary* for 16, 17 June, 429). The Foreign Secretary's hopes of some recovery in Italy did rise after the first shock (to Buckingham, 27 June 1800, Buckingham, III, 86); but not for long. See II, 626 for an earlier episode with the King of a not dissimilar nature.

1. Minute of 26 June (above). The otherwise possibly rather curious inclusion of this item gains strength from the fact that, notwithstanding the result of Stuart's objection (pp. 359–60 above), Dundas's instructions to Abercromby had left the question of a Russian garrison uncomfortably open (see P.R.O., W.O. 6/21) – a point made clear, or admitted, to Grenville only a week before the Cabinet meeting (19 June 1800; *H.M.C., Dropmore*, VI, 250). Exactly what the 'original' understanding over Malta had been was a question which would become of major importance in the next few months.

Vorontsov in point of fact had recently asked the Tsar for permission to retire, ostensibly on grounds of ill health, from a post in which he was having to convey instructions he increasingly disliked; and that had just been granted. He continued however to live and in the event to perform his duties in England – his name indeed is remembered in Woronzow Road and Almshouses in St John's Wood in London.

2. See pp. 346–7 above for the position at the beginning of May. The final phase is covered in Grenville's despatches in F.O. 7/58–9, and in Minto's which, shown of course to Pitt, were kept by him and survive in his papers in P.R.O. 30/8/339. The growing urgency is brought out in Grenville to Minto, 3, 20 (Private), 27 (Private and Secret) June 1800 (*H.M.C., Dropmore*, VI, 242–3, 251, 256). Cf. p. 193 above for Ireland.

3. Pitt to Grenville, 4 July 1800 (*H.M.C., Dropmore*, VI, 262).

through the House with a vote of credit the next day.[1] Grenville still hoped to exclude the secret articles from the Emperor's ratification. But he failed, and taken all round Thugut obtained much of what he needed: his £2 million, and much of the backing he sought if northern Italy could be regained.

The extent of Austria's success turned on the apprehension in London of her loss. As the Opposition did not fail to point out, this was not an auspicious moment to seal a fresh connexion with an ally who might crack at any point.[2] But it was precisely the fear of such an event that actuated the British Government. Ministers were deeply anxious to prevent a unilateral withdrawal, and the most hopeful – the only – course to that end was to assist Austria's capacity for war while cementing her obligation not to negotiate a separate peace. As so often in fact, weakness profited where strength had met greater resistance. The first advance from the loan, to suit Thugut's wishes, was made in specie instead of bills of exchange, and Minto was instructed, following a further Cabinet, to accede to the armistice and if necessary to joint peace talks, and told further that in this latter case payments might be continued in order to strengthen the bargaining position.[3] Meanwhile the Government pursued its dual purpose, seeking a new treaty of defensive alliance, provided for in the Convention,[4] and all practicable means of fostering Austria's recovery and keeping her in the war.

Austria for her part made it quickly known that she could not fill an active role. The armistice signed in Italy was extended in mid July, after French advances in southern Germany, and this might have to lead to peace talks at some point. Nevertheless she did not sue for peace herself. The French were kept in play, following a further overture from Paris, and

1. The Convention was officially backdated to 20 June at Thugut's request (see Duffy, 'War Policy', 411, 412n1 for the possible reason), and appears as such in *The Consolidated Treaty Series*, 55, 235–45, where the French text of the public and secret articles is given. For the English text of the former alone, as shown to Parliament, see *inter alia P.H.*, XXXV, cols. 431–3. Minto's part, and his worries – not without cause, as Grenville's distinctly grudging response showed (no. 27, 17 July 1800; F.O. 7/58) – emerge in his despatch to Grenville, no. 36, 24 June 1800 (P.R.O. 30/8/339, where Wickham's letters to the Foreign Secretary for this period can also be found), and in a letter to Wickham, 25 June 1800 (*Life and Letters of Elliot*, III, 131–2). For the speed of communication to Parliament see Pitt to Grenville, 13 July (*H.M.C., Dropmore*, VI, 268) and same to George III, 14 July 1800 (*L.C.G. III*, III, no. 2192); for the subsequent proceedings, in the course of nine days, *P.R., 3rd ser.*, XII, between 379 and 575.

2. Tierney's speech, op. cit., 569–71.

3. Cabinet Minute, 16 July 1800, and correspondence between Grenville and George III, 16–17 July 1800 (*L.C.G. III*, III, no. 2193); Grenville to Minto, no. 27, 17 July 1800 (F.O. 7/59). The King remained unhappy.

Cf. p. 51 above for the remittance in specie. Such a transaction was uncommon, after the experiences of 1795–6 (see II, 524–5, 617–18). But it did at any rate have the merit of costing less than bills of exchange in commission and transfer charges (Duffy, loc. cit., 419n2, citing an account to the Treasury in Pitt's papers in P.R.O. 30/8/339).

4. By a secret article XI.

an emissary from Vienna in fact went so far as to sign a peace agreement there on his own. But the Emperor, while vacillating, disavowed it; he ratified the British Convention; and while the threat of peace talks continued, he kept in touch with London as the agreement required. The situation, not unnaturally, was shaky. The old divisions at Court were hardening, and the old resentment of Britain was taking a stronger hold. By the end of the summer Minto had to report that the 'jealousy, envy and indisposition towards the supposed monopoly of trade and specie enjoyed by England', long known indeed throughout Europe and fanned assiduously of course by France, now had 'complete possession of the Austrian people'.[1] Every point sought by London provoked 'a battle', with Thugut's opponents quite as much as himself, for the Foreign Minister, no great Anglophile but opposed to a second surrender to France, was now fighting for his influence and increasingly hard pressed. He managed to have the peace 'agreement' in Paris officially disavowed; to block the recall of the now openly pacific Archduke Charles; to hold, with growing difficulty, the Emperor's ear. He had indeed to threaten resignation in July. But still, in those summer months and somewhat surprisingly, the alliance held.

What could be done militarily to raise its morale; and equally to strengthen British interests themselves? The two, it could be represented, were not necessarily or diametrically opposed, for if joint peace talks had to be undertaken on Austria's behalf more might be salvaged for the one partner if the other could be shown to be improving its position. At the end of June Abercromby was on his way, a reinforcement was – inadvertently – following, sizeable forces were gathering to besiege a reputedly strong garrison in Belleisle, and others were in reserve for the assault on Holland.[2] Half of Maitland's detachment for the Mediterranean was now countermanded and returned to Houat, and Maitland himself was brought home for talks while Ministers reviewed the situation. For the moment the plans held good. But Dundas was thinking of 'several new ideas',[3] and towards the end of July he produced a new assessment.

The ideas strictly speaking were new in application rather than in essence. For they carried a stage farther those of his own last memorandum, in March;[4] and they already existed, as it were in embryo, in contingent orders and troop dispositions which had survived the rejection of his suggested main design. He had indeed continued to devise, or prepare, a pattern which could serve his colleagues' preferences while capable of

1. To Grenville, no. 67, 7 September 1800 (F.O. 7/60).
2. Pp. 360–2 above.
3. Dundas to George III, 1 July [1800] (*L.C.G. III*, III, no. 2184).
4. See pp. 353–5 above.

serving his own if the opportunity came. In the confused weeks between his success in cutting down the Mediterranean expedition and his sudden turn on the eve of Marengo, he went some way towards showing his real hand. The battle for a change of strategic direction had, apparently, been lost. But he was the Minister who issued the operational instructions, and those to Abercromby were scarcely such, in tone and in content, as Grenville for example would have given. The General was to concentrate on Malta, leaving lesser formations to stage raids and demonstrations in aid of the Austrians and of French royalists if the latter emerged. But if such undertakings seemed not worth while, or the Austrians failed in Italy or withdrew from the war, he should consider, after Malta, the capture of Tenerife. Dundas's intentions indeed were underlined by his simultaneous treatment of an appeal by Portugal for reinforcements against an alleged new Spanish threat of invasion. He not only turned it down at once, but authorised Abercromby to take any of the troops already there whom he might need for his own purposes.[1] The mainland of southern Europe, except in emergency, was clearly taking second place. And neither was his treatment of north-west Europe as simple as it might appear. He sub-scribed to – he encouraged – the gathering of a force of 25,000 men on Belleisle. But when the need for such numbers was questioned, in the light of his own earlier argument that a British contribution on the Continent could be only 'indirect', he replied that the island was well placed to serve a range of opportunities: to cover an arc in western France as far as Biscay, and even 'if, as may be the case, you should find it necessary to detach expeditions to South America or to distant objects'. This last possibility was rendered the more practicable by the inclusion in the force for Belleisle of some regiments available for service outside Europe.[2] All in all the juggling was skilful, as Dundas sought to prepare for an alternative to a strategy he deplored and would continue to resist.

The memorandum, of 22 July, returned to the charge, concentrating on Europe itself as an opening step.[3] The build-up at Belleisle had lost much of its point now that Austria was, at best, on the defensive and, in his view, the royalists' prospects were firmly reduced. Brest itself could be block-aded without risking an expensive and hazardous assault – a change from the bolder plan pursued so eagerly the year before.[4] Why not therefore

---

1. See Mackesy, op. cit., 98–100. Cf. pp. 354–5 above for Tenerife.

It should however be stated that Dundas was not alone in doubting that Portugal would be attacked. Both the British Legation in Lisbon and Grenville himself were sceptical of Spain's strength and also of France's ability, even after Marengo, to provide enough support (P.R.O., F.O. 63/32, 33).

2. Grenville to Dundas, 15, 17 April; Dundas to Grenville, 16 April 1800 (B.L. Add. Ms 40101). See Mackesy, op. cit., 102, and pp. 354–5, 361 above for the exercise in calculations. Belleisle was also well placed in Dundas's view to cover Ireland against any further French attempt.

3. 'Secret Memorandum', 22 July 1800 (B.L. Add. Ms 40102). I have not found Pitt's copy.

4. Cf. pp. 225–6 above.

switch attention to the Spanish ports?[1] After taking opinions, he favoured an opening assault on the arsenal of Ferrol, just beyond the Bay of Biscay, which might be undertaken with some of the reinforcements destined for Belleisle. Beyond that lay the possible targets, for which Abercromby's force might suffice, of Cartagena in the Mediterranean and Cadiz on the Atlantic coast; and beyond them again his old favourite, Tenerife.[2] Such a progression – whatever the sequence – could best be accommodated by sending on the troops available from the capture of Ferrol to join Abercromby at Gibraltar, with the prime target of the main naval base at Cadiz.

Dundas could not refrain once more from a wider survey. We should now stop thinking 'only' of the Austrians and the French royalists. It was time to give priority to weakening our enemies' possessions overseas. That would make the strongest impression available to drive them towards peace, and if in the negotiations we adopted our familiar principle of *uti possidetis*[3] we must acquire some equivalent to offset the partial cession of British gains in the West Indies. Concentrating, as his plans already suggested, on Spain, he proposed two transatlantic targets: Cuba, rich in produce and strategically important, and, in South America, the area of the River Plate. Entry into the latter in particular, opening extensive new markets, might even lead to the removal in peace talks of 'all pretences for commercial Wars' by an agreement to open all European colonies to 'the commerce of all'.

This vision, so favourable to current views of the British economy, did not persuade Dundas's colleagues to embark on the appropriate strategic course. They were prepared however to endorse the first stage of the more limited programme, and on 24 July the Cabinet approved an assault on Ferrol if St Vincent gave it 'a reasonable prospect of success' with 12,000 troops and part of his Channel fleet. Thereafter, whatever the

1. These months were in fact to mark the end of the now fading plans for a major assault on north-west France. In late May, Pitt, Grenville and Dundas seem to have been prepared to encourage royalist hopes; by mid September even Windham had to admit that 'all idea of Royalists' had disappeared (Windham's diary, 31 July, 18 September 1800; B.L. Add. Ms 37924).

2. Dundas stated that Ferrol had been 'suggested'. The author of the idea may have been Sir James Pulteney, formerly Murray, who had been York's adjutant general (chief of staff) in Flanders in 1793–5 and his second in command in Holland in 1799, and was currently destined for the command of operations from Belleisle. It was put to Spencer, who consulted St Vincent, cruising, now with the Channel fleet, off Ushant. The Admiral was doubtful; he thought the port 'the least vulnerable' in Spain, and inclined rather to Cartagena or Cadiz, and strongly to Tenerife, using Abercromby's troops (correspondence in *Private Papers of Spencer*, III, 357–61). Dundas however, gratefully citing him in favour of these last targets, drew on Pulteney for the opinion that Ferrol, while strong on the seaward side, was vulnerable to a landing nearby.

3. Cf. II, 628: 'a principle under which property not expressly provided for in a treaty terminating hostilities is to remain in the hands of the party who happened to have possession of it when hostilities ended' (David M. Walker, *The Oxford Companion to Law* (1980), 1269).

outcome, the force should proceed to Gibraltar, joining Abercromby, who would be ordered there from the Mediterranean with his own 'disposeable' troops, for a combined attack on Cadiz and the Spanish ships in port. Thereafter, again whatever the result, some of the forces should proceed to the Canaries, to capture Tenerife and perhaps some neighbouring islands, while the rest returned to base at the Rock.[1]

Dundas might well have reflected that he had gained as much as he could hope for at this point. If so, he had reckoned once more without the King. George III had been reviewing troops near Bagshot on the day the Cabinet met. Returning to Windsor, he was greeted by its Minute. The result was a note to Dundas which sent that statesman hurrying round to Pitt and Grenville with a view to calling another meeting at once. Neither was in town; Pitt was at Holwood, and going on to stay with Charles Long at Bromley;[2] but he responded with equal haste when he read the royal message. For the King was angry. He was already displeased with his Ministers for their behaviour over the message to Minto, and with Dundas for despatching the order to Maitland without waiting to inform him, let alone consult.[3] This latest, unheralded news added further insult. Not only did it seem alarming; overturning a settled policy for which preparations were supposed to be under way. It was a fresh slight from Ministers apparently disposed increasingly to ignore him; a decision, he was told, to be followed by 'immediate' action, without proper regard for his military and still more his sovereign rights.[4] His note was a reminder.

> . . . Not having heard of an expedition against Ferrol and on what ground of supposed success it is to be undertaken, nor what force will remain in this country after sending so large a force out of it, I cannot give any answer till I have received the date on which to form an opinion.[5]

It was a sharp sign of disapproval. Furthermore, it contained an accompanying comment on Ministers' propensity to issue 'orders and counterorders . . . too frequently', the result of an approach both unprofessional in detail and – ironically, as Dundas himself had been objecting – failing

1. Minute, 24 July 1800 (*L.C.G. III*, III, no. 2202).
2. Cf. p. 89 above.
3. P. 361 above. Dundas moreover may well have been still in disfavour following his quarrel with the King in the winter, which rankled with them both, over Leveson Gower's military appointment (see p. 357, n4 above).
4. The Cabinet Minute recommended that further troops from England should be immediately embarked. For the King in person as head of the army see II, 484.
5. To Dundas, 25 [so dated] July 1800, 10.15 pm (*L.C.G. III*, III, no. 2203). I put the qualification because I suspect from an opening sentence and the correspondence which followed that the date should be the 24th. If so, it was a rare mistake by a meticulous man.

to assess the range of problems as a whole.[1] Coming particularly after the episodes of the past few weeks, it looked serious enough for Pitt to take a hand himself.

The Minister's immediate intervention was marked by tactical good sense. Eschewing a further Cabinet, which might have either raised the temperature or yielded too much, he wrote direct to Windsor quietly but firmly stressing the importance of speed to exploit the remainder of the summer, while he counselled Dundas to do likewise in a tone of moderation and skirting any dangerous constitutional ground. He should rather point out the need for 'striking some blow' which could be quickly effective, and thereby reduce the pressures of 'impatience' that might otherwise lead to a clamour for peace which the King himself would certainly not like. The plans for Belleisle and the French coast would take at least as large a force. Strength at home, from the figures, would be adequate. And the Cabinet was specifically referring the verdict to professional opinion, in the shape of Pulteney (who would be the land commander) and St Vincent for the fleet.[2] Dundas followed this line, 'in his own name and that of Mr Pitt'; and the King, relieved on reflection that the full Cabinet was not to be involved, and not wishing to enter 'a paper war', dropped his opposition.[3] It was a fortunate outcome in the sense that it avoided a confrontation. But the episode left a further mark on those centrally involved. George III's resentment had been heightened, as had his doubts of his Ministers' competence,[4] while Dundas, 'astonished and hurt', had wanted at first to send a sterner reply. And Pitt, while dissuading him, was also upset. If their advice was not accepted after explanation, he wrote to his colleague, there was only one course left. The King must be invited 'to find servants whose judgments he can trust more than ours'.[5]

1. Cf. for Dundas p. 354 above. The application however was by no means always the same in either case. Thus on this occasion the King drew attention to a possible paucity of military strength which would be left in England at a time of continuing unrest (cf. p. 295, n1 above) – exactly as he had done on an analogous occasion, against Dundas's wishes, in 1795 (II, 597n2). For another earlier criticism see II, 318, Ch. XIV p. 351, above. His remark this time about orders and counter-orders was caused by the instruction to Maitland to despatch his troops to the Mediterranean (to Dundas, 2 July [1800]; *L.C.G. III*, III, no. 2184).

2. See pp. 367–9 above.

3. Pitt to George III, 27 July 1800, from Bromley (*L.C.G. III*, III, no. 2204); same to Dundas, 25 July 3 pm, from Holwood, 26 July 10.30 pm, 27 July 1 pm, from Bromley (op. cit., pp. 383n1, 385n2); Dundas to George III, 25 July 1800 11 pm (op. cit., no. 2203); same to same, no. 27 July 10 pm; George III to Dundas, 28 July 7.10 am, 7.23 am (all op. cit., no. 2205). 'Mr Pitt', the King wrote at the end, 'shewed his usual penetration in thinking it ['my note wrote in a hurry'] not intended for to be laid before a Cabinet meeting'.

4. A point amply made in the reply to Dundas on the 28th at 7.10 am (above), which seized the opportunity to lecture the Secretary for War on the need for well digested arrangements – as the stagnating plans for Belleisle could show.

5. To Dundas, 25 July 3 pm (n3 above). He made it clear that he would 'most decidedly join' in this.

The atmosphere was therefore troubled as the troops and ships were prepared. Perhaps the more affected by it, their orders were strong on precautions. The commanders were to be guided by their expectations of 'a reasonable prospect of success'. They had discretion to 'relinquish the attempt as too hazardous'. They were to make sure of re-embarkation if necessary, and not risk the destruction of the force.[1] These provisos for Ferrol were inserted with the greater operation against Cadiz also in mind.[2] They were scarcely calculated to foster initiative; and perhaps the less likely to do so when the General was Pulteney, respected for his intelligence but not for his powers of decision.[3] Assembling off Brittany in mid August, the troops reached Ferrol on the 25th, and following a successful landing were soon threatening the town. But after assessing the defences the General ordered a withdrawal, and the expedition sailed on to the south. The navy at once condemned him, the army was disposed to exonerate. At least, it could be agreed, he remained at full strength for the main part of the design.

That in turn was being prepared at Gibraltar in September, where the two forces, from the north and the east, joined towards the end of the month. By the beginning of October they were lying off Cadiz: an impressive sight with over a hundred transports, covered by the Mediterranean fleet with 22 ships of the line and 37 frigates and sloops. Deliberations took place, in growing confusion, through the following week. A summons to surrender was issued; a landing was mounted, and then called off while the first wave was heading for the shore; the weather, already uncertain, worsened; and on the 8th the armada sailed away. It was hard at first to make out precisely what had happened. Plague was known to be rife in Cadiz, and that could be advanced in explanation. But as details emerged from indignant participants it became ever more obvious that co-operation between the army and the navy had broken down. Two experienced commanders, Abercromby and Admiral Lord Keith, Commander-in-Chief in the Mediterranean, had in fact entirely failed to grip the enterprise. It seemed that St Vincent might have been right when he commented sardonically after Ferrol, 'Good Lord deliver us from all conjunct operations, unless they are commanded by Sir Charles Grey or Sir Charles Stuart'.[4]

The news occasioned some weary disgust at home, after a season of inertia and muddle ending in humiliation against a Power we were

1. Mackesy, op. cit., 132.
2. P. 369 above.
3. Cf. II, 330.
4. To Spencer, 7 September 1800 (*Private Papers of Spencer*, III, 368). Sir Charles Grey and he himself (as Sir John Jervis) had of course produced a notable run of success in the West Indies six years before (II, 356). Stuart might be thought a more questionable example, by St Vincent's own reckoning indeed at one time. But his qualities had been harnessed satisfactorily with the Mediterranean fleet in the Admiral's own day, for the seizure of Minorca in 1798.

accustomed to despise.[1] Such feelings for the year were summed up by the veteran soldier and proconsul to whom Pitt had always shown marked respect. 'What a disgraceful and what an expensive campaign have we made', wrote Cornwallis from Ireland. 'Twenty-two thousand men . . . floating round the greater part of Europe, the scorn and laughing-stock of friends and foes'.[2] The latest chapter was indeed a dispiriting performance. Not all its authors however were, or professed to be greatly depressed. Dundas himself, who had proposed the programme, seemed indeed content to write it off. He would have been happy, he claimed, to have countermanded the orders for Cadiz if he could have done so once the programme was launched; as it was, not much time had been lost there, and time was of the essence after the Cabinet's earlier waverings had delayed any action until late in the year.[3] Such lack of worry was at first sight surprising – and not least considering his careworn state.[4] But by the time that the report came in, matters in point of fact had moved on. The Ministry could point by then to a success elsewhere, welcome in itself and now as a distraction;[5] and, more fundamentally, as the Spanish attempts were under way so too were more extensive affairs which, in Dundas's view, put them in the shade. For the Cabinet had meanwhile been arguing a further plan of operations; and this was resolved, to his satisfaction, before the news of Cadiz was received.

II

The spring and summer of 1800 may be said to have witnessed the nadir in the British management of the war. There had been years – 1796 to '98 – which saw virtually no active engagement in Continental operations.[6] But none had then been planned on a serious scale – in 1797 none had been required – and there was some minor compensating effort in the Caribbean. The navy moreover supplied a contribution, at the Nile, as the army could not do.[7] The difference now lay in the contrast between intention and action: between the incessant Ministerial debates and the nullity that followed. The continuous indecision in the higher counsels and the

1. See eg II, 631.
2. To Major-General Ross, 6 November 1800 (*Correspondence of Cornwallis*, III, 300–1).
3. Dundas to Windham, 29 October [1800] (B.L. Add. Ms 37847): 'Cabinet deliberations', he wrote, 'which I subscribe to, as I suppose they are a necessary Evil, but it falls always heavily against the Person who happens to hold the Pen on such occasions' (cf. II, 531, 532). He was acknowledging congratulations from his colleague on the commanders' decision not to land at Cadiz in the presence of plague. Windham had written on the 22nd (loc. cit.), when the report was received.
4. See p. 357 above.
5. P. 394 below.
6. The only British troops stationed on the mainland, in Portugal, saw no action, though a detachment did so in the capture of the island of Minorca.
7. See pp. 143–4, 150–2 above.

hesitations of some of the commanders, the paralysis in planning and the faintness of attempts to implement the orders that finally emerged, made a combination with no exact parallel in any of the previous campaigns. There had been plenty of failures before, in London and in the field; but never such sequential reversals of design and undisguised loss of nerves on the spot. To observers, the capacity and direction of the system could show the signs of wholesale disarray. Despite every intent, 'not a single British soldier had been in action in Europe' when Marengo was fought; and the same applied to the mainland, broken only for a day, over three and a half months.[1]

A contrast indeed can be drawn in this sense with the experience of 1799. That had ended in failure; but the failure of a purposeful attempt to impose a grand design – a genuine concept – and of a substantial if truncated combined operation. The two periods however, marking the resumption in London of a full Continental strategy, may be taken together for the light they throw on the Ministry's conduct of such a war. Together they exemplified the complications, more sharply perhaps than at any other point: the constraints in an alliance whether fluctuatingly close, as with Austria, or fluctuatingly distant as with Russia. It is not a simple matter to restrain the disruptive tendencies present within a combination of states. Bonaparte himself remarked that the wider a hostile alliance the better he was pleased. But a narrower Coalition, of prominent Powers,[2] can equally project its discords, with contingent effects from neutrals rather than associates on strategic purpose and plans. The point need not be laboured; it has been a theme of these chapters, as has the course of the argument in London for persistence in the face of such facts. Their strength remained formidable, alike when the consequences had to be broadly suffered in the First Coalition and when an attempt was pursued in the Second to achieve a closer military pattern in the framework of a more specific diplomatic consensus.[3]

The effects were all too clear in the last two years of the century. The problems posed by separate interests were not in themselves wholly responsible for the disappointments in the febrile atmosphere of the late summer of 1799; nor again wholly for the feeling of helplessness in London in the first half of 1800, when, as Grenville complained, Ministers laboured after every incoming despatch.[4] But the discrepancies were prominent, and intensified as usual by the uncertainties of communications – by the length of time borne so often everywhere in waiting for news by horse and sail, the more so in winter now that the

---

1. The phrase is Mackesy's, op. cit., 114. And see p. 372 above.

2. As the Second was in comparison with the First; cf. II, 650.

3. Cf. Ch. VII above for the emphasis in London on a consensus of aims and claims to accompany the nascent Second Coalition, and VIII for the attempted imposition of an operational strategy on a combination of separate Alliances.

4. P. 356 above.

traffic had to go so largely by Hamburg and the Elbe.[1] The massive freezes of 1798–9 and 1799–1800[2] only underlined more sharply the importance of a factor which must never be ignored. Particularly in periods when the pace of events quickened, up-to-date information could be vital if responses, let alone decisions, were to make good sense.

The impact of these problems was heightened moreover in London by another form of pressure, whose effect had not been felt so acutely before: by the financial and social alarms, first experienced seriously in 1795–6,[3] which were now combining in a more threatening way. Pitt himself was increasingly anxious to escape from the costs of a full Continental war. At the same time a Continental war seemed the only path to timely victory; the sole alternative in fact to a struggle, confined broadly to a maritime strategy, which might be annually rather less expensive but could drag on for years.[4] It was this above all that swung him behind Grenville, to Dundas's rising distress: the fears of the Chancellor of the Exchequer weighed hard on the First Lord of the Treasury. A loose, slow-moving Alliance, as experienced in the First Coalition, should not be accepted if possible in the Second. But – an argument of course entertainable against the strategy itself – this placed an exceptional burden on military capability in a century in which outright victory had seldom been expected from a single campaign.[5] Bonaparte, it was true, seemed to be setting a different example; as the Revolutionary armies indeed had threatened to do in 1792. It was not one however to be achieved easily by a traditional, disparate combination. Even if the Allies could claim their successes in the field at different times, an unusually ambitious end was being asked of the means.

Given their own results in the field moreover, the British land forces themselves stood in poor repute, abroad and at home. Bundled out of Holland and seemingly futile against the French and Spanish coasts, the army's fortunes, not renowned throughout the European war, had reached a new level of depression. As things turned out in point of fact, it proved to be their lowest ebb. Before another year was over, Abercromby had fought a contested landing as the prelude to a success, and the new century, despite early failures, would see a quickening rise in achievements until the culmination under Wellington at Waterloo. It was no use pretending in 1800 that the army was in good shape. But neither officers nor men, nor even the framework of their service, were as uniformly bad as they were apt to be painted. Some advances in training and administration, if mostly still marginal, were taking place: in methods of manoeuvre, regulation of promotions (bringing however their own greater rigidity), means of recruitment, design of some equipment. Above all, a start was

1. For which see II, 548. And cf. in general I, 167.
2. Eg pp. 204, 207, 348 above.
3. II, Ch. XI section 1, XII *passim*, XIII section III, XV, 617–22, 638–41.
4. Cf. pp. 200–1 above.
5. Cf. II, 540.

being made to providing some proper professional education, in institutions from which the later cluster of military colleges would emerge.[1] The Horse Guards under York was not immune from the era of 'improvement': amidst the obstinate prevalence of custom and entrenched rights of diffused authorities, the Department was taking notice of the experiences of 1793–5. It was not Wellesley alone in Flanders who had then seen what not to do;[2] the lessons were not wholly lost within the commands themselves. There were signs that might yet herald – slowly, unevenly, in the face of constant frustration – a return to the renown of British arms in the days of Cromwell and Marlborough, and Chatham.[3] Lack of ultimate success since then, in America – itself bequeathing some irrelevant tactics for Europe – and now in the two Coalitions, obscured the fact that, if competently trained, the men could give a good account of themselves. Cornwallis, York, Abercromby were all prepared to claim as much. And if the men's officers were amateurish, largely idle and impatient of discipline, they too proved capable of building on an acknowledged courage and spirit as they learned. The potential turned largely on the system's capacity to hold and train formations together. Thereafter, matters would of course depend on how the troops were handled in the field. The Generals so far in this war, as Cornwallis observed, made 'a melancholy list', and senior officers as a whole were not held in high regard by the outside world. Grenville spoke for others when he called them 'inefficient . . . instruments',[4] and while there were a few exceptions – Grey and Abercromby spring to mind in the older generation, Charles Stuart and John Moore in the younger – it was tempting to say that these proved a rule. Even so, their greatest successes had been gained overseas in semi-independence: in the first two cases in the West Indies, the last two in Mediterranean islands.[5] Distance from Whitehall of course could favour enterprise; and proximity was certainly no advantage now. As the King remarked, 'orders and counter-orders which are too frequently given puzzle the services'.[6] For if the British aim in Europe placed high demands on the instruments available, their effectiveness in turn, within the prevalent limits, was conditioned largely by the aim.

The army in this instance was the immediate concern: the head of the arrow, the sharp point of the nation's capacity. In many, less instantly visible, ways the Government's grasp on the war, over a period overall disappointing, had in fact strengthened. From the end of 1796, when the

1. See II, 482–92 for the situation before 1797.

2. II, 330n4.

3. Cf. Richard Glover, *Peninsular Preparation* . . . (1963), 1.

4. II, 567 for Cornwallis in 1795; *H.M.C., Dropmore*, VI, 233 for Grenville in 1800. The two older Grenville brothers however were perhaps unduly in the habit of regularly denigrating the army as a whole.

5. Respectively II, 356, 614; p. 326 above; II, 347 for Corsica, where both Stuart and Moore distinguished themselves. See also II, 491.

6. To Dundas, 2 July 1800 (*L.C.G. III*, III, no. 2184). See p. 369 above.

peace talks collapsed, one senses indeed something of a new atmosphere: a sharper sense of purpose, and readiness to exploit all the weapons that could be used. Operational intelligence, that vital element, seems still to have languished, as was shown for Holland in 1799 and Brest – and Ferrol – in 1800.[1] But there were advances over a range of areas, the products of experience and of resolve: in assembling and handling the great maritime convoys for instance, in the treatment of intercepted neutral trade, in naval blockade, in managing subsidy payments, in devices of economic warfare. One has also an impression of greater energy, and possibly innovation, in some greyer areas: in the support of resistance movements in Europe, and in introducing subversion direct. Such activities fell within the aegis of the Alien Office, that repository of miscellaneous services and responsible, directly, to Portland as a Secretary of State. Such activities were known only to a very small circle; and in detail doubtless then not to all.[2] But in so far as they were set on foot or supported, they may have been a sign of a harder – a more ruthless – approach which lay within a growing professionalism in a struggle viewed now as of mortal concern.

Growing competence at several levels in the management of the means is however distinct from, if linked with, the conduct of policy itself. The higher direction was sorely tested by the concatenation of strategic pressures. Coming as they did in conjunction with – indeed partly stemming from – the domestic tensions, and as a final proof to Dundas that strategy itself called for reassessment, the impact was deeper than any felt hitherto in the war. No system in such circumstances could have emerged unscathed. The damage to confidence and cohesion in this instance arose from the strain on the inmost group which had been able so far to show a broadly common front. Both Grenville and Dundas deplored the need to consult the 'large Cabinet' increasingly.[3] But it was the very form of strategy favoured by the first, involving foreign policy so constantly and closely, and the challenge later posed by the second, that combined to heighten that requirement. And the same applied to the monarch once the Cabinet was drawn in. When a Minute became necessary he had almost always to be shown it,[4] and here in circumstances that encouraged comment and could allow ready intervention. A degree of stress was being placed on central relationships which they were not accustomed to bear.[5] It was small wonder that the response became increasingly confused.

1. Cf. eg pp. 326, n1 above.
2. This, naturally difficult, subject is at present being examined by Mrs Elizabeth Sparrow; eg in 'The Alien Office, 1792–1806' and 'The Swiss and Swabian Agencies, 1795–1801' (*H.J.*, vol. 33, no. 2 and vol. 35, no. 4 respectively).
3. Pp. 320, 372n3 above.
4. See I, 628 for the Cabinet's role in foreign affairs, and 629 for the practice, indeed the origin, of the Minute; but also II, 207n4 for at least one possible exception to the normal procedure.
5. Not at any rate in wartime since the later years of the War of American Independence, and then neither Ministers nor the King himself had been happy about the situation (cf. I, 140).

This applied much more to the year 1800 than to 1799, when the policy pushed so hard by Grenville had derived directly from the British view of the Second Coalition and was adopted by his colleagues without deep dispute. Dundas then found no support for his own attempt at an alternative, as yet unspecific,[1] and the difficulties, confined for the most part to the inner circle itself, related to the implementation rather than the shape of operations. But the following spring and summer were different, and there are some pointers, if slight, to the attitudes of some other Cabinet members. Chatham seems broadly to have shared Dundas's thoughts, and Spencer naturally sympathised with his concern at least for seapower in the Mediterranean; Windham on the other hand was normally opposed to anything, in or outside Europe, that detracted from whole-hearted support for the French royalists.[2] Others again, with less cogent interests, may have felt less direct or persistent concern. But of course it was not merely or indeed primarily a matter of arguing an ideal strategy; the situation demanded answers to urgent questions, and Dundas's own point of vantage had, however reluctantly, to take this prominently into account. He was not at leisure to promote *in vacuo* the prospects of a fundamental change, and, like the rest, he could shift his ground in response to an apparent sudden change of scene.[3] His hands in fact were largely tied after the Cabinet ignored his ideas on the eve of the Continental campaign, and his unwilling compliance with the fact was expressed in his ingenious secondary measures.[4] Until Marengo at least that was all he could do, and he was not wholly free in its immediate aftermath. And Grenville for his part, still determined in purpose, was swayed in the choices for its execution by a state of affairs on the Continent whose own indeterminacy dictated successive British plans. Such a sequence was proving hard to break, and yet an outright departure in Dundas's direction would reduce the likelihood of aiding victory within the short time desired, and thereby of influencing the subsequent European peace. Nor, as the Foreign Secretary saw it, were victory and peace in fact at all unattainable. From the early winter of 1799 to mid June 1800 the prospects could be argued from his information as pointing, in Pitt's words, 'the one way'.[5] And what indeed, one may ask, might have happened if the Austrians had won at Marengo, as they very nearly did? Could Bonaparte have survived politically; and if not, would the French have sought terms? What lines might the Austrians, and the Russians, have then followed in the absence of a close British involvement, to which subsidies and naval operations alone could scarcely have supported a claim? 'The permanent Interests of Great Britain'[6] did not appear to

1. Cf. pp. 143–5, 319 above.
2. See pp. 351, 353n3 above for Chatham; 351, 361 and n2 for Windham.
3. Pp. 354–5, 361.
4. Po. 354–6 above.
5. On 3 February 1800; p. 342 above.
6. P. 354 above.

Grenville to lie only, or primarily, in trade through distant seas. His confusion over military movements, unlike Dundas's, had not stemmed from a half-heartedness but rather reflected a steadiness of aim.

What was Pitt's position in all this? In one respect it was clear. Throughout 1799 and the first six months of 1800 he sided with Grenville against Dundas in the choice between a European and a more exclusively maritime policy.[1] When however it came to the consequences for action in the later period, like both Grenville and Dundas he changed his mind more than once. That said, however, there was a certain difference between his case and theirs. For Grenville and Dundas each viewed the immediate decisions against the background of his final intent; one does not have the impression with Pitt that this was so. As sceptical in the end as Dundas of the value of an attack on Brittany, he acquiesced in it – and without ulterior motive – for want, one feels, of something better.[2] When an alternative seemed to offer in the Mediterranean, he was attracted and initially approved; but again not decisively, and with qualms revealed at once by the brief French sortie from Brest.[3] Every one was puzzled, and dithered, in the dismal months preceding Marengo. But one senses more keenly with Pitt than with either of his two associates a mood of drift in the face of events. Of course he played a part in the preparations: early in the year he had plunged vigorously into the plans for north-west France,[4] and he naturally took his share in the discussions throughout. But his efforts were then engaged as much in finding enough common ground to pacify his two colleagues, and at the worst to holding Dundas to his post,[5] as in the hope of gaining control over the obstinate problems. He was adept at the first exercise: at fastening on the features of a case that embraced different elements, and placing them in a pattern that might comprehend them all. But he could find no adequate 'practical vision' for the second here.[6] As he turned his eyes at this time to the map in the corner of his room,[7] he could not draw from it a solution that had escaped his colleagues.

There was indeed plenty of cause for bafflement. But Pitt's mood of indecision – almost of a state of limbo while awaiting an outcome – merits further review. One may suggest a combination of possible reasons. There was much wearing business at home to occupy him from the autumn of 1799. The Irish situation still demanded attention as the preparations for the Union advanced. He was working hard on the

1. Chs. VIII, XI; and earlier see 148 above.
2. Cf. pp. 350, 358–9 above.
3. Ch. XI, sections III, V above.
4. Pp. 325–6 above.
5. Pp. 356–8 above.
6. See I, 319.
7. '. . . what consolation does Pitt point out after looking at the map in the corner of his room by the door?'; Canning to Hookham Frere after Marengo, quoted in Mackesy, op. cit., 168. And cf. I, 354 for an earlier glimpse of maps in use.

improvements to the Income Tax which then ran into trouble. Above all he had to grapple with the great dearth and its ramifying dangers; and if the worst part of that crisis was still to come after the second bad harvest, most of the measures, including controversial experiments, had been effected by then.[1] He was bearing a heavy load. But that does not provide an answer in itself. His powers of assimilation were legendary, and he was well used to applying them, speedily if belatedly, when the need came.[2] After sixteen years in high office he was accustomed to carrying a package of burdens. But that very fact could tell its own tale, and it must be open to doubt whether he was able to do as comfortably now. By and large he seemed to have weathered the pressures in 1799 pretty well. But his health had become thoroughly suspect, and in July and again in October 1800 it suffered a serious collapse.[3] He struggled on as the scene in England darkened and the problems from Europe persisted, and as the autumn went by he appeared to be on the mend. His resilience was notable. But a general deterioration may well have been lessening his capacity for impressing himself on many spheres of activity at once.[4]

The conditions in this particular sphere moreover were such as to underline the trend. For the contrast between 1799 and the spring and summer of 1800 was pronounced, particularly perhaps for someone with Pitt's cast of mind. In the earlier year there was a pattern, comprehensive and intricate, on which to fasten. The formlessness for much of 1800, at least once the initial plan for Brittany disappeared, gave him no focus on which to concentrate his thoughts. He was not usually discouraged by intellectual complications; he stood accused in fact of dealing in them himself.[5] But the perplexities of this situation hardly allowed of any such treatment. Strategy seemed simply to be living from hand to mouth.

Such a state of affairs was not one in which Pitt's talents shone. It was indeed the reverse. His readiness to see all sides of a question as a basis for a balanced answer left him vulnerable when the question could not be given proper shape. He was not always inclined then in point of fact to go on trying too hard; and disappointment, above all in a case where he had been enthusiastically involved, left a more visible mark. Indeed, at such a point he was liable to lose interest; and while that was not possible in war to the same extent as in peace, the same process of initial energy followed by a measure of withdrawal could be the more sharply observed. His

1. See Chs. VI section IV, IX section I, X section I above.
2. Cf. p. 37 above.
3. P. 82 above.
4. I put it like this because, as emerges from pp. 409–10 below, he could still command a decisive impact on a difficult strategic decision when the problems finally narrowed to a point.
5. '. . . a fondness in every difficulty for complicated expedients'; Grenville's 'Commentaries of my own Political Life' (I, 202n3). He was generalising there from an earlier example, the Irish Propositions of 1785.
Cf. the titles of Chs. VIII and XI above for the comparison between the two years.

interventions were apt, from one cause or another, to be spasmodic; and although of course this can apply to any prominent hard pressed figure in government, the need for persistence in such conditions could be at odds with a mercurial temperament. In the context of war moreover two factors could combine to underline the effects. As Dundas told him, the sanguine 'tendency which I think belongs to your disposition, and which . . . on many occasions . . . produces the most happy consequences, is to be carefully guarded against in the examination and execution of military plans'.[1] He had soon become aware that he 'distrust[ed] extremely any Ideas of my own on Military Subjects',[2] and it seems unlikely that experience had seriously shaken his misgivings. He had indeed no natural feeling for the friction of war – for measuring its elements or absorbing its contingencies – and, working in harness with two increasingly disgruntled but to him indispensable associates, he was now being pulled in contrary directions. Grenville's certainty and Dundas's doubts alike bore down on his own indecision, in a time of distracting troubles and of his own tenuous health.[3] He agreed with elements in both of their themes, and neither could count on his wholehearted compliance; the atmosphere suffered accordingly, and so did his peace of mind. Grenville's personality – his singlemindedness and what Dundas called 'persistent importunity'[4] – always had an effect when his cousin was not sure of the ground. Dundas for his part stood in a different relationship, the closest Pitt enjoyed with any senior colleague. He had long gained the Minister's confidence, and been at his right hand for six wartime years, 'every act of his being as much *mine as his*'.[5] They still talked over their 'business of state' in their morning rides and evening walks at Wimbledon;[6] but while his departure could not be allowed, and he remained affectionately loyal, that statement of identical views no longer held good. These personal pressures deepened a central loss of will in this sphere.[7] The lack of focus in the planning process was augmented by the echo it found in Pitt himself.

1. To Pitt, 4 January 1800; cf. p. 326, n5 above.
2. A remark of 1794; II, 489. Others agreed that he would be right to do so. Liverpool observed that 'Pitt was very ignorant of those subjects' (*Glenbervie*, I, 160); and the effect in this area of business had been noted by the General whom it affected particularly at this time. 'In Mr. Pitt', Abercromby told his son, '. . . you saw . . . very nearly a great man in Cabinet. If his mind was equal to his abilities and talents, he would deserve the name of a first-rate statesman' (Dunfermline, *Lieutenant-General Sir Ralph Abercromby*, 217).
3. That impression may have spread. It was said for instance that on one occasion, in March 1800, he simply left a meeting with the two men at which they were airing their differences (see *A Prime Minister and his Son . . .*, ed. E. Stuart Wortley (1925), 329–30).
4. Mackesy, op. cit., 39.
5. See *H.M.C., Dropmore*, II, 595.
6. Dundas's account of their habits, given almost a decade later (*Diary of Farington*, IX, ed. Kathryn Cave (1982), 3458).
7. It will be clear that I do not subscribe to the view that Pitt may have been content in this matter to hold a balance of power between his two colleagues; in effect to divide and rule (cf. Mackesy, who himself is inclined to reject such a conclusion, op. cit., 39, 176). My impression in fact is strongly otherwise.

III

And then Marengo came, raising its urgent queries not only for the shape of possible operations but also for the stance to be taken if Austria should seek to leave the war. Familiar questions were revived in both respects at an unpromising time. The Emperor might of course end by repeating the story of 1797, and find himself opting under pressure for a unilateral peace.[1] In that case we could not hope to influence a European settlement; hence the Cabinet's immediate resolve to make it absolutely clear that we would wish to take part in any negotiation directed to a 'general peace'. At the same time, that must carry an implication which partly accounted for the King's concern. His dislike of an offer, however understandable, which might only encourage an Austrian move[2] was accompanied by a deeper fear. For when it came to the point, a complete distinction between the handling of a 'Continental' and of a 'Maritime' peace – a concept introduced in the past by London[3] – might prove hard to maintain. Bargaining on the first, in talks which we were committed and anxious to join, could not but interact with bargaining on the second. That had been clear when we ourselves sought investigatory talks with France in 1796;[4] but with their sudden collapse, and Austria's later action, the issue was not brought to a point. The linkage might well indeed be thought beneficial to our ally, bringing a counterweight from distant British gains to bear on European failure. But would it thereby be beneficial to Britain itself? And might the results influence the Government in London in its own attitude to a continuing war? This last matter would of course turn on a wider assessment, and George III had his suspicions.[5] But it might be posed in this context as it had not been posed before. An approach from Vienna to Paris moreover, always half expected in the Foreign Office, now looked really on the cards. For though Thugut, that still suspect champion, managed to stay in his post, his domestic opponents could well be gathering for his fall.[6]

The King's misgivings were soon confirmed. In mid July, when the Convention with Austria was returned after its ratification in London, the Cabinet took the occasion, in commenting on some of the provisions in the light of possible peace talks,[7] to repeat and enlarge on its position of

1. See p. 363 above.
2. Ibid. for the exchanges on 26–7 June and for the 'general' peace.
3. P. 134 above.
4. See II, Ch. XV, section III.
5. This emerges from his first response, in a reply focusing on the probable effect on *Austria* of any communication of the Cabinet's wish (to Grenville, 27 June 1800; *L.C.G. III*, III, no. 2181).
6. See pp. 346–7, 352–3 above for Vienna, 335–6, 342–3, 363 for London. As late as mid-August, Wickham, so influential with Grenville, was still denigrating Thugut's good faith (15 August, *H.M.C., Dropmore*, VI, 297; and cf. Grenville to Minto, 19 August 1800, op. cit., 300–1).
7. The secret articles, and arrangements for payments (pp. 364–5 above).

three weeks before. A further Minute was sent to Windsor, which Grenville took care to stress conveyed a unanimous opinion. Minto should be instructed that

> under the present circumstances his Majesty will not oppose the Austrian Armistice, if judged absolutely necessary for the interests of the Court of Vienna . . .; but Lord Minto is to declare, if any occasion should arise, that his Majesty does not judge it proper to agree to any armistice on his part. . . .
>
> But that the basis on which his Majesty proposes in such case to treat for peace, is that of an uti possidetis, from which he is not disposed to relax for the sake of any continental arrangements other than such as may relate to Holland and the Netherlands . . .[1]

The Foreign Secretary's own lack of enthusiasm, or caution, was evident in some of his accompanying remarks. Peace, Grenville told Minto officially, would be highly unsatisfactory at this point. Talks were unwelcome unless Austria was really driven to extremities; and he underlined Britain's refusal to agree to an armistice on its own part – 'the circumstances of a naval war are not such as to admit of such equal arrangements in this respect or [to] take place with regard to military operations'.[2] His personal feelings were conveyed also to the monarch, and, taken in conjunction with the tighter phrasing of the Minute compared with its predecessor, might have been expected to conciliate the latter in some degree. So it did; but the degree was slight. George III acknowledged that his Ministers might be resolved 'not to accede to any but reasonable terms'.[3] But he repeated his profound hostility to their central proposal; and his apprehension must indeed have been heightened by Grenville's own line of reasoning, which he made regretfully but unmistakably clear.

For the Foreign Secretary was now brought to a conclusion that was in fact inherent in a policy which had hitherto sustained him on the opposite course. More strongly than any other Minister, he had – he still – pinned

---

1. 16 July 1800 (*L.C.G. III*, III, enclosure in no. 2193. Drafts – one corrected – are in Grenville's hand in B.L. Add. Ms 59306, with 'Points' to be discussed, and a list of those present. There were two absentees from the meeting: Chatham and, possibly deliberately, Windham; cf. pp. 385–6 below). The armistice referred to could have been either that in Italy, or the prospect of that possibly imminent in Germany, which had in fact been signed on the ground on the 15th.

Cf. for a British armistice pp. 363n3, 368 and n3 above.

2. No. 27, 17 July 1800 (P.R.O., F.O. 7/59). Privately, he did not expect much from a joint negotiation itself. We might still have to reserve 'the right of beating out our own terms of peace, in our own way', and 'The appearance and name of treating jointly is much more than the real aid we can derive from our ally' (same to same, Private, 25 July 1800; *H.M.C., Dropmore*, VI, 276).

3. Grenville to George III as in n1 above, in phrases which sound genuine rather than merely placatory; George III to Grenville, 17 July 1800, 6.41 am (*L.C.G. III*, III, no. 2193).

his faith to full continental Coalition warfare, as the only satisfactory path to the kind of victory he sought. If that strategy were to collapse, he could find no comfort in a substitute. He did not indeed believe that Parliament and the country would support a maritime war without allies unless the Government had first been ready to seek a 'reasonable' Allied peace. But in any case he doubted the efficacy of such an alternative: 'in a contest single-handed, although the means and resources of the country are abundantly sufficient to ensure the attainment of fit and honourable terms, Lord Grenville does not see the possibility of our compelling the enemy, by our separate exertions, either to destroy the present usurpation in France, or to restore tranquillity and independance to the Continent of Europe'. For his part, he would be prepared to 'persevere to the very last extremity, and to take every possible chance of a change of fortune'. But – and this was his message for the King – it would be irresponsible for the Cabinet to 'ground . . . advice on . . . feelings'. Without allies there could only be compromise, and if Austria decided to treat, British interests demanded joint negotiation, which was 'unavoidable' and should be secured.[1]

George III could not persist further – manoeuvring only to propose Thomas Grenville as the envoy if talks should come about – and Minto's instructions were dated the same day.[2] On 9 August the envoy made his announcement in Vienna. The consequences were swift and very largely unforeseen. The first came at once. On the 10th the Emperor invited Britain to join in a negotiation with France, which would be held at Lunéville near Nancy. Such immediacy was unexpected; but the response showed at any rate that he was listening to Thugut rather than others who were anxious for a unilateral peace, and that indeed Austria under the armistice remained in a state of war.[3] By and large then, it seemed that the Cabinet's decision had been timely, even though the pace of events was to

---

1. To George III, 16 July 1800, 11 pm (p. 382, n1 above). It will be noticed that this conclusion was not vitiated if the consequences of such a negotiation were unacceptable for Britain (cf. pp. 381–2 above). If linkage proved too unsatisfactory – even though, as Grenville in fact surmised, it might help Austria – the Government would 'reserve' an independent course which would still be aimed at peace.

The Foreign Secretary's position was given in some detail in a paper, nd but endorsed 'of Lord Grenville written in 1800', in Pitt's files (Dacres Adams Mss, formerly P.R.O. 30/58/8). It stressed the need in a joint negotiation 'to model the Continental Peace according to any separate interests of our own, distinct from those which Austria may pursue'.

2. P. 382, ns 1–3, above. George III's suggestion was obviously designed to pre-empt any other which might place the talks in hands less close or sympathetic to the Foreign Secretary. Cf. pp. 202, 253–4 above for Thomas himself.

The mutual exasperation between the King and Pitt was now undisguised. On 26 July, by which time George III was objecting to the Cabinet's unheralded plans for the attacks on Spain, the Minister remarked, 'it is really provoking to find a disposition equally to object to all means of making peace or making war' (to Grenville; *H.M.C., Dropmore*, VI, 279. And cf. pp. 369–70 above).

3. Minto to Grenville, nos. 40, 47, 51, 55, of 9 July, 2, 7, 10 August 1800 (P.R.O. 30/8/339).

be deplored. But a second and more embarrassing consequence followed very soon. On 24 August the French Government, requesting further information on Minto's statement, proposed a truce with Britain, as an extension of that obtaining with Austria, which in effect would be and was quickly described in London as a naval armistice.[1]

The move was skilful, for by connecting a prospective with a current truce, the terms to be reached for the former could be linked with those already in existence for the latter. The British would be placed in effect under an obligation to Austria prior to the negotiation for peace itself. The French spokesman was already at hand: a Monsieur Otto (by birth a Bavarian) who was resident in London as agent for the exchange of prisoners of war. He was now given full powers from Paris, and the proposition was soon made clear. Three Austrian forces, in addition to those still in the field, were blockaded in the fortresses of Ulm, Philippsburg and Ingoldstat, and under the armistice could be victualled for fourteen days at a time so long as the defences were not strengthened. In the field itself, both sides could reinforce up to specified limits. Bonaparte maintained that since the British were to be involved with their ally in the peace talks, they in turn should agree concessions, obviously maritime, under a truce, as Vienna had given and received by land. If this offer was refused, France would not permit Austria to shelter under her armistice while the negotiation at Lunéville was under way.

This looked like an ultimatum, and on 29 August Otto confirmed as much, with a closing date of 3 September.[2] Such a period was inadmissible, and so, it was decided, was the principle, equating as it did 'the circumstances of a naval war' with those for 'military operations' and demanding as of right a preliminary agreement never hitherto thought 'necessary' to a negotiation for peace.[3] The reasons for the French approach indeed were obvious at that precise moment; for over and above the broad disadvantages to Britain of a truce at sea, there were some applying immediately in the Mediterranean. Bonaparte made his offer, or demand, at a point when the lengthy blockade of Malta had at last brought the French garrison to extremes. On 4 September in fact it surrendered,[4] and he was clearly trying in August to forestall the prospect by ensuring supplies. The same applied moreover to his old army in Egypt, which, after several twists and turns of fortune, was still in occupation and

---

1. Louis Guillaume Otto to Grenville, 24 August 1800 (B.L. Add. Ms 59036).

2. Otto to Grenville, 24 August; Captain George to same, 29 August 1800 (printed in *P.H.*, XXXV, cols. 540–1, 543–4; see p. 385, n3 below). Captain Rupert George was designated at the start as an agent of Government to receive and transmit answers to the French representations. He was already in regular touch with Otto as the Commissioner on the naval Transport Board (see II, 496) responsible for the exchange of prisoners. His new responsibilities however were shortly transferred to more senior officials.

3. Instructions to Captain George, 28 August, enclosed in Grenville to George III, sd (*L.C.G. III*, III, no. 2230, and see also *P.H.*, XXXV, cols. 542–3).

4. Cf. p. 359 above.

cut off from home. On all counts, therefore, British interests would best be served by an outright rejection. Nevertheless, as Pitt explained to a colleague, it was not as easy as that.[1] The question as he saw it was 'a delicate one'. 'All' the benefits of a naval armistice would go to France.

> But the absolute refusal of such a measure would, I conceive, clearly produce the immediate renewal of hostilities between France and Austria, and probably drive the latter, after some fresh disaster, or from the apprehension of it, to an immediate separate peace on the worst terms. We should thereby not only lose the benefit of a joint negotiation, at which we have so long been aiming, but should also give up the present opportunity of negotiating for ourselves in a manner much more creditable and satisfactory than would result from any direct and separate overture which we might make at a later period . . .

This reasoning led the Cabinet to probe farther, as it proved at some length.[2]

The course of the subsequent exchanges can be briefly described.[3] The Cabinet meeting, on 4 September, lacked three members: Loughborough and Windham, who were with the King taking the sea air at Weymouth, and Dundas who was down at Cheltenham for his health.[4] No attention was paid to the ultimatum, or to a fresh one now said to expire on the 11th. But the Ministers consented to lift the blockade on French naval ports[5] – though not on Flushing or Cadiz, as Bonaparte wished in order to involve Dutch and Spanish interests – provided that no warships left and no warlike stores entered; and to place Malta and Alexandria on the footing of the German fortresses. This Counter-Project was conveyed on the 7th. Otto's reply was received on the 16th. It was found unacceptable, for the volume of rations for Malta was to be higher than that for the fortresses; those for Alexandria were to be carried in a specified number of vessels which would not be subject to inspection; and reinforcements of men were to be specified for Egypt, as they were for the armies in the field under the Austrian armistice. A further ultimatum was given for good measure, threatening assaults on The Two Sicilies. By this time, however,

---

1. To Loughborough, 5 September 1800 (Stanhope, III, 240).

2. Minute of 4 September 1800, in B.L. Add. Ms 59306. Grenville later claimed that the response to the French approach was taken 'simply and plainly in the sole view of preventing France from suddenly renewing hostilities in Germany' (to Wickham, 26 September 1800; *H.M.C., Dropmore*, 332); and see also same to Minto, no. 41, 8 September 1800 (P.R.O., F.O. 7/60).

3. The correspondence was laid before Parliament in November and may be followed in, *inter alia*, *P.H.*, XXXV, cols. 540–83. The Foreign Office file of the contents is P.R.O., F.O. 27/55; Grenville's own, B.L. Add. Ms 59036. H.M. Bowman, *Preliminary Stages of the Peace of Amiens . . . November 1799–March 1801* (1899), 45–60 provides a detailed account, though one lacking full evidence from the British side.

4. Cf. p. 382, n1 above.

5. And thereby in practice also of Belleisle.

the Cabinet's tactics, whatever the views on policy of some individual members, were settling into a pattern. The campaigning season would end effectively in November, and if the Austrians could be saved until then or thereabouts they might perhaps be preserved until the spring.[1] If a satisfactory result was not reached at Lunéville, they might then be ready for a further campaign, and meanwhile the war weariness in France, reported persistently, might become acute. On 20 September a fresh British Note was returned, and the exchanges continued over the next week, under sustained and admittedly 'dexterous' pressure from Otto.[2] Neither side however was now prepared for further significant compromise; events were moving once more on the Continent; the Cabinet decided at the end of the month to bring the business to a close; and by 8 October the idea of a naval truce was dead.[3]

The Government's procrastination would soon prove to have been in vain. It also proved damaging to its own well-being. For the decision to parley with Otto deepened and extended the divisions, with the King and within the Cabinet itself. The connexion moreover was underlined, for two of the Ministers absent on 4 September were then with George III and both were out of sympathy with what had been done. Nor in one case was that sentiment uninfluenced by the King's own response, as he noted the names of those responsible while 'most unwillingly' sanctioning their desire. The Lord Chancellor Loughborough, by his office peculiarly the guardian of the King's conscience in Cabinet, and long celebrated for a lack of that political commodity himself, echoed the royal reluctance while acquiescing in the Ministry's move. Windham for his part expressed more genuine feelings more openly, at Weymouth and again on his return.[4] Soon however a like voice of greater power was heard. Dundas, down at Cheltenham, was aghast at what he learned. Returning more 'abruptly' than he had intended, he informed the King of his 'disapprobation', saw Pitt as soon as he could, and a week later circulated his colleagues.[5] He had

1. Grenville to Wickham, as in p. 385, n2 above.

2. As both Pitt and Grenville privately acknowledged (*H.M.C., Dropmore*, VI, 329).

3. Windham's diary for 30 September 1800 (B.L. Add. Ms 37924); Canning's for 7 October 1800 (Canning Ms 29d).

4. George III to Grenville, 6 September 1800, 6.50 pm (*L.C.G. III*, III, no. 2235); Loughborough to Pitt, sd 'evening' (the relevant part printed in op. cit., 409n1), which also indicates Windham's expressed views; Windham's diary, 17–25 September (B.L. Add. Ms 37924). Cf. I, 104 for this aspect of the Lord Chancellor's position in Cabinet; op. cit., 116n3, 621, II, 176–9 for glimpses of Loughborough's past. A good idea of his reputation may be gained from *GEC*, XI (1949), ns to 174–5.

5. Dundas to [Grenville], 9 September 1800 (Dacres Adams Mss, formerly P.R.O. 30/58/3, partly printed in *L.C.G. III*, III, 412n2); same to George III, sd (*L.C.G. III*, III, no. 2242; copy of same to Loughborough, 14 September; 'State of the Cabinet', 22 September 1800 (both in B.L. Add. Ms 40102). The last is printed in *English Historical Documents 1783–1832*, ed. A. Aspinall and E. Anthony Smith (1959), 110–11.

left London before Otto's approach was considered, when the latest thinking had been that an early prospect of joint peace talks was to be
deplored.[1] His own opinion on the subject was known moreover, and it
was abundantly clear: any such negotiation would almost certainly end in
'an unsafe and dishonourable peace'.[2] Now things apparently were wholly
changed: we were toying with the idea of a disadvantageous truce in aid of
a subsequently hazardous settlement – and this at a time when a sizeable
force might well be used free from Continental demands. He could only
'wonder' at some of Grenville's speculations,[3] and his mounting exasperation boiled over at the current 'state of the Cabinet'. There was no basic
consensus on policy from which strategic decisions could follow. 'Some of
us' thought that the peace of Europe and the security of Britain could be
obtained only by a Bourbon restoration, and that everything was 'mischievous' which did not hold that aim in view. Some, while not going so far, still
thought we should not treat with a revolutionary Government, and that
the Consulate could be so described. Some on the other hand thought
that, whatever its foundation, it had established itself de facto and could
be accepted as a party to negotiations. Some thought that a negotiation in
this instance should be conducted only in conjunction with our allies, and
particularly with Austria. Some by contrast thought that 'the time is past'
when 'the interior Government of France' could be influenced by force of
arms; that such efforts might in fact be counter-productive and that 'we
may lose much and can gain nothing by implicating our interests with
Austria': rather, our only solid ground lay in ourselves. Such 'jarring'
differences of view could not be treated in the abstract; they were entering
'daily . . . into every separate discussion . . . on . . . the subject of either
peace or war'. It was therefore to be 'earnestly hoped', the paper ended,
'that Mr. Pitt will take these observations under his serious consideration
before it is too late'.[4]

This was a robust indictment, and it did not spare the two men who
mattered. For the first time in a series of objections, it entrenched directly
on the Foreign Secretary's preserves. And the conclusion was eloquent.
Dundas was appealing, almost despairingly, to Pitt himself. He was indeed
deeply worried by the man he could not reject. He had shrunk from
applying too much pressure in their recent meeting when he found the
Minister 'very much agitated on the subject'.[5] Now he was trying to
influence others to help bring his fears to bear. He dreaded the drift which

1. Cf. p. 384 above; and also for that matter p. 363 and n3.
2. Dundas to Spencer, 25 August 1800 (quoted in Feiling, *The Second Tory Party*, 215). Cf.
same to Loughborough, 14 September (as p. 386, n5 above), 'We have nothing to gain and
much to lose by entwining ourselves round the desperate fortunes of Austria'.
    Dundas seems to have left London on 27 August.
3. To Loughborough as n2 above.
4. *English Historical Documents* as in p. 386, n5 above. Excerpts are given, but with some
differences, in Stanhope, III, 342–3.
5. To Loughborough as in n2 above.

he saw around him, and all the more keenly since he knew that Pitt was
bent on peace if possible and that his view of the possible might go too far.
The policy of exploring a naval armistice could be defended in itself. But
there were areas in any such exercise into which he must not be allowed to
stray. '. . . when aiming at peace', Dundas recalled the next year, 'there is
no sacrifice which at times he has not been ready to make';[1] and while the
Cabinet's ideas at this point were not in fact unduly compliant,[2] a strict
watch might be necessary to keep him on the rails. Others too were aware
of this intense desire for peace: Rose, Canning, Windham noted it from
different points of vantage, and the last thought Pitt 'well disposed . . . to
concede to a great extent'.[3]

The end of exchanges with Otto left Dundas's paper to his colleagues in
the air. And the particular issue was soon overtaken.[4] The second French
ultimatum declared in London was of course given also in Vienna: the
armistice by land would end on 10 September if the British did not accept
the naval terms, and on the 5th the Emperor went to Germany in person
to take command. One member of his suite was a certain Count von
Lehrbach, a diplomat of experience in the German states and hitherto
counted as a supporter of Thugut. Now however he persuaded his master
to accept a continued armistice in return for the cession of the three
beleaguered fortresses, and a Convention to this effect was signed at
Hohenlinden, near Munich, on the 20th. Thugut himself had been kept
in ignorance. He resigned, and Lehrbach became Minister for Foreign
Affairs, only to be removed himself when the British Government
objected to his appointment. That proved not to be much of an allevia-
tion. The Emperor was annoyed by the protest: he believed that Thugut
was behind it; and the evanescent Lehrbach was replaced by a new Vice-
Chancellor in the familiar form of the suspect Cobenzl.[5] Thugut did not
entirely disappear: he was retained in charge of Italian interests, and as
recipient of general business when his rival left for Lunéville. But his
power was gone, and with it the best hope of residual sympathy in Vienna
for the British connexion.

This was not evident at once. Cobenzl was anxious to gain a negotiating

1. To Spencer, 17 November 1801 (quoted in Feiling, op. cit., 165–6).
2. There is a 'Sketch of a Plan for Peace – 1800 – settled at the Cabinet (at the time of
the discussions with . . . Otto) . . .' in Grenville's papers, B.L. 59067A. It is printed in
Pellew's *Life of Sidmouth*, I, 257–60, and had been Pitt's copy – a paper distinct from that
sent probably for his personal consumption, for which see p. 383, n1 above. The proposals
recognised Dundas's own familiar insistence on retaining the Cape of Good Hope and
Ceylon (II, 628n2; p. 61 above).
3. See Mackesy, op. cit., 138–9 for the first two – Canning's feelings, of disapproval in
this instance, are shown strongly in addition in his diary for 5 September (Canning Ms
29d) –, and Windham's diary, 17 September 1800 (B.L. Add. Ms 37924). Pitt's own final
sentence in the passage quoted on p. 385 above might indeed be taken, though not in so
many words, as pointing to an acceptance now of an almost certain prospect of peace.
4. For what follows see also Duffy, 'War Policy', 430–50.
5. Cf. pp. 153, 200, n2 above.

ally who might shore up Austria's position, and reassuring messages were sent at first to London. But his instructions allowed in point of fact for the conclusion of a separate peace; and the British for their part, disgusted by the Convention, news of which reached them on 28 or 29 September, no longer had hopes of the Emperor and dismissed the prospect of a naval armistice.[1] 'No good can be expected from Vienna', George III pronounced; and that conclusion was 'becoming daily more prevalent' among his Ministers.[2] The Government did not precipitate a break: it declined to 'give the example to Europe of abandoning, even under such circumstances, those to whom we are bound by treaty' – a splendid sentiment, if perhaps somewhat diminished by the experience of four years before.[3] Rather, there was a fading away: no mention of renewing the Convention of June, due to expire in the coming February, which must be left for decision according to events; no further financial advances without express orders in each case.[4] The French for their part delayed the passports for a British envoy to Lunéville, and Cobenzl went to Paris by invitation on his own. He duly informed London, and reasserted Austria's loyalty to the Alliance. But Pitt and Grenville were now inclined to be sceptical, and had little faith in what might ensue.[5]

Their pessimism, as it turned out, was still premature. Bonaparte was driving too hard, his terms were too harsh, and Cobenzl returned to Lunéville to await his British colleague. Furthermore, encouraged by reports of their armies in the field, the counsellors in Vienna were taking fresh heart. It remained hard to guess how the pendulum would settle. A sudden French incursion into Tuscany, breaking the armistice, was accepted passively: 'there is literally no Government whatever in this Empire', Minto dejectedly exclaimed.[6] Nevertheless the derided institution resolved in November to renew the fight. Hostilities opened on the 28th. On 3 December, at Hohenlinden – name of ill omen – the Austrians suffered a crushing defeat. On Christmas day they signed a fresh armistice, and two days later the Emperor informed George III that he

1. Cf. pp. 384–5 above. The first report of the Convention was learned from the French newspapers (see *Diary of Windham*, 433, for the 28th but also London newspapers of the 29th and 30th, and correspondence of those dates between Starhemberg and Grenville in *H.M.C., Dropmore*, VI, 333–5). It seems to have been credited at once (ibid, and eg George III to Dundas, 5 October 1800, in *L.C.G. III*, III, no. 2256), although the official report from Minto arrived only on 8 October (no. 78, 24 September 1800; F.O. 7/60).

2. George III to Dundas, 5 October; Dundas to George III, 9 October 1800 (*L.C.G. III*, III, nos. 2256, 2259; and see also George III to Grenville on the latter date, no. 2261). Grenville himself had reverted to his not infrequent pessimism (eg to Minto, 10 October 1800; *H.M.C., Dropmore*, VI, 346).

3. Grenville to Minto, no. 45, 10 October 1800 (F.O. 7/60). Cf. II, 645–6.

4. Same to same, nos. 45, 48, of 10, 31 October (F.O. 7/60, 61 respectively); Pitt to Grenville, 30 October, 2 November 1800 (*H.M.C., Dropmore*, VI, 368, 372).

5. Pitt to Grenville, 30 October (as in n4 above); Grenville to Minto, no. 47, 31 October 1800 (F.O. 7/61), and cf. n4 above.

6. See his nos. 96–8, 29 October–4 November 1800 (F.O. 7/61).

could no longer meet his Allied engagements. The fact was accepted without recrimination; it had been half expected for all too long, and the Alliance indeed died on a more amicable note than it had achieved for most of its life.[1] On the last day of the year a negotiation opened between Austria and France, and peace was signed at Lunéville on 9 February 1801.

IV

The climate throughout Europe in the autumn, while these events were unfolding, was almost uniformly depressing where it did not threaten worse. Following Marengo, Bonaparte stepped up the pace of a wide diplomatic offensive which added to the yields from the victory itself. From Lisbon to Naples, from Berlin to St Petersburg and the Baltic states, there was no relief for London in prospects for the Continent or, with one qualified exception, visible improvement for those of a maritime war.[2] Some light might be discerned from distant Constantinople.[3] But it was circumscribed and fitful, and fell mostly on regions viewed largely as contingent to those of central concern. The one area within Europe itself still containing a British military presence was moreover a liability rather than an asset. Troops remained in Portugal, consonant with the treaty of 1793,[4] to give support in case of invasion, from Spain and/or France. But this was a purely defensive function, and its degree of priority was becoming awkward. British aid had in fact been quite substantial – some 5,000 men, including French émigrés, and some £200,000 over the past four years.[5] But there was little improvement to be seen in Portuguese readiness or co-operation; the Portuguese Government had treated abortively with France at a low point in British fortunes; and it was known to be looking, not unnaturally, towards Paris again. The ancient alliance retained mutual advantages. They had been wearing thin, however, for some time: trade had shrunk in recent decades, the pre-war years had seen a protracted dispute over commercial relations, and these were not benefiting now from conflicts of opinion over Portugal's maritime relations with Spain. The 'Commercial and Monopolizing Calculation of the British Cabinet' was resented in Lisbon as elsewhere on the

1. See Grenville to Minto, no. 3, 30 January 1801 (F.O. 7/62). He had earlier observed – to the King, in what he knew would be an acceptable opinion – that the event was by now not 'on the whole unfavourable' to British interests (6 January 1801; *L.C.G. III*, III, no. 2319).

2. Discussed in section V below.

3. Pp. 150–1 above.

4. See II, 280.

5. For the former see II, 634 and pp. 152, n3, 152, 294, n3 above; for the latter, Sherwig, *Guineas and Gunpowder*, 136–41, 166. The year of highest allocation was 1798, when, taking the first rather than the alternative table of figures in op. cit. 166, the sum accounted for over half the total devoted to 'allied states' (see p. 100, n2 above).

Continent;[1] and the Portuguese also became aware, if they were not already, that their ally's military commitment was far from absolute.

There had indeed been one proof of this, in 1798, when the British force had been reduced for the occupation of Minorca. The fact was made much plainer in the last quarter of 1800, when the obligation was tested more seriously and did not survive. A certain scepticism had grown up in London of reiterated Portuguese alarms.[2] Nonetheless, renewed reports of Spanish and French preparations as the summer progressed became serious enough to cause genuine concern. The Foreign Secretary became anxious to act, in a way that would honour the treaty of 1793 and also pose a counter threat to the weaker of the two Powers; and when the issue came to a point, which it did late in September, he gained the Cabinet's initial agreement. Fifteen to sixteen thousand men should be sent, from Abercromby's and Pulteney's forces based on Gibraltar.[3] Such a move however could not be made in isolation from the other operational options; indeed it was proposed in a critical phase of that tortuous debate. And as the whole question was examined more extensively it provoked a series of meetings which ended, despite Grenville's severe opposition, in favour of a different demand.[4] The undertaking was not abandoned at once: rather the numbers were cut, at first to 8,000 and then to 5,000, with a reinforcement from Dutch troops in England to replace part of the augmented force. But thereafter the mood hardened, as the weeks went by and urgent danger seemed to recede. Priorities were shifting over a wider scene. In November the Portuguese were told that the existing British force would be wholly withdrawn, to strengthen the defences against the spread of unrest at home; and at the end of the year its departure was confirmed for 'more immediate and pressing Services'.[5] So far from being envisaged as a scene of action, let alone reinforced, Portugal was taken finally as a source of reserve.

1. Robert Walpole to Grenville, no. 15, 7 April 1800 (P.R.O., F.O. 63/32; and cf. p. 366 above). A sharp quarrel between the capitals continued throughout 1800 (F.O. 63/32–4) over cargoes to Spain from South America carried in Portuguese ships, despite the fears of a Spanish invasion and the fact that Portugal was an 'auxiliary' wartime ally of Britain. See pp. 64, 151 above for the Portuguese talks with France in 1797.

2. Cf. p. 367 above.

3. Agreement was reached at some point from 23 to 26 September (cf. Mackesy, 153, who opts for the 23rd). Cf. p. 389 above for Grenville's sense of obligation to allies. Windham, who sympathised with him in that, noted his accompanying hope of unsettling Spain or even detaching her from France by an offensive in conjunction with Portugal (diary for 24 September 1800, B.L. Add. Ms 37924); and see also Grenville to Pitt, 23 September 1800 (*H.M.C., Dropmore*, VI, 329).

4. For which see pp. 401, 407–10 below. Draft of a Cabinet Minute on 3 October, in Dundas's papers with draft changes in Grenville's hand (B.L. Add. Ms 40102); Grenville to John Hookham Frere [newly appointed Minister to Lisbon; and see pp. 92, 111 above], nd, probably 4 October 1800 (F.O. 63/34).

5. See p. 294, n3 above for the impact of the unrest in England. Grenville to Charles Arbuthnot [chargé d'affaires in Lisbon], 19 November; same to Frere, no. 4, 15 December 1800 (P.R.O., F.O. 63/34). Warnings of withdrawal had been given slightly earlier, one to try to force Portugal's hand in the dispute over her conduct of

In the event the winter passed in the Peninsula without disaster. That was reserved for 1801; meanwhile the Tagus remained open to the British fleet. Farther east, within the Mediterranean, the navy's situation held promise but also doubt. The central facilities there lay in Naples, and The Two Sicilies were potentially in trouble: the Government had fled Palermo after the debacle in Rome,[1] the King would not return unless he had to, and Anglophil advisers were under a cloud. Nor could Austria or perhaps Russia now be called on for effective support against France: the former was powerless after Marengo, particularly since Tuscany had been overrun, and the latter's mood, though still not unfriendly in this case, had changed in relation to the war.[2] In this state of affairs, Bonaparte in point of fact had his own ideas for Italy. He was wooing Spain with an offer of a new dependent 'Kingdom of Etruria', in return for the transfer of the transatlantic territory of Louisiana; and while this arrangement with one branch of the Bourbons gained preliminary acceptance in October, he had already told London of his conditional intention for the other.[3] Naples thus hung under a menace from someone who had shown his capacity to deliver. And relations with Britain itself, maintained uneasily in these dispiriting conditions, were suffering from a dispute occasioned by the Allies' one success, the expulsion of the French from Malta. That achievement indeed, which was to prove of historic importance and replace Naples itself for British use, had some immediately troubling as well as favourable implications. It raised its awkward questions for Britain's relations with Russia; it also had a consequence for those with The Two Sicilies, whose interest in the island's affairs, recognised by its allies two years before, seemed now in danger of being ignored. There was a controversial incident at once, when the blockading force – the only Allied force present – raised the British flag to fly on its own on taking possession: a matter on which the British envoy himself in fact felt so strongly that he took up the cudgels with his Government.[4] The new alternative base was causing problems at this point by its very attractions for the exercise of seapower, above all now in a region where interests in Europe met those in Africa and the Near East.

Turning back beyond the Alps, the scene in the autumn became gloomier the farther north one looked, and it was transformed for the

---

maritime affairs. Doubts of the extent of her danger moreover seem to have surfaced even while the Cabinet's discussions were taking place – at least according to Dundas (to George III, 28 September 1800; *L.C.G. III*, III, no. 2252). They had grown belatedly stronger, perhaps conveniently, by November.

1. See p. 205 above.
2. See pp. 389, 348–50 above. Russia appeared to be still prepared after Marengo to try to defend Sardinian and Sicilian interests at a general peace (see Garlike, in Berlin [p. 201, n5], to Grenville, no. 55, 31 July 1800; P.R.O., F.O. 64/57); but that was all.
3. P. 385 above.
4. See p. 384 above for the fall of Malta; *The Paget Papers . . .*, ed. The Right Hon. Sir Augustus Paget, I (1896), 265–75 for the British envoy's representations.

worse in the last two months of the year. The German states, naturally on edge under the Austrian armistice, were in disarray after the battle of Hohenlinden; nervously despondent, defiant or hopeful as their readings of French intentions might suggest. Domestic divisions in some became more acute, for instance in Bavaria which was of concern to Britain for its supply of troops;[1] many were watching reactions from Prussia as Austria sank in the scales; and Prussia, again not surprisingly, was sniffing the wind. So far as London was concerned, the picture in Berlin had in fact appeared the same for much of the year: Prussia remained a highly cautious neutral, probing and withdrawing as short-term advantage seemed to dictate. The one near certainty was that she would fight to preserve northern Germany from a French incursion. Otherwise she drifted more noticeably into Russia's orbit, dallying with approaches from St Petersburg as the Tsar swung away from his allies, making an agreement with him in July to use good offices in a mediation for peace, and putting out feelers for that object – as she had done earlier – to Austria and France. Britain too was included, and the more actively as Otto's activity became known. But the atmosphere, already clouded, became more troubled as the autumn passed. The Prussians intervened, unhelpfully it was thought in London, in a dispute between Spain and Sweden over an incident in which British men-of-war had been concerned; they put a wholesale stop – for their own needs – on the export of grain to England when that was sought in the continuing dearth;[2] and in November 1800, in another incident involving a British man-of-war, they occupied the port of Cuxhaven at the mouth of the Elbe, commanding the approach to the entrepôt of Hamburg. This last action at once aroused a strong response in London.[3] For it confirmed Ministers' suspicions, already alerted by the backing of Spain, that Prussia was upping the stakes for a role in an all too familiar development which could end as a thrust at the heart of Britain's capacity for war.

The exercise of belligerent maritime rights over neutrals is almost always a cause of contention, and it was bound to be so in the chequered course of the Revolutionary War. It the mid nineties the British could congratulate themselves on having escaped the worst possible effects.[4] Negotiation,

1. See pp. 249, n1, 318, 346 above.
2. See p. 281 above. Grenville to the Earl of Carysfort [envoy in Berlin], no. 11, 14 October; Carysfort to Grenville, no. 32, 28 October 1800 (P.R.O., F.O. 64/58), *et seq.* in 64/59. Carysfort was close to the Foreign Secretary by marriage (as a brother-in-law), politics and tastes.
3. The news was conveyed on 13 November (Carysfort's no. 39, loc. cit.) and received on the 23rd. A British warship with a Prussian prize had been driven into the Elbe by bad weather, thus, it was claimed, violating the neutrality of northern Germany, which the King of Prussia was committed to protect. Prussia was also claiming on the same ground a 'jurisdiction' over the river Ems which was said to underline the 'demarcation' agreed in 1795 as a limit to any French move eastwards from Holland.
4. See II, 504–7 for what follows immediately.

and indeed common prudence, had produced certain if minor easements; their own trade was not significantly hampered, while that of the enemy was at least inconvenienced; diplomatic ties were nowhere broken off; above all – the most obvious danger – the Armed Neutrality of the American War had not been revived. Something of a crisis had blown up with Denmark and Sweden in 1794. But it had passed, thanks in part to helpful Russian influence, and matters remained largely, though uneasily, quiescent over the next three years. In 1798 and '99 however there were some angry encounters, the worst of which occurred at the end of the latter year when a Danish escort opened fire during a search of her convoy off Gibraltar. The resulting dispute was still unresolved when there was another incident, this time in the Channel, in July 1800. Shots were exchanged, the Danish warship and convoy were taken into port, their Government claimed satisfaction and restitution, and a 'lively and peremptory exchange of state papers ensued'.[1] At the same time, the British Government did not wish to bring the case to extremes. Denmark was generally more favoured than Sweden, whose sympathies were seen as lying often more clearly with France,[2] and Grenville and, particularly, Pitt were disposed to compromise if possible, while Spencer helpfully agreed that his cruisers should not be 'very particular in looking out for neutral convoys for the present'. Moderation nonetheless could not exclude firmness: we should show that we did not mean to abrogate our necessary rights. An answer was found by sending a special envoy to Copenhagen, with conciliatory instructions to seek a settlement but armed more cogently with the despatch of a naval squadron to the Sound.[3] On this basis, and under a readiness to use force if required, a reasonably satisfactory agreement was reached on 29 August.[4] But by then the affair had produced one unforeseen result. On the 27th, approached by the Danes for support and angered by the presence of the British men-of-war, the Tsar

1. In the happy phrase of the old *Cambridge Modern History* (IX (1907), 45). An excellent account of Denmark's position in this, and in all that followed over the next six months, is given in Ole Feldbaek, *Denmark and the Armed Neutrality 1800–1801* (1980).

A Swedish vessel was involved as well in the affair.

2. Though not always, and the position of course was usually affected largely by current relations with Russia. Cf. eg pp. 235, 321 above.

3. He was Whitworth, armed also now with his peerage (see p. 206 above). His instructions were drafted on 30 July (P.R.O., F.O. 22/39) and dated 2 August. Pitt then wanted an alteration designed to ameliorate a phrase of Grenville's (see *H.M.C., Dropmore*, VI, 288) and this was sent to catch Whitworth on the eve of leaving, reaching him however only while he was negotiating in Copenhagen (Feldbaek, op. cit., 52). See also Cabinet Minute of 30 July, enclosed in Grenville, 1 August 1800 (*H.M.C., Dropmore*, VI, 287).

Pitt was also advising caution in August with the Swedes, involved as they were together with the Danes in the incident in the Channel (Windham's *Diary*, 430, for the 13th).

4. The captured ships were restored and the Danes consented not to form convoys for the time being, except in the Mediterranean for protection against the Barbary corsairs. The whole question of convoy was reserved for future discussion. The text of the Convention is published in, *inter alia*, Sir Francis Piggott and W.T. Omond, *Documentary History of the Armed Neutralities of 1780 and 1800 . . .* (1919), 412–13.

invited Denmark and Sweden, together now with Prussia, to establish a fresh Armed Neutrality on the lines of that in the American War; and the next day he ordered an embargo on British vessels in Russian ports, the restraint of their crews, and the sequestration of British property.[1]

This last news, of action suddenly taken, caused particular alarm. Russia might not be a partner on whom to count for a prime role in European operations; but her alliance at the start of the war had 'completely destroyed' the threat of 'an armed neutrality', and her value had since been incontestable in influencing the smaller Baltic states.[2] The embargo itself was soon removed by the settlement in Copenhagen.[3] But it marked a worrying extension of Paul's sense of hostility; and the relief proved shortlived. There were hopes in some quarters, though scarcely at the Foreign Office, of a return to more friendly relations.[4] But on 6 November the measure was reimposed.

The immediate cause on this occasion lay in warmer waters. Four days earlier the Tsar had learned belatedly of Malta's surrender, and of the fact, which had caused trouble with The Two Sicilies, that the British flag had been raised on its own. As Grenville forecast, he was 'exasperated' once more.[5] A violent temperament was by now undoubtedly under frightening strain. But there was more to it than that, and in this instance Paul had reason to feel aggrieved. The British action could indeed be suspected as revealing a policy which ran counter to past indications. The Tsar could point not only to tacit Allied acceptance of his 'protectorship' of the Knights, but also to the agreement, as he saw it, at the time of the Anglo-Russian Convention of December 1798 that Malta would be garrisoned and a wartime protectorate established, on the Order's behalf, under the authority of the three interested Allied Powers.[6] Russia furthermore had been given to understand that if she so wished – and she

---

The settlement however was not secured without threat. The British Government, having envisaged the possible use of force from the start in sending the naval squadron, had agreed orders as recently as 26 August giving discretion to open hostilities if agreement was further delayed (Cabinet Minute, enclosed in Grenville to George III, sd; *L.C.G. III*, III, no. 2230; and see also no. 2228). Whitworth in fact quitted Copenhagen at a late stage for the squadron on his own judgment, while bomb vessels moved into position off the city.

1. There is a translation of his Declaration to the other three Powers, dated 16 August 1800 (O.S.), in P.R.O., F.O. 65/47. See also Piggott and Omond, op. cit., 416–19. Prussia had not been a member of the previous confederacy, for which see I, 49–50.

2. See *H.M.C., Dropmore*, VI, 331 for the news reaching London on 26 September. Cf. Ch. VIII *passim*, pp. 348–9 above for the inherently optimistic expectations of Russia's role in Allied operations in the west; II, 276 for the judgment in 1793, which was George III's.

3. In point of fact it was not put into execution until 4 September, and seems to have been discontinued six days later.

4. Eg Carysfort and Grenville in their private correspondence, *H.M.C., Dropmore*, VI, 306, 318, 345, 355–6, 373.

5. Grenville to Carysfort, 7 November 1800 (op. cit., 373).

6. Pp. 208, n1, 359 above.

did – she could provide the garrison herself. That had been Grenville's own position until recent months,[1] and Dundas himself seems to have changed his mind only in the spring. Earlier in fact he had accepted and indeed approved of a Russian presence in the central basin.[2] The change now stemmed from developments, actual and potential and affecting extensive areas, which were coming into sight in London and being brought progressively to bear.

For if the Tsar could suspect British motives, the British were fast growing nervous of the Tsar, and their rising feeling dictated a fresh look at their position in the Mediterranean. It seemed clear that Russia was pulling out of the war on the Continent in any active sense; having sent ships into the Adriatic, her activities there were sometimes disturbing her allies; and if her attitude to the Coalition were to change actively for the worse, a helpful influence or presence farther east could be replaced by a possible threat.[3] Malta's possible role was suddenly emerging in response to new concerns. The island had been of very little interest before Bonaparte landed in Egypt, and even then Dundas himself, fearful as he was of a threat to India, concentrated on support from Turkey and others for the overland passages, and on British movements in and through the Indian Ocean, rather than on a fresh naval base to the west while Naples was in use.[4] It was in fact Russia's growing ambivalence quite as much as France's enmity that had at length focused attention more closely on the problem. The Tsar, now so dangerously unreliable, should not be permitted 'to seize upon the whole Watch Towers of the Levant and the Adriatic'; Malta stood 'the foremost in that description'; and although such reasoning was discounted by a Foreign Secretary anxious to keep an ally still in play, that object seemed increasingly unobtainable as the months went by.[5] Rumours grew of French approaches to St Petersburg to which Paul was lending an ear, and at the beginning of August the Cabinet decided to prohibit any Russian force that might join the blockade from entering the island until the British commander received further instructions. By October, when news of the French surrender reached London, the attitude had hardened, and Dundas was able to state categorically that Russian troops, if present, should 'on no account' be admitted.[6] There was no explicit policy for the future: this was a holding

1. See p. 360, above for Stuart's resignation over the question in April, and 364 for the policy, communicated to the Russian Minister in London, as it still stood in June.

2. Ibid. above.

3. See section III above for the Continent; 348, n2 for the Russian presence in the Adriatic, where reports from the British consul in Corfu (P.R.O., F.O. 42/3–4) supplemented others from cruising men-of-war and information received from Constantinople (F.O. 78/21–2, 24, 28–9).

4. Cf. pp. 142–3, 148–52 above.

5. Dundas to Grenville, 16 April 1800 (copy in B.L. Add. Ms 40101). Cf. pp. 359–60 above, and see also same to same as late as 10 June (*H.M.C., Dropmore*, VI, 250).

6. Same to Abercromby, 1 August, 6 October 1800 (P.R.O., F.O. 49/2, the first published in *The Keith Papers* . . ., ed. Christopher Lloyd, II (1950), 135–8). The second

operation, directed to the present. Justification was sought in technicalities affecting the agreement in December 1798.[1] Vindication could be claimed better by assessing the weight of strategic advantage against that of a decision which would certainly intensify but would not in itself have incited the Tsar's demonstrable wish to be free of the Coalition.

For matters, as seen from London, were now virtually beyond recall; even moving perhaps beyond neutrality itself. 'As for Russia', Grenville remarked at the end of October, '. . . we are all but at war with that near and natural ally of this country';[2] and though now lacking direct information in the absence of an envoy and a chargé d'affaires,[3] he knew from other sources something of the contacts between St Petersburg and Paris. Bonaparte had earlier made a good impression on Paul by returning Russian prisoners of war without seeking compensation, and also by offering him Malta if and when the garrison surrendered. He maintained unofficial approaches; talks were opened more directly in October; and by then indeed the Tsar was considering a joint attack overland on India. It is arguable that his action in the Baltic was designed largely to farther his Mediterranean interest; for the embargo, damaging Russia in the long run, would scarcely affect the northern trade in the depths of winter.[4] He still maintained contact with London; some hints of possible discussion were received in December.[5] But these were greeted cautiously pending a more solid indication; and before that could be furnished the die was finally cast. On 16 December the formation of the Armed Neutrality was announced, with Russia, Denmark, Sweden, and Prussia as members,[6] and a month later a Russian diplomat was sent to treat for an alliance with France.

---

instruction followed a letter to Dundas from Grenville earlier in the day (B.L. Add. Ms 40101). Despatches from Corfu (F.O. 42/4) suggested from time to time that Russian warships might shortly be despatched, and according to the Foreign Secretary 2,000 men had in fact reached Naples.

1. See *H.M.C., Dropmore*, VI, 199; Norman E. Saul, *Russia and the Mediterranean 1797–1807* (1970), 147 & n66. The Foreign Office decided to stand on the pretext that the agreement on the island at that time had been verbal and so not to be taken as on a par with the clauses ratified in the Convention itself (p. 208, n1 above).

2. To Minto, 31 October 1800 (*H.M.C., Dropmore*, VI, 370).Cf. II, 22, p. 321 above for the old concept of the natural ally.

3. The Secretary of the Legation having been refused leave to stay after Whitworth left. For good measure, the consul at St Petersburg, reaching Russia on return from an abbreviated leave in England, was ordered on 17 September to quit the country at once (Stephen Shairp to Grenville, 1 October 1800; F.O. 65/47).

4. Cf. Saul, op. cit., 148.

5. See eg a Cabinet Minute of the 15th enclosed in Grenville to George III, sd (*L.C.G. III*, III, no. 2297). As often in what proved to be terminal developments, these weeks saw a crop of confusing reports.

6. The texts of the Conventions are published in Piggott and Omond, op. cit., 439–43, 447–62. That with Prussia was dated 18 December.

The British Government learned of the second embargo on 27 November. It responded at once. A Privy Council was held the next day at which merchants trading with Russia were forbidden to pay or be paid by bills of exchange. This was the most effective weapon to hand, in both the immediate and the longer term; obviously inconveniencing British houses but striking harder at their Russian counterparts.[1] Meanwhile Ministers awaited the outcome of the Tsar's proposal for the Armed Neutrality. Their stance was made clear to Prussia, perhaps still the best hope of bringing persuasion to bear. After a stern reference to the occupation of Cuxhaven, which must be viewed against the prospect of a 'Northern League', a categorical warning was given by way of a general deterrent.[2]

> The Rights of this Country [in relation to neutral vessels] are grounded on such principles of justice and reason that they cannot be shaken: the Maintenance of those Rights is necessary to our existence as a Naval Power, and any endeavour to enforce by arms a contrary system, may be productive unquestionably of some temporary embarrassment to this Kingdom but must totally annihilate the foreign Commerce and consequently the domestic industry of all those Countries who shall engage in such a Confederacy.
>
> . . . the object of such a Confederacy will not be attained but by a struggle, in which Great Britain, contending for her Existence, will exert Her utmost efforts . . .
>
> The claims of Great Britain will never be relinquished on her part till Her Naval Power be annihilated . . .

Pitt repeated this language two months later. We had rights under 'the law of nations' and 'positive treaties' alike 'upon which not only our character but our very existence as a maritime power depends'.[3]

The prospective outcome had been settled by then. The members of the Armed Neutrality themselves viewed the 'league' with varying

1. Correspondence between Grenville and George III, 27 November 1800 (*L.C.G. III*, III, no. 2287); George III to Pitt, 28 November 1800 (Stanhope, III, Appendix, xxii). *L.C.G. III*, III, 443n1 is inaccurate. The adverse imbalance between the number of Russian vessels in British ports and British vessels in Russian ports was an additional argument for the measure, which in fact was urged speedily by some – though not all – of the British merchants themselves (see William Glen Johnston to Grenville, 27 November, with Grenville's endorsement for Pitt's concurrence, but also Samuel Thornton (for whom p. 274, n5 above) to Pitt, 28 November 1800; both in F.O. 65/47). Consul Shairp (p. 397, n3 above) made the same suggestion independently (to Grenville, 1 December 1800; loc. cit.).

2. Grenville to Carysfort, Most Secret, 3 December 1800 (F.O. 64/59). For Cuxhaven see p. 393 above.

3. In a debate on 2 February 1801 (*P.R., 3rd ser.*, XIV (1801), 52–5). He was referring to the treaties with Denmark and Sweden respectively of 1661 and 1670.

It may well have been in preparation for this debate (see *H.M.C., Dropmore*, VI, 433–4) that the Minister compiled or more likely was given extensive notes on the 'Conduct of Russia respecting Neutrals since 1793' (P.R.O. 30/8/196; 10ff., nd but after 1799, not in Pitt's hand). Cf. II, 276n2.

degrees of enthusiasm. Prussia, on the margin, was far from anxious to be seen in London as an actual enemy, deprecating a hostile interpretation of her action over Cuxhaven.[1] Nor were the Danes keen for a further demonstration of Britain's response to their claims. Their Government was upset by the Tsar's linkage of that question with his interest in Malta; it viewed with suspicion the developing ties with his fellow monarch of Sweden; and was anxious to avoid an extension of Paul's plans for Baltic defence into possible co-operation with France.[2] In Sweden too there were similar doubts, and an emissary was sent to London in December to try to settle the prize case of the summer.[3] The British were ready to play on these symptoms of reluctance, notably in Berlin and Copenhagen. In February 1801 indeed Grenville suggested that Denmark might like to consider an alliance, which would embrace Sweden as well.[4] This, as it proved, would be followed up in due course. But only after the clash had occurred. For the formation of the Armed Neutrality could not be disavowed; the expressions used to Prussia, repeated to the other members, meant what they said; and as soon as the news was formally received in London, the first steps in retaliation followed. On 14 January 1801 embargoes were placed on Russian, Danish and Swedish ships in British ports, and from the 16th to the 28th successive Orders in Council were issued prohibiting commercial transactions with those countries, though not with Prussia. Preparations for armed action were also in hand. The seizure was ordered of Danish and Swedish islands in the West Indies, while at home the Channel fleet would be made available and, as one of the Grenville brothers prophetically observed, the matter had come now to the point at which 'Sir Hyde Parker and Lord Nelson will be our best plenipotentiaries, as soon as the Baltic will thaw enough to receive them'.[5]

While these last soundings were being taken, there was no longer any doubt about the Tsar. His attitude was unmistakable by December, and the proofs emerged in the next month. On 14 January he cancelled the

1. F.O. 64/59–60 and *H.M.C., Dropmore*, VI, *passim* for November 1800–January 1801. Unlike Denmark and Sweden she did not sign reciprocal instruments of adherence to the confederacy (see Piggott and Omond, op. cit., 452), but only one with Russia which could be interpreted as being in line with her agreement, on 28 July 1800 (see p. 393 above), to exercise good offices in a mediation for peace.

2. For which cf. pp. 396–7 above.

3. See p. 394, n1 above. The visit of Baron Ehrensvärd can be followed in P.R.O., F.O. 73/28; see also *L.C.G. III*, III, nos. 2297, 2326.

4. See Jupp, op. cit., 261. He had initially been slow to express British reaction to the events of November and December, out of a desire not to appear to seek an accommodation and also a hope that Denmark and Prussia might withdraw from the confederacy of their own accord (Feldbaek, op. cit., 105).

5. Thomas Grenville to Buckingham, 13 January 1801 (Buckingham, III (1855), 117). See *Private Papers of Spencer*, IV, 274, 275–6 for Parker. Nelson almost certainly learned of the prospect from his senior Admiral on 16 January.

See also Windham's diary for 8, 11, 25 January (B.L. Add. Ms 37924), Grenville to Dundas, 13 January (B.L. Add. Ms 40101), Dundas to George III, 14 January 1801 (*L.C.G. III*, III, no. 2325) for these steps and consequential measures to be taken in ports overseas.

pension he had been granting to Louis XVIII, then resident in Russia, and required him to leave the country at once. The next day he despatched his envoy to Paris to negotiate definitely for peace.[1] On the 27th he made known his impatience for a French draft as soon as possible, and suggested that Bonaparte should make a diversion on the English coast. It seemed possibly only a question of time – of very little time – before Russia exchanged her alliance with Britain for an alliance not for neutrality but actively with France.

V

The affairs of the North, as this last decision showed, were perforce linked in London with developments elsewhere. That in fact had been indicated as early as September. For the report of the agreement with Denmark followed on the heels of the Portuguese call for reinforcement; that appeal was sent at a time when Dundas was making his case for a strategy beyond Europe; and if naval resources were tied up more extensively in the North Sea and the Baltic, and in covering supplies and operations, perhaps quite prolonged, in Iberia, he might well find it harder to gain consent for a major shift of emphasis.[2] He was thus relieved by the outcome in Copenhagen in August, reluctant to give 'a single thought' to Portugal, and likewise to lock up excessive forces on either side of the Irish Sea.[3] Although confined in the event immediately to raids on the Spanish Atlantic coast,[4] he was still able to plan for a more considerable future.

The result indeed emerged and was settled in principle while those ventures were under way. Before Dundas went down to Cheltenham late in August, he had followed up his paper of 22 July[5] with a renewed proposal for consequent operations. Surveying his two favoured targets, Cuba and the River Plate, he settled for the former in the first instance, drafted instructions for Abercromby, and applied to the Cabinet again. It is hard to tell how much credence he found there: doubts were raised about the adequacy of the force, but also about the strength to be left at home; and the question was in abeyance when he left London.[6] On his return in

1. See p. 397 above.
2. See p. 394 above for Denmark, the news from which reached London by or on 5 September (*The Morning Post* and, differing slightly, *The Times* of the 6th, and George III to Spencer, sd, in *Private Papers of Spencer*, IV, 273); 391 above for the appeal from Portugal, which was relayed from Lisbon on 2 August and received on the 23rd (P.R.O., F.O. 63/33). Defence there, it may be recalled, might, in Grenville's mind at least, be replaced by a joint offensive with Portugal into Spain.
3. For his feelings on the last two subjects respectively see Dundas to Huskisson, 3 September 1800 (Mackesy, op. cit., 142–3), and a memorandum of 14 August 1800 (S.R.O., Melville Ms GD 51/1/725/1).
4. Pp. 367–8, 371 above.
5. P. 367 above.
6. Dundas to George III, 18, 26 August 1800 (*L.C.G. III*, III, nos. 2223, 2229). I have not found an account of the discussions, which may have taken place by the 25th (see

mid September, however, his attention fastened on a quite different object. On the 18th he recommended to his colleagues that the expedition should be aimed at Egypt.[1]

This sudden switch must seem surprising at first sight. After all, Egypt had not figured in Dundas's memoranda to the Cabinet over the past six months.[2] But one contributory reason for a move may have lain in the prominence now accorded to Portugal. During his stay in Cheltenham that appeal had been gaining sympathy, and if it succeeded it could reduce or even cancel the free use of the combined forces so arduously assembled and hitherto preserved. There would thus have been a fortuitous incitement for him to press for an alternative. But that in itself could not provide an argument for the choice to be made.

Despite its absence from his recent priorities, Egypt had certainly not left Dundas's thoughts; nor had it been allowed to escape the Cabinet's attention. On the contrary, it had been a persistent preoccupation with him, and a source of acute embarrassment for a time to the Ministry as a whole. This last awkwardness stemmed in point of fact not from Bonaparte's success but rather from his failure after the promise of his landing in 1798. Early victory over the Mamelukes and effective occupation of the country still left him, after Nelson's action, open to the threat of Allied attack; and a move into Syria in 1799 to forestall a Turkish attempt in the spring, halted by Sidney Smith in his much applauded defence of Acre, ended in a withdrawal which checked any immediate hopes of exploiting his conquest. After beating off a Turkish seaborne assault in June, he slipped away in August to his European future.[3] The army however remained, and with it the problems he had created.

For what should be Britain's policy, now as before? To leave the force to decay? Or try to destroy it? Or if that looked impracticable, to see it removed? A considered answer from London, to be resolved in the light of strategic priorities, was pre-empted in the event by the state of affairs on the ground. For the local British authorities very soon decided the choice of options themselves; moving without instructions, and, for good measure, in a direction already abandoned by the French. Shortly before he left, Bonaparte had offered terms to the Porte to evacuate his troops, and he told his successor, General Kléber, to repeat them if necessary

---

Canning to Pitt of that date, Canning Ms 30). The draft instructions to Abercromby gave Guadeloupe, the Canaries, Porto Rico and the Plate as other choices if required (dated 'August', copy in Dacres Adams Mss, formerly P.R.O. 30/58/3). By the time he returned from Cheltenham, Dundas had the benefit of qualified approval for Cuba from Cornwallis in Ireland, whose military position had to be considered and whose opinion of course always carried weight (7 September 1800, addressee not stated in *Correspondence of Cornwallis*, III, 292–3).

1. Windham's diary, 17, 18 September 1800 (B.L. Add. Ms 37924); memorandum by Dundas, 19 September 1800 (Eng. Ms 907, John Rylands Library, Manchester).
2. See pp. 353–5, 366–8 above.
3. P. 333 above.

unless reinforcements arrived by the spring. Kléber did not wait that long. After driving off a second Turkish landing, he took up the running in the autumn, and very soon found that the idea was well received. The Turks told the Russian and British envoys that they would like to see the back of the French; their wish was accepted, and by the end of November 1799 the necessary passports were agreed.

That however was not the end of the matter. Even if such a policy was to be followed, there were terms to be worked out, and the need for British sanction was paramount for safe passage from the Mediterranean fleet. The process of diplomacy was not eased by the state of the British representation at Constantinople.[1] Agreement on the passports was given by the acting Minister, Spencer Smith – Sidney Smith's brother –, who in one rank or another had been in charge over the past four years. But a new Ambassador, Lord Elgin,[2] had at last been appointed and was on his way; and when he arrived, in November, he did not approve of what was being done. The terms proposed were too lenient; and in any case why bargain for departure rather than surrender?[3] A British General had been sent out at the start of the year, with artillery and stores, to work with the Turks. They now authorised him to go to Syria in earnest of a further assault, while Elgin sought consent directly from the Governor General in India for a force to be sent to the Red Sea. Spencer Smith was resentful of all this, he deployed considerable powers of frustration, and a bitter row ensued, which in due course resulted in his recall.[4] Involving a reluctant Foreign Secretary who was also his cousin, it ended indeed by reaching the Cabinet, having embittered and confused relations with an Embassy distant from timely control. That was not helpful; but the pattern of authority contained a greater seed of weakness. For while Spencer Smith was controversial, it was not he but his brother who caused the greatest alarm. After a career which might in fact have given warning, Sidney Smith had come out to the Mediterranean endowed with a pair of appointments which in themselves might have hinted at trouble. Posted by the Admiralty to the command of a ship in the fleet, specifically destined for the eastern basin, he also carried credentials from the Foreign Office to act as a diplomat jointly with Spencer.[5] In those particular hands, so

1. A good account of what follows is to be found in Edward Ingram, *Commitment to Empire . . .* (1981), ch. IX, section III.
2. See p. 153 above.
3. A way out of this choice was suggested by the Russian Ambassador: passports should be granted, the French allowed to depart, and then stopped and made prisoner on the way home.
4. The problem was compounded by a pattern of dual responsibilities. Spencer Smith was charged specifically, among his other duties, with the interests of the Levant Company; and its long established and semi-independent regional power, in some ways more immediately relevant than the authority of the King's representative, provided information not otherwise accessible which he now refused to show to his superior.
5. It was hard to tell, as subsequent debate showed, if his powers could be termed those of a 'Special' (or sometimes 'Extraordinary') mission, or were more general. The

armed, the trouble was almost assured. Capable, venturesome, extravagantly vain and in perennial search of glory – a notable example of an unusual but not unfamiliar wartime type – the Captain (now Commodore) was still in the area of Acre with a small squadron, where he was indeed, contrary to orders, issuing passports on his own.[1] Conveniently on the spot, and happily continuing to deploy his diplomatic identity, he soon took charge of the talks which Kléber had opened with the Turkish authorities on the Egyptian coast. In December Elgin found to his astonishment that 'a Naval Officer commanding [an] inconsiderable force' was in danger of committing his Government to an agreement reached 'exclusively' by himself.[2] This indeed was so, and the danger was soon turned into established fact. On 24 January 1800 Sidney Smith approved the signing of the terms which he had largely drafted for the Convention of El Arish.

The report of a negotiation in Constantinople for the issue of passports had reached London on 8 December. It produced a prompt reaction. Dundas was about to leave – as it seemed at that point – on his usual winter visit to Scotland, and we do not know if he was consulted.[3] But Grenville took the matter to Cabinet, a decision was taken quickly, and the King's approval followed at once. Ministers' information of course was then confined to this point, and orders were sent to Lord Keith, St Vincent's successor in the Mediterranean fleet, that British consent was not sanctioned, no passports were to be granted, and if any French were met at sea they were to be returned to Egypt. It was too late. The instructions reached Keith at Minorca on 8 January 1800 – Elgin only on 25 February –, and it was not until 22 March that Ministers knew of the Convention

former were of course not unusual in these wartime years (cf. II, 332, 343, 582; pp. 54, 202, 254, n2 – more doubtfully – above), and carried credentials where there was a valid authority to receive them (exceptions being for instance Macartney's mission to the French Pretender, and Wickham's second mission to the borders of Switzerland after having to remove his Legation from Berne). Ministers later claimed that this was the correct interpretation, applying only to limited operational requirements in a possibly fast-moving situation in the Near East, and supplied only because at the time of the grant there was no Ambassador in Constantinople.

1. His immediate naval superior (though the interpretation of the chain of command was itself open to question under challenge) had instructed him – strictly, knowing his man – 'never to give any French ship or man leave to quit Egypt' (*The Dispatches and Letters of Lord Nelson . . .*, ed. Sir Nicholas Harris Nicolas, III (1846), 296, for 18 March 1799). *DNB* gives some idea of Smith's spirited and rather tiresome career; Mahan (*The Influence of Sea Power upon the French Revolution*, I, ch. X), a good account of his personality and reputation.

2. To Sidney Smith, 22 December 1799 (P.R.O., F.O. 78/24). He seems to have learned of the Captain's intervention by the 17th.

3. Ingram, op. cit., 358n6 suspects not. In the event Dundas did not leave until the 13th (see Stanhope, III, 204–5).

itself.[1] They were faced by a dilemma. On the one hand, acceptance would certainly have bad effects on their two major allies. Thugut could complain, and at a delicate moment, that the British had ensured the return of an army to swell the strength against Austria on the eve of the new campaign; the Tsar was likely to protest at an agreement at which no Russian representative was present, and which might allow the Turks to leave the war and resume their hostility to Russian designs. On the other hand, total denial would undoubtedly offend the Porte; and Government could not but admit that its own good faith was involved. Sidney Smith had had the residual sense not to put his own hand to the document; but he had been present, he had largely composed it, and given the impression that he was so entitled.[2] The Cabinet met on 27 March in an angry mood. But Ministers were driven to the conclusion that though they would confirm the disavowal of the Convention, and that no active assistance must be given to implement the results, Britain would not 'break' it or obstruct the Turks in its observance, and indeed would advise them and the Russians to honour the terms.[3]

There was an unpleasant aftermath. Keith had informed Kléber in January that no passports would be given, and added – it could be held provocatively – that troops could leave Egypt only as prisoners of war.[4] Kléber thereupon denounced British perfidy, reopened hostilities, and defeated a Turkish army – a few days in fact before the Cabinet met. In June 1800 he was assassinated, and his successor showed no interest in reopening the talks. Matters had thus reverted to their original state, before El Arish had arisen, and the Government in London was free to consider the Convention void. It only remained for Pitt and Dundas to

1. Of which Elgin received the news, with details, only on 14 February (to Grenville, nos. 18, 20, both of 16 February 1800, endorsed with date of receipt; F.O. 78/28). For the Government's earlier action see Elgin to Grenville, no. 5, nd, with endorsement of date of receipt (F.O. 78/24); *Diary of Windham*, 419 for 12 December 1799; Cabinet Minute, sd (*L.C.G. III*, III, no. 2089); George III to Grenville, 13 December 1799 (op. cit., no. 2090); Grenville to Elgin, no. 8, and same to Admiralty for Commander-in-Chief Mediterranean fleet, both of 15 December 1799 (F.O. 78/24). The Admiral was at the centre of the instructions because, as was pointed out to the Ambassador, it was not diplomats but the responsible naval and military commanders who granted and settled the terms of 'capitulations'. For Keith's receipt of the orders see *The Keith Papers*, II, 205; for Elgin's, his no. 23 to Grenville in F.O. 78/28 (where the latter's despatch is given the date of the draft, 13 December).

Dundas intended to leave London probably on 10 December; see his parting shot to the King when requesting permission on the 8th (*L.C.G. III*, III, no. 2087).

2. And not only to enemies and allies. The Governor General in Bengal, on receiving the news of the Convention from him, addressed him in form as Your Excellency (see *Private Papers of Spencer*, IV, 97–9). For the signature see p. 403 above.

3. *Diary of Windham*, 422; Cabinet Minute, 27 March 1800 (B.L. Add. Ms 59306); correspondence of Grenville and George III, 27, 28 March 1800 (*L.C.G. III*, III, no. 2120).

4. See *The Keith Papers*, II, 205.

endure a series of debates in the Commons, in which they defended uneasily every action and person concerned.[1]

The affair had shown the underlying problems which Egypt could pose for the Allied Coalition, and thus for British strategy in a period when both Russia and Austria were very much in play. Grenville was bound to see it in this light: 'a most mortifying event' that 'might well put a less peevish man than Thugut out of honour with his allies'.[2] He was quite content to see the French left where they were – 'a much greater comparative advantage than could result from any other employment'.[3] Dundas of course, on the contrary, never lost hope that they could be removed; and while he could not but bow to the general disapproval of Sidney Smith's behaviour, he continued to set on foot his own efforts to defeat the enemy outright. It did not look, in 1799 or again in the first half of 1800, as if this could be attempted from the West. He therefore placed the greater emphasis on Turkish operations which might be supplemented by a British blockade or – better – assault mounted from the East. Plans for the latter indeed had been in his mind ever since the winter of 1798; and in point of fact it was set on foot, primarily as a measure of advanced defence of India itself, by a small expedition in the spring of 1799 to Perim, at the mouth of the Red Sea, which was covered thereafter by a squadron in that area sent from England via the Cape.[4] While Dundas continued to deplore his colleagues' neglect of the object,[5] he could at least pursue such an undertaking largely undisturbed, tacitly supported by the East India Company, itself in discussion with the Governor General in Bengal. The reliance on Turkey, on the other hand, exposed him more directly to contact with Grenville, and thereby to a further divergence of views. For the basic disagreement on strategy had specific diplomatic consequences here. The Foreign Secretary saw the Turkish alliance primarily as an offshoot of our alliance with Russia; a means of

1. *P.R., 3rd ser.*, XIII, 168–9, XIV, 675–712, XV (1801), 192–5, 422–39, for 18 November 1800, 27 March, 1 May, 2 June 1801. There was a debate in the Lords on 23 December 1800 (see op. cit., XIII, 376–7, 560–6). Ministers however were still not clear as late as June 1800, before they knew of Kléber's death, what action Keith should take if a vessel was encountered with returning French troops on board (see *The Keith Papers*, op. cit. 202). Dundas later remarked that 'the words had almost stuck in my throat' in the House when he defended the original refusal to allow the evacuation (to Spencer, 27 September 1800; *Private Papers of Spencer*, IV, 126).
2. To Minto, 28 March 1800 (*H.M.C., Dropmore*, VI, 186). And cf. same to Whitworth, no. 10, 8 April (F.O. 65/46), same to Dundas, 2 June 1800 (P.R.O. 30/8/140).
3. To Elgin, no. 8, 15 December 1800 (F.O. 78/24).
4. See Ingram, op. cit., 99–100, 103, ch. VIII, sections III–IV, 342. The earliest plans in London involved the ubiquitous Maitland, at that time recently returned from the Caribbean (see p. 257, n3 above).
5. '. . . the total forgetfulness we seem to labour under with regard to Egypt' (to Pitt, 24 November 1799; *H.M.C., Dropmore*, VI, 39).

holding the two natural antagonists in a triple partnership with Britain which would exclude French influence and counter thrusts to reduce the Ottoman Empire. Dundas for his part saw the same partnership from, as it were, the other side of the glass; as the desirable, perhaps necessary, guarantee of the overland defences of India, through Persia and Afghanistan or Syria and Arabia, which might disappear if Turkey's alliance with Russia was replaced by the normal state of mutual hostility or, in the worst case, if either broke away from the Coalition. The two Ministers thus had a common immediate end in view, but for divergent reasons; for Dundas's approach held implications of historical importance which at this stage found no echo – rather aroused suspicion – in Grenville.[1] As the Secretary for War – the chairman of the India Board of Control – pursued his policies through the Near and Middle East, from the Red Sea isthmus and Damascus and Aleppo to Teheran and Kabul, Mecca and Baghdad, he was encountering an essentially different and recently sharpening perspective,[2] focused on Constantinople as a capital in Europe, which prevailed firmly within the Foreign Office and broadly in the Cabinet itself.

The most immediate impact of El Arish, however, fell on the Porte. The Turks of course wanted the French out of Egypt; that was largely why they sealed an alliance with Britain. But in so doing they counted largely on their new ally to forward the result. They themselves had much else on their minds – they were preoccupied at least as much with Russia's Balkan activities – and their hostility to France, and its revolution, was strictly defensive. They were thus far from pleased by Britain's withdrawal from a means of attaining their object in the Convention; and the repeated failure of their own operations, carried out partly by unreliable feudatories,[3] did not encourage them to wholehearted further effort. Such an atmosphere did nothing to foster an already questionable usefulness: the army in Syria was now said to be destitute of supplies and 'in a state of general insurrection',[4] and the sprawling provinces of the Empire were barely under control. These facts, and perhaps some sense of guilt and caution, suggested the case for greater British involvement. Pitt had observed on the first decision over passports that 'as we are determined to prevent the Turks from getting rid of these troublesome visitors, we are bound to make some effort for enabling the Turkish force to act against them with effect';[5] and while the latter part of the equation looked different by the summer of 1800, as hopes of the Porte's capability

1. This question will be considered more fully as a theme in Ch. XIII, section III below.
2. Cf. II, 28–9.
See I, 192 and Ch. XV, particularly 456–7, for the central significance of the Board of Control in the progress of Dundas's career.
3. Cf. p. 151, n1 above.
4. A report in April 1800; see Ingram, op. cit., 364, and also 386.
5. To Dundas, 12 December 1799 (Stanhope, III, 204). Designed partly perhaps to assuage; see p. 402 and n4 above.

declined, some independent action, it was held, must be borne by the resources of India.[1] That however proved to be an aspiration by no means shared fully in India itself, and such action as followed came from chance rather than design. A British expedtion from Asia did indeed land in Egypt in the spring of 1800; but it was a small self-propelled venture, with no instructions from London or Calcutta and only a limited aim. The force at Perim,[2] after an unhappy stay, had moved in September 1799 to Aden; but finding that territory also inhospitable, set sail in the following January for Suez. Its hope was to capture the port and establish a base for closer blockade. But the attempt, made in March 1800, failed; an assault farther south was considered but rejected; and at the end of May the troops, withdrawn to southern Arabia, re-embarked disconsolately for Bombay. Meanwhile the Governor General in Bengal, involved in his own needs and ambitions and not greatly impressed by the argued threat from Egypt, declined categorically to send a reinforcement. While the Turks called on Britain in September for a serious effort to help expel the French, there was thus no real question by then of its coming wholly from the East.

Such was the background, though the final movements of the force from Arabia were not known, when the subject of an Egyptian expedition reared its head in London once more. Coming as it did with the discussion on Portugal,[3] the two questions were debated together, urgently and fiercely, over the next two weeks. Dundas followed up his proposal of 18 September with a 'detailed minute' the next day.[4] Its whole emphasis lay on the need for speed. He was able to start, as he noted or claimed, from a new and significant premiss: 'a general concurrence' that in any peace talks France should not be left in possession of Egypt. There was therefore – and Dundas was writing with Otto obviously in mind[5] – a corresponding obligation to decide on action (not merely a continued disavowal of El Arish) at once. If the French remained in situ moreover for much longer, they might themselves contrive to settle with Turkey to exclude our interests if and when peace came; and we had also to bear in mind the prospect – 'not improbable' and 'equally to be deprecated' – of Russian 'interference' at some point in Egyptian affairs. The British public itself was unlikely, if it came to the point in the course of a negotiation, to carry on the war for the sake of Egypt alone. All the more necessary to gain the prize quickly; and it was a valuable one, more so in his view than any perceptible

1. Stanhope, III, 204–5.

2. See p. 405 above; and for what follows Ingram, op. cit., ch. VIII, sections III–IV, ch. IX, section V.

3. P. 391 above.

4. See his letter to Grenville, 20 September 1800 (*H.M.C., Dropmore*, VI, 326–7), and p. 401 and n1 above.

5. Cf. pp. 386–7 above.

Continental alternative. Portugal, reconsidered, could expect to find protection in other ways: so long as the French continued to be engaged by Austria they would not have the troops to spare, and if there was a joint peace negotiation we would take trouble to provide safeguards. On the other hand, if the worst happened and Bonaparte entered the country after a separate peace with the Emperor, there was effectively nothing we could do, and we should not therefore raise Lisbon's hopes. And neither should we raise Vienna's, by proposing any '*particular*' form of help. We had done our fair share; we could make no further difference; and for his part he now felt 'an aversion to waste more blood' in that cause.[1]

This was a skilful document, aimed at the point of the 'concurrence' that Dundas had found. He was careful indeed not to dwell on the two factors which were now increasingly linked in his mind. There was no direct mention of the threat to India, on which he knew that he stood in a minority, and indeed alone in the degree of his fears. And the reference to Russia was brief; it was focused on Egypt, and the possible broader effects in Asia were implicit or at most indirect. He went out of his way in fact to accept that such dangers were not necessarily immediate: the pressing need was to have acted in advance of any forthcoming talks. And in concentrating on the latter prospect he might expect to find a sympathetic ear in Pitt. For as he would have guessed, and was very soon aware, Dundas was going to have a fight on his hands.

Its extent was apparent indeed by the time that he launched his appeal to the Minister, at the end of his ensuing memorandum on 'the state of the Cabinet'.[2] Grenville's preference for Portugal had then just been strengthened by a fresh report that Spain was going to invade; Camden added his doubts of Dundas's proposal in a letter to Pitt; Spencer, responsible for the navy's role, feared the winter weather on the Egyptian coast; Windham quite simply wanted 'all' the troops in question to be sent home.[3] The Admiralty's argument seemed to carry conviction[4] – at any rate conveniently to other objectors – and the Secretary for War set to work to dispute it. He was not unhopeful: Spencer had proved co-operative in the past provided he would stand up to professional advice, and Dundas tackled that problem as far as he could on its own ground, canvassing some knowledgeable naval officers and the Levant Company, having log books searched, enlisting the aid of the Secretary of the Admiralty himself, who had once been his own Under Secretary.[5] He

1. Dundas to Pitt, 19 September 1800 (found by Holland Rose, but not by me, in the Pretyman Mss – possibly as a copy of the 'detailed minute' itself – and paraphrased in his II, 387); memorandum of 22 September 1800 (pp. 386, n5–87 above).
2. N1 above. Cf. pp. 387–8 above.
3. See Mackesy, op. cit., 152; Windham's diary for 18, 22 September 1800 (B.L. Add. Ms 37924).
4. Loc. cit., 22 September.
5. Evan Nepean, at the Home Office. Cf. p. 35 and n3 above for the impression of the First Lord's undue attention to some of his Board.

managed to reduce, indeed largely dispose of the initial obstacles; but not entirely, and others were brought to the fore.[1] Over the next few days in fact his case lost ground in general. By 25 September the Cabinet resolved to send a substantial reinforcement to Portugal, leaving only some 5,000 men after garrison duties were met.[2] The opposition was not wholly consistent: Windham for example disputed with Grenville as well as with Dundas. But it was strong enough to carry the day, and the plan for Egypt seemed to have been 'abandoned'.[3]

And then the tide began to turn. Not all Ministers shared to the full the Foreign Secretary's concern for Portugal; doubts began to be felt, as so often before not least by himself, about Lisbon's credibility,[4] and on 30 September these were openly expressed. By then, too, the talks with Otto had effectively ended. And perhaps most telling, the first report had just been received of the Franco-Austrian Convention of Hohenlinden, leading the Cabinet to take 'the new situation on the Continent' into review.[5] The result was not decisive. The force for Portugal suffered its first reduction, and any prospect of aid for Austria from the Mediterranean was summarily ruled out. But that did not mean that Egypt was accepted on the basis that Dundas sought; Ministers resolved rather to send troops to Minorca to await a decision. The response enraged him. He played what could have been his last card, declined to issue the necessary orders, and stayed away from a further Cabinet the next day.[6] Whether or not that did the trick, the decision followed. On 3 October it was resolved that a force of not less than 15,000 men should 'compel' the French to evacuate Egypt 'without delay'.[7]

The end was still hotly contested. As Dundas told the King, 'it was scarcely to be expected' that there would be 'no difference of opinion', and Grenville and Windham in fact went so far as to record their dissent.[8] According to one participant, Pitt in person saw the business through.

1. Mackesy, op. cit., 154–5.

2. See p. 391 above; George III to Dundas, 29 September 1800 (*L.C.G. III*, III, no. 2252).

3. Spencer's word (quoted by Mackesy, op. cit., 155). And see Windham's diary for 25 September (B.L. Add. Ms 37924).

4. Cf. p. 391 above.

5. Windham's diary, 30 September 1800 (B.L. Add. Ms 37924) for all three factors. See pp. 388–9 above for the Convention and the report; 385–6, for the termination of Otto's talks. Austria's 'shamefull conduct' also played a considerable part in swinging the Duke of York, as Commander-in-Chief, to Dundas's side (York to Dundas, 29 September 1800; W.B. Hamilton, 'Some Letters of George III' [unpublished in *L.C.G. III*, III] (*The South Atlantic Quarterly*, LXVIII, No. 3, 423–4)).

6. Windham's diary as in n5 above; Dundas to Pitt, 1 October 1800 (Dacres Adams Mss, formerly P.R.O. 30/58/3).

7. Draft Cabinet Minute, 3 October 1800 (B.L. Add. Ms 40102).

8. Dundas to George III, 4 October 1800 (*L.C.G. III*, III, no. 2256); Minute of 3 October (n7 above). Such a record was highly unusual; cf. II, 555. The Foreign Secretary did however contribute amendments to the draft, largely accepted, before inscribing his dissent in his own hand. The King himself thoroughly disliked the idea of the expedition, adding significantly to Dundas's worries (see *L.C.G. III*, III, nos. 2256, 2259; *Glenbervie*, I, 233).

The whole Cabinet was present apart from the Lord Privy Seal, Westmorland,[1] and the balance of opinion was nearly even. But, so Liverpool stated a little later, the Minister, knowing that he was in favour, 'called out (contrary to custom) . . . "I wish to hear Lord Liverpool's sentiments"'; and in summing up he counted three members who had not spoken as being in effect for the expedition.[2] His own attitude counted for at least as much; and it was, in its extent, peculiarly his own. For, as Dundas knew perhaps even better than most and had played on in the latest presentation, it rested very largely on his desire, so recently shown once more, for peace.[3] He was correspondingly disposed to support the operation which might yield the speediest advantage in discussing terms. And time may well have figured also in the general view. Cuba and the Plate were far away, and transatlantic expeditions lengthy affairs. Such a strategy moreover had proved expensive in manpower. Furthermore, it took no real account of the *eastward* direction of the quickening pace of change. For if the focus in London was shifting from the Continent as viewed hitherto, it was fastening on what was none the less the Continent's periphery. Dundas himself could not prise loose from the fact that the keys to the East would be turned, and British action still moved, by events in Europe. France had to conquer Austria, Russia's aspect to harden, before the Government's strategy would alter. It was as those possibilities became probabilities – as Grenville's case weakened after Marengo and seemed to be in ruins in the very course of the Cabinet's talks, and Dundas's fears of the Tsar became increasingly acceptable[4] – that he could return to his own preference over other possibilities advanced in an earlier context, and jettison the Americas in favour of the Egyptian coasts.

The orders could now be sent. They envisaged a dual assault. Dundas aimed at a target of December for a landing by Abercromby's force, to be followed by one in February mounted from India and launched from the Red Sea. He had warned the Governor General early in September that he must prepare for such an expedition, and he now did his best to hasten

1. For whom see II, 221, 401, 423. He had been given the post in February 1798, filling the vacancy left by Chatham seventeen months earlier (op. cit., 379, 463). So far as weight of argument was concerned, his absence, which seems to have been frequent in 'the summer' (Camden Ms U840 0197), was no great loss.

2. *Glenbervie*, 159–60.

3. Cf. p. 388 above. On Liverpool remarking for instance that for his part he had been against the talks with Otto throughout, Pitt 'in anger said, "And I was decidedly for it"' (*Glenbervie*, 160).

4. Cf. p. 396 above for the effect on the instructions in August and again in October for Malta. The news of the island's surrender, received on 6 October, followed neatly on the decision for Egypt; even if Windham saw in it an argument – not pursued – for the need to find reinforcements for the expedition, which would probably delay it until the spring (to Spencer, 11 October 1800; *Private Papers of Spencer*, IV, 131–2). It was in August and September, too, that Dundas began to hear from his own sources of the Tsar's growing interest in an overland attack on India.

the process.[1] His timetable proved optimistic. Abercromby left Gibraltar on 5 November with some 16,000 men and the Mediterranean fleet. But it was not until March 1801 that the assault took place. The interval was a period of intense anxiety for its progenitor, conscious of the hazards that might be encountered and exposed to the consequences of a hard and lonely fight, after months of growing strain, against powerful colleagues and a notably unsympathetic King. As the old year gave place to the new, all seemed still to be in the balance.

A balance could scarcely be discerned by then over the wider prospect. The Coalition was in tatters, and its surviving dependants were at serious risk. Only the Turks remained as major allies, largely ineffectual and increasingly morose. Portugal and Naples still formed outposts on a mainland dominated now by France; but both could – and would – all too easily disappear. A potentially hostile neutral League in the north was led by a nominal ally who might turn into an enemy. To all intents and purposes, after eight years of warfare Britain stood alone. At home there was a widespread desire for an acceptable peace, interlaced with disaffection in the worst rise in bread prices that had ever been known. A time indeed might be close when Bonaparte could once more contemplate invasion. As the new year opened, the scene looked very grim.

And yet, at this low point, there was movement that would yield results. The dockyards were preparing a fleet for the Baltic, for 'Nelson and the North'; and Abercromby was pointed towards a strike against a significant but vulnerable French force at a point which its first commander had seized on as a key to the war. Both undertakings held a resonance. One represented the old tradition of enforcing the claims of belligerent sea-power; the other the arrival, introduced by Bonaparte, of what would become an expanding British theme. After the sorry tale of the recent past there would indeed soon be successes to cheer. But when they were proclaimed Pitt would not be in office.

1. Cf. p. 407 above. Earlier approaches, at intervals over the past two years, could now be replaced by a virtual command. See Mackesy, op. cit., 159–61 for that and the plans and instructions for Abercromby.

Part Three

CHAPTER XIII

War and Empire

I

The sombre balance struck at the turn of the century was certainly promoting active thoughts of peace, which would be a unilateral 'maritime peace' if Austria left the war and proper terms could thereafter be agreed.[1] The trend of the reasoning, now accepted in Cabinet, was not the product of unrelieved despair, as indeed the course of the recent talks with Otto had shown: it was possible even to see the struggle as one 'that had made this country the terror & the admiration of Europe'.[2] Not all Pitt's colleagues were as anxious for a settlement as he was himself; and while he for his part was eager to discover if that could be found, he would be content, if the result did not endure, to have gained a pause in which to husband resources which would then be required once more.[3] Arguments supporting a good bargaining position, and beyond that a basic capacity for strength, were in fact produced on either side of a low point. Less than twelve months later, most of the senior Ministers who had been in charge of hostilities at that time were pointing to the achievements of what they saw as an effective struggle;[4] and in the year before the Second Coalition foundered, the joint Secretary of the Treasury published a statement of the country's ability to sustain and indeed flourish in an expensive war. George Rose's pamphlet followed his initial *Brief Examination into the Increase of the Revenue, Commerce, and Manufactures of Great Britain* through the peacetime period 1783 to 1792; the fresh survey, covering the succeeding years to 1799, could retain his title with the change of dates, and it earned a steady succession of editions from a public hankering to be reassured.[5] He wrote when the income tax had just been introduced and before its initial disappointing yield was known, and immediately after a year in which the pace of the rise in war expenditure was temporarily eased;[6] while the

1. See pp. 382, 384 above for a distinct maritime peace; p. 194, n3 for a proper dating of a new century.
2. Thomas Grenville to Spencer, 9 October 1801 (B.L. Add. Ms. temp Althorp G42).
3. This is developed further in Ch. XVII, section I below.
4. Context and some detail here, again, are contained in sources given more appropriately below in p. 559, n1.
5. Cf. p. 270, n3 above.
6. See Ch. IX, section I; pp. 99–100 above.

retrospective Ministerial assessments were made in an altered political climate and to some extent in the light of a crop of belated operational gains. Nevertheless they were applied to a longer period and a larger scene; and the two sets of claims in their separate ways were not mere propaganda – both were deeply felt – and can be viewed strictly on their merits. Their significance indeed lay beyond the immediate case. Rather, in their bearing on the moment they pointed to the bases and parameters of Britain's conduct of this most costly and demanding of French wars.

The economic pointers cannot yield all that can be sought. Rose attributed the 'favourable state of the country', in his terms, to 'its established credit, its productive industry, the unequalled extent of its commerce and navigation, and the consequent unrivalled power of the navy.'[1] The combination was justifiably formidable; but it left some particularised questions perforce largely in the air. Measurements of statistics have been subject to more sophisticated methods since his judgments were given. He was working on figures which were often unreliable, and sometimes known to be so;[2] and economists in any case have since widened and elaborated the criteria required to read the interactions between an economy and a war. The resolution of such problems indeed is never simple, and liable – in many cases bound – to be imprecise. Quite apart from contemporary statistical inadequacies, how far can one give an accurate interpretation of the mutual impact of factors – and not all themselves statistical – which go to form a mosaic of results? In this instance one can cite short or middle term gains for some industries – shipbuilding, iron, cotton manufactures –, but likewise constrictions and losses to others – for example to activity in building, often taken as a yardstick of prosperity. And how far precisely can one attribute the rates of increase or decrease to the war itself? How far too should one lay stress on distinctions between periods within the long struggle? Trends for a decade, or for the whole length of the two wars, can differ significantly from those for shorter terms; and no one could foretell exactly when Britain would emerge from an experience which in the event helped make her the predominant Power of the nineteenth century. Over the full period itself, furthermore, improvements in one sector could have adverse or complicating effects on others. In agriculture for instance, still the largest national industry, an increase in output which helped keep England fed in highly critical conditions was accompanied by rises in prices and wages which helped fuel a more general inflation. Again, substantial investment from profits in land or trade or manufacturers was put into Government stocks required to service the war; but perhaps at some expense to financial resources that might sometimes have gone into other forms of growth. Over that longer period moreover the pace of growth itself, in both overseas trade and an

1. *A Brief Examination* (1799), 76.
2. Cf. for one important inherited example Ehrman, *The British Government and Commercial Negotiations with Europe*, 211–15.

aggregate of manufactures, has proved under recent microscopes to have been less dramatic than was earlier thought. Britain, enjoying on balance a strong economy with roots for expansion before the Revolutionary War, emerged from the Napoleonic War actually and prospectively the greatest economic force in Europe. It is the more necessary to bear in mind that the passage was not along a consistently upward road. As a leading expert has concluded, 'It is possible to draw both a black and a rosy picture of the economic condition of England during the [two] French Wars'.[1]

Two comments may be made on the mosaic for our own purposes. First, we are concerned here with the state of affairs at a point which was only a third of the way to the conclusion. And we may also perhaps, crudely, make some distinction within the process between effects of the war on the economy and effects of the economy on the capacity for war. The latter, while in essence subsumed in the former, may perhaps be allowed a more restricted treatment. One might start from the primary factor of the size of population, whose growth through the century, if not as explosive in the last two decades as once surmised, was a reality underlying the prolonged advance later called the Industrial Revolution. With a probable 5 to $5^{1}/_{4}$ million people in Britain and Wales around 1700 and perhaps a further half million by around 1750, there may have been $7^{1}/_{2}$ to 8 million in the 1780s, and the census of 1801 reported 8,893,000, with a further 1,608,000 in Scotland.[2] From the experience of its successors, these last figures were by no means exact; too high for Scotland and low for England and Wales. But despite the approximations throughout, and allowing for increases in life expectancy among the very young and the old, there were clearly more men to bear arms and, with women, to produce the necessary supplies than there had been in earlier conflicts, even in the War of American Independence. The disproportion in this respect between Britain and the great Continental states, so marked early in the century, was closing to some extent. If there were more mouths to feed in the island, there were more hands available for the diverse needs of war.

While of fundamental importance, the rise in numbers however takes us only part of the way. Even if Irishmen and foreign mercenaries eased operational burdens, severe constrictions remained in relation to strategic choice; and these were underlined by, indeed followed from the range of occupations in which the rising population was engaged. As Pitt was warned at the start of the war, Britain was not like Austria or Russia, with

1. To quote François Crouzet, in 'The Impact of the French Wars on the British Economy'; in *Britain and the French Revolution* . . ., ed. H.T. Dickinson (1989), 207.

2. E.A. Wrigley and R.S. Schofield, *The Population History of England 1541–1871* . . . (1981), Appendices 5, 6; M.W. Flinn *et al.*, *Scottish Population History* . . . (1977). It is worth noting that the first census produced a total for England and Wales which on the face of it was close to the calculations made for 1800, only a year before the census itself. Ireland (a source of manpower for the armed forces) probably contained some $4^{3}/_{4}$–5 million people at the same time.

large reserves of men 'having little Else to do than to come forth for War when wanted'. Agriculture and trade in all its aspects could not be encroached on too far; rather in fact they marked the bounds of recruitment.[1] But the balances in manpower between the various sectors give rise to more significant consequences than those for the overall size of the armed forces themselves. Perhaps the most remarkable aspect of the economy in the late eighteenth century was the favourable ratio of productivity to labour on the land. It has long been claimed that the industrial revolution rested on the shoulders of the agricultural revolution: whether or not that was so, and however the term revolution is defined, a growth in agricultural efficiency at any rate assisted a growth in manufactures from one critical resource. For it was not only that the country was maintained broadly, if not always reliably and with one great exception in the case of wheaten bread, at a level of self-sufficiency which helped defer the Malthusian nightmare; it was also the fact that this was done by a third of the nation's working force – in contrast to two thirds and sometimes more in Europe –, allowing a correspondingly larger pool of labour to be used productively on other work. There was almost certainly an element of slack in the enlarging economy of the past few decades. That could be taken up and expansion continued by the forces available for employment, not least – a further contrast with Europe – in a nexus of expanding towns. The social effects – mobility itself – could arouse keen political fears.[2] But the distribution and flexibility as well as the size of the working populace underpinned the capacity to tackle direct demands for hostilities – for vessels and the yards in which to build them, cannons and rifles and their ammunition, uniforms and boots, camp equipment and transport – on an unprecedented scale. Such pressures may have distorted natural processes for the nation's development in the longer term. They were also a fostering agent as they served the immediate end.

There were further effects. The test of the economy as the engine for war lay in its ability to power the finance. It must generate but also deploy the resources to pay as far as possible by taxes and to fund the loans needed to defray the costs which taxation could not meet. Capacity and consent were alike required. The profits accruing broadly over a period to the landowning interest in particular helped support a broad rise in its income as a share of the national aggregate. It accordingly possessed an enlarged facility to sustain Government's finances: not one, obviously, of decisive significance within the whole spectrum of public involvement – of the sums produced also from trade, and manufactures, and the private consumption stemming from all sectors –, but distinctly important

1. Duke of Richmond's 'Minutes of Conversation with Mr Pitt Wednesday 10 April 1793' (P.R.O., W.O. 30/81); see II, 267. One might assume in the context that he included manufactures in trade.
2. Cf. II, 130–1.

coming from the quarter that carried the main political weight. For the embodiment of the governing order of the country in a Parliament which engrossed fiscal responsibility concentrated power for the support required from a pluralistic spread of interests. Over the past century a combination had developed in Britain as a weapon of war: of significant but dispersed taxation not however emanating from diverse authorities, together with a unique system of public credit which was the envy of European states. In its greatest trial so far it was surviving, in amended but familiar form, not least by a voluntary acceptance[1] itself set effectively in the institutional frame. Pitt in 1792, Rose in 1799, stressed the connexions between the parts of what they saw as an organic whole.[2]

> What is it which has produced, in the last hundred years, so rapid an advance, beyond what can be traced in any other period of our history? What but that, during that time, . . . a general calm has prevailed throughout the country . . .: and we have also enjoyed, in greater purity and perfection, the benefit of those original principles of our constitution, which were ascertained and established by the memorable events that closed the century preceding? This is the great and growing cause, the operation of which has given scope to all the other circumstances . . . It is this union of liberty with law which . . . affords to property its just security, produces the exertion of genius and labour, the extent and solidity of credit, the circulation and increase of capital . . .
>
> In looking on the . . . state of the country, of its established credit, its productive industry, the unequalled extent of its commerce and navigation, and the consequent unrivalled power of its navy, our countrymen will . . . impute the advantage we enjoy to a Constitution fitted to produce them . . .

The process in short was two-way. A 'spirit of useful industry' would 'confirm' men's 'attachment' to the Constitution;[3] the spirit and framework of the Constitution were necessary ingredients of the economic activities themselves.

Well and good. Such tributes to congruence indeed prefigured the teleological view of English history which, secure in the end after wartime victory and further peacetime strain, was to become orthodox in the course of the next century. Seen more immediately however, Rose's eulogy in 1799 could scarcely command the ready assent given to Pitt's seven years before. The pattern of the elements sustaining the war was certainly discernible, and they would be combined to mounting effect over a generation. But when the pattern of the war itself appeared to be

---

1. See for one revealing but extreme occasion II, 639–41.
2. Pitt's conclusion in his budget speech of 17 February 1792 (*P.H.*, XXIX (1817), col. 835; for the text see II, 52n2); Rose, *A Brief Examination*, 76–7.
3. Pitt again, on another occasion in 1792; see II, 87.

unravelling, it was the pressures rather than the underlying strengths of the economy that caught the eye. Landowners, as an order, may have been enabled by profits to support the public funds. But what was attracting their attention at this point was the new tax on income in addition to rises in more familiar duties, and a disastrous corn harvest. The volume of shipping, in numbers and tonnage, was continuing to grow, more sharply in 1800 itself than in any previous wartime year; and so, as far as could be seen in a much less exact reckoning, was that of exports and the aggregate of overseas trade. But many merchants' eyes were fixed anxiously on losses from capture, on delays and frustrations from convoys, on levels of insurance premiums, on uncertainties for traffic with neutrals caused not least by diplomatic disputes. Manufacturing too was certainly increasing in aggregate value, and altogether in the tale of short-term business cycles the period 1798 to 1800 has been designated one of recovery and peak between troughs in 1797 and 1801. But it also saw a further growth in inflationary pressures, from the impact indeed of Government's expenditure before the sudden effect of bread prices towards the close; the terms of trade with Hamburg as the available Continental exchange worsened notably from 1799; and bankruptcies in England, while reflecting individual misjudgments and mischances in an active economy, were near the top end of the figures recorded over the past five years.[1] The propertied orders, settled or aspiring, had visible causes for disquiet, and for the consequent serious grumbling as the prospect of peace receded once more. And to Pitt sitting in the Treasury, the flow of revenue which sustained capacity seemed disturbingly liable to slacken if consent waned too far under persistent demands. A broad economic tide might be running recognisably on the flood; but an overlying adverse current could also be detected, and as can happen in such a conjunction, navigation could be at risk.

It was thus possible to find reasons for confidence or equally for alarm. In a sense they were complementary as far as Pitt himself was concerned, for he looked to the former without much question to restore the nation's inherent strength when afforded a chance of recovery from the latter.[2] In considering such an opportunity, as he was now doing given tolerable prospects, a major factor was of course Britain's position beyond the seas. An increasingly indigenous feature of this country's treaties with other Powers through the century, acknowledged as such in the past few years in the proposals for a distinct 'maritime' settlement within a general peace, it

1. Sources for this paragraph may be found in Notes on Sources, p. 870 below.

2. Cf. the claim in the closing stage of the War of American Independence, which he had seen abundantly justified in the following ten years, comparing British commerce to 'a spring of mighty power, which always exerts its force in proportion to the weight of its compression'; made in 1782 by George Chalmers, later Secretary of the Committee of Trade (I, 164).

could be taken at this point as the heaviest counterweight to the negotiating weakness of the Coalition. Whatever the costs and in some cases
the reverses, Britain could point to a long list of wartime conquests
outside Europe: Tobago, part of St Domingue (though abandoned later),
St Pierre et Miquelon, Pondicherry in 1793; Martinique, Guadeloupe
(abandoned), St Lucia, the Saints, Mariegalante, Descada in 1794;
Ceylon, Malacca, the Cape of Good Hope in 1795; the Dutch dependen-
cies in the East Indies, and Demerara, Essequibo, Berbice in 1796;
Trinidad taken and Madagascar secured in 1797; Minorca in 1798;
Surinam in 1799; Goree, Curaçao, Malta in 1800. Some of these might
indeed have to compensate for the Allies' failures on the Continent itself;[1]
a short-term necessity whose limits should be carefully watched. But
beyond the current situation, whose outcome was still in doubt, and the
more prolonged involvement perforce in the affairs of Europe, there lay
Britain's own conspicuous 'permanent Interests' as they had been shaped
in the past hundred years. It was they that were supplying 'the present
Strength and pre-eminence of this Country' from the 'Resources arising
from its Commerce, and its Naval Power which are inseparably connected'. The leading proponent of the consequences for the conduct of
the war itself could take for granted that this was an 'obvious' fact.[2] So his
audience could readily accept; though not necessarily his conclusions for
the immediate strategy. It was a tribute to developments in the past two
decades that this could be done without demur.

For much in point of fact had emerged since the end of the American
War. The loss of the mainland colonies, not surprisingly, had shaken attitudes at home. It had appeared to undermine the familiar foundations of
Britain's Atlantic supplies and trade. It raised to a new level questions,
already broached, for colonial policy and forms of governance. It seemed
to threaten a prospect of geographical contraction – as close indeed as
Ireland – replacing expansion in both war and peace.[3] It posed large
problems; and something of the effect could still be seen. Dundas, the
guardian of the 'permanent Interests', found it wise to take into account
current doubts of the merits of territorial gains in promoting his ideas for
pursuing overseas trade. The 'acquisition' of markets did not necessarily
mean the acquisition of fresh possessions: in his favoured case of Spanish
America he 'disclaim[ed] all Plan of Conquest or Colonization' – all that
would be required would be 'Commercial Stations' from which to set
business on foot.[4] How, one might wonder, did that strike his colleagues as
they saw how far Britain had moved in India from the settlement at

1. Cf. pp. 61, 143 above.
2. Dundas's 'Memorandum' for the Cabinet of 31 March 1800 (p. 353 above); and see
also his 'Secret Memorandum' of 22 July (p. 367 above). An interesting confirmatory
comparison may be found a year later from an enemy source; see the report by Otto from
London in April 1801 quoted in Duffy, *Soldiers, Sugar, and Seapower*, 387–8.
3. Cf. I, 158–61, 196.
4. Cf. p. 354 above.

Madras – a progression moreover which had 'arisen almost without our seeking it'?[1] But this was a line of thought, surfacing more powerfully later in the 'indirect' or 'informal imperialism' of a more peaceful age, that never disappeared amid the pressures and actions of the prolonged Great War.

A developing concept of Empire indeed contained connexions which could run through differing sets of conditions. In the 1790s it was hard to foretell what directions commerce might take. For the fact that the forebodings of the early eighties had been happily confounded over the next few years[2] had not wholly removed anxieties for the economy's future. Alongside the triumphalism of Rose, for public consumption, can be set the more private assessment by Dundas of possible prospects for trade.[3] Offering great promise, these nevertheless could by no means be taken for granted. The rewards of the 1780s, preserved by and large successfully in the nineties, might be expected to persist in many respects. The marked rise, instead of a reduction, in favourable traffic with the new United States could probably continue until a distant day when their own manufactures would start to pose a challenge; and business with Europe, declining in the last peacetime years as a proportion of the British total, was still rising in value and should also prove favourable when peace came again, on the basis of existing commercial treaties[4] and in a situation in which Continental states would be unlikely, after their convulsions, to deploy their stocks of capital as effectively as ourselves. At the same time, limits could be foreseen in this country's current expansion, and moreover within the markets which had been augmenting its strength. The British West Indies, taken as a whole, had probably reached the peak of their prosperity, and their appetite for manufactures might in fact decline. India held out promise for a time, but its attraction as a market was confined by its own foreseeable economic level: its greatest value lay rather in the annual remittances which accrued to capital in Britain itself. Large uncertainties thus lay ahead. Fresh outlets for manufactures must be sought, as existing outlets must of course be exploited. We enjoyed a position and potential for world-wide activity which no other Power could currently match: a 'pre-eminence' indeed, but one whose sustenance needed a watchful flexible thrust.

Much of course must turn in the first instance on the outcome of the war itself. Our advantages must be preserved against loss or undue diminution. And here the wheel came full circle in the emphasis on existing possessions. If we did not necessarily wish to engross new blocks of territory for the simple sake of territory, we must nonetheless retain the most significant of our elements of strength. This was one leg of a

1. See I, 420.
2. I, 161–3.
3. Memorandum of 31 March 1800; p. 354 above.
4. See I, Ch. XVI, section II.

'colonial' policy of which the other was the capture of enemy possessions, sometimes of particular advantage as trading posts or strategic points of communication, but generally in the belief that losses would seriously weaken the owners – a reverse image in fact of the British case.[1] Assumptions for the future must be determined on the basis of what was already in our power. Prospects could not be envisaged realistically except from a starting point already known.

That was a broad approach. When it came to specifics, war turned out, as so often, to be a solvent of questions in various ways that could not be foreseen. Commercial effects followed in due course from strategic demands and incentives, some already latent, some now emerging, which produced or encouraged shifts of emphasis in spheres of influence as well as of power. In both respects their impact fell also on a pattern of imperial governance; and here a lengthy and complicated dual process was taking place. On the one hand authority was perforce devolved farther in detail over enlarging distant regions; on the other however it was held firmly within a sovereign system that was discouraging subsidiary constitutional checks on the executive and legislature at home. A vivid example of this latter trend lay in the Crown's closest possession of all, in Ireland, where of course particular considerations applied.[2] But wherever possible there was a certain wartime uniformity of approach, and Burke's earlier 'mass of heterogeneous governments, all more or less free and popular in their forms' though held 'in subservience', was a description more appropriate to an earlier 'First Empire' than to the development of 'the Second'.

For as the Great War progressed on its span of some twenty years, one may reasonably introduce a concept of imperial rather than purely colonial history. The word Empire itself had been and still was one of diverse usage, when indeed it was used. It had referred to 'the British Empire in Europe': the three kingdoms, controlled by England, comprising the British Isles and Ireland – an application that could echo still in claims for a distinctive identity in Scotland, and likewise in the passionate debates in the Dublin Parliament shortly before its demise.[3] Or it had served certain English historic pretensions on the seas. Or it included, within a concept of a maritime–colonial complex, specifically the British transatlantic islands and the mainland colonies of North America. Or there was 'the British Empire in India' or 'in the East', which for purposes of policy or administration were now tending to replace the purely commercial 'East Indies'.[4] Such applications could coexist. But while the term in its ultimate coverage, to denote all territories in British dominion across the

1. See Dundas's speech in the Commons of 25 March 1801 (*P.R., 3rd ser.*, XIV, 576–7; and cf. Pitt earlier (II, 356).
2. Pp. 181–2 above.
3. For which see pp. 184–6 above; and cf. 159 and n4.
4. For instance Pitt himself was reported to have spoken of 'the imperial dominion of our territories in the East' when seeking to introduce his bill for India in 1784 (*P.R.*, XII (1785), 545).

globe, was still unformed at the turn of the century in both precision and scope, that meaning could be better understood fifteen years later even if it was not yet regularly or indeed readily employed. Semantics by then in fact could recognise the extent of a major consolidation and expansion, and an accompanying, if temporary, evolution stemming largely from the same wartime pressures towards a firm and in essence a common type of central control.

II

Such developments of thought did not mean a notable increase in the provision of armed support for overseas territories after the first phase of the Revolutionary War. Across the Atlantic indeed, rather the reverse. Operations in the Caribbean and on the nearby coasts of central and south America had declined in scale after the massive designs of 1795–6.[1] A broad stalemate followed in the islands which had been the first concern of Ministers at the outbreak of war; and the capture of the small Dutch possessions of Surinam and Curaçao in 1799–1800 marked the only recent gains in a theatre by then subordinated to the demands in Europe. A naval force of course was always present, merchant convoys were accompanied by their escorts, blockading squadrons off the enemy's ocean ports watched for escapes that might threaten the west. Military replacements and minor reinforcements continued to be sent. But their strength was small compared with the expeditions in the middle of the decade; and despite opposition from the local legislatures and among the civil administrations, further thought was given to native levies, particularly after the high wastage of white troops.[2] While defence remained important for the West Indies' sustained contribution to the British economy, the shift in operational priorities moved the islands towards the fringe of events.

That however was true only in degree; operations could always shift again. And the continuing strategic needs had their effect on considerations of forms of government. Conditions in a region whether of central or subsidiary warfare were not conducive to debate on established systems, a subject viewed warily in any case after the experience of the revolted mainland colonies. Nor could Ministers be reassured by more recent experience farther north, for the well-intentioned Canada Act of 1791 proved disappointing from the start in important respects. The attempt to reproduce the spirit of the British constitution through adaptation was not a success; and the partition of the colony into an Upper Canada, British-speaking and broadly Protestant, and a Lower Canada, partly French-speaking and predominantly Roman Catholic, never really

1. Cf. for the rest of this paragraph pp. 144–5, 421 above.
2. See II, 355, 359–61, 564–5.

got off the ground though the machinery survived for almost fifty years.[1] Formatively for the shorter term elsewhere, relationships deteriorated in Quebec within the legislature and with the executive, and by 1807 the Colonial Office in London concluded that 'it had been a mistake to grant Lower Canada representative government'.[2] There was thus no incentive by example to contemplate changes favourable to the Assemblies in the 'old' British islands – on the contrary, Governors in the Caribbean should wield effective control. Nevertheless, questions of governance in the region could not be wholly ignored; and as in fact had happened with Canada following the secession of the neighbouring American colonies, these arose directly from the fortunes of war.

A pattern was set as early as 1794, with the seizure of French territory in St Domingue. The instructions to the new Governor indeed formed the basis of all such future arrangements, allowing for the local variations, when enemy centres of colonial power were occupied.[3] So far as possible the territory in each case was to be ruled according to its 'ancient Laws and Institutions' – in the case of the French before 1789 – with right of appeal for the former to the British Privy Council. But authority lay fully in the Governor, who should be assisted by a small body (in St Domingue, from among 'the proprietors' – the planters) for advice and consultation only; all existing councils or legislative assemblies were abolished. The British trade and navigation laws were to apply as in the British West Indies. The Roman Catholic religion was to be maintained, taking due care to guard against alienation of allegiance by the clergy; and the oath taken by Catholics on appointment to an office was to be administered in the form prescribed by the Quebec Act of 1774. In brief, there should be as little disturbance to the civil administration as possible – a key proviso – under authoritarian wartime conditions, when the future of the territory moreover must remain unknown. This was a pattern which could be reproduced where necessary throughout the globe. In the particular instance of the Caribbean, however, the context might be jeopardised by a controversial issue affecting the occupying Power itself.

The attempts to abolish the slave trade had been stymied since 1792.[4] Wilberforce's undimmed resolve, impelling him to a series of annual Parliamentary efforts over the next four years, encountered a strong

1. See I, 360–71.
2. Quoted in John Manning Ward, *Colonial Self-Government, The British Experience 1759–1856* (1976), 26.
3. Starting with the Cape of Good Hope in 1795; see Vincent Harlow and Frederick Madden, *British Colonial Developments 1774–1834, Select Documents* (1953), 83n1.
There was one exception to prove a rule: Tobago, captured in 1793, had twice been ruled by Britain before and been granted a representative system. It was accordingly restored.
4. See I, 402, and for the background op. cit., Ch. XIII, section IV.

combination of reasons and pretexts for obstruction. While never losing sight of his goal, he varied his tactics on occasions. The great debate which had failed to achieve immediate abolition had led the Commons to vote in a delaying device for a gradual approach, so as to end the trade at the beginning of 1796. But that itself had been frustrated by the Lords calling for further evidence, and in 1793 he moved for the lower House to restate its object, in the hope of inducing the peers to hasten their deliberations. A few months later he also revived an earlier idea, to forbid British slavers trading with foreign colonies; and he brought a further motion to this end in 1794. All the proposals failed: the first by 53 to 61 in the Commons; the second, after passing the first reading by 41 to 34, losing the third by 29 to 31; the last, having finally got through the House by 74 to 33, suffering an apparently unchangeable doom in the Lords. A renewed attempt at outright immediate abolition fared worse early in 1795; defeat in the Commons by 61 to 78.[1] The margins there had some-times been narrow; but the thin attendances suggested the mood – a certain weariness of the subject after its reiteration in recent sessions, and a marked reluctance to meddle with it further in the shadow of the late native rising in St Domingue and the unknown impact of a sweeping change on British possessions in an area now swept also by French mes-sages of hope and increasingly a cockpit of war.[2]

The extent of passive disinclination could be seen in the fact that nothing was being done meanwhile to bring any closer the Commons' declared aim of abolition in 1796. Wilberforce tried again in February with a direct motion. The timing might not have seemed propitious, for the Ministry only a few months before had strictly forbidden local inducements for negro military recruitment to include, as one had done, any promise of prospective emancipation in return.[3] Once again the effort failed, though once again narrowly: an opposing attempt to adjourn the debate indeed was defeated, but so in due course was the motion itself, by 70 to 74.[4] So, later, was an attempt to tackle conditions in the slave ships, which aroused so poor an attendance that it was twice counted out.[5] But if there was plenty of room for discouragement, the size of the minority for the main motion still gave some ground for hope, and while the abolitionists' committee was now becoming passive its Parliamentary leader persisted in the fight. In 1797 he was initially outmanoeuvred by a 'gradualist' success in referring improvements

1. *P.R.*, XXXIV (1793), 616, XXXV (sd), 637, XXXVII (1794), 587, XLI (1795), 26.
2. See I, 399–400.
3. II, 358–60, 564–6.
4. *P.R.*, XLIV (1796), 323. This last may well have happened from bad luck. The bill had in fact passed its second reading with unusual ease by 63 to 31 (op. cit., 321); but the attrac-tion of a new comic opera on the evening of the third reading proved too much for some of the abolitionists, to Wilberforce's natural anger and evangelical sorrow.
5. Op. cit., 703, 713. The motion, which was allowed to be introduced by 99 to 63, built on legislation in the 1780s and a further proposal in 1795.

in conditions on the islands to the local legislatures, with the aim of reducing the trade to a point at which fresh imports of slaves would eventually die away. But he was nonetheless given leave to introduce his customary motion, which was lost by 74 to 82; and a repetition in 1798 met the same fate but only by 83 to 87.[1] In 1798–9 the tactics broadened, on the more limited precedent of 1793–5, to embrace a range of measures 'in a kind of ascending order of actual or potential effectiveness'.[2] One of the movement's most committed adherents, William Smith, fathered a bill – the Slave Carrying bill – to revive and extend Wilberforce's past efforts. Another, Henry Thornton, introduced a Slave Trade Limitation bill to forbid export from much of the West African coast – a prospect designed largely to protect the new benevolent settlement of Sierra Leone.[3] And Wilberforce himself moved as usual in 1799 for immediate comprehensive abolition. Their fates differed. The first passed both Houses;[4] the second, having succeeded in the Commons by 59 to 23, was lost in the Lords by 61 to 68; the third failed in the Commons by the depressing margin of 54 to 84. Circumstances, it seemed, needed to change if abolition was to be achieved: Wilberforce indeed confessed in 1799 that he found such a prospect unlikely while the war continued; and in 1800, for the first time in nine years, he refrained from raising the subject again.[5]

The debates in the Lords on those bills that reached them in 1799 were closely fought, and the consequent attention was much increased by the prominently hostile part played by the royal Duke of Clarence. Seen normally by his father as a tiresome and politically unreliable younger son, it was obvious that he spoke here with the King's favour, and the Court's dislike of anything to do with suppression of the trade was all too clearly marked. The peers in any case had long been recalcitrant, delaying or defeating Wilberforce's own motions; and Pitt, stung to anger, resolved to try to bring the question to a point. He would take it to the Cabinet – 'regularly', according to a report – and bring forward a motion in the next session 'with ministerial authority'. This was a return with a vengeance to the spirit of the later eighties; and on an identical subject, when he had threatened to resign if his colleagues obstructed a bill on conditions in slave ships. But nothing in fact happened. He approached Liverpool, of the Committee of Trade, and also raised the matter at a Cabinet meeting; but faced by opposition, he seems to have found relief in giving one

1. *P.R., 3rd ser.*, I (1797), 468; V (1798), 575.
2. Roger Anstey, *The Atlantic Slave Trade and British Abolition 1760–1810* (1975), 330.
3. For which see I, 403–4.
4. Enacted as 39 Geo. III, c80; preceded by a lesser measure in 1798, 38 Geo. III, c88.
5. See *P.R., 3rd ser.*, VIII (1799), 187, IX (sd), 557; *The Senator*, XXIII (nd), may be added for the debates on limitation. Thornton's measure had run out of time in 1798; a fact of which he reminded Pitt in the course of the debate in 1799, in a note in the House (nd; P.R.O. 30/8/310) urging him to whip up attendance at an important moment in the passage of the bill.

member a 'severe dressing' before being obliged to drop the idea of involving the Government as such.[1]

The episode is instructive. For it suggested, indeed by its exceptional nature, a more regular pattern which by now was widely discerned. As the decade wore on in fact, Pitt was less prepared than he had been in this whole subject to press against obstruction in person, or indeed do much more than speak in support. The declarations themselves remained unequivocal – in 1795 he did not hesitate to counter Dundas's annual gradualist arguments, and later in the year was willing to confer 'satisfactorily' with Wilberforce, after some strain in their personal relations, over the 'West Indian subject'.[2] But the climate thereafter cooled. The Minister voted to count out the first of the ill attended discussions on conditions in slave ships in 1796;[3] and while the two men had a 'tête-a-tête' a week later on the then forthcoming general election, and early the next year were at one in the crises of the Bank and the fleets, Pitt tried to persuade his friend to accept an amended version of the gradualist proposal for amelioration of conditions in the islands – a diversionary issue on which Wilberforce felt deeply hurt. Meeting with no success, he 'stood stiffly' with the old unaccommodating cause, and the next two years continued to produce mixed impressions: an intervention by the Minister in the House to postpone debate on Smith's bill in 1798, and again on Thornton's in 1799; but also support for the latter in the face of the Lords' manoeuvres, an impressive speech on Wilberforce's motion for immediate abolition, and the hope, expressed privately, of progress with the 'Slave Trade business' in the following year.[4]

Pitt's attitude proved hard for some at the time and for many later to accept. Historians in the nineteenth century – Brougham, Macaulay, Lecky – condemned a conduct which would be seen more starkly in the final stage. Wilberforce himself however did not do so when he came to sum up; and while the intensity of his admiring affection was such as to forbid final censure, one may note that his judgment was shared from a less obvious source, a firm ally here but more normally a political opponent, the Foxite MP William Smith.[5] Wilberforce indeed did not waver in

1. The report of Pitt's opening attitude comes from Canning (see Josceline Bagot, *George Canning and His Friends*, I (1909), 151, and also Anstey, op. cit., 303–4). Wilberforce tells the story of the dressing-down; the victim was '*Emmanuel*' – possibly Loughborough? (*Life*, II, 337). For the Minister's behaviour over Dolben's bill in 1788 see I, 394–5.

2. See *P.R.*, XXXIV, 625, XXXVII, 328, XLI, 23–6 for successive years; II, 380 for the personal strain; *Life of Wilberforce*, II, 110–11 for the meeting in October 1795 in the hope of including the subject in a forthcoming Address to the King.

3. See p. 426 above; this was on 11 May – 'Counted out – 36, with Pitt by the West Indians', Wilberforce recorded sadly (op. cit., 147).

4. See op. cit., 196, 286, 331, 337, 340; and also John Pollock, *Wilberforce* (1977), 176 for the Minister's hope of achieving agreement for abolition in a general peace treaty when that came.

5. Speech in the Commons of 10 June 1806 (see Anstey, op. cit., 302n54). For one of his contributions to the cause see p. 427 above.

retrospect. 'I *solemnly declare*', he wrote, almost a decade after the Minister's desertion of the motion, '. . . my firm conviction that Mr. Pitt was a sincere friend to the Abolition'.[1] Blame should be attached to his 'dilatoriness and proscrastination, his great vices'.[2] But these were particularly serious in this instance because they bore on an inherently thorny situation, in which advantage must be taken of any chance to advance. For the nub of the problem lay in the fact, as the Minister of course knew well, that abolition of the trade was not conceived by normal constitutional usage as being a measure of Government.[3] It could be held, like Parliamentary reform, to lie beyond the bounds of Cabinet responsibility in the primary relationship of that body to the King; to be rather a personal enthusiasm and treated in that light. Wilberforce himself found this a 'narrow view' when one considered the bearing of the question on the commercial interest of the country, and he wished that Pitt could have succeeded in overcoming it and involving the Ministry directly in legislation. But he recognised that in the general practice

> what shall and what shall not be a Government question is not an arbitrary arrangement, nor is it dependent on the Minister's will, it turns in fact on the answer to the question: 'Is the credit or stability of an administration at stake?'

In the case of a motion for abolition of the slave trade 'every one was perfectly at liberty to vote as he should see fit'.

This was perfectly valid, as far as it went. Canning, himself taking up the cause in the late nineties, argued on the same lines. Abolition was not a question on which Government should 'impose a restraint upon liberty of conscience': something that 'Mr Pitt never ventured to think advisable' here, and on which he allowed his closest intimates freely to differ from himself.[4] The convention was very strong. Its strength indeed accounted partly for an alternative treatment that could be sometimes tried.

For within the question as a whole there was always a distinction to be drawn between its various aspects. Outright abolition, immediate or delayed, was obviously a matter for statute: certain more limited measures however – referring to conditions in the ships, regulations for conquered territories, amelioration in 'old' British possessions – might be dealt with

1. To Thomas Harrison, 22 October 1814; quoted in Pollock, *Wilberforce*, 175.

2. Ibid.

3. Memorandum by Wilberforce, nd but dictated for his memoirs. The original was formerly in the Wrangham Mss, a collection now being catalogued in the Bodleian Library. An excerpt, not in itself reflecting the full weight of the argument, was published by his sons in *Life*, I, 165; fuller passages are given in Anstey, op. cit., 300–2.

Cf. for the rest of this paragraph, with particular stress on a similar situation in the case of Parliamentary reform, I, 224, 610, 632–3, 638; and see p. 427 above.

4. This was written in 1802; quoted in Patrick C. Lipscomb, 'Party Politics, 1801–2: George Canning and the Trinidad Question' (*H.J.*, Vol. XII, No. 3, 457). Cf. I, 230 for the conduct of some of Pitt's friends on other questions in earlier days.

as administrative matters by Orders in Council. Such an occasion first arose, or was accepted, on the occupation of Trinidad in 1797. The attempt to deny a partial import of slaves into captured foreign colonies by legislation had failed four years earlier.[1] But there was a chance of a different approach now, and furthermore of checking a transfer from British islands to the recently reconquered island of St Vincent as well.[2] This last had unfortunately been approved, and an Order in Council issued for the purpose. But Wilberforce intervened with Pitt, and after a pause it was rescinded and fresh supplies stopped to both islands in 1798. The decision did not work in practice as intended; in 1800 the abolitionists reckoned that 'new' lands were taking some three-quarters of all the British imports of slaves. A precedent however had been set, and moreover in a way that should appeal to the planters' interest, to beware of sinking capital investment in territories whose future might be open to bargaining at the peace. In 1805 indeed preventive action was taken by a similar Order for the captured Dutch colony of Guiana, and all importation of slaves was then forbidden to conquered foreign colonies.[3]

The question of Trinidad itself would return to trouble Pitt, in conditions that made it a political matter; and it cannot be said moreover that he acted quickly in either 1798 or 1805.[4] His problems and his vacillations became the more apparent in fact as the old century gave way to the new. Some temporary relief was then forthcoming, for the abolitionists reduced their activity for a few years. Changed circumstances in 1801 led Wilberforce himself to stay his hand while he hoped for the peace which might include international abolition in a treaty; in 1802 he tried again in Parliament, but too late in the session to stand any real chance of success;[5] in 1803 Government's attention was so fixed on a threat of invasion that he judged it proper to let the issue lie. It was 1804 indeed before he tried seriously to renew his main effort. Political conditions seemed to hold better promise, and late in May – countering signs that some of his opponents might agree to a period of 'suspension' in lieu – he introduced once more a motion for immediate abolition. This time he was rewarded in the Commons with markedly easy success: 124 to 49, 100 to 42, 69 to 33 on the successive stages.[6] But of course the peers were waiting. Grenville, a champion of the cause in the Lords, advised against proceeding there before the summer recess, in order to improve the odds in the longer period available in the next session; his counsel was approved,

---

1. P. 426 above.

2. For which see II, 564, 614.

3. Anstey, op. cit., 332–3, 368; and cf. also 375–6 and n39. Wilberforce argued as a 'very powerful' reason to move in this instance by '*an Act of Government*' the encouragement it would give to an inclination among Dutchmen themselves to abolish the trade (to Pitt, nd, endorsed 1805; P.R.O. 30/8/189).

4. *Life of Wilberforce*, II, 333, 358–9.

5. P. 428, n4 above for 1801; *P.R., 3rd ser.*, XVIII (1802), 745 for the next year.

6. *P.D.*, II (1812), cols. 475, 557, 871.

independently, by Pitt; and Wilberforce felt that he should consent. He waited accordingly to February 1805.

But at that point he met with a great disappointment. Pitt had recently been in the midst of acute political difficulties, which however might be receding and must not be allowed if possible to recur. He was particularly concerned to avoid risks of dissension, at least in the near future. He wished his friend to postpone the question; and when that was refused he stated in the Chamber that he would not speak in the debate. A resurgence of obstruction in point of fact already seemed likely, after the abolitionists' significant success the year before. Some of Wilberforce's associates were unduly complacent; their opponents had been hard at work; and Pitt's remark doubtless made its impact on a depressingly habitual thin House. The motion was lost on the second reading by 70 to 77: a blow, Wilberforce wrote, which struck 'a damp into [my] heart'.[1] He did not give up lesser action, however, and Pitt, under pressure, later moved to help. His agreement to prohibit further imports of slaves to conquered colonies had earlier turned on securing the object by administrative order – 'very strong on this, and against any vote by Parliament' – and it was by such a means that he was eventually brought to act.[2] The move was his final contribution to a cause that had once enlisted a fiercer loyalty. Its limited achievement, as things turned out, came as the abolitionists' fortunes were about to rise.

For in point of fact, at this low point in the long years of disappointment Wilberforce's main aim stood on the verge of success. An end was at hand, and when it came the process was easy and swift. It was complete indeed within fourteen months of Pitt's death. In the summer of 1806 a revived Foreign Slave Trade bill,[3] prohibiting the import of slaves into British possessions in foreign ships, passed through both Houses; so did resolutions against the slave trade in principle; and the Government obtained Parliament's consent to approach other Powers for combined abolition. And then in March 1807 the British trade was comprehensively abolished. These successive steps moreover met with no real obstruction. The concentric walls seemed suddenly to collapse. The Foreign Trade bill passed its final division in the Commons – taken now deliberately at a low key – by 35 to 13, and in the Lords by 43 to 18. The votes on the resolutions of principle were respectively 114 to 15 and 41 to 20. The Address to the King for an approach to other Powers received unanimous backing from both Houses. And the bill for abolition itself, having first passed the Lords by 100 to 36, did so triumphantly in the Commons by 283 to 16. The majorities amazed the abolitionists themselves. Their renewed efforts seemed to bear witness to an astonishing change. How had that occurred, and what light did the outcome throw on Pitt's assumptions over the years?

1. To Lord Muncaster, 4 March 1805 (*Life of Wilberforce*, III, 214). For the vote see *P.D.*, III (1812), col. 674; for Pitt's remark, col. 668.
2. Op. cit., 348, 358–9; *Life of Wilberforce*, III, 184 for a conversation as early as July 1804.
3. Cf. pp. 426–7 above.

Several factors combined. In 1806 there appeared once more to be at least some movement towards peace, and peace, it was agreed, would provide the best chance of securing an end to the trade. But in any case, however that might be, and while the traffic continued, the course of the war was providing a good premiss for the abolitionists' final opening move to exclude the foreign element. This may indeed merit some slightly closer inspection in its own right, as a part of an ensuing success which itself has been given a different and more comprehensive explanation. The slave trade after all had been a major factor in the evolution of a commercial empire, and its deliberate abolition might accordingly be thought to have responded to a perceived change in economic circumstances. Did the decision not in fact occur at a convenient point, in a context of recent overproduction but also of a gathering structural decline in the profitability of the West Indian plantations? It is a stimulating argument.[1] But it has not stood up to analysis; indeed the trend of policy might be found explicable on opposite grounds. For the economic influences in 1806–7 can be claimed rather to have been at work in a short-term contrasting sense: in protection of perceived advantages which could be currently at risk. The years before the war had shown some signs of a relative reduction in the role of the British West Indies as an outstanding jewel in the home country's commercial crown: a stabilisation in place of an increase in their exports of sugar and coffee, though those of cotton markedly rose, and the sharp increase in British traffic to the markets of the new United States. But that state of affairs gave way in turn to a renewed upward trend during the war itself, in years when the expansion of British foreign trade turned so prominently on the re-export of colonial goods, as well as on export in their worked-up state.[2] From 1793 to 1802 the former indeed rose in official value by 187.2 per cent over that for 1788–92, as against an increase of 57.7 per cent in the export of domestic products, and accounted for some 40 per cent of the (increased) sum of exports and re-exports compared with 26.8 per cent in the earlier period. Sugar, coffee and cotton in combination remained vital to this world-wide process of growth, and trade between Britain and the Caribbean accounted now, directly and indirectly, for over a third of the British global value compared with a fifth twenty years before. That might not continue to be the case in the longer run, when British manufacturing processes would demand markets subject to greater enlargement than those of the islands themselves.[3] But in the years immediately preceding abolition such speculative thoughts, with their strategic implications, were scarcely a matter of public review. The emphasis in London lay rather on the need, while conditions permitted, to damage the foundations of foreign competition in important primary products,

1. See Notes on Sources on p. 871 below.
2. Cf. I, 389; p. 144 above.
3. Cf. Dundas in 1800, p. 354 above.

particularly from certain conquered territories which might have to be returned at a peace.

It was on this aspect of the wider question that the abolitionists fastened successfully in the last stage. Wilberforce had at one time feared any proposal that might sidetrack his main cause. But in the event the limited measures paved his advance, as some of his colleagues had in fact hoped.[1] The piecemeal denial of imports of slaves to conquered possessions, ending in a successful Foreign Trade bill, was designed to guard a British interest in export markets at least for so long as the war with France endured. It was an aim moreover that could be linked with others to reinforce a now strengthening naval domination – with a closer limitation in particular on the cargoes allowed to be carried in neutral bottoms, to which the French were having to turn increasingly for their overseas trade. And it was one that, so far now from potentially obstructing abolition, could on the contrary promote connexions, already discernible, between the two sides in the main debate.

For as the years passed, common attitudes were more easily acknowledged beneath the surface of the Parliamentary speeches. The evidence produced by the abolitionists had certainly induced a wide uneasiness of conscience: moral justification of the trade was weakened, gradual suppression approved, and the defenders founded their arguments more strictly on economic and political grounds. Dundas himself as a gradualist never tried to assert the humanity or justice of the traffic; and this feeling undoubtedly deepened and spread as time went by. Experience of the system, it has further been suggested, from officers returning from the large expeditions may also have had an effect, together with the heavy losses of white lives from disease and the resultant attractions of native recruitment.[2] Some convergent attitudes lay behind the figures of the divisions in the Commons. And the divisions themselves – despite lack of detailed evidence – suggest that the strength of opposition need not always be taken as hard and fast. The majorities against outright abolition were sometimes very narrow, and the small numbers normally involved indicate a widespread indifference which, apparently solid as it were in repose, might nonetheless prove a shaky defence if pressure were to be applied. Such a deduction might be supported moreover by the pattern of the one majority for which we have a list of names: in the defeat of Wilberforce's motion for abolition in 1796 by 74 to 70 votes.[3] Taking the attribution of connexions at their broadest, only some 15 Members were to be found in the lobby out of a West India interest in the House which might be counted at an upper figure of 34; to that one might add eight from constituencies benefiting from the slave trade or from businesses so

1. See pp. 427, 431 above.

2. Duffy, *Soldiers, Sugar, and Seapower*, 391–2; and see p. 424 above, though also 426 for the implication of recruitment.

3. P. 426 above. See *P.R.*, XLIV, 323–4. The list in point of fact yields 77 names, one more (allowing for the tellers) than the recorded vote. Anstey (op. cit., 296–8, 306–15), who analyses the details, decided to ignore the small discrepancy.

involved; and a further three from seats under the patronage of Sir James Lowther, who had property in the islands. Of the rest, it has been pointed out that 23 had colonial links, all but one of which however related to the East[1] – nabobs, retired officers or officials or their own close connexions –, some 11 of those being Members with a loyalty to Dundas; and the residue of 28 was made up, less precisely, of some placemen including Scots who again might reflect Dundas's influence, some Members perhaps with less specific ties with the Caribbean or the trade, and a few whose votes may have been given to please electoral patrons. In numbers this might be said to represent a core vote, subject to additions but also to erosions, which was not conspicuously larger than the abolitionists' vote itself; in composition it pointed to a range of allegiances – self-interest, often combined with a version of the national interest, a generalised feeling for imperial order, a willing compliance with a patron's views. The effects were for long sufficient to bolster the specific planters' connexion. But they proved vulnerable when an overspill of conscience could be the more easily entertained after the acceptance of a preliminary measure of protection. The subsoil in fact was showing evidence of shifting. But that was not enough in itself to account for the outcome, let alone its speed. The final development came about thanks to a strictly political change. For the Ministry which saw the end of the slave trade was ready and waiting to secure that result. Its two major figures, by then Grenville and Fox, new in office and unequivocal in aim, carried enough weight to disregard a continuing minority in a coalition Cabinet of 'all the talents' – and were glad also to combine their followers over an issue on which most would agree. Abolition still could not be taken in 1807 as a measure of Government: it was moved, naturally, by Wilberforce in the Commons, and in the Lords by Grenville speaking once again as an individual. But he spoke there also on the preceding occasions, and as First Lord of the Treasury on the Address to the King;[2] and the Foreign Trade bill was introduced in the Commons by the Attorney General. The new direction of influence was felt at once. The Commons followed the leaders, and the peers were no longer recalcitrant, the more so when disapproval from the Court, if detectable, was no longer so loudly heard. The problems which Pitt had encountered, and continued to envisage, were summarily dispersed. Why, one may ask, had he himself not persisted more boldly towards the end?

As things turned out however, it was precisely towards the end that Pitt felt most circumscribed. If he had been faced by problems within the Cabinet in the nineties, these were increased after 1800 by the course of political events. A new era opened then in Parliament, in which a long-lived stable Ministry gave way to others less well placed in a more confused scene. Various influences opposed to immediate abolition loomed larger in his life, and he was not prepared to upset them too far; his

1. The exception relating to Canada.
2. Cf. p. 429 above.

manoeuvres on the question in those years took form from the last stage of his own career. But this was not the whole story, for while the obstacles may have grown rather than diminished, they brought to the fore an already visible reluctance to accord priority to this single cause.[1] The trade had its part to play on a wartime stage on which the slave islands held a significant if reduced strategic role, and its well entrenched supporters in and outside Parliament might not be easily overcome. In the midst of guiding a Government in a conflict of ever rising proportions, the Minister was not inclined to devote himself beyond the occasions required. His sympathy, as Wilberforce and Smith asserted, remained engaged in principle. But he was always liable by temperament to drop a subject which had become inconvenient or uncongenial – Parliamentary reform and Ireland spring to mind[2] – and it was his friendship with Wilberforce and a sense of private honour that held him for as long as they did to what he came to see as an awkward distraction. Patience – the quality he found the most necessary in a Minister – wore thin; caution – usually alert in testing his assorted following – became progressively more profound.[3] By the later nineties, too, he was obviously under more strain, and that increased markedly with worsening health as he faced his heavy burdens at home and abroad. By the close he had no energy to spare. When he finally abandoned the effective pursuit of the object he had once espoused so ardently, he was no longer willing to make an effort to throw his influence into the scale. It was sadly ironic that this happened when a time had come which allowed others less encumbered by the recent past to exert themselves at once for convincing success.

Questions arising from the slave trade in conquered territories proved to be the sharpest disturbers of wartime relations between Ministers in London and the British Caribbean colonies themselves.[4] They also cast their shadows over the longer term. There was no question for the moment at any rate of creating Assemblies where those had not been known: as the British Governor argued from the former Spanish Trinidad, that would be to 'generate the seeds of lasting Fermentation'.[5] But the problem of how best to foster cultivation there while denying foreign import of slaves led in 1802 to a commission of inquiry being sent from home. This was a failure: the members were recalled and a report was called for in 1804 on the laws and governance of the island, from which to decide on the future. In the upshot the Colonial Office preferred

1. Cf. I, 322: 'good Ministers are hopeful men. But they do not devote themselves in the highest office to crusading for a single cause'.
2. Cf. II, 87–8; I, 215–16, pp. 43, 162–3 above respectively.
3. Cf. I, 88; op. cit., 234.
4. See pp. 424–5 above.
5. Sir Thomas Picton to Lord Hobart [Secretary of State], 26 June 1801; quoted in Ward, *Colonial Self-Government*, 87.

the precedent of Quebec, where the Governor administered with a Council; but nothing further happened, and in 1810 the Ministry of the day resolved to leave matters as they were. Meanwhile however one decision had been taken in 1802 itself: no further grants of land in Trinidad should be made to British planters in the Caribbean without reference to Parliament. The intervention did not please them, or by extension their legislatures; and neither did the fresh pressures, favoured at the time by the gradualists in Westminster, for the further amelioration of conditions for the slave populations in Jamaica and elsewhere. This last theme became more prominent as the humanitarian impulse at home was transferred increasingly, after the war, from the trade to the survival of slavery itself. Important constitutional questions were focused for a region which contained both Crown and unrevised Legislative colonies; and the reforming 1830s and '40s inherited a problem, raising even the spectre of local defiance, bequeathed by a then reduced economy to a changing age.

III

In 1800, however, it was easier to take an audit of empire for the West than for the East. Despite the loss of the mainland to the south of Canada, and the first hard evidence of a threat to the slave trade, the island colonies remained an economic unit in a familiar complex of wealth and power. Matters were different in the far-flung region which for the British centred on India. The paucity and possibly temporary nature of possessions beyond the subcontinent allowed little scope for a settled coherent Navigation System;[1] within India the consequences of trade, administrative, diplomatic, military, were continually developing, often faster than approved at home; while authority in London lay in a diarchy of the Company and the Government whose own relationship was evolving at a pace reflecting fresh pressures from events. The balance of trade itself with 'East India' (the 'East Indies'), as measured directly in the Customs' books, could appear less favourable than that with the Western possessions. In 1797–8 the official values of imports from either region were much the same – £5,982,000 from the West Indies, £5,785,000 from the East; but on the same basis the respective exports were worth £4,612,000 and £1,640,000 and the re-exports £489,000 and £75,000.[2] Bullion – Mexican silver itself available partly from Caribbean trade with Spanish America[3] – had to be sent to help pay the costs of the Company's sepoy troops, stemming initially from arrangements with the Indian rulers,

1. For hopes and the achievements see I, 423–36, II, 561–2.
2. Mitchell & Deane, op. cit., ch. XI, table 11.
3. And see I, 460–1 for more extensive but frustrated ideas from Pitt and Dundas to attract Spanish bullion to India in the eighties.

which lay at the root of the whole gradual process of tax collection and acquirement of influence that, often unavoidably, sometimes deliberately, was being drawn into territorial control. It was not a simple matter to gauge overall the weight of advantage to be had from India; or surprising that Dundas, the prime champion of the need to protect the British position, focused on the value, when compared with such trade figures, of remittances for capital formation at home.[1]

The canvas in point of fact was broader than that. The remittances themselves from individual Company members and servants had given rise, particularly in the earlier days, to a new element in society; the nabobs' conspicuous consumption seemed to confirm the faith in the fabled treasures of the East. It continued, if less flamboyantly, accompanied by the produce of lesser returns from the holders of civil and military posts; but in addition the Company as an institution could recover something in the last decades of the century of the pristine vision of wealth from lands beyond India itself. Largely excluded by earlier comers, Portuguese and Dutch, from the first rewards of the old European dream, denied direct entry above all to the spices of the Moluccas, the British had had to rest content with their scattered settlements in parts of the subcontinent. But the subcontinent in time yielded a reward. For the East India Company was able at least to mitigate the loss on its annual budget by the trade with China, centring on raw cottons in exchange for teas, which comprised essentially at this stage direct regional transactions.[2] Owing its growing success to two unconnected processes – Pitt's massive reduction of duties on tea in 1784, which soon knocked out foreign competition, and the structure of the Company, which still allowed Private and Country trade by its members alongside and here in excess of its own[3] – this looked in rising scale to the future. Currently however it was a significant factor not represented properly in the narrower ledger, and it made its impact on aspects of an enlarging scene. The Company's regional activities, of which those with China were the most considerable, buttressed its validity. They propelled the hopes of expansion along the south-east passage to a wider commercial world. And they reinforced the need to secure the focal stake in the area, in an age of crisis through much of Asia and one of European war.[4]

Those two lines of pressure were seen to meet, under a fresh impetus, at the very end of the century. The decline and in one case the dynastic replacement of the great imperial regimes, Mogul in Delhi, Savafid in Isfahan, Ottoman in Constantinople, had witnessed compelling changes

1. Cf. pp. 354, 422 above here with I, 118.

2. The respective contributions to Britain's trade with the Far East of domestic manufactured goods and of regional produce and products is a source of debate among economic historians. In this still relatively early period the latter would seem to have been much the more important.

3. See I, 243–5, 411–13, 415–16.

4. Op. cit., 162, Ch. XIV section III; II, 562, 628, 647.

in authority from the centres towards regions of semi- or complete independence, spread from Egypt and the lands north of the Arabian peninsula to Afghanistan and the Punjab and the princely fiefdoms in India itself. The process had a significance deeper than an opportunistic filling of a vacuum. Fundamental developments were at work, in shifts of economic forces – the Orient was not as stagnant as Europeans were apt to assume – and fiercely searching religious dissensions, which could underlie and spur the transformations of military and political power. The effects proved substantial for world history. The perspective for the British at this point, however, was defined sharply by the world they knew.

Unusually sharply, indeed, in these particular years. The insertion of the East India Company into a dissolving Mogul empire had been followed by conflict, and this would persist in a future in which European rivals would play no part on the ground. But in the last quarter of the eighteenth century French influence remained a factor to be reckoned with in the centre and south, and from the eighties, it could be held, most strongly as an element in Tipu Sultan's ambitions from Mysore. He had been checked, with a substantial loss of territory, in 1792;[1] and the French themselves were ejected from their base in Pondicherry in 1793. But the European war revived his hopes; he got in touch with France's nearest point of contact, in Mauritius; and an unwise proclamation from the Governor there in 1797, reported in Calcutta in June 1798, allowed the British to prepare, diplomatically and militarily, for a pre-emptive strike. Rumours came to hand also of the sailing of an enemy naval force; and the news of Bonaparte's landing in Egypt, received in October, proved a decisive signal. After some negotiation, held in play while British preparations were on foot, operations began in February 1799 and in May Tipu was killed in his capital of Seringapatam.

The victory marked the opening of a new stage in the story of the British dominion in India: the effective end of French rivalry, a precursor of other problems and renewed advance. Nor was this adventitious. For a new Governor General had arrived. His predecessors since Hastings, Cornwallis and then the Company official Sir John Shore, did not seek expansion for its own sake; they were concerned rather to consolidate and, Cornwallis notably, pursue financial and administrative reform, and while further territory accrued from Tipu's defeat that had not been a deliberate earlier object. Now, however, a different spirit was abroad. For continuing quarrels between Shore in Bengal and the more forceful subordinate Governor of Madras[2] were worrying London, replacements were needed, and in the autumn of 1797 a successor was found, to Shore's own relief, for the senior post. At first indeed Cornwallis was asked to return to Calcutta and accepted out of duty until he had a disagreement with the Company's

---

1. I, 443.
2. Robert Hobart, formerly the Chief Secretary in Ireland (II, 221), who returned to England in 1798 in 1799, as Lord Hobart, married Eleanor Eden (p. 192, n1 above).

Directors, and then Ireland called;[1] and Dundas thought of himself, but could not be spared. In default however the nomination fell on Lord Mornington, a member of the Board of Control, intended initially for Madras with the reversion of the Governor Generalship after Cornwallis. The choice was not popular with either the Company or Dundas. But it held, for it came from Pitt. Mornington was a friend, a year younger than the Minister, one of the habitués of Holwood;[2] clever and active and ambitious and increasingly impatient for more scope. He had somewhat compromised his chances at home moreover by marrying a French mistress who had borne him five children in advance. Setting off in November, he reached India in May 1798 to embark on a career which within seven years would cause the maps to be redrawn.

That saga cannot be told here. When it closed, in 1805, 'the Company's scattered possessions had been transformed into a great empire, and the Company, with the Mogul emperor himself under its protection, stood forth as unquestionably the Paramount Power in India'.[3] British territory had been extended to Mysore and along the Carnatic to the southern Cape Comorin and inland to Travancore; along the Indian Ocean between Malabar and Goa and to Surat beyond Bombay; in the far north, flanking Oudh, to 'the ceded provinces' along the river Jumna; while Oudh itself, Jaipur, Berar, Hyderabad had been placed in differing degrees under protection. The whole had been effected by a blend of diplomacy, peaceful annexation by coercion, and war; and over the same period the Governor General's dominance was imposed on the Presidencies of Madras and Bombay, to concentrate, as the Directors in London complained, 'all . . . political powers' on himself – 'an exercise not warranted by law' – forming 'one Government, through every part and ramification of which his authority was practically and constantly to pervade'.[4] It was a heady mixture, and one not to every one's taste at home. Brilliant by and large as was the personal achievement, it ended not surprisingly in his recall.[5]

Much of the trouble lay indeed in the personality itself. Mornington, the eldest of the five Wellesley brothers four of whom gained peerages, was in many ways a highly attractive but undoubtedly a difficult figure, with an innate exalted conception of his place and worth. Ardent, imaginative, casting an image of splendour on his policies and his surroundings,

1. See pp. 168–9 above.
2. For a glimpse of him there with the early group of friends see I, 592–3.
3. Sir Penderel Moon, *The British Conquest and Dominion of India* (1989), 276.
4. Quoted op. cit., 277. This admonition in the draft of the despatch was deleted by the Board of Control. But there was no dissent from the conclusion that strictly speaking this exercise of power was illegal under Pitt's Act of 1784 – which in general had strengthened the Governor General's authority (see I, 189–91) – both in relation to the lesser Presidencies and to the Governor General's own council in Bengal.
5. Or effectively so. He had intended to leave, at a time of his choosing, but in the upshot was left no real choice.

charming and inspiring to a talented young staff – a kindergarten devoted to 'the glorious little man' – and in general to those who served his policies well, he was also unable to work easily or charitably with equals, and his sensitivity to his own requirements, practical and emotional, allowed little room for dissent or suspected lack of appreciation. 'Narcissus-like', throughout his life 'he brooded upon his beautiful reflection';[1] not unlike his distant successor Curzon, who was fascinated by him, he was a great (a greater) proconsul who failed in successive stages to bend his contemporaries to his will. The chinks soon appeared, and at an early time of glory. Created an Irish marquess, as Marquess Wellesley, in reward for extinguishing Tipu, he was disgusted – 'my double gilt Potatoe' – and discouraged to a degree whose effects he never managed entirely to shake off. He had expected something higher – the Garter, which he had mentioned, or a marked step in the British peerage, giving him a seat with promotion of rank in the House of Lords – and his vulnerability in such matters, intense even by the standards of a society where they were of real importance, clouded his regard thereafter for those who in his view had let him down.[2] His friendship with Pitt endured – their mutual affection was real – and it fell in due course to the Minister to explain privately and with genuine kindness that Wellesley's repeated wish to leave – by then he had announced his resignation three times – would be met, and at once.[3]

For the disagreements between the Governor General and London – at first with the Company, later the Government as well – had grown in almost every direction since the promising days of 1799. There were in fact discrepancies of aims, always underlying and increasingly visible, within the triple institutions (for in practice distance could so promote Calcutta in the short term) which in their troublesome interactions were responsible for Britain's place in the East. The creative tension which

1. Iris Butler, *The Eldest Brother*, 24.
2. For the potato see Wellesley to Pitt, 28 April 1800 (P.R.O. 30/8/188). Pitt's letter with 'the innocent offer', as Rosebery called it, is printed in his *Pitt*, 211–12 and the subsequent attempt to heal the wound op. cit., 213–17. The new Marquess's distress at his 'disgrace' was painful, leading him at first to ask to come home (see eg letters to Dundas in *Two Views of British India . . .*, ed. Edward Ingram (1970), 258–9, 266, 281–2).
The title of Mornington was that of an earldom in the Irish peerage (of which the Governor General was the second holder), and thus ineligible for a seat in the British House of Lords; which however he could claim since October 1797 on the grant of a British barony following his appointment. He will be referred to hereafter by his better known title of Wellesley. Some of his bitterness sprang from the fact that Cornwallis had been given both the Garter (at the start of his Governor Generalship), and a British marquessate (near the end). There was of course no comparison between the two men's positions in the national life; and a technical complication could also be cited which differentiated Cornwallis's latest step in the peerage from Mornington's hope, or expectation, now (*GEC*, IX, 237nc).
3. 21 December 1804 (Rosebery, *Pitt*, 219–21). The relationship on Wellesley's side may be followed in letters in P.R.O. 30/8/188 and Dacres Adams Mss, formerly P.R.O. 30/58/4–5.

characterised the Company – the balance of its primary purpose of trade with the varied functions which that imposed – was tipped in these years increasingly in favour of stability as a forward policy was revived on the ground. Seen from the great building in Leadenhall Street, the necessary aim should be to contain expense; and Wellesley in that respect was far from satisfactory, from the costs of his own idealised splendour to the much greater problems of the expansion of power. He could rightly point to increased revenues, gained from administrative improvements and the territories conquered or annexed. But the income was swallowed in the end by costs: in 1805–6 the annual deficit exceeded £2 million and by then the debt on the Company's books, £17 million in 1798, had risen to one of £31½ million. The Directors were naturally worried, and at times infuriated; as they were also by the Governor General's persistent campaign to concentrate all business on himself. Their rising animosity, complicated as always by internecine feuds reflecting competing Company interests, could be amply aired in Parliament, at the annual reviews of finance and as occasion offered. It was also a persistent factor in Wellesley's dealings with Government itself.

That meant, over a critical period, with Dundas as head of the Board of Control. Pitt for his part was involved in major issues and, particularly from the two colleagues' incessant contact and his own friendship with Wellesley, sometimes in minor ones as well; and he kept a close eye when occasion arose on the state of the Company's debt. But to all intents, as had been the case since 1784, Government's management of affairs in India lay in Dundas's hands.[1] Like Scotland, it was his fief; and the blend of his policies was his own – not in sum either that of the Company or of the Governor General. Pitt and he were at one in the place they held for India in the framework of national interests. Before the war they had proclaimed British 'sovereignty' in the subcontinent in relation to other European Powers,[2] and the course of the war itself naturally hardened this assertion of right. The 'imperial dominion' there was of prime importance, the focus for the whole position in the Far East; to be upheld and, as Pitt aspired from the turn of the century, not to be a bargaining point – unlike Western conquests – in any terms of peace.[3] To Dundas, the exponent of a war for 'colonial resources', the importance of 'that extensive empire' could not be overstressed.[4] It was the counterpoise to French power; and as that grew in Europe in the middle nineties he placed

1. See I, 192. In the later eighties Pitt attended quite a high proportion of the Board's meetings (op. cit., 457). But that proved to be something of an exception to a rule.

2. Eg in the pre-war negotiation with France for a commercial Convention in India, Eden [Auckland] was instructed in a paper drawn up by the two men together that 'We' were 'treating as the Sovereigns of the country, they [the French] as possessing a commercial interest protected by us' (I, 441–2).

3. P. 423, n4 above for his phrase.

4. See in particular his letter to Mornington of 31 October 1799 (*Two Views of British India*, 206–7); 'extensive empire' occurs in same to same, 27 September 1799 (op. cit., 180).

his faith the more in the regions beyond. Such a strategy, the offspring of commercial enterprise, brought economic benefits later over a wide sphere. At the same time, consonant with his speculations on the advisability of outright territorial possession,[1] he did not believe that that course was invariably necessary in India to achieve the required ends. British security must of course be guaranteed, but more than one road could lead to that goal. He was indeed hostile to a rigid prospect applied to the subcontinent; determined in fact to 'prevent' it, whatever the pressures.[2] The answer should be to choose horses for courses. Where our interests were so threatened that direct possession was required – in Mysore for instance and the Carnatic – there should be no hesitation; in some other cases – of the lands for instance within the loose Maratha confederation, where the circumstances led sometimes to war and sometimes to a watchful peace – influence and alliances could be preferred; in others again – for instance in Hyderabad and the far north – effective annexation which left the existing authority in possession of the title deeds. It could also be desirable, as a defence against any French designs, to obtain a transfer of power from another European state: an ambition focused on the surviving Portuguese enclaves of Goa and Diu on the western coast. The pattern in short rested on circumstances. It was shaped towards a comprehensive design, but the elements in a formative stage could respond to fluctuating needs.

These were affected moreover in the case of India by a highly visible form of pressure. For the pattern in this instance reflected not only the general approach which Dundas sketched for the Cabinet in 1800, but its reinforcement from the persistent problem, occupying Pitt as well as himself, of the Company's debt.[3] He hoped constantly for a chance to build up the revenues in a period of quiet. But he was as constantly thwarted by developments which frustrated in particular the reduction of military costs. Troop reinforcements were sent when necessary from England or Ireland; but not with much pleasure, and he watched with dismay the rise of the forces in the subcontinent, from a strength of 80,000 in 1796 to over 142,000 by the end of 1800.[4] The costs admittedly

1. P. 354 above.
2. To Charles Grant (see I, 458n3), 31 July 1800; John Rylands Library English Ms 907. He was talking, in the context, of commercial pressures from within the Company, which he would not admit in opposition to his basic 'principle'.
3. His letters to Mornington show, sometimes with dramatic force, his intense anxiety to 'reduce the great load of debt, by which our affairs in India are encumbered . . . our only mortal foe' (*Two Views*, 313–14).
Cf. Pitt's own view, typical of more hopeful early days but formed in this instance partly by the same preoccupation: 'Ambition and trouble were companions but too often; and they had proved particularly harmful to our interests in India. Indeed they were what ought most studiously to be avoided there' (speech in the Commons, 17 July 1784; *P.R..*, XVI (1784), 10).
4. *Two Views*, 315–16; and see op. cit., 10 for other figures. Fortescue, *History of the British Army*, IV – Part II (1906), Appendix C, gives establishments for the King's troops in India under the annual Estimates.

were proportioned between the home Government, the Company, and local charges and revenues; but this in itself was an awkward arrangement for both authority of command and quality of men, making it desirable to gain an improved balance favouring 'King's troops'[1] over 'Company' Europeans, which in turn increased the desirability of a policy where possible of restraint. Dundas and Wellesley held many beliefs in common: on the need to enlarge British exports to India carried in British rather than neutral shipping, thereby also reducing the volume of Indian goods shipped directly to other European states; on the indispensability of ensuring a lasting exclusion of other European Powers from influence or possession – the French must not return, or the Dutch to Ceylon, and the Portuguese remnants might well be displaced; on the superior morality of British administration, whose wide influence should be applied and its own abuses rooted out – a legacy in particular from the recent Governor Generals, Cornwallis and the evangelical Shore, and sincerely felt now in Calcutta as in Downing Street.[2] The two men assured each other of their mutual aims and fundamental harmony. But the qualifications and differences in policy and in the interpretations of the Governor General's powers, falling in either case also on the relation with the Company, cast a deepening shadow which was not lifted as the years went by.

The political map in India was a given premiss for the intruding European Powers. They could seek to exploit or reduce the indigenous instability as their own interests dictated or allowed, and the changes were bearing witness at this time to what would become a transforming process. But the pattern of fluctuation itself looked back to origins and incentives which had owed little or nothing to the extraneous forces. Nor had the subcontinent stood earlier in the same relation as the transatlantic theatres to the European wars. The East as a whole in fact had been viewed from a far distance as a distinctive issue, whose results might be important but whose operations were unrelated to those of the main strategies except in intermittent calls on resources of ships and men. The Dutch and the British fought in the East Indies, the French and the British in India, as a result of their Western conflicts. But while it can be argued that central India had been penetrated, as Canada had been won, 'on the plains of Germany', the reverse had never been contemplated. No significant thrust had yet been made from Europe towards the subcontinent as a threat which might act eventually as an indirect means of victory in a Western war itself.

This however had now happened, or at least could be seen in that

1. Cf. I, 451–6.
2. Which since 1794 had harboured Dundas, as Secretary of State, as well as Pitt (I, 575).

light. Bonaparte's occupation of Egypt and advance into Syria could be interpreted as a first step towards realising such an aim.[1] One cannot of course tell what might have followed had he persisted; whether indeed he would have done so against the chance, enforced as it proved, of returning to gain power at home,[2] or alternatively been able to elicit sufficient strength from there or elsewhere. But the spectre had been raised at any rate for the British figure most closely involved. Dundas's vision of a coming danger to India failed to arouse his colleagues, and the outcome of the expedition laid it, uneasily, to rest. But the effect outlasted the initial alarm. The landing of a French army in 1798 and its existence on the edge of Asia, even if cut off, until 1801[3] advanced – one might say generated – attitudes to the Near and Middle East and the trans-Himalayan region which, lacking coherence in London and Calcutta and among representatives on the ground, nonetheless laid foundations for a process of fundamental consequence beyond the current wars.

Faced by a new French threat indeed, and initially in such hands, the implications of power in India began to appear in a fresh light. Its defence must be secured: that was already manifest in the swift occupation of the Cape of Good Hope and Ceylon when the Dutch left the war in 1795.[4] Now the focus shifted to freshly appropriate areas, some within the ambit, partial or complete, of India itself, and almost all – and this was the most significant new factor – impinging on Britain's diplomatic concerns. The Red Sea and the Persian Gulf, Arabia, Syria, Persia, Afghanistan loomed with unaccustomed immediacy on the horizon. Some of these regions had seen British couriers or traders before; the latter indeed regularly in the Syrian Levant through the Levant Company, though the peacetime traffic had more recently been declining compared with French efforts. Ships had also penetrated the straits of Bab-el-Mandab and Hormuz, and the overland route had been used for despatches, increasingly from the 1780s. But once beyond the environs of the Syrian coast none of this had entered seriously into London's calculations, or since Warren Hastings's day into those of Calcutta.[5] Inconsiderable though the results were now of the sudden rise in attention, it marked a rapid approach to a different age.

There were four possible lines of advance in theory for a French threat to India. If they could establish themselves in Syria they could either take a northern route from Aleppo across the desert to Baghdad and thence through Persia, possibly in co-operation with a Russian force, into Afghanistan; or, from the same base, they could proceed along the Euphrates to Basra at the head of the Persian Gulf and thence along the coast, perhaps under certain circumstances with maritime support. Or

1. Pp. 145–6 above.
2. P. 146 above.
3. Pp. 401–7 above.
4. II, 561–2; and cf. I, 454.
5. See I, 438–9 for signs and limits of interest, including in Egypt; and also p. 402, n4 above for the continuing status of the Levant Company.

they could cross the Suez isthmus and, given sympathy or support from the local power, head down the Red Sea, establishing a base at Aden and a forward point at Muscat for the shortest crossing to the mainland coast; or alternatively, if circumstances permitted, for a sea passage direct to an Indian port of their choice, Portuguese Surat or Goa or (for a time Tipu's) Mangalore. Circumstances, as it transpired, did not permit: rather they became adverse, when Bonaparte was checked at Acre and Tipu was eclipsed at Seringapatam. But the possibilities could not be ignored while an army remained unconquered in Egypt, and British responses, in alliances or influence or strongpoints, had to be considered in turn.

In the southern region these must rest on the habitual faith in seapower, deployed in this instance, despite the thinness of naval resources in the East, to dominate the entrances to the Red Sea and the Gulf. Various prospects could be envisaged – Perim, Sokotra, Aden for the first, Aden, Hormuz, Kishm for the second – and some were briefly tried; all in any case must be held in view as long as any likelihood of a threat remained, whether as staging posts for an offensive from India against Egypt or a denial to a French offensive. And this meant an involvement, with an unfamiliar prominence, in political developments in Arabia; in the relations between the sherif of Mecca, the Sultan in Constantinople, and the simmering military power of the fundamentalist Wahabi sect in the Nejd, itself a constant threat to both, the former directly in his guardianship of the Holy Places, the latter in his Mesopotamian lands centred on the virtually autonomous principality of Baghdad. The Sultan figured likewise in his suzerainty over the governor of Basra, that focal point for the possible French line of advance from Syria. A new pattern of problems was perforce taking shape, if sketchily, on the fringe of south-west Asia, and extending, with potential for some complications to the new Turko-British alliance,[1] into the margins of the Ottoman Empire.

And not only the margins, or with the Ottoman Empire alone. Turkish and British interests, propelled into a closer connexion by Bonaparte's adventure and Nelson's counter stroke, had elements in common but with strong shades of difference.[2] Constantinople's loose suzerainty over its sprawling possessions, in Europe as in Asia, was exercised in circumstances that did not always suit London's concerns; while the Porte had had its reasons for not wishing to jettison all hopes of French sympathy or even support. Its main preoccupation remained, as had long been the case, the growing power of Russia, and the sudden advent of a triple alliance hinging on Britain did not remove that distrust. The feeling was not confined to prospects in Europe – to those for the Balkans and adjacent waters – which for the British themselves were now suggesting the need for a more direct concern in the continental Eastern Question. For Russian ambitions were directed equally into the Caucasus and beyond,

1. For which see p. 209 and n2 above.
2. For this paragraph cf. pp. 150–1, 396–7, 401–6 above.

where the independent kingdoms in Georgia bordered the dominions of Persia and the Turks themselves. No love was lost between St Petersburg and Teheran; and while there was currently no war in the region as there had been earlier, the record of hostility suggested that the former might seek in due course to reduce the latter's empire. That in its turn could have effects for the Gulf and the Indian Ocean. Turks and British therefore, each for their own reasons, had an interest in good relations with Persia; but the Porte was naturally suspicious of British influence among its eastern territories, and from 1798 the British were obliged to consider with some respect the aims of a Power which they were hoping to convert from a limited to a full ally.

The same applied, if somewhat less directly at that point, to Russia herself; and indeed the complications from that quarter soon began to overshadow those with the more marginal partner in Constantinople. For the barely predictable course of Anglo-Russian relations over the next few years, swinging from promising to almost disastrous and then to promising again,[1] posed uncertainties for policy in the middle regions between Europe and India which were unfamiliar in London and hard to resolve. Both there and in Calcutta, however, it seemed expedient to consider some pattern of defence. As in other matters there was some discrepancy of view, for Dundas and Wellesley once more were not in tune. Surprisingly perhaps at first sight, the Governor General was less impressed by danger from Egypt than was the distant head of the Board of Control.[2] He was markedly disinclined to spare resources from India for the plans conceived to eject the French,[3] and he held his own view of the course to be pursued beyond the Indus plain. For there was one more piece to be placed in the jigsaw. East of Persia lay Afghanistan, straddling a main overland route and under its formidable ruler Zeman Shah closely affecting the British position in north-west India. Zeman's relations with the Maratha confederacy, which itself stretched as far south as Hyderabad, were in fact crucial to Wellesley's own policies, and played an important part in his more extended plans. The Afghan was to be seen as a threat to the territories lying beyond Bengal, and as such to be kept at bay by a combination if possible of Maratha and British action farther to the west – annexation of Oudh and treaties with Sind and with the Sikhs – and by a diplomatic approach to Persia, which was unlikely to welcome any expansion by her neighbour. Dundas on the other hand preferred to see Zeman as a likely ally; not necessarily in his view as an irreconcilable alternative to Persia, but as the favoured choice. Resting on the proposition that the Persian regime would be driven more strongly by its relations

1. See for this Ch. XII, sections IV, V above, and for the later developments XIX–XXI below.

2. This attempt to summarise a highly complicated subject leans largely on the detailed work of Edward Ingram, particularly his *Commitment to Empire . . . 1797–1800* (1981) and *Britain's Persian Connection 1798–1828* (1992).

3. P. 407 above.

with Russia than by any with Britain, and thus reluctant to bind itself too closely in agreements affecting the overland route or the Gulf, he sought influence or a treaty with Afghanistan. Although therefore a British envoy was sent direct from Calcutta to Teheran, there were other plans in London, to despatch the resident in Baghdad to Kabul, which in the upshot were frustrated by Wellesley himself.

Nothing in any case had come of either project before an immediate French threat was removed, and after Wellesley's departure the pace was reduced. The issues however did not go away. They were revived only a few years later on suspicion of a further French threat by the overland route, and by that time in active co-operation with Russia; and yet again, with Russia herself as the suspect, after another four decades. Dundas's and Wellesley's successors found themselves rehearsing much the same arguments as those of the last years of the previous century; and indeed the indecisive conjectures at that earlier time held a prophetic significance. Coming at the point when the Eastern Question in Europe was foreshadowing for Britain a direct relationship with an emerging Near and Middle Eastern Question in Asia, the problems marked the uncertain advent of a phase of policy, strategic and diplomatic, which reached a sustained peak in the Victorian era and lasted effectively almost to the First World War. It was only in the final few years before 1914 that the defence of India did not take its accustomed first place in military assumptions at home, and attention began to be paid to the possible return of involvement with land forces in a European war.

A massive development was thus in the wings. But it was in the wings rather than on the stage. For while the problems first thrown up by the enemy in Egypt bulked large in the correspondence between the two authorities most intimately concerned, they were of marginal significance to the central British conduct of the current struggle. Letters passed; the Company's small secret committee was involved in exchanges with the Board of Control;[1] a handful of men were concerned in the formulation of ideas and the means to put them into effect. But there were no British resident representatives, let alone envoys to the rulers, in Arabia or the Asian central states, and the Embassy in Constantinople was kept largely in the dark over designs affecting the Sultan's periphery.[2] The Foreign Secretary himself was and remained dismissive of an overland threat 'in a quarter where nature has separated us by limits more insuperable than the *oceanus dissociabilis*, which Horace speaks of'.[3] Middle Asian questions ideally, in fact, could be kept separate from the normal conduct of

1. See I, 190.
2. Ingram, *Commitment to Empire*, 211.
3. To Dundas, 20 September 1798 (*H.M.C.*, *Dropmore*, IV, 319); a not untypical dig at a colleague whose classics were not up to his own.

Foreign Office business, and were certainly not to be discussed with Allied governments in their capitals without specific permission.[1] Grenville looked on the complication introduced by Bonaparte as probably transitory and in any case irrelevant in the short term; more likely to fail than succeed, and even if successful in the environs of Egypt unlikely to alter the focus or effect a vital change in the main fortunes of the war. Nor was Pitt for his part greatly impressed, as his verdict on strategy confirmed over the next two years. Victory must be sought in Europe, as the most certain way to a convincing peace with whose terms Britain must be intimately concerned. This of course was not to pose options, for either man, in starkly contrasting terms. For some years there were enough resources to employ without excessive strain in both Continental and colonial operations; the alternatives were never as clear-cut in practice as they could be represented in theory; distant possessions claimed protection, gains where possible should be made; regional connexions could not be ignored; strategy bends to circumstances which can distort guiding rules. Pitt by now was working in the context of what he saw as the needs, financial, political and diplomatic, for as opportune a result as could be achieved. At the same time his and Grenville's argument could stand in its own right for the sake of the overseas achievements themselves. For a favourable balance on the Continent could be held to provide the ultimate security not only for the offlying island itself but also for the system of power and wealth deriving from overseas trade and possessions as a whole. The commercial and territorial treaties of the past affecting such regions had not been drawn in isolation from a central reality which was reflected in even as it was modified by their contents. Within the parameters as he viewed them in the shifting conditions of the Second Coalition, the Minister and the bulk of the Ministry were not ready to weigh the scales in favour of a colonial warfare so largely shaped by European rivalries whose own outcome, they believed, it could not decide in reasonable time.

In the later 1790s, therefore, there was no serious shift in strategic thought – if such a designation can be attached in its detail to the indecision and operational futility which followed the collapse of a European grand design. The questions then arising from the defence of India might be argued rather to have marked a final phase in a different transition: in the 'swing to the East' which has been seen as a governing feature in the development of a second British empire. The nature – the very existence – of such a process can be open to dispute: in trade itself there was an addition rather than a transfer of value.[2] But the themes raised by India now very largely related to dominion; and these were weightier than the

---

1. It was 'by no means proper that the Court of St Petersburg should be mixed in any discussion relative to His Majesty's interests in India' (Grenville to Whitworth, no. 72, 27 August 1798, P.R.O., F.O. 65/44); and this applied equally to Constantinople. Ingram, who quotes the despatch (op. cit., 245), assigns the instruction at least in part to this cause.
2. Cf. I, 161-3.

counterparts applying to colonies in the West. In so far as there was a swing it was one concerned at this time most noticeably with assessments of power; and here the glimmerings of involvement with indigenous conflicts and conditions in large tracts of the Asian world introduced a dimension hitherto scarcely known. The time would come when the British would claim to be the greatest of Asian Powers. The Caribbean colonies by then were no longer of great note on a recognisably imperial map.

Such a map however was only in outline in London as yet in governmental terms. Dominion in India was something different from authority in colonies which had their own Department separate from the Board of Control. Nor was a strict concept of 'colonial' as an alternative to 'continental' warfare, or of self-contained imperial interests, effectually applied. Early in the new century Pitt and Bonaparte could be depicted dividing the globe between them, with Bonaparte confined to Europe and Pitt carving the larger slice of Ocean and the lands largely hidden beyond.[1] The contrast, thus starkly presented, contained a fundamental truth, recognised and sustained in London through the Revolutionary and Napoleonic Wars. That did not mean that it governed the British strategy which emerged in the course of the first long stage.

1. A caricature of February 1805 – before Trafalgar was fought.

449

CHAPTER XIV

Government and Parliament

I

O ver much of the last six years of the century, from 1795 to 1800, the pressures on Pitt were unusually intense. The pace and scope of the issues, at home and abroad, quickened to a point that made setbacks and successes almost equally draining; and the former were the more depressing because the latter had sometimes seemed so closely in sight. The accumulation of business itself mounted on a scale not experienced in any of the three preceding wars, which had all lasted for much the same length of time as the current conflict.[1] But it was the combination of the dangers that brought a new dimension, in a period which saw a major run on the Bank of England and a stop on the convertibility of the pound, collective mutinies in the home fleets, one in the midst of rumours of invasion, an armed rising in Ireland and signs of organisation for widespread disaffection in England, the military collapse of a second Allied Coalition. These were public strains, falling heavily on a Minister who had achieved a focal position in exceptional degree. And for Pitt himself they were underlined, from that very position, by the growing dissension on strategy between his two most intimate colleagues, increasingly affecting the personal foundations of his conduct of the war.

Grenville and Dundas had never been particularly close by nature: the temperaments, tastes and backgrounds were too far apart. Theirs was rather a working partnership tuned in the exigencies of the struggle – both for instance seem to have found Spencer at the Admiralty more congenial than either did the other.[2] Nor did they stand – they had never stood – in an entirely similar relation to Pitt: Grenville, associated firmly with his cousin and recognising his gifts, could nonetheless call on an inherited standing of his own denied at Westminster to Dundas.[3] But

---

1. Taking Preliminary treaties for the subsequent Definitive peace as the yardsticks in each case.

2. Despite an awkward start – mainly on Spencer's side (pp. 121, n2, 248, n1 above) – Dundas's feeling for his colleague is expressed in his letter of 15 February 1801 in B.L. Add. Ms temp. Althorp G221. Grenville took for granted a preference arising doubtless from the First Lord's normally greater compliance with his own views, but also from a compatibility of interests and social station which seemed to him entirely obvious.

3. Cf. I, 132–3.

these facts, and some mutual jealousies, had not seriously detracted from a combination which had effectively survived controllable disputes and differences of emphasis; and if Grenville was now more critical of Pitt, in his strong disapproval of the policies for handling the dearth of bread, and Dundas, denied his main aim for strategy and unable to stop talks for a naval armistice, was also – and probably more deeply – worried and dissatisfied,[1] their co-operation remained of high consequence to the health of the Ministry and in some degree of the Minister himself.

The damage, patched over for some time but increasingly disturbing, was a factor contributing to the use made of the Cabinet as a body in the later campaigns. 'Cabinet practice is notoriously elusive',[2] and not least in the often formative periods of war, with their tension between a postulate of collective responsibility and a need for effective control. In the current form of the system the postulate itself had limited application. That there was a system in principle was generally recognised. Dundas stated the wartime doctrine on lines that had been stated before: 'The operations are canvassed and adjusted in Cabinet and become the joint act of His Majesty's Confidential Servants . . . the Secretary of State who holds the Pen does no more than transmit their Sentiments'.[3] And if a theoretically clear definition was produced for such a purpose, a similar process of discussion and chain of execution could be acknowledged for a wide range of politics, within the frame at any time of a Ministry's accepted scope.[4] Important subjects were certainly offered from the middle of the 1790s: legislation needing careful attention aimed at curbing varied forms of unrest; policy for Ireland, culminating in the far-reaching question of Union; treaties of alliances that moreover now included financial subsidies; as well as strategic issues in the war itself. Other matters of course might be raised though not collectively pursued, including those deemed to fall outside the bounds of the conventions – the slave trade in this period springs readily to mind. The treatment was highly uneven. Parameters and processes of authority were hedged about by uncertainties; Cabinets functioned largely within grey areas, surrounding claims to personal inclusion, interpretations – central to the body's development – of collective relationships with the King, the rights and powers of individual members in their functions and loyalties as holders of posts which

1. Respectively Chs. X section I, XI section IV, XII sections II, III.

2. I.R. Christie, 'The Cabinet in the Reign of George III', in *Myth and Reality in Late-Eighteenth Century Politics . . .* (1970), 55.

3. To Pitt, 9 July 1794 (P.R.O. 30/8/157; see II, 532, where (with 531) his point of vantage at that time is taken into account). A more recent, exasperated, confirmation can be found in p. 372, n3 above. The phrasing of 1794 echoes definitions to the same effect from Germain and from Sandwich in the American War (Christie, op. cit., 91), and see also Piers Mackesy, *The War for America 1775–1783* (1964), 12.

4. Eg Dundas again, before he was in the Cabinet, on the Project for a commercial treaty with Holland in 1788 covering the Far East, which was 'more Proper for the general Consideration of His Majesty's Ministers, . . . as it bears upon their General System of Politicks and Connexion with Holland. It is not merely an India Question' (I, 428).

owed nothing in origin to a committee unknown to the Constitution.[1] Nonetheless membership was the goal of the ambitious politician; more important in itself for a hopeful candidate, as Pitt told Canning, than the possession of an appropriate marginal post.[2] By the end of the century in fact there was an established instrument, free to meet and discuss when it wished, holding a position by accumulating usage of acknowledged if undefined and fluctuating weight in reference to the more ancient twin poles of Crown and Parliament, and operating, in the manner of committees, as persons and circumstances decreed.

Precedent springing from practice is supremely important to such a model. By the middle nineties there was a process of recognisably Cabinet meetings, which the demands of war and simultaneous domestic pressures tended to escalate at times. Much is obscure. Sometimes we hear of a 'Council' rather than of a 'Cabinet Council' being held, which nevertheless is clearly not a Privy Council in some form. Sometimes a gathering of named Cabinet Ministers may not have amounted to a formal meeting – indeed may even have been the reverse, specifically to avoid such an outcome. The Cabinet dinners, by now a normal routine, were sometimes accompanied openly by meetings, doubtless of varying degree of formality and at times perhaps including a few other guests.[3] We can gain some information, not only from correspondence and diaries and memoirs but also, despite their shortcomings, from the London daily newspapers which in the 1790s followed the occasions – as earlier but now with rather greater consistency and detail – giving names of attendants and at times the main subject and the duration. Mention of such a source of course at once raises serious qualifications.[4] It does not tell us what went on at a meeting, and some of the detail at least can be questioned or proved wrong. A Minister for instance may be said to have been present who could not have been there, and the added statement at times that 'the result was sent to the King' (usually at Windsor) does not necessarily mean the despatch of a Cabinet Minute: a much rarer event, quite recent in origin and sparingly used.[5] The journals' references and reports nevertheless provide a useful glimpse of business, not least to set against those formal submissions. On the basis of selective reading for the years 1797 to 1800, and excluding 'Councils' other than 'Cabinet Councils' and all dinners not specifically associated with a meeting, I have gathered some

1. Cf. I, 180–2, 628–31.
2. In 1805 (p. 820, n3 below).
3. Cf. I, 581 & n2 for the 1780s, II, 432–4 for 1793–4. The custom seems to have been well entrenched over the next decade, and thereafter to have become almost a recognisably constitutional (and highly unsatisfactory) way of doing business; see Aspinall, *The Cabinet Council 1783–1835*, 181–6 for the early part of the nineteenth century.
4. See I, 605–8; but also pp. 113–14 above.
5. Professor Christie has found very few Minutes sent before 1779, and Aspinall (op. cit., 195) only 74 from the whole period 1783 to 1801, with an unusual peak of thirteen in 1800. See I, 629 & n5.

35, 26, 14 and 31 meetings respectively: a total of 106, which may be on the low side even taking into account meetings so specified which in fact were possibly informal consultations between selected members. The regularity and detail of reports may hint, at any rate sometimes, at notice from some official quarter; if so, this could bear on a comparison with a possible 66 meetings for the period covering the six years of normal functioning from the opening of 1784 to the middle of 1790.[1] The higher total, and the contrast with the likely number of Minutes, alike point to an acceleration in a process. As Fox indeed observed a few years later, with rather typical emphasis but freshly renewed experience, the 'Cabinet Council' could meet for different purposes: 'For affording the members an opportunity of consulting with each other and stating their ideas reciprocally on points connected with their several departments, but with no intention of communicating the result to his Majesty', or 'On other occasions . . . to advise His Majesty in person'.[2] The bare outline of the record, despite – and in – its ambiguities, goes some way towards confirming a development which would have been impelled by the pressure of the times.

Much however remained the same. The sequence of meetings tended to follow a familiar chronological pattern. The bulk occurred when and shortly before Parliament was sitting; the summer recess usually showed very few. There was a crop of the latter in 1800 from August into September and October, when a combination of urgent and mostly controversial matters, largely of a kind yielding Minutes to the monarch – the quarrel with Denmark, Otto's approach for a naval armistice, decisions on competing operational plans ending with Dundas's proposal for Egypt, the first impact of a second failed corn harvest[3] – had to be faced. But even then members could not always be rounded up, and the months of leisure had not been similarly disturbed in the three preceding years. It also seems unlikely that there was a regular programme as yet during the session itself such as existed, we are told, in the early nineteenth century – several meetings a week, and at one time at least almost daily in the run-up. The arrangements altogether probably remained distinctly flexible

1. Ie excluding the exceptional period of the Regency crisis in which the normal ingredient of an active sovereign was absent; see I, 628–9. I must make clear the selectivity of my readings: *The Morning Chronicle*, *The Morning Post*, *The Times*, *The True Briton*. The fact that reports of meetings not infrequently occurred in more than one of those journals can of course often mean that 'the major source of press reports was items in other newspapers' (Jeremy Black, *The English Press in the Eighteenth Century*, 87). But not so obviously when they appeared on the same morning; and a sarcastic comment in *The Morning Chronicle* of 8 September 1797 is perhaps suggestive at least for one type of occasion: 'It is a question whether a Cabinet Council or a Cabinet dinner, is of the most importance to the nation, but to remove all dispute, they are generally announced together'.

2. Speech in the Commons in 1806; quoted in Pares, *King George III and the Politicians*, 168–9: see I, 632.

3. The last, though, not the subject of such a Minute. Cf. II, 532 for the first two years of the war.

and ad hoc.[1] Nonetheless, particularly if the Cabinet dinners in London are taken additionally into account, Ministers were well accustomed to collecting together over the greater part of the year.

If war is an extension of diplomacy by other means, that in itself was an extension of a major subject for discussion; for 'despatches from the Continent' seem to have provided the staple summons for a meeting as they had done in peace.[2] Conversely, however, the circumstances could produce an opposite tendency, to limit consideration to a very few. The size of the Cabinet was not large by subsequent standards, or indeed in the light of the position only a few years later. But a figure of 10 to 11 after 1794 (with 13 for part of that year) was noticeably higher than the 8 with which Pitt started, and when the matter to be dealt with was delicate or awkward, or speed was of the essence, the effective Ministers were apt to deplore the encumbrance of the 'great awkward' body.[3] Given its current habits and means of business this was not surprising,[4] and there was no structure of delegation to directly subordinate committees – that emerged only in the first quarter of the twentieth century. As so often therefore – as is endemic in committees – much was left to an inner group, and the main demands in this instance gave its normal members a distinct identity for several years, which cast its influence over the range of business beyond the war itself. The emphasis varied: Grenville for example might have more to say than Dundas about the economics of dearth and relief, or the Irish question after the rising of '98 had been crushed; Dundas more than Grenville on the regional prospects for overseas trade. But it was rare for both to be silent, or less than prominent, on a major issue, and the fact helped bridge gaps and hold within bounds that widely deplored but recurrent phenomenon, all too easily induced by the structures, a 'Government of Departments'.[5]

The cohesion and distinctiveness of such a group, however, were not absolute. Examples have been taken from these years of matters reserved from the majority of the Cabinet, usually with its tacit consent but not infrequently without,[6] and dealt with confidentially by the same few members – most often Pitt and those two colleagues, joined for the purpose with whoever else might be involved. Secrecy sometimes dictated, and diplomatic or political convenience could argue for exclusion;

---

1. Richard E. Willis, 'Cabinet Politics and Executive Policy-Making Procedures, 1794–1801' (*Albion*, vol. VII, no. 1, 9).

2. Cf. I, 628–9; p. 356 above.

3. See p. 320 above.

4. The mechanical constraints for instance on intercommunication should not be overlooked (see eg I, 576) and confidential clerks were few (eg I, 174, II, 514).

5. See eg North to Fox in 1783 (*Memorials and Correspondence of Fox*, II, 38); Spencer Perceval to Huskisson, 21 August 1809 (*English Historical Documents 1788–1832*, ed. Aspinall and E. Anthony Smith, 129). Cf. I, 304, and 309 on the Secretaries of State.

6. See eg Aspinall, 'The Cabinet Council, 1788–1835' (*Proceedings of the British Academy*, XXXVIII, 149), 210–11; Willis op. cit. 3, 14–15.

partially indeed even of a Minister – one can instance Windham – who was administratively concerned. But confidentiality could also affect the treatment of the most important figures themselves: for instance, in striking degree, in the struggle between Pitt and Grenville over policy in the peace negotiation at Lille.[1] This was certainly exceptional. Nonetheless it underlined the lesson that Pitt, once engaged, did not 'choose to suffer it to be doubtfull who is the effectual Minister'.[2]

For the balance and tone of a Cabinet responded very largely, within its developing frame, to the personality and performance of the member who by this stage was emerging more definitively as First or Prime Minister. In Pitt's case there was no room for doubt.He had never been greatly interested in the Cabinet as such: it was a given political fact, a necessary context for the conduct of policy, tangential to the small groups of intimates and officials with which he preferred to work. His instinctive response, as he put it politely when questioned on the outlook for the expanded Cabinet in 1794, was that 'he placed much dependence on his new colleagues, and still more on himself'.[3] The dominance was not – could scarcely be – as even over almost two decades as its undoubted existence conveyed. The abiding impression of his capacity was clear, and was set in marble by his followers after his death.

> Mr. Pitt must have felt, and his colleagues must have felt also, that he had such comprehensive talents and powers that he was himself essentially the Government in all its Departments – that he could form a Government almost of himself, and each of his colleagues must have felt that Mr. Pitt could do without him, though he could not do without Mr. Pitt.

So wrote a disciple and successor to an associate who had also known the great man.[4] And the terms carry, as they carried, conviction. 'Only connect'. Pitt was the indisputable source of connexion, the centre of reference for other Ministers. The acquired range of his knowledge of business, and the rarer capacity to perceive and construct relationships and linkages, gave him a status among his colleagues which none seriously presumed to share. And the connexions carried farther. His prolonged superiority in Cabinet bolstered, as it drew on, his standing with the fundamental authorities from whose constitutional tension and partnership the Cabinet itself had emerged. He bore a formidable reputation both in Parliament and at Court; and the triple accomplishments sustained one another,

1. Pp. 57–61 above.
2. Cf. I, 133, for December 1783.
3. II, 415.
4. Spencer Perceval to Huskisson, 21 August 1809 (*English Historical Documents 1783–1832*, 129). Cf. for the middle nineties the information given to a new MP, later Speaker: 'He will not suffer anybody to arrange his papers, and extract the important points for him' (Charles Abbot's diary for 17 March 1796; *Colchester*, I, 45).

multiplying the effect. The whole represented a remarkably rounded achievement, which mounting adversities now had not overturned.[1]

The terms of the tribute, even so, were well defined; 'even under these circumstances', it ended, 'I have understood . . . that Mr. Pitt himself could not in all Departments control expenditure as he wished'. Nor were the limits confined to that.[2] The talents of an individual cannot extinguish on their own the workings of a rooted administrative system. Nor do they ensure that exchanges over policy in Cabinet itself will always be plain sailing. Pitt was not the easiest of chairmen, whether or not he called a meeting himself.[3] A prime connector in the range of business, he was scarcely a connector of people: the charm which could fascinate in the right company was not readily conspicuous with assorted colleagues. His social manner had relaxed somewhat. But the awkwardness and chill were not far absent beneath the acquired handshaking and loud laugh, and he never threw off that 'shyness of . . . disposition', as Richmond once described it, 'which when there has been any little rub knows not how to bring matters to rights again'.[4] Nor was he as consistently decisive as the imperious attitude suggested; the recent vacillations were not confined to military judgment, exceptionally acute as these had recently been.[5] Some of his colleagues indeed were apt to complain of his yielding too much to the influences of companions with 'minds not of sufficient . . . Calibre to lead a Mind like his'; and his own congenital approach was not of a piece – he could indeed have echoed his father, who once confessed of himself that 'he was an odd mixture of a creature the most obstinate on the one head and the most diffident on the other'.[6] When he could or did not wish to make up his mind he could prove highly irresolute or evasive; and in such circumstances the cards could be played very close to his chest. It was hard to tell sometimes how far he was being swayed and how far his responses were tactical. It could also be very hard to gain a view when a lack or loss of interest resulted in papers being put aside and momentum delayed.[7] Sometimes opaque, easily deflected by those in his confidence but in the last resort, when sufficiently concerned, looking to himself alone, temperamentally distant with those beyond his circle, and not dis-

1. Cf. I, 633 for the earlier, and pp. 35–9, 378–80 above for more recent and vulnerable years.
2. See I, 303; 309–11, 317–20.
3. Cf. op. cit., 309 for the frequency of summons by the Foreign Secretary.
4. To Pitt, 15 December 1794 (*H.M.C., Bathurst*, 707). Cf. II, 406 and n5 for the cultivation of a superficial heartiness.
5. Pp. 378–80 above.
6. Eg copy of Spencer to Dundas, 13 November 1801 (B.L. Add. Ms temp. Althorp G44), alluding to their common 'Experience'; and cf. Redesdale to Charles Abbot, 5 May 1804 – 'I know his disposition to yield to inferior minds', apt to be one 'of all great men' (P.R.O. 30/9/15/1). The comment was in fact quite a common one; see I, 322. Chatham's remark was reported by the Duke of Devonshire, in *The Devonshire Diary, . . . Memoranda on State of Affairs 1759–1762*, ed. Peter D. Brown and Karl W. Schweitzer . . . (1982), 93.
7. Cf. I, 323–4, 215–16; p. 429 above.

posed to suffer a challenge, his leadership was unquestioned but the atmosphere was not warm.

This was well known, and tales of dissatisfaction were of course well aired. Their effects had been exaggerated at points along a lengthy course. The opening two to three years in the eighties saw some difficulties, largely from the Minister's inexperience, and uneasiness grew with the mounting weight of the issues in the latter years of the following decade. But the emphasis among Pitt's associates was for long on his preponderant formidable virtues; exceptions were mostly episodic; and of the two most persistent doubters Thurlow was forced to go and Liverpool, co-operating throughout partly out of loyalty to the King, contained his reservations, as he made his contribution, in a steady attention to his duties. Over the central years in fact, say from 1786 to 1795, rising success followed by the rising pressures promoted a broad consensus;[1] and the subsequent problems, coming to a head at the very close of the century, were those inexorably of policy, compounded rather than generated by personalities under growing strain. The interaction in that period however gave more genuine substance to the impression of discontent; made the more serious in the end by its extension to an intimately associated quarter, as the King – the focus of so large a share of any Cabinet's attention – began to stir under its tendency to take his consent for granted in fast-moving events.[2] It was of this most recent phase, though the comment was apparently applied, wrongly, to the wartime Ministry as a whole, that a later Secretary of the Treasury could write that he did not believe 'there was ever a less united Cabinet, and nothing prospered except Mr. Pitt's never-to-be-equalled management of the House of Commons'.[3] The times indeed were then out of joint, Pitt himself seemed increasingly unable to grip the state of overseas affairs, and in 1800 was even perhaps on the verge of a nervous breakdown. Such a picture was not complete. The Minister retained his authority and sense of direction in handling the simultaneous domestic problems arising from the great dearth; his breakdown, if such it was, lasted only briefly; and hopes of the war itself rose, as they fell, intermittently in 1798 and '99.[4] Operational plans moreover were on foot in 1800, one choice forced through by himself,[5] which in due course would bring their rewards. Nevertheless a partial vacuum developed at this low stage in the country's fortunes which brought his colleagues collectively, and thereby the King, into a detailed prominence they could well have done without.[6]

---

1. For these suggested markers see I, 633, II, 441–2, 523–4, Ch. XIV sections I, III.
2. Eg pp. 369–70, 381–3 above; and see Willis, op. cit., 13–17.
3. Charles Arbuthnot to Wellington in 1834, quoted in Aspinall, op. cit. 203n4. It is hard to be sure to which exact period it was applied.
4. Ch. X, section I, pp. 81–3 above for the first two.
5. Pp. 409–10 above.
6. See p. 387 above for Dundas's list of disagreements.

II

'Government' in the eighteenth century 'shared the values of politics'. The interpenetration could be variously traced to express the unifying forces of the state. In the work of administration itself during an age of largely autonomous institutions, the link existed in a system of patronage 'which held the political nation in the service of the Crown, and turned service under the Crown into a political asset'.[1] Given the scale of business, the product hitherto had survived its periods of strain. How well would it cope now against a double challenge, from a possible domestic threat to the old order and, within that order, from the demands of a war that would endure almost unbroken for almost twenty-five years?

By the end of the 1790s strains could certainly be seen. In the face of disaffection, they spread across the patterns of authority lying beyond the central executive, to the Courts of law and into those areas where support for Government was qualified by the varieties of local response. Within the central management itself, particularly of the war, the pressures fell on Departments that were small in size, affected – though not dominated – by the casualness and jobbery arising from patronage,[2] and limited in their effect by the conscious dispersal of powers. Something has been seen of the widespread efforts, with their own constraints of theory and of practice, to apply the regulations on prices of bread and the laws against sedition.[3] The focal machinery of government for its part encountered a combination of demands which Pitt and others feared at moments might even threaten the foundations of the state, but in the event proved containable once more within the time span of the decade.

For both elements – the time span and the combination – should be recognised. We must recall that we are concerned with a period which turned out to be a stage in a process; we are not discussing the impact of the Napoleonic as well as of the Revolutionary War.[4] On the other hand, the amalgam of pressures was novel in degree to a point not repeated in the renewed hostilities: the prospect of a serious invasion was then quashed in the opening phase, and while Government's finances were under pressure and discontent in the country persisted, there was no crisis comparable to the closure of the Bank of England and the mutinies in 1797 and the combination of the dearth and unrest from 1799 to 1801. These tests took the accepted defences of domestic order about as far, it seemed, as they could go. And if the impact of operations was not felt so dramatically on its relevant areas of administration, their familiar responses were likewise under heavy stress by the end of the decade. Rather as in the case of the wars of William III and Queen Anne, much

1. I, 180.
2. Cf. op. cit., 173–4, 177–9.
3. II, Chs. V, XII; Ch. X above.
4. Cf. pp. 417, 419–20 above.

experiment now in the first period laid a groundwork for improvement in the second.

Nonetheless the demands of the 1790s were not such as to force major changes to the system. The war did not last quite long enough for revisionary incentives to be tried. The size of the regular land forces in particular was notably higher by the close of the French Revolutionary War than by that of the American War of Independence: some 150,000 effectives in 1801 compared with some 115,000 in 1782.[1] But the graph had not moved steadily through the wartime years, and the numbers achieved were lower – markedly lower – than were allowed by the annual Parliamentary votes. Thus in 1795 and 1799, the peak years of recruitment for the regular army, its effective size (including Ordnance artillery) was respectively some 124,000 and 115,000 men while the sums granted were for some 213,000 and 257,000; and in 1801 itself for some 289,000.[2] The limits in fact were not so directly financial as practical. The results of recruitment for the army were remarkable – far more so than in the American War: some 210,000 additions over nine years, compared with some 77,000 in the six years to 1774–80.[3] But these had to be balanced against, and for some years were overbalanced by losses (largely from disease) and desertions; and the hope of preserving significant forces for action beyond Britain and Ireland rested on a major enlargement of auxiliary troops to reinforce home defence. Again, much was done. The militia and Fencibles were said to stand in 1801 at some 104,000, and Volunteer effectives including the horsed yeomanry at perhaps over 92,000 (the latter as against some 147,000 on paper).[4] Much too was attempted by the standards of the day, and something achieved, to improve these forces and their use: by better, if still flawed, regulations for pay, for a limited transfer of direction from the Home Office and the Lords Lieutenant to the Secretary of State for War, and a partial freeing of British militia for service in Europe and in Ireland.[5] But traditional barriers survived the efforts, themselves guarded, towards a more comprehensive pattern: jealous authorities, watchful peers and MPs, administrative inadequacies, constraints from other demands on available numbers. The machinery for the part-time soldiers was consciously diffuse, the spirit, favourably or resentfully, amateur: a mixture of draft by

1. For the land forces, deducting the embodied British militia and Fencibles and the Irish establishment in each case, see Mackesy, *The War for America*, Appendix, 524–5, Fortescue, *History of the British Army*, IV-Part II, Appendix D, 940. Figures to the nearest thousand.

2. Fortescue, op. cit., Appendices D and C, 938–40; subtracting embodied militia and Fencibles where relevant.

3. Mackesy, op. cit., 526; Fortescue, op. cit., Appendix D, 940.

4. Western, *The English Militia*, 222 cites Dundas's calculation of 82,000 for that force in 1799; Fortescue, op. cit., gives his conclusions on real strength for the militia, 889, and the Volunteers, 893.

5. See pp. 123–6, 223–4 above, and in particular Western, op. cit., ch. IX, sections II, III.

selective compulsion and substitution and of voluntary duty itself the product of inducements as well as encouragement, of social approbation and social pressures; the whole resting perforce, if sometimes uneasily, on a confidence that the people could be armed against invasion – or disaffection – in a form which in practice could disguise only sketchily the unfilled needs against external attack. The problems of manpower for the land forces, regular and auxiliary, remained unsolved at the end of the first of the two French wars. They had indeed to be freshly addressed even before the second began.

The problems for the navy of course were rather different. While its control and organisation ashore showed their own degrees of dispersed authority, the Admiralty enjoyed an inherited precedence, and conditions imposed a higher degree of co-ordination.[1] In the event it managed to collect a fair proportion of the numbers whom it asked the Commons to finance. Granted money for 73,000 'seamen' in 1794 it in fact claimed to have found some 74,000, and against allocations for some 92,000 in 1800 it could muster some 94,000.[2] They were not necessarily available where most needed, or at all easily produced in a conflict that saw a large expansion of the fleet. The processes relied on the familiar methods – bounties to volunteers, contracts with maritime institutions some in return for exemptions from impressment, the press itself from the ports, as regulated by the new Impressment Service, and from British merchantmen;[3] and the same were applied, increasingly as the war went on, to coloured colonials and to foreigners. The latter's numbers in fact accounted for a small but noticeable part of the complement in many British men-of-war: Nelson's *Victory* herself at Trafalgar had on board 71 men from twelve sources outside Britain and Ireland – eight per cent of the company; and the proportions could be rather higher than that.[4] The calls for men were unceasing, and often hard to satisfy from the nature of the case as ships came and went, often depleted by casualties and desertion and again at short notice, among their stations at home and overseas. Such limitations were those of quantity. But the navy's most acute shortage lay in quality: in the persistent want of proper seamen as distinct from those so called in the Parliamentary Estimates. The pool of maritime manpower was extensive; but it fed the streams of a mercantile economy, and there were never men enough, or always conveniently placed, to fill the unpopular service of the wartime fleets. Pitt's Quota Acts of 1795–6 were designed to help

---

1. Cf. I, 171, 494.
2. Michael Lewis, *A Social History of the Navy 1783–1815* (1960), 119–20. On the other hand there was a shortage of Marines in both years – in 1794 by over 4,000 on a grant for some 12,000, in 1800 by over 3,000 on a grant for some 23,000. All figures to the nearest thousand. The evidence however is sparse, and the Admiralty indeed, from the nature of its recruitment, had to cope with a variety of genuine difficulties in providing accurate numbers.
3. II, 496–7.
4. Lewis, op. cit., 129.

meet both the needs – for numbers, requiring landmen as well as seamen, and for skills – by enlistment under improved bounty; and they were soon judged a reasonable if variable success. The quality by and large was thought acceptable; in the first year they supplied more than double the intake from impressment over the two preceding years; and while the level of recruitment then declined, and they became a whipping boy for the mutinies of '97, earning a largely adventitious notoriety,[1] they continued to provide a modest proportion of many ships' companies until the end of the war. Their contribution joined the others, persistently piecemeal – from Irishmen whether in Ireland itself or scattered in British ships and ports,[2] from the foreigners, mostly neutrals, from the home-grown products of the press – which together as the years went by accounted increasingly for the crews who manned the ships that established the strategic command of the seas.

Pitt himself was prominently involved at times in the series of measures to raise men for the forces. He personally moved the bills for the naval Impressment Service in 1793, the military Volunteers in 1794 and the Quota scheme in the next two years, intervened to suspend exemptions from the press in 1798, and was concerned in the efforts for improved direction and use of the militia in the same year; and early in the next decade he plunged into dispute on fresh plans for military manpower.[3] Some of these instances – the support for the Volunteers, and the later controversy over a force for reserve – had a strong political connotation over and above the administrative content. And so too had a further associated initiative, which focused less on the problems of naval manpower – perennially unsolved – than on the record of naval administration as a whole.

Pitt entered this last arena for mixed, or complementary, reasons which led him into a broad defence of the workings of the current system. It is unlikely that in different circumstances he would have paid the subject such prominent public attention: on the contary it was one that he had earlier kept within the confines of Government as strictly as he could, when, as had happened in peacetime, it had come under examination. The reforming decade of the 1780s had seen a series of inquiries into the navy's finances, as part of a wider scrutiny of Government Departments: by, among others, the Commission for Examining the Public Accounts, established by North, the Commission for Auditing the Public Accounts and the Commission of Enquiry into Fees, both set up by himself.[4] Some useful results had been obtained quite promptly by the reports of the first two bodies. But the searches of the third were more extensive, and they gave support and cover to proposals, on which in fact they were partly

1. II, 497; pp. 19–20, 25–6 above.
2. Ibid. and p. 32.
3. II, 487, 497; pp. 123–6 above. The later dispute will be followed in Chs. XVIII section II, XIX section IV below.
4. For what follows see I, 88, 302, 308–9, 314–17.

based, emanating within the system itself from the reforming Comptroller of the Navy, Sir Charles Middleton. The Minister had been sympathetic. But pressure of other business and then mischance and a waning of interest intervened, and he himself had taken care at the outset to see that the Commission was responsible to the King in Council and not, as the Commission for Examining had been, directly to the House of Commons. There were administrative attractions in this course, in what might be difficult conditions. At the same time the arrangement made it easier for the findings to be ignored and further work to be dropped. That in fact was what happened; the completed reports on the various offices were still not published when war broke out, and meanwhile Middleton's own experience – he resigned in 1790, though remaining in charity with Pitt – seemed to be conclusive. It proved however not to be so. For in 1797 a fresh investigation took place, by the Commons' Select Committee on Finance.

This last was a further major undertaking, as deep and wide-ranging as its predecessor and drawing, as that had done, on the experience of a fresh increase in demands and responses. The pressures were not felt evenly in the various sectors. But their combination for the navy was substantial, given the many constraints – of men for ships and yards, of suitable docks, of the different types of timber native and imported, of hemp and canvas, victuals for sizeable floating populations constantly on the move: of the multifarious needs in fact of what was still, as it had been through the century, the largest and most widely spread industrial undertaking in the country. The fleet had entered the war in unusually good shape, and was able to settle quickly onto a war footing. At the start of 1793 it mustered 291 ships of the line and 99 smaller vessels, amounting to 390 in all; for 1794 the figures were 300, 120 and 420 respectively; for 1801 373, 362 and 735. On the same respective dates 20, 63 and 71 per cent of the ships of the line, and 40, 80 and 86 per cent of the frigates, were in commission for sea service: witnesses (allowing for the losses, and distinct from repairs and captures) to the broad limits of construction of larger units, as also to the capacity for effective mobilisation.[1] Other statistics also suggest the attainable levels of construction and availability of resources. Some 6,000 tons of warships was launched in 1793 (some 4½,000 from the royal dockyards), some 22,000 (6,000) in 1794, and 12,000 (4,000) in 1801 after two years of lower figures. Likewise there were some 1,300 of the range of tallest masts in store at the start of 1793 and some 1,200 for 1801, 5,000 and 7,000 tons respectively of hemp, 12,000 and 48,000 bolts of canvas, 52,000 and 97,000 copper sheets, some 58,000 and 42,000 loads of timber of all kinds. On virtually the same dates in the two years the royal yards contained some 8½,000 and 11,000 artificers

1. Roger Morriss, *The Royal Dockyards during the Revolutionary and Napoleonic Wars* (1981), 12 table 1, 16–17 tables 2, 3. Cf. I, 313 for the peacetime performance. Figures to the nearest 500 tons.

and labourers and 3 and 3¹/₂,000 shipwrights.[1] The whole represented an overall substantial, though not startling, progressive enlargement of capacity for war, whose problems on shore became a prominent target at intervals in an age of conscious reform.

The Select Committee proved very thorough, reporting on every naval establishment.[2] The impact was beneficial, in both the short and the medium term when subsequent reformers built, though in partly contrasting ways, on the latest findings. Informed pressure from outside was indeed of high value; for the authorities were well placed to obstruct. The technical complexities enabled them, often justifiably, to fend off unpalatable criticism; and the Admiralty at the summit of its professional Boards tended to regard itself as special and distinct among the Departments.[3] Although directed by a Privy Council committee in 1792 to comment on the detailed evidence and opinions of the Commission on Fees, it did not do so, and when the Select Committee followed up five years later the reply was only in general terms. 'How far this may be deemed a Satisfactory Explanation', the affronted members noted, was for 'the Judgement of the House'.[4] Changes were necessary, as indeed was recognised within the naval 'civil' branches themselves. But, as elsewhere, there were strong vested interests, and in this instance with practical responsibilities; experience bred genuine caution; the usage of the service was easily invoked and amateur criticism instinctively rejected. Life in any case could be comfortable and profitable. 'That degree of laziness natural to office', as Pitt remarked of Government agencies in general at the start,[5] could be seen in many nooks and crannies familiar since the age of Pepys; and so too could abuses that likewise infuriated officers and men afloat. Examples could be culled perhaps most plentifully from the dockyards, those focal points of management; and the Select Committee paid due attention to them, and to the wider questions of procedures and problems. Much was examined afresh. The latest investigation proved quite as impressive as its predecessors over the past fifteen years.

Its conclusions nonetheless were by no means wholly condemnatory. In their explanation of the need, from the Admiralty's inadequate response, to delve so fully into detail, the inquisitors added their wish to be abreast of the 'many useful Regulations and Improvements . . . made, particularly in His Majesty's Dock Yards of late Years'.[6] And in point of fact a good deal

1. Morriss, op. cit., 28 table 5, 86 table 13, 80 table 10, 106 table 17. The figures for 1801 in table 13 are given for mid February rather than the usual 1 January. Allowing for the many mutations affecting naval statistics, those for the intervening years are broadly compatible.

2. See its 17th, 18th, 31st–35th Reports, to be found most conveniently in *House of Commons Sessional Papers of the Eighteeth Century*, ed. Sheila Lambert (nd), vols. 107–114.

3. Notably so for instance under Howe in the eighties; I, 315.

4. 17th Report; *Sessional Papers of the Eighteenth Century*, vol. 109, 147–8. And see also 31st Report; op. cit., vol. 112, 8.

5. Speech of 17 July 1784 (*P.R.*, XVI, 7).

6. 31st Report; *Sessional Papers*, vol. 112, 8.

had been done, in its own ways. The naval transport system was tidied up in 1794–5 with the creation of the Transport Board; the work of the Navy Office was reorganised in 1796 on lines recommended by the Commission on Fees and Middleton; medical services were greatly improved, not least by stricter discipline in hygiene, from the early years of the war; supervision of the Treasurer of the Navy's accounts and cash balances had earlier been marginally tightened, though only marginally as would be proved;[1] and in the dockyards, as the Select Committee acknowledged, reforms were unevenly being applied. There were, as there generally were, active men at work among the dross. In particular, the appointment in 1796 of the ingenious and energetic Samuel Bentham to the new post of Inspector General of Naval Works introduced a period of experiment and improvement – if one also of some organisational conflict – which included the construction of two docks at Portsmouth, the first built, as distinct from planned, for many decades.[2] The process of change in the extensive naval system was modest compared with that of the ensuing Napoleonic War. But it gave its successor a recognisable birth, and it was significant compared with the record since its nearest counterpart in the two French wars of a century before. The climate of opinion – of attitude – was developing among 'the civil ingredients of naval power'.[3] And as the Board of Admiralty sat at its great table in the panelled room with the wind vane on the wall, the conduct of the resulting operations, themselves the fruit of hard experience, was steadily increasing in effect.[4] The French remained strategically dangerous; they could threaten invasion of Ireland or Britain, and the war on trade claimed heavy losses, rising to a peak in 1797, and particularly in the West and East Indies.[5] But the convoys, instituted in 1793 and made compulsory in 1798, grew in size and their organisation and defence were greatly improved; exports more than doubled, and imports increased by over 60 per cent, between 1792 and 1799; and the Royal Navy was the victor in the set battle pieces. Seapower, under continuous pressure, was making itself felt progressively, with sufficient, if arguably just sufficient, resources and management ashore. When Pitt entered the lists a few years later there were achievements to applaud, as well as the highly visible continuing need to improve.

The other elements of the armed forces could likewise show some adaptation to some of the demands. Partially, slowly, encumbered by administrative structures and political demands, specific advances were being made. Some could be claimed, despite its persistent bad reputation, by the Ordnance, largely the legacy of Richmond's time as Master General until early in 1795.[6] Much of the drive was lacking thereafter. But

1. I, 301–2, II, 495–6; Morriss, op. cit., *passim*.
2. Op. cit., 46–53.
3. Op. cit., vi.
4. Cf. II, 497–500.
5. The annual average overall in the war amounted to about 500 ships.
6. Cf. I, 312, and more particularly II, 492–4.

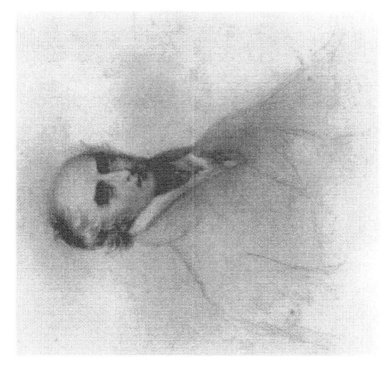

Marquess Wellesley. *by J. Pain Davis*

William Wilberforce. *Unknown*

Pitt and Napoleon, 1805, by *Gillray*

one important process was secured: supply of small arms – the most widely needed weapons – was eventually regained by the Department from its competing colleagues buying muskets at short notice for their own frequently short-term ends. Home production from private industry increased – a proposal in 1794 for the Ordnance to go into manufacture itself came to nothing – and procurement from the Continent (an early exception to the more normal picture of Britain as the arsenal for the alliances) was gradually reduced. Provision in other respects – of field artillery and gunpowder – was more adequate in quantity, and for the latter in quality: William Congreve at the Government's powder mills saw to that.[1] The results overall were no more than moderate. The British were regularly outgunned by the French, serving the greatest gunner of them all, and the Ordnance as a ministry of supply suffered incessant complaint, as it always had done, from its military and naval customers. Much of that was justified. Nonetheless the central office was not exceptionally incompetent under one of the most reliable Secretaries in Government service – R.H. Crew, whose calibre places him in the company of officials such as Irving and Frewin at the Customs –, and in fact it earned qualified approval from the Select Committee of 1797.[2] It certainly did useful work in its other capacities, of mapping and education and research. The Trigonometrical or Ordnance Survey, set on foot in 1791, saw its first map published four years later by a private printer; and the discovery that its own facilities were inadequate for such a task led to a first, if typically qualified, step in 1794 with the provision of a 'Drawing' (but not engraving) 'Room' in the Tower which was united with the Survey itself in 1801. The latter's work went on slowly throughout the decade on a financial pittance. But it went on, and the quality was good. So too, against the same background and thanks in part to private efforts, did work on the development of powder and ammunition. Richard Watson, self-taught while professor of chemistry at Cambridge before moving to the Regius chair of divinity and a Welsh bishopric, had earlier increased the explosive power of shot, and his method was now improved by the Department; and through the later 1790s Captain Henry Shrapnell of the artillery was experimenting, partly at his own expense, with the invention that would bear his name and, like Congreve's rocket conceived slightly later, remain a British monopoly in the Napoleonic War to the envy of other Powers.[3] Such lines of activity argued a basis of official education – as in some other Government offices[4] – which indeed was fitting for an institution responsible for design of weapons. The Royal Military Academy at Woolwich had been in existence for over fifty

1. See Richard Glover, *Peninsular Preparation*, ch. 2.

2. 21st Report; *Sessional Papers*, vol. 109. For Irving and Frewin see I, 179, 324.

3. Glover, op. cit., chs. 3, 8. Glimpses of the Bishop of Llandaff in various other aspects of public life appear in I, 235, 389, 492, 621, II, 59, 65. Shrapnell spelt his name thus, though his invention dropped the final letter.

4. See I, 178 for the Post Office.

years when the war opened, and its syllabus was impressive, providing
'probably . . . the most thorough, all-round scientific education to be had
in England, if not in Britain, at the time'.[1] That was at least in theory, and
in Richmond's day at any rate it appears to have been so in practice.
Founded originally for the training of engineers, it now also included
artillery cadets, all tested by public examination on passing out for their
commissions; and the overall numbers were enlarged in 1793 and again in
1798, on the latter occasion to cater for the East India Company's forces as
well. So far so good. The difficulty however was to translate principles into
effective action. There were not many opportunities for British artillery to
perform systematically on the Continent after the first two years of the
Revolutionary War. But its shortcomings were conspicuous in the next
decade in the operations in the Peninsula, most notably perhaps when
both gunners and engineers proved almost useless in siege work – in
bombardment and sapping and mining. Nor did the Academy or any
other official source provide manuals of instruction; those came from
private hands. Amateurism continued to flourish in the Ordnance, in the
office and among the troops. One can only claim that perhaps it was
coming to play a minor part.

The same could scarcely be said of the infantry and cavalry. The fact
was recognised openly at the time, and indeed when performance, at least
of the former, was undeniably on the mend. It was not untypical of the
navy, and certainly of himself, that St Vincent should have thought the
army could be abolished and replaced by Marines. But soldiers too, and
Ministers, were disparaging; and the French for their part held their
opponents in contempt.[2] Much of this was born of the unduly depressing
experiences encountered in the past few years, in which even the steady
qualities of British troops in battle, formerly commanding high respect,
seemed to have deserted them at times. Generalship and discipline
appeared to be at a low ebb, and while the state of the Commissariat
for supply, coming under the Treasury (and the eye of the First Lord),
coped not too badly after the disastrous winter of 1794–5,[3] the condition
of planning was viewed with increasing derision. Seeds of recovery, it
has been argued, were being sown in the later 1790s: in drill and manoeuvre and tactics, some items of equipment, regulation of rank, plans for
education;[4] and these last indeed were potentially if belatedly of high

1. Glover, op. cit., 189; see 187–93, and 211–13 for the syllabus in the early nineties.
2. For Ministers see eg Grenville in 1800 (p. 375 and n4 above), and Windham, recently
Secretary at War, still felt much the same seven years later. See Glover, op. cit., 2–4. Within
the service itself the experienced Major Charles James was by no means alone in stating
that the army was good only for 'a war of mere descent and alarm', in the 1810 edition of
his *New and Enlarged Military Dictionary* – and this after the Peninsular victories of Vimeiro
and Talavera. Wellington himself made similar comments, in a European context, at
much the same time (II, 330, 379).
3. I, 482–3 and n2.
4. See pp. 374–5 above.

importance. The regular army had no equivalent to the Woolwich Academy for the Ordnance: some young aspirants to commissions in the past had gone to a handful of private military establishments at home, others to the Continent, usually to France or Prussia. There were few British manuals of the military art in its more extensive branches,[1] though translations had been made of foreign specimens, and practice was limited to regimental routines and to movements at battalion level. The result was a serious lack of competent Generals – Cornwallis lamented their 'melancholy list'[2] – and above all of staff work in either the Adjutant or the Quartermaster General's departments.[3] This latter deficiency worried some senior officers; but nothing was done in face of the traditional fears of too effective a standing army, and it was the very end of the century before matters began to move. In 1798, however, they benefited from the arrival of one of those peripatetic professional soldiers who had always been a feature of European warfare, often gaining high qualifications on the way. The Frenchman Francis Jarry – called indifferently General and Monsieur in London – had served on the staff of Frederick the Great and ended as head of the Prussian Ecole Militaire; more recently he had held a command in the army that defeated the Prussians at Jemappes. He may have been known to York when the young Duke was sent to learn his trade in Germany; at all events the Commander-in-Chief was glad to accept his offer, on emigrating to England, to set up a military school for instruction in the higher reaches of the art of warfare. It was a modest start in a private house at High Wycombe, and it was soon in trouble, for the lectures, delivered for good measure in French, proved too much for most of the pupils. Rescue however came from an enterprising British soldier, Colonel Le Marchant, who set to work with York's official neutrality but sympathetic support to modify the syllabus and attract public interest. In 1801 his plan for an official institution could be approved by a military committee, and in June the Royal Military College was officially established. Much had to be done, and in such matters the effects are apt to be slow. A foundation nonetheless had been laid, and a junior branch for possible cadets, sited nearby at Marlow, was confirmed in 1802. Both trod difficult and wary paths. But the seeds of the Staff College at Camberley and the Military College at Sandhurst had been sown.

There were thus signs of improvement at the Horse Guards under York. The effects were slender – barely observable – by the end of the Revolutionary War, and the commissioned ranks of the British army by and large retained their amateur culture in the European campaigns

---

1. And little notice taken; a relevant exception, Thomas More Molyneux's investigation into *Conjunct Operations*, published in 1759, fell on deaf ears in the 1790s (A.D. Harvey, *Collision of Empires* (1992), 131).

2. P. 375 above.

3. The two assistants to the latter in the campaign of 1793–4 in the Low Countries were Hanoverians.

down to Waterloo. They acknowledged, some deplored, but many were rather proud of the fact, which they and their compatriots took for granted as the product of its particular context. The old suspicions persisted of a professional armed force on home soil: that was something more permissible elsewhere, in distant theatres and of course at sea – sailors had long regained their standing, as soldiers had not, from apprehensions of threat under the Stuarts. The feeling remained instinctive and strong. At the same time it had now to take account of a new element, or at least a sensation that was novel in degree. For an increase in land forces in the country could not be avoided if sedition, as conceived in the nineties, was to be held down. The size of the militia was raised; the Volunteers were encouraged and the numbers responded; the regulars were housed in the new barracks whose expense, under the new Barrack Master General, soon began to get out of hand.[1] Policing in general indeed now formed 'a Branch, and not an immaterial one, of the Public Expenditure':[2] the pre-war dislike of such regulation persisted, but one way and another the practice was enlarged. The Bow Street runners, few in numbers, were more active outside London than before; the powers of the police in the capital were extended in 1800 to a force on the Thames with a new office in Wapping; magistrates were brought more closely into touch with the Home Office as unrest heightened in the great dearth.[3] The machinery of co-operation was fully used over this wide sphere, within the parameters of acceptance, between the civil and the military authorities and among the former themselves.

Such efforts gained their best measures of success of course when prior information was received: a commodity for which they required direction and aid.[4] The prime deterrent to purposeful disaffection, as distinct from the climate of discontent, lay in hard intelligence; and here the Government seems to have moved with confidence and effect. This was indeed in stark contrast to the provision of operational military intelligence, which had not advanced significantly under the war Departments from the situation in the opening campaigns.[5] But in a clandestine sphere there was less need to consult Departmental interests, or public sentiment. For control was concentrated in the Alien Office, that discreet offshoot of

1. See II, 195, 490, p. 294 above. The Commons' Select Committee of 1797 found the 'Barrack Department' standing 'upon a very large and extensive Establishment' (20th Report; *Sessional Papers*, vol. 109, 391).
2. As the Select Committee put it (28th Report; op. cit., vol. 112, 7–8).
3. P. 313 above for the runners, and see Ch. X, section II in general. The Act for the Thames police, passed in July, was 39 & 40 Geo. III, c87; some light is thrown on discussion in 1800 in the diary of Charles Abbot, that expert on legislation, in P.R.O. 30/9/32.
4. See for instance the assertion by a later Home Secretary to that effect, reflecting as one example on the course of events in the discovery of the Irish revolutionaries in 1798 (Lord Pelham to George III, 30 July 1803; *L.C.G., III*, IV, no. 2774); pp. 117, 165 above.
5. See II, 485, 542, 577–8; p. 376 above.

the Home Office which was responsible directly to the Secretary of State and applied its inspection of émigrés to a variety of roles. Covering the inseparable problems of Ireland and Britain, it could claim a remarkable level of achievement: 'a systematic collection of intelligence' which, recalling the situation a decade before, amounted to 'the speedy development of an efficient secret service'.[1] Its tentacles spread beyond home territory: in particular to a 'police office' in Hamburg, a meeting point for Irish revolutionaries, which was equipped through the British resident with powers to arrest. That however in its turn was not its sole function, within an integrated organisation. The 'police' officer, a German mercenary agent previously employed by several European states, also managed to penetrate the local republican 'secret committee' directed from France.[2]

For the Alien Office was concerned from the start with foreign as well as domestic intelligence; and not only with intelligence but – the exact reverse of its purpose at home – subversion as well. The detail is intricate to follow, though it is yielding much of its pattern. The essentials however have been becoming increasingly clear. The setback to Wickham's plans from Switzerland in 1797, the failure of the French risings in 1799, had not extinguished British hopes of supporting a counter-revolution.[3] Money was not lacking, for contacts that were kept tightly secret: only a handful of officials and Ministers were aware of the extent of both. The amounts of 'Pitt's gold' indeed appear to have been quite exceptional, sent through special accounts in banks in London and Hamburg, themselves employing in part letters of credit on French banks; over £3,600,000 was recorded in Wickham's account for the first half of 1800 – a sum larger than the provision for Allied subsidies in the budget for that year –, and if this may have included some payments still owing it by no means stood on its own. On the contrary, much must have been spent on a fresh organisation in Paris of which he was at first kept ignorant: an 'English committee' of royalists which, despite their usual internecine quarrels, managed within the next few years to achieve in effect 'the saturation ... of the Paris police'. Bribery on a large scale revived hopes, no longer of political weight in the Assembly or military risings linked to a strategic design, but focused rather on a decisive single event. For the prime object of the committee was the assassination of Bonaparte, which should open the way to a well planned coup; its hand lay behind the successive attempts through the autumn of 1800, culminating in the bomb which missed him in a Paris street on Christmas eve. That led to a setback. But the 'gold' continued to flow, the committee to function, the preparations for Bonapare's removal to develop. The dimensions of London's support, suspected in France and

1. Roger Wells, *Insurrection*, 40, summing up his ch. 2; and see also Elizabeth Sparrow, 'The Alien Office' (p. 119, n3 above), 383. Cf. by earlier contrast II, 136–8.
2. Sparrow, loc. cit., 376–7.
3. See Ch. VIII, section I above for the place of such plans as a strategic weapon; Sparrow, 'The Alien Office', 367–75, 377–80, 383–4 for what follows.

emerging in part there over the following years, were successfully hidden from official British records for more than a century and a half.

The case may not have provided a sole example of its kind around the turn of the decade. There are some indications that the chargé d'affaires in the Legation in Berne may have had advanced knowledge of the murder of the French delegates to the expiring Rastadt Congress in April 1799; a crime which fastened on Austria and confirmed her split with France in March.[1] Since he was the rash James Talbot, already ostensibly in trouble with the Foreign Office, this may well have been so.[2] More cogently, the assassination in 1801 of Tsar Paul, that dangerous threat whose removal in any case was contemplated in St Petersburg, has sometimes been ascribed to British 'direction', and one recent authority is prepared to agree.[3] Such suspicions, in a grey area, raise the question how far the relevant Ministers knew of and approved any such plans. The three concerned would have been Portland as Home Secretary, Grenville, and Pitt himself; with Dundas perhaps less intimately or persistently concerned. All, one may conclude, must have known of the intention to try to kill Bonaparte – it was the basis now of any likely timely counter-revolution, itself the object for which large sums continued to be supplied. At the beginning of 1799 Talbot's contacts with royalist plans to murder the Directors in Paris had earned him the Foreign Secretary's stern and seemingly disgusted reprimand – an idea '*wholly abhorrent*' to '*the character of a civilized nation*'. But a more private letter from Canning as Under Secretary, specifically mentioning Grenville, mitigated the effect, and the offending diplomat was next sent as chargé d'affaires to Sweden, always a potential trouble spot, and as it turned out at a delicate time.[4] Grenville was in charge of secret funds – some more secret than others – and in personal touch with some of the French counter-agents; he certainly was well aware of the policy and its means in this case. So, too, must Portland have been; he was very much the responsible Minister for the Alien Office, whose presence indeed in such a capacity was seen by the senior officials as essential.[5] And Pitt for his part must have been closely in touch: he authorised the payments from the Treasury; he was quite used to the offer of bribes – he had seen their potential advantage fully in 1797;[6] he was also used to meeting Frenchmen bringing plans or information from across the Channel. He must surely have approved. Whether, or how far, the same situation held good for Russia it may be more difficult to say. There may be suggestive evidence without the same degree of probability.

1. See pp. 209, 153 above.
2. Sparrow, 'The Swiss and Swabian Agencies, 1795–1801' (p. 221, n3 above), 881–2. For Talbot see pp. 219, 222 and n1 above.
3. Sparrow, 'The Alien Office', 384. See p. 555 below for the event.
4. See p. 222, n1 above.
5. Sparrow, 'The Alien Office', 380.
6. Pp. 66–8 above.

In the event the results of the efforts at subversion, of whatever kind, were negligible. The timings of French risings proved to be beyond British control;[1] a great deal of money was spent to no visible purpose; Bonaparte survived, and if Paul did not he might well have been deposed in any case, and his disappearance proved to have only a temporary effect. Britain failed to set Europe ablaze, once that prospect seriously suggested itself. The whole subject however of the Alien Office and its work at home and abroad can throw light on more than one aspect of the Government's arrangements for handling the war. It threw into sharp relief, against the pace of limited advances in larger scale administration, a boldness and acceptance of high costs for the experiments abroad, and a rapid development of the skills that harried and penetrated the hard cores of domestic disaffection. It showed the possibilities, in a covert area under the aegis of powerful Cabinet Ministers, of co-operation between Departments which normally asserted their territorial rights, and the remarkable extent to which secrecy could be maintained. And, by no means least, it revealed the determination – the ruthlessness – with which Pitt and this small group of colleagues were ready to fight the later stages of a war which he was increasingly anxious to bring to an end.

The adequate provision of resources, human and material, may underpin success in war: it does not guarantee it. Nor in a sense, before the advent of mass warfare for this country, was that expected. In the eyes of contemporaries the credit fell naturally, as it always had done, on other qualities – enterprise, ingenuity, courage, leadership in the field and at sea; often indeed shown the more heroically when the provision failed to meet the need. The processes of management themselves could show little of the heroic flavour: nothing for instance to place against Carnot's inspiring organisation for victory in revolutionary France. But that very contrast was a cause for satisfaction; we were not revolutionary here; patterns of administration in Britain for this latest of eighteenth-century wars did not see a radical tilt in the balance of liberty and efficiency. Worrying though the problems of supply of men became to both Government and Parliament, and the changing and potential dimensions of the whole conflict increasingly to Pitt, there was an instinctive consensus that strength came less from official dictation than from the nation's own resources, themselves nurtured in constitutional values and practices which should not be too rashly disturbed.[2]

Pitt's personal primacy reinforced his status as First Lord of the Treasury to affect issues often lying beyond his Department's scope. That range in itself of course was wide; the Treasury stood at the apex of the most extensive sector of Government, and controlled more appointments

1. See pp. 223–6 above.
2. Cf. 419 above.

than any other group of Departments and Boards.[1] The design to some extent and still more the tone of civil administration responded to the First Lord's approach – passive or active – as finance did to that of the second Lord, the Chancellor of the Exchequer. This was never more so than when the two offices were united in one hand, and that hand was his. The approach remained basically the same after war had succeeded peace: Pitt sought improvement, where possible through improved institutions. At the same time he was not attracted to structural change as such, desirable though that proved more than once in the financial sphere; he had tended to work where he could through detail – in patronage often by a non-renewal of posts as they fell in;[2] and the mounting distractions and atmosphere of war deepened that inclination. He found less time in fact for civil reform unless it seemed really necessary; his attention nonetheless – as always, and perhaps now partly as a substitute for less welcome undertakings – continued to fasten on keeping costs low, in so far as he could. That of course could itself demand his personal efforts, and it was naturally not always possible in areas in which the volume of business grew. As the Commons' investigations conceded, 'the Public Service . . . called for Supplies greater than at any former Period of our History'.[3] Even so, the numbers of the staffs in the central offices were kept small. Pretyman, working presumably from calculations by Rose, claimed a reduction – it would seem a net reduction – of 441 revenue posts of all categories between December 1783 and February 1793; Rose himself asserted that by 1799 '747 fewer persons' in the Excise alone than at the first of those dates were managing a revenue of double the size. That result had been gained by the abolition of one office of taxation (the Salt Office) and further reductions of sinecures.[4] While there was a gross increase in working appointments in the Treasury's sphere, the steady process of reform had not dried up in recent years.

Figures covering a more comprehensive range of Departments are not so conveniently available, and carry their own complications; but some of the clearer examples may be cited. Taking 1797–8 as the yardstick, the Treasury itself had a staff, including five Board members at the top and porters and the like at the bottom, of 59 of whom three of the officials were part-time: a total of 15 more than in 1784. The Home Office boasted a Secretary of State and two Under Secretaries served by 18 persons on the same basis; the Foreign Office (likewise progressively substituting salaries for fees) a total of 21 with a further 13 'annexed'; the Secretary for War, a wartime creation with one Under Secretary, commanded a staff of 10; and the three Departments could call on 30 messengers held in theory in common. This gave an aggregate of 95. Other important offices told

1. I, 282.
2. Cf. I, 283–6, 289–90, 298–9, 307–8, 320.
3. 8th Report (*Sessional Papers of the Eighteenth Century*, vol. 108, 208). 'Supplies' of course meant financial, as the context, of an inquiry into the Taxes Office, made clear.
4. Cf. I, 318 and n3 with Rose's *Brief Examination . . . from 1792 to 1799*, 46–7 and n.

much the same story: the Admiralty had a staff of 47 below the seven-man Board; the War Office, not including the officials of the Paymaster General and the Commissary General of Musters, one of 44 below the Secretary at War and one Deputy Secretary (an increase of 24 from 1782); the Privy Council's office had 21, its offshoot Committee of Trade 17 below the eight Commissioners. Even the Navy Office, with its respresentatives mustered collectively in the yards as well, accounted for staffs totalling 126 under its 22 central and local Commissioners.[1] These are statistics for selected institutions, and some at least need supplementing in various degrees – they were collected for a financial inquiry and some posts fell under other financial accounts, temporary clerks and others came and went in the busier areas. Havens of sinecures and pluralism diminished only slowly in various quarters, largely in the more ancient offices and outworks – the Exchequer could display its medieval processes and places into the early railway age.[2] But allowing for errors and omissions and obscurities across a wide spectrum, it remains the case that the network of government at home and overseas centred on groups of office-holders in London whose numbers were few for the tasks in hand. Under Pitt, a war by this time of unexampled expense did not spawn a great extension of bureaucracy – a word one may use here to contrast what was happening to the traditionally much larger bureaux in France.

The bulk of the structural alterations themselves came from movements in finance: most notably the reconstruction in the Mint following the Committee on Coin's – Liverpool's – initiative in 1798, and the expansion of the Taxes Office as a result of the Income Tax introduced at the end of that year. The former followed a familiar pattern when there seemed to be no grave urgency – the exercise ended effectively in 1812. The latter was put in hand quickly: the extra Surveyors and Inspectors – the paid officials of the inherited system – were needed at once if the extra revenue was to be gathered in.[3] Both showed strong reflections of their public and personal contexts. After his troubled experience with the Triple Assessment Tax,[4] Pitt was determined to meet renewed fears, this time of a more threatening impost. The salaried staffs with their fresh powers – a disturbing thought – would be firmly responsible to Commissioners similar in nature to those of the old Land Tax; taken from the gentry and civic authorities whose 'independence of influence' in this sphere paralleled that of their traditional functions as JPs. And the powers themselves were circumscribed in the initial Act, to a point in fact which led to such widespread evasion of payment that he was forced to try to strengthen them in 1800, only to be roundly defeated on the most

---

1. Reports as relevant from the Commons' Select Committee of 1797–8; *Sessional Papers, passim.* Cf. the lists of *Office-Holders in Modern Britain*, vols. 1, 4–8 (Institute of Historical Research, University of London, 1972, 1974–9).
2. Cf. I, 299–300.
3. Pp. 14–16, 262, 266–7 above.
4. Pp. 102–9 above.

objectionable parts of the bill.[1] The Minister achieved a great deal – more than could have been imagined a few years before. Brought in stages by necessity to propose a measure he felt obliged to adopt, he overcame its intense unpopularity through his political standing and power. He was able to shape its management broadly on the lines he wished, concentrating on the Taxes Office, the most professional of the fiscal departments in its processes and relative costs. Even so he had to watch his step very carefully, and when he went too far he was brought up short. The whole issue, of exceptional sensitivity and importance, underlined past experience. It pointed to the scope he could command, particularly in finance, from the confidence he usually enjoyed; it also emphasised the limits, to which he was sensitive and generally preferred to contest so far as he could less by confrontation than through patience,[2] adroitness and skill.

Such an approach placed a premium on retention of control, not least on timing, a quality on which Pitt set increasing if often haphazard store. The effects could indeed be a cause of resentment to those who thought they had gained his support. Within and outside the confines of Government, advisers or projectors of schemes for improvement deplored his procrastination or failure to move after they had reason for earlier hopes.[3] While natural, the charges were frequently unfair. It was obviously hard for a Minister as focal as he had become to give enough sustained attention, and when correspondence failed or meetings were put off in these years he was often entitled to plead pressure of business. That also became, more than of old, the pretext for his habitual unevenness of temperament. But there was a further consideration to bear in mind. For, taught by experience, Pitt was disposed to steer clear of premature open intervention in cases where he reckoned he might forward rather than himself promote the object. One instance may perhaps illustrate the combination of factors.[4] In the mid 1790s there was a revival of a long-running battle, intermittent over half a century and visible earlier than, that to develop the Port of London, increasingly congested by an ever rising tide of business. This now took the form of proposals, from different and soon rival sources, to build deep-water docks and warehouses at Wapping and the Isle of Dogs. Pitt kept and was assiduously kept in touch; he was seized of the projects' importance, he sought opinions from officials, his files contain an accumulation of papers; and in the end, after the first stage gained statutory approval in 1799, he laid the

1. Pp. 263–6 above.
2. Cf. I, 88.
3. To take one prominent example, see eg p. 429 above for Wilberforce's view. And cf. p. 475 below.
4. What follows is an interpretation of the papers in Pitt's files P.R.O. 30/8/255 6. I cannot pretend to a proper knowledge of the historical background of the case, which is complex, and look forward to its detailed elucidation, as well as to a full account of the current process, by Professor H.G. Roseveare. Meanwhile I am most grateful to him for providing me with a basis on which to venture my own, I hope informed, deductions.

foundation stone with a flourish the next year.[1] He had watched the discussions – the quarrels – between the interests concerned, and was prepared actively to assist a bill.[2] At the same time he had not followed up his officials' initial findings, his interest in fact had seemingly lapsed, and at a very late point the different progenitors were badly worried by his continuing delays. A meeting, pressingly requested in April and again in May 1798, and agreed for July, took place finally in November. The distraction of his 'various Engagements' could be blamed, and a congenital inclination to put a given question farther down the pile.[3] But it is also noticeable that the Minister had waited through a substantial period of acute disputes between the two principal parties concerned, the City Corporation and the West India Planters and Merchants, until each appeared ready to allow the other's preference to be considered simultaneously by Parliament. Thereafter matters went ahead with his more active involvement – he took part in 'arbitration'[4] – and a fundamental advance was secured. It was an instance in which good judgment, in the midst of unpredicted delays, helped gain the result.

Timing was not the only weapon of control. Pitt, like any Minister, sought where possible to keep a controversial subject out of hands he might not manage to restrain. That had been demonstrated in the 1780s with first the appointment and then disuse of the Commission for Enquiry into Fees.[5] It was shown again in the 1790s, and particularly as the decade progressed. His emphatic emphasis on Orders in Council rather than statutes in questions affecting the slave trade, and his establishment of a Privy Council committee to deal with the coinage, are instances in point.[6] For Pitt by then was wary of potentially awkward intervention by Parliament into questions where administrative treatment could be employed; and in 1798, when the issue of the coinage seemed to demand

1. Leading the procession from the City and at the ceremony itself proclaiming 'loudly, "May the Dock and Canal prove an additional support to the Trade, Commerce, and Prosperity of the Port and City of London, the Emporium of the World"' (*The Morning Post*, 14 July 1800; and see also *The Times* of that date for a day spent 'with great conviviality').

Legislation opened with 39 & 40 Geo. III, c47, and the final Act, passed in July 1799, was 39 & 40 Geo. III, c69.

2. In which Government was necessarily concerned, not only from the range of the programmes which demanded the equivalent of several public bills for local undertakings, but also because the Treasury committed itself to buying out the proprietors of the existing Landed Quays.

3. The quotation comes from a note by the City Remembrancer, nd but after May 1798, reminding Pitt of the requests for the meeting with a deputation of a joint committee of both parties (P.R.O. 30/8/256).

4. Charles Abbot's diary for 9 and 10 May 1799 (*Colchester*, I, 177–8). For an earlier significant allusion, coming at the point it did from a source close to the Minister, to the hope that 'private interests' would not 'prevent the accomplishment of so great a good', see Rose's *Brief Examination* published early in that year.

5. See I, 308.

6. Pp. 429–30, 16 above.

investigation, he had a particular reason for taking the path he did. He had only recently seen a Select Committee of the Commons which he himself had proposed, to reassure opinion on the state of the finances following the suspension of credit in 1797, converted in essence into one with powers of examination throughout the whole range of public expenditure.[1] The outcome was unexpected, and while he professed to welcome it and in due course gave the findings his support – indeed using them to fend off a suggestion for a further Parliamentary inquiry[2] – the process was not what he had sought. For this was the committee whose 36 reports, appearing regularly and promptly, furnished far-ranging evidence on the executive which perforce appeared publicly at once.[3] The House in fact, following part of the way in a direction suggested by Opposition, had effectively wrested an advantage from Government in favour of itself.

III

A Select Committee of the House indeed could be a formidable instrument. Used in the first half of the century chiefly for the scrutiny of private bills bearing on local and individual interests, it became in addition 'a regular part of Parliamentary action' in examining and framing comments in the national sphere.[4] The process, long under way, was encouraged by the rise in Government business in the 1780s and '90s;[5] and the impact was increased, for the House as a whole though less than for its committees, by the form of procedure for such bills, requiring fourteen stages on the way to enactment some of which (practice varied) could involve debate in committee or the Chamber itself.[6] The effect on the legislators' work and time was thus compounded; the greater the number of Government bills, the greater the likely proportion of delay from the

1. See ibid., pp. 461–2 above.
2. *H of P*, III, 2.
3. Cf. p. 16 above for this last point.
4. P.G.D. Thomas, *The House of Commons in the Eighteenth Century*, 265. I use the word national rather than public because as the century wore on many bills, private by nature, were transferred to the public domain – to an extent that led the House in 1796 to distinguish them as 'Public Local and Personal Acts'. The Courts however, for good legal reasons, ignored any distinctions between the various categories (Sheila Lambert, *Bills and Acts* . . . (1971), 179).
5. Though not so steeply as the rise in the number of 'public' bills might suggest at first sight; see preceding note. 'Private' and 'Public Local and Personal Acts', as later designated, continued to account for at least half, and generally more, of the numbers of statutes passed (*The Statutes At Large* for 1767 to 1800, as a check on Pitt's period in office from 1784 against the preceding equivalent of years; and cf. for bills from 1776 Orlo Cyprian Williams, *The Clerical Organization of the House of Commons*, 318–19).
6. Williams, op. cit., 63 for the stages, and for limits in practice. Cf. I, 168–9 for the greater weight placed on the preparatory committees in relation to the House itself. But altogether, in the view of a leading contemporary expert, the general business of the Commons was trebled between 1760 and 1801 (see *H of P*, I, 334).

nature of their passage, unless the executive could bring to bear its own devices of control. The consequences were far from insupportable for either party: Members by and large could retain their leisurely pace and levels of attendance, while the, sometimes recondite, niceties of the procedures often allowed Ministers considerable scope. The relationship between those concerned remained on its familiar footing. But the context had altered somewhat since Pitt had entered office in 1783, and signs could be detected by the time of his death of a recognition of the fact.

Faced by a need to meet a growing load, and not unaffected by the spirit of an age of improvement, Parliament itself indeed was starting to respond in various directions. Printing for the House had been on the increase since the later seventies, and notably from 1780; the Clerk of the House, the celebrated John Hatsell, published his *Precedents of the Proceedings* in four volumes from 1781; the Speaker was brought into line with growing practice when his inadequate fees were replaced in 1790 by a more appropriate salary, and a few years later he was given possession of an official residence in Palace Yard; procedures, as always, were modified by judgments on specific cases. The Speaker himself throughout the decade, Addington, was sympathetic to useful advance; and perhaps his most telling contribution in the longer run was to support the exertions of a Member elected in 1795, who at one remove proved to be his successor in the Chair. For the years around the turn of the century saw a sustained programme of improvements which owed much to a single man, Charles Abbot; a politician dedicated to the rationalisation of business, including (with unusual foresight) the arrangement and promulgation of records. In the Parliamentary sphere indeed he was a counterpart to those skilled Departmental officials with whom Pitt always liked to operate; and in fact the Minister was soon calling him in aid for the preparation and passage of bills – the measures for the Poor Laws and the Assessed Taxes for instance in 1797, the Thames police in 1800 – and discussing some of Abbot's own proposals over a wide field.[1] The eager novice had some early successes in his strictly administrative ventures: he secured a committee to identify expiring Acts by a comprehensive search, which reported in 1799 and set on foot a massive plan to tidy up the statute book as a whole and make it available to public offices and Courts of law. He also had his failures: he could not carry a proposal to indicate by marginal reference the contents of clauses in public bills, or to embark on an 'improved style and diction' in such Acts. But his great period came after he was elected Speaker in 1802, a position he retained for fifteen years. Limits were set to the number of private bills to be presented, while work on their passage was speeded up; the *Votes and Proceedings* were printed in a shorter mode and finally

1. See II, 472–3, p. 468, n3 above with Abbot's diary for 19 June 1800 (P.R.O. 30/9/32). Evidence on his relations with Pitt on various matters in the '90s may be found in *The Diary and Correspondence of Charles Abbot, Lord Colchester*, ed. by his Son Charles, Lord Colchester, I (1861).

'compressed'; the abortive proposal for itemising clauses in public bills was now approved; the titles of Acts were framed more succinctly; expiring Acts, now identifiable, were listed for annual review; the *Journals* of the House up to 1801 were reprinted, and indexing followed; so were past sessional papers, as far as could be found, for the use of Parliament and Government offices, and agreement was gained for the same practice in future; the reports of the Select Finance Committee of 1797, of which he had been chairman, were given similar distribution. When he had finished, the Commons' records were available as never before.

Improvements percolated in other ways: a library was formed for Members' use; the Speaker's residence was largely rebuilt and Members were regularly entertained; working areas of the House itself were refurnished; reporters' attendance in the gallery was given further regulation. When Abbot received a peerage, he began to turn his attention to the House of Lords. Nor were his unremitting labours confined to Parliament's internal concerns. In 1800, with Addington's encouragement and a fair wind from Government, whose own attention had been aroused recently by its interest in past plans for defence,[1] he was able to press for a committee of inquiry into the preservation of the public records, which led to an official Commission that in turn approved a revised small establishment at the State Paper Office intended (as had long but ineffectively been approved in principle) to calendar and index the contents. Before he was denied the activities of an ordinary Member, in which he had taken an attentive part, he had moreover left his mark on the Treasury itself; the Finance Committee of 1797 ranged through the Department's preserves as widely as the terms allowed, and in 1799 he obliged the Board to make available its accounts for the year, a practice which became an annual event. Unpopular in the quarters he disturbed, and indeed not greatly liked by his fellows – his personality was awkward –, he was a figure to whom both the House and the state owed more than to many of greater note.

The Commons were thus becoming rather better equipped to meet the increased work – a pressure which would soon rise further after the Union with Ireland in 1801.[2] But the remedies could hardly keep pace. Legislature and executive in fact were suffering alike, in their degrees, from a similar process; and the fact was beginning to impinge, if marginally, on the balance between them. The day in the Chamber was still conducted, as it had been in the seventeenth century, by the 'procedure of an opposition', strengthened furthermore by a greater freedom, more openly recognised from the 1780s, to put questions to Ministers.[3] In return

1. For which see p. 121 above.
2. Both Hatsell and Abbot were worried at the start by the implications of this latter event, and after a time by the results (Williams, op. cit., 150; *Diary of Colchester*, I, 326–30; *H of P*, I, 334). And see Peter Fraser, 'The Growth of Ministerial Control in the Nineteenth-Century House of Commons' (*E.H.R.*, LXXV, no. CCXCVI, 446).
3. The quotation is from Fraser, loc. cit., 450; and see *H of P*, I, 340–1.

however Ministers were receiving their own assistance from emerging practice and, further, from a succession of Speaker's rulings determined by the observable need for reasonable dispatch. A restriction began to be placed on the right to move a matter of controversial nature without giving previous notice, which was upheld by Abbot in 1806 and, despite wide doubts, buttressed five years later by the introduction of certain 'order days' in the week on which Government's notices took precedence. It was an early signpost to a future that would see the diminution of the private Member's standing in the normal course of proceedings, as the volume of administration grew and the House settled gradually and at length inexorably into the concept and pattern of party politics.

As those developments clarified in outline, so did the growth of a revived search for the Speaker's own political independence. His election had been controlled throughout the century without disguise by the Ministry; the custom indeed had grown up that he should be proposed by the Leader of the House, though when Pitt nominated Addington in 1789 he seems to have listened to advice from Hatsell that it would be best at least to appear to leave the choice to the Members.[1] Abbot himself, despite the reservations he aroused in the Treasury and moreover in George III, had always been broadly a King's Friend: a supporter, as he stated from the start, of whichever Administration was carrying on the King's Government.[2] The occupant of the Chair – seldom of a prominence to raise him to the more puzzling complexities of high office – embodied the singular character of the assembly over which he presided, that balance of tension and co-operation with the executive that pervaded all its quarters in different degrees.[3]

These signs of movement were dawning in the second half of the 1790s at a time when Pitt's own situation was entering a new phase. From 1797–8 in particular the conditions became ever more testing. He was perforce largely on the defensive; strategic choices were increasingly baffling, domestic challenges multiplied. Nonetheless, at the turn of the century his Parliamentary position seemed to be basically unshaken: indeed to all appearance stronger if anything than before. No rival for his place was in sight, and on the great issues of confidence the debates yielded massive divisions in support. This was a fact for all to see: abroad as at home. What lay behind it? If his management of the Commons in such a setting was 'never-to-be-equalled', as memory claimed,[4] what were the ingredients that sustained the feat?

Fundamentally they were much as they had been at an earlier point in the decade. One, not of his making, had indeed been reinforced. Fox had done more by 1797 than could have ever been imagined to bolster

---

1. See Philip Laundy, *The Office of Speaker* (1964), 15.
2. *H of P*, III, 4.
3. Cf. I, 40, 46–7.
4. P. 457 above.

the Minister's standing: with the King, in Parliament, and on balance probably with the political public. Over the next two years he did little to dispel the resulting real distrust. His readiness to support men charged with seditious or treasonable practices – notably O'Connor and the other plotters in 1798 –, his appearance in company with Horne Tooke and the reiteration of the toast to the sovereignty of the people, the impression that had mounted in respectable circles after 1792, went far to efface his attempts to prove his patriotism in a year of high alarm.[1] Nor did his withdrawal from attendance in the House do his party or his cause any good. The leadership was left to lesser figures, subject to greater chances of dissension and an uncertainty – for the absentee did not give up his seat – only deepened by a single reappearance;[2] while his followers in the country lost a spokesman, as indeed did those critics of the Ministry – by no means always the same – who sympathised in part with what he stood for from dislike of the latter's conduct. Whether present or absent, in short, Fox now found himself in a position in which for the time being he was more likely to strengthen than damage Pitt.

The New Whigs were thus ineffective in their suspect concept of a 'formed' Opposition, and unattractive as a focus for the more familiar answer of a combination of interests. The other elements of the Coalition of 1783 – the Old Whigs and the Northites – were pretty well absorbed in the Government they joined in 1794 and from which their chief representatives – even Windham – gave no signs of breaking away. The times were too grave for men in Cabinet lightly to contemplate a split; the circumstances that provoked grumbling discouraged a political crisis; and without example or guidance backbenchers in the main were not disposed to mount a serious revolt. That had been shown in the spring and summer of 1797,[3] and the factors involved were broadly the same three years later. The lesson was relearned that a self-styled 'Armed Neutrality', claiming independence, could not hope to succeed on its own as an initiator of change.[4] When it came to the point it needed others grouped around more specific loyalties, and given such majorities defections must come largely through Ministers or the King themselves. Both however, and for similar reasons, stood as before in support of Pitt. The Cabinet had become more unhappy and George III was fretting. Doubts were rising among those in the know about the Minister's health and state of mind.[5] But a replacement still seemed almost unthinkable to his colleagues; his own thoughts on the matter were not vouchsafed;[6] his status remained unchallenged, the familiar balance of authority was

1. Pp. 115–17 above. And cf. 33 for the earlier period.
2. See pp. 42, 105 above. Fox's stance, in point of fact as much discouraged as freshly provocative, is admirably depicted in L.G. Mitchell's *Charles James Fox* (1992), 141–56.
3. Cf. pp. 35–42 above.
4. Pp. 43–4 above, and cf. I, 615, 655–6.
5. Pp. 34–6; 353–8, 367–70 above.
6. Unlike, at least momentarily and only in secret, in 1797 (pp. 46–50 above).

maintained. Vacillating as his grip might now be on the problems of strategy and operations, he remained an arbiter whose approval was as necessary as ever and whose judgment in the last resort could prevail.[1] This was scarcely a situation favourable to a determined Cabinet revolt or even a unilateral move by the King; and it would have caused the greater shock from Pitt's reputation with the Commons themselves.

For while desertions from the Government benches in the House turned materially on the attitudes of leaders and patrons, the process was by no means automatic. If the recipients of loyalties – or some of them – were powerful, they in turn had to recognise differing degrees of obligation. Private patrons of seats varied markedly in the areas of freedom they allowed – or some indeed could impose on – their Members; Government itself could not count invariably on the beneficiaries; political leaders – even the most eminent, like Pitt – could seldom command large personal followings; a shifting pattern was built up at any time from a mosaic of reciprocal relationships.[2] Government was carried on politically by arrangements between different elements, often varying in firmness according to the issues concerned. The elements themselves were composed, around their nodal points and again in varying proportions, of influences from below as well as from above.

During these latest years, of danger and steep fluctuations between promise and disappointment, Pitt did not lose command of the House. His bearing was as chilling as ever. But in stern and anxious days it could be uplifting as well; for particularly in the great set pieces his eloquence gained an added dimension. Powerfully directed to convince in a 'state-paper' style, it could now also, increasingly, inspire. In his physically awkward way – 'his action like a Taylor drawing his thread' – he had always brought a lofty dignity to his office; he now disclosed a passion, rarely seen in calmer times, which could bring the assembly to its feet in a like response.[3] Under the sterner threat of invasion he was identified with the island's inviolability; the impression of 'a ruler of the people' deepened in a period when his performance in Government was coming under growing dispute.[4] Less spectacularly, he continued to deploy his telling potency in the incessant debates of which he had a disproportionate share, and the exploitation of procedural niceties – even if not always up to the standard of experts such as Hatsell and Abbot – which was the fruit

1. Eg for 1799 Ch. X, section I, pp. 232–3, 247 and for 1800 p. 387 above.
2. Cf. I, Ch. II, sections II, III; op. cit., 619.
3. The description was Wilberforce's, in some notes on Pitt's oratory (Bodleain Library Add. Ms C254); and cf. Stanhope, IV, 413. His speech on the slave trade in 1792 was an earlier revelation of passion (I, 400–1). See op. cit., 611 for the state-paper style.
The impression – though it would be rash to try to be too chronologically exact – may moreover have been conveyed through the country with growing effect as newspapers developed their coverage of news in these eventful years; cf. pp. 113–14 above.
4. I, 611 for the quotation, which came retrospectively from Brougham, whose attention to politics was in fact dawning from just this period.

of long experience. By early training and it seemed by nature he had been a child of the House from the first, and he had not shed the faculties with which he had been endowed.

From this position he could sometimes lead Members along paths which they instinctively disliked. But not always, or as far as he would wish; the story of the new income tax was a leading example.[1] Other prominent instances come to mind: in 1795, the abandonment of purchases of wheat from overseas by Government through an official contractor; in 1797, the abrupt withdrawal of Pitt's bill for poor relief at a preliminary stage; in 1800, the failure of a first attempt to apply to London the powers of the Assize in permitting variations in the quality of bread.[2] The fact was that despite the advantages on which Ministers could normally call, and were heightened in his case thanks so largely to himself, he could not take Parliament for granted. He had not been able to do so on all occasions before 1794; he was not able to do so in his final years in office, beyond the turn of the century; and he could not do so in the years which saw the plenitude of his numerical power. A setback even on an issue conventionally of confidence need not of course lead to resignation, of either a Minister or a Ministry. 'Divisions did not in themselves decide the fate of governments, only of questions',[3] and Pitt of all men, looking back on his beginnings, was aware of that. But a string of defeats in the lobby, on matters involving a vote, whether by the House or the House in Committee, was not to be taken lightly. It could unsettle the troops; and according to circumstances it could unsettle the King.

Nor were divisions the sole verdict, or hazard, to be considered. As has been suggested,[4] the temperature in the Commons could more often be taken at earlier points or in less direct ways. A debate, obviously, could provide amendments proposed on a public bill at one of its stages, in a preparatory committee or a full Committee of the House, which the Government could decide to accept without a further test of strength; and sentiment and opinion could make themselves felt before that stage itself was reached, by signs when notice was given of leave to bring in a motion or initially while a plan was in draft. Such indications have been truisms in any of the past three centuries at least. But they may need reiteration or emphasis when a Ministry has enjoyed an exceptional, let alone a crushing, majority. The regulations of the House permitted – one can say encouraged – a variety of means for Members to bring pressures to bear; by direct exploitation of procedural forms, by the system of committees, and not least in that latter respect by the use to be made of petitions from the public.[5] For these were obvious weapons to employ against an Administration. They had to be presented in each instance by a Member

1. Pp. 262–7 above.
2. See II, 464–7, 471–5; pp. 286, 288 above.
3. R.G. Thorne, in *H of P*, I, 339.
4. Eg pp. 41–2, 45, 433–4 above.
5. Cf. pp. 478, 476, 39–40 above.

– that was 'an absolute obligation' – and they could cover both legislation, actual or intended, and matters of high policy: a range extending largely, though not fully – it excluded *proposed* taxes –, over that of 'the forum of the nation' itself. Witnesses might have to be heard in particular cases and inquiries set on foot; in any event, unless the House decided to refuse a reading, debate might be provided. The ancient right had not been touched in essence by the repressive Acts of 1795 – the Treasonable Practices and the Seditious Meetings and Assemblies Acts; so long as the promulgation and language did not run counter to their terms, it remained the prime instrument through which subjects of the Crown, individually or collectively, could address Parliament direct.[1] Pitt had made that clear at the time.[2] He might have found it hard to do otherwise, and in any case he was not so disposed; by upbringing and experience he was far from underrating the moods and expressions of opinion 'out of doors', and moreover if the channel could carry hostile messages it could do the same for others of support.[3] They were not all necessarily self-generating, whatever the content; for while petitions formed a link from people to Parliament, they also provided one in reverse. The appeals and their counters could be set in motion by Parliamentarians, of both Houses, themselves: quite often in purely local battles – the fights for power within a constituency –, on rarer but significant occasions to air grievances of greater note. Even so, such organisation had to be based on the interests concerned; and the outcome, however obtained, could not be dismissed. Above all, a wave of petitions on a subject of national concern was to be taken seriously. In 1797 it was almost certainly a factor hostile in intent – if not wholly unwelcome – which bore on Pitt's decision to seek a renewal of talks for peace.[4]

A good deal thus lay behind the heavy majorities so regularly produced towards the end of the decade – more than might perhaps be deduced from their persistent size. The political resources on which the Minister could draw ensured recurrent victory when really required. But that did not mean he could safely ignore feelings within the ranks that supplied it: votes were not necessarily to be given uniformly on different subjects, loyalties could be strained, signs of revolt could appear above the surface which normally disguised them, as they did unexpectedly on Grey's motion in 1797 for Parliamentary reform.[5] And when brought to the point, Pitt himself was far from immune from such influences. His bearing might belie the fact – the erect unseeing entry as he took his seat, the high indignant stare with which he could favour supporters as well as opponents – and his methods of treatment deepened the impression: the

1. Thomas (op. cit., 17-20) and Fraser (op. cit., 448–51) describe the position for their respective periods, within broader surveys of individual and minority tactics.
2. Cf. II, 455–6.
3. See p. 40 above; I, 153 for the heartening lesson of 1784.
4. P. 45 and n6 above.
5. P. 42 above.

persistent carelessness of individual wants and claims, the intense reluctance to conciliate personally for conciliation's sake. It was an unusual style of leadership, rather disconcerting from its elevated plane. Nonetheless, unlikely as it might appear, he was careful by and large to take currents of attitude into account, and he challenged or overrode them outright only when he thought it must be done. In politics as in administration, he achieved results by choice from working with the grain.[1] By conviction, instinctive and reasoned, he was a Parliamentary politician and statesman. And this feeling for the sense of the House reinforced its own widespread recognition of his talents in securing for him the dominant status he continued to enjoy.

Beyond the Commons' home in the former chapel of what was still the royal Palace of Westminster, through a gallery and the Painted Chamber where the King opened the sessions, lay the White or Parliament Chamber used since the early fifteenth century by the Lords. These arrangements were not solely of antiquarian interest. They epitomised in physical form the living reality of Parliament in completion: the three elements that formed the 'beautiful Combination' of the Constitution.[2]

The ethos of the upper House was markedly different from that of the lower. The peers liked to think of themselves as the upholders of constitutional equipoise, 'the balance', in Fox's words at a well-disposed moment, 'that equalized and meliorated the powers of the other two branches, and gave stability and firmness to the whole'.[3] This could indeed sometimes be so. On the one hand there did appear to be a natural alliance between the Houses in counter balance to the Crown, while on the other the peerage looked on itself as the Crown's natural body of support, 'the ancient source of counsel and still the most splendid Estate of the Realm'.[4] In practice in the 1790s its scales were weighted heavily towards stability: their Lordships sought the equipoise for the most part in a concept of defence against the threat of excessive change. And while attention and power were now obviously focused increasingly on the Commons, their own powers and types of influence, direct and indirect, collective and individual, gave them significant means of making their contribution felt.

The direct powers of course entered the process of legislation itself. The Lords could initiate bills, and indeed were so used sometimes by a Ministry – in the 1790s the Aliens Act and the Treasonable Practices Act were notable if unusually important examples. The working members spent much of their time, as always, in amending the bills sent up to them:

1. Cf. I, 325; and also 88.
2. See I, Ch. I, section I for the geography. Maurice Hastings, *Parliament House* ... (1950), shows a plan.
3. Quoted, from a speech in May 1791, by Michael W. McCahill, *Order and Equipoise, The Peerage and the House of Lords, 1783–1806* (1978), 1.
4. Cf. I, 43–5.

their most consistently useful function, correcting, supplementing, sometimes quietly adjusting to second thoughts from the drafters themselves. And the House could impose delay, at times causing tension when that became serious or the Commons conceived that their own rights were being infringed. The protraction could come of course from the amount of amendment genuinely required. It could also exploit technicalities to support opposition in principle, a fact that would emerge more clearly in the course of the debates.

Two things are noticeable about these processes in the 1790s. First, the number of public 'general' bills amended or lost in the Lords was quite small.[1] The former were certainly greater in the period 1791 to 1800 than they had been from 1784 to 1790: the figures were 103 amended and 34 lost compared with 35 and 34 respectively. Given the rise in business, mainly that sent from the Commons, this was nothing much in quantity. But secondly, the figures relating to *Government* bills – measures introduced to either House by Ministers or of particular interest to them – show an interesting divagation from those for public general measures as a whole. From 1791–1800 they were 53 amended and 3 lost compared with 8 and 12 respectively from 1784 to 1790. In other words, one might suggest, the two respective columns for amendments reflect the developing pace of Ministerial legislation within the period, while those for its losses indicate the Lords' reluctance to oppose such measures to the point of defeat. One might note further that the figures relating to public general bills in aggregate rose from 1796 to 1800 by comparison with the preceding five years – sharply for amendments to 63, and for losses to 17; but that those for Government bills remained more modest for amendments – 39 – while only one measure was lost, for reducing the militia in 1799.

This degree of support for Government was largely, though not invariably, ensured, beyond the broad inclination of the peerage as an order, by the numbers of its members holding high offices of various kinds. Even if important bills seldom started their lives in the upper House, it contained most – for a time all but one – of the Cabinet Ministers: Pitt was the sole exception for his first five and a half years, he had only one companion – first, briefly, Grenville, and then Dundas – for the next five, and thereafter only two when Windham was added in 1794. Peers were also represented in certain non-Cabinet posts: among the Postmasters General and Masters of the Mint, as well as the largely absent Lords Lieutenant in Ireland. And to this weight of influence – Grenville, assisted by Hawkesbury, was an effective Leader of the House from 1790, and the Portland Whigs brought their acres from 1794[2] – could be added for numbers the 'cohorts' presumed to be attached to the Crown. 'The

---

1. Losses including bills voluntarily withdrawn and those lapsing from lack of time in a session.

For what follows see McCahill. op. cit., 41–2 and Appendix A; for the designation of public bills p. 476 and n4 above.

2. Cf. for Lord Chesterfield's comment in 1792 I, 635n2.

thanes, high priests and household cavalry'[1] were often lumped together as dependent and dependable troops for any Ministry enjoying the confidence of the King; and normally, under such conditions, this was broadly the case. The first two groups could show certain affinities.[2] The 16 Scottish representative peers owed their election, by their fellows, in practice very largely to the Government of the day, and this was so to an exceptional extent in the second half of the 1790s in the capable hands of Dundas at his peak. By the end of the decade indeed his fief seemed almost personal; but although that situation still endured when the personal circumstances changed, it was in conditions which underlined the fact that loyalties were fixed in the end on the source of enduring patronage.[3] Meanwhile there was a reliable body of generally solid strength, and while a peer of Scotland might follow a line of his own on some occasions, and local balances of power had to be taken into account, the elected representatives by and large lived up to their English reputation. The 26 bishops too owed their presence, and hopes of further preferment, to the Crown; in their case from a blend, or sometimes compact, of patronage between the First Lord of the Treasury and the King. That in itself could bear on their behaviour if the former was parted from the latter, as in fact had been proved more than once; and there were always some who aimed – with George III's approval in principle, but as a well defined minority in practice – at a state of broad independence. The prelates' attendance moreover was apt to be irregular – even Pretyman, well placed in London as Dean of St Paul's, spent much time during the sessions in his diocese in Lincoln[4] – and they were not merely cynical or uniformly docile. In matters of direct interest to the Church, their effect could be felt quite as much before as during the debates; and that was the visible tip of an influence which in any case helped mould the context of legislation itself. The roots of Anglicanism ran deep, its tone and effects were pervasive. The Establishment of Church and State was not a one-way affair.[5] The ecclesiastics in the House of Lords stood for more than their votes. Nevertheless – or consequentially – in unsettled times those showed them as a body to be a force on which Government could call.

The conduct of the household cavalry was likewise predictable, so long as the King and his Ministers were agreed. There were at least 20 peers holding Household appointments at any given time, and those of the

---

1. Op. cit., 622.

2. What follows draws in places on work by Michael McCahill, in *Order and Equipoise*, particularly ch. 3, and 'The Scottish Peerage and the House of Lords in the Late Eighteenth Century' (*Scottish Historical Review*, 11), published since my remarks on the subject in I, 623–4.

3. Three times in the next decade Dundas did in fact rally supporters, in both Houses, to his standard in *opposition* to the Ministry of the day. But that was part of a wider process (for the first see Ch. XVIII, section III below) and at points when he and they could scent victory or were aware of the King's own preference.

4. See I, 13, and for George III on 'his' bishops being 'party men' op. cit., 623.

5. Eg II, 61–8, 161–3.

senior functionaries carried a political importance not far below that of senior Ministers themselves. In the 1780s it was possible for *The Royal Kalendar* to include some of the latter in its list of the Court, while conversely some of the former had recently been treated as political creations, subject to replacement when a Ministry fell.[1] The question lay in a grey area of uncertain size and bounds, the monarch watching jealously for undue intrusion on his comfort and prerogative, the politicians for undue extensions of influence exploiting sources close to himself. There was always a latent possibility of conflict surfacing from persistent undertones of contest. But the impact on the Parliamentary balance was normally the reverse; one in which King and Cabinet in combination fortified the resources of the Crown.

These elements of strength provided a significant numerical proportion of the upper House: roughly 62 members out of a total of 238 in 1784, and 296 in 1800 on the eve of the accession of 28 Irish representative peers.[2] They were also valuable in aggregate, as they had been in the 1780s, in their comparative regularity of attendance on important occasions.[3] Some Scots and bishops might be absent by geography or duties – though the former were expected to be reasonably available in the months of business – but they and the courtiers turned up in sufficient force when required. While they were not all or always purely Ministerial fodder – they had their reciprocal influences on their patrons and leaders, and could share their loyalties to the Crown between its own constituent elements – they supplied an ample focus of Ministerial support within the wider reaches of the House. They were better drilled than any of its elements other than the core of Opposition: better than the penumbra of King's Friends, or the semi-independent connexions based on mutual interests and family relationships, or of course the amorphous bulk of consciously independent peers – and that core itself was much shrunken after 1794. Pitt's personal ascendancy in this setting could not draw on his presence, and the great magnates in particular were not so ready to grant it. Their proprietary attitude to Government and politics was as securely confident as ever. But they were not now as confident about the times around them, the current Minister seemed indispensable, and apart from the remains of the Foxite circle they did not offer an organised challenge. The Lords required management, as always; they were not to be taken wholly for granted in the detail of business; but, within the walls of their Chamber, they were indisputably a bulwark of the Ministry and the Crown.

And not only within those walls. Individual peers, operating like other private patrons from their properties and interests, played an essential

1. See I, 169, 623.
2. For whom cf. p. 174 above. A.S. Turberville, *The House of Lords in the Age of Reform 1784–1837* (1958), 42; Appendix VI gives numbers of temporal peers in December 1783, to whom must be added the bishops. Cf. I, 43 for 1780.
3. Cf. I, 623–4.

part in local affairs which themselves demanded Parliamentary support. From the forwarding of – or objections to – a private bill, to the encouragement – or otherwise – of an economic policy or the mounting of a public petition on a national issue, the notabilities and representatives of their 'countries' brought their pressures to bear on the legislature.[1] Many of their internecine contests, in which success marked a proof or fresh step in the vital matter of local standing, were conducted almost wholly on that footing and had little to do with wider loyalties. In others however the factors were merged; certainly in the case of public petitions, perhaps the clearest signs apart from elections of the balance of influence within a constituency. For of course the constituency lay at the hub of whatever need was to be served, and influence to the point of unchallenged possession held a prominent place among the properties of a politically minded patron. The map was always changing, as gains and losses were recorded and compacts made or brought to an end, and its contours are the harder to delineate precisely at any given time, let alone for a period. But within those parameters one fact was unchallengeable. If the Lords cut a minor figure in the direct process of legislation, their impact could be felt at an earlier point among the Commons themselves. When Pitt first entered Parliament in 1780, it was reckoned that 52 peers (out of 119 private patrons) 'controlled' 113 (out of 221) seats; in 1793, from a propagandist but well researched list, the respective numbers were put at 71 and 163; in 1802 (in lists unaffected by the recent Union with Ireland) the peers' 'patronal' interests have been calculated, on a careful survey of degrees of influence as well as of outright nomination, at 98 and 224. In an assembly of 558 members until 1801 and 658 thereafter, these various estimates accounted very broadly for about a third of the House.[2] To the effects can be added others from less well definable factors. Many MPs, whether or not sitting in such seats, were related closely or quite closely to peers: no fewer than 67 legitimate sons in 1780, together with much larger numbers boasting a family connexion, altogether amounting to perhaps two-thirds of the Membership as a whole.[3] That figure may have shrunk to some extent over the next twenty years, with an increase of 'non-élite'[4] members of the lower House which had been noticeable since the 1770s and continued steadily thereafter; and other factors too should be weighed in mea-

---

1. Cf. for the phrase op. cit., 31.

2. Op. cit., 43; Turberville, op. cit., 246; James J. Sack, 'The House of Lords and Parliamentary Patronage in Great Britain, 1802–32' (*H.J.*, 23, no. 4, republished in *Peers, Politics and Power: The House of Lords, 1603–1911*, ed. Clyve Jones and David Lewis Jones (1986), to which this reference applies), 353. E. Porritt's *The Unreformed House of Commons* (1903, I) puts the proportion higher.

The figures in 1793 were published by the Burkean *Annual Register* (see p. 3 and n1 above) from a calculation by the Friends of the People.

3. See I, 43 for 1780; *H of P*, I, 282–4 as an indication for the 1790s and beyond.

4. Ian R. Christie, *British 'non-élite' M.P.'s 1715–1820* (1995) particularly Ch. 3 and Appendix A.

suring the Lords' influence. Such an aggregate of patronage and family ties somewhat reduced its effects by its very size: by no means all the men so included agreed with, or always thought much about, their noble relatives' opinions. Nor in fact were those nominated by private patrons, as many of them were, necessarily held on a short lead: Pitt himself, in his opening guise as Member for Appleby, was given a wide latitude by the most notorious borough-monger of his time;[1] and while this was exceptional from such a source, it was not unusual, in varying degree, from a range of rather more characteristic 'proprietors'. Nonetheless, while the mutual relationship need not be crude, there was a dependence, from strict to virtually nominal, attaching to a patronal seat, and throughout the lower House the links with the Lords could affect its proceedings and colour its tone.

Any First Lord of the Treasury had accordingly to watch the upper House, more particularly perhaps if he himself was in the Commons. 'Pitt's peers', his additions and promotions, brought its share of criticism at the time and a veritable chorus in the decades after his death. He had recent precedents on which to call: from 1776 to 1783 inclusive there had been 36 creations and promotions in the British and the Irish peerage. But these were exceeded in the British peerage alone in the next seven years – 45 such grants from 1784 to the general election in 1790 – and they continued to the end of the century.[2] By then the size of the British peerage had in fact risen by virtually a half: by 65 such new titles with seats in the House of Lords,[3] 11 British creations from existing Scottish titles – an addition to the 16 Scottish representative peers –, 22 from existing Irish peers (not entitled as a body before 1801 to be represented at Westminster), and 4 new royal dukes. That made a total of 102 to be added to the 208 temporal peers in the House when the Minister took office. There were also 26 elevations within the existing British peerage (which of course did not add the recipients to the numbers in the Chamber), discounting the British titles bestowed on Scottish and Irish peers which could be higher or lower or equivalent in rank to those already held.[4]

It was not surprising therefore that such a process should have aroused

1. I, 25–6.

2. Op. cit., 624–5. My figure there, of 119 creations and promotions during Pitt's periods in office as First Minister until his death, can be revised upwards to 133 if grants by special remainder or limitation (see below) and some creations from existing courtesy titles are taken more fully into account. The figure of 212 temporal peers in 1783 should also be changed to 208 (as below).

3. I put it like this because there were also 2 creations for women (of whom one was already an Irish baroness by descent) – as there had been in 1761 for Pitt's mother, five years before his father decided to become a peer himself.

4. Turberville, op. cit., Appendix III, whose detail, rather than the figures op cit. Appendix VI, provides the basis for my calculation.

In Pitt's years in office after 1800 there were a further 4 creations (of which one was by special limitation and one to a royal dukedom) and 1 elevation.

acute suspicions. Pitt was accused of debasing the character of the upper House with a flood of social inferiors – immortalised much later by Disraeli with his 'fat graziers' and the products of 'the alleys of Lombard Street . . . the counting-houses of Cornhill' – and, more to the point, of exploiting that exclusive assembly for an undue political influence. The prosecution's arguments were flawed: the social charge was wide of the mark – there had been 'fat graziers' from the squirearchy before, and not a single recruit was snatched from Lombard Street or Cornhill[1] – and the Lords had long been used to guard a Minister's flank or provide a comfortable political retreat. But if the indictments were in part mis-directed, a justifiable case remained. In their quantity and continuity the changes in the peerage were exceptional and could not be ignored.

The figures need a closer look. Of the 102 creations 10 were made by special remainder or limitation, in instances where the claims of geneal-ogy and law were stronger than those of political value; 5 for services in war – the veteran Heathfield, Cornwallis, Duncan, St Vincent, Nelson – carrying little if any political connotation, 4 of them being loosely attached and St Vincent in fact of doubtful use to Pitt;[2] 1 (Kenyon) on appointment as Lord Chief Justice, a practice now settling towards a convention, although he was in any case sympathetic to Pitt. The 4 royal dukes, younger sons of George III, were the monarch's creation. And these gradations of connexion with the Ministry itself, shown in such cases in untypical contexts, were not in point of fact untypical of the scene as a whole. For it is by no means always easy, once more, to dis-tinguish too exactly the proportions of support for the current Government and for the Crown in its comprehensive sense. The new accretions to the British peerage shared the broad assumptions of the majority of the order they joined. This applied to all the categories from which they were chosen – from whichever class of grant, and for which-ever cause; and it included the most directly important group for our purpose, that of the constituency patrons, which could be said on a wide measurement to number 20 with control or serious influence in 41 seats.[3] Here Pitt might expect indeed to gain a reasonable measure of strictly Ministerial benefit; and he might also hope to count on a small body of personal attachment – Carrington, Mornington, Camden, William Grenville and his brother Buckingham when the latter was in a good mood, possibly the brothers Hood and Bridport in acknowledgment of old family favours. Other beneficiaries, even within the Ministry

1. Cf. I, 624–5.
2. The war produced the germ of an idea which in certain cases might have become an alternative to a peerage for naval and military commanders. Shortly before Pitt died he was in touch with the College of Arms over the possible institution of an Order of Merit; indeed he was looking at a draft of the statutes (Hawkesbury to Pitt, 12 December 1805 (P.R.O. 30/8/143); Sir Isaac Heard to same, 21 November, 9, 16 December 1805; loc. cit., 144)).
3. McCahill, *Order and Equipoise*, Appendix F.

itself – Auckland (from an Irish peerage bestowed earlier), Hobart, Hawkesbury later elevated to Liverpool –, might look more freely to their own interests, as could servants of the state (sometimes with political connexions) such as Malmesbury and Macartney. Experience alone could show; and in Pitt's case it did, in due course at different times with distinctly variable effects.

This rather mechanistic approach, however, is not a full answer to a question in which personalities as well as backgrounds and circumstances always play their part. For Pitt himself was not as consistently purposeful as the first impression of his lists might suggest. Neither he nor the King in point of fact wished the House of Lords to expand too far. George III, as the fount of honour, disapproved of too great a largesse; and the Minister for his part confessed in the mid eighties to 'a larger addition to the British Peerage than I like, or than I think quite creditable'. A 'variety of circumstances' had led to an unusual display of such patronage in his opening years.[1] His good intentions cannot be said in the event to have lasted long: notable political occasions – the Regency crisis, and the junction with the Portland Whigs – produced fresh waves of gratitude, and there was a further consolidation in the less favourable span of 1796–7. The process ironically brought its own disadvantages, as was pointed out – Camden for instance observed, as the King had done earlier, that the growing size of the upper House made it less rather than more governable, and Rose noted that transfers from the Commons could open the door to inconvenient replacements.[2] Pitt was unlikely to have been blind to these considerations. They may indeed have supplemented his temperamental distaste for the incessant applications, which themselves were encouraged by the volume of the grants. The trouble was, he found, that rather too often the latter were 'unavoidable'.[3] And this in turn reinforces the strong suspicion that he did not really worry very much about the composition of the House of Lords. If he was notoriously negligent about meeting requests and demands of all types for ribbons or places, he could also be carelessly profuse when it came to the creation of peers.[4] He respected the order's weight in the country and its constitutional role. But he had no great feeling for it as a caste, and he viewed the great magnates in particular with a sardonic eye. 'They see', he commented as the Old Whigs made approaches in 1794, 'that their titles & possessions are in danger, & they think their best chance for preserving them is by supporting Government & joining me'.[5] A measure of indifference – what Rose called a 'most uncommon share of good nature' – should not be eliminated from his

1. See I, 626–7.
2. Op. cit., 627.
3. Ibid, and for what follows.
4. The story of a Grenville cousin – not even recommended by his acquisitive clan – may be an example, though told many years later; see *GEC*, V, 666n(b) for Glastonbury.
5. Pretyman's recollection of a conversation, in which he put these words into double quotation marks, in the unpublished ch. 18 for his biography; see II, 408.

response to the more serious amalgam of pressures which led him to employ and demonstrate his influence where it would count.

For in the 1790s as in the '80s Pitt stood out in public as the dominant partner in such an exercise. Possible fissures in the structure of patronage did not emerge in a decade in which he and George III remained yoked together. The earlier harmony, or mutual abstinence, was showing signs of strain as the King's doubts increased over the direction of the war. But he could not press them too far, and in the Parliamentary sphere the Minister was too much in command of the Commons for him to be challenged on his handling of the Lords. His performance in that matter was not his most attentive, and it may furthermore have been disproportionate to the need. His prodigality with peerages indeed may be set against his stricter treatment of sinecure places. The process, persistent and sometimes haphazard, was, as he said, not particularly creditable. There could be no doubt however that the responsibility was his.

At the end of 1800, dismal as the year had been, there seemed to be no obvious reason why the political situation should change. Opposition in the Commons was at a low ebb. The Lords were not going to cause trouble. The Cabinet, though divided, was not looking for a new leadership. The monarch's misgivings on the course of operations were marginal in their effects. Pitt's standing, when it came to the point, remained incontestable; indeed if it had declined in some respects it was higher in others as the country faced and had so far survived its domestic trials. Whatever the sentiments he aroused, he occupied the centre of the stage: a figure of keen personal attention in Europe, and of an authority at home whose very lapses shaped the process and pattern of decisions. Unless his health were to collapse he seemed set to continue, if he wished, for an indefinite time. And then within a few weeks the whole scene was upset.

Notes on Sources

For Volume III and Volume IV

The researches of Stanhope and then Holland Rose (see Abbreviations) set a framework for all later studies of Pitt. Even where not mentioned specifically in these Notes, it is axiomatic that their works should be consulted. One recent compilation may also be cited here: A.D. Harvey's *William Pitt The Younger 1759–1806 A Bibliography* (1989).

CHAPTER I

The French landing in Wales, which precipitated the financial crisis of February 1797, is the subject of E.H. Stuart Jones, *The Last Invasion of England* (1950), and David Salmon, 'The French Invasion of Pembrokeshire in 1797' (*West Wales Historical Records*, 14). Edouard Desbrière, *Projets et Tentatives de Debarquement aux Iles Britanniques, 1793–1805* (4 vols., 1900–2) remains a classic. For the Bank of England see Sir John Clapham, *The Bank of England, A History 1694–1914* (2 vols., 1944), W.M. Acres, *The Bank of England from Within, 1694–1900*, I (1931), I.P.H. Duffy, 'The discount policy of the Bank of England during the suspension of cash payments, 1797–1821' in *Ec.H.R.* (see Abbreviations), *2nd ser.*, XXXV, no. 1; for provincial banking, L.S. Pressnell, *Country Banking in the Industrial Revolution* (1956). N.J. Silberling, 'British Financial Experience, 1790–1830' (*Review of Economics and Statistics*, I), E. Victor Morgan, *The Theory and Practice of Central Banking 1797–1913* (1943), Frank Whitson Fetter, *Development of British Monetary Orthodoxy, 1797–1875* (1965), and the first two chapters, by J.K. Horsefield, in *Papers in English Monetary History*, ed. T.S. Ashton and R.S. Sayers (1953), provide general surveys. A.E. Feaveryear treats of *The Pound Sterling, A History of English Money* (2nd edn., 1963), and Peter Mathias discusses copper coin in ch. 10 of his *The Transformation of England, Essays in the Economic and Social History of England in the Eighteenth Century* (1979). Sir John Craig is the historian of *The Mint, A History of the London Mint from A.D. 287 to 1948* (1953). P.K. O'Brien, 'Government Revenue 1793–1815, A Study in Fiscal and Financial Policy in the Wars against France' (D.Phil. thesis, University of Oxford, 1967) is of fundamental importance in its comprehensive treatment. A further notable unpublished study is Richard A. Cooper, 'British Government Finance, 1793–1807' (Ph.D. thesis, University of North Carolina, 1976).

Two significant contemporary publications on the crisis are Francis Baring's *Observations on the Establishment of the Bank of England* (1797), and Henry Thornton's *An Enquiry into the Nature and Effects of the Paper Credit of Great Britain* (1802) which was edited in 1939 by F.A. von Hayek. The reports of the Committee of Secrecy of the Lords and Commons contain the main elements of Pitt's correspondence and meetings with the Bank of England and his evidence before the Committee itself; they may be found in *H.L.J.* (see Abbreviations), XLI, pp. 186–262 (and in *P.H.* (Abbreviations), XXXIII (1818), cols. 294–324), and *Reports from Committees of the House of Commons*, XI (1803). These last, XII–XIII (1803) contain the report of the Commons' Select Committee on Finance of 1797.

Pitt's papers hold scattered material. P.R.O. (see Abbreviations) 30/8/101, 276 include some of his correspondence with the Bank of England; 107, a letter from Charles Abbot as chairman of the Commons' Finance Committee; 110, 115, 178 proposals from Auckland, Walter Boyd, Sir John Sinclair respectively; 152, letters from Lord Liverpool; 183, one from Samuel Thornton; 196, ff. 209–12v, Pitt's own notes on causes of the crisis, and ff. 237–40v on the current situation in Ireland; 197, f. 189v, some on copper coin; 276, ff. 129–37, notes in another hand relating to his evidence before the Commons' Committee of Secrecy; 326, letters from Camden in Ireland which include much on its finances. Liverpool's papers on coin and the Mint are principally in B.L. (see Abbreviations) Add. Ms 38423, and there are a few on the crisis in 38354. B.L. Loan Ms 72, vols. 54, 55 contain correspondence on coin from his son Hawkesbury. The Dacres Adams Mss for 1797, formerly P.R.O. 30/58/2, include one letter from him to Pitt. For guidance to the proceedings of the Privy Council's Committee on Coin see M.S. Giuseppi's *Guide to the Contents of the Public Record Office* (revised edn. 1963), II, and the List & Index Society's vol. 35.

There are two good accounts of the main naval mutinies, from rather different points of view, in Conrad Gill, *The Naval Mutinies of 1797* (1913), and G.E. Manwaring and B. Dobrée, *The Floating Republic* (1935). Both contain some primary material in appendices. They may be supplemented by James Dugan, *The Great Mutiny* (1966). Selections from Spencer's papers are published in *Private Papers of George, Second Earl Spencer, First Lord of the Admiralty 1794–1801*, II, ed. Julian S. Corbett (1914). For the background of naval life see above all N.A.M. Rodgers's *The Wooden Walls, An Anatomy of the Georgian Navy* (1986). The position in the army is discussed in the Hon. J.W. Fortescue's *A History of the British Army*, IV-Part II (1906), and Alfred H. Burne, *The Noble Duke of York, The Military Life of Frederick Duke of York and Albany* (1949). Roger Wells, *Insurrection, The British Experience 1795–1803* (1983) argues the political dimension, and Marianne Elliott, *Partners in Revolution, The United Irishmen and France* (1982) the Irish.

The Windham Papers . . ., II, ed. Lewis Melville (1913) and *The Diary of the Rt. Hon. William Windham*, ed. Mrs Henry Baring (1866), *H.M.C.* (Abbreviations), *Dropmore*, III for William Grenville, *The Life of William Wilberforce, by his Sons Robert Isaac Wilberforce . . . and Samuel Wilberforce*, II (1838), *Correspondence of Charles, First Marquis Cornwallis*, ed. Charles Ross, II (1859), *L.C.G. III* (see Abbreviations), II (1963), give scattered published indications of reactions from Ministers and others less fully engaged than Spencer. Among ms sources for those most centrally concerned, Pitt's papers are patchy for the mutinies: P.R.O. 30/8/102, 146, 173, 259 have items from Bridport, Howe, and George Rose, and the Dacres Adams Mss formerly P.R.O. 30/8/2, from Bridport and from Spencer. Spencer's own papers in B.L. temporary Althorp Ms G197 add something to the published *Private Papers* above. For Dundas, the Melville Castle papers in S.R.O. (see Abbreviations), GD 51/2 are relevant. B.L. Add. Mss 37844–6 give glimpses of Windham's alarm.

Parliamentary debates for the year are published in *P.R.* (see Abbreviations), *3rd ser.*, I–IV (1797–8), *The Senator*, XVII–XIX (nd), *P.H.*, XXXII–III (1818).

CHAPTER II

Politics in the first half of 1797 attracted much comment scattered through private diaries and correspondence and in the London newspapers, particularly *The Morning Chronicle* and *The Morning Post* in opposition and *The True Briton* and *The Times* (the latter rather uncertainly) in support, not least for the petitioning movement and for Cabinet and other Ministerial meetings. *H of P* (see Abbreviations), I–V are indispensable. The episode of the 'armed neutrality' is examined by Arthur Aspinall in *L.C.G. III*, II, xxi–xxix, and see also his edition of *The Correspondence of George Prince of Wales 1770–1812*, III (1965). Sinclair's role is discussed in Rosalind Mitchison, *Agricultural Sir John, The Life of Sir John Sinclair of Ulbster 1754–1825* (1962). Albert Goodwin, *The Friends of Liberty: The English Democratic Movement in the age of the French Revolution* (1979), J.E. Cookson, *The Friends of Peace, Anti-War Liberalism in England 1793–1815* (1982) examine the background of the uneasiness that produced the wave of petitions. See Note on Sources to Ch. I above for the Parliamentary debates. Pitt's papers, in P.R.O. 30/8, P.R.O. 30/70, and the Dacres Adams Mss, are rather disappointing, though 30/8/170 suggests something of his attitude in letters concerning John Reeves.

The Minister's thought of resigning to be succeeded by Addington is mentioned in the Hon. George Pellew, *The Life and Correspondence of the Right Honble Henry Addington, First Viscount Sidmouth*, I (1847), and in Bishop Tomline [Pretyman's] 'Estimate of Pitt together with Chapter XXVII from the Unpublished Fourth Volume of the Life', ed. by Lord Rosebery in *The Monthly Review*, XII, no. 3 for August 1903 and republished privately in the same year. The episode is recounted in greater detail by Mrs Pretyman in Stanhope Ms U1590 S5 C41, in the Stanhope Mss on deposit at the Centre for Kentish Studies, Maidstone. Versions of drafts for the Bishop's chapter are in B.L. Add. Mss 45107 (H) and 45108 (F) and Tomline Ms 35.1–13 at Pembroke College, Cambridge.

British interests and diplomacy in Europe, excluding the process of the negotiation at Lille for which see below, may be followed in the Foreign Office papers in P.R.O., F.O. 7/48–50 (Austria), 9/14, 31/9, 33/13, 68/11 (states in Germany), 22/27–8, 97/117 (Denmark), 28/17, 42/2, 67/24–5, 70/10, 79/15, 81/2 (states in Italy), 29/12–14 (Army in Germany), 43/2 (Thomas Graham in Italy), 63/24–6 (Portugal), 64/43–6, 95/6 (Prussia), 65/36–8 (Russia), 73/25, 97/399 (Sweden), 74/20–1 (Switzerland), 78/18 (Turkey). For the enemy states F.O. 37/59, 38/2 cover Holland, 72/45, 95/7 Spain, 27/51–2 intelligence on France. Grenville's own papers in B.L. Add. Mss listed by countries (and see A.D. Harvey, *Lord Grenville 1759–1834 A Bibliography* (1989), 24) contain much of the same material. Michael Duffy, 'British Diplomacy and the French Wars 1789–1815' in *Britain and the French Revolution, 1789–1815*, ed. H.T. Dickinson (1989) is an excellent introduction; his 'Pitt, Grenville and the Control of British Foreign Policy in the 1790s' in *Knights Errant and True Englishmen, British Foreign Policy, 1660–1800*, ed. Jeremy Black (1989), an interesting study; his D.Phil. thesis Oxford (1971) 'British War Policy, The Austrian Alliance 1793–1801' an authoritative account of relations for which *The Cambridge History of British Foreign Policy*, ed. Sir A.W. Ward and G.P. Gooch, I (1922), Appendix, contains a précis of selected documents. Some light is shed on intelligence and subversion in *The Correspondence of the Rt. Hon. William Wickham from 1794, ed . . . by His Grandson William Wickham* (2 vols., 1870), from material now largely in the Hampshire R.O. (Abbreviations); the study by Harvey Mitchell, *The Underground War against Revolutionary France, The Missions of William Wickham*

1794–1800 (1965) has been superseded in part by Maurice Hutt, *Chouannerie and Counter-Revolution . . .* (2 vols., 1983) and also by articles with important fresh material by Elizabeth Sparrow, 'The Alien Office, 1792–1806' and 'The Swiss and Swabian Agencies, 1795–1801' in *H.J.* (see Abbreviations), 33, no. 2, 35, no. 4 respectively.

Pitt's moves for peace from April to June 1797 are documented in Stanhope (Abbreviations), III, Appendix, J. Holland Rose, *Pitt and Napoleon*, Part II (1912), *H.M.C., Dropmore*, III, *L.C.G. III*, II. Canning's diary in Canning Ms 29d in the Harewood deposit at the City of Leeds Archives Office, and Windham's *Diary* (see Ch. I above) are also useful. So too is Peter Jupp's *Lord Grenville 1759–1834* (1985) for that subject and the subsequent negotiation at Lille, and for the latter one should also note Ephraim Douglas Adams, *The Influence of Grenville on Pitt's Foreign Policy 1787–1798* (1904). I have drawn very largely for the talks themselves on a detailed unpublished survey by Dr Anthony Smith, to which I am greatly obliged. The despatches are in P.R.O., F.O. 27/49–50. Malmesbury's private correspondence is published, quite extensively here, in *Diaries and Correspondence of James Harris First Earl of Malmesbury . . ., ed. by His Grandson . . .*, III (1844), and see also op. cit., IV, 128; and *The Private Correspondence of Lord Granville Leveson Gower (first Earl of Granville) 1781 to 1821, ed. Castalia, Countess Granville*, I (1916) augments that of his principal. The Grenville papers in B.L. (see above) add little here to *H.M.C., Dropmore*, III and the F.O. papers. Canning Mss 29d, 30, 58, 63 and the less central 34a, 62, 69; Leveson Gower's papers in P.R.O. 30/29/6, 384; Pitt's in P.R.O. 30/8/120 (Canning), 140 (Grenville), 155 (Malmesbury), 195 (notes of October), and in the Dacres Adams Mss formerly P.R.O. 30/58/2 for Canning, Grenville, and Malmesbury, provide some added information. So do letters from him in the Camden [Pratt] Mss in the Centre for Kentish Studies, U840 C102, C106, and some to him in the Stanhope Mss loc. cit., U1590 S5 03, 06. Windham's correspondence in B.L. Add. Mss 37844, 37846, 37876–7 shows the Secretary at War's unvarying views. Dundas's early support for a negotiation appears in draft in S.R.O., Melville Castle Muniments, GD 51/1/526. P.R.O. 30/8/147 (for Huskisson), more substantially 115 for Walter Boyd – not supplemented materially in this instance by S.R. Cope, *Walter Boyd, A Merchant Banker in the Age of Napoleon* (1983) –, 364 (for Chatham), throw some further flickering light on the French approach for a douceur to reach a settlement, as does *L.C.G. III*, II.

CHAPTER III

Letters relating to 'Pitt's One Love Story' were published, under that title, in *Pitt: Some Chapters of his Life and Times. By the Right Hon. Edward Gibson, Lord Ashbourne* (1898). The whole correspondence was gathered together by Lord Rosebery in *Letters Relating to the Love Episode of William Pitt . . .*, in *The Monthly Review*, I, no. 3 of December 1900, and reprinted privately at the same time. The contents may be followed in B.L. Add. Mss 46491, 59704, which reached the Library in 1948 and 1976 respectively. Letters between Auckland and Pitt in P.R.O. 30/8/110 and a later note in Stanhope Ms U1590 S5 C60/19, B.L. Add. Ms 46519, *A.C.* (see Abbreviations), III, shed light on the two men's relations over the rest of the year.

Personal finances are as hard to construe for 1797 as for any other time. Pointers in a confused situation can be gained from Thomas Coutts's letters to

Pitt in P.R.O. 30/8/126 and, more fully, in the Bank's Ledgers and Private Ledgers, and from investigations by others rather than by Pitt himself. There is important material in *The Diaries and Correspondence of the Right Hon. George Rose . . .*, ed. the Rev. Lewis Vernon Harcourt, I (1860) and B.L. Add. Mss 42772–3, in the papers of Pitt's private secretary Joseph Smith, lately in the possession of Mr W.H. Saumarez Smith, and some in Pretyman's deposited at the Suffolk R.O. at Ipswich (Pretyman Mss) and in the Stanhope collection at Maidstone. Pitt's own papers contain references to expenditure and borrowing, particularly in P.R.O. 30/8/196–7, 201–3, 213–14, 219 Part 6. They, and Joseph Smith's, include purchases of books. A list of his library at Walmer, strewn about the rooms on his death, is in Pretyman Ms 562:21.

Information on health to 1801 is widespread, suggestive and in the last resort baffling. It will be discussed again for Chs. XVI and XXII below. I have been much indebted throughout this volume to an article by R. Guest Gornall MRCP, 'The Prime Minister's Health, William Pitt the Younger', in *The Practitioner*, 179 (1957), and to expert assistance in correspondence with Mr T.G.J. Brightmore FRCS. Pitt's doctor Farquhar wrote an account after his patient's death, which was published by Rosebery to accompany his article on *the Love Episode* in *The Monthly Review* which was then reprinted (see above); the full title in fact was *Letters Relating to the Love Episode of William Pitt together with an Account of his Health by his Physician Sir Walter Farquhar*. Some letters from Farquhar to Pitt are contained in P.R.O. 30/8/134, and there is much scattered material elsewhere among which one may mention in particular P.R.O. 30/8/203 for consumption of wine, the Saumarez Smith Mss for lists of medicines, B.L. Add. Ms 41852, B.L. Loan Ms 72 vol. 54, Pretyman Mss 435/42, 44 at Ipswich, Camden Ms U840 226/4, and references of varying significance in Stanhope, III and Appendix, *A.C.*, III, IV, *Life of Wilberforce*, II, *Diaries and Correspondence of Rose*, I, *P.R., 3rd ser.*, VI (for the summer of 1798), *The Diary of Joseph Farington*, ed. Kenneth Garlick and Angus Macintyre, III–IV (1979).

Pitt's interest in architecture – illustrated by a sketch of the library for Henry Thornton's house in Clapham, with which he is credited, in E.M. Forster's *Marianne Thornton . . .* (1956), but focusing on his patronage of Soane for alterations, actual and envisaged, to Holwood – is noticed in Dorothy Stroud's *Sir John Soane Architect* (1984) and in Howard Colvin's *A Biographical Dictionary of English Architects 1660–1840* (2nd edn., 1978). There are two letters from Soane to Pitt in P.R.O. 30/8/179; more interesting material is to be found at the Sir John Soane Museum in Lincoln's Inn Fields in London, in plans, designs and views for Holwood in drawer 2, sets 9 and 9A and 14/1, journals nos. 1 and 3, Ledgers B, C, D, and one document of 1807 in Private Correspondence. For the complementary area of landscape gardening, Humphrey Repton's memoirs in B.L. Add. Ms 62112 are useful (as they are for Pitt at home); and there is a financial 'memorandum' in the Saumarez Smith Mss. Holwood is mentioned in Repton's *Observations on the Theory and Practice of Landscape Gardening*, and there is a brief account of the house and grounds in Sidney Gammon, *The Story of Keston, in Kent* (1934). Pitt's occupations at Walmer, which were more extensive later, are covered more fully in Ch. XVI below; but one may note here some mentions in his correspondence – eg to Rose in B.L. Add. Ms 42772 and from Dundas in the Dacres Adams Mss formerly P.R.O. 30/58/2. The London and Kentish newspapers are helpful for his movements, which they followed assiduously in these years.

Material on the Minister's circle in the later nineties is, again, widely scattered.

But there is plenty to be found on Canning, very largely emanating from himself in his own papers and those of his friends as well as in the correspondence and diaries of others. Letters from him to Pitt fill P.R.O. 30/8/120; the Canning Mss in the Leeds City Archives Office holds his diary (Ms 29d), and relevant correspondence and papers include Mss 30–1 (for Pitt), 34a, 58, 62–7, 69, 76–7. Selections are printed in Josceline Bagot, *George Canning and his Friends*, I (1909). Dorothy Marshall, *The Rise of George Canning* (1938) is excellent, as is Wendy Hinde, *George Canning* (1973). Both cast light on Hawkesbury also, for whose youth see C.D. Yonge, *The Life and Administration of Robert Banks, Second Earl of Liverpool . . .*, I (1868) and Norman Gash, *Lord Liverpool* (1984). Gabrielle Festing, *John Hookham Frere and his Friends* (1889) conveys something of the atmosphere of the younger men in their regard for Pitt.

CHAPTER IV

Pitt's proposals for the Triple Assessment and his handling of the issue are treated at length in the unpublished theses of O'Brien and Cooper (Ch. I above), and more briefly in Cooper, 'William Pitt, Taxation, and the Needs of War' (*The Journal of British Studies*, XXI, no. 1). Stephen Dowell, *A History of Taxation and Taxes in England from the Earliest Times to the Present*, II (1884), William Kennedy, *English Taxation 1640–1799, An Essay on Policy and Opinion* (1913), with Arthur Hope-Jones, *Income Tax in the Napoleonic Wars* (1939) for an introduction to a sequel, are useful. The question of the real impact of taxation in this country, particularly as compared with France, falls more easily to Ch. IX below. The Parliamentary debates for the year, extensive on finance, are covered in *P.R.*, *3rd ser.*, IV–VII (1798–9), *The Senator*, XIX–XXI (nd), *P.H.*, XXXIII. *L.C.G. III*, III, Stanhope, III, Appendix, Buckingham (see Abbreviations), II, *H.M.C.*, *Dropmore*, III, Camden Ms U840 0190 A, show Pitt in action with the King and Ministers over the Voluntary Contribution. W.R. Ward, *The English Land Tax in the Eighteenth Century* (1953) gives the background for its sale, and P.R.O. 30/8/282 and the Dacres Adams Mss formerly P.R.O. 30/58/2 contain some of Pitt's papers on that subject. His approach to the Triple Assessment itself may be seen in P.R.O. 30/8/197, 273 (or 302), 282. *H.M.C.*, *Dropmore*, III, 382–4 contains his forecast of yields. Some letters from Rose to Pretyman in Pretyman Ms 435/44 are concerned with the problems of persuading the Commons and the public.

Jeremy Black, *The English Press in the Eighteenth Century* (1987) is a helpful survey of a wide period, and the same author writes on 'The Challenge of the Revolution and the British Press' in *The Press in the French Revolution: Studies on Voltaire and the Eighteenth Century*, ed. Harvey Chisick (1991). Other useful sources for a subject which attracts much attention for the wartime years are A. Aspinall, *Politics and the Press c. 1780–1850* (1949), *A History of The Times . . .*, I (1935), Ivon Asquith, 'Advertising and the Press in the Late Eighteenth and Early Nineteenth Century' (*The Review of English Studies*, XXII, no. 85), Ian R. Christie, 'British Newspapers in the Later Georgian Age, James Perry and The Morning Chronicle' and 'James Perry of the Morning Chronicle', in his *Myth and Reality in Late-Eighteenth Century British Politics and Other Papers* (1970). Donald Read, *Press and People 1790–1850, Opinion in Three English Cities* (1961) is one example of a concern with the provinces which is a fruitful field of study. Notices of some editors may be found in *The Annual Register*, *The Gentleman's Magazine*, *DNB*.

Light is thrown on Pitt's relationship with *The Anti-Jacobin* in his letters to Canning in Canning Ms 30 at Leeds; extracts from the journal are printed in *Poetry of the Anti-Jacobin*, ed. L. Rice-Oxley (1924), and there is material in Emily Lorraine de Monthuzin, *The Anti-Jacobins, 1798–1800, The Early Contributors to the Anti-Jacobin Review* (1989), which is concerned more largely with a successor to the original.

An extensive literature has been building up in the past thirty years on the nature and dimensions of loyalism and discontent. It will be followed more conveniently in the Note on Sources to Ch. X below, but one should mention here some publications on measures against disaffection, and their reception in the law courts. The management of Government's intelligence is discussed in Kenneth Ellis, *The Post Office in the Eighteenth Century* (1958), R.R. Nelson, *The Home Office, 1782–1801* (1969), Clive Emsley, 'The Home Office and its sources of information and investigation 1791–1801' (*E.H.R.* (Abbreviations), no. CCCLXII), Roger Wells, *Insurrection* (Chapter I above), Elizabeth Sparrow, 'The Alien Office, 1792–1806' (Ch. II above), with the Irish dimension in Marianne Elliott, *Partners in Revolution* (Ch. I) and Stanley H. Palmer, *Police and Protest in England and Ireland, 1780–1850* (1988), and sidelights in W.J. Fitzpatrick, *Secret Service under Pitt* (2nd edn., 1892). J.R. Western, 'The Volunteer Movement as an Anti-Revolutionary Force, 1793–1801' (*E.H.R.*, LXXI, no. 4) is no less useful for the later than for the earlier years. Leon Radzinowicz, *A History of English Criminal Law and its Administration from 1750* (4 vols., 1948–68) is the prime general account. F.K. Prochaska looks into 'English State Trials in the 1790s: A Case Study' (*The Journal of British Studies*, XIII, no. 1); Clive Emsley works on a wide canvas in 'Repression, 'terror', and the rule of law in England during the decade of the French Revolution' (*E.H.R.*, C, no. 397) and 'An Aspect of Pitt's 'Terror': prosecutions for sedition during the 1790s' (*Social History*, 6, no. 2); Douglas Hay brings a different emphasis to bear in 'Prosecution and power: malicious prosecution in the English courts, 1750–1850' (*Policing and Prosecution in Britain, 1750–1850*, ed. Douglas Hay and Francis Snyder (1989)). State trials are published in *A Complete Collection . . .*, compiled by T.B. Howell and T.J. Howell . . ., XV–XVII (1819–20).

Plans against invasion may be found in P.R.O., W.O. 56–62, 64–71, particularly in 64 and 70. Pitt's interest in them emerges from P.R.O. 30/8/245. An account of the land forces, regular and auxiliary, is given in Fortescue, IV-Part II (Ch. I above), which is corrected and supplemented in Piers Mackesy, *Statesmen at War: The Strategy of Overthrow 1798–1799* (1974), J.R. Western, 'The Recruitment of the Land Forces in Great Britain, 1793–99' (Ph.D. thesis, University of Edinburgh, 1953) and *The English Militia in the Eighteenth Century, The Story of a Political Issue 1660–1832* (1965). Linda Colley, in *Britons, Forging the Nation 1707–1837* (1992), ch. 7 and Appendix 3, examines the social contexts and regional responses, as does J.E. Cookson in 'The English Volunteer Movements of the French Wars, 1793–1815' (*H.J.* (Abbreviations), 32, no. 4) and some separate studies of local corps. Christopher Oprey is valuable on 'Schemes for the Reform of Naval Recruitment, 1793–1815' (M.A. thesis, University of Liverpool, 1961). *Correspondence of Cornwallis*, II (Ch. I above) and *Private Papers of Spencer*, II (ibid) throw light on measures of defence, the latter not least for his colleague Dundas's views, which also emerge vigorously in letters to Pitt in P.R.O. 30/8/157 and B.L. Add. Ms 40102, and to Windham in B.L. Add. Ms 37877. Difficulties over the militia and volunteers may be followed in B.L. Add. Mss 40101–2, *H.M.C., Dropmore*, IV, Buckingham, II.

The Younger Pitt

P.H., XXXIII is the best single source for Tierney's speech which led to Pitt's challenge and the duel on Putney Heath. Sir George Clark, *War and Society in the Seventeenth Century* (1958) and J.C.D. Clark, *English Society 1688–1832* . . . (1985) are among the many who have considered the institution of duelling itself.

CHAPTER V

The search for a Quadruple Alliance or a substitute is followed in *The Cambridge History of British Foreign Policy*, I (Ch. II above), John M. Sherwig, 'Lord Grenville's Plan for a Concert of Europe, 1797–1799' (*The Journal of Modern History*, XXXIV, no. 3), E.D. Adams, *The Influence of William Grenville on Pitt's Foreign Policy*, Michael Duffy, 'Pitt, Grenville, and the Control of British Foreign Policy', Jupp, *Lord Grenville* (all Ch. II). Karl F. Helleiner, *The Imperial Loans, A Study in Financial and Diplomatic History* (1965) and John M. Sherwig, *Guineas and Gunpowder, British Foreign Aid in the Wars with France* (1969), examine the question of the Austrian Loan, which is related in further detail to its diplomatic setting in Duffy's admirable 'British War Policy, The Austrian Alliance' (Ch. II above). See also Karl A. Roider, *Baron Thugut and Austria's Response to the French Revolution* (1987). Andrei Lobanov-Rostovsky, *Russia and Europe, 1789–1825* (1947), T. Naff, 'Ottoman Diplomacy and the Great European Powers 1797–1802' (Ph.D. thesis, University of London, 1960) are helpful for their subjects which are linked in one aspect in Norman E. Saul, *Russia in the Mediterranean 1797–1807* (1970).

The link is further important for the revival of a British naval presence on the southern flank of Europe, discussed by Piers Mackesy in *Statesmen at War* (Ch. IV above) and, from its own point of coverage, Edward Ingram's *Commitment to Empire: Prophecies of the Great Game in Asia 1797–1800* (1981). Ingram has also assembled some relevant articles in *In Defence of India, Great Britain in the Middle East 1775–1842* (1984). Other sources on that extensive theme will be found for Chs. XI & XII, XIII below. Nelson's fortunes in the summer of 1798, discussed to exhaustion in naval histories and biographies, are placed in a context by A.B. Rodger in *The War of the Second Coalition 1798–1801, A Strategic Commentary* (1964). Fortescue's treatment of operations in the Caribbean, in his *History of the British Army*, IV-Part I (1906), is superseded by Michael Duffy, *Soldiers, Sugar, and Seapower, The British Expeditions to the West Indies and the War against Revolutionary France* (1987). The secular issue for British strategy of the balance, or choice, between seapower and a direct contribution to Continental warfare, treated in the classic works of Mahan, *The Influence of Sea Power upon the French Revolution and Empire* (2 vols., 1892) and Admiral Sir Herbert Richmond, *Statesmen and Sea Power* (1946), has been given new approaches in recent years in such studies as Paul M. Kennedy's *The Rise and Fall of British Naval Mastery* (1976) and Nicholas A.M. Rodger, 'The Continental Commitment in the Eighteenth Century' in *War, Strategy and International Politics, Essays in honour of Sir Michael Howard*, ed. Lawrence Freedman . . . (1992). Some elements of seapower itself are underlined in Michael Duffy, 'The Establishment of the Western Squadron as the Linchpin of British Naval Strategy' in his edition of *Parameters of British Naval Power* (1992) and Daniel A. Baugh, 'Maritime Strength and Atlantic Commerce' in *An Imperial State at War, Britain from 1689 to 1815*, ed. Lawrence Stone (1994). We await the forthcoming volumes of a new comprehensive naval history of Britain by Rodger; meanwhile G.J. Marcus, *A Naval History of England*, 2 (1971) is a serviceable account. Some older narratives are listed in my II, 661.

There are useful publications of European documents in A. von Vivenot and H.R. Zeissberg, *Quellen zur Geschichte der deutschen Kaiserpolitik Österreichs während der französischen Revolutions-Kriege* (5 vols., 1873–90), *Arkhiv Kniazia Vorontsova* . . ., ed. P.I. Bartenev (40 vols., 1870–95), *Correspondance de Napoléon Ier: publiée par Ordre de l'empereur Napoléon III* (32 vols., 1858–70). For the texts of treaties see *The Consolidated Treaty Series*, 54, ed. Clive Parry (1969). Sources for Britain include *L.C.G. III*, III, *H.M.C., Dropmore*, IV, *Private Papers of Spencer*, II (Ch. I above) and IV, ed. Rear Admiral H.W. Richmond (1924), *Diary of Windham* (Ch. I above), and for the scene as watched by Mornington in India *The Despatches, Minutes, and Correspondence of the Marquess Wellesley, K.G., during his Administration in India*, ed. M. Martin, I (1836).

Relevant Foreign Office papers are P.R.O., F.O. 5, series II/22 (United States), 7/51–3 (Austria), 14/1 (Brunswick), 63/27–9 (Portugal), 64/47–51 (Prussia), 65/39–41 (Russia), 70/11 (The Two Sicilies), 78/19–20 (Turkey), 81/13 (Venice). There is intelligence on French plans and naval movements in F.O. 28/18 (Genoa), 42/3 (Ionian Islands), 79/16 (Tuscany). P.R.O., W.O. 1/219–20 contain despatches from the British force in Portugal. Papers for Holland and Switzerland are listed for Chs. VII–VIII below. Pitt's papers in P.R.O. 30/8 are disappointing; the Dacres Adams Mss formerly P.R.O. 30/58/2 have letters from Portland and from Canning in October 1798. Dundas's voluminous correspondence for the period is covered expertly in Ingram's *Commitment to Empire* (above); his letters to his Under Secretary William Huskisson in B.L. Add. Ms 38735 also reveal his state of mind. Grenville's unpublished papers add marginally to *H.M.C., Dropmore* and the F.O. files: in B.L. Add. Mss 59023, 59048, 59057 (for Portugal), 59031, 59038–9 (Naples), 59044, 59076–7 (Russia), 59049 (United States), 59081 (Turkey). 59306 has his surviving list of Cabinet Minutes and associated memoranda. His subordinate Canning's mss at Leeds are occasionally helpful (29d, 30, 67). There is a letter from Pitt to Windham in September 1798 in B.L. Add. Ms 37844; two to Rose indicating the Minister's state of mind in August and early September, in B.L. Add. Ms 42772, and others from Rose to Pretyman at that time in Pretyman Ms 435/44. The Bishop's account of Downing Street on receipt of the news from Nelson at the Nile is also to be found loc. cit. Stanhope Ms U1590 S5 048 has a letter to Pitt from Mornington on the victory's possible effect.

CHAPTER VI

Lecky's great *History of Ireland in the Eighteenth Century*, III–V (1892 edn.) for long towered over the scene for Ireland. Much work has been done since, for which David Dixon, *New Foundations: Ireland, 1660–1800* (1987) is a good introduction. In the multi-volume *New History of Ireland* the relevant volume is IV, ed. T.W. Moody and W.E. Vaughan (1986), in which L.M. Cullen contributes to the economic treatment and R.B. McDowell to the political. Both have published valuable studies: the former *An Economic History of Ireland since 1660* (1972), the latter *Irish Public Opinion 1750–1800* (1944) and *Ireland in the Age of Imperialism and Reform 1760–1801* (1979). See also, more recently, *Nationalism and Popular Protest in Ireland*, ed. C.H.E. Philpin (1987), and *Cultures et pratiques politiques en France et en Irelande, XVII–XVIII siècle* . . ., ed. Louis M. Cullen and Louis Bergeron (1991). E.M. Johnston, *Great Britain and Ireland 1760–1800* (1963) is helpful on the administrative and political structure. Marianne Elliott, Stanley H. Palmer and also Roger Wells (Chs. I, IV above) are required reading for the final years of the century; Thomas Pakenham, *The Year of Liberty, The Story of the Great Irish Rebellion of 1798* (1969) tells the story of their centrepiece, and Desbrière (Ch. I above) covers the scene from France. G.C. Bolton examines *The Passing of the Irish Act of Union* (1966).

Among biographies, A.W. Malcolmson provides an important study of the influential *John Foster, The Politics of the Anglo–Irish Ascendancy* (1978). Jupp's life of *Lord Grenville* (Ch. II above) is very useful, and so is H.M. Hyde's *The Rise of Castlereagh* (1933). Primary published sources include Cornwallis' *Correspondence* (Ch. I above), *The Correspondence of the Right Hon. John Beresford, . . .ed. the Right Hon. William Beresford*, II (1854), *Memoirs and Correspondence of Viscount Castlereagh, Second Marquess of Londonderry, edited by his Brother, Charles Vane, Third Marquess of Londonderry*, I–IV (1848–9), *L.C.G. III*, III, *H.M.C., Dropmore*, IV–V, Buckingham, II, *A.C.*, II, *Life and Letters of Sir Gilbert Elliot, First Earl of Minto, from 1751 to 1806, ed. by the Countess of Minto*, II (1874). Stanhope, II, Appendix, Ashbourne (Ch. III above), J. Holland Rose, *Pitt and Napoleon* (Ch. II above), contain significant letters and papers; *Correspondence of the Prince of Wales* (Ch. II above), IV (1967), those on the offer of himself for Lord Lieutenant.

The debates in Dublin are covered in *Reports of Debates in the House of Commons in Ireland* [1796–1800] (1797–1800); those at Westminster in *P.R., 3rd ser.*, VII–IX, XI (1799–1801), *The Senator*, XXI–XXIV (nd), *P.H.*, XXXIV–XXXV (1819). Maurice Hastings, *Parliament House . . .* (1950) alludes to the physical alterations introduced to the British House of Commons by the Union, described more fully in Orlo Cyprian Williams, 'The Topography of the Old House of Commons' (unpublished; a copy is held by the Department of the Environment).

Unpublished material abounds, on either side of the Irish Sea: on this side in the Home Office files in P.R.O., H.O. 100/66–100, 123/4–5, 19–21, augmented by Pitt's papers in P.R.O. 30/8/320–30 and the Dacres Adams Mss formerly P.R.O. 30/58/2–3, and by Camden's in Camden Mss U840 C98, 102, 106, 112, 0107–0110, 0153–0209. Of interest also are B.L. Add. Mss 59254–5 (Grenville), 33103–6, 119 (Thomas Pelham), 34455 (Auckland), 37844–5, 37847 (Windham), Canning Ms 29d, Pretyman Ms 435/44.

CHAPTERS VII & VIII

The material on negotiations for a new Coalition is covered largely in the Notes on Sources for Ch. V above, to which may be added for background to the later phase T.C.W. Blanning, *The Origins of the French Revolutionary Wars* (1986), ch. 6, and Norman Frank Richards, 'British Policy and the Problem of Monarchy in France, 1789–1802' (Ph.D. thesis, University of London, 1954). Texts of treaties are taken from *The Consolidated Treaty Series*, 54 (Ch. V above). D.C. Elliot, 'The Grenville Mission to Berlin, 1799' (*The Huntington Library Quarterly*, XVIII) is helpful for a critical year, and of the works cited earlier Duffy's thesis on the Austrian alliance and Mackesy's *Statesmen at War* are essential reading for policy in these Chs. A useful balance for Mackesy is provided by Paul W. Schroeder in 'The Collapse of the Second Coalition' (*The Journal of Modern History*, 59, no. 2). Maurice Hutt, 2 (Ch. II above), Wynne Lewis, *The Second Vendée, The Continuity of the Counter-Revolution in the Department of the Gard, 1789–1815* (1978), Jacques Godechot, *The Counter-Revolution, Doctrine and Action 1789–1804* (transl. 1972), are authorities for France; Simon Schama, *Patriots and Liberators, Revolution in the Netherlands 1780–1873* (1977) sets the scene in the other region from which much was expected in 1799. Fortescue, IV-Part II (Ch. I above) disparages the British Government's handling of the Dutch expedition; Alfred H. Burne, *The Noble Duke of York* (ibid), and *Lieutenant-General Sir Ralph Abercromby, 1793–1801, A Memoir by his Son, James, Lord Dunfermline* (1861) argue the case for the British commanders. Richard Saxby, 'The Blockade of Brest in the Revolutionary War' (*The Mariner's Mirror*, 78, no. 1) supplements works cited in Ch. V above. Parliamentary debates are covered in Ch. VI above, with the addition of *P.R., 3rd ser.*, X.

Primary published sources for the Continent include von Vivenot and Zeissberg, and *Arkhiv Vorontsova* (both Ch. V above), and Hermann Hüffer, *Quellen zur Geschichte der Zeitalters der französischen Revolution*, I (1900). See also *The Paget Papers: Diplomatic and Other Correspondence of . . . Sir Arthur Paget, 1794–1807*, ed. Sir Augustus B. Paget, I (1896), for Bavaria, and *The Life and Letters of Sir Gilbert Elliot*, III (Ch. VI above) for Austria. Wickham's *Correspondence*, II (Ch. II above) sheds light on his overt as well as his covert diplomatic activities. *H.M.C., Dropmore*, IV–V – supplemented by Holland Rose, *Pitt and Napoleon* (Ch. II above) – contain material of central interest; *Diary of Windham, Private Papers of Spencer*, II (Ch. I above), III, ed. Rear Admiral H.W. Richmond (1923), *L.C.G. III*, III, may also be consulted.

Manuscript material is voluminous. P.R.O., W.O. 1/179–82, 6/20,25 are concerned with the Dutch expedition, 1/408 with the missions of Malcolm and of Maitland to Flanders, 1/411 with Home Popham's to Russia. Foreign Office files are in P.R.O., F.O. 5, Series II/22, 25A (United States of America), 7/53–7 (Austria), 9/17–18 (Bavaria), 14/1 (Brunswick), 33/17–19 (Hamburg), 37/59, 38/4 (Holland and Flanders, Frontiers of Holland), 64/52–5 (Prussia), 65/40–5 (Russia), 70/11–12 (The Two Sicilies), 73/27 (Sweden), 74/22–8 (Switzerland), 82/2 (Württemberg).

The most useful volumes in Pitt's papers are P.R.O. 30/8/12 (Hester Countess of Chatham), 101 (Countess of Chatham), 102 (Sir Charles Grey), 106 (York), 119 (Camden), 122 (Chatham), 140 (Grenville), 147 (Huskisson), 160 (Admiral Mitchell), 191 (Vorontsov), 197 (memoranda), 240, 243a (army), 335 (France), 336 (Holland), 339 (Empire and Austria); and the Dacres Adams Mss formerly P.R.O. 30/58/2 contain letters of interest from Windham, Chatham, and particularly Grenville. Stanhope Ms U1590 S5 09/53 in the Centre for Kentish Studies has a memorandum in Pitt's hand on a landing at Brest. Of other collections, Spencer's papers contain a series of letters from Thomas Grenville in Berlin (B.L. Add. Ms temporary Althorp G33), and G208–13 supplement his published private Admiralty correspondence. There is some material in Dundas's papers in B.L. Add. Mss 40101–2 and S.R.O., Melville Castle Mss GD 51/1/529, 548; in Huskisson's, B.L. Add. Mss 38735, 38759, 38764; and Windham's, B.L. Add. Mss 37844, 37846, 37877–8. Canning Ms 63 has Grenville's interesting letter on the question of the Foreign Secretary's going in person to Holland. Grenville's own private correspondence is published extensively in *H.M.C., Dropmore*, IV; but further material from his voluminous papers (many duplicating the F.O. volumes) may be found particularly in B.L. Add. Mss 59028–9, 59033, 59045, 59052, 59061, 59076–7, 59306 (Cabinet Minutes). There is more in his correspondence with his brother Thomas in the Stowe Mss at the Huntington Library in California; but this has been combed and noted so fully by Mackesy (Ch. I above) that it would be otiose to particularise here. Little of importance for the period can be gleaned from Thomas's papers in B.L.; but see Add. Mss 41852, 41854–5.

CHAPTERS IX & X

The theses of Patrick O'Brien and Richard Cooper (Ch. I above) are prime sources for Ch. IX. See also O'Brien, 'The Political Economy of British Taxation, 1660–1815' (*Ec.H.R.* (Abbreviations), XLI, no. 1), O'Brien and Peter Mathias, 'Taxation in Britain and France, 1715–1810 . . .' (*The Journal of Economic History*, 5, no. 3), and Cooper, 'William Pitt, Taxation, and the Needs of War' (Ch. IV above); also Dowell, Kennedy, and for the Land Tax W.R. Ward (Ch. IV), and for the background of central management J.E.D. Binney, *British Public Finance and Administration 1774–1792* (1958). Arthur Hope-Jones, *Income Tax in the Napoleonic Wars* (Ch. IV above) greatly advanced knowledge of the subject, and A. Farnsworth, *Addington, Author of the Modern Income Tax* (1951) – a claim discussed in Ch. XIX below – is useful here on Pitt's abortive second bill of April 1800. Henry Beeke, *Observations on the Produce of the Income Tax* (1799, enlarged edn. 1800) supplies an interesting contemporary view of early yields, whose figures may be obtained from B.R. Mitchell and Phyllis Deane, *Abstract of British Historical Statistics* (1962; enlarged edn. 1988) with comment on them in Phyllis Deane and W.A. Cole, *British Economic Growth 1688–1959, Trends and Structure* (1962), Appendix II. Parliamentary debates are important, in particular *P.R., 3rd ser.*, VII, X, XII, XV (1799–1801), *P.H.*, XXXIV. Pitt's papers in P.R.O. 30/8 contain much material: in 136 (Fordyce), 170 (Mitford), 183 (Samuel Thornton), 196–7, 235, and, within the series of files on finance 272–305, particularly 273–4, 278–82, 304. P.R.O. 30/8/341 includes a misdated memorandum; Dacres Adams Mss formerly P.R.O. 30/58/8, one undated on the redemption of the Land Tax. The Treasury Board Minutes for the period occupy P.R.O., T 29/73–7. Some remarks of interest occur in Pretyman Mss 435/44, 45, B.L. Add. Ms 42772 (Rose), B.L. Loan Ms 72 vol. 54 (Hawkesbury), the published diaries of Rose, I (Ch. III above), and of Charles Abbot, *The Diary and Correspondence of Charles Abbot, Lord Colchester, ed. by his Son, Charles, Lord Colchester* (1861), I.

Selected publications on loans and credit and monetary policy are mentioned in the Note on Sources for Ch. I. The rest of Pitt's files P.R.O. 30/8/272–305 are necessary to gauge his knowledge of the state of duties and stamps, and 275 contains papers on the National Debt. E.L. Hargreaves, *The National Debt* (1930) remains useful on that subject, as indeed does J.J. Grellier, *The History of the National Debt, from the Revolution of 1688 to the Beginning of the Year 1800 . . .* (1810). The same author's *The Terms of All the Loans which have been Raised for the Public Service during the Last Fifty Years* (1799), and William Newmarch, *On the Loans Raised by Mr. Pitt during the First French War, 1793–1801 . . .* (1855) are valuable.

Dearth, disaffection, and the connexions between them attract much attention. The complexities of the problems are observed in R.B. Outhwaite, *Dearth, Public Policy and Social Disturbance in England, 1550–1800* (1991). Bearing them in mind, and while I cannot agree with the balance of Roger Wells's political conclusions in his study of *Insurrection* (Ch. I above), his *Wretched Faces, Famine in Wartime England 1793–1801* (1988) has furnished a basis on which to discuss the dimensions of shortage and of the discontent in the years around the turn of the century. Some earlier works on agricultural matters are noticed in my II, Notes for Ch. XII, to which should be added the Cambridge *Agrarian History of England and Wales*, vol. 6, *1750–1850*, ed. G.E. Mingay (1989). Much has been written on the question of unrest since E.P. Thompson published the first edition of *The Making of the English Working Class* in 1963. Some of it may be found in the Notes on Sources for my II, Chs. IV & V; and I would repeat or add here, highly selectively from a substantial literature, John Stevenson, *Popular Disturbances in England, 1700–1870* (1979) and, more specifically, in ch. 3 of *Britain and the French Revolution, 1789–1815* (Ch. II above), John Bohstedt, *Riots and Community Politics in England and Wales 1790–1810* (1983), Ian Gilmour, *Riot, Risings and Revolution, Governance and Violence in Eighteenth-Century England* (1992). Local and regional attitudes and responses are of course of central importance, and have been increasingly investigated – examples can be found through bibliographies; a wide introductory survey is available in A. Charlesworth, *An Atlas of Rural Protest in Britain, 1548–1900* (1982); and three urban studies may serve as illustrations, J. Ann Hone, *For the Cause of Truth, Radicalism in London 1796–1821* (1982), John Money, *Experience and Identity, Birmingham and the West Midlands 1760–1800* (1977), C.B. Jewson, *The Jacobin City, A Portrait of Norwich in its Relation to the French Revolution 1788–1802* (1978). All three embrace broad fronts in the debate between the respective cases for the strengths and influences of loyalism and radicalism; the latter ranging from hostility to the Government, through movements for political and social reform, to revolutionary feelings and activities. Clear opposing conclusions are reached by Roger Wells in *Insurrection* (above) and Ian R. Christie in *Stress and Stability in Late Eighteenth-Century Britain, Reflections on the British Avoidance of Revolution* (1984); and see also studies of policing and of the Courts cited in Ch. IV above. But the debate moves on. Books and articles by Emsley and by Cookson (Ch. IV above), Linda Colley, *Britons, Forging the Nation 1707–1837* (ibid), take their place with eg R.R. Dozier, *For King, Country and Constitution: The English Loyalists and the French Revolution* (1983), Robert Hole (as one example of the denominational factor), *Pulpits, Politics and Public Order in England, 1760–1832* (1989), and chronologically more narrowly in ch. 1 of *The French Revolution and British Popular Politics*, ed. Mark Philp (1991), H.T. Dickinson, 'Popular Conservatism and Militant Loyalism, 1789–1815' in his edited *Britain and the French Revolution* (above), David Eastwood in 'Patriotism and the English State in the 1790s' (*The French Revolution and British Popular Politics*, above). J.C.D. Clark, *English Society, 1688–1832, Ideology, Social Structure and Political Practice during the Ancien Regime* (1985) is a central document in the rediscovery of the confessional state. Mark Philp, 'The Fragmented Ideology of Reform', together with Eastwood and with John Dinwiddy, 'Interpretations of Anti-Jacobinism' (all in Philp's edited volume, above) bring a note of scepticism to balance the more enthusiastic advocates for the effects of traditionalist teachings. In a different framework, C.R. Dobson, *Masters and Journeymen, a prehistory of industrial relations, 1717–1800* (1980), John Rule, *The Experience of Labour in Eighteenth-Century History* (1981), John V. Orth, *Combination and Conspiracy: A Legal History of Trade Unionism, 1721–1906* (1991) are important. David Eastwood, *Governing Rural England, Tradition and Transformation in Local Government 1780–1840* (1994) demonstrates from the point of vantage of the main instruments of social order the role of applying poor and price laws and conventions; themes treated in works, cited in the context of the dearth of 1795 but for the most part equally applicable here, in my II, Note on Sources to Ch. XII. The ever continuing discussion among economic historians, economists and econometrists over the standard of living of the population is best followed in the latest current articles and reviews in the appropriate journals.

Parliamentary proceedings are highly important for policies in Ch. X. *P.R., 3rd ser.*, VIII–XV may be compared with *The Senator*, XXIII–XXVI (nd), the last particularly for the Combination Acts which *P.H.*, XXXIV–XXXV ignore. *H.C.J.*,

54–6 and *H.L.J.*, XLII (Abbreviations) are useful for the passage of legislation, and *Sessional Papers of the House of Commons in the Eighteenth Century*, ed. Sheila Lambert, vols. 131, 121 (1975) are of great interest.

Correspondence and diaries for this Ch. include the *Life* of Wilberforce (Ch. I above), III, his *Private Papers*, ed. A.M. Wilberforce (1897), *A.C.*, IV, *H.M.C.*, *Dropmore*, VI, *H.M.C.*, *Kenyon*, *Diary and Correspondence of Colchester*, I (above). Manuscript material is plentiful. In Pitt's papers, P.R.O. 30/8/291 (corn), 308 (relief of the poor) are particularly helpful, and 148 (journeymen), 152 (Lord Liverpool), 177 (Lord Sheffield), 178 (Sir John Sinclair), 193 (Arthur Young) convey specimens of opinions and advice, as do the Dacres Adams Mss formerly P.R.O. 30/58/3 for Grenville. This last also has a letter from Hawkesbury on the London Bread Company, on which see also Liverpool's thoughts on economic principles in B.L. Add. Ms 38311. Further sources are B.L. Add. Ms 42772, Pretyman Ms 435/44 (Rose and Pretyman), Harrowby Mss vol. XXXIV at Sandon Hall in Staffordshire (Pitt on importation of corn), P.R.O., P.C. 2/153, B.T. 5/11–12, H.O. 42/48–56.

CHAPTERS XI & XII

The locus classicus for the study of British strategy after the failure of the expedition to Holland in 1799 is Piers Mackesy's *War Without Victory, The Downfall of Pitt 1799–1802* (1984); taking over chronologically from its predecessor (Ch. I above), overtaking A.B. Rodger (Ch. V above) for the same years, and superseding Fortescue's comments in his IV-Part I (ibid), though this last remains important for detail. Biographical studies for commanders include Lord Dunfermline's of his father Abercromby (Chs. VII & VIII above) and Walter Frewin Lord, *Sir Thomas Maitland* (1897); Home Popham's contribution in Russia is followed in Hugh Popham, *A Damned Cunning Fellow* . . . (1991); Mahan (Ch. V above), I, ch. X remains well worth reading on Sidney Smith in the Mediterranean. For works on the navy see the Notes to Chs. V, VII & VIII, to which may be added R.C. Anderson, *Naval Wars in the Baltic During the Sailing-Ship Epoch, 1522–1850* (1910) and *Naval Wars in the Levant, 1559–1833* (1952). Duffy's *Soldiers, Sugar, and Seapower* (Ch. V) deals succinctly with the war's closing phase in Central American waters; C. Northcote Parkinson considers the *War in the Eastern Seas, 1793–1815* (1954).

Parliamentary debates on Bonaparte's peace message of December 1799 may be followed in *P.R., 3rd ser.*, X, *The Senator*, XXIV, *P.H.*, XXXIV, the last being the most comprehensive. Coverage for the period is as in the Note to Chs. IX & X.

For the place of counter-revolution in France see Chs. VII & VIII above. For policy in general, add to *The Cambridge History of British Foreign Policy*, I (Ch. II), Jupp, *Lord Grenville* (ibid), Sherwig, *Guineas and Gunpowder*, Duffy, 'British War Policy', Roidier, *Baron Thugut* (all Ch. V); H.M. Bowman, *Preliminary Stages of the Peace of Amiens* . . . *November 1799–March 1801* (1899); D. Gregory, *Minorca, The Illusory Prize: A History of the British Occupancy* . . . *between 1708 and 1802* (1990); Guy Stanton Ford, *Hanover and Prussia 1795–1803, A Study in Neutrality* (1903); Hugh Ragsdale, *Detente in the Napoleonic Era, Bonaparte and the Russians* (1980), Lobanov-Rostovsky, *Russia and Europe* (Ch. V), Ole Feldbaeck, *Denmark and the Armed Neutrality, 1800–1* (1980), the same author on 'The Foreign Policy of Paul I: An Interpretation' (*Jarbücher für Geschichte Osteuropas*, IV, pt. 2), Roderick E. McGrew, *Paul I of Russia, 1754–1801* (1992), Saul, *Russia in the Mediterranean* (Ch. V), M.S.

Anderson, *The Eastern Question 1774–1923, A Study in International Relations* (1966), Naff, 'Ottoman Diplomacy and the Great European Powers, 1797–1802' (Ch. V), T. Stanford Shaw, *Between New and Old, The Ottoman Empire under Selim III* (1971), Schroeder, 'The Collapse of the Second Coalition' (Ch. VIII above).

The question of Egypt has attracted increasing attention. Its ramifications for British policy in Asia will be noticed in that for Ch. XIII below. But one should mention here François Charles-Roux, *L'Angleterre et l'expédition française en Égypte* (2 vols., 1925), as an introduction to Ingram's important study *Commitment to Empire* (Ch. V). The biographies of Dundas by Cyril Matheson, *The Life of Henry Dundas, First Viscount Melville, 1742–1811* (1933) and Holden Furber, *Henry Dundas, First Viscount Melville, 1742–1811* (1931) are naturally relevant; and see further J. Holland Rose, 'The Political Reactions to Bonaparte's Eastern Expedition' (*E.H.R.*, XLIV, no. 1), Edward B. Jones, 'Henry Dundas, India, and British Reactions to Bonaparte's Invasion of Egypt, 1798–1801' (*Proceedings of the South Carolina Historical Association*, 1973).

Documents bearing on strategy are published in *Private Papers of Spencer*, IV (Ch. V above), *The Keith Papers, Selected from the Letters and Papers of Admiral the Viscount Keith*, II, ed. Christopher Lloyd (1950), *The Dispatches and Letters of Vice-Admiral Lord Nelson*, III, ed. Sir Nicholas Harris Nicolas (1846), Sir John Barrow, *Life and Correspondence of Sir William Sidney Smith*, II (1848), *The Diary of Sir John Moore*, I, ed. J.F. Maurice (1904). *L.C.G. III*, III, and two additional letters published by W.B. Hamilton in 'Some Letters of George III' (*The South Atlantic Quarterly*, LXVIII, no. 3), illustrate the King's fast-growing unease; and see also *The Diaries of Sylvester Douglas Lord Glenbervie*, I, ed. F. Bickley (1928). For diplomacy see the Note to Chs. VII & VIII above. Sir Francis Piggott and W.T. Omond, *Documentary History of the Armed Neutralities of 1780 and 1800* (1919) is helpful.

Despatches are contained in P.R.O., F.O. 7/57–62 (Austria), 9/18–21 (Bavaria), 22/35–9, 97/118 (Denmark), 27/54–6 (France, 55 being for Otto), 31/10–11 (German States), 33/19–21, 97/241–2 (Hamburg), 38/5 (Frontiers of Holland), 42/3–4 (Ionian Islands), 43/3–4 (Italian States and Rome), 49/2 (Malta), 63/31–5 (Portugal), 64/55–60 (Prussia), 65/44–7 (Russia), 67/28–9 (Sardinia), 68/13–14 (Saxony), 70/12–15 (The Two Sicilies), 72/46 (Spain), 73/27–8, 97/399 (Sweden), 74/25–35 (Switzerland), 78/21–30 (Turkey), 79/17–18 (Tuscany), 81/13 (Venice), 82/2 (Württemberg). P.R.O., W.O. 6/21 includes instructions for expeditions, and 6/55 orders to Minorca. P.R.O., Adm. 2/139–40 are equally relevant, and the Board's Minutes are in Adm. 3/123–5. Pitt's files hold correspondence and papers in P.R.O. 30/8/101 (Chatham), 119 (Camden), 120 (Canning), 140 (Grenville), 157 (Dundas), 195–7, 243 (memorandum by Dundas), 339; and there is further material in the Dacres Adams Mss formerly P.R.O. 30/58/3 and 8. Within a range of scattered sources, Grenville's unpublished papers in B.L. under countries and correspondents, and in Add. Ms 59306 for Cabinet Minutes, again complement *H.M.C., Dropmore*, VI; there are papers for Dundas in B.L. Add. Mss 40101–2, John Rylands Library Manchester Eng. Ms 907, S.R.O., Melville Castle Mss GD 51/1/725/1 (as well as duplicated papers widely spread among the recipients' collections); for Spencer in B.L. Add. Mss temporary Althorp G38–40; for Huskisson in B.L. Add. Mss 38736, 38759; for Canning in Canning Mss 29d, 30; for Rose in Pretyman Ms 435/44; for Windham in B.L. Add. Ms 37924, and in 37844–6, 37878–9.

CHAPTER XIII

Ministers' retrospectives on the Government's wartime achievement are given in Ch. XVII below. George Rose's defence of its economic and financial performance, *A Brief Examination into the Increase of the Revenue, Commerce, and Manufactures of Great Britain from 1792 to 1799*, was published in the latter year, to run quickly into succeeding edns. I have found the following of particular help amid a range of publications in past decades: E.R. Wrigley and R.S. Schofield, *The Population History of England 1541–1871* . . . (1981), M.W. Flinn, *Scottish Population History from the 17th Century to the 1930s* (1977), *Land, Labour and Population in the Industrial Revolution*, ed. E.L. Jones and G.E. Mingay (1967), particularly for A.H. John's ch. on 'Farming in Wartime: 1793–1815'; Judith Blow Williams, *British Commercial Policy and Trade Expansion, 1750–1850* (1972), Ralph Davis, *The Industrial Revolution and British Overseas Trade* (1979); N.F.R. Crafts, *British Economic Growth during the Industrial Revolution* (1985) – including some significant corrections to Mitchell and Deane's tables (see Ch. IX above) and following a series of articles –, Phyllis Deane, 'War and Industrialisation' in *War and Economic Development, Essays in Memory of David Joslin*, ed. J.M. Winter (1975), W.A. Cole, 'Economic Growth Revisited' (*Explorations in Economic History*, 10, no. 4); A.D. Gayer, W.W. Rostow and A.J. Schwartz, *The Growth and Fluctuation of the British Economy, 1790–1850* (2 vols., 1953), T.S. Ashton, *Economic Fluctuations in England 1700–1800* (1959), Julian Hoppit, 'Financial Crises in Eighteenth-Century England' (*Ec.H.R.*, Second Series, XXXIX, no. 1) and *Risk and Failure in English Business 1700–1800* (1987), P.H. Duffy, *Bankruptcy and Insolvency in London during the Industrial Revolution* (1985); J.L. Anderson, 'Aspects of the Effect on the British Economy of the Wars against France, 1793–1815' (*Australian Economic History Review*, XII, no. 1), Glenn Hueckel, 'War and the British Economy, 1793–1815: A General Equilibrium Analysis' (*Explorations in Economic History*, 10, no. 4), François Crouzet, 'The Impact of the French Wars on the British Economy' in *Britain and the French Revolution*, ed. Dickinson (Ch. II above) and *Britain Ascendant: Comparative Studies in Franco–British Economic History* (1990), Patrick Karl O'Brien, 'The Impact of the Revolutionary and Napoleonic Wars, 1793–1815, on the Long-Run Growth of the British Economy' (the Braudel Center *Review*, XII, no. 3).

The British concept of empire in its initial stages is illustrated in Daniel Szechi and David Hayton, 'John Bull's Other Kingdoms, the English government of Scotland and Ireland' (*Britain in the First Age of Party 1680–1750, Essays Presented to Geoffrey Holmes*, ed. Clyve Jones, 1987), and in more familiar guise in Richard Koebner's *Empire* (1961). A stimulating survey of a crucial period is to be found in C.A. Bayley, *Imperial Meridian, The British Empire and the World, 1780–1830* (1989); an economic analysis of fundamental importance in P.J. Cairn and A.G. Hopkins, *British Imperialism and Expansion, 1688–1814* (1993). For the themes followed in this Ch. there is material in John Manning Ward, *Colonial Self-Government, The British Experience 1759–1856* (1976), *Imperial Reconstruction 1763–1840, Select Documents on the Constitutional History of the British Empire and Commonwealth*, II, ed. F.W. Madden with D.K. Fieldhouse (1987), A.F. McFadden, 'The Imperial Machinery of the Younger Pitt' in *Essays in British History Presented to Sir Keith Feiling*, ed. H.R. Trevor-Roper (1964), D. Mackey, 'Direction and Purpose in British Imperial Policy, 1783–1801' (*H.J.*, 17, no. 4).

Notes on Sources

The question of the slave trade has of course long received continuing attention, some of which is cited in the Note on Sources to my I, Ch. XIII. Eric Williams's *Capitalism and Slavery* (1944) has given rise to 'A Critique' by Roger T. Anstey (*Ec.H.R.*, *2nd ser.*, XXI, no. 3) and *British Capitalism and Caribbean Slavery: The Legacy of Eric Williams*, ed. Barbara L. Solow and Stanley L. Engerman (1987). Other contributions have been J.R. Ward, *British West Indian Slavery, 1750–1834, The Process of Amelioration* (1988), Seymour Drescher, *Econocide, British Slavery in the Era of Abolition 1760–1810* (1977), and further on figures David Richardson, 'Slave Exports from West and West-Central Africa, 1710–1810 . . .' (*The Journal of African History*, 30, no. 1). The process of the abolition of the trade itself is followed closely in Anstey's *The Atlantic Slave Trade and British Abolition 1760–1810* (1975), and see Alan M. Rose, 'Pitt and the Achievement of Abolition' (*The Journal of Negro History*, XXXIX, no. 3), P.C. Lipscomb, 'William Pitt and the Abolition Question: A Review of an Historical Controversy' (*Proceedings of the Leeds Philosophical and Literary Society*, XII, Pt. IV). David Turley, *The Culture of English Antislavery 1780–1860* (1991), and Seymour Drescher, 'Whose Abolition? Popular Pressure and the Ending of the Bristol Slave Trade' (*Past & Present*, no. 143) investigate the influences, some of them changing, within the country. Pitt's own papers on the Caribbean, which are not particularly revealing, are in P.R.O. 30/8/148–52: he talked, with Wilberforce (but see loc. cit. 189, Dacres Adams Mss formerly P.R.O. 30/58/4) and others, more than he discussed his ideas on paper; and see the biographies of Wilberforce, by his sons (Ch. I above), by Robin Furneaux (1974), and John Pollock (1977). Papers for the other main British possession in the Western hemisphere, Canada, are in P.R.O. 30/8/346–7.

In addition to Ingram, *Commitment to Empire*, and to Naff and Stanton and Shaw on the Ottoman Empire (all Chs. XI & XII above), I have drawn for the East on John Marlowe, *Perfidious Albion: The Origins of Anglo-French Rivalry in the Levant* (1971), J.B. Kelly, *Britain and the Persian Gulf, 1795–1880* (1968), M.E. Yapp, *Strategies of British India, Britain, Iran and Afghanistan 1798–1850* (1980), Ingram, *Britain's Persian Connection 1798–1828* . . . (1992). Lobanov-Rostovsky (Ch. V above), Feldbaeck, McGrew (Chs. XI & XII) discuss Russia's aims, as do J. Lee Schniedman, 'The Proposed Invasion of India by Russia and France in 1801' (*The Journal of Indian History*, XXXV) and John W. Strong, 'Russia's Plans for an Invasion of India in 1801' (*Canadian Slavonic Papers*, VII). P.J. Marshall, the pre-eminent authority for India itself within the British context in the 18th century, provides an introductory survey in *Problems of Empire, Britain and India 1757–1813* (1968). Sir Penderel Moon, *The British Conquest and Dominion of India* (1989) is a fine account. Iris Butler, *The Eldest Brother, The Marquess Wellesley, The Duke of Wellington's Eldest Brother* (1973) portrays the principal British figure in the subcontinent in these fateful years. His policies are displayed in *The Despatches, Minutes, and Correspondence of the Marquis Wellesley* (Ch. V above); his relations with London more confidentially in *Two Views of British India, The Private Correspondence of Mr. Dundas and Lord Wellesley, 1790–1801*, ed. Edward Ingram (1970). The treatment in Furber's biography of Dundas (Chs. XI & XII above) is strong on Indian affairs; and the bulk of that statesman's ms sources – in S.R.O. and N.L.S. (Abbreviations), the John Rylands Library at Manchester, the former India Office Library (now B.L.) in London – compared with Pitt's in Dacres Adams Mss formerly P.R.O. 30/58/4–5 reflects a balance that neither man abused.

CHAPTER XIV

Arthur Aspinall, *The Cabinet Council 1783–1835* (1952) and Richard Pares, *King George III and the Politicians* (1953) are basic studies for the Cabinet to which may be added I.R. Christie, 'The Cabinet in the Reign of George III' in his *Myth and Reality in Late-Eighteenth Century Politics* (Ch. IV above) and, focused more directly on the period of this Chapter, E. Willis, 'Cabinet Politics and Executive Policy-Making Procedures, 1794–1801' in *Albion*, VII, no. 1. There are useful documents, from Parliamentary debates, correspondence, diaries and memoirs, in *English Historical Documents 1783–1832*, ed. A. Aspinall and E. Anthony Smith (1959), Part I, B, and, above all, in *L.C.G. III*, II–IV. Pitt's papers in the P.R.O. 30/8 series contain no file comparable with Grenville's of (selected) Cabinet Minutes in B.L. Add. Ms 59306, and impressions of his dealings with his colleagues and position as First Minister derive from the proceedings and statements and allusions in the range of sources used for other Chapters. Evidence of Cabinet meetings and attendance from London newspapers in these years is interesting, though far from conclusive.

The administration of the armed forces has naturally attracted much attention. C.M. Clode, *The Military Forces of the Crown, Their Administration and Government* (2 vols., 1869), and Fortescue's *History of the British Army*, IV-Part II (Ch. I above) should not be neglected. Richard Glover, *Peninsular Preparation, The Reform of the British Army 1795–1809* (1963), J.R. Western, *The English Militia in the Eighteenth Century*, J.E. Cookson, 'The English Volunteer Movements of the French wars' (both Ch. IV above) – together with some stimulating articles on specific corps –, throw valuable lights on the land forces, regular and auxiliary, and Glover extends the examination by Arthur Forbes of *A History of the Army Ordnance Service* (1929). David Gates investigates a significant specific question in *The British Light Infantry Arm, c 1790–1815: its Creation, Training and Operational Role* (1987).

Michael Lewis gave a pioneering rigour to *A Social History of the Navy 1783–1815* (1960), and some other, administrative studies are cited in my II – Christopher Oprey, 'Schemes for the Reform of Naval Recruitment, 1793–1815' (Ch. IV above), Clive Emsley, 'The Recruitment of Petty Offenders during the French Wars' (*The Mariner's Mirror*, 66, no. 3), N.A.M. Rodger, *The Admiralty* (1979), articles by P.K. Crimmin on its staff and on relations with the Treasury in *The Mariner's Mirror*, 55, nos. 1 & 3, Bernard Pool, *Navy Board Contracts, 1660–1832 . . .* (1966), Christopher Lloyd and Jack S. Coulter, *Medicine and the Navy, 1200–1900*, III (1961). Paul Webb follows the 'Construction, Repair and Maintenance in the Battle Fleet of the Royal Navy, 1793–1815' in *The British Navy and the Use of Naval Power in the Eighteenth Century*, ed. Jeremy M. Black and Philip Woodfine (1988). R.A. Morriss, *The Royal Dockyards during the Revolutionary and Napoleonic Wars* (1981) is an authoritative study to which Jonathan Coad, *Historic Architecture of the Royal Navy . . .* (1983) is an architectural complement. Michael Steer, 'The Blockade of Brest and the Victualling of the Western Squadron, 1793–1805' (*The Mariner's Mirror*, 76, no. 4), examines a specific problem.

One contemporary published source of primary material joins the Departmental unpublished files to underpin secondary accounts of central administration in general: the important 36 reports of the House of Commons Select Committee on Finance of 1797, which were printed in series from 1798, collectively in vols. XII and XIII of the *First Series of Reports* in 1803, and may now be found in *Sessional Papers of the House of Commons in the Eighteenth Century*, ed.

Sheila Lambert (Chs. IX & X above), vols. 107–114. They were particularly searching on the navy, particularly the dockyards. But they covered almost the whole of the Government's financial responsibilities, for which some secondary authorities are noted below, providing on the way many of the figures which George Rose used in his *Brief Examination* of 1799 (Ch. XIII above). One office however which escaped survey was the Alien Office, annexed to the Home Office: an institution whose secrets, of British, Irish and European intelligence and British subversion on the Continent, have recently been under investigation, by Roger Wells, by Marianne Elliott (both Ch. I above), and most interestingly for Europe by Elizabeth Sparrow, whose searches continue but have already yielded two articles as given in Ch. II above; and see also, in this grey area, J.J. Kenny, 'Lord Whitworth and the Conspiracy against Tsar Paul I: The New Evidence of the Kent Archives' in *Slavic Review*, xxxvi. On the more regular main civil Departments, Henry Roseveare examines *The Treasury* . . . (1970), R.R. Nelson *The Home Office 1782–1801* (Ch. IV above), Charles Ronald Middleton *The Administration of British Foreign Policy 1782–1846* (1977). The lists of *Office-Holders in Modern Britain*, I, III–VIII, compiled by J.C. Sainty (I–VI) and by J.M. Collinge (VII–VIII) (1972–9) are of very real value. Pitt's surviving papers in P.R.O. 30/8/255–6 are of interest for the development of the Port of London.

The practice and procedure of the House of Commons in the greater part of the century are covered in P.G.D. Thomas, *The House of Commons in the Eighteenth Century* (1971), while O.C. Williams examines *The Clerical Organization of the House of Commons 1661–1850* (1954) and Sheila Lambert the legislative procedure of both Houses in *Bills and Acts* . . . (1971). The five volumes of *H of P* for 1790–1820 (Abbreviations), ed. R.G. Thorne, are of course essential reading, and among the notices of the Members themselves the editor's own contribution on Pitt is a masterpiece in miniature. Two recent complementary studies may be mentioned, the latter too recent for me to use properly: the more general by Peter J. Jupp, 'The Landed Elite and Political Authority in Britain c 1760–1850' (*The Journal of British Studies*, 29, no. 1), and Ian R. Christie, *British 'non-élite' MPs 1715–1820* (1995). Philip Laundy, *The Office of Speaker* (1964) is a general account; Charles Abbot's *Diary and Correspondence of Lord Colchester* (Chs. IX–X above) of some use for that indefatigable holder of the Chair, and the ms of the diary starting for our purposes in P.R.O. 30/39/32, together with 39/12 (2), 25 are more so. See also his entry in *H of P*, III (again by Thorne). Patrick Howarth, *Questions in the House, The History of an Unique British Institution* (1956) is of interest. Peter Fraser, 'The Growth of Ministerial Control in the Nineteenth-Century House of Commons' (*E.H.R.*, LXXV, no. CCXCVI) has observations relevant to the immediately preceding period. Wilberforce noted some particulars of Pitt's oratory, to be found in Bodleian Library Ms C254.

The House of Lords has attracted fresh attention in the years since A.S. Turberville's *The House of Lords in the Age of Reform 1784–1837* . . . (1958): in Michael W. McCahill, *Order and Equipoise, The Peerage and the House of Lords, 1783–1806* (1978), and in articles by himself, by David Large, by G.M. Ditchfield, and by James J. Sack – on the Scottish peers, the 'party of the Crown', Parliamentary reform, Parliamentary patronage, creations in the peerage – assembled in *Peers, Politics and Power: The House of Lords, 1603–1911*, ed. Clyve Jones and David Lewis Jones (1986). Maurice F. Bond has produced the authoritative *Guide to the Records of Parliament* (1971). The topography of the old Palace of Westminster before its destruction is described in Maurice Hastings, *Parliament House*, and in greater detail with the stated emphasis in an unpublished account by Orlo Cyprian Williams, 'The Topography of the Old House of Commons' (both Ch. VI above). Pitt's files in the P.R.O. 30/8 series contain miscellaneous papers and lists in 234–5, 238. Correspondence on the proposed Order of Merit appears in 143 (Hawkesbury), 144 (Sir Isaac Heard).

CHAPTER XV

Pitt's correspondence with the King on his resignation was published in 1827 as the second part – his first bearing on the question in 1795 of membership of Parliament for Irish Roman Catholics – of a volume (assembled by Henry Phillpotts, Bishop of Exeter) entitled *Letters from His Late Majesty to the Late Lord Kenyon on the Coronation Oath, with His Lordship's Answers: and Letters of the Rt. Hon. William Pitt to His Late Majesty, with His Majesty's Answers, Previous to the Dissolution of the Ministry in 1801*. Stanhope republished the latter in his III, Appendix, xxiii–xxxii. The ms material, some original, some transcribed, had been in the possession of the 1st Lord Kenyon, Lord Chief Justice, and remains in that of his descendant at Gredington in Shropshire. Pitt's copies of his own letters are in P.R.O. 30/8/101; the originals of the King's answers may be found loc. cit., 104.

Pretyman's draft account on the events centring on 3–4 February 1801, for the unpublished volume of his Life of Pitt, is in B.L. Add. Ms 45107, and again with some variations in 45108; and notes and memoranda on the whole affair are scattered in his papers. The most useful single account of earlier proceedings in Cabinet is that of Camden, in Camden Ms U840 0197 at Maidstone. This has been printed with a commentary by Richard Willis in *Bulletin of the Institute of Historical Research*, XLIV, no. 110, itself discussed with a different conclusion by Charles John Fedorak in 'Catholic Emancipation and the Resignation of William Pitt in 1801' in *Albion*, 24, no. 1. Other members of the Cabinet have left us less on the various stages of the business affair: among those who likewise resigned, Grenville noticeably so, though there is an interesting undated letter to Pitt in the Dacres Adams Mss formerly P.R.O. 30/58/4; Dundas's attitude and exertions may be seen from a few scattered documents, among them letters to Pitt loc. cit. and in P.R.O. 30/8/157, and a hopeful list for a new Cabinet under Pitt in B.L. Add. Ms 40102; Spencer's papers in B.L. yield nothing notable of his own; for Windham see his diary in B.L. Add. Ms 37924. For those who did not resign with Pitt, there are letters to his brother Chatham from the King in P.R.O. 30/8/364, from Addington loc. cit. 369 and P.R.O. 30/70/4, and Pitt himself in Ashbourne, *Pitt: some Chapters of his Life and Times* (Ch. III above); for Portland see Malmesbury's diary (Ch. II above), for Liverpool and Loughborough Glenbervie's (Chs. XI & XII), for Loughborough again that of Rose (Ch. III above), I. Addington's position emerges to some extent from that of Charles Abbot [Colchester], I (Chs. IX & X), and is discussed in Pellew's *Life of Sidmouth* (Ch. II above); his papers in the Devon R.O. at Exeter are of course essential from his own point of view. The King's illness is treated in ch. 6 of Ida MacAlpine & Richard Hunter, *George III and the Mad-Business* (1969). His views emerge clearly above, and in *L.C.G. III*, III, with Aspinall's notes. The position of his heir has been well summarised by Aspinall in *Correspondence of the Prince of Wales*, IV (Ch. VI above); a problematical surmise of his attitude to Pitt's future in the event of a Regency is raised by a document now in the Royal Archives as RA 3/77.

Reactions from men less closely involved – Canning, Pretyman, Auckland, Thomas Pelham – emerge likewise in the diaries of Malmesbury, Rose, Glenbervie. They show how normally well-informed figures were living on a mixed diet of fact, rumour and speculation. Canning's sentiments as distinct from knowledge – his diary in Canning Ms 29d is empty for this period – may be gauged in a letter to Pitt of March (Stanhope Ms U1590 S5 02/1). Pretyman corresponded with his wife and received letters from Rose (Pretyman Mss 435/45, 44). Auckland's own exertions in self-justification may be seen in *A.C.*, IV. Published diaries and correspondence within the political and social world, and the London newspapers, convey the atmosphere in the course of the baffling drama.

CHAPTER XVI

Pitt's finances, for which sources for earlier years are given in Ch. III above, began to yield depressing information shortly before and immediately after he resigned. Correspondence and papers between Rose and Pretyman in the latter's Ms 435/44 and the former's B.L. Add. Ms 42772–3, Rose's published diary (Ch. III), some accounts in Stanhope Ms U1590 S5 C44, lists of income and expenditure in the Saumarez Smith papers, illustrate the process of examination which led to the loan subscribed by a circle of the Minister's friends, for which see Stanhope, III, 348 and Pretyman Ms 108/45. Further evidence survives in Pitt's own papers, P.R.O. 30/8/202–3, 218–19.

The Saumarez Smith Mss continue to be valuable for the next three years, as do Coutts's ledgers (Ch. III above) over the whole period. The sale of Holwood, as one measure of economy, is covered in Stanhope Mss U1590 S5 C44, 60/6. The Saumarez Smith papers provide some information on purchases of books; Pretyman Ms 561:21 contains the list of those at Walmer at Pitt's death. Walmer itself begins to figure more prominently in the financial records at this time. A good account of life there is given in ch. V of The Marquess Curzon of Kedleston, *The Personal History of Walmer Castle and Its Lords Warden* (1927); but some details can also be gained, at a period when memories could still be tapped, from Stephen Pritchard, *The History of Deal and Its Neighbourhood* (1864), itself corrected in places by John Laker, *History of Deal* (1917). Other accounts occur in John Lyon, *The History of the Town and Port of Dover* (2 vols., 1813), R.S. Elvin, *The History of Walmer and Walmer Castle* (privately printed, 1894), Ernest Law, *Walmer Castle Illustrated – with a Catalogue of the Pictures, Prints and Furniture* (1906); and there is a good official *Guide* (first published in 1952). Pitt's biographer Stanhope printed for private circulation in 1866 *Notes and Extracts of Letters referring to Mr. Pitt and Walmer Castle 1801–1806*, and this was published in *Miscellanies. Collected and Edited by Earl Stanhope. Second Series* (1872). Reminiscences of life at the Castle were published in *Memoirs of the Lady Hester Stanhope . . .* (3 vols., 1845). They must be treated with the caution required for this source throughout; but her contemporary descriptions may be found in letters to Francis Jackson in Stanhope Ms U1590 C240, published in the Duchess of Cleveland's *The Life and Letters of Lady Hester Stanhope* (1914), and thereafter to William Dacres Adams in Dacres Adams Mss formerly P.R.O. 30/58/9. The best account of her, and her half-brothers', relations with Pitt is in Aubrey Newman's *The Stanhopes of Chevening* (1969); a sidelight on him as for once a disapproving uncle to a member of the family, in Stanhope Ms U1590

S5 C30. The retired Minister's enthusiasm for his military duties as a Colonel of Volunteers is shown in Curzon and in Cleveland above and can be glimpsed in *The Diary of Sir John Moore*, II, ed. J.F. Maurice (1904) and the General's *Life* by John Carrick Moore, II (1813). Some letters to Pitt's subordinate officer Carrington, in Bodleian Library Mss Film 121, convey the flavour. Peter Bloomfield, *Kent and the Napoleonic Wars* (1987) and P.A.L. Vine, *The Royal Military Canal* (1972) discuss his involvement in the wider regional issues of defence, glimpsed also in letters to the Secretary of State for War and the Secretary at War in B.L. Add. Mss 40862, 45040. Other, social, aspects of life at Walmer may be found in Moore's diary, in Canning's for 1802–3 (Canning Ms 29d), and in Kentish newspapers. A highly coloured impression of Pitt's (sole) visit to the Pretymans at the Bishop's palace emerges from his hostess's account in Pretyman Ms 435/29.

By this time Walter Farquhar was well installed as Pitt's physician, and his retrospective diagnosis was published in *The Monthly Review* of December 1900 by Rosebery and given private circulation (Ch. III above). Some of the doctor's correspondence is printed in Stanhope's *Miscellanies. Second Series* (see above), and there are a few further letters in P.R.O. 30/8/134, which can be supplemented from Stanhope Ms U1590 C419/8. There are lists of medical supplies in the Saumarez Smith papers. Canning's diary (Canning Ms 29d) for September 1802 shows the position on a visit after Pitt's severest attack, and reports on a reduced consumption of wine in the autumn appear in Pretyman Ms 435/44. There have been various diagnoses of the causes of Pitt's apparently congenital constitutional weaknesses. Pretyman's own thoughts are given in drafts for the unpublished part of his biography (Ch. XV above). I have learned much from Dr R. Guest Gornall's article in *The Practitioner*, and in correspondence with Mr T.G.J. Brightmore FRCS (both Ch. III above).

The young Lord Haddo's letter to Pitt announcing his choice of him and Dundas as guardians under Scots law is in P.R.O. 30/8/107. Later letters from Pitt are in Aberdeen's papers in B.L. Add. Ms 43227, and see also Muriel E. Chamberlain, *Lord Aberdeen: A Political Biography* (1983).

CHAPTERS XVII & XVIII

Pellew's biography published in the 1840s (Ch. II above) did not carry enough guns to counter the widely received tradition that Pitt's successor was a nullity as First Minister: one deriving largely from the fact that he was not Pitt, crystallised by Canning's sarcastic attacks, enshrined in Whig historiography after the war, and not disturbed by subsequent studies – Stanhope (III–IV), Rosebery, Holland Rose (II) – of Pitt himself. Certainly Addington was not a great Minister; he could not emerge from his predecessor's shadow; but more recent examination suggests that the verdict may have been exaggerated, and without favouring excessive revisionism one should take into account Philip Ziegler's biography, *Addington . . .* (1965), the entry on Addington (by R.G. Thorne) in *H of P*, III, C.D. Hall, 'Addington at war: unspectacular but not unsuccessful' (*Historical Research*, LXI, no. 3) and *British Strategy in the Napoleonic War 1803–15* (1992), and above all Charles John Fedorak, 'The Addington Ministry and the Interaction of Foreign Policy and Domestic Politics 1800–1804' (Ph.D. thesis, University of London, 1990). Family background is provided in E.M.G. Belfield . . ., *The Annals of the Addington Family* (1959).

In a period in which Pitt's intentions while out of office were a lively subject of rumour, and were indeed hard to forecast, the reliability of different sources poses particular problems. Some recent studies of the political scene are most helpful. A.D. Harvey, *Britain in the Early Nineteenth Century* (1978) draws on his own Ph.D. thesis for Cambridge (1972) 'The Grenville Party, 1801–1826', and there are other studies of Addington's opponents in J.J. Sack, *The Grenvillites 1801–1829: party politics and factionalism in the age of Pitt and Liverpool* (1979), Richard E. Willis, 'Fox, Grenville and the Recovery of Opposition, 1801–1804' (*The Journal of British Studies*, XI, no. 1), Peter Jupp, *Lord Grenville* (Ch. II above).

Private diaries and correspondence, bearing on a retired but increasingly central figure whose own correspondence as often was uneven, provide the evidence for his developing attitudes over the three years. The reactions to Pitt's defence of the Preliminary peace treaty from former colleagues who had resigned with him emerge from letters in *H.M.C., Dropmore*, VII (and marginally in B.L. Add. Mss 60487A, 69067), in B.L. Add. Ms 37877 and *The Windham Papers*, (Ch. I above), II, the Dacres Adams Mss formerly P.R.O. 30/58/4, B.L. Add. Mss temp Althorp G42, 48, 221–2 – with 293 for Lady Spencer – for Spencer's papers. The texts of the peace treaties are in *Consolidated Treaty Series* (Ch. V above), 56 (1969). Signs of Pitt's rising uneasiness in the first half of 1802 are to be seen in the Grenville brothers' correspondence – *H.M.C., Dropmore*, VII and the political letters in B.L. Add. Mss (see A.D. Harvey's bibliography in Ch. II above, 24), Buckingham (Abbreviations), III and the Stowe Ms at the Huntington Library, California, Thomas Grenville's papers in B.L. Add. Mss 41851–2, 41856; in the Dacres Adams Mss as above; Canning Mss 29d, 30 and his letters to a favourite correspondent, Granville Leveson Gower, in P.R.O. 30/29/8; Addington's papers in the Sidmouth Mss at the Devon R.O., 152M C1802; Pretyman Ms 435/44 and B.L. Add. Ms 42772, for the hopeful watch kept by the Bishop and George Rose. Canning's activities may be followed in Marshall's biography and Wendy Hinde, *George Canning* (both Ch. III above), and P.C. Lipscomb, 'Party Politics 1801–1802: George Canning and the Trinidad Question' (*H.J*, XII, no. 3).

The same primary sources, published and unpublished and adjusted for date, apply through the rest of the year and 1803. To them may be added in rising proportion a number of publications: the *Diaries and Correspondence of Malmesbury* (Ch. II), IV, Rose (Ch. III), I–II, Abbot, I (Colchester – Chs. IX & X above), Glenbervie, I (Chs. XI & XII above), *L.C.G. III*, IV (1968), *H.M.C., Bathurst, Life of Wilberforce* (Ch. I), III, *Life and Letters of Sir Gilbert Elliot* (Ch. VI above), III. Of the further ms sources one may mention Hawkesbury's reports to Liverpool (B.L. Loan Ms 72, vol. 55), Bathurst's unpublished papers (B.L. Loan Ms 57, vol. 2), Dundas's – Melville's – (P.R.O. 30/8/157, B.L. Add. Ms 40102, John Rylands Library Eng. Ms 907 as well as those in S.R.O. and N.L.S.), Huskisson's (B.L. Add. Ms 38737), Mulgrave's (the Normanby Mss at Mulgrave Castle, Yorkshire). Canning Ms 31 holds copies, presumably from Pitt, of the latter's correspondence with Addington in the spring of 1803, for which see also Sidmouth Ms 152M C1803. For details of publications in the pamphlet war starting later in that year see p. 622, n1 above.

The growing rift, culminating from the turn of 1803–4 in Pitt's attacks on the Ministry and ending in his return to office in May, brings Fox's position to the fore; see *Memorials and Correspondence of Fox*, ed. Lord John Russell, III–IV (1857) and ch. 10 of L.G. Mitchell's *Charles James Fox* (1992), together with E.A. Smith,

Lord Grey, 1764–1845 (1990) and the studies of Grenville and the Grenvillites above. For the Prince of Wales see Ch. XV above and for Moira also *H.M.C., Hastings*, while *The Letters of Richard Brinsley Sheridan*, ed. Cecil Price, II (1966) contains some interesting material. The specific causes of Pitt's onslaught on Addington, the manning of the land forces and reforms to the civil administration of the navy, are set in context for the former in Glover, *Peninsular Preparation* (Ch. XIV above), Fortescue's *History of the British Army* (Ch. I above), and the latter's *The County Lieutenancies and the Army, 1803–14* (1909) and Western for the militia (Ch. XIV above), and for the latter in Roger Morriss, 'St Vincent and Reform, 1801–04' (*The Mariner's Mirror*, 69, no. 3) as well as his work on the dockyards (Ch. XIV above), *Letters of Admiral of the Fleet Earl St Vincent, while First Lord of the Admiralty, 1801–4*, ed. David Bonner Smith (2 vols., 1922–7), Jedediah S. Tucker, *Memoirs of Admiral the Right Hon⁴. The Earl of St Vincent*, II (1844), *Letters and Papers of Charles, Lord Barham . . . 1758–1813*, ed. Sir John Knox Laughton, III (1911). Pitt's papers in P.R.O. 30/8/240, 243–5 include some material for the land forces and in 257 for the navy. The prelude to the return itself yields some evidence in *Secret Correspondence connected with Mr. Pitt's Return to Office in 1804 . . .*, which was privately printed by Lord Mahon (Stanhope) in 1852. As the subtitle made clear, the compilation drew chiefly on the mss in Melville Castle. These are now in the S.R.O., and their account of events can be supplemented from the diary and letters of Alexander Hope in the Hope of Luffness papers, S.R.O., GD 364, which are also useful for his earlier contacts with Pitt. The Dacres Adams Mss formerly P.R.O. 30/58/5 are interesting, and there is some material in the Normanby Mss boxes J, VII bundle 13, 37. Michael W. McCahill, 'The House of Lords and the Collapse of Henry Addington's Administration' (*Parliamentary History*, VI, Part I) brings out the importance of the Upper House in the spring of 1804. The introduction to *H.M.C., Dropmore*, VII by the editor, Walter Fitzpatrick, is a well argued energetic case for Grenville over a controversial period.

Further information on the final stage is to be found in *H.M.C., Bathurst*, almost certainly from Pitt's conversation. Horace Twiss, *The Public and Private Life of Lord Chancellor Eldon . . .*, I (1844) is useful, as are the sources already cited on the Grenvillites and Foxites. Stanhope, IV, prints in the text and Appendix letters between Pitt and the King from the Dacres Adams Mss. Macalpine & Hunter (Ch. XV above) give an account of the recurrence of George III's illness.

Parliamentary debates are of high importance particularly from the late autumn of 1803–4. *P.R., 3rd ser.*, XIV–XVIII (1800–2), *4th ser.*, I–III (1803–4) cover the period March 1801–August 1803. The publication then ceased, and Cobbett's *Parliamentary Debates* (*P.D.*, see Abbreviations) began their life, opening the famous series 'Under the Superintendence' of T.C. Hansard as the edition of 1812 stated, with I–II (1804) covering November 1803–July 1804. *The Senator, 2nd ser.* had meanwhile ceased publication after covering January 1801–June 1802 in I–V (nd). Cobbett's later *P.H.*, XXXV–XXXVI (1819–20) cover March 1800–August 1803.

CHAPTER XIX

Sources for Ch. XVIII supply much of the political information here. For the formation of the new Ministry and attitudes to it one may cite in particular Stanhope IV, the diaries of Rose (Ch. III), Colchester, I (Chs. IX & X), *Glenbervie*,

I (Chs. XI & XII), *Malmesbury* (Ch. II), IV, Twiss, I for Eldon (Chs. XVII & XVIII), *H.M.C., Bathurst, L.C.G. III,* IV, *Correspondence of Prince of Wales,* V (1968) with Aspinal's notes, to which one may add *Correspondence of Leveson Gower,* I (Ch. II above), *Letters to 'Ivy' from the First Earl of Dudley,* ed. Samuel Henry Romilly (1905). Among unpublished ms material (and much is published) the Dacres Adams Mss formerly P.R.O. 30/58/5 – and marginally 8 – are of interest, as are P.R.O. 30/8, eg 112 for Bathurst, 119 for Camden, 120 for Canning, 133 for Euston, 146 (Hope, on Moira), 160 Duke of Montrose, B.L. Loan Ms 57, vol. 2 (Bathurst), Canning Mss 29d, 30, Camden Ms U840 C209/3, Normanby Mss box 37, Pretyman Ms T435/44.

Most of the sources for financial affairs repeat publications cited for Ch. IX above. O'Brien and Cooper are fundamental, and Farnsworth's claim for Addington's contribution to Pitt's income tax calls for attention. Mitchell & Deane, Hope-Jones, Newmarch are of value; the diaries of Rose, II and Colchester, I shed light on Pitt's opinion of his predecessor as Chancellor of the Exchequer. The Parliamentary debates (below) are important, but need supplementing by *The Times* of 14 July 1803 for Pitt's speech of the day before. P.R.O. 30/8/173, 197, 275, 303–4, Sidmouth Mss 152M C1802 OT 14, C1803 OT 29 are relevant, as is B.L. Add. Ms 31229 for Vansittart.

The study of foreign affairs, like that of finance, benefits from two unpublished theses: by Fedorak (Chs. XVII & XVIII above) and by G.B. Fremont, 'Britain's Role in the Formation of the Third Coalition against France' (D.Phil., Oxford, 1991), both providing necessary background and bibliographies from Addington's period, for which Norman Gash, *Lord Liverpool* (Ch. III above) gives a further well balanced judgment on Hawkesbury as Foreign Secretary. The older account of policy by Holland Rose in *The Cambridge History of British Foreign Policy,* I (Ch. II above) retains its value, and he also edited *Select Despatches from the British Foreign Archives, relating to the formation of the Third Coalition against France 1804–5* (1904). Russia, the other party most actively involved, is well served by published documentation; in Simon Vorontsov's correspondence in London, *Arkhiv Kniazia Vorontsova* (Ch. V above), X, XV, and, for those qualified, more comprehensively in *Sbornik Imperatorskago Russkago Istoriceskago Obscestva,* LXVII for relations with France and *Vneshniaia Politika Rossi XIX i nachala XX veka. Dokumenty rossiiskogo Ministerstva del Ministerstvo Inostrannykh del SSSR,* I, II (1960) for policy in general. Patricia M. Grimsted reproduces 'Czartoryski's System for Russian Foreign Policy, 1803: A Memorandum' (*California Slavic Studies,* V, no. 1), the *Memoirs of Prince Adam Czartoryski and his Correspondence with Alexander I* are edited by Adam Gielgud (II, 1888), and M. Kukiel, *Czartoryski and European Unity, 1770–1861* (1955), Grimsted, *The Foreign Ministers of Alexander I . . . 1801–1825* (1969), and – particularly – W.H. Zawadzki, *A Man of Honour . . .* (1993), are most useful. See also M.S. Anderson, *The Eastern Question* (Chs. XI & XII above), Lobanov-Rostovsky, *Russia and Europe, 1789–1925,* Saul, *Russia and the Mediterranean, 1797–1807* (both Ch. V above). Sources for Prussia are contained in *Briefwechsel König Friedrich Wilhelm's III . . . mit Kaiser Alexander I,* ed. Paul Bailleu (1900), and *Preussen under Frankreich von 1795 bis 1807 . . .,* ed. Bailleu (1887). For Austria see *Österreich und Russland in dem Jahren 1804–5,* ed. Adolf Beer (1875), August Fournier, *Gentz und Cobenzl: Geschichte der österreichischen Diplomatic in dem Jahre, 1801–1805* (1880). For France herself see the *Correspondance de Napoléon I* (Ch. V above), and also *Lettres inédités de Talleyrand à Napoléon, 1800–1809* (1889). Harold C. Deutsch, *The Genesis of Napoleonic Imperialism* (1938) is a good study. Some light is thrown on Francis Jackson in Berlin in letters to his brother (*Diaries and Letters of Sir George Jackson, from the Peace of Amiens to the Battle of Talavera*, ed. Lady Jackson, I (1872)), and on Arthur Paget in Vienna in *The Paget Papers* (Chs. XI & XII above). The former's relevant papers are in P.R.O., F.O. 353, the latter's in B.L. Add. Mss 48389–414; Granville Leveson Gower's for Russia in P.R.O. 30/29. Harrowby's papers as Foreign Secretary are in the possession of the Earl of Harrowby. Pitt's files containing correspondence on Europe and the United States are P.R.O. 30/8/332–45. There are letters from Vorontsov loc. cit. 191 and from Novosiltsov 163. Foreign Office papers are in P.R.O., F.O. 5/33, 36, 39, 41–3 (United States), 7/63–72 (Austria), 9/22–9 (Bavaria), 22/41–5, 118 (Denmark), 27/57–70 (France), 28/18 (Genoa), 31/11–13 (German States), 33/21–6 (Hamburg), 37/60–1, 38/6–7 (Holland and Netherlands, and Frontiers), 42/4–5 (Ionian Islands), 49/3 (Malta), 63/35–45 (Portugal), 64/60–6 (Prussia), 65/48–56 (Russia), 67/30–3 (Sardinia), 68/15 (Saxony), 70/16–23 (The Two Sicilies), 72/46–54 (Spain), 73/29–32 (Sweden), 74/36–8 (Switzerland), 78/31–45 (Turkey).

Pitt's activity in plans for defence has been noted while he was out of office (Chs. XVII & XVIII above). One may add for his return P.R.O. 30/8/157 (for Melville), 240, 245, 250, with background for Fulton's 'experiment' in *The Keith Papers* . . ., ed. Christopher Lloyd (Chs. XI & XII above), III (1955) and 'Congreve's Rockets, 1805–1806', ed. Christopher Lloyd and Hardin Craig, Jnr (*The Naval Miscellany*, IV, ed. Christopher Lloyd, 1952). His political difficulties, shown at once in his proposals for the land forces, are illustrated clearly in the Parliamentary debates, *P.D.*, II (see Chs. XVII & XVIII above). Relations with Grenville, deteriorating further after a newspaper leak, are followed in Jupp, *Lord Grenville* (Ch. II) and the other sources cited for Chs. XVII and XVIII above, and see also B.L. Add. Mss 37846, 37882, 37884 for Windham; those with the King and with his heir in *L.C.G. III*, IV and *Correspondence of Prince of Wales*, V – and see Stanhope Ms U1590 S5 04/5 for Tierney –, the diaries of Rose, II (Ch. III above), Malmesbury, IV (Ch. II), Glenbervie, I (Chs. XI & XII), the Dacres Adams Mss formerly P.R.O. 30/58/5; those within the Ministry similarly and in Camden Ms U840 C309, P.R.O. 30/8/146 (Alexander Hope), 160 (Montrose), 120 and Canning Ms 29d, B.L. Loan Ms 72, vol. 24 (Hawkesbury) with Stanhope Ms U1590 S5 010/16, P.R.O. 30/70/4 for a letter from George Villiers, Pretyman Ms 435/44. For the Minister's efforts to improve his situation one may cite in addition *Memoirs and Correspondence of Fox*, IV, *H.M.C., Dropmore*, VII, Buckingham, III, *H.M.C., Hastings*, Pellew (Ch. II above), II, the published diaries of Colchester and P.R.O. 30/9/33, P.R.O. 30/8/143 (Hawkesbury), B.L. Add. Ms 31229 (Vansittart). The studies by Harvey and Sack (Chs. XVII & XVIII) continue to be of great use.

CHAPTER XX

The authorities cited in Ch. XIX for foreign affairs apply again here, particularly for Russia on which the main weight of British policy was concentrated in the first eight months of 1805. I therefore confine references for this Ch. to some specific items. Bonaparte's letter to George III at the start of the year with a suggestion of peace, and the British reply, are in P.R.O., F.O. 27/71, the King's response to Pitt is printed in Holland Rose, *Pitt and Napoleon* (Ch. II above), Part II, drafts of the British reply are in the Dacres Adams Mss formerly P.R.O. 30/58/6. Pitt's survey, in answer to the Tsar, of a European peace and its maintenance is in F.O. 65/60, and there are working drafts, mostly in his hand, in the Dacres Adams Mss formerly P.R.O. 30/58/8. The text was made available after a decade in *H.C.J.*, 70, and the bulk was published in C.K. Webster, *British Diplomacy 1813–1815; select documents dealing with the reconstruction of Europe* (1921). E. Ingram, 'Lord Mulgrave's Prospects for the Reconstruction of Europe' (*H.J*, XIX, no. 2) claims credit for the Foreign Secretary. Stephen R. Graubard, 'Castlereagh and the Peace of Europe' (*The Journal of British Studies*, III, no. 1), F.H. Hinsley, *Power & the Pursuit of Peace* (1963), chs. 8, 9, are among those who trace the legacy of ideas. Foreign Office papers for 1805 in the P.R.O. follow numerically on those given for the period of Ch. XIX; to the private papers cited loc. cit. may be added Leveson Gower's letters to Pitt in P.R.O. 30/8/152 and letters to him from the Minister in P.R.O. 30/29/384, Pitt's corresponcence with Novosiltsov in Dacres Adams Mss formerly P.R.O. 30/58/6 and letters to Harrowby in Harrowby Mss vol. X, some letters from Harrowby to Pitt in P.R.O. 30/8/142, Mulgrave's papers as Foreign Secretary in the Normanby Mss. Figures for financial provisions of the treaties of alliance with Russia, Austria, and Sweden are examined in Sherwig, *Guineas and Gunpowder* (Ch. V above). For the terms of the agreements themselves see *Consolidated Treaty Series* (ibid), 58 (1969), and *Select Despatches . . . relating to the Third Coalition* (Ch. XIX above) for the Provisional treaty with Russia. The engagements with Sweden are followed in Raymond Carr, 'Gustavus IV and the British Government' (*E.H.R.*, LX, no. CCXXXVI) as well as by Fremont (Ch. XIX above) who gives the most detailed account of British diplomacy in these months throughout.

For the Parliamentary events of the period see *P.D.*, III–V, *P.H.*, XXXVII. As in foreign affairs, and for the same reason, I concentrate on particular sources for domestic politics. Dissatisfaction with Pitt is reflected in correspondence in P.R.O. 30/29/8, The Dacres Adams Mss formerly P.R.O. 30/58/6, Camden Mss U840 C116, 244, *H.M.C., Bathurst*. His quarrel with George III over the choice of a new Archbishop of Canterbury can be followed in Stanhope, IV, *L.C.G. III*, IV, Rose's *Diaries* (Ch. III), II, Ashbourne, *Pitt, His Life and Times* (ibid). The great upset of the investigation into Melville's conduct takes up much space in *P.D.*, III and IV; the text of the Tenth Report of the Commission of Naval Inquiry is printed there, as also in the Commons' *Parliamentary Sessional Papers* for 1804–5 (Chs. IX & X). See also Stanhope, IV, Matheson, *Life of Henry Dundas* (Chs. XI & XII above), P.R.O. 30/8/157, *Life of Wilberforce* (Ch. I), III, *H.M.C., Bathurst* and B.L. Loan Ms 57, vol. 2, *Diaries of Colchester* (Chs. IX & X), I, Canning Ms 29d, B.L. Add. Ms temp Althorp G294 – Lady Spencer's curious tale in the preceding August –, B.L. Add. Ms 31229 (Vansittart to Lord Hardwicke); *H.M.C., Dropmore*, VII, Harvey and Sack (both Chs. XVII & XVIII above) for the Grenvillites; *The Creevey Papers*, ed. John Gore (1963), *Diaries of Malmesbury* (Ch. II above), IV, *Letters to 'Ivy'* (Ch. XIX above), *H of P*, IV (Whitbread). The Commission's Eleventh Report and Pitt's response are covered in *P.D.*, V; and see a letter from Bathurst to Camden, 11 April misendorsed 1802 but 1805 (Camden Ms U 840 C226/5). The subsequent problems precipitated by the appointment of Middleton (Barham) to the Admiralty – see *Letters and Papers of Charles of Barham*, III (Chs. XVII & XVIII above) – and Addington's (Sidmouth's) resignation provoked a flurry of correspondence and ideas for rearrangements: one may draw attention to Pellew (Ch. II above), II,

The Younger Pitt

Diaries of Colchester, II, B.L. Loan Ms 72, vol. 55, Dacres Adams Mss formerly P.R.O. 30/58/6, *Memorials and Correspondence of Fox*, IV (Chs. XVII & XVIII), Jupp, *Lord Grenville* (Ch. II), Camden Ms U840 C95/3, *H.M.C., Bathurst* and B.L. Loan Ms, vol. 2, *H of P*, I.

When writing his biography, Stanhope collected information from survivors on Pitt in his later days. Most of it was published, but one interesting account was not, of a conversation in 1810 between Dacres Adams and the King, and this may be found in Stanhope Ms U1590 C405/15. Hester Stanhope often spoke of her uncle and her remarks were reported in the *Memoirs*, II (Ch. XVI above). Stanhope, IV gives glimpses of some carefree relations with children and the young; *The Diary of Joseph Farington*, VI, ed. Kenneth Garlick and Angus Macintyre (1979) contains the painter Thomas Lawrence's report of one less unbuttoned social occasion, and also has some interesting comments from portrait artists on him as a subject. We catch a sight of the Minister in action towards the end with an embarrassing deputation, in *The Irish Catholic Petition of 1805, The Diary of Denys Scully*, ed. Brian MacDermot (1992).

CHAPTER XXI

The Trafalgar campaign is a tale oft told. Nelson's return to England after the long chase, and the consultations in London, are covered in Carola Oman's *Nelson* (1947) and in *The Barham Papers*, III (Chs. XVII & XVIII above) which are also of course of value throughout. Both, together with P.R.O. 30/8/111 and Dacres Adams Mss formerly P.R.O. 30/58/6 for Barham, indicate Pitt's involvement. Stanhope Ms U1590 S5 C60/15 contains an account of the Minister's farewell of the Admiral in Downing Street, and see *Diaries of Malmesbury*, IV (Ch. II above) for his reception of the news of the battle and Nelson's death.

The balanced study of *British Strategy in the Napoleonic War* by Christopher D. Hall (Chs. XVII & XVIII above) deals briefly with plans in 1805 for the southern flank of Europe which receive definitive treatment in Piers Mackesy's *The War in the Mediterranean 1803–10* (1957). P.R.O., F.O. 70/22–7, W.O. 6/56 bear on the local scene; F.O. 65/57–9, with 42/7 for the Ionian Islands, together with Saul (Ch. V) and sources for Ch. XX above, on the all-important exchanges with Russia.

For the expedition to the Cape of Good Hope see the documents edited by W.G. Perrin in 'The Second Capture of the Cape of Good Hope 1806' (*The Naval Miscellany*, III, ed. W.G. Perrin, 1928), L.C.F. Turner, 'The Cape of Good Hope and the Anglo-French Conflict, 1797–1808' (*Historical Studies Australia and New Zealand*, 9, no. 36). Fortescue's *History of the British Army* (Ch. I above), V (1910) examines – as for other operations – the provision of the force and the outcome, and *Memoirs and Correspondence of Castlereagh* (Ch. VI above), VI (1851) apply to his period as Secretary of State for War and the Colonies. The capture of Buenos Aires by Home Popham is set in context by John Lynch, 'British Policy and South America, 1782–1808' (*The Journal of Latin American Studies*, I, no. 1); his past efforts of persuasion in that direction can be seen *inter alia* in N.L.S. Ms 67a (for Melville) – and see Hugh Popham's biography (Chs. XI & XII above) –, those of Miranda in P.R.O. 30/8/190, 395, and other, anon examples loc. cit., 395, N.L.S. Ms 1075, S.R.O., Melville Castle Mss GD 51 series. A letter to Pitt from Mulgrave in December 1804, in Stanhope Ms U1590 S5 03/7, gives an impression of the official interest.

The heightening pace of the search for an Allied Coalition embracing Prussia yields a complicated story, followed carefully by Fremont (Ch. XX above). Stanhope, IV and Holland Rose, II are also useful, as is the latter's edition of selected documents in *Third Coalition* (ibid). The relevant Foreign Office papers are F.O. 7/74–9 (Austria), 97/74 (Bavaria), 22/46–7 (Denmark), 64/68–71 (Prussia), 65/58–9, 62 (Russia), 73/34–5 (Sweden). A crucial complement lies in the private correspondence between Pitt and Harrowby in Harrowby Mss vols. XII–XIII, P.R.O. 30/8/142, Dacres Adams Mss formerly P.R.O. 30/58/6, P.R.O. 30/70/4, and between Harrowby and Mulgrave in Harrowby Mss vol. XI. For other private ms material (Leveson Gower, Paget, Jackson) see, as for published, Ch. XX above. The diaries of Rose, II and Malmesbury, IV, and *H.M.C.*, *Bathurst* in particular, give further glimpses of Pitt's hopes and expectations; some notes by him in the Dacres Adams Mss formerly P.R.O. 30/58/8 relate to the expedition designed for Hanover, for which see also Fortescue, op. cit., V.

The Minister's hopes of a coalition in domestic politics, frustrated by the King in September 1805 but not entirely abandoned, can be followed in *Rose*, II, *H.M.C.*, *Bathurst* with P.R.O. 30/8/112 and B.L. Loan Ms 57, vol. 2, the Dacres Adams Mss formerly P.R.O. 30/58/6, Harrowby Mss vol. XII, B.L. Loan Ms 72 vol. 55, the Bankes Mss at Kingston Lacy, Dorset in the possession of the National Trust.

CHAPTER XXII

Some of Pitt's thoughts at the end of 1805 on political appointments – to Ireland and to the Cabinet – appear in P.R.O. 30/8/112 (Bathurst), 119 (Camden), 120 (Canning) for whom see Marshall, *The Rise of Canning* (Ch. III above), the diaries of Rose, II, Malmesbury, IV (Chs. III, II above).

For the Minister's time at Bath see accounts in *The Bath Herald*. B.L. Loan Ms 57, vol. 2 and P.R.O. 30/8/174 (Richard Ryder) show friends at work to find him rooms. Reports and memories were gathered by Stanhope for his IV and also in his *Miscellanies. First Series* (2nd edn., 1863); see eg Stanhope Mss U1590 C404/14, 405/15. There is a particularly interesting contemporary series to Mulgrave from his brother Major-General Edmund Phipps in the Normanby Mss, bundle 31. P.R.O. 30/8/112 (Duke of Beaufort) and *H.M.C.*, *Bathurst* contain some correspondence on Pitt's projected visit to Badminton. There are letters from Farquhar to his patient in P.R.O. 30/8/134, and his retrospective account of his visit was first published by Rosebery in *The Monthly Review*, I, no. 3 in December 1900 (Ch. III above).

The final period, at Bowling Green House in Putney (of which Stanhope made descriptive notes in 1872; Stanhope Ms U1590 S5 C60/23), of course produced much correspondence from those closely involved, let alone from those on the margins. Hester Stanhope was frequently in touch with Adams (Dacres Adams Mss formerly P.R.O. 30/58/9, and see also Stanhope Ms U1590 C419/9), and Adams sent news to his brother-in-law Courtney of his own visits (Dacres Adams Mss formerly P.R.O. 30/58/11, and see also Stanhope Ms U1590 C66/7). Tomline (Pretyman), reappearing on the scene, reported continually to his wife (Pretyman Mss 435/26–7, 44, 110), Rose (Ch. III above) II, noted the Bishop's information at the time, Ashbourne, *Pitt* (ibid) published an extract of his subsequent memorandum, and his full account for the unpublished part of his Life of

Pitt first appeared in *The Monthly Review*, XII, no. 3 in August 1903. Canning resumed his diary after a lapse of three months (Canning Ms 29d). For Wellesley's visit see Iris Butler, *The Eldest Brother* (Ch. XIII above). Stanhope published in IV James Stanhope's account, the ms of which is in Stanhope Ms U1590 C60/4, and amended for future editions his own first reading of Pitt's last words (letter to *The Times*, 24 April 1862). For other, less impressive versions see p. 829, n2 above.

CHAPTER XXIII

For the proceedings in Parliament on Pitt's death see *P.D.*, V–VI; also *H of P*, I (for Abbot), V (Windham). For his lying in state and funeral, *The London Gazette*, London newspapers, Pretyman Mss 435/15, 123, P.R.O. 30/8/364 (Chatham).

The lengthy process of clearing up the finances may be followed principally in the Pretyman Mss (435/26–7, 39, 45, 123, 503:3, 10, 562:1, 21, 22, 1820–3, 1826, 1828), P.R.O. 30/8/369 (Chatham), together with the Saumarez Smith Mss, Coutts's Bank ledgers, Stanhope Mss U1590 S5 C42 (for Coutts), 06/54 (Thomas Steele), Rose (Ch. III above) II. Adams's capture of Pitt's books from Walmer is recalled in Stanhope Ms U1590 C405/15; as are the circumstances of the distribution of Hoppner's portrait of Pitt in Stanhope, IV, 2nd edn. (1862–3), with results listed in Ashbourne, *Pitt* (Ch. III above), Appendix. *The Pitt Clubs, A short historical guide* (nd) by J.B. Lewis enumerates and traces authoritatively those constituent if almost entirely posthumous elements in a legacy whose longer-term context is discussed in J.J. Sack, *From Jacobite to Conservative, Reaction and orthodoxy in Britain, c. 1760–1832* (1993).

Index

For Volume III and Volume IV

Names and ranks of persons are given as far as possible in the style by which they were generally known in the period of this volume.

Abbot, Charles (1st Baron Colchester) 43n, 260n, 301n, 303n, 468n, 475n, 477–9, 481, 528n, 581n, 608n, 655n, 845

Abercorn, 1st Marquess of 85, 776–7, 832

Abercromby, Major General Sir Ralph: in West Indies 144; commands in Ireland 163–5, 168–9; and invasion of Holland 236, 245–8, 253, 254–7; Mediterranean command 360–2, 364n, 366–371, 391; military successes 374–5; on competence of army 375; on Pitt's qualities 380n; Dundas drafts instructions for 400; commands expedition to Egypt 410–11, 555; death in Egypt 555

Aberdeen, 4th Earl of (*earlier* Lord Haddo) 547, 552 & n

Aboukir Bay 146

Acre 401, 403

Act for the Union of Great Britain and Ireland (1801) 192–4, 478, 501

Adams, William Dacres 605n, 771–2, 822, 825, 831n, 836

Addington, Dr Anthony 554n

Addington, Henry (1st Viscount Sidmouth): Pitt favours as successor 46–9, 519n, 524; reconciles Pitt and Auckland 74n; and Pitt's attachment to Eleanor Eden 80; and Pitt's drinking 81, 83n; Pitt visits 82, 88; influence on Pitt's art interests 85n; personal relations with Pitt 89–90, 589n, 596–7, 607, 623; Speakership 90, 477–9, 554, 596; destroys Pitt papers 94, 509n; proposes Voluntary Contribution 107; and *Anti-Jacobin* 111; and Pitt-Tierney duel 127–8; dislikes reply to Bonaparte's peace overtures 341n; and Pitt's resignation 495–6; opposes Catholic emancipation 505, 514, 531, 587n, 764; George III asks to form government 508–9, 513, 519n; in Opposition and formation of Ministerial Coalition 518n; on reasons for Pitt's resignation 519n; forms Ministry 523–4, 553–4; relations with George III 524, 751; and George III's illness and incapacity

525–6; summoned by Prince of Wales 527–8; and Pitt's promise to George III on Catholic emancipation 529; Melville's scorn for 531; and Pitt's prospective return to office 532–3, 576–82, 584–603, 605n, 640, 642–3, 645, 649–50, 665n; and Pitt's personal finances 536; overlaps with Pitt 540; background 554–5; 1801–2 peace settlement (Treaty of Amiens) 556–65, 569, 724n; Pitt supports as leader 565–72, 576, 601–2, 619, 852; offends Pitt 569; overrules Hawkesbury as Foreign Minister 569; and abolition of slave trade 570; financial management and budget 570, 579, 640–1, 676–7, 679–85, 693; and 1802 election 574; and Bonaparte's Continental annexations 575; promised peerage and Lords Speakership 588, 589n, 592; and conduct of war 599, 610, 612, 614 & n, 692, 702, 797; Pitt's Commons attacks on 605–9; and 1803 resumption of war 608; Parliamentary support for 611, 666, 668; loses support 620; and 'pamphlet war' 621–3; Pitt criticises Ministry 636–8, 640–1, 645; and Pitt's criticisms of national defence 636, 645–6, 709; Pitt's increasing contempt for 636 & n; performance as Minister 643–4; proposed exclusion from Pitt's new government 648 & n; government falls (1804) 652–3, 655n, 661–2; and Harrowby 670; seeks wartime allies 686; considers seizing New Orleans 690, Starhemberg on 690; and attack on neutral Dutch ships 704n; and army strength 709–11, 713n; on Commons attacks on Pitt's Additional Forces bill 712; on difficulties in Pitt's Cabinet 718; joins Pitt's 1805 Cabinet 722–25, 745–9, 764, 783; peerage 723–5; reconciliation with Pitt 724; Alexander I mistrusts 726n; Russians disapprove of appointment to Cabinet 737n; and Pitt's quarrel with George III 750; on Melville and Naval Enquiry Commission Report 754–5, 756n; supporters' votes 763;

with Pitt 524; visits Pitt at Walmer 541; on back-benches 552n; and Pitt's reaction to Peace of Amiens 567; and Addington's criticism of Pitt 569; attacks Addington 570–1, 642; and Pitt birthday celebration 571; hopes and plans for Pitt's return 572, 576–9, 581, 600–2; attitude to Long 587; proposed position after Pitt's return 592, 672; and Patten's censure motions 606; on Grenvillites 620; and Pitt's attitude to Addington Ministry 622n; on Pitt and Opposition 624; on Pitt's Commons speech on navy 632n; in Pitt's 1804 government 673–4, 723, 748; relations with Grenville 674; and evacuation of Portuguese fleet to Brazil 692n; dislike of Pitt's 1804 Ministry 722; and Hiley Addington 725n; and differences within Pitt's Cabinet 746n, 747; dismay at Pitt's Cabinet appointments 748–9; on Melville and Naval Enquiry Report 755, 756n; Nelson meets 789; visits Pitt in Bath 821; and Pitt's final illness 825n, 826–7; on Pitt's last words 829n, 854; and Pitt's death 830–1; and memorialising of Pitt 837; and successor government to Pitt 840–1; and posthumous tributes to Pitt 842; Pitt wishes to bring into Cabinet 819–20

Canterbury: Archbishopric 749–51

Cape of Good Hope 54, 61, 67, 143, 388n, 425n, 444, 557–9, 563, 789, 793–6

Cape St Vincent, Battle of (1797) 17, 28, 99, 149

Capetown 794

Caracas 795

Caribbean *see* West Indies

Carlisle, 5th Earl of 617–18, 674n, 757

Carnot, Lazare 471

Carrington, 1st Baron: friendship with Pitt 85, 88–9, 99n, 490; and subscription for Pitt 536, 537n, 834; and Kent Volunteers 543; Pitt's debt to 834; and successor government to Pitt 840

Carthew, John 90n, 495n

Cartwright, John 308

Cartwright, William 833

Carysfort, 1st Earl of 529n, 617n

Castlereagh, Viscount (*later* 2nd Marquess of Londonderry): relations with Pitt 91, 772, 774; duel with Canning 129; foreign policy 135; as Irish Chief Secretary 172–3, 180, 183, 501; and Irish Union 176, 178–81, 184, 186–7, 190n, 193 & n; and Irish Catholics and Dissenters 177n, 191, 192n, 497n, 498, 503, 506, 510, 514, 521; temperament 183; resigns 524; on back-benches 552n, 557; visits Pitt at Walmer 575; favours Pitt's return to office 588, 590, 640, 649; Pitt's liking for 622n, in Pitt's 1804 government 666, 671–2, 673n, 674, 676, 767, 819; and Russian alliance 688n; threatens resignation 718; at Congress of Vienna 731–3; and Melville in Naval Enquiry Report 756, 760; Nelson meets 787; on Cape of Good Hope 794; and news of

Third Coalition 818; and Pitt's final illness 824, 838; on Fox at Commons Address for Pitt's death 833; and successor government to Pitt 840–1; and posthumous tributes to Pitt 842

Cathcart, 10th Baron 798

Catherine II (the Great) of Russia 148n, 154, 206n, 210, 658n

Catholic Relief Acts (Ireland, 1790s) 171

Cayenne 335 & n

Census Act (1800) 291, *see also* Population

Cereals *see* Corn

Ceylon 54, 61, 67, 388n, 444, 557–8, 563

Chantrey, Sir Francis 837

Charlemont, 2nd Earl of 777n

Charles I 260, 263n

Charles, Archduke of Austria: commands in Campaigns in Italy 50, 806–7; and Leoben truce 51; supports Russians in Switzerland 209, 211–13, 237–41, 248, 251, 324; and Austrian Mediterranean strategy 346; seeks peace 366; withdraws after Ulm 813, 816, 817n

Charlotte, Princess (Wales's daughter) 710–12

Charlotte, Queen 194, 715

Chatham, 1st Earl of 37, 83, 85, 515, 550, 703, 704n, 709n, 832–4, 853

Chatham, 2nd Earl of: and French peace overtures 58; appointed Lord President of Council 73; military advice 236n; serves in Holland 253, 255; and army preparations 351; supports Dundas's strategy 377, 518; and 1800 truce proposals 382n; and Catholic emancipation 502, 511, 512n; and Pitt's resignation 509n; in Addington's administration 553 & n; absent from Pitt birthday dinner 571, 572n; proposed as First Lord of Treasury 584; and Pitt's accommodation with Addington 623n; favours Pitt's return to office 640; in Pitt's 1804 government 671–2; favours Pitt alliance with Addington 722; and Pitt's final illness 826–7, 830n; as Pitt's executor 828, 835; inherits Pitt's papers 836; and successor government to Pitt 838–9

Chatham, Hester, Countess of 88, 128, 255; death and burial 546, 588n, 832n; portrait 837n

Chesterfield, 5th Earl of 84

Chilver, S. 83n

China: trade with 437

Chouans 226 & n, 318, 325, 359n

Church of England: and national morale 109–10; and Church of Ireland 173, 177–8; and Lords 486; and Catholic emancipation 497, 499, 506, 508

Church of Ireland 173, 177–8

Churchill, Sir Winston S. 140

Cinque Ports: Pitt's Lord Wardenship of 69n, 75–6, 88, 91, 125, 536n, 537; Volunteer Corps 543; *see also* Walmer Castle

Printed in Great Britain
by Amazon

28102081R00322